We Gather Together

We Gather Together

The Religious Right and the Problem of Interfaith Politics

NEIL J. YOUNG

OXFORD
UNIVERSITY PRESS

OXFORD
UNIVERSITY PRESS

Oxford University Press is a department of the University of Oxford. It furthers the University's objective of excellence in research, scholarship, and education by publishing worldwide. Oxford is a registered trade mark of Oxford University Press in the UK and in certain other countries

Published in the United States of America by Oxford University Press
198 Madison Avenue, New York, NY 10016, United States of America

Library of Congress Cataloging-in-Publication Data
Young, Neil J.
We gather together : the religious right and the problem of interfaith politics /
Neil J. Young.
p. cm.
Includes bibliographical references and index.
ISBN 978–0–19–973898–4 (cloth : alk. paper) 1. Religious right—United States—History—20th century. 2. Christian conservatism—United States—History—20th century. 3. Christianity and politics—United States—History—20th century. 4. Evangelicalism—United States—History—20th century. 5. Catholic Church—United States—History—20th century. 6. Church of Jesus Christ of Latter-day Saints—United States—History—20th century. I. Title.
BR525.Y68 2015
261.70973'09045—dc23
2015009831

1 3 5 7 9 8 6 4 2

Printed in the United States of America on acid-free paper

For Nate

Contents

Acknowledgments

AT THE COMPLETION of writing a book, one realizes how many people and institutions have supported what so often felt like a solitary task. I am grateful to the financial support provided to me by the Graduate School of Arts and Sciences at Columbia University, where this book began as my dissertation, in addition to the Columbia University Summer Research Fellowship and the Howard and Natalie Shawn Summer Research Scholar Fellowship. My research and travels were supported by the following awards: the Annaley Naegle Redd Student Award in Women's History, Charles Redd Center for Western Studies, Brigham Young University; the Cushwa Center for the Study of American Catholicism Research Travel Grant, University of Notre Dame; the Gerald R. Ford Foundation Research Travel Grant, Gerald R. Ford Library; the Kenneth Spencer Research Library Travel Grant, University of Kansas; and the Lynn E. May, Jr., Study Grant, Southern Baptist Historical Library and Archives. At Princeton, the University Committee on Research in the Humanities and Social Sciences provided two separate research grants for trips to archives in California and Illinois.

For a historian, librarians and archivists are the saints who do God's work. I appreciate the kind assistance I received at the Church History Library of the Church of Jesus Christ of Latter-day Saints; the Harold B. Lee Library at Brigham Young University; the J. Willard Marriott Library at the University of Utah; the Billy Graham Center Archives; Special Collections at Georgetown University; the Southern Baptist Historical Library and Archives; the American Catholic History Research Center and University Archives at the Catholic University of America; the University of Notre Dame Archives; the Archives of the Archdiocese of Chicago; the Spencer Research Library at the University of Kansas; the Bentley Historical Library at the University of Michigan; the Gerald R. Ford Presidential Library; the Jimmy Carter Presidential Library; and the Ronald Reagan Presidential Library. I am indebted to the staffs at all the archives I visited, but Taffey Hall and Bill Sumners at the

SBHLA; Helmi Raaska at the Ford Library; and Rebecca Schulte at the University of Kansas deserve special mention for their indefatigable efforts on my behalf.

In the course of researching this book, I crossed the nation and back, relying in many places on the generous hospitality of friends. Matt and Jenny Timion happily shared their home with me for the two months I spent in Salt Lake City. Kristi and Ed Thomas kindly welcomed me in Atlanta and threw a rousing dinner party that may have not been entirely on behalf of my visit. Jody and Todd Stanley graciously hosted me in Nashville. Jennifer Palmer and Tamar Carroll made my time in Ann Arbor far warmer than the weather allowed. In Chicago, Meghan Donnelly Slocum opened her doors to me not once but twice. Patrick Cooper and Nick Dobelbower hosted me at least as many times in Washington, D.C. And Jason Hamilton and Ben Mandelker took turns letting me crash at their apartments in Los Angeles, both making sure I had fun dinner plans (and a steady stream of LA's best frozen yogurt) awaiting me after a long drive back from the Reagan Library in Simi Valley each day. Along the way, other friends provided me with resting stops and brief excursions from the research trail. Thanks to Ginny and Peter Gentles, Mandy Humphreys, Lynsley Smith, and Ryan Scott for these restorative detours. Ryan's witty emails were welcome distractions from the isolation of research and writing. He has been a constant friend on whom I have depended for nearly twenty years. Drew Stoudt and Yosbel Ibarra have given me use of their guest room in Miami Beach so often that I could probably call it my winter writer's retreat, although the real pleasure of visiting them was that I never seemed to get much work done. Becca Roberson Turett, in her typical caretaking fashion, made sure I remained alert on my drives to the archives, supplying a hearty pile of books-on-CD that kept me awake on long road trips. Shane Dawson gave Molly, my West Highland terrier, all the love and care she needed while I was away from New York. His friendship and support for me during my graduate school years often made the impossible seem achievable.

Invaluable teachers have shaped my intellectual development. I'm not sure there's a finer high school history teacher than the incomparable Renee Bell. Her classroom at Winter Park High School constantly demonstrated how exhilarating the study of American history could be. I am a historian because of the incredible professors I encountered as an undergraduate at Duke University, most especially to Peter Wood, Raymond Gavins, Claudia Koonz, and John H. Thompson, who told me I was "just weird enough" to make it as an academic. Sydney Nathans was a dream advisor for a young student to have. Sydney taught me the art of historical research and the thrill of working in the archives. I still remember how his probing questions about evidence and argumentation during long office visits sharpened my analytical skills and allowed me to see I had the stuff to become a historian. At Columbia, I profited from the mentorship and instruction of Barbara Fields, Eric Foner, Alice Kessler-Harris, and Herb Sloan. Sarah Phillips deepened my thinking with her insightful questions about my dissertation. When I realized, quite unexpectedly, that I wanted to pursue American religious history, Randall Balmer was the best guide anyone could imagine. Courtney Bender helped me see both my academic studies and the world around me with new eyes. Her outstanding course on the sociology of religion transformed my graduate school experience and gave me a new intellectual passion. I am thankful for all the time she spent with me refining my writing and asking me the important questions about my work. Elizabeth Blackmar is a graduate student's hero. Her historiography course shaped how I read and write history, and her excellent scholarship has served as a model for my work. My advisor, Alan Brinkley, believed in this project before I realized it existed. A research paper I wrote under his direction during my first year at Columbia grew into this project, prodded by his enthusiasm and vision. To be regarded so favorably by such an outstanding scholar as Alan both humbled and sustained me as I wrote. I am grateful for his steady encouragements.

At Princeton, I delighted in the incredible community of historians who welcomed me into the profession. I am especially grateful to Kevin Kruse. One could hardly imagine a more kind and exemplary model of what a historian and colleague should be than Kevin. Kevin carefully read my dissertation and more than one version of the book manuscript, greatly improving it with his insightful comments and expert suggestions. Thanks also to Wallace Best, Margot Canaday, Gillian Frank, Hendrik Hartog, Judith Weisenfeld, Sean Wilentz, and Julian Zelizer for commenting on all or portions of this manuscript, and for making my time at Princeton so personally and intellectually rewarding. Sections of this manuscript also benefitted greatly from lively discussions and questions during presentations at Princeton with the Workshop in American Studies, the Religion in the Americas Workshop, and the Center for the Study of Religion. My students at Princeton inspired me with their enthusiasm and boundless inquisitiveness. I am especially grateful for those in my writing seminar whose comments on Chapter 2 greatly strengthened it as they pinpointed and remedied—with trademark undergraduate conviction—a persnickety structural problem. I only wish the semester's schedule had allowed for them to workshop all of the book's chapters. Julia Vill, whose senior thesis I advised, shared with me the thick stacks of original documents she had uncovered while researching the pro-life movement in Minnesota and chatted endlessly with me about the important cast of anti-abortion activists who came out of her home state.

Outside of Princeton, a diverse and accomplished group of scholars provided invaluable feedback for this work at conferences and on other occasions, including Julia Azari, Paul Boyer, Darren Dochuk, R. Marie Griffith, Susan Hartmann, Melani McAlister, Steven P. Miller, Sara M. Patterson, Axel Schäfer, S. J. Thomas, and Daniel K. Williams, and the tremendous participants in the International Colloquium on New Perspectives on American Evangelicalism and the 1960s held at Keele University.

The anonymous reviewers for Oxford University Press have greatly improved the quality of this book with their penetrating comments and clear-sighted suggestions. In light of all this assistance, any errors this book contains are my own. At Oxford, Theo Calderara has been an ideal editor to shepherd a first-time book author. Theo saw the potential in my dissertation, helped me reframe its focus, and guided me through extensive revisions of the manuscript. Thanks also to the production and marketing teams at Oxford—and especially to Marcela Maxfield, who answered every email entreaty with promptness and good humor. My talented sister-in-law, Margo Russell, kindly took my author's photo.

I am fortunate to be too rich in friends to thank all who have so immeasurably added to my life. Even after all these years, my friends faithfully continued to ask about the book's progress and never seemed bothered that they still had to inquire about it. My writing accountability partner, Nicole Hemmer, deserves much of the credit for this book's completion. Daily email check-ins from Niki kept me (mostly) on schedule, and our frequent conversations on everything from modern American conservatism to reality TV always enlightened and entertained me. Her friendship and camaraderie as we both completed our books made all of this much more bearable.

My family strengthens me with their encouragement and love. Leola and Janice Young, my grandmother and aunt, respectively, filled me with home cooking and family love in Memphis before I headed west for my first research trip. I only wish that Grandmother and my other grandparents were still here to see this book in print. I'm not sure I will ever have a more enthusiastic cheerleader than I do in Jackie Hughes. Aunt Jackie provided me with a generous gift that helped purchase the car I drove across the nation and back. Her financial support helped make this book possible, but her love and friendship have sustained me far longer. My sister and brother-in-law, Lee Ann and Boone Fleming, made every trip home to Orlando fun-filled, and they have provided me with one of life's greatest gifts in the births of their children, Reese and Jackson. There's not a role I cherish more than being their uncle. Bob and Mary Young, my parents, have showered me with every advantage in life. Their tales of childhoods in a segregated South instilled in me from my earliest days an interest in the past and confronted me with the historian's task of understanding "change over time" before I even realized it. I am thankful for their unending love and devotion.

This book would not have been possible, or as worthwhile, without the sustaining support of Nate Russell. Nate entered my life just as I was beginning work on my dissertation almost ten years ago. His presence has been felt on every page of every draft; his warmth has infused its every word. Nate has been more than a partner to me, shouldering far more than the equal burden that such a word implies. His constant encouragement and his steadfast enthusiasm for my work lifted me up each day. He never once complained about the heaps of religious ephemera and presidential papers scattered constantly throughout our home. Instead, Nate tiptoed around the piles and enthusiastically cheered each of my own tiny steps forward as I wrote. With our two dogs, Molly and Buddy, Nate has given me the greatest refuge of home and the deepest comfort of a life together. He always believed that this book would be completed. And now it is. This is for you, Nate.

Neil J. Young
New York City, February 2015

We Gather Together

Introduction

For where two or three are gathered in my name, there am I in the midst of them.

MATTHEW 18:20 (King James Version)

That they all may be one; as thou, Father, art in me, and I in thee, that they also may be one in us: that the world may believe that thou has sent me.

JOHN 17:21 (KJV)

Be ye not unequally yoked together with unbelievers: for what fellowship hath righteousness with unrighteousness? and what communion hath light with darkness?

2 CORINTHIANS 6:14 (KJV)

LATE IN 1970, the Interreligious Council of Southern California, a newly formed group of Catholic, Protestant, Orthodox, and Jewish leaders, issued a Thanksgiving proclamation "in the name of the entire organized religious community."[1] Such organizations had been sprouting up since mid-century, a reflection of the era's pluralist values. The newest offering out of Los Angeles had explained itself, in part, as an effort to "join forces in meeting the perils of our time."[2] With a war in Vietnam and a nation erupting over the civil rights movement, those perils seemed profound. Religious leaders also worried about urban poverty, increasing drug use and sexual promiscuity, and the breakdown of the American family. Banding together as a united front against these ills and the growing trend of secularism seemed only logical, but not every Christian supported it. When asked how evangelicals would respond to the Interreligious Council's claim to speak for all of Southern California's religious members, a Methodist leader of the group admitted, "I don't think they'd agree with that."[3] A reporter covering the group noted not only that major evangelical denominations like the Southern Baptist Convention and the Churches of Christ were missing from the organization, but also observed the LDS Church had failed to join up. "Any attempt to say they have 'got it all together,'" the reporter concluded about the organization, "would be misleading."[4]

"Interreligious" and "interfaith" activity reflected the pluralist spirit dominant at mid-century, a civic virtue of religious inclusion and equality that transformed the nation's idea of itself. What had been a "Protestant country" was now "tri-faith America"—the nation of, as a best-selling book of the time had it, *Protestant, Catholic, Jew*.[5] At the same time, these activities were shaped by the ecumenical movement, a theological and organizational cause among Protestant liberals for Christian unity with roots back to the late nineteenth century that had grown particularly strong by the middle of the twentieth century. Conservative Christians—evangelicals, Mormons, and Catholics alike—while often indifferent to pluralism, more strongly rejected ecumenism as an attack on authentic Christianity, grounding their objections in their specific understandings of the faith. In critiquing ecumenism, their beliefs and convictions distinguished them not only from the ecumenical trend but also, given the exclusivist nature of those beliefs, from each other.

While liberal believers sought ecumenism, conservative Catholics, evangelicals, and Mormons countered with internal self-examination, updated apologetics, occasional dialogue, and renewed separatism. They appreciated one another's efforts—they thought it necessary to attack the ecumenical monolith from all sides—but they passed on joining forces. Indeed, since their challenges to ecumenism sprang from their own particular theological claims and traditions, a coordinated religious response was impossible. The impulse to defend a particular theological viewpoint at least affirmed that there was a truth that could be understood and believed, something that seemed all the more urgent in an age of religious pluralism and moral relativism. But it also meant that those competing truth claims had to be reckoned with and vanquished in turn. In the end, Mormon, evangelical, and Catholic anti-ecumenists had to contend with each other's anti-ecumenical arguments and their underlying suppositions as much as liberal ecumenism's. What these conservative Christians were ultimately advancing was what they had always defended: their unique and exclusive conception of the truth and their mutually exclusive claims to the mantle of authentic Christianity.

But as the nation's civic ethos shifted from pluralism to secularism in the 1970s, at least as far as conservative Christians saw it, anti-ecumenists reassessed their relationships with each other, recognizing their shared cultural positions and moral convictions. Separately, conservative evangelicals, Mormons, and Catholics decried the breakdown of the traditional heterosexual family; fretted about changing gender roles and the strength of the women's movement and feminism; denounced sexual permissiveness, abortion liberalization, and the normalizing of homosexuality; and inveighed against government encroachments on individual rights, free enterprise, and religious liberty. In doing so, they again perceived themselves as outsiders fighting the cultural and political consensus. But this political crisis, they reasoned, was different. Because it was not, at heart, a conflict over theology, it allowed for more cooperation among them. In the late 1970s, a band of political actors, including some ministers and religious leaders, worked to unite these disgruntled conservative Christians into a potent political force, a Religious Right for a nation where everything seemed to have gone wrong.

"I am seeking to rally together the people of this country who still believe in decency, the home, the family, morality, the free-enterprise system, and all the great ideals that are the cornerstone of this nation. Against the growing tide of permissiveness and moral decay that is crushing our society, we must make a sacred commitment to God Almighty to turn this nation around immediately," the minister turned political activist Jerry Falwell wrote on the eve of the 1980 election.[6] Falwell, an independent fundamentalist Baptist pastor, sought to do something revolutionary. He claimed he would bring together people of different faiths—evangelical and fundamentalist Protestants, traditionalist Catholics, Mormons, even Orthodox Jews—to attack common political causes. Deeming themselves and their movement "pro-family," in the 1970s Christian conservatives involved themselves in politics, some for the first time. They aimed to fight back against what they saw as an assault on the most basic institution of civilization—the family—and to preserve their belief that America remain a Christian nation against the onslaught of a secular attack. Political observers at the time (and scholars hence) marveled that Falwell and other Religious Right activists had assembled a conservative ecumenical coalition so quickly. But conservative Catholics, Mormons, and evangelicals had been wrestling with questions of Christian unity and interfaith relationships since mid-century. In a secular age, ecumenism might mean something different than it had during the heyday of tri-faith pluralism, these conservative Christians believed. Yet there were still core convictions to be defended, eternal truths that could not be negotiated. Navigating that tricky balance between political opportunity and religious orthodoxy, between political alliance-building and uncompromising evangelistic outreach, proved daunting. Their efforts yielded electoral victories but legislative disappointments, and produced some closer inter-Christian relationships but also hardened religious lines. These developments remade the nation's political and religious terrain and reshaped American society.

This book, which ranges from the 1950s to the present, examines the religious conversation among Mormons, Catholics, and evangelicals about the relationships between and among them, the subject of ecumenism, and the meaning and nature of "true" Christianity. This conversation—always internal, often external, sometimes a dialogue, frequently a debate—both shaped and was shaped by the rise of the Religious Right as an influential force in American politics and society.

Scholars have viewed relations among American religious groups in the twentieth century through the "tri-faith" lens.[7] Much of the focus has been on how liberal ecumenism shaped relations with American Catholicism.[8] Less investigated are conservative Christian responses to ecumenism. Conservative evangelicals, Mormons, and Catholics opposed ecumenism as an unchristian (and sometimes anti-Christian) movement that threatened the ultimate truth and authentic Christian message each tradition argued it alone possessed. My book examines these three groups—these three critics of the ecumenical movement—and replaces the traditional Protestant-Catholic-Jew formulation with an evangelical-Catholic-Mormon focus.[9] These three groups understood the ecumenical movement, rightly, as a fundamental issue of Christianity, one that called into question foundational though contentious matters regarding Christian identity and beliefs, including salvation, scriptural authority and Biblical truth, church governance, and evangelism. It was Catholics, Mormons, and evangelicals who responded to the ecumenical movement with a defense of the Christian faith—a Christian faith, of course, that each made synonymous with their particular and unique theology, traditions, and scriptural interpretations.

It was also Mormons, Catholics, and evangelicals who formed the three main pillars of the Christian Right, a major force in the modern conservative movement and a critical new base for the Republican Party.[10] For more than twenty years now, historians have produced a robust scholarship on the rise of the Christian Right.[11] Despite the diverse titles, a general consensus emerged: that the formation and success, if limited, of the Religious Right depended on the sublimation, abandonment, and erasure of denominational distinctions, historical divisions, theological disputes, and institutional exclusivity among different and historically antagonistic religious groups in pursuit of political victory and the defense of traditional morality and the idea of a Christian nation.

This book complicates that narrative of an easily achieved, harmonious political coalition by stepping back from the "culture wars" of the 1970s,

1980s, and 1990s to examine the longer religious history of interfaith dialogue and relations among evangelicals, the LDS Church, and the Catholic Church since the middle of the twentieth century. Long before Jerry Falwell and other political operatives suggested these religious groups drop their denominational divisions and theological objections to unite against political liberalism, these three faiths had been thinking deeply about each other and the very question of Christian unity. The emergence of the Religious Right was not a brilliant political strategy of compromise and coalition-building hatched on the eve of a history-altering election. Rather, it was the latest iteration of a religious debate that had gone on for decades, sparked by the ecumenical contentions of mainline Protestantism rather than by secular liberal political victories.

Although the Catholic Church had, along with the LDS Church and evangelicals, resisted the ecumenical movement, it softened its anti-ecumenical position with the Second Vatican Council (1962–65). Vatican II also impacted the LDS Church and evangelicals. In seeking to engage and minister to the wider world, the Catholic Church eased its isolationist tendencies and reached out to other religious communities to share in the burdens and battles of a broken world. Since "ecumenical" was the word of the day, it adopted the language to describe these efforts, but the Catholic Church meant something different by it than their liberal Protestant colleagues did. Still, LDS and evangelical leaders lashed out at the church's about-face and stiffened their own anti-ecumenical resolve all the more. They also, evangelicals especially, attributed sinister motivations to the Catholic Church's newfound ecumenical push, a view that was in line with their long history of anti-Catholicism. Catholic ecumenism, they believed, was the latest strategy, now sanctioned and supported by unwitting Protestant ecumenists, to gain complete control of Christendom. Yet even as they decried Vatican II as an act of Catholic aggression, evangelicals acknowledged that it also brought promising reforms, particularly the council's emphasis on the Bible in the life of lay Catholics. From this small but, in evangelicals' estimation, monumental start, evangelicals began in the 1970s to imagine and then tentatively pursue closer connections with some Catholics even as they maintained and refined their critique of the church. Mormons countered that no reform could achieve what the restoration of the gospel through Joseph Smith had accomplished, and LDS leaders mounted another attack on ecumenism, condemning all associational ties even as they found themselves alongside Catholics and evangelicals on the political battlefields of the decade and beyond.

While the ecumenical movement initially appeared ascendant, it actually masked deep problems in mainline Protestantism that were fully exposed by the 1970s. The decline of mainline Protestantism and the rise of nondenominational conservative Christianity altered the American religious landscape and required new ways of understanding interfaith relations. In his landmark book, *The Restructuring of American Religion* (1988), Robert Wuthnow argued that American Christianity had undergone a "restructuring" in the years since World War II. In the 1950s and 1960s, denominational differences within Protestantism became less and less important as signifiers of theological and social divisions. The more important divisions were now *within* rather than *among* denominations, as evidenced by the internal splits and external mergers of various Protestant denominations. Wuthnow contended that this realignment divided Protestantism into two camps: conservative evangelical and liberal mainline. This conservative-liberal divide also affected Protestant relations with non-Protestants, drawing evangelicals closer to Catholic traditionalists and Mormons, on the one hand, and uniting liberal Protestants and Jews on the other.[12]

As outsiders to the mainline Protestant establishment, skeptics of the ecumenical movement (at least, for Catholics, until after Vatican II), and major players in conservative politics, the Catholic Church, the LDS Church, and evangelicals have recognized each other as close neighbors on religious and political terrains since the 1950s. That recognition came with its own set of questions and concerns, as this book demonstrates, but it brought evangelicals, Mormons, and Catholics into conversations with one another about theology and politics that shaped the "restructuring" of American Christianity and influenced the course of American politics and modern conservatism. Usually this meant dialogue rather than multi-party exchange, but even the one-on-one relationship often was shaped and informed by thoughts of the other. Evangelicals and Catholics drew closer, in part, in reaction to the growth of the LDS Church and in response to the theological assertions of Mormonism, particularly its claims to be a branch of Christianity and the divinity of its new scriptures. And when the LDS Church critiqued the Second Vatican Council, it augmented its dismissal of Catholic reform by also rejecting the traditional Protestant interpretation of the Reformation that was so central to evangelical identity and beliefs.

All of this took place alongside and in relation to wider political developments. From the school prayer controversy of the 1960s, to the abortion battles of the 1970s and 1980s, to the religious liberty debates of today, evangelicals, Mormons, and Catholics found common cause and pursued similar ends, sometimes together but more often separately. Historians, however, have highlighted the former at the expense of the latter. The historian Kenneth J. Heineman chastised scholars who have chosen "to ignore theological and cultural divisions among social conservatives and to depict the Religious Right as a monolithic movement."[13] This book aims to rectify that. The Religious Right was no monolith; it was a diverse and intricate network that contained, endured, and suffered internal tensions, denominational divisions, and often competing agendas. While evangelicals, Catholics, and Mormons formed the Religious Right's base, the Religious Right also stood distinct from and sometimes in conflict with the political endeavors and convictions of the Catholic Church, the LDS Church, and influential evangelical leaders and institutions. By placing the Religious Right in the context of the much longer history of relations between these groups, the theological and cultural divisions underlying their political cooperation become clear.

Finally, a word of explanation: As a history of anti-ecumenism, conservative interfaith dialogue, and the rise of the Christian Right, this book examines the three main players in that story—Mormons, evangelicals, and Catholics. In doing so, I am all too aware of noted scholar William R. Hutchison's warning that religious historians not succumb to the futile idea that we can "fit it all in."[14] In writing the history of three religious groups and their interactions with each other, I have selected important moments, institutions, and actors while recognizing that a lot has been left out. Perhaps no task felt more daunting than accounting for American evangelicals, a diverse and wide-ranging group near impossible to qualify.[15] Throughout, I have sought representativeness rather than made any pretense of comprehensiveness. My study draws heavily on evidence from the influential evangelical magazine *Christianity Today*, the powerful Southern Baptist Convention, and the important National Association of Evangelicals, along with leading evangelical figures like Billy Graham, Carl Henry, Francis Schaeffer, and Jerry Falwell. But I have also drawn from smaller evangelical outlets including the Lutheran Church—Missouri Synod, the Evangelical Theological Society, and Wheaton College, and lesser-known evangelical names like Walter Martin and Robert Dugan. While I focus mainly on what Steven Miller has termed "moderate" evangelicals or what Molly Worthen has deemed evangelicalism's "mainstream," I also include discussions of other groups that fall under the evangelical label, like fundamentalists, Pentecostals, and charismatics.[16] I have combed religious publications, denominational archives, parachurch organizational records, and presidential papers to understand evangelicals of all stripes. I have read dozens of sermons from infamous and unknown ministers alike; I have inspected hundreds of letters from their followers; I have skimmed thousands of pages of religious pamphlets and periodicals. All of this is not to provide an exhaustive portrait of American evangelicalism—an impossible task—but rather to sketch some of its major components, historical patterns, and points of convergence, but also its lingering and often intensifying fault lines and divisions. In documenting the instances of unity and divergence within modern evangelicalism, I also refine and complicate the book's larger argument about the shifting relationships of Catholics, Mormons, and evangelicals and the uncertain promises and perils of conservative ecumenism.

****

Given their histories and their deep theological convictions, the possibility of a conservative ecumenism uniting conservative Catholics, Mormons, and evangelicals to affect American culture and politics was an ambitious, though unlikely, prospect. But the Bible—the foundational text they all shared and, as they each believed, the blueprint for the social order—offered them a metaphor of how they might work together, even if there were also scriptural warnings about associating with others, the very admonitions that had shaped their response to the liberal ecumenical movement. "A threefold cord is not easily broken," Ecclesiastes reads.[17] Standing together, bound by a common purpose and shared concerns, Mormons, Catholics, and evangelicals might have become an unbreakable force. But their union more closely resembled a loose braid than the indestructible cord: separate threads brought together in tension, they overlapped in some places and rested closely but independently beside each other in others. At different moments, though, stray strands of that braid slipped away, sometimes in defiance, at other times out of necessity. The braid could allow some of the strands to stray while retaining its own shape, loosening but still holding form. Yet each stray strand carried the potential for an ultimate unraveling. This is the story of that braiding and of its unraveling.

1

That They All May Be One

ONE NIGHT IN late 1953, Billy Graham awoke in the middle of the night with a start. Not wanting to bother his wife sleeping beside him, he retreated to his study where he began to write. There in the darkness, the young revivalist imagined a new light for the world: *Christianity Today*, a magazine for evangelical Christians.

The time was ripe for such an endeavor. The country had found religion. During the Second World War, Americans increasingly sought answers to their most troubling questions about the brutalities of the battlefield and their fears of a maniacal dictator in Germany by turning to the church. Sanctuary pews filled and membership rolls ballooned even more after the war when Americans encountered the new danger of Communist aggression and a Cold War that disturbed any hopes for a return to tranquil peace and good living after the victory in Europe. By 1960, almost 70 percent of Americans belonged to a church—up from 47 percent in 1930.[1] At mid-century, Americans seemed generally like-minded in staving off Communism, atheism, and secularism with a heightened religiosity, and the government rushed to reflect those sentiments in its policies and practices. Congress added "under God" to the Pledge of Allegiance; "In God We Trust" became the country's official motto and a slogan imprinted on its currency. "Our form of government has no sense unless it is founded in a deeply felt religious faith, and I don't care what it is," president-elect Dwight Eisenhower remarked in 1952. "With us of course," Ike continued, "it is the Judeo-Christian concept."[2]

A national religious identity strengthened by government action might strike Americans today as exclusivist and discriminatory, but the Judeo-Christian image expanded mid-century Americans' national conception beyond the long-standing notion of their land as a "Protestant nation," a historical mythology that had abetted all sorts of trials and tragedies in America's short history. This new tolerant ethos prevailed, a powerful cultural disposition that upheld pluralism as among the nation's greatest values. What the historian Kevin Schultz has termed "tri-faith America" then replaced the idea of a national Protestant hegemony. In rebuke of the totalitarianism, fascism, and Communism ravaging other parts of the world, the tri-faith rhetoric granted Catholics, Jews, and Protestants an equal status and stake in American public life and traditions, three pillars upholding the nation. Transcending (or at least sublimating) divisions of race and class, the tri-faith myth organized Americans into three religio-cultural groups and deemed them all equal guardians and inheritors of America's most inclusive and democratic values.[3]

The tri-faith ideal was a totalizing national self-conception fitting everyone into the tripartite model, as Schultz has shown, but that didn't mean all Americans accepted it as a ruling metaphor for the nation or for themselves. Although pluralism didn't erase anti-Catholicism (or any other religious bigotries), it went a long way in permitting greater Catholic cultural, social, and political influence and power in the nation's public life. Still, many Catholic leaders at first hesitated to board the tri-faith bandwagon. Catholic theology and history with their blend of exclusivity and self-protection provided a powerful countervailing force, dulling the gleam of pluralist inclusivism. Mormons, cultivators of their own "peculiarity" and chosenness, bristled at being lumped into the "Protestant" category, a classification that flew in the face of LDS theology and self-identity. Generally skeptical of most trends that originated outside of their purview (liberal Protestants were by and large the architects of the tri-faith outlook), evangelicals saw tri-faith religion for what it was: not religious but cultural—an equalizing social identity for the purpose of national cohesion rather than a hallmark of authentic faith. Already immersed in a decades-long project of self-scrutiny, theological differentiation, and institutional buttressing in response to mainline Protestantism's modernizing, evangelicals rejected the pluralistic vision as a religious smokescreen blurring the nation's descent into secularism.

The civic code of tri-faith pluralism was distinct from but resonant with the religious trend of ecumenism, an organizational, ideological, and theological current gathering momentum in mainline Protestant circles at midcentury. Growing out of joint missionary efforts in the nineteenth and early twentieth centuries with a decidedly evangelical purpose of worldwide conversion, the ecumenical movement soon shifted its zeal for proselytizing to Social Gospel efforts for justice and humanitarian intervention. That focus culminated in the creation of the World Council of Churches (WCC) in 1948, an organization that united more than one hundred churches to bear their prophetic voice on world events, believing a coordinated Christian response had to confront the moral crises of the day.[4] Outside of the WCC, the ecumenical conversation played out in mainline Protestant denominations, religious journals, seminaries, and churches, a wide-ranging movement that ran the gamut from those who cheered interdenominational cooperation to others who prayed for the permanent joining together of one worldwide Christian church.

Heightened religiosity, tri-faith pluralism, and a budding spirit of ecumenism and Christian unity: these were major themes of mid-century American religious life, but many conservative religious Americans rejected (or at least distrusted) these trends, especially the ecumenical movement. Evangelicals from a broad range of denominations and traditions argued that ecumenism prized unity over doctrinal soundness, a prioritization that sacrificed the unique Christian gospel of salvation for a weak and meaningless commitment to harmony and "moral influence." At the same time, some evangelicals at mid-century sought to strengthen their position through their own associational ties, linking together through institutions like the National Association of Evangelicals (NAE) and in the pages of Graham's new magazine, *Christianity Today*, an endeavor launched to challenge the ecumenical movement and confront the nation's shapeless and affected piety with a clear and unflinching expounding of evangelical theology. Other evangelicals, particularly fundamentalists, continued to bang the separatist drum. How evangelicals distinguished these unifying efforts from mainline Protestantism's ecumenical aims informed their theological critique of ecumenism and shaped their relationships with each other and with outsiders.

Conservative Protestants were not alone in resisting ecumenism. Both the Catholic Church and the Church of Jesus Christ of Latter-day Saints strongly opposed the ecumenical movement at mid-century. Within the Catholic Church, some influential voices like John Courtney Murray tried to support ecumenical efforts, but more powerful authorities stanched those developments. Catholics rightly understood that much of the early impetus for ecumenism grew out of Protestant desires to unify against Catholic power. That sentiment of liberal ecumenism was dissipating, softened by the civic value of tri-faith pluralism and, soon, by John F. Kennedy's convincing church-state separation speech (1960) and the reforms of the Second Vatican Council (1962–1965), but Catholics remembered that not that long ago ecumenists had called for a united Protestant front to prevent a Catholic takeover of the nation.[5] With this fresh memory (and a longer anti-ecumenical theological tradition), Catholics understandably continued their inward focus and spurned ecumenism. Similarly, Mormons generally maintained the isolationist spirit that had characterized the church for more than a century. No mid-century Protestant ecumenist made any overture to Mormons, but neither did the LDS Church seek out relationships beyond Mormonism. Yet new developments within the church, particularly the faith's explosive expansion and changing theological beliefs and institutional practices during David O. McKay's presidency, required that Mormonism confront the ecumenical movement.

However much evangelicals, Catholics, and Mormons may have wanted to ignore the ecumenical movement, it was impossible to overlook one of Protestantism's major emphases at the middle of the twentieth century. Given liberal Protestantism's decline since the 1970s, it may be difficult to recall how thoroughly dominant the Protestant establishment once was, even in the ascendant pluralist milieu. Mainline Protestant churches continued to grow, expanding into the rapidly developing American suburbs with the construction of new churches, institutions, and agencies. Thousands of Americans read *The Christian Century* and listened to pastors like Norman Vincent Peale of New York City's Marble Collegiate Church. At the elite stations of the nation—from Congress to the White House, from university campuses to major news organizations—stood white men that most likely belonged to a mainline Protestant congregation and advocated its values. The National Council of Churches and its political and theological liberalism provided the representative voice of Protestantism—and therefore the religious voice of the nation. Groups like the National Association of Evangelicals and the fundamentalist American Council of Christian Churches (ACCC) seemed like cantankerous upstarts, scraping out some hidebound position at the margins.[6]

Consequently, mainline Protestantism's increasing advocacy of ecumenism elicited resistance from evangelicals, Catholics, and Mormons. Evangelicals refused to acquiesce to a liberal monopoly of Protestantism or to allow liberal Protestantism to become the only face of Christianity. Liberals could claim the prestige pulpits of First Presbyterian and First Congregational. They could dominate the denominations and control the seminaries. There were ways to combat these developments, after all, and evangelicals responded by creating their own institutions, schools, and seminaries, splitting orthodox congregations away from liberal churches, and strengthening the evangelical convictions of denominations like the Southern Baptist Convention (SBC) and the Lutheran Church—Missouri Synod. Evangelicals were happy—or at least amenable—to present the gospel from the margins of Protestantism, calling out to those who would accept their message of salvation and truth over the privileged but erroneous liberal theology that occupied center stage. But evangelicals had to maintain that alternative position to dominant liberal Protestantism if they were to offer their distinctive message.

For this reason, they stridently resisted ecumenism, which they believed would absorb and suppress the evangelical witness, paving over meaningful theological differences for the purposes of a meaningless unity.[7]

Mormons and Catholics often saw the ecumenical movement as a strange preoccupation within Protestant circles, and for most of the 1940s and 1950s this was true. Mid-century ecumenism hardly concerned them, and at first Catholics and Mormons did not give it the attention that evangelicals did. Still, the force and visibility of the ecumenical conversation in the 1950s became impossible to ignore. And responding to a major theological argument of the age—one that made claims about the nature of Christianity and the organization of its churches—often proved necessary for both Catholics and Mormons. Obviously, Catholics and Mormons hardly worried about how ecumenism might remake Protestantism, but the theological claims of the movement required some sort of internal response in Catholic and Mormon circles. Lay Catholics and Latter-day Saints heard constantly about the ecumenical movement—it garnered consistent coverage in national media outlets, not just Protestant publications. Leadership in both churches responded accordingly, speaking out against ecumenism and reinforcing the unique claims and the separatist disposition of their faiths. Separately, but with an awareness of each other, Catholics, evangelicals, and Mormons confronted the ecumenical movement, challenged its concept of church unity and moral witness, and asserted their individual accounts of ultimate truth against the broad tenets of ecumenical Christianity. It wouldn't be the last time these three faiths found themselves opposed to a major national development, religious or otherwise. But how evangelicals, Catholics, and Mormons responded to the ecumenical movement and the question of Christian identity and purpose would shape their relationships with one another and their ideas about their place in American public life for the next sixty years.

New Evangelicals and the NAE

Amid the upsurge of mid-century religiosity, the men who founded the National Association of Evangelicals envisioned a "grand strategy" of uniting evangelical forces spread across denominations into an organization that would champion an orthodox biblical message and an active Christian social ethic.[8] The new organization was also a project in self-conscious identity formation and differentiation. By nearly every measure, the men who established the NAE—like Harold Ockenga, pastor of Boston's Park Street Church, and the theologian Carl Henry—were fundamentalists. However, they wanted to drop the term's emotional and historical baggage, so they began calling themselves "New Evangelicals" or "neo-evangelicals" to separate themselves from the separatists—not only in their own minds but, most importantly, in the minds of the American public. The gospel meant "good news," after all, and the neo-evangelicals wanted to present a hopeful and inclusive message to the world.[9] These men had no doubt that their vision represented true Christianity. At the NAE's first convention in 1942, Henry boasted to the crowd gathered in St. Louis, "We unhesitatingly declare that evangelicals have the 'keys of the kingdom.'"[10] Between liberal and fundamentalist Protestantism, the NAE staked out its ground, believing not only truth but also numbers were on its side. "Between these poles of thought . . . is found the great body of evangelicals," the NAE's executive committee explained.[11]

The Federal Council of Churches (FCC) (renamed the National Council of Churches in 1950) represented the liberal corner of Protestantism. Founded in the early years of the twentieth century by Protestant ministers who wanted to unite the mainline denominations, the FCC advocated a program of social activism, liberal theology, and ecumenical conviction.[12] The American Council of Christian Churches, on the other hand, with its biblical orthodoxy and ardent, almost mean-spirited, defense of the faith, had just been created in 1941 by a group of fundamentalists that included the firebrand preacher Carl McIntire of Collingswood, New Jersey, who believed liberalism had thoroughly corrupted the churches. The ACCC banned from its membership any churches that had joined the FCC. Its members came instead from independent churches and small denominations like the Bible Presbyterian Church and the Bible Protestant Church, breakaway sects that had left mainline denominations over theological disagreements and remained mostly cut off from the larger world.[13]

The NAE's founders, working at the same time as the creation of the ACCC but mindful of the FCC's historical legacy, meant to distinguish their group from the exclusivist negativity they believed McIntire's organization generated and the "drift into the sandbars of heterodoxy" they charged the liberal FCC with promoting.[14] Throughout the first decades of the twentieth century, a skirmish within Protestantism drew battle lines between liberal and conservative interpreters of the scriptures. "The Great Apostasy," as the conservative churches likened the developments within liberal and mainline Protestantism, had brought about the "Battle of the Century," as various preachers, churches, and denominations fought over what constituted true Christianity, the church, and the Christian mission on earth.[15] McIntire and his fundamentalist compatriots launched some of the fiercest and ugliest defenses of traditional Christianity—it wasn't beneath McIntire to brand the

Christians working for the FCC as "pagan forces"—but neo-evangelicals wanted to present a more positive protection of the faith that would invite rather than repulse potential converts to conservative Christianity.[16]

The NAE's Statement of Faith, with its insistence on salvation found only in Jesus Christ's atonement and in the infallibility of the divinely inspired Bible, distinguished it from the lenient theology of the FCC that prized ecumenical unity over purity. But the Statement of Faith also affirmed "the spiritual unity of believers," believing the Bible called for true Christians to come together through the fundamental beliefs they held in common rather than endlessly splinter over tiny theological disagreements as fundamentalism seemed to encourage.[17] This expansive yet strict theology attracted a wide range of conservative Protestant denominations and churches to the NAE at its founding. Representing the Reformed, Pentecostal, Holiness, and Free Church traditions, these early members of the NAE demonstrated the vibrant diversity within American evangelicalism at mid-century. While each of them had their own unique worship practices, liturgies, and organizational arrangements, they all shared the basic proposition that what the world needed was the saving grace of Jesus Christ found in the unchanging truth of the Word of God. This loose aligning required orthodoxy only where it mattered and permitted, even encouraged, variance for all the lesser details of belief and practice. The model got off to a slow start. By 1945, only fifteen small denominations participated, giving the group less than 500,000 members—a shadow of the potential fifty denominations with some fifteen million followers that had sent representatives to the group's 1943 constitutional convention in Chicago. By the mid-1950s, the NAE's membership had grown to forty denominations, plus individual church memberships from forty other denominations. Bible colleges, seminaries, youth groups, benevolent societies, and evangelistic organizations also belonged to the NAE, bringing its total membership to over two million.[18]

But other evangelical denominations and fellowships stayed away from the NAE. As if to confirm NAE's ideas about fundamentalists, McIntire forbid any groups belonging to his organization from also joining the NAE, just as he had previously banned them from participating with the liberal FCC. Restorationist churches, like the Churches of Christ and the Independent Churches of Christ, could not abandon their loose fellowship model that prized congregational autonomy for an organization that smacked of denominational trappings. On the other hand, strong evangelical denominations, like the Church of the Nazarene, Lutheran Church—Missouri Synod, and the Southern Baptist Convention, stayed out of the NAE in part as a statement of their own denominational loyalty. The nation's second-largest Protestant denomination at the time with five million members in 1940, the SBC would have been a boon to the fledgling organization. Several prominent Southern Baptist pastors had assisted the group's founding and served as officers of the organization, but Convention leaders saw the NAE as a "northern" organization, making it sufficiently suspect to a denomination still rooted almost entirely in Dixie, not to mention the SBC's tradition of going alone on religious matters. The SBC had its own agencies, publishing enterprises, and an enviable membership roll, plus a fierce denominational allegiance and strong regional identity. The NAE seemed redundant and superfluous to Southern Baptists.[19]

Henry and the NAE's founders had achieved a significant accomplishment through the creation of their organization, a flexible coalition linking a wide range of theologically conservative denominations and churches together on a scale not seen before. Henry's writings had also positioned him at the forefront of evangelical intellectual life. Yet that world remained relatively small even as the larger evangelical movement mushroomed around mid-century. This swelling body of Christians needed direction, especially as many of them found their home denominations sliding into liberalism and ecumenism. *Christianity Today* would step into that void, offering an orthodox yet irenic voice and articulating an evangelical, extra-denominational identity while attacking ecumenism to a massive national audience of conservative Christians.

Evangelical Spiritual Unity and the Case against "Church Unionism"

Billy Graham had big plans for his little magazine. Graham and his neo-evangelical allies welcomed the nation's increased interest in faith, but only so far as it provided a more receptive heart for the evangelical message. Religion alone could not provide the true salve for America's woes, nor could it offer eternal salvation to individuals. Americans needed to encounter the salvific message of the evangelical gospel, not any of the watered-down theology of ecumenical Protestantism, the errant doctrines of Catholicism or, even worse, the heresies of religious cults attracting new members across the country, particularly Mormonism. *Christianity Today*, Graham hoped, would cut through the religious fervor of 1950s America with the authentic message of true Christianity. An early planning document outlining the magazine's editorial objectives listed tackling the "problem of false sects and how to answer their false teachings" and "disclos[ing] the doctrinal fallacies of Roman Catholicism, its political ambitions and its threat to religious freedom."[20] Additionally, though Graham certainly believed that fundamentalist Protestantism spread a biblical message of salvation, he wanted *Christianity Today* to avoid fundamentalism's "strong separatist or negative attitude," as he later recounted.[21]

While Graham expected evangelical denominations to be particularly receptive to his new publication, he also knew that evangelically minded ministers existed throughout mainline Protestant denominations—many of the denominations that had been unwilling to join the NAE. To these he particularly imagined the new magazine offering a biblically oriented base of support as their denominations moved deeper into liberalism. Graham and the magazine's cofounders worried about the state of American seminaries and the young ministers coming out of them. "At the present time," a memorandum written during the magazine's planning stages explained, "the overwhelming majority of theological seminaries are [*sic*] turning out men with an <u>impaired</u> faith in the scriptures and therefore with neither the ability nor the inclination to take the Sword of the Spirit as God would have them use it." A memo sent to possible contributors to the magazine explained that *Christianity Today*'s purpose was "to reach ministers whose theological training has been inadequate, weak, and erroneous. Especially is there a desire to restore their confidence in the Scriptures as the very Word of God."[22] *Christianity Today* would act as a seminary in newsprint, providing a conservative interpretation of scripture for the young ministerial student and the established pastor.

To combat the liberalizing trend in the seminaries, *Christianity Today* would devote itself primarily to defending biblical inerrancy (the idea that the Bible was perfect in its entirety) and plenary inspiration (the belief that every word of the Bible was authored by God). Such doctrines, accepted unquestioningly throughout most of the church's history, had erupted as controversial subjects in the early decades of the twentieth century in light of such events as the Scopes Trial and the embrace of German higher criticism (a method that interpreted the historical context of religious texts) by many Protestant church leaders. Although modernism appeared to be winning the theological battle of the twentieth century, *Christianity Today*'s founders felt that the Cold War 1950s offered a "climate of uncertainty [in] which we may have a strategic opportunity . . . to reorient to Christian compass-bearings." While fears of Communism rushed many Americans back to church pews, Graham and his friends worried about what they would hear inside those walls. "As Protestants," they explained, "we are not today preparing ourselves for the flood of Russian atheistic propaganda that is certain to exercise an enormous influence upon Western Christendom in this generation."

Christianity Today would combat Communism from both within and without American Protestantism.[23] For conservative evangelicals, the ecumenical movement smacked of totalitarian groupthink and an anti-individual agenda that too closely resembled the Communist message, despite the fact that leading ecumenists had championed a united church, in part, as a defense against Communism.[24]

While *Christianity Today*'s organizers wanted to use the magazine's pages to advance evangelicalism's critique of liberal Protestantism, they also intended the publication to continue distinguishing evangelicals from their fundamentalist rivals. During the magazine's planning stages, Marcellus Kik, an associate editor and respected Canadian theologian, wrote to the other organizers that he wanted the magazine's first editions to "show the difference between the evangelical position and that of the fundamentalist. We must hammer at that continually."[25] Liberal Protestants of the time saw evangelicalism and fundamentalism as interchangeable, synonymous terms—names for a retrograde Christianity that clung to tradition and superstition. But evangelicals asserted their differences from fundamentalists so that they might be distinct in Americans' minds—and their own. In delineating themselves from fundamentalists, evangelicals sought to establish their identity in part by ridding themselves of the negative traces of fundamentalism.[26] In positioning themselves between the separatist fundamentalists and the ecumenist liberals, evangelicals advanced a defense of "spiritual unity" that both borrowed from and critiqued the ideas and values of fundamentalism and liberalism.

Carl Henry led the two-pronged assault against fundamentalism and Protestant liberalism. As a convert to evangelical Christianity, Henry offered a compelling biography for the cause. Unlike other leading evangelicals (like Graham) who had grown up in the faith, Henry's religious journey made him a particularly powerful testimony for the evangelical message but also a pointed critic against rival Christian representations. Born in 1913, Henry grew up on Long Island, the son of German immigrant parents who changed their family name from Heinrich during the rabid anti-German years of World War I. The oldest of eight children, Henry received no religious instruction at home from his Roman Catholic mother or his Lutheran father, neither of whom practiced their faiths. Henry's father battled alcoholism throughout his life, and during Prohibition he operated a small distillery out of their home. But Henry heard the gospel at the age of twenty and became a Christian. After his conversion, Henry decided to pursue a new career path. He had already distinguished himself as the nineteen-year-old editor of the *Smithtown Star*, a Long Island weekly newspaper, but now Henry felt called to the ministry, and he wanted to attend a Christian college in preparation. Henry headed west to the suburbs of Chicago, where he enrolled at Wheaton College, long reputed as the "evangelical Harvard." At Wheaton, Henry became close friends with fellow undergraduate Graham as well as Harold Lindsell, who would become an influential evangelical author and also an editor at *Christianity Today* during the 1960s. Gordon Clark, an esteemed philosophy professor and devout Calvinist, made a huge impression on the young student.[27]

After college, Henry earned separate doctorates at Northern Baptist Theological Seminary in Chicago and at Boston University while also helping launch the National Association of Evangelicals in 1942. In 1947, the same year that Henry helped open the evangelical Fuller Theological Seminary in Pasadena, California, with other NAE leaders, Henry published a brief yet influential book, *The Uneasy Conscience of Modern Fundamentalism*, which secured his place as one of America's foremost evangelical thinkers and helped crystallize the neo-evangelical identity.[28] In his book, Henry espoused biblical orthodoxy against modern liberalism while also attacking fundamentalism's abandonment of the culture—a twin barrage that would characterize his lifelong defense of evangelicalism. Both liberalism and fundamentalism harmed the gospel, Henry contended. Liberalism did so by retreating from the authentic and inspired exclusive message of the Bible for the heresies of historicism and scientific rationalism, making mainline Protestantism all the less discernible from the secular world. Fundamentalism, on the other hand, retreated from the world that God had called Christians to engage, taking its saving message from those who most needed to hear it because of some ill-founded notion that it was more important to remain untainted by the world rather than to be a light in the darkness. Evangelicalism, Henry argued in *Uneasy Conscience*, had to stand in the gap—in the world but not of it, as the scriptures prescribed, spreading the gospel truth.[29] In the book's introduction, Harold Ockenga offered a prayer: "May this brief thesis be the harbinger of a new articulation of the growing revolt in evangelical circles on ethical indifferentism. . . . Here then is a healthy antidote to Fundamentalist aloofness in a distraught world."[30]

Henry continued to define evangelicalism against fundamentalism and liberalism in the pages of *Christianity Today*. Tapped by Graham to serve as the magazine's first editor, Henry had been suggested for the position by Graham's father-in-law, L. Nelson Bell, a former medical missionary to China and an influential southern Presbyterian.[31] In just the third issue of the magazine, Henry began a two-part series on the perils of "Independency," meaning fundamentalism, and "Church Unionism," referring to theological liberalism, both of which he characterized as "extremist." This had been a powerful argument justifying the NAE's founding nearly fifteen years before, but the opportunity of a national magazine meant the message could now reach a much larger audience. Church Unionism, characterized by the National Council of Churches (NCC), prioritized ecumenism over doctrinal soundness, Henry charged. Desiring unity rather than theological purity, Henry wrote, the NCC and other advocates of ecumenism "leave to whatever interpretation a particular group . . . may wish to put upon" key creedal beliefs.[32] "The ecumenical movement," Henry underscored in part two of his series, " . . . elevates the doctrine of the unity of the body above every other doctrine. There is a driving emphasis on this unity accompanied by a rather pale and anemic concern for basic Christian doctrine."[33]

On the other hand, fundamentalism turned doctrinal devotion into dogmatism. While Henry and the other editors of *Christianity Today* certainly advocated a defense of the basic doctrines of orthodox Christianity, they believed fundamentalism had "incorporated secondary doctrines into its creeds with an absoluteness that is incredible."[34] The evangelicals of *Christianity Today* did not have a theological disagreement with fundamentalism, as much as an organizational and temperamental critique. Evangelicals disparaged the separatist outcome of fundamentalism's use of theology rather than the theology itself since it closely resembled their own. "Independency tends to produce a divisive spirit," Henry explained, "It refuses to cooperate even with those with whom it is in essential theological agreement. . . . The movement sometimes arrogates to itself judgment belonging to God." Fundamentalism, while theologically sound, was organizationally heretical. "True believers," Henry lamented, "are separated one from another" by the divisiveness that fundamentalism encouraged.[35] Henry desired a pan-evangelical association that would sublimate denominational and doctrinal distinctions in favor of a unity built on shared belief in the basic Christian gospel message, but fundamentalism obsessed over the tiny theological details and championed splintering and independency as a sign of the true faith itself.

Liberal ecumenism, on the other hand, demonstrated no discrimination, opening itself to any groups with seeming disregard for actual beliefs. "They regard outsiders as members of the body," Henry wrote of liberal ecumenicists, including ". . . . some whose lack of adequate credentials ought to exclude them from an apostolic fellowship." Yet Henry pointed out that this apparent tolerance masked ecumenism's true intolerance of conservative orthodoxy. "Ecumenicity," Henry wrote, "tends to be just as intolerant as Independency, although this intolerance is expressed in a somewhat different fashion. Whereas Independency draws narrow lines, defining beliefs in such a detailed and technical fashion that it rules out many, ecumenicity also draws lines which are narrow and intolerant." Ecumenicists were really hypocrites, Henry reasoned, because they demanded that conservative Protestants drop their exclusive theology in order to fit into the ecumenical mold. For Henry, the Catholic Church posed as a menacing example of ecumenism's absolute aims. "The concentration of power in the hands of the few is a corrupting device," Henry warned. Ecumenicity's "ultimate form is the pope of Rome, or another pope like him."[36]

Christianity Today positioned evangelicalism as the true form of Christianity by contrasting it to liberal Protestantism's departure from theological orthodoxy, and by characterizing fundamentalism as a historical invention rooted in a particular moment, whereas evangelical Christianity's lineage extended back via the Reformation to the Apostolic Church of the New Testament. Fundamentalism's most "serious deficiency" was "its departure from the New Testament theology of the Church. If anything is clear in the New Testament, it is the teaching of the unity of the true body of Christ. A transcendental outlook detaches Independency from the present historical scene in relation to the heavenly and otherworldly side of life. This detachment produces more and more fragmentation, and encourages militant opposition to efforts looking toward an undivided Church."[37] While liberal ecumenism dismissed the exclusive message of salvation and atonement through Christ's crucifixion and resurrection, fundamentalism departed from the biblical injunction of unity among all true believers. Both, in other words, were historic aberrations of Christ's church. "If modernism stands discredited as a perversion of the scriptural theology," Henry explained in another editorial in the summer of 1957, "certainly fundamentalism in this contemporary expression stands discredited as a perversion of the biblical spirit."[38] "True biblical Independency," Henry reminded his readers, "is essentially a group enterprise, banding together men of like mind and spirit for the preservation of what they believe to be true."[39]

This was the delicate balance of independency and spiritual unity evangelicals sought to achieve at mid-century. Throughout the 1940s, 1950s, and 1960s, parachurch organizations like the National Association of Evangelicals and *Christianity Today*, along with other groups like the Billy Graham Evangelistic Association, Youth for Christ, and Bill Bright's Campus Crusade for Christ, shared—and to some extent even surpassed—the influence of denominations in the lives of conservative Protestants, augmenting and articulating an evangelical identity and establishing an institutional network while resisting ecumenical invitations. Through these organizations and publications, and through Billy Graham's revivals in overflowing stadiums and religious broadcasts like Charles Fuller's *Old-Fashioned Revival Hour*, millions of Americans came to understand what it meant to be a Christian outside of any denominational identity. They had learned that they were sinners; that Jesus had died for their sins; and that forgiveness and eternal life came through asking Jesus into their hearts—by becoming "born again."[40] They also understood that this was not a private, personal experience, but a message that they were called to share with others. Through Graham's sermons, the articles in *Christianity Today*, and the books coming out of evangelical presses like Zondervan and William B. Eerdmans, they learned that the Bible was God's perfect and true Word that they must study daily in order to apply its truth to their lives and to make sense of the world around them. Many of them recognized themselves as evangelicals, but more of them simply called themselves "Christians." Because of this, they were less committed to the denominations they might have been raised in and more compelled to the evangelical message they found in various churches and organizations.

Importantly, evangelical leaders advanced arguments about "spiritual unity" rather than, as ecumenists spoke of, the "unity of Christians"—an important distinction at mid-century for the way it advocated evangelical identity and independency while also rejecting ecumenism. Spiritual unity purposefully implied a singular theological conception of Christianity—the distinct and exact theology of evangelicalism. Unity of Christians, on the other hand, could connote the unification of all types of the faithful. This was no doubt a pluralist vision, enshrined in the Constitution, rooted in the nation's self-conception, and in some ways rearticulated by the ecumenical movement, but it was unequivocally at odds with the evangelical postulation of true Christianity. This theological commonality of mid-century evangelicalism helped stitch together a loose but powerful interdenominational alliance, but that alliance constantly asserted its spiritual unity among institutional diversity as an explicit rebuke of the growing ecumenical movement. In doing so, evangelicals found some of their strongest anti-ecumenical allies among the non-Protestant Christian faiths they criticized even more often than they did among their liberal Protestant brethren.

The "True Church," the "Only True Religion," and Catholic Anti-Ecumenism

American Catholics stood at a crossroads in the 1950s, with many advantages opening up alongside persistent challenges. Within the faith, promising signs emerged. The church showed no shortage of workers, as men and women accepted the call to religious service in abundance. Parochial schools and other church institutions like hospitals, seminaries, and universities all experienced record growth. Catholic publications provided a rich theological and intellectual space to showcase various perspectives within the church. During the first half of the twentieth century, Catholics increasingly had entered political office at the local, state, and federal levels. Like other white Americans, American Catholics profited from the economic boom of the post–World War II years that brought with it rising educational achievements, income levels, and socioeconomic standing. This increasing prosperity, and with it the move to the suburbs typical of aspirational whites of the time, helped many Catholics distance themselves from their immigrant, ghettoized past. And Catholic families continued to expand their church through bountiful reproduction, an act now supported not only by Catholic teaching but also by the aggressive pronatalism of the Cold War years.[41] By 1960, the Catholic Church counted over forty million members in America, representing nearly a quarter of the country's population and making Catholicism by far the largest faith in the nation.

As hopeful as these signs appeared within the parish walls, American Catholicism still occupied a tentative position in the nation at large. Though no longer victims of the violence and unbridled hatred that so many of their nineteenth-century forerunners had endured, American Catholics in the 1950s still suffered numerous slights and indignities from their Protestant counterparts. Will Herberg's landmark sociological study, *Protestant, Catholic, Jew,* had found that of the three titular groups, Catholics demonstrated the most homogeneity: clustering in northeastern urban centers, supporting the Democratic Party, and attending Catholic schools, all of which constituted a "self-contained Catholic world."[42] This seeming uniformity, the historian Patrick Allitt has noted, only bolstered anti-Catholic sentiments and provided fodder for works like Paul Blanshard's *American Freedom and Catholic Power,* written in 1949.[43] Blanshard depicted a people brainwashed by their leader in Rome and unable to ever display full loyalty to the United States because of their higher fealty to the church hierarchy. "The Catholic problem," Blanshard gloomily wrote, "is still with us."[44]

Despite some negative reviews, Blanshard's book benefited from an anti-Catholicism still common enough in 1950s America, even as the tri-faith model was taking hold.[45] Forty thousand copies sold within the first three months of its publication, and the Book of the Month Club blessed it with a recommendation.[46] Blanshard's book remained on the *New York Times'* best-seller list for seven months.[47] *The Christian Century* praised Blanshard for striking "valiant blows in defense of that heritage of liberty," but thought Blanshard had overemphasized the distinction between the Catholic faith and the church policies espoused by its leaders. "The distinction is well meant and wisely made, but it cannot be applied rigidly," *Christian Century* argued, "The Roman Catholic doctrine of the church, culminating in papal infallibility, is inseparable from politics and secular society." Church policies that insisted on state support and enforcement of doctrine "are not incidental characteristics," but rather "*are* Roman Catholicism—not its accidents but its essence."[48] A reviewer for the *Christian Science Monitor* found the book "measured, coolly reasoned, and backed by a broad range of careful, scholarly research." "The effects of this book are likely to be historic," the review concluded.[49]

Given the response to *American Freedom and Catholic Power* plus a lingering, if now merely smoldering, anti-Catholic attitude, most Catholics, priests and laypersons alike, remained inwardly focused during the 1950s, finding comfort and consolation within the Catholic Church and community. Official Catholic doctrine also did little to encourage outward focus or close ties between church members and non-Catholics. The Vatican still taught that salvation came only through the Catholic Church, church law continued to bar Catholics from attending religious services at non-Catholic churches, and Catholic clergy generally turned down invitations to appear alongside Protestant ministers at community events or public talks to avoid any suggestion that the Catholic Church regarded other faiths as its equal. Some Catholic leaders, like John Ford and Joseph Fenton, even went so far to suggest that the Constitution's religious protections found in the First Amendment might be denied to non-Catholics if Catholics ever became the majority.[50] Such moves hardly encouraged warm Catholic-Protestant relations, but they were consistent with over four hundred years of Catholic isolationist policies, reflected the exclusive claims of Catholic theology, and revealed the lingering consequences of American anti-Catholicism.

Still, Catholic leaders often wanted to keep abreast of developments within American Protestantism, but often that desire served to reconfirm Catholic suspicions of their fellow Christians. Following the announcement of a new magazine for evangelicals, the National Catholic Welfare Conference (NCWC) suggested the editors of various Catholic publications subscribe to *Christianity Today* "as a responsible Protestant magazine," but they quickly regretted the endorsement. "The early issues . . . were read with much interest," Rev. John Kelly, director of the NCWC, wrote to *Christianity Today*'s editors. "It was, therefore, quite a surprise to us, to read in later issues irresponsible statements on Catholic teaching and practices." By the time of Kelly's letters, only a few issues had even been published, but the damage had been done. In just *Christianity Today*'s eighth issue, C. Stanley Lowell, associate director of

Protestants and Other Americans United for Separation of Church and State (POAU), warned against the population of thirty-three million Catholics in the United States, "which has become in the hands of the hierarchy a gigantic battering ram to breach the wall of separation." "If the Protestants do not unite in determined opposition to this drive," Lowell ominously concluded, "another decade will see the end of Church-State separation here." Rev. Kelly cited this article and also advertisements in the magazine from Christ's Mission, an evangelical ministry for ex-Catholic priests, in his letter to the editors, explaining that if such trends continued, the NCWC would retract its endorsement.[51]

In a series of letters to Kelly, Carl Henry explained that *Christianity Today* had no "anti-Catholic bias," but that it would "touch points of disagreement with Roman Catholicism either in the sphere of doctrine or practice." Readers of the magazine had submitted "constant inquiries" about Catholic theology, policies, and events in the news, Henry explained, and the editors felt responsible for accurately responding. "Be assured again that our perspective is not anti-Catholic," Henry wrote to Kelly, "We have not criticized Catholicism any more vigorously than we have criticized Protestantism, and we have sought to preserve that criticism on the plane of principle and to guard it from any deterioration to the point of bias." Henry shared the correspondence from Kelly with Lowell, who responded he had "never before witnessed an overt attempt by the hierarchy to censor a Protestant publication."[52]

Whatever détente Catholic leaders imagined *Christianity Today* had promised quickly evaporated in a round of critical articles about Catholicism in the magazine's first full year of production. One writer described the Catholic Church's "political aims and ambitions" as "no less total and arrogant than are those of Communism," a scathing indictment at the height of the Cold War, but a perspective that Carl Henry and NAE leaders had endorsed fifteen years earlier. "It must always be remembered," the article continued, "that the only effective safeguard against the domination of Darkness, whether civil or ecclesiastical or both, is the promotion of that vital evangelical religion whereby men's hearts and minds are enlightened and liberated by obedience to the Word of God."[53]

The following summer, the Catholic Church launched a punch at Billy Graham. The evangelist opened a six-week revival in New York City in May, but with packed crowds at the nightly Madison Square Garden services, Graham soon extended the revival until Labor Day. By summer's end, more than two million New Yorkers had listened to Graham at the Garden or at outdoor revivals he conducted in Times Square and Yankee Stadium. Millions more throughout the country watched the revival on ABC's weekly telecasts. After the crusade's first night, the *New York Times* provided two full pages of coverage including a complete transcript of Graham's sermon.[54] The front page article in the *Times*, "Billy Graham Opens His Crusade Here," carried a large photograph of the event. Graham, his back to the camera, stood at the stage's edge, his arms raised, as he so often did when he preached, to emphasize an important point. Before him, and taking up most of the photograph, stretched the massive audience of 18,500 listeners.[55] It was a scene that would be repeated in New York throughout the summer of 1957.

In anticipation of those crowds, the Catholic Church had prohibited its members from attending or listening to the revival. Before the revival began, New York's archdiocese commanded its priests to deliver a nine-sermon series on basic Catholic doctrine to counter Graham's evangelical message. The Catholic sermons stressed that Christianity did not mean merely finding a relationship with God or joining any available church, but adhering to right doctrine contained in Catholicism's historic creeds and interpreted by its authorities.[56] Rev. John Kelly, the recent combatant of *Christianity Today*, labeled Graham a "danger to the faith of all who listen to him," calling his teachings "false" and "incomplete." Kelly forbade Catholics to attend the revival, listen to the services on radio or television, or to read any of his sermons or books. *Christianity Today* reckoned that Kelly's denunciation of the revival "must be considered the most complimentary . . . on the record."[57] But as the summer revival wore on, the magazine fretted there was "little doubt but that America is gradually becoming a Roman Catholic country. This is not surprising, however, for the strategies of Rome give her considerable earthly advantage." In contrast to Graham, who offered the simple Christian message to his audience, "The Pope must look to his legions because he can no longer look to the gospel." "The Roman Catholic Church *will* continue to grow," the magazine predicted, "She will infiltrate government, education, and labor. But let us not fear. Rome *has* her limits. The Lord says to worldly wisdom, as he says to the tides of the sea, 'Thus far shall you go, and no farther.' Rome can coerce the film industry to use priests and Christopher medals in movie plots; she can lobby senators with effective cunning; and she can rule over the treasuries of the world. But these are strategies of worldly wisdom. They have *nothing* to do with the gospel. . . . Rome is a genius in worldly wisdom. But worldly wisdom is one thing, the gospel is another." "If we honor the Word of God," *Christianity Today* promised, "we have no reason to fear Roman Catholicism. . . . The Pope will continue to look to his legions. But let us look to the power of the gospel."[58]

Given these exchanges with both mainline and evangelical Protestants, the Catholic Church maintained its opposition to the burgeoning ecumenical movement throughout the 1950s. Before the decade began, the convening of the WCC in Amsterdam in 1948 allowed the church to make its anti-ecumenical position clearly known. The WCC brought together 148 churches, mostly Protestant along with a few Eastern Orthodox churches, in a global association for Christian unity, but Rome had prohibited any Catholics from attending. A year later, the Vatican issued an "Instruction" on ecumenism that eased some of its restrictions, encouraging ecumenical work from its bishops but requiring that it only take place within the Catholic Church. Participation in ecumenical conferences and meetings remained forbidden. While the "Instruction" had encouraged bishops to engage in what it called "reunion work," American Catholics largely read the document as a continuation of the church's ban on ecumenical endeavors. (American Protestants, on the other hand, largely interpreted "reunion work" as calling for their churches to submit themselves to Rome.) When the WCC gathered for its second meeting in Evanston, Illinois, in 1954, no Catholics attended. A pastoral letter from Chicago's Cardinal Samuel Stritch had made it clear that Catholic bishops were to avoid the assembly. He even went so far as to prohibit priests from attending as reporters.[59]

Though most Catholic bishops and priests ignored the ecumenical movement, a few Catholics, most notably the Jesuit scholar John Courtney Murray, sought a different relationship for the Catholic Church and the nation by advocating interfaith partnerships and articulating a complimentary association between Catholic theology and American Constitutionalism. Murray had been born in 1904 on Manhattan's 19th Street. At the young age of sixteen he joined the Jesuits, remaining until his death in 1967. In the late 1930s, Murray had accepted a position at the Catholic seminary in Woodstock, Maryland, where he served out his professional career. Though based in a rural college town, Murray preferred the excitement of big cities like Washington, D.C., and New York, where he frequently traveled for meetings and conferences. Two of Murray's closest friends, *Time* magazine cofounder Henry Luce and his socialite, eventual Catholic-convert wife, Clare Boothe Luce, represented the urbane sophistication Murray enjoyed cultivating throughout his life. (Luce would put Murray on the cover of his magazine in 1960—a rare spot for a Catholic theologian.)[60] At one point, Murray reportedly described the Jesuit vow of poverty as "less a sacred promise than a regrettable fact."[61]

Perhaps it was Murray's personal interactions with a life beyond the Jesuitical seminary that fostered his desire to rethink church teaching on Catholic engagement with the American nation and the larger Christian community.

But for all of Murray's worldly delights, particularly golf and cocktails, he was certainly no secularist. Indeed, it was likely his own involvement in public life that exposed him to national developments he found particularly troubling. Murray worried that America was stumbling deeper into secularism, and he charged that the Supreme Court was hastening this development with decisions like *Everson v. Board of Education* (1947) and *McCollum v. Board of Education* (1948) that concerned religion and public education. These decisions, in the words of the majority opinion for McCollum, affirmed that the First Amendment "had erected a wall of separation between Church and State."[62] By not supporting religion, the court had not only misinterpreted Jefferson's famous phrase, Murray argued, but also thrown its support to the forces of secularism. The court had not established neutrality, as advocates of church-state separation now contended, but instead had thrown the balance "to the subsidization of secularism, as the one national religion and culture, whose agent of propagation is the secularized public school."[63] In Murray's view, the wall of separation had meant that government would endorse no religion over another, but the court's decisions signaled that the government would now privilege—and finance—non-religion over all religions.

In light of such court decisions and Cold War fears about an attack on religion launched by Soviets abroad and liberals at home, Murray recommended that Catholics band with like-minded Protestants to defend religion's place in the public square. When compared to the growing threat of secular humanism, Murray explained in 1949, "I consider [the] Catholic-Protestant polemic to be an irrelevance."[64] The Catholic Church disagreed. The warning from the Holy Office in 1948 against attending the WCC meeting followed by the "Instruction" the following year both regarded ecumenism negatively. *Humani Generis*, an encyclical released in 1950, added to the church's disapprovals of Catholics working with those outside the church.[65] The encyclical, describing itself as "concerning some false opinions threatening to undermine the foundations of Catholic doctrine," lamented the fact of "principles of Christian culture being attacked on all sides," but this sad state still could not justify the Catholic Church weakening its witness through associations with other churches. The ecumenical movement was a "danger . . . which is all the more serious because it is more concealed beneath the mask of virtue." Those who advocated ecumenism as a way of "joining forces to repel the attacks of atheism" also intended to remove those barriers that challenged their irenic project. Ecumenism would require "dogmatic relativism" at the same time as it denied the "Teaching Authority" of the Catholic Church. The Catholic Church's historic critique of Protestantism thus merged with its developing rationale against ecumenism: the more ecumenists downplayed institutional authority—namely the Catholic claim of being the "true church"—for the nebulous goal of Christian unity, "the more severely do they spurn the teaching office of the Church, which has been instituted by Christ."[66] Ecumenism undermined the saving message that the Catholic Church alone offered.

Closer to Murray, the American priests Joseph Fenton and Francis Connell, both of the Catholic University of America, used the pages of the *American Ecclesiastical Review* to attack Murray's proposal for Catholic ecumenical engagement in the early 1950s. Whereas Murray saw ecumenism as a solution to the growing secularism of the age, Fenton and Connell believed it to be a symptom of that threat. Catholics, especially the professional middle class, had moved too far away from the healthy isolationism of the immigrant, ghettoized faith, Fenton and Connell contended. Enjoying economic prosperity and professional mobility, these Catholics had lessened their devotion to the church, moved into Protestant-majority suburbs, and even sent their children to non-Catholic schools. In such a setting, further encouragement of ecumenical relations with Catholics needed to be quashed lest Catholics come to believe that different faiths had equal access to ultimate truth.[67]

Fenton and Connell's vigilant war against indifferentism—the idea that religious differences have little or no importance—represented an ardent defense of Catholicism's exclusive truth claim. Worried that Murray's ideas diminished Catholic exceptionalism, Fenton and Connell blasted the Jesuit for his promotion of ecumenism throughout the 1940s and 1950s. Writing in the *American Ecclesiastical Review,* Fenton reminded Murray of "the truth that societies as well as individual men are obligated to worship God according to the directions of the true religion, and the no less important truth that Catholicism is the only true religion."[68] But Murray was no Catholic indifferentist, even if Fenton and Connell suspected so. In fact, Murray continually affirmed a rather narrow conception of ecumenism—what two historians have characterized as "strategic ecumenism."[69] In his public and private writings, Murray consistently limited ecumenism to the joint political demonstration of Protestants and Catholics in affirming the nation's Christian tradition and the general advocacy of religious faith against the secularist tide. But Murray made just as clear his opposition to ecumenical dialogue on theological issues, calling it an impossible prospect given Protestantism's rebellion from Rome and its disagreement on basic doctrines.[70] Writing to a Rochester housewife in 1956, Murray made clear that his ecumenical openness still retained Catholic exclusivism: "We must keep distinct the precept of 'love thy neighbor' from the quite different question, which is the true Church of Christ? We are indeed bound to love all men, not least those whom we believe to be in error with regard to the nature of the Church. At the same time, we must be careful to state . . . the theological truths about our Church."[71]

While Murray's views of ecumenism received little support among his Catholic cohorts at the time, his larger writings on religion and the American state provided him both with a censure and, later, an ultimate vindication. Again, Murray saw in rising secularism the impetus for rethinking Catholic teaching about religious freedom and church-state separation.[72] From his perch as editor of the scholarly journal *Theological Studies* and from his frequent pieces in the Jesuit magazine *America*, Murray hammered out a defense of religious liberty on the basis that it preserved the only true guard against secularism, as religion would flourish in a free marketplace. Murray, as many conservative Protestants did, feared an overbearing state that would either coerce a particular religious devotion or forbid any faith expressions. Of course, Protestants feared that not only an atheistic state posed this threat but also the Catholic Church, and Catholic authorities did little to assuage such fears as they denounced Murray for his support of religious liberty. By the mid-1950s his Jesuit superiors in the United States and Rome believed he had gone too far in his critiques of the church. They censured Murray and ordered him to stop writing on religious freedom and church-state relations.[73] Dutifully, but with sadness, Murray obliged, turning his writing to other topics, but Murray had not been silenced forever. In the end, his ideas would prove triumphant.[74]

Prophet David O. McKay and Mormon Anti-Ecumenism

David O. McKay, like many prominent Mormons, could trace his family history back to some of the LDS Church's earliest years. Both sets of grandparents had been converted in 1850 and left their homes in the Scottish highlands and in South Wales, respectively, settling among the Saints in Utah. Thousands of Mormon converts who learned of Joseph Smith's restored gospel from missionaries made the same journey from the British Isles and from Scandinavia, crossing the Atlantic Ocean and then joining the thickening caravan trail of American Mormons heading westward. In Utah, McKay's grandparents worked alongside other Saints, building God's kingdom on earth that they called Zion. There were often tough years of famine and drought—building paradise in a great desert proved no easy task—and violent clashes with non-Mormons and federal officials frequently disrupted the idyll, but the Mormons were a resilient and industrious people and they clung to their faith and to each other as they struggled to build their Eden.[75]

McKay had trained to be a teacher at the University of Utah where he played on the school's first football team, served as class president, and graduated as the Class of 1897's valedictorian. He worked in education for a few years, but in 1906 at the age of thirty-two he received a life-changing call from LDS headquarters to join the Quorum of the Twelve Apostles, the dozen men who help run the church and report to the First Presidency, the three highest leaders in Mormonism. At the time, McKay was the youngest man in the Twelve. However, in 1951 upon the death of LDS Church President George Albert Smith, McKay was the longest-serving apostle in the Quorum. Mormon tradition meant McKay's seniority made him the next LDS president. After meeting for prayer and reflection around the blue altar in the Salt Lake Temple, the apostles unanimously sustained McKay as the new leader of the LDS Church.[76]

McKay would soon turn seventy-eight years old, but his promotion to the head of the LDS Church meant that his busiest days were ahead of him. He embraced them with gusto. Rising at 4:30 each morning, McKay was often busily working at his desk before six o'clock, his car usually the first one in the church parking lot. McKay's biographers correctly credit him with bringing about the rise of modern Mormonism—transforming the LDS Church from a regional sect into an international religion—and this depended as much on institution building as it did on any theological reform.[77] When McKay assumed the LDS presidency in 1951, Mormonism remained a highly centralized religion, dominating its historic base in Utah and the wider Intermountain Region. Missionaries had converted thousands to the LDS faith, but church teaching up through the early twentieth century encouraged converts to move to Utah. In the 1920s, the church changed course, urging new members to remain in their homelands and build up the LDS Church around the globe. On this thin global network, McKay transformed the LDS Church into an international phenomenon. He increased missionary efforts and poured money into church construction abroad. The efforts proved fruitful. During McKay's presidency, LDS church membership almost tripled from 1.1 million Mormons in 1951 to nearly 3 million by the time of his death in 1970.[78] Thirty percent of that expansion had come from missionary work, with particular growth in Latin America and Asia.[79]

The missionary emphasis and successes during the McKay years not only strengthened Mormonism but also negated some of ecumenism's own justifications at the time. Protestant ecumenists often pointed to the challenges and setbacks of the mission field as a reason for uniting. Mission work for mainline Protestants at mid-century had in many ways become the work of humanitarian aid rather than salvation.[80] How much more efficient and successful might they be, ecumenists contended, if they coordinated their efforts and combined their resources? What was the purpose of denominational missions when you were trying to improve the material lives of others rather than convert them to a particular form of Christianity? But LDS missionaries traveled the globe to bring people into the faith. The mission field was not an opportunity for service (though the LDS Church deeply engaged in humanitarian work as well) but a competition for souls. "There must surely be something distinctive to justify their presence in all parts of the world," McKay explained of his Mormon missionaries.[81] In countries where Protestantism or Catholicism reigned, Mormon missionaries brought those Christians Christ's restored church. Where Christianity had not taken hold, LDS sought to convert others to Mormonism before they could become Catholics or Protestants. Mormon missionary work's booming success in the 1950s and 1960s further strengthened the church's claims about its exclusive message. Thousands were accepting the unique Mormon message. Their very numbers demonstrated Mormon ascendancy and vitality even as some ecumenists recommended Christian unity to combat the stagnancy in many denominations. Other Christians had to advocate ecumenism, Mormons argued, because they lacked the potency that came with being Christ's one church on earth. Unity was merely a way of keeping a dying patient alive.

While the successes of the LDS Church under McKay helped stave off the ecumenical threat, McKay also transformed Mormonism's image. For one, he looked much different than his presidential predecessors, all of whom, dating back to the second LDS president Brigham Young, had worn heavy beards, stern expressions, and dark suits. McKay was beardless and a broad smile typically covered his face. A shock of white hair atop his head only added to his already tall stature, and McKay's habit of wearing double-breasted white suits with matching white shoes gave him an almost heavenly appearance. Most of McKay's predecessors had come from polygamous households. McKay's father, however, had taken only one wife even though they had married far before the LDS Church renounced polygamy in 1890, so McKay lacked the familial baggage that had inhibited previous presidents' ability to present a new image of Mormonism to the world. If nineteenth-century Mormonism had conjured up images of deviant lifestyles and controlling authorities to its critics, McKay's church exceedingly stressed free agency and individual autonomy, though at times these remained more wishful dreams than lived realities.[82]

Perhaps the most significant though underappreciated transformation during McKay's tenure concerned the status of the presidency itself. As Mormonism grew from its Utah base, church leaders worried about how closely

Mormons remained obedient to the church's directives. What was needed, they decided, was a return to the days of the pre-Utah statehood LDS Church, when Mormon officials led a theocracy of spiritual and political power over their followers. This could be accomplished again, it was determined, by altering Mormon perceptions of the church president. Beginning in the 1960s, the LDS Church began to encourage among its members an adoration of the church's hierarchy and, most importantly, an understanding of the church president's prophetic status.

Faithful Mormons have not always seen their president as a prophet. Before 1955, every mention of the Mormon leader in the church's *Deseret News* articles referred to him as "President." The honorific "Prophet" was reserved only for Joseph Smith, the founder of the LDS Church in 1830, and prophets from the Bible and the Book of Mormon. Then, during the presidency of David O. McKay, church publications began to refer occasionally to President McKay as "Prophet." By the late 1960s, "President" had become interchangeable, if not synonymous, with "Prophet," thanks to routine references to the latter in both church publications and at General Conferences, the semi-annual church conventions held each April and October. In the *Church News* section of the *Deseret News*, headlines like, "Honors For a Prophet" and "The Beloved Prophet, Seer, and Revelator," increasingly ran above articles about McKay.[83] (This trend dramatically increased in the three years following McKay's death when from 1970 to 1973 three different men assumed the LDS presidency. In stressing the prophetic status of each man, the church seized the opportunity to recast a rocky institutional period instead as a stable, divinely appointed succession of authority.)[84]

The espousal of McKay's prophetic status represented the most significant development of his presidency, and it had enormous theological, institutional, and political consequences for Mormonism. It also entailed a rewriting of history, as the prophetic status now given to McKay was also bestowed on all of his predecessors. The LDS Church, Mormons now understood, had always been led by prophets. Additionally, the prophetic emphasis shaped Mormon attitudes and actions concerning ecumenism. To be led by an active Prophet of God rather than simply an administrative head heightened the exclusivity of Mormonism and mitigated any ecumenical impulses. As thoroughly as McKay helped modernize Mormonism's image and its institutional practices, he equally resisted the ecumenical urge exciting so many other religious leaders of his era. Generally, the LDS Church ignored the ecumenical discussion taking place predominately in Protestant denominations, churches, and seminaries, perceiving it as an issue that did not concern Mormonism. The ecumenical movement made no direct overtures to the LDS faith for unity—most Protestants across the theological spectrum still did not believe Mormonism was part of the Christian faith so there was no reason to seek its association. Yet the issue of ecumenism contained implications that the LDS Church could not entirely ignore. If ecumenism sought to unite or at least build stronger connections among Christians, did Mormons have no interest in that endeavor? Considering that some of its advocates often justified ecumenical efforts on the basis of opposing Communism—something LDS leaders, particularly McKay, vigorously and frequently attacked—how could Mormons ignore the invitation to participate in a broad Christian coalition against its evils? More generally, what did the church want its members to know about this movement and how did its goal of unity square with Mormonism's theological exclusivity?

Church talks and publications seldom directly addressed the ecumenical movement; the frequent emphasis on the LDS Church's status as the "one true church" during the McKay era provided an implicit rebuke to ecumenism. The LDS Church alone was Christ's restored church on earth, Mormons were reminded. Joseph Smith had brought that restoration about when as a young boy confused by the various churches seeking adherents in his hometown, he asked God which one to join. "None of them, for they were all wrong," God had responded, directing him instead to the golden plates buried in a hillside that Smith would translate into the Book of Mormon.[85] Mormonism's very existence repudiated traditional Christianity. What purpose did it serve to align or communicate with those who lacked the truth? Why associate with the very denominations whose errors and apostasy had required Mormonism's creation? "Jesus Christ is the only one who has the authority and right to establish his church among men," McKay had written in 1923 in response to the small ecumenical movement beginning to form in some Protestant denominations. The church's magazine reprinted excerpts from that piece in 1961 as ecumenism caught fire again.[86] Christ had established his church before his ascension and reestablished it through Joseph Smith because man's efforts had led it so far astray. Ecumenism was just another example to Mormons of the futility of Christian efforts outside of the one church that Christ had established. "There are not many roads that lead to heaven. There is one and one only, and that is the road that we profess to travel and should be traveled," contended J. Reuben Clark, Jr., one of the members of the church's First Presidency, in 1960.[87] Clark warned against ecumenism's dangerous "trend of thought" that suggested "it does not make very much difference to what church we belong, what creed we may have."[88] But his sermon title, "All Roads Lead to Rome," implied, just as evangelicals had, that Roman Catholic domination would be the ultimate consequence of ecumenical activity.

For decades, Mormons had lived in relative isolation, carving out their own Zion in the Utah desert safe from the persecutions and proselytizing of others. By the 1950s, Mormonism extended far beyond the Beehive State, with robust communities throughout the West and a growing national and international presence. Of course other faiths existed in Utah. The Catholic Church had established its first diocese in the state in 1891, and there were notable Methodist, Presbyterian, Baptist, and other Protestant communities as well. Close to home and around the world, Mormons made increasing contact with other religious groups during the McKay presidency. But that contact only reinforced anti-ecumenical sentiments in the church. Certainly, the LDS Church would be a good neighbor to fellow churches in Salt Lake City, and McKay's presidency reached out to the Catholic Church and Protestant congregations in the area with a friendliness unmatched by previous church administrations. These gestures, however, served to underline Mormonism's dominant status in Utah. The LDS Church signaled its toleration of other churches in its midst while it reasserted its standing as Utah's de facto church. Contact between the LDS Church and other faiths was not ecumenical, but hierarchical.[89] Asked what he thought of ecumenism, McKay scoffed at the notion that Christian unity could be achieved outside of an institutional framework or rigid theology. "They can all be united if they are baptized in the Mormon Church," McKay responded in 1962. "I am not hopeful of the ecumenical movement."[90] Outside of the state, the church kept to itself, busy with its evangelizing efforts and building up tight Mormon communities that could protect the faith. Across Mormonism, church teachings countered ecumenical trends and strengthened the faith's own separatism. Routinely, church leaders emphasized Mormons' historic status as a "peculiar people" and warned them against abandoning their unique virtues and convictions in order to be accepted by outsiders.[91] Though this teaching largely had cultural and political significance in terms of Mormons' relationship with other Americans and the nation, it drew from a particular theology of Mormon exclusivity that undercut any cross-religious ties or ecumenical engagement. As the ecumenical movement grew and even as conservative Christians sensed their increasing social and political isolation, that Mormon theology of exclusivity and anti-ecumenism proved unwavering and increasing.

Conclusion

Ecumenists often argued that a unified Christian front provided one of the nation's best defenses against Communism, but some of ecumenism's toughest critics, namely evangelicals and Mormons, routinely tied Communism with Catholicism when they spoke of the greatest threats facing both the country and their particular faiths. In 1956, as a Hungarian freedom revolution against the Soviets tried to take hold, David O. McKay declared in a meeting with LDS Church officials that there were "two great organized forces" seeking "to undermine the high principles of the Restored Gospel." "One is Communism, which is moving aggressively over the face of the earth . . . and is against the [LDS] Church," McKay explained. "The other is the Catholic Church."[92] Another time, on a visit to dedicate an LDS chapel in California, McKay declared there were "two great anti-Christs in the world: Communism and that church," he pointed as they drove by a Catholic church. "Remember that," he told those with him.[93]

Evangelicals made similar associations. At its founding, the National Association of Evangelicals had identified Communism and Catholicism along with secularism as reasons for creating the organization. In a 1952 article for the organization's magazine, Carl Henry reaffirmed that position, calling them "Three Threats to Our American Way of Life."[94] Those "three threats" persisted as a popular trope in evangelical circles well into the 1960s. Speaking at the Southern Baptist Convention's 1964 meeting, G. Earl Guinn, a Baptist college president, warned against the three "Contemporary Threats to Freedom"—Communism, secularism, and "Catholicism's Conquest of America," which carried out its "carefully formulated plan" of taking over the country through high reproduction rates, the "successful conquest" of the news media, and the "organized and relentless drive for public funds" for Catholic schools and hospitals.[95]

The Catholic Church's own anti-Communism did little to alleviate such barbs thrown against it. Tellingly, anti-Catholics failed to see the Catholic Church as another bulwark in the war against godless Communism, but rather they spotted eerie similarities between the two.[96] Both thrived on authoritarianism and individual subservience to a hierarchy, evangelicals and Mormons argued. Both were foreign invaders—American Catholics didn't even worship in their own language, Catholicism's critics scoffed—that sought to overtake the nation and destroy the principle of religious liberty. The "religious culture" of Catholicism, a Presbyterian minister in upstate New York argued, "produces the type of mind that is conducive to Communism." "I cannot understand," the minister continued, "why any responsible Protestant religious leader would even think of talking union with the Catholics."[97] The Catholic Church could not be an ally against Communism; it was simply a different danger that must also be opposed. Doing so required every "true American," in the words of an NAE pamphlet, to oppose any further

Catholic influence on the nation and for evangelicals to band with "the Jews, the Mormons, the Unitarians and the atheists who as American citizens are as gravely endangered as we. Unless such a united front can be presented against the united forces of Catholicism we are defeated before we start."[98]

That united front against Catholicism never materialized beyond a symbolic front, but the NAE pamphlet suggested that evangelicals could at least imagine ecumenical scenarios if it entailed anti-Catholic purposes. Why evangelicals could envision partnering with such disparate groups as Mormons, Jews, and atheists to oppose Catholicism at the same time they routinely disparaged linking with moderate and liberal Protestants in ecumenical endeavors reveals both the depths of mid-century evangelical anti-Catholicism and the peculiar consequences of evangelicalism's exclusivist theology. But it also suggested the nascent notion that evangelicals might associate with other faiths for political purposes in spite of a firm insistence against religious unity. Better to imagine political partnerships with clearly differentiated other faiths—against one particular faith, no less—than to water down theological distinctions within Protestantism that would jeopardize evangelical orthodoxy for a supposed unity. A monumental transformation of the Catholic Church accomplished through the Second Vatican Council (1962–1965) would soon strengthen evangelical and Mormon fears that the ecumenical movement provided cover for Catholicism's scheme to dominate Christianity. Evangelical and Mormon responses to Vatican II, however, demonstrated that for these religious conservatives the best means to resist Catholicism's advance came not through banding together against the Vatican, but rather through doubling down on their own exclusivist messages and separatist convictions.

2

Separated Brethren

ON THE MORNING of October 11, 1962, millions of viewers around the world turned their televisions to the live coverage of the Second Vatican Council's opening assembly. An hour-long procession of 2,500 council fathers, draped in all-white vestments with matching white miters on their heads, snaked across the grand square of the Vatican and into the soaring majesty of St. Peter's Basilica. At the end of the parade, carried aloft in an ornate portable throne by a dozen sturdy attendants dressed in red, came Pope John XXIII, the visionary of this great meeting. While the spectacle and pageantry represented to many Catholics both the seriousness and grandeur of such an occasion, for the church's critics it evidenced again Catholicism's most outrageous excesses. Just a few weeks before Vatican II commenced, the evangelical magazine *Christianity Today* had predicted the first day of the council "will doubtless be marked by pomp and ceremony such as only the Roman penchant for spectacle can produce." "To the 550,000,000 on Roman Catholic rolls," *Christianity Today* continued, "the deliberations will be sacred sessions. To other millions they will be a saga of sacrilege."[1]

Sacred sessions, they were in part. But the council had gathered for the serious, if ungainly, business of institutional and theological reform, guided by John XXIII's frequent invocation of the word *aggiornamento* to describe his hopes for the council. The Italian word meant "bringing up to date," and it permeated the discussions at Vatican II. Throughout the sessions, the council sought to bridge the past with the present, updating the church so that it might assume a more effective and prominent position in the modern world even while retaining its enduring traditions and teachings.[2]

A reassessment of the church on this scale required an army of considerable size. Vatican II would meet for about ten weeks of every fall from 1962 to 1965, but between the sessions—and from John XXIII's announcement in 1959 to the opening session in 1962—there was still more work to do. During the sessions, 2,200 bishops hailing from 116 countries traveled to Rome, making it the largest such meeting in the history of the world. Those from Europe and the Americas dominated the meetings, representing 36 and 34 percent of the bishops gathered, respectively. Less-represented corners of the globe, like Asia and Africa, bristled at the predominance of Western authorities, but even among the bishops of Europe and the Americas there was hardly unanimity of purpose. North America, claiming only 7 percent of the world's Catholics, enjoyed an overrepresented presence at the council with its bishops making up 12 percent of the total. Already in the habit of meeting regularly back in the States—a tradition not observed by the bishops of most other nations—the American bishops met weekly during Vatican II's sessions.[3] They would prove an indomitable force by the council's end.

The American bishops helped secure some of the church's most significant reforms, but for outsiders Vatican II's ecumenical spirit proved most significant. Having resisted the ecumenical movement, the Catholic Church now opened itself up and encouraged deeper connections with other Christian faiths—although with some important caveats attached. American liberal Protestants generally greeted the ecumenical developments with excitement and relief, but evangelical and LDS leaders scoffed at the Catholic Church's plans to dialogue with other churches, seeing far more sinister ambitions beneath the talk of openness. The Catholic Church had joined the ecumenical conversation, if not the movement, through the reforms of the Second Vatican Council. In response, Mormon and evangelical leaders both recommitted their faiths to resisting ecumenism, now made stronger in their minds by the support of the Catholic Church, and strengthened their particular messages against the developments from Rome.

An Ecumenical Council

On the afternoon of October 28, 1958, a trail of white smoke began to lift above the rooftop of the Sistine Chapel. Those gathered in St. Peter's Square waiting for such a sign broke into enthusiastic chants of "Viva il Papa!" Upon hearing the crowd, thousands more poured into the Vatican plaza eager to hear the news. A new pope had been chosen. Pope John XXIII, formerly Angelo Giuseppe Cardinal Roncalli of Venice, had been elected the 262nd head of the Roman Catholic Church on the eleventh ballot after three days of voting.[4]

Had Catholics speculated about their new pope's intentions for the church, few would have predicted his call to convene a Second Vatican Council or his declaration of its ecumenical nature.[5] The First Vatican Council, held in 1869 and 1870, had defined papal infallibility as dogma, and many felt that there would never be the need for another council since the first had declared the pope held all the answers to any problems the church faced. But less than three months after his election, Pope John XXIII stunned the church with his announcement on January 25, 1959, calling for a council. John XXIII's statement outlined two broad goals for the council that would open in 1962. First, the council would promote "the enlightenment, edification, and joy of the entire Christian people." Second, the council would offer "a renewed cordial invitation to the faithful of the separated communities to participate with us in this quest for unity and grace." This latter goal, even if only vaguely expressed, marked a departure from Catholic tradition, underscored by papal decrees in the twentieth century, which had forbidden ecumenical interactions. Coming at the end of the "Week of Prayer for the Unity of the Churches," the pope's pronouncement of an ecumenical council perhaps should not have been so surprising, but it represented a significant break with the church's past. Pope Pius XI's 1928 encyclical *Mortalium Animos*, for instance, had denounced the ecumenical movement after Protestants held the World Conference on Faith and Order in Lausanne, Switzerland, in 1927, and had implored those who called themselves Christians to return to the one true church.[6] Other ecumenical gatherings, like the World Council of Churches conference in 1948 and its 1954 sequel, had received similar responses. So Catholics, bishops and laypersons alike, greeted Pope John's call for an ecumenical council with astonishment and confusion. At first, some understood the pope to be proposing a meeting between Rome and other Christian churches to negotiate their merger, but it eventually become more apparent that the ecumenical council would instead focus on the Catholic Church's own preparations for uniting the Christian faith.[7] As Cardinal Tardini, the Vatican's secretary of state, clarified nearly a year after the pope's announcement, the council would be entirely an "internal affair" of the church and not an opportunity for "giving and taking" with Protestant advocates of Christian reunion.[8]

In preparation for the council, the church asked its bishops to send proposals for the meeting's agenda. Many of the responses from American bishops directly engaged questions on ecumenism, most of them positively, a surprising development given how recently the bishops had ignored and often opposed the movement.[9] Some bishops encouraged the church to proceed cautiously lest the church in its eagerness for ecumenism issue scriptural interpretation that "smacks of Protestantism or Indifferentism," as one bishop warned. This same bishop stressed that rather than promoting unity between the church and other Christian communities, the council needed to strengthen unity within the church among its clergy and members "against the enemies of Holy Church and perverse men enjoying the name Christian."[10] One bishop painted things in even starker terms. "The history of Christianity shows," Bishop Bartholome of St. Cloud, Minnesota, wrote to Rome, "that it is more difficult to bring heretics back to the unity of faith than it is to bring pagans to life in Christ."[11]

Despite some reservations, most American bishops optimistically welcomed the church's ecumenical turn. In eager anticipation, leading Catholics hosted conferences and published papers exploring the new ecumenical focus.[12] As the American bishops prepared to attend the council they issued a pastoral letter, "Statement on the Ecumenical Council," that emphasized the Catholic Church's reconciliation with the larger Christian community as among the most important ways the council could bring about renewal.[13] Even as the American bishops called for "ultimate Christian unity," however, they remembered the history of their church, "which was born and has grown to maturity in an atmosphere not always friendly."[14] The bishops also acknowledged that the goal of Christian unity struggled against the considerable impediment of theological differences. "Christians in this country, of several hundred divisions," the bishops warned, "should be particularly conscious of the wide, deep, and inveterate divisions, especially in the field of Christian teaching, which separate the many religious groups here and throughout the world."[15]

No sooner had Pope John revealed his plans for an ecumenical council than evangelicals launched a response, attacking it as Rome's next move in its plan to pull all Christian churches back under its control. (Similar arguments regarding the Catholic Church's plans for political domination via John F. Kennedy's 1960 presidential campaign coexisted with and shaped evangelical assessments of Vatican II as a Catholic ploy for ecclesiastical domination.)[16] One headline in *Christianity Today* shortly following the pope's announcement bleakly warned, "Rome Projects Strategy for a World Church."[17] Vatican II, one writer for the magazine contended, demonstrated that "we as evangelical Protestants need to be aware that Jesus Christ is challenging us to demonstrate that we as the people of God are the real Body of Christ, the Church invisible, to which both radical Protestant and Roman Catholic are incited to return, not in slavish submission but in believing, apostolic faith."[18] Liberal Protestants, however, heralded Vatican II's ecumenical emphasis, enthused that the Catholic Church appeared to be embracing a movement they felt they had long shouldered alone. If liberal Protestants worried about anything, it was that the Second Vatican Council would not go far enough in embracing true ecumenism—the very opposite of evangelical concerns of the council. In nervous anticipation of the event, *Christian Century* predicted it would be "an impressive denominational spectacle, but nothing yet said or done indicates that it will be an *ecumenical* council."[19] Evangelicals envisioned a Catholic Church stealthily using ecumenical talk to increase its global dominance and continue its creeping takeover of America through swallowing up large chunks of a compliant and confused corner of Protestantism. Liberal Protestants, instead, braced for the disappointment that Vatican II would not go far enough in committing the Catholic Church to true ecumenism.

The push for institutional unionism among Protestant ecumenists perplexed evangelicals who contended that one of the Reformation's chief purposes had been to break up the Catholic Church's totalitarian hold on the Christian faith. Now the ecumenical movement unwittingly seemed to be pushing Protestantism back into the control of Rome. Protestant ecumenists were foolish, evangelicals argued, if they believed anything but Catholic domination would be the end result of any ecumenical efforts.[20] Ecumenicity's "ultimate form is the pope of Rome," Carl Henry had cautioned in 1956.[21] In its project of hardening and securing evangelical theology, *Christianity Today* found that Vatican II and ecumenical calls for unity and compromise provided a perfect means for underscoring its hardline message of biblical authority, scriptural inerrancy, and *sola fide* salvation. A reader of the magazine agreed. "It would be well," Benjamin Sharp of New York wrote to *Christianity Today* in response to a series of articles attacking the council, "if the evangelicals of our time would open their eyes to the prophetic significance of the Bible and recognize that all this breathless hunt for some kind of agreement and understanding . . . is not of God nor of his Christ."[22]

Pope John had made clear that the council concerned his church's internal renewal, but evangelical observers saw less generous motivations in the pope's overtures. Writing in *Christianity Today* not long after the pope announced the upcoming council, G. C. Berkouwer, the Dutch Reformed theologian and frequent contributor to the magazine, argued that the Catholic Church's relationship vis-à-vis Protestantism did not really depend on the particular viewpoint of any given pope, but rather owed itself to the church's very structure itself. Given this, it was "impossible for any pope to speak about unity without the background of the pretentions [*sic*] of Rome as the Catholic, the one and only Church." Rather than opening up a dialogue among Christians, the pope truly meant for "the rest of us to *return*. . . . For this reason the coming council ought not to be seen as signifying a change in Rome."[23] The evangelical magazine *Eternity* agreed that whatever changes the council produced would only be "practical and non-doctrinal aspects—*but not one iota as far as her doctrines or dogmas are concerned*. . . .

and many of her dogmas are in flagrant opposition to evangelical truths."[24] Readers of *Christianity Today* were warned to doubt the pope's pronouncements, but they were also encouraged to see his words as a "challenge to us for searching our own hearts." While the Catholic Church advocated reunion in the disguise of dialogue, *Christianity Today* called for evangelicals to think about the "true" nature of Christian unity—one found only through a spiritual unity based on adherence to the message in the Word of God rather than an allegiance to any earthly church.[25] As the council opened, the National Association of Evangelicals offered a more pointed definition of Christian unity as "found only in the Holy Scriptures and in the apostolic heritage carried forward by the Reformation."[26] Even as they decried the Catholic Church's insistence on itself as the sole repository of truth and the only locus for Christian unity, evangelicals contended that they were the only heirs of the true Christian tradition (and, therefore, truth itself)—a truth that had been corrupted, not carried, by the Catholic Church and had been recovered by the defiant acts of a German monk more than four hundred years before.

Given the ecumenical push that seemed to be coming from Rome, many evangelicals wondered what the Second Vatican Council meant for them and their faith. "One thing it means," *Eternity* made clear, "is that evangelicals will have to become more aware of their differences with Roman Catholicism."[27] A reader of *Christianity Today* agreed that the occasion of Vatican II marked "*the* time to analyze the differences between Romanism and Protestantism."[28] To that end, *Christianity Today*, *Eternity*, and other evangelical outlets devoted numerous pages to outlining those distinctions across a broad spectrum of theological, historical, and institutional divergences. Within the catalogue of disagreements, however, "three major areas of conflict," as *Eternity* magazine described, emerged time and again in evangelical evaluations of the Catholic Church on the eve of Vatican II. These three remained the issue of Rome's authority, the role of the "cult of Mary," and the question of the doctrine of salvation. Still, *Eternity* contended, even these three main conflicts boiled down to one basic disagreement regarding the nature of the Bible. For evangelicals, the magazine reminded, the Bible held sole authority while Catholics looked to their church.[29] Adhering to different authorities, evangelicals and Catholics stood at an impasse regarding reconciliation, no matter the aims of the Second Vatican Council. "The Catholic Church will certainly not compromise its position on papal and ecclesiastical authority," *Eternity* argued. "And we as evangelicals must never compromise our position on the authority of the Word of God."[30]

The Decree on Ecumenism

If Pope John XXIII had truly meant Vatican II to demonstrate *aggiornamento*, perhaps nothing could better represent that spirit than the first issue the council extensively debated. The Liturgical Commission reviewed many aspects of the liturgical celebration, like music, sacraments, and the Eucharist, but discussion of the use of vernacular languages in the Mass overwhelmed the proceedings. Many, especially those representing the church in places where Catholicism had enjoyed a briefer history, like Asia and Africa, and also most of the American bishops, believed the church could no better update itself than by abandoning the requirement of the Latin Mass in favor of services conducted in the local language. In ending the Latin Mass, these bishops contended, the Catholic Church would become less a distant relic of Europe and instead a living presence in the local community. The proposals initiated extended and animated discussions, but in the end the council, during its second session in 1963, overwhelmingly approved the end of the Latin Mass when it issued *Sacrosanctum Concilium*, "The Constitution on Sacred Liturgy."[31] The decision seemed to settle the question of what direction, in the words of Vatican II's historian John O'Malley, the council should take—"confirm the status quo or move notably beyond it."[32] By allowing the vernacular to enter the Mass, the council had shown its seriousness in updating the church for the modern era. Additional reforms and declarations of Vatican II would further demonstrate the grand transformation at work.

Looking back on the first session, John XXIII reflected that it had blown a breath of "fresh air" into the church.[33] That spirit would continue, but John XXIII would not live to see it flourish in the remaining sessions. Battling stomach cancer, the pope finally succumbed to the disease in the summer of 1963. The new pope, Paul VI, emerged in a close election with the support of key conservatives like Cardinal Francis Spellman of New York. The question that remained, however, was what direction the Second Vatican Council would take under his leadership.

When the council met for the third session in 1964, the bishops showed they would remain committed to Pope John's ecumenical vision for his council. Shortly after the 1964 session began, the bishops turned their attention to *Unitatis Redintegratio*, the "Decree on Ecumenism." The council had been convened for the very purpose of uniting the Christian faith, so the document predictably affirmed that intention throughout. Compared to other decrees under consideration, the document on ecumenism largely avoided the controversy and debate that other Vatican II proposals endured. In late 1964, the bishops overwhelmingly voted 2,137 to 11 to support the decree.[34]

More than any other document, the "Decree on Ecumenism" established Vatican II's new notion of seeing other Christians as "separated brethren" rather than the heretics church teaching had long regarded them as. Throughout the document, the church affirmed the "common heritage" Catholics had with other Christians and granted that separated brothers and sisters had rich spiritual lives that evidenced the work of Christ.[35] Rather than living in complete error as previous church doctrine had maintained, these Christians simply lacked the "fullness" of the Christian life found only through unity in the Catholic Church. Additionally, the decree admitted the presence of truth in other churches' theologies, a necessary acknowledgment for regarding those Christians as separated brethren with some understanding of truth. Yet, "when comparing doctrines with one another," the decree reminded, Catholic theologians "should remember that in catholic doctrine there exists an order or 'hierarchy' of truths, since they vary in their relation to the foundation of the christian [*sic*] faith."[36] The Catholic Church possessed the fullest understanding of truth and showcased its most complete expression, but other Christian faiths approximated that truth to varying degrees. The notion of "the fullness of catholicity" found throughout the "Decree on Ecumenism" broadened the church's relationship with other Christians while still reaffirming its own status as the true church.[37] In essence, Vatican II permitted that non-Catholics could lead lives that expressed essential gospel truths and deep Christian conviction but that they lacked the "fullness" of the faith found only in adherence to the Catholic Church and its teachings.

Notably, the "Decree on Ecumenism" altered church doctrine on the nature of separation. Occurring nearly thirty times in the document, the phrase "separated brethren" represented an important change from the previous descriptive "heretics," and this alteration signaled the church's softened judgment of non-Catholics.[38] (This transformation was not lost on evangelical watchers of Vatican II, though they still viewed the new designation with suspicion. The Southern Baptist college president, G. Earl Guinn, noted that being regarded as separated brethren was a step up from being seen as "lepers outside the gate," but he suggested that legacy persisted.)[39] While the decree affirmed that "certain rifts" were "damnable," in other separations and divisions "people on both sides were to blame." This was a startling admission with both theological and historical consequence, a rewriting of both doctrine and the past that imagined separation from the Catholic Church as not always a sinful action but perhaps sometimes Catholics' fault too. Furthermore, the decree lifted the guilt of sin from those who had been "born into these communities." Absolved from the sin of separation that could only be attributed to their heretical ancestors, these Christians were now accepted "with respect and affection as brothers and sisters" by the Catholic Church.[40] Perhaps most radically, the decree suggested that other Christians could partake in the "mystery of salvation" even though remaining outside of the church, but this acknowledgment came with a caveat. Since only the Catholic Church provided the unity that Christ had desired for his believers, "it is through Christ's Catholic church [*sic*] alone . . . that the fullness of the means of salvation can be obtained."[41]

The decree compelled all Catholics—not just the bishops or priests—to ecumenical work. This work, as the decree imagined it, would involve shared worship experiences and theological discussions, but also service work to promote peace; protect the vulnerable; minister to the victims of war, famine, and disease; and attack the ills of poverty, illiteracy, and "the unequal distribution of wealth."[42] For Christians, the bishops explained, working together demonstrated the mission of Christ. "Cooperation among Christians vividly expresses that bond which already unites them," the decree explained, "and it sets in clearer relief the features of Christ the Servant."[43] But such cooperation was tempered by the church's tentative permissions to its members regarding their religious interactions with people outside their faith. For instance, the decree stated that "in certain circumstances . . . it is allowable . . . that Catholics should join in prayer with members of other christian [*sic*] churches and communities."[44] This was a bold step and one liberal ecumenists and conservative evangelicals alike applauded (though for different reasons), but the directions also qualified Catholic ecumenism and suggested an air of danger if not taking place "under the attentive guidance of . . . bishops."[45]

Both evangelicals and Mormons complained that ecumenism depended on liberal Protestants smoothing over theological differences and abandoning hard truths for the project of Christian unity. But the "Decree on Ecumenism" demonstrated that the Catholic Church did not believe the ecumenical movement necessitated an abandonment of Catholicism's distinctive doctrine and made clear that ecumenism could never devolve to indifferentism. Rather, the decree conceptualized ecumenism in quite opposite terms than its liberal Protestant advocates did, seeing it as an opportunity to come together to discuss and wrestle with the definitive theologies of those involved. This then required not tolerance and compromise but instead truth and conviction. Catholics involved in ecumenical work, layperson and priest alike, had to be firmly rooted in their faiths, respectful of difference but firm in their knowledge of Catholic teaching. The decree warned against a "false irenicism which harms the purity of catholic [*sic*] doctrine."[46] Catholics should see the ecumenical movement as an opportunity to clarify non-Catholics' understanding of Catholicism. In that process, other Christians could come to a "deeper realization" of Catholic truth.[47]

Some historians have noted that the "Decree on Ecumenism" did not implore other Christian communities "to return" to the Catholic Church as other church documents, such as *Mortalium Animos* in 1928 and *Ecclesia Catholica* in 1949, had.[48] Although those words did not appear in the decree, their implicit message still remained throughout. The document's first lines asserted this desire: "The restoration of unity among all Christians is one of the principal concerns of the Second Vatican Council. Christ the Lord founded one church and one church only."[49] If the command "to return" was missing, the implication that Christian unity could only be achieved under the auspices of the Catholic Church was not. The document even justified ecumenical activity as the means by which Christians would come back to the church. "Little by little," the document explained, "as the obstacles to perfect ecclesiastical communion are overcome, all Christians will be gathered . . . into the unity of the one and only church."[50] As the document closed, it returned to this point, calling "the reconciliation of all Christians in the unity of the one and only church of Christ" a "holy objective."[51] However radically Vatican II had revolutionized the Catholic Church, it could not upend the foundational logic that guided the church. Its status as "the one and only church" required certain consequences, among them that any true Christian unity would ultimately involve the reconciliation—the *return*, to use the missing word—of all Christians to the Catholic Church.

The "Decree on Ecumenism" essentially confirmed the suspicions of critics who charged ecumenism would in the end result in a return to a pre-Reformation Catholic monopoly of Christianity. While the "Decree on Ecumenism" may have removed the commanding language of "return," it nevertheless presented it as the implicit, proper, and even inevitable outcome of ecumenism. Evangelical critics of the council agreed on this interpretation. On the day before the bishops voted in favor of the Decree, *Christianity Today* published a scathing piece on Vatican II and the ecumenical movement that had, in the magazine's opinion, "been given a tremendous thrust" by the council.[52] Citing the schema on ecumenism that the bishops were about to vote on, *Christianity Today* noted the document did not recognize Protestant churches as churches, but instead as "communities." "Obviously," the magazine concluded, "to dissolve and absorb these 'Protestant communities' is the aim of Catholic ecumenists."[53]

The Church in the Modern World

While the "Decree on Ecumenism" directly engaged the council's ecumenical directive, that spirit emanated throughout other documents produced by the meeting. In the latter sessions, the American bishops emerged as more influential directors of the council's proceedings, steering the church in ways that strengthened its ecumenical outlook. Most important to the American bishops, they worked at the Second Vatican Council to transform the Catholic Church's relationship with the outside world. Catholicism's historic parochialism, which had roots in its theological position as the "one true religion" but also in its historical condition, particularly in the United States, as an aggrieved and targeted faith, had resulted in a separatist institution justified by Catholic doctrine. The Vatican had, for example, strengthened its separatist philosophy with the 1864 *Syllabus of Errors*, which dismissed the idea that "the Roman Pontiff can and ought to reconcile and harmonize himself with progress, with liberalism, and with modern civilization."[54] But the Second Vatican Council upended this notoriously isolationist tradition. In addition to the "Decree on Ecumenism," other conciliar documents produced during the council moved the church away from separatism.

None was more important in revolutionizing the church's relationship with the outside world than the "Pastoral Constitution on the Church in the Modern World." Also known as *Gaudium et Spes*, this text urged the end of the church's defensive stance to the outside world and stressed the connections the church felt to people around the world—the "deep solidarity with the human race and its history."[55] That solidarity of humanity made the Catholic Church sensitive to the plight and poverty of all persons, whether church members or not. And with that awareness came a responsibility for the church to work for the betterment of those people. While the church had historically served as a sanctuary from the corruptions of the world for its members, the "Pastoral Constitution" now instructed its bishops and parishioners to go out into that fallen world and make things better. Some of the German bishops, most notably the theologian Joseph Ratzinger who would later be named Pope Benedict XVI, objected to the "Pastoral Constitution" as overly optimistic and lacking firm theological support. Ratzinger and others published articles critical of the text in the summer of 1965, but most of them eventually joined the overwhelming majority of 2,309 bishops who voted for the document (against only seventy-five in opposition) later that fall.[56]

The "Pastoral Constitution" outlined a set of worries in the world—"Some More Urgent Problems," as the document called them.[57] These listed issues to which the church was to turn its attention, and they appear like a checklist of the political issues the American bishops would engage in the 1970s and 1980s, as Timothy Byrnes has pointed out.[58] First and foremost was the state of the family and marriage. From the marriage relationship came new life, and the "Pastoral Constitution" reminded Catholics that they were "forbidden to use methods disapproved of by the teaching authority of the church" for birth control. Life, the document instructed, existed "from the moment of conception: abortion and infanticide are abominable crimes."[59] The "Pastoral Constitution" also commanded the church to work on issues of economic development and the fostering of peace, matters to which the American bishops devoted great resources and energies in the years ahead. But none would energize the American bishops like the issue of abortion.

The "Pastoral Constitution" authorized the bishops' political activities, gave them a series of issues they might take up, and provided them with the positions they should hold. The church's endorsement of political activity marked a historic shift, but the "Pastoral Constitution" served as a reminder that the church's original purpose remained. "Christ did not bequeath to the church a mission in the political, economic, or social order: the purpose he assigned to it was religious," the council instructed. But a new sense of what that religious mission was emanated from the Second Vatican Council. The church had expanded its vision and its conception of how it ought to act in the world. "This religious mission," the council fathers wrote, "can be the source of commitment, direction, and vigor to establish and consolidate the human community according to the law of God."[60] Political activism, then, was a direct outgrowth of religious duty and service, not a disconnected new preoccupation of the church.

Lastly, the "Pastoral Constitution" reached out to other groups of people who shared the church's views and asked them to work with the church to achieve results—a development that owed itself directly to the council's ecumenical emphasis. In the "Declaration on Religious Liberty," the council had defended "the right of religious groups not to be prevented from freely demonstrating the special value of their teaching for the organization of society and the inspiration of human activity in general," and the "Pastoral Constitution" hinted at a willingness for the Catholic Church to work with other like-minded institutions and people.[61] These other groups included fellow Christians from "communities who are not yet living in full communion with us; yet we are united by our worship of the Father, the Son, and the Holy Spirit and the bonds of love." But it also included "those who respect outstanding human values without realizing who the author of those values is."[62] This ecumenical and coalitional vision of the church's religious mission to engage social and political issues would be challenged in the years ahead both internally and externally by theological differences and historical tensions, but the willingness to engage and work with other groups was significant, even if the limitations of that possibility remained unrealized at the moment.

While documents on ecumenism and the church's place in the world had enjoyed relatively minimal debate and smooth passage through the council, the council's document on religious freedom endured a more difficult course to its adoption. Heavily backed by the American bishops, the "Declaration on Religious Liberty" attracted fierce resistance from European conservatives. The tension between U.S. constitutional principles and the church's own teachings that defended the linking of church and state had always allowed American Catholics to be targeted as un-American anti-democrats, but most American bishops had opted to suffer the consequences of affirming, or at least not challenging, Catholic teachings. Those who sought to push the church to support religious liberty, most notably John Courtney Murray, earned stern rebukes from Rome and from other American Catholic leaders. But the 1960 election altered many American bishops' views about religious liberty as John F. Kennedy faced steady anti-Catholic bigotry and constant questions about how his church's teachings would affect his presidency. Weary from the campaign and the challenge of convincing the American people that no Catholic president would overthrow church-state separation and submit his presidential authority to the pope, the more than two hundred American bishops who participated in the Second Vatican Council presented a unified front to the council on the matter of religious liberty.[63]

Though he had once been repudiated and silenced, John Courtney Murray greatly shaped both the spirit and policies that emanated from the Second Vatican Council. Murray had been excluded from the council's proceedings at first, but given that he had become a leading expert on religious liberty, Cardinal Francis Spellman of New York invited Murray to the second session of the council to serve as his *peritus*—or "expert"—on the topic as the council drafted its "Declaration on Religious Liberty."[64] Standing at 6 feet, 4 inches tall, Murray had always been an imposing physical presence, but now his ideas about ecumenism and religious liberty cast an enduring shadow over the proceedings of the Second Vatican Council.

As the bishops debated, wrote, amended, and rewrote the "Declaration on Religious Liberty," it garnered special attention from outside observers of Vatican II. Evangelicals skeptically questioned whether the Catholic Church would achieve any substantive reforms on religious liberty, knowing that the European bishops were resisting an endorsement of church-state separation. Additionally, evangelicals charged that Catholics meant something entirely different by religious liberty than how most Americans—meaning Protestants—used the term. "When the Roman Catholic Church talks about religious liberty," one *Christianity Today* article explained, "it is talking about the right to preach and practice Catholicism in Communist countries such as Poland." "But when Baptists talk about religious freedom," the article pointed out in contrast, "they are talking about equal rights with Catholics in Spain and Portugal."[65] Liberal Protestants, however, failed to join evangelicals in assuming the Catholic Church could not develop an acceptable document on religious liberty. Instead, they looked to the Declaration with great anticipation, seeing in it, as the *Christian Century* described, the hope that it would "contribute greatly to ecumenical rapprochement."[66] What the bishops produced in the "Declaration on Religious Liberty" surprised most observers, especially American evangelicals. The Declaration stated that "the human person has a right to religious freedom," and this right was "to be recognized in the constitutional law whereby society is governed," reversing the church's historic position on religious freedom and also providing a tacit endorsement of American constitutional principles.[67]

Considering this development, evangelical leaders were forced to acknowledge the important transformation this represented, but they resisted a full endorsement. "On the surface," the declaration appeared revolutionary, *Eternity* admitted. "But as you study the document closer, you begin to have mixed feelings about it. . . . As you read it critically, it seems to favor religious liberty only if the Catholic church [*sic*] is recognized as the one true church."[68] *Christianity Today* also observed the document's significance, but even in doing so they reminded their readers of the Catholic Church's bad history on the matter and suggested evangelicals retain a healthy skepticism of the church's declaration. "If one wonders why it took the Roman Catholic Church until 1965 to become what the secular press is designating as 'modernized,'" one editorial sneered, "the answer lies in the way the Roman Catholic Church has viewed itself. Believing itself to be the true representative of God on earth . . . and the power to which all other temporal powers are subject, it too often functioned as God and denied the right of error to exist in its presence. Since nothing is a greater terror to freedom than something that thinks itself divine, the history of the Roman church has been muddied by its use of coercion and even persecution to further its aims."[69] After Vatican II's close in late 1965, *Christianity Today* pointed out that many evangelicals, such as Barry Garrett, a Baptist newsman and frequent critic of the Catholic Church, believed that the "Declaration on Religious Liberty" had not gone far enough in defining religious freedom. For instance, while the document had declared that no person should be coerced into religious belief, it still contended that people had to embrace Catholicism as the "one true faith" once they understood its claims, the very point *Eternity* magazine also contended lurked beyond a surface reading of the document.[70] This, *Christianity Today* suggested, meant Catholicism continued to pose a problem for the future of American pluralism, especially if liberal Protestants increasingly entertained ecumenical talks with the Catholic Church. Protestant ecumenists did express regret that the Declaration included words regarding the "one truth faith," but unlike evangelicals they saw this language as a regrettable flaw in an otherwise "exceptionally good document," as the *Christian Century* editorialized. "Seen in the context of the great good achieved," the magazine continued, "the harm that was done diminishes in importance."[71] American evangelicals could not agree. Instead, they saw the Catholic Church's inclusion of an exclusive truth claim in a document about religious liberty as proof of Catholicism's inherent inability to be reformed and as a sign of its true domineering intentions when it came to ecumenism.

Emboldened by his vindication in Rome, John Courtney Murray emerged from the Second Vatican Council as a reinvigorated advocate of ecumenism and religious liberty. After the council, Murray spent the time until his death in 1967 traveling the country and spreading Vatican II's message of openness and social engagement to Catholic audiences and to interfaith gatherings.[72] *Christianity Today* described his appearance at a conference on Vatican II at the University of Notre Dame in 1966 as seeming "tired and worn out from his years of work and suffering for this cause."[73] In a lecture in Chicago, Murray explained the new obligation Catholics had to work with others for the improvement of the nation. "The ecumenical dialogue from now on," Murray told his audience, "necessarily must be an essential element in the life of the Church, in the lives of all our Churches. We not only have a charter; we have a mandate."[74] Writing in the academic journal *Religious Education*, Murray reaffirmed that though the ecumenical movement had originated in Protestant churches, the Catholic Church had to ensure that ecumenism emanated from within the church rather than remaining a movement to which the church merely responded. This would require Catholic innovations of both theology and bureaucracy, but it was critical that the church make ecumenism central to its mission.[75] Murray would live to see little of the new church that the Second Vatican Council had created. But his influence on the revolutionary remaking of the Catholic Church had been monumental. Once scorned, Murray's ideas now stood at the heart of the modern Catholic Church's relationship with the larger world.

Evangelicals Respond to Vatican II

Though there had been some important changes in the Catholic Church's position on religious liberty, Vatican II reaffirmed other Catholic teachings that evangelicals could not endorse, such as papal infallibility and authority, Mariolatry, and salvation through grace and works—the three issues *Eternity* magazine had identified at the council's start as unbiblical Catholic positions that evangelicals could not countenance. "In light of these statements . . . ," one *Christianity Today* article contended as the council began its last session in 1965, "we must conclude that Rome has not fundamentally changed. There are important changes in climate, in approach, in emphases, even in aspects of truth; but the system as such has not changed."[76] Characterizing Catholicism as a "system"—a human-made authority replete with flaws and falsehoods as contrasted to the unquestionable truth of the evangelical gospel rooted in the authority of the Holy Scriptures—had been a frequent aspect of evangelical criticism of the Catholic faith at mid-century. By calling the Catholic Church a "system," *Christianity Today* also placed Catholicism in the magazine's larger conversation with the other systems of Communism and liberalism it had been taking on for the past decade. "We are afraid of a superchurch," the magazine worried in a separate article, "just as we are afraid of a superstate."[77] The Second Vatican Council, with its pomp and formality, its often inflexible bureaucracy, and its rigorous and protracted debates over Catholic teachings and traditions rather than, in the minds of evangelicals at least, the Holy Scriptures themselves, underscored again for evangelicals their conviction that the Catholic Church stood as an institutional monstrosity that strangled the gospel and possibly threatened America's democratic experiment, much like Communism threatened to do. Just after the first session of Vatican II had begun, one writer for *Christianity Today* concluded exactly what the outcome of the council would be. "The church will seem less an intransigent institution to non-Catholics after the captains and kings have departed," the writer predicted, "yet . . . it will not have changed its essential nature one iota."[78]

This essential nature, evangelicals argued, owed to the Catholic Church's view of itself rather than the Holy Scriptures as sole authority over the life of the believer. Indeed, evangelical beliefs about the Bible—and specifically their beliefs about Catholicism's relationship to the Bible—appeared throughout their reactions to all of the council's decisions. In their critiques of Vatican II declarations and statements on issues of authority, the papacy, the Virgin Mary, and even religious liberty, evangelicals tied their particular disagreements with each issue to larger claims about the Catholic Church's erroneous interpretations and use of the Bible. But while their own interpretation of the Bible served as the consistent cudgel with which evangelicals attacked Vatican II, they still saw one promising development in Vatican II's emphasis on the Bible, and they highlighted this change throughout the council and in the years that followed.

The decision to use the vernacular in the Mass meant Catholics would hear biblical scriptures in their native tongues. Vatican II also suggested priests give more attention to the scriptures in their sermons and encouraged Catholics to read their Bibles more often and participate in Bible studies. In response, evangelical publications urged their readers to join Bible studies with Catholics.[79] Although they viewed Vatican II's ecumenical aims with suspicion in general, evangelical leaders suddenly celebrated this spirit of the council when they understood it might work to their advantage in regard to the Catholic Church's increasing openness with Bible study. "How thankful we can be for Rome's ecumenical vision," *Eternity* proclaimed during Vatican II's last session without any hint of the consistent skepticism evangelicals had shown throughout the council. "This has opened lines of communication," the magazine continued, "that have previously been closed. Rome dialogues out of security, but every orthodox Protestant should welcome this unprecedented opportunity to witness."[80]

The Southern Baptist Convention also responded to the ecumenical push from Vatican II with a series of pamphlets aimed at assisting the Southern Baptist in converting Catholics to evangelical Christianity. These pamphlets were produced during the late 1960s by the Department of Work Related to Non-Evangelicals, later renamed the Department of Interfaith Witness, an arm of the Home Mission Board established in 1966 that worked to share the Southern Baptist understanding of Christianity with other Christian faiths. Notably, at almost the same moment Catholic bishops were establishing the Commission for Ecumenical Affairs near the end of Vatican II in order to work with other ecumenically minded organizations like the World Council of Churches and the National Conference of Christians and Jews, Southern Baptists responded to the Second Vatican Council's ecumenical endorsement with a missionary organization specially tailored to proselytizing Catholics and other "non-evangelicals."[81] "Basic to the work of this department," one Southern Baptist magazine explained, "is the conviction that each person called nonevangelical should be regarded as an individual personality and only secondarily as a Mormon or Catholic or Christian Scientist."[82] Yet the department produced dozens of pamphlets and articles outlining the theological shortcomings, heretical claims, and blasphemous beliefs of these specific faiths along with detailed instructions on how a Southern Baptist might reach out to others and share the evangelical message with them as subjects of their particular religion.

One pamphlet produced by the department noted that the positive effect of Vatican II's emphasis on opening up the Catholic Church to other Christian faiths was the opportunity it allowed Southern Baptists to develop "friendly relations with Catholics with the ultimate view to sharing our understanding of the Christian faith."[83] Another pamphlet warned, however, about the temptation to ignore theological differences that an ecumenical movement might encourage. "Unqualified optimism as to the possibilities of agreement in doctrine is unwarranted at this stage. . . . Where complete disregard for doctrinal matters is a climate of ecumenical relations," the pamphlet advised, "it is to be questioned whether it is a *Christian* unity that is sought or merely a social and human fellowship."[84]

Though the Catholic Church intended Vatican II's ecumenical efforts to bring all Christians back into its fold, evangelicals argued, the church's reforms regarding the Bible "might just accomplish under God much more than Rome either expects or hopes," *Christianity Today* editorialized, because the Catholic Church failed to recognize the very power for transformation that the Bible contained.[85] In joint Bible studies, evangelicals imagined, they could point their Catholic friends to the gospel without interference from Catholic authorities. And Catholics who committed to private devotionals would encounter on their own the biblical truth that might bring about changes similar to those that had happened when Martin Luther had buried himself in the Holy Word more than four hundred years before. "Something is bound to happen when people begin reading the Bible," *Eternity* magazine declared.[86] "The Word of God does not return void," *Christianity Today* concurred. "It is still the power of God unto salvation, able to divide the thoughts and intents of the heart. Not even the rigidity of Roman Catholic tradition nor her structured monolithic power can in the end resist the movements of the biblical Word and its power to renew and reform. Protestants should remember the Reformation; what the Word wrought once, it can work again."[87]

Throughout Vatican II, the bishops had debated the document on scriptures that was finally promulgated by Pope Paul VI, John's successor, near the close of the council's last session in 1965. The "Dogmatic Constitution on Divine Revelation," or *Dei Verbum*, meaning "Word of God," as it was officially known, had attracted close evangelical attention throughout the proceedings because as a constitution it would redefine Catholic doctrine.[88] Given the other decisions and pronouncements on the Bible issued throughout the council, evangelicals hoped the final document on Divine Revelation would substantially alter Catholic Church doctrine regarding scripture, but the Dogmatic Constitution drew mixed reactions. Parts of the text read "like an evangelical document," *Eternity* magazine noted, but "other portions may provoke violent disagreement."[89]

That disagreement centered on the Catholic Church's balance between sacred tradition and sacred scripture. As the Constitution on Divine Revelation reaffirmed, tradition and scripture "are closely bound together, and communicate one with the other. . . . Thus it is that the church does not draw its certainty about all revealed truths from the holy scriptures alone. Hence, both scripture and tradition must be accepted and honored with equal devotion and reverence."[90] Claiming that tradition, which one evangelical critic of Vatican II argued "might better be called sacred interpretation," stood alongside the Bible proved impossible enough for evangelicals to accept, but that the Constitution's chapter on sacred tradition came before the one on sacred scripture revealed in clear print that the Catholic Church in reality saw itself "above the Scriptures and not subservient."[91]

In sanctifying tradition, evangelicals argued, Catholic Church leaders had fallen prey to the twin errors of blasphemously regarding themselves as divine agents of truth while also subjecting the scriptures to the "human and sinful limitations" of their own interpretive abilities.[92] For evangelicals, the reaffirmation by Vatican II that tradition and scripture stood on par together, as the Constitution on Divine Revelation declared, "as the supreme rule of its faith," meant that the Catholic Church had not lessened in any way its long-standing insistence on its own ultimate authority.[93] To claim that tradition stood alongside scripture, evangelicals argued, was in reality to declare that scripture remained subject to human authority. Scripture either held sole authority over the life of the believer, evangelicals reasoned, or it was always subservient to the authority of flawed human actors. The very act of equating scripture with tradition, evangelicals argued, was in fact an assertion of the Catholic Church's supremacy over the Bible and the institutional practice by which it justified the teachings and traditions evangelicals most opposed as unbiblical, including papal infallibility, the veneration of Mary, and the theology of salvation through grace and works.

Restoration and Revelation vs. Reformation

As evangelicals had, Mormons viewed the Second Vatican Council with a great skepticism that drew upon and revived long-standing LDS critiques of Catholicism. That the Catholic Church would seek to reform itself struck one esteemed LDS intellectual as almost laughable. "To one familiar with the Catholic polemic of bygone years with its pounding emphasis on the great, monolithic, unchanging, universal, victorious Church, all this sounds very new, surprising, and changed indeed," wrote Hugh Nibley, a professor of history and religion at Brigham Young University, in the LDS Church's official magazine. "Isn't it rather late in the day to try to decide what the Church is all about?"[94] Nibley ventured that new discoveries of historical documents had caused the Catholic Church to seek reform because they had exposed how deeply corruption existed throughout the church's past. Vatican II's emphasis to return the church to Christ underscored, in the opinion of Mormon observers, Catholicism's abominable ways, but also the impossibility of its reform project. The Catholic Church insisted that it maintained the continuous legacy of Christ's church, but Vatican II's purpose of reform and renewal proved how far it had gotten away from the original church. This contradiction between Catholicism's insistence on its unchanging nature and Vatican II's unwitting admission, in Mormon opinion, of how much the church had deviated from its origins through the centuries heightened Mormon objections to Catholicism and, more importantly, reaffirmed the LDS theology of restoration and revelation. Anti-Catholic and anti-popery sentiment had been at the heart of Mormonism's founding in the 1830s and appeared throughout the Book of Mormon. While no longer expressing the harsh and unbridled views of early nineteenth-century America, Mormon responses to the Second Vatican Council still used developments within Catholicism to justify and reinvigorate Mormonism's theological raison d'être.

Generally, the LDS Church did not watch the proceedings of Vatican II with the close eyes that evangelicals gave the council. In fact, most commentary the church published appeared in the years immediately following Vatican II, rather than as a play-by-play documentation of events that evangelical outlets gave the meetings in Rome. While Mormons had little respect for the Catholic Church, they manifested that attitude more commonly by generally ignoring the council. In part, this reflected Mormonism's traditional inward-focused bearing, but also its historic disinterest in the theological debates and skirmishes outside of Zion. Focused on its own self-preservation and development, Mormonism had little time or reason to engage in close observation of other faiths. Indeed, its failure to do so reflected in some ways Mormonism's own desire throughout much of its history to be equally ignored and left to its own purposes, free of the harassment and persecution that it frequently faced. Given that history, Mormons were predisposed to view Vatican II at a distance, if at all. But the burgeoning and increasingly vocal ecumenical movement, made all the more prominent by the Second Vatican Council, and David O. McKay's more outwardly focused and internationally minded leadership of the LDS Church meant Vatican II could not go entirely unobserved by Mormons.

Mormons greeted some of the developments coming from Rome with measured approval, including the statement on religious liberty and the council's liturgical reforms. Unlike evangelical evaluations of these changes that elicited protracted theological and political commentary, Mormon reactions tended toward indifferent recognition or mildly supportive expressions. The council's liturgical reforms, including the abandonment of the Latin Mass, and other changes regarding priestly vestments and worship practices adopted shortly after the council struck one Mormon observer as a return to more simple worship from the ritualism that had built up through the ages.[95] Mormon leaders generally greeted the "Declaration on Religious Liberty" positively, granting that the Catholic Church had finally embraced the principles of individual liberty and freedom of conscience that the Reformation had brought about.[96]

Notably, Mormon reaction to the religious liberty statement lacked the suspicion and skepticism found in evangelical responses to the document. Though Mormon theology and scriptures sharply inveighed against the doings of Rome, this critique usually focused more on Catholic theology and worship practices than on the church's political or social involvements. Still, just a few years earlier, Mormons had largely opposed John F. Kennedy's bid for the White House. As the *New York Times* explained, Mormons worried about a candidate who belonged to the church that Mormon theology considered the "abominable church, whore of the earth."[97] LDS Church president McKay publicly backed Nixon over Kennedy, an influential endorsement for Mormon voters. Critics expressed outrage at McKay's endorsement, and the LDS Church scrambled to clarify that McKay had spoken "as a Republican and a personal voter," but that distinction was likely insignificant to many faithful Mormons.[98] Throughout Utah, the LDS hierarchy expressed opposition to Kennedy, while reminding church members of their "freedom of choice" on political matters. Meanwhile, LDS training manuals for the priesthood continued to outline the dangers of a "worldwide Catholicism."[99] But while evangelical arguments against Kennedy's election in 1960 easily found their way into their responses to the Second Vatican Council, Mormon evaluations of Vatican II, particularly the "Declaration on Religious Liberty," remained curiously disconnected from the attitudes and arguments revealed so plainly in Mormon opposition to Kennedy in 1960. Perhaps the LDS Church's marginal and often-maligned status softened Mormon critiques of Catholic political involvement, or maybe Mormons figured a more visible Catholic Church would lessen the Protestant stranglehold on the public square, but

Mormon leaders saw no sinister undertones in the "Declaration on Religious Liberty." Similarly, Mormon observers acknowledged that Vatican II's reforms would "strengthen measurably the role and position of the Roman Catholic churches in America," but this was not so much a warning or lament, as typical from evangelicals, as it was a simple observation.[100]

Though many of Vatican II's developments caused little of the concern for Mormon watchers as they had for evangelical observers, Mormon criticism of the council centered on its ecumenical emphasis just as much as evangelical responses had. Writing in the LDS Church's magazine, Mark Petersen, a high-ranking official, characterized the council's ecumenical push as no less than "astonishing."[101] This astonishment, however, revealed important differences in Mormon and evangelical assumptions about Catholicism. Evangelicals expected Catholic ambition to work toward bringing all Christians back under Rome's control. Mormon anti-Catholicism, however, lacked this doomsday expectation of the Catholic Church's intentions. While evangelicals offered dark predictions about Catholicism's plots, Mormons expressed simple surprise at Catholicism's turn to ecumenism.

But this surprise did not reveal a weakening objection to ecumenism from LDS leaders. Instead, Vatican II provided a new opportunity for Mormon officials to recapitulate their opposition to the decade's ecumenical movement. Yet Mormons did not want their avoidance of ecumenical councils to suggest an unconcern with the divisions in Christianity. Those divisions, Mormon leaders reminded LDS faithful, had been foretold by the Bible and created the confusing diversity of denominations that had sent Joseph Smith to God for direction of which one to join. God had answered that he was to join none and instead should establish the LDS Church, so Christian division had been at the heart of Mormonism's creation and also persisted as a threat to the unity God wanted his people to find in the LDS Church.

Though evangelicals contended that divisions within Christianity allowed for variations of worship styles and doctrinal distinctions, Mormons acknowledged that "the very reason for which the ecumenical councils are being called are [*sic*] evidence that the division in the first place was wrong and even apostate in its dimensions." That apostasy meant that Christian division was lamentable but, as evangelicals had, Mormon critics of ecumenism scoffed at ecumenists who called for Christian unity. Yet unlike evangelicals, who had called for spiritual unity over church union, Mormons insisted unity could only be found in the LDS Church—an explicit institutional claim that outflanked even the Catholic Church's own exclusive claim. "There is indeed a need for unity," Boyd K. Packer, a high-ranking LDS leader, told a large gathering of Mormons. "But we would be mistaken to assume that each of the multiplicity of Christian churches is part of the so-called 'body of Christ' . . . and that putting them all together would make the full 'body of Christ.'" "They are not component parts, but are imperfect and distorted copies of the whole," Packer continued. "To pretend that bringing them together will constitute bringing into one whole all that is essential for the salvation of mankind would be to mislead one another." Flawed entities could not become a perfect whole. "No more will be accomplished through uninspired reorganization and attempted unification of the Christian churches than has been accomplished through the uninspired separation of them," Packer explained. Because of this, the LDS Church would continue to abstain from the ecumenical movement and would keep sending its missionaries into Christian communities to share the gospel truth that only Mormonism could offer.[102] In the ecumenical age of Vatican II where Christians sought to repair the divisions among them, the LDS Church asked "both Catholics and Protestants to listen to the authentic features of Mormonism."[103]

While many evangelicals had hoped that Vatican II would bring about important reforms in the Catholic Church, as the proceedings drew to a close they recognized that whatever reforms an institution that saw itself as the ultimate authority carried out would never be enough. "What the church of Rome needs is not 'reform,' which amounts to pruning away some of the historical accretions," the influential evangelical theologian and journalist Klaas Runia wrote near the end of Vatican II, "but 'reformation,' that is, new, completely new, understanding of the Gospel itself."[104] The reference to reformation was, obviously, not merely descriptive, but pointedly historical. Evangelical critiques and commentators of Vatican II constantly invoked Martin Luther and the events of the sixteenth century in their interpretations of the council. The Catholic Church's message of reform and the actual changes put into policy and practice elicited evangelical observation that only the ultimate reform of the church could complete Luther's reformation of it.

That the Catholic Church would undergo a full-scale reformation remained unlikely, evangelicals acknowledged, but owing to Vatican II's changes regarding the Bible, evangelicals believed that some individual Catholics, if not the church itself, might undergo their own personal reformations. "It is possible that forces are being let loose in the Roman church that only God can control," *Christianity Today* predicted.[105] In 1972, on the tenth anniversary of the opening of the Second Vatican Council, *Christianity Today* looked back on the historic event and praised the council for unleashing the power of biblical truth within the Catholic Church, but stressed the "swelling Catholic interest in the Scriptures offers hope for perplexed souls, if not necessarily for structures."[106]

This idea among evangelicals that the increased attention on the Bible in Catholic circles would reform and renew some individual Catholics rather than the church itself would shape evangelical-Catholic relations in the years ahead. As the 1970s opened, conservative Christians worried about the fate of a nation that had undergone the transformations of the 1960s and now faced what they saw as new assaults on tradition through things like the passage of the Equal Rights Amendment in 1972 and the federal legalization of abortion in 1973. In light of these developments, some religious conservatives began to suggest that they band together across denominational and theological divides to preserve the nation's Judeo-Christian heritage and to protect the family. "The feeling may . . . be growing among both Protestants and Roman Catholics," *Christianity Today* commented at the end of 1973, "that the issues separating them are becoming less important than their common perils in an increasingly secular and atheistically dominated world."[107]

That ecumenical aligning for the sake of politics proved to be a complicated, challenging, and often unsuccessful project, but even the discussion of building bridges for political gain between traditionally antagonistic groups, especially Catholics and evangelicals, was historically significant. As evangelical leaders first began to suggest a Catholic-evangelical alliance to oppose abortion and other political and social ills, they imagined a grassroots association of individual Catholics and evangelicals, rather than any partnering of religious institutions. In part, this reflected the evangelical conviction that Christians rather than churches should be engaged in civic affairs and political matters, but it also revealed the lingering distrust and discomfort evangelicals felt about the Catholic Church itself. As *Eternity* magazine explained, "if we can not [*sic*] have fellowship with the *institution*, we can sometimes have fellowship with its members."[108] The Second Vatican Council had been instrumental in this new and developing relationship between evangelicals and Catholics even as it allowed evangelicals to reconfirm and recapitulate their critiques of the institutional church.

While the evangelical image of reformation permitted a hopeful if also doubtful evaluation of Vatican II, the Mormon concept of restoration forestalled any positive interpretations. The possibility of a true reformation of the Catholic Church always existed, evangelicals argued, even if it remained unlikely. Who was to say what God might accomplish? There had been a mighty reformation before; there could be another one. But, Mormons argued, there could be only one restoration. That restoration had happened already, bringing Christ's church back into existence in the early nineteenth century, and LDS Church sermons and publications used the Second Vatican Council to repeatedly make that point.[109] "There can only be one Church of

Jesus Christ in all the world," a high-ranking Mormon told the faithful as Vatican II approached.[110] Reformation had multiple potential results. Each individual brought into the Christian faith had experienced, in a way, the reformation of their own soul, reconciled to God through the atoning work of Christ. Institutions, therefore, might undergo a reformation as well. The possibilities were endless. But *restoration* was singular. Only one truth existed; only one church could contain that truth, and Christ had carried out his work of restoration in creating the LDS Church. While reformation spread the evangelical message outward utilizing diverse churches, different worship styles, and minor variations of orthodox theology, restoration permitted only one outcome. Endless churches could spread the evangelical gospel. Only one church could offer the exclusive and restored truth of Mormonism.

For Mormons, Vatican II confirmed the need for restoration. The pope himself had called for it, they pointed out, when his First Encyclical had declared, "We are concerned to restore to the Church that ideal of perfection and beauty that corresponds to its original image."[111] "When Mormons have spoken of a restoration of the gospel," the LDS Church's official publication responded, "other Christians have been quick to take offense and demand in outraged tones, 'Restoration? When was it ever lost?' But now no less a person than the Pope of Rome declares that there must be a restoration affecting 'the whole structure of the Church'!"[112]

In addition to the opportunity the council gave them to disapprove of the Catholic Church, Mormon leaders also used Catholicism's moment of reform in Vatican II to critique evangelicals' model of reformation through their emphasis on restoration and revelation. There had been one restoration, Mormon leaders taught, but it had brought about the possibility of new revelation through Christ's restored church. "A reformation cannot lead them back, but this new revelation can," Hugh B. Brown, First Counselor in the First Presidency, told his audience at an LDS conference in 1964, and he meant both the historical example of the Protestant Reformation and the present reform efforts of Vatican II. "We Latter-day Saints have that new revelation," he continued. "We have a new prophet and new scriptures also, which, added to the Bible, now point the way." Revelation had brought restoration, and restoration had allowed for continual new revelations where God spoke through his chosen mouthpiece on earth. Evangelical and perhaps now Catholic emphasis on looking to the Bible alone simply doomed them to repeat the historic errors of misinterpretation and misapplication that had required God to restore his church. "That restoration is Mormonism," Brown asserted.[113] His church restored, God now actively directed it through the revelations of David O. McKay. But the restoration had been definite, making "ecumenical councils unnecessary" and ending the need for "further debates over differing creeds and dogmas," another LDS leader explained.[114]

Aside from the metaphors of reformation, restoration, and revelation, both evangelicals and Mormons contended the Second Vatican Council's developments had pushed the Catholic Church in directions that affirmed their respective faiths. For evangelicals, the council's emphasis on scripture and various reforms concerning the laity struck them as developments of a particularly evangelical nature. Mormons argued that the Second Vatican Council meant the Catholic Church now esteemed so many of the things that the LDS Church had been attacked for since its founding days, including its emphasis on inspiration and revelation. "Need we remind the reader," the LDS magazine *The Improvement Era* asked, "that from the beginning its claim to continuing revelation was considered to be the most obnoxious and dangerous aspect of Mormonism?"[115] But now the Catholic Church too had declared direct revelation, rather than scholasticism, stood on equal footing with the Bible in discerning the will of God. Vatican II's declaration that official church statements ought to be considered as revelations struck Mormon observers as curiously similar to LDS beliefs about the prophetic message of its own leaders. In fact, they pointed out, the pope had even taken to calling one of his predecessors a prophet.[116] Additionally, the council's commitment to recovering true beliefs and practices that had been lost or corrupted through the years vindicated and validated one of Mormonism's most central claims. "As everyone knows," *The Improvement Era* argued, "the world was mightily offended by the assertion of the Latter-day Saints that the Christians had lost many of the ancient rites and ordinances and was scandalized and amused by their preoccupation with rites and ordinances they considered essential to salvation."[117] For Mormons, Vatican II's reforms and policies affirmed the basic principles of Mormonism. Every conciliar mention of renewal and each policy emphasizing inspiration and revelation struck Mormons as the Catholic Church's attempt to accomplish what Joseph Smith had already brought about and how their church leaders directed God's one true church each day. "It is astonishing how many of the changes that are taking place in Catholic and Protestant doctrines and ordinances are in the direction of those very things that have heretofore been peculiar to Mormonism and that have always brought persecution and derision on the heads of the Saints in the past," *The Improvement Era* pointed out.[118]

Conclusion

Whatever promising reforms they may have spotted, both evangelicals and Mormons believed the Second Vatican Council ultimately recommitted the

Catholic Church to its own erroneous beliefs and practices. In some ways, Vatican II had unwittingly affirmed their respective traditions, evangelicals and Mormons both pointed out, but the bulk of the council still served to strengthen the distinctively Catholic theologies and traditions that prevented the Catholic Church from holding the true gospel. While the Second Vatican Council exhibited signs of recognizing evangelical and Mormon truths, the overall errors that the council affirmed strengthened evangelical and Mormon convictions that they alone offered a complete and exclusive gospel message. And it made starkly clear again why both evangelicals and Mormons rejected ecumenical efforts even now that the Catholic Church cautiously endorsed ecumenism. Looking back on his magazine's consistent critique of the Second Vatican Council, Carl Henry praised *Christianity Today* in an internal memo for having "boldly disputed the claims of the papacy as formulated by Vatican Council I and left unchanged by Vatican II."[119] For evangelicals, Vatican II's ecumenical energies helped draw in and strengthen conservative Protestants to an evangelical identity. Noting the Catholic Church's new commitment to ecumenism, the Southern Baptist G. Earl Guinn recommended at the SBC's 1964 annual meeting that Baptists "find ways of cooperating with other Christian groups. Many of us believe that we can work together on matters of common interest without all becoming alike or Romanizing Protestantism." Though Southern Baptists had represented some of the most separatist elements of evangelicalism, turning down offers to join even the National Association of Evangelicals, so feared was the ecumenical push coming out of Vatican II that it led Southern Baptists like Guinn to reconsider Baptist independency in favor of joining other evangelicals to accomplish shared goals and to resist "Catholic aggression."[120]

The National Association of Evangelicals also rejected any talk of partnership with the Catholic Church throughout the decade. One resolution passed by the NAE in 1964 acknowledged the "significant changes in the posture of the Roman Church" thanks to Vatican II's emphasis on openness and confessed the Catholic Church's new disposition required a "reciprocation of friendliness" from evangelicals. Still, the resolution stressed that whatever changes in attitude the Catholic Church had developed mattered little while "we observe no basic alterations in doctrine giving promise of recognition of the great truths of the Reformation, upon which any real cooperation involving evangelicals must be based."[121] The basic theological premise of Catholicism prevented ecumenical ties. A separate resolution passed that same year outlined the narrow terms upon which evangelicals could agree to any ecumenical associating. Christians, the resolution explained, were united in belief, not by institutions, after experiencing true conversion. "Visible unity will never be sought for its own sake; nor founded upon any other rock than that which is Christ," the resolution continued in a clear strike against the Catholic Church's teaching of its authority as the basis of unity. "When of the Spirit, motions toward unity will always be of conviction and not compromise. . . . Not all activity in the name of Christian religion accomplishes these ends."[122] Unity, then, meant the spiritual union of those bounded together by the evangelical gospel. Spread throughout Protestantism—and even the occasional born-again Catholic—the evangelical Christian insisted that, as a tract on ecumenism put out by the NAE in 1964 explained, "pulling together vast numbers of so-called Christians regardless of whether or not they have been born again, simply because they bear the name of Christian can never be interpreted as true oneness in Jesus Christ." The pamphlet also made the argument common among evangelicals that the ecumenical movement "will not reach its logical goal until all Protestant and Orthodox churches are united with the Roman Catholic Church. Leaders who deny this will find that they have started something which may not be stopped before it reaches Rome." Instead, evangelicals were urged "to do all in their ability to establish fellowships with others of like Christian faith for the carrying out of the commands of our Lord and Saviour [*sic*]." Two years later, the NAE adopted yet another resolution against ecumenism and assured evangelicals "prayerful support in their efforts to resist pressures toward an unbiblical conformity and to present a pure Gospel of redeeming grace to their countrymen."[123] Amid the push for ecumenical ties and despite the allure of closer association with those who stood opposed to the secularization of both American culture and religion, evangelicals were encouraged to link themselves only with other evangelicals as a fulfillment of scriptural obligation and a rejection of the false bids for Christian unity.

For Mormons, Vatican II's ecumenism, signaling yet another foolish endeavor of the fallen churches, only hardened their exclusivity and autonomy against the calls to unity. "The Church certainly does not stand alone in the defense of righteousness, but it does stand alone as God's authorized representative on the earth to bring about the salvation of all those who would hear and turn to the teachings of Jesus," LDS leaders editorialized in the church magazine a few years after Vatican II.[124]

Yet at the same time Vatican II recommitted evangelicals and Mormons to anti-ecumenism, events in the American political system suggested Catholics, Mormons, and evangelicals might regard one another as cultural and political allies against the forces of secularism and in defense of a Christian nation. Two Supreme Court decisions that banned Bible reading and prayer in public school classrooms in the early 1960s alarmed religious conservatives of all faiths and elicited strident responses. Given the court's decisions, the cultural developments of the 1960s, and the further liberalization of mainline Protestant theology, seen in the most extreme example in the "God is dead" theology circulating among a small group of liberals, evangelicals, Catholics, and Mormons began to acknowledge how much they shared in common. Some even dared wonder if they should form stronger ties to combat what they saw as attacks on Christianity and its role in public life. But developments in the school prayer battle soon revealed the fault lines among a potential conservative ecumenical alliance and reheated long-simmering tensions and suspicions among theological rivals.

3

Our Father

"ALMIGHTY GOD," THEY said aloud, "we acknowledge our dependence upon Thee, and we beg Thy blessings upon us, our parents, our teachers and our country." Every morning, in school districts throughout New York, students recited the prayer as their school day began. But a group of Nassau County parents had objected to the prayer and taken their protest to court. Although state law allowed their children to not participate, the parents opposed the New York State Board of Regents' creation and authorization of the prayer on First Amendment grounds. By 1962, their case had reached the Supreme Court, which handed down a decision stunning many Americans, 79 percent of whom had recently told Gallup pollsters that they approved of religious exercises in the country's public schools.[1] *Engel v. Vitale* banned organized prayer in public schools. One year later, the court followed with a joint decision in *Abington Township School District v. Schempp* and *Murray v. Curlett* prohibiting Bible-reading exercises in public schools and declaring the recitation of the Lord's Prayer in public schools an unconstitutional act.[2]

Opponents of the Supreme Court's prayer and Bible-reading decisions frequently described the rulings as an attack on God. Such a charge resonated with millions of religious Americans who worried about the secularization of public life and believed the court was determined to destroy any expression of the nation's Christian heritage. By the 1960s, the assumption that the nation's political institutions originated from biblical principles and Judeo-Christian traditions had become a particularly powerful guiding idea for religious conservatives, and it undergirded their responses to the federal government, especially Supreme Court decisions. The court's decisions launched a movement to return prayer to the nation's classrooms, but that cause soon faltered under the weight of denominational divisions, differing interpretations of scripture, and persistent anti-ecumenical convictions that the politics of a school prayer amendment quickly exposed.

At the same time, liberal trends regarding the theology of God enervated just as powerful conservative responses as any court rulings had. Though endorsed by only fringe elements of liberal Protestantism, these theological developments represented some of the worst fears of ecumenism's staunchest critics, who had predicted the ecumenical movement would ultimately dismantle Christianity's most orthodox foundations. Yet while conservative evangelicals, Mormons, and Catholics found themselves making similar attacks against theological liberalism, they did not see the moment as calling for an orthodox ecumenical counterweight to the ecumenical movement and liberal Protestantism. Instead, they decided that such falsehoods demanded a truthful response found only in the exclusive message of their particular faiths. Both the school prayer and "God is dead" controversies brought evangelicals, Mormons, and Catholics together momentarily to lament the rise of secularism and assert the nation's Christian heritage and foundations, but the alliance was short-lived and merely symbolic, quickly replaced by more strident criticisms of the ecumenical movement and more assertive declarations of their own unique messages. Recognizing the mushrooming LDS Church as a religious threat and a heretical cult rather than a conservative co-combatant against liberalism's advance, Catholic and, particularly, evangelical leaders mounted attacks on Mormonism through the 1960s that placed Mormonism outside the Christian tradition and helped the slow but steady advance of Catholic-evangelical relations.

School Prayer

In colonial days, private institutions taught their students a religious curriculum closely tied to their sponsoring church. With the founding of public schools in the early nineteenth century, most of that sectarian teaching had been stripped away, but practices like daily Bible reading and reciting the Lord's Prayer remained in many classrooms, promoting a general Protestant identity. Waves of Catholic immigrants helped increase Protestant unity; school boards across the country implemented required readings from the King James Bible and the recitation of Protestant prayers in response to the influx of Catholic schoolchildren. Some school systems even taught from blatantly anti-Catholic literature. In response, many Catholic children enrolled in the Catholic school system their church had founded as a refuge from the aggressively Protestant public schools.

But for those Catholic children who remained in the public schools, discrimination, intimidation, and even violence often greeted them. No place was worse than Philadelphia. There, Catholic parents objected to the required

Protestant hymns and prayers and the daily readings from the King James Bible—a version that canon law prohibited Catholics from reading in part because it lacked all the books that the Catholic version included and had ties to the Church of England. When the Philadelphia school board ruled that Catholic schoolchildren could excuse themselves from such exercises in 1844, local nativists began to riot in defense of their Bible. By the time calm was finally restored, at least fifty-eight people had been killed and nearly one hundred and fifty others injured. No other place endured the level of violence that the Philadelphia Bible Riots of 1844 displayed, but throughout the country Catholic schoolchildren often suffered greatly for not participating in their classroom's religious activities.[3] In 1859 in Boston, for example, school officials severely beat a young Catholic boy who refused to recite the Protestant version of the Ten Commandments. A few years earlier, a mob had tarred and feathered a Jesuit priest in Maine who encouraged his congregants to refuse to participate in the King James readings the local school system required each day.[4]

After the Civil War, schools prioritized nationalism over Protestantism in their curricula, emphasizing lessons on democracy, capitalism, and patriotism. One study of textbooks found that nearly every religious reference had been removed from those volumes used in the late nineteenth century. By the twentieth century, as Stephen Solomon has noted, the religious content of public schools had dwindled down to a short scripture reading or offering of the Lord's Prayer. Some states passed laws to ensure at least this much remained. For instance, in 1913 Pennsylvania required that its public schools read ten Bible verses each morning. Other states followed Pennsylvania's lead. Still, twelve states declared Bible reading in their public schools unconstitutional—though not one state in the nation prohibited saying the Lord's Prayer.[5] One-third of the nation's school systems, in fact, mandated some form of prayer to begin the school day at the time of the Supreme Court's first ruling in 1962.[6] By the mid-twentieth century, scripture reading and morning prayers took place in school systems mostly in the Northeast and South, with little participation in the Midwest and West.[7]

Even if less than half of the nation's school systems held some sort of devotional activity by then, reaction from the American public to the Supreme Court's decisions was swift and overwhelmingly negative.[8] A Gallup poll taken in 1963 found 70 percent of Americans opposed the decisions.[9] Remarkably, reactions from religious leaders were more mixed. Episcopal Bishop James A. Pike of California said the Supreme Court had "just deconsecrated the nation."[10] But most mainline Protestant denominations and the liberal National Council of Churches were joined by Jewish leaders in supporting the decisions. The Catholic Church denounced the rulings.

Though Catholic leaders had often challenged the Protestant devotionals in public schools during the nineteenth century, a century later the Catholic Church opposed the Supreme Court's decisions, signaling both Catholicism's security as part of the "tri-faith America" religious establishment and also its more recent concern that secularism, rather than Protestantism, posed the greatest threat to the faith.[11] Cardinal Francis Spellman, Archbishop of New York, declared himself "shocked and frightened" by the court's rulings.[12] Spellman charged the court's decision "strikes at the heart of the Godly tradition in which America's children have for so long been raised," despite the unwelcome tradition of anti-Catholicism public school religious exercises had once shown.[13]

The LDS Church also condemned the decisions at first. Church president David O. McKay attacked the court for cutting "the connecting cord between the public schools . . . and the source of divine intelligence, the Creator himself."[14] After the *Schempp* case, McKay added that the Supreme Court was "now leading a Christian nation down the road to atheism."[15] If Mormons, like Catholics, had once worried about Protestant incursions on their faith, the church's regional dominance in the Intermountain West and its influence over the public school system there now allowed Mormon scriptures and prayers to flourish in the classrooms of Utah and other heavily LDS areas.

Perhaps surprisingly, reactions from evangelicals were mixed. The evangelist Billy Graham described the Supreme Court's actions as "another step toward the secularism of the United States."[16] In his typical alarmism, the fundamentalist Billy James Hargis ranted on his popular radio show, "I do not think there has been a more serious blow against Christian freedom."[17] Many evangelicals argued that given the nation's attitude toward the Soviet Union, the decisions smacked of hypocrisy. "It is one of the ironies of the American government and its people," a Pennsylvania man wrote to *Christianity Today*, "to be fighting atheistic communism within and without national boundaries, while at the same time condoning a secularized educational system that banishes God from the universe he created, and is designed to inculcate into the minds of American youth atheistic beliefs identical with Russian ideology."[18] The title of a 1964 book popular in some evangelical circles written by a Florida Baptist minister—*The Supreme Court Decision on Bible Reading and Prayer: America's Black Letter Day*—spoke to the despondency some evangelical Christians felt toward their government and hinted at the apocalyptic worries lurking below the surface of their political objections.[19]

Other evangelicals felt differently. Notably, the Southern Baptist Convention supported the decisions in keeping with their historic commitment to religious freedom. Reacting to *Engel*, the SBC's president Dr. Herschel H. Hobbs hailed it as "one of the greatest blessings to those of us who believe in the absolute separation of church and state."[20] Carl McIntire, president of the fundamentalist International Council of Christian Churches, agreed that the *Engel* decision was "sound." "The prayer was offensive to Bible-believing Christians," McIntire explained, "because it was not made in the name of Jesus Christ. . . . It is not tolerable that the State should presume to dictate an official prayer to God satisfactory to all religions, but most assuredly not satisfactory to Jesus Christ."[21] *Christianity Today* shared the concern that the New York prayer was a diluted offering to God rather than an explicitly Christian expression: "Christians adhering to the New Testament view of prayer, that God's answer is pledged only to petitions offered 'in Jesus' name,' might further have deplored the promotion of a religion-in-general doctrine of intercession implied in the New York devotional. Biblical Christians therefore could have considered themselves discriminated against as much as atheists."[22] The tri-faith committees of mainline Protestants, Catholics, and Jews appointed by state governments to write the prayers gave more reason for evangelicals to accept *Engel*. Many evangelicals believed a state-sanctioned prayer produced by an ecumenical consensus would never be heard by God.[23]

Although mindful of its diverse evangelical readership, *Christianity Today* leaned more to endorsing the Supreme Court's decisions. (The evangelical magazines *Eternity* and *Moody Monthly* both voiced approval of *Engel*.)[24] Often that support revealed *Christianity Today*'s—and evangelicalism's—frequent suspicions about Catholicism's theocratic aims. "In keeping with their Church's traditional objective of union of Church and State, and their current desire to narrow the contrast between public and parochial schools," the magazine editorialized just a few days after the *Engel* decision, "Roman Catholic spokesmen deplored the Supreme Court action as leading to godlessness in education."[25] A separate article in the same edition explained, "Catholic reaction was largely predictable, for the hierarchy has never shown enthusiasm for the principle of the separation of church and state."[26]

After the *Engel* decision, evangelicals who backed the ruling stressed the principle of church-state separation. The National Association of Evangelicals issued a 1,300-word statement agreeing with Justice Hugo Black's majority opinion that the New York prayer had been banned because of its authorship by a government body.[27] "Evangelical opinions were mixed. . . ." *Christianity Today* acknowledged, but boasted that, "As the days passed . . . support grew for the view that the position on church-state separation implicit in the Supreme Court action was—as CHRISTIANITY TODAY had editorialized . . .—both defensible and commendable."[28] Yet the magazine granted that it would look to the upcoming cases out of Maryland and Pennsylvania for "an enunciation . . . of guiding principles that will prevent both anti-religious government and sectarian government. If the Supreme Court is unable to draw a consistent line between the wholly godless state and a state religion, then the nation needs a new team of umpires."[29]

After the ruling in 1963, some evangelicals who had supported *Engel* now began to change their position in light of *Abington School District v. Schempp* and *Murray v. Curlett.* The removal of Bible reading from the classroom angered evangelicals more than a ban on rote prayer because of the importance of scripture to evangelical belief and identity. Now taken together, it was hard for evangelicals to not see the school prayer and Bible-reading decisions as a willful assault on the nation's Christian heritage and a major advance for secular forces.[30] The NAE's president described the new decision as "another step in creating an atmosphere of hostility to religion. Rather than serving to protect against the establishment of religion, it opens the door for the full establishment of secularism as a negative form of religion." The fundamentalist Carl McIntire switched his earlier support for *Engel* and now called for a constitutional amendment to allow school prayer and Bible readings.[31]

While waiting for the Supreme Court's decision on *Schempp, Christianity Today* reminded its readers that the "public schoolroom in a republic dedicated to the separation of church and state should be used for evangelistic purposes by neither Protestant, Catholic, nor Jew [*sic*]; by neither atheist nor theist."[32] Yet after the court's joint ruling in *Schempp* and *Murray* in the summer of 1963, the magazine blasted, "We can expect atheistic forces to utilize the Supreme Court decision to further the case of irreligion." It did acknowledge, however, that public schools "were never intended to carry the burden of instilling devotional attitudes in the younger generation. . . . Writing or sanctioning of prayers is surely not a governmental responsibility, religious practice and commitment is not to be secured through legal proscription, and coercion has no place in achieving conformity of religious ideas and practices."[33]

Catholic reaction to the rulings further tempered *Christianity Today*'s response, though not nearly as much as they shaped Southern Baptist responses to the rulings. Earlier that spring, as the nation awaited the court's decision, the magazine had chastised those "who oppose religious elements in civic life simply on anti-Catholic grounds. . . . It is always pertinent to base how much of our program springs from genuine church-state concerns, and how much from sectarian bias that is dignified with the motive of pluralistic sensitivity."[34] But after the *Abington* and *Murray* rulings, *Christianity Today* noted that the Catholic Church was citing the decisions as proof that secular humanism had taken over the public schools, thereby justifying their requests of public funds for parochial schools, a position thoroughly opposed by evangelicals in the 1960s. "It is significant," *Christianity Today* editorialized, "that the loudest Roman Catholic condemnation of the recent Supreme Court decision came from areas such as Boston, New York, and Los Angeles, where Romanism has invested heavily in public schools. We must remember, however, that no *official* establishment of humanism yet exists in the public schools." If there was any silver lining to the Supreme Court's decisions for evangelicals, the magazine delighted, it came in the implicit limitations of Catholic political objectives: "The court ruling that compulsory religious devotions are illegal in public schools strengthens the obstacles to government aid to parochial schools."[35]

While religious leaders and organizations debated the rulings' consequences, politicians supported by an overwhelming public majority leapt to strike a blow at the decisions. Senator Sam Ervin of North Carolina lamented the "Supreme Court has made God unconstitutional."[36] A day after the *Engel* decision, a Republican congressman from New York, Frank Becker, declared it "the most tragic decision in the history of the United States" and offered a constitutional amendment to overturn the ruling.[37] Twenty-two senators and fifty-three representatives introduced their own constitutional amendments that year. Senator James Eastland convened a Judiciary Committee forum for those who opposed the court's decision, though the National Association of Evangelicals and several other religious groups submitted statements urging moderation and opposing any constitutional amendment.[38]

The following year, during the 88th Congress, 146 different resolutions sought to overturn the *Schempp-Murray* decision via a constitutional amendment. Representative Becker once again emerged to lead the fight. Recognizing that the many different resolutions prevented any one measure from collecting enough votes to pass, Becker gathered a bipartisan group of sixty representatives to hammer out a new amendment. The Becker Amendment read, "Nothing in this Constitution shall be deemed to prohibit the offering, reading from, or listening to prayers or Biblical scriptures, if participation therein is on a voluntary basis, in any governmental or public school, institution or place."[39] For the Judiciary Committee hearings on the amendment, Becker brought in an assortment of religious figures to express their support, including Catholic Bishop Fulton Sheen, fundamentalist Carl McIntire, and the NAE's Robert Cook, but Cook undercut any pluralistic pretense the amendment's backers might have wanted to display when he admitted that he interpreted the "Biblical scriptures" language of the amendment to mean only the Christian Bible.[40] Sheen proved unreliable as well. In front of the committee, the bishop voiced his disapproval of the Supreme Court's decisions, seeming to indicate his support for an amendment, but confusing his position as he noted that the "problem of pluralism" would likely cause different faiths to push for the use of their particular scriptures in the classroom. Outside the committee's hearing room, Sheen was clearer, stating to a group of reporters that he opposed a constitutional amendment.[41] Other Catholic bishops testified more plainly against the amendment to the committee. Although the Catholic Church took no official position on an amendment, some saw this silence as an endorsement of the status quo.[42]

Other religious leaders from diverse backgrounds appeared before the committee to challenge the amendment. Representatives from the liberal National Council of Churches, the moderate Baptist Joint Committee on Public Affairs, and the conservative Lutheran Church—Missouri Synod all testified against the amendment. The editor of Louisiana's Southern Baptist newspaper, *Baptist Messenger,* explained to the committee that Southern Baptists opposed the amendment because of their historic commitment to church-state separation and concerns that "it would leave the door open for prayers and Bible reading to be determined by the predominant religion in a given locale. This, in turn, would escalate religious conflict in America." Outraged by the editor's testimony, Billy James Hargis fumed in his magazine, "It is difficult to understand why a Southern Baptist preacher would join in with the communists, liberals, far-left National Council of Churches, etc., to destroy this move to return prayer and Bible reading to the public schools."[43]

But destroy it, they had. Testimony from conservative evangelicals against the amendment helped convince committee members that there was no religious unanimity on school prayer even in the most conservative religious circles. During the committee hearings, *Christianity Today* had reiterated its commitment to religious liberty and church-state separation and concluded the amendment "does not merit support."[44] The magazine most worried that "by removing present limitations upon state-prescribed religious exercises . . . the amendment is dangerous. Under it there is nothing to prevent such practices as the devotional reading of the Bible and the Book of Mormon . . . or the recitation of the 'Hail Mary.'"[45] Increasingly, evangelicals cited fears of extrabiblical scriptures and sectarian prayers as a reason to drop their backing of the amendment. As a generalized outrage at the removal of God from the classroom had given way to the pesky policy questions of what an amendment would look like, evangelicals recognized that a constitutional remedy might pose far graver theological concerns than schoolchildren should have to face. In the end, most evangelicals decided they were more concerned about their children having to read from the Book of Mormon or pray the

Rosary than they were that they could no longer officially pray as a class each morning.

The Catholic Church also had its concerns now that the hearings were "throwing a more penetrating light on the amendment," a pamphlet produced by the church's political organization observed. "There are, for example, problems of non-denominational prayer in a pluralistic society," the pamphlet noted. Describing Bible reading and prayer in schools as products of a dominating Protestant culture, the church now conceded that the Supreme Court had "endeavored, though awkwardly, to react realistically to the new culture, rather than to perpetuate the Protestant tradition in American culture."[46]

Upon deeper reflection, the LDS Church also changed its course. Although President McKay originally had denounced the decisions as leading the country into atheism, other Mormon leaders and theologians demonstrated a more thoughtful and rather neutral stance as the debate proceeded, ultimately interpreting *Engel* as a "strike at the undesirability of state-imposed and state-prescribed prayers" rather than the removal of God from public schools.[47] This interpretation, as presented in the church's magazine, prompted one Mormon reader to praise the LDS Church for its "entirely proper and expected" decision to "not add a statement of its position to the many declarations proclaimed by other faiths."[48]

The court's decision banning devotional Bible readings in schools may have made Mormon leaders more receptive to the decisions as a whole—quite the opposite reactions many evangelicals and Catholics initially had toward *Schempp*—because of the LDS Church's complicated relationship with the Bible. While the Bible was an important scripture to Mormons, it stood alongside other holy texts like the Book of Mormon. Mormon teachings in the early 1960s routinely pointed out the incomplete and imperfect nature of the Bible. "I knew I could not go to the Bible," President J. Reuben Clark, Jr., had told an LDS General Conference in 1960 about his search for Jesus' words. "We do not believe the Bible is absolutely correct."[49] The basis of Mormonism—the need for new revelations and additional scripture—was rooted in the Bible's own inadequacies, LDS leaders reminded. According to Mormon doctrine, the Bible itself admitted its own incompleteness and called for a new revelation—what Joseph Smith had delivered more than a hundred years before. The Bible alone was an unreliable guide, according to Mormon logic, because it confessed more truth was needed. "There are so many statements in the Bible that prove that there should be a restoration of the everlasting gospel . . . ," one Mormon leader explained in 1961, "that one could not possibly believe in the Bible and believe in the perpetuation of the truth."[50]

The Bible for Mormons, therefore, was controversial and certainly not uncontested. As LDS leaders frequently pointed out, scholars had found "4500 different manuscripts of the Bible, and . . . estimated that there were 120,000 variations."[51] Those variations, like the multiple denominations, pointed both to Christianity's fallen status and the Book of Mormon's perfection through which God had restored his church. While Mormons were encouraged to study and revere the Bible, that reverence was not for an infallible, inerrant word of God, as evangelicals believed, but as a guide toward truth, revealed most perfectly in the Book of Mormon and the LDS prophets. Instead, they were to remember that, as the church's Eighth Article of Faith taught, the Bible was the "word of God as far as it is translated correctly."[52] Smith himself had undergone the project of correctly translating the Bible, beginning to remove the errors and corruptions and reconcile the discrepancies that had accreted through history, but he had not completed his task. Because of this, "an entirely accurate and reliable translation of the Bible is not available," Mormons were reminded.[53] Smith's version, however, was titled the Inspired Revision, and that title, rather than "translation," spoke to Smith's overall approach to the scriptures. In 1965, just months after the Becker Amendment hearings and in the midst of the nation's debates about the Bible's role in public life, the LDS publication *The Improvement Era* issued a four-part series on "The Inspired Revision of the Bible" that closely examined the "Prophet's correction" of the King James Version.[54] Since Smith's task remained incomplete, the Inspired Revision had not become official scripture, but LDS leaders pointed out that Smith's task stood as proof of the Bible's imperfection and also, importantly, "a monument to the knowledge, spiritual insight, and inspiration of the Prophet."[55] Studying the Inspired Revision along with Smith's other translations and revelations, LDS leaders assured Mormons, "will result in a deeper appreciation for the divine mission and appointment of the Prophet Joseph Smith."[56] For Mormons, the Bible pointed the way toward Joseph Smith, his revelation, and his prophecies.

As Congress debated the Becker Amendment, LDS Church officials questioned the biblical wisdom of their fellow Americans, a sentiment that weakened Mormon support for the amendment. "Since men have strayed so far in the past with the Bible in their possession," one LDS leader asked a Mormon audience at the height of the Becker Amendment debates in 1964, "is it likely that this same Bible by itself can bring them back to Christ?"[57] While evangelicals worried that the Becker Amendment might permit readings from the Book of Mormon in classrooms across the nation, LDS leaders instead questioned the prevalent Christian logic that Americans' devotion to the Bible—in the classroom or anywhere else—was the remedy for the nation's ills since the Bible remained incomplete. Instead, the LDS Church accepted the court ruling as "the law of the land" that "breathes resentment, not against prayer, but against *state-required* and *state-authored* prayer."[58] Dallin H. Oaks, a professor at the University of Chicago Law School who would later become a high-ranking LDS official, reasoned in a long piece for the church's magazine that even if the court's decisions allowed secularism to take greater hold in the public schools, "a one-minute state prescribed religious ceremony at the beginning of the school day would certainly be insufficient to offset" that influence. This sentiment was soon shared by many religious conservatives.[59] Yet although evangelical and Catholic leaders were largely backing away from supporting the Becker Amendment or any other constitutional enforcement of school prayer and Bible reading, they did not demonstrate the generous view that Mormon leaders took of the court's decisions more generally. While evangelicals and some Catholics argued that the court's decisions inculcated secularism in the classroom and curriculum, Oaks argued the cases worked as a defense against the threat of secularism. Trusting that the court's ruling meant "the religion of secularism could not be established," Oaks argued the cases made it "unlawful for any public-school time to be used either to derogate religion or to promote secularism. This is because the use of school time for either of those purposes would be an establishment of secularism, agnosticism, or atheism just as the use of school prayers was held to constitute an establishment of denominational religion."[60]

Overall, most LDS leaders came to see the court rulings as both a correction against government-prescribed religion and a weapon that could be used against any attempts to incorporate secularism in public education. Importantly, whereas evangelical and Catholic leaders tended to see the removal of prayer and Bible reading as an automatic advance for secularism, LDS officials agreed with the court's claims of neutrality. Accordingly, while some Mormon leaders would occasionally decry the court's prayer and Bible decisions in sermons that worried about the spiritual state of the nation, no LDS leaders traveled to Washington to speak for or against the Becker Amendment.

In the end, public support for the Becker Amendment also dropped precipitously. At the beginning of the hearings, mail to Congress demonstrated nearly complete support for the amendment. As *Christianity Today* had noted, "If volume of mail is any indication, this so-called prayer amendment is for many citizens of greater importance than the civil rights bill."[61] But by the hearings' end, more than 50 percent of the letters expressed opposition. Support fell out within the committee, and it allowed the amendment to die without a vote.[62]

Meanwhile, the death of the Becker Amendment may not have mattered in much of the country. Many schools in the South and East continued to openly flout the court's rulings by continuing to offer Bible readings and prayers each morning. Grassroots organizations throughout the country like the Florida Back to God Movement, Iowans for Moral Education, and the Fort Wayne Prayer Group also rose up and kept the issue of school prayer active among concerned evangelicals.[63] For now, fights over school prayer remained largely local, but the energies and anxieties elicited by the removal of prayer and devotional Bible reading from the public schools—like so many other festering issues of the 1960s and early 1970s—simmered in communities across the nation, a slow boil of anger and outrage that would eventually erupt.

The school prayer controversy also provided one of the first glimpses at the shifting terrain of American religious life, suggesting potential new allies and possible reconfigurations. A Midwestern evangelical, for instance, might recognize she had more cultural convictions and anxieties in common with a conservative Catholic than she did with her neighbor who attended the mainline Methodist congregation in town. A Catholic priest working in the Intermountain West might grow to appreciate the LDS Church's strong stance on prayer in public life, not to mention Mormonism's fierce devotion to the traditional family. Yet the recognition by conservative Christians across the denominations of a mutual worry about their nation and its direction met up against the hard reality of politics where the sacrifices and compromises required for political change sketched the limits of ecumenical politics among them. Unwilling to give up particular theological convictions and religious practices and worried that the wrong wording of a school prayer amendment might actually expose their children to religious beliefs and language they didn't want their children to hear or say—that is, the very religious beliefs and language of each other—Mormons, Catholics, and evangelicals allowed school prayer to die because many felt there wasn't a better option. Instead, many of them voiced their moral outrage at this latest political transformation within their country, while quietly feeling relieved that their children wouldn't have to pray a Hail Mary or read from the Book of Mormon. Not insignificantly, what had really died was not God in the classroom but rather a vestige of ecumenical pluralism in the form of a prayer, abandoned by evangelicals, but also Mormons and Catholics, who revered their unique convictions more than hollow pieties.

The Death of God

In the fall of 1965, *Time* magazine reported on a new wave in Protestant theology, the "God is dead" movement. *Time*'s article highlighted four scholars it called the "death-of-God" theologians, but the piece—and the accompanying fallout—centered on Thomas J. J. Altizer, a young religion professor at Emory University. Altizer had called on Americans to "recognize that the death of God is a historical event; God has died in our time, in our history, in our existence."[64] Unlike atheists who denied God's existence and had no connection to organized religion, these "Christian atheists," as they called themselves, hailed from Protestant seminaries and denominations. Altizer was an Episcopal layman and had published his treatise in Princeton Theological Seminary's journal, *Theology Today*.[65] Altizer and his co-conspirators weren't seeking to destroy Christianity, but they contended the church's success in the modern age depended on acknowledging that God no longer existed and developing a theology unconnected to the divine.

Time's article, not surprisingly, quickly stirred up controversy. Emory, a Methodist university, felt the immediate effects of Altizer's words when alumni canceled contributions to the school's just-launched $25 million fundraising campaign.[66] *Christianity Today* pronounced, "'Christian atheism' is the newest twist in a sick theological world. . . . No one will deny these men the right to be atheists; but . . . for God's sake let them be atheists outside of institutions supposedly training men to spread the gospel that God is alive and that faith in his Son means life from the dead."[67] After that article, the magazine devoted its December 17, 1965, issue to the "God-Is-Dead Stir," with a cover-page declaration, "What the 'death of God' theologians are really saying is that they have not found him."[68] Throughout the magazine, various writers railed on a liberal Christianity that had allowed such heresy to bubble up from its seminaries, denominations, and churches. Because of this, one editorial concluded, "Never has the burden of presenting historic Christian theism fallen so heavily upon the shoulders of a vanguard of evangelical theologians."[69]

Outrage reached new heights, though, when *Time* published a follow-up six-page cover-piece on the "Godless Christian thinkers" just before Easter in 1966. The grim cover page displayed none of the colorful brightness usually accompanying Holy Week. Instead, an all-black page showcased a red-letter headline: "Is God Dead?" It was the first issue of *Time* to use only words on its cover, and the starkness reflected the dark story within the magazine's pages.[70] "A small band of radical theologians has seriously argued that the churches must accept the fact of God's death, and get along without him," the magazine reported.[71] Taking their pulpits just days later, ministers from across the theological spectrum denounced the death-of-God theology in their Easter sermons.[72] "I know God is alive. I talked to him this morning," Billy Graham quipped a month later as the controversy continued.[73]

Christianity Today, the magazine created to challenge the liberal theology of mainline Protestantism, was unimpressed by progressive Christians' protestations over the death-of-God theology in large part because they initially tended to dismiss the controversy rather than engage it as a serious theological crisis. "The living God cannot be imperiled by men who say he is dead, and he needs no defense by those who say he lives," *Christian Century*, *Christianity Today*'s liberal rival, editorialized in the spring of 1966 as the "God is dead" debate intensified, striking just the sort of anemic apologetic evangelicals had come to expect of mainline theology.[74] After the strident Easter-day response to the *Time* magazine cover, most mainline Protestant leaders regarded the "death of God" controversy as little more than "hullabaloo," as one influential Methodist ecumenist put it in his denomination's theological journal.[75] But some mainline leaders started to engage the "God is dead" theology more substantively. A handful of liberal seminaries held talks and offered new courses on the theology. Some mainline ministers pointed to the idea in sermons as something their congregants should take seriously. While most still regarded the "God is dead" theology as ultimately invalid, many saw in it as an opportunity to discuss the question of religion's relevancy to modern culture and the challenges of Christianity in the secular age with their congregations and denominations. Paul Lehmann, a professor at Union Theological Seminary, voiced a growing feeling in liberal Protestant circles that the death-of-God theologians "share with many of us an acute sense of recognition of the fact that the language of the Christian tradition has lost its obvious power to convey meaning."[76]

Evangelicals pounced on such responses, blaming liberal Protestantism and its intellectual legacy for giving rise to such heresy. "Religious professionals took the lead in crucifying Jesus of Nazareth," wrote Carl Henry, "now they are conspiring to kill the Living God also." Amid the trend of interfaith cooperation, Henry blasted the "ecumenical Sanhedrin" that was willing to "embrace almost every theological novelty" yet "ignores traditional evangelical views or disdains them as heresy."[77] The Presbyterian theologian Addison H. Leitch pointed out that denying God's existence was hardly a new idea. "First of all," he commented, "we should note that the argument is a very old one. . . . The battle of the Israelites was to push into general thinking of the ancient world the fact of God, and they had plenty of opposition."[78]

While evangelicals acknowledged that opposition to God had a long history, in the 1960s they worried about an increasing antagonism to the Christian tradition across the nation. Still, it was one thing for secular culture—Hollywood, the universities, the Supreme Court—to shun God for the lure of secular humanism. But the rise of an atheistic theology from within Protestantism outdid evangelicalism's darkest predictions about the church. Though evangelical and mainline Protestantism had diverged through the twentieth century, developments within both traditions—not least the emergence of the "God is dead" theology—revealed how wide the divide now existed within Protestantism. That distance also exposed new proximities, making the 1960s, as scholar Robert Wuthnow has argued, a decade of both "social and religious upheaval."[79] Upheaval laid the groundwork for realignments—the "restructuring" of Wuthnow's thesis—and evangelicals took the tentative first steps toward the advocates of conservative Catholicism. At the beginning of the decade, *Christianity Today* had remarked with some surprise, "At this point it is necessary to insist that there is a much broader area of theological agreement between evangelical Protestantism and Roman Catholic theology . . . than there is between evangelical Protestantism and modern liberalism." Still, while evangelicals appreciated the orthodoxy they believed the Catholic Church espoused, *Christianity Today* stressed to its readers that "deep cleavages" that "constitute an impassable gulf" remained between evangelicalism and the Catholic Church. "But, great as they are," the article concluded, "they are not as great as those which separate evangelicals from all forms of contemporary liberalism."[80] Some voices within American Catholicism agreed that the "death of God" controversy required a reevaluation of the relationships among Christians, particularly Catholics and conservative Protestants. "It's important to distinguish between those problems which divide the Churches and those which they all face in common," Monsignor William Baum, secretary of the Bishop's Committee on Ecumenical Affairs explained. "Faith—the crisis of belief underlying the 'God is dead' movement—is a matter for common concern."[81]

Christianity Today's appreciation of the Catholic Church in the 1960s demonstrated how far it believed mainline Protestantism had diverted from the gospel message more than it did any endorsement of Catholic theology. Throughout the decade, and especially during the Second Vatican Council, the magazine continued outlining in elaborate detail how Catholicism fell short of evangelicalism's exclusive truth. After a majority of voters in 1960 had looked past Kennedy's Catholicism to elect him president, the magazine lamented the election revealed "the widening public judgment that *all religion is irrelevant* to political attitudes and acts." While many Americans believed this demonstrated the nation's values of fairness and decency for all, *Christianity Today* criticized an "American mentality [that] rapidly is losing any distinction of *true* versus *false* religion, and is dismissing this contrast as based on unbrotherliness and intolerance."[82] The election of Kennedy, then, hadn't signaled a triumph of the pluralist experiment; it had exposed America's indifference to the falsity of the Catholic faith.

But the decade provided several moments for evangelicals and conservative Catholics to find themselves on the same side of issues confronting the nation—the concern over the school prayer and Bible-reading decisions, for instance, and the shared alarm over a culture that tolerated and even embraced the sexual revolution, the women's rights movement, and the rising prominence of homosexuality. When the initial rebuke most mainline Protestants offered the death-of-God theology was followed by a call from many of them for discussion and debate, the Catholic Church's opposition to any insinuation that God had died once again put evangelicals in closer alignment with the Catholic Church than with their Protestant counterparts. "The atheistic propaganda is spectacular not only for its scope and savagery," Carl Henry bemoaned, "but also for its entrenchment in Protestant institutions."[83] From Rome, Pope Paul VI in an address at St. Peter's Basilica denounced the God-is-dead theology, calling it the result of "an atheistic mentality, far from any religion."[84]

Still, whatever appreciation evangelicals may have felt for the Catholic Church's strong stance against the God-is-dead theology did not engender any ecumenical sense among them but instead a recommitment to using the controversy for aggressively distinguishing the evangelical message. In an internal memorandum for *Christianity Today*, Carl Henry argued evangelicals had to seize the death-of-God controversy as an opportunity not for cross-denominational partnering with like-minded defenders of the living God, but as a chance to present the distinct message of evangelicalism's exclusive truth. A Gallup poll taken late in 1967 revealed that 97 percent of Americans believed in God, buttressing mainline Protestant reluctance to make much of the "God is dead" talk coming from some in their corner.[85] But poll results like this only heightened evangelicals' convictions that they had to engage the "death of God" controversy in order to assert and secure the evangelical conception of God in the American mind. Amid the clamor, Henry contended evangelicals would "lose the battle for the minds of men if they do not enter aggressively and definitively into this intellectual debate over who and what God is."[86] Harold O. J. Brown, an influential theologian, also argued the moment demanded evangelical exceptionalism rather than ecumenical bridge-building. "The loss of the vision of God, the pitiable smallness of what passes for theology today," Brown wrote, "must be counteracted by those of us who would hold the Word of God, *who are the legitimate heirs* of the prophets, apostles, and martyrs."[87] At its annual meeting in 1966, the Southern Baptist Convention cited the God-is-dead movement as an impetus for their decision to aggressively expand the SBC into the "unchurched" northern industrial centers. "Something must be done to challenge effectively the autonomy of un-Biblical thought" prevalent in northern Protestant circles, one speaker at the convention declared.[88] So in whatever ways the controversies of the 1960s produced a recognition among evangelicals and conservative Catholics of their close alignment—especially in contrast to their distance both from secular culture and liberal Protestantism—these moments also helped sharpen the distinctions among religious traditionalists, especially evangelicals, who ultimately used the opportunity to highlight their distinctive account of truth rather than to dilute their message by emphasizing cross-denominational commonalities.

Although the "God is dead" moment had also led some Catholic leaders to stress alliance among Christian traditionalists against liberal theology and secularism, the controversy ultimately recommitted them to defending Catholic orthodoxy and the church's singular authority while revising its ecumenical vision. In 1967, at the first Synod of Bishops—a gathering of nearly two hundred bishops established by Pope Paul VI to serve as an advisory body—the bishops addressed some of the church's problems, including the threat of atheism. In anticipation of the event, the Congregation for the Doctrine of the Faith, headed by Alfredo Cardinal Ottaviani, the Second Vatican Council's most conservative voice, distributed a document for discussion among those attending. Titled "On Dangerous Opinions of Today and on Atheism," it warned of the growth of atheistic humanism and asserted the truth of Roman Catholicism and the power of the papacy. "Does not the church have the duty to reaffirm the authority of its magisterium," the document asked, in light of the growing movement away from religious faith.[89] Once assembled, the Synod recommended the church move away from a philosophical response to the "God is dead" movement to one that favored action through bringing Catholics and atheists together for discussion.[90] In part, this reflected the bishops' desire to build upon Vatican II's open and dialogical emphasis, but the recommendation also undercut an ecumenical response to the "God is dead" controversy and growing atheism. The Catholic Church determined to engage atheists directly rather than link with fellow Christians against a general scourge of atheism. As Vatican II had often conceptualized ecumenism, the Synod of Bishops also affirmed a vision of ecumenism that advocated Catholic dialogue with a particular group with the purpose, in part, to assert Catholic orthodoxy rather than some expression of pan-Christian unity.

More broadly, the "God is dead" moment allowed the Catholic Church to chastise some of its liberal bishops and also curb the more progressive momentum coming out of Vatican II, especially the ecumenical vision, which

Pope Paul VI greeted skeptically. To worshipers gathered in Vatican Square in April 1968, Pope Paul denounced the "God is dead" philosophy and reprimanded church leaders who in light of Vatican II's reforms sought to throw off Catholic teachings at their discretion.[91] Rather than characterizing the "God is dead" theology as an external threat of secular forces, Pope Paul seized the opportunity to link this humanistic philosophy with liberal ranks within his own church for the purposes of reasserting the magisterium's authority and weakening the modernizing trend. Conceding that some church areas had needed updating and revision, Paul nonetheless reaffirmed that two aspects of the church—the absolute truth of the faith and adherence to church law and its leaders—remained above reproach. Lest any confusion owe to the ecumenical nature of the Council, the church's dogma remained unchanged. The "truths of the faith" could never be forsaken or altered to please other Christian denominations, Pope Paul clarified.[92] Later that year, Paul again condemned the "God is dead" theology coming from some Protestant circles. Pivoting from that example, the pope also criticized "excessive haste" in the ecumenical movement that was moving too quickly to establish Christian unity at the expense of "theological truth." Recent participation by some Catholics, laypersons and priests alike, in interfaith services, ecumenical gatherings, and interdenominational Eucharist celebrations drew the pope's strong reprimand and rebuke because they had occurred without the church hierarchy's approval. While Catholics were right to desire the unity of all Christians, Pope Paul conceded, he reminded them that "the road to Ecumenism is long and hard, because it cannot avoid the path of theological truth." Rather than an initiative that lay Catholics and individual priests could direct, ecumenism could only be led by the church hierarchy and had to conform to church rules. These rules were not merely suggestive advice, but a set of "very definite rules" and "a real instruction, an outline of the discipline to which those who want to serve Ecumenism must submit."[93] Grassroots ecumenism or Protestant-led interfaith initiatives posed a danger to true Christian unity and right doctrine, the pope asserted, and he intimated that in an age of religious indifference an unchecked ecumenical movement might eventually succumb to the "God is dead" forces. While evangelical and Mormon critics often predicted that the ecumenical movement would ultimately result in the reabsorption of all Christians to a Catholic monopoly, the Catholic Church inveighed against a non-Catholic-directed ecumenism that would eventually degenerate into the sort of theological relativism and religious indifferentism that had birthed the death of God in the first place.

The pope's charge that the "God is dead" movement had originated from liberal ranks within the Catholic Church resembled evangelicals' blame of liberal Protestants for having hatched such heresy, though the latter diagnosis was more accurate. Mormon leaders, on the other hand, argued that Christianity itself, weakened by the denominational divisions which demonstrated its apostasy, encouraged doubt of God's existence. The very nature of modern Christianity, LDS officials declared, made fertile ground for atheism to take hold. Catholic and evangelical leaders had praised each other's defenses against atheistic theology even while asserting their exclusive understanding of God's truth, but Mormon accounts of the "death of God" controversy tended to present its Christian origins not as an aberration within some churches but rather as the extreme form—and natural outgrowth—of Christianity's fallen status.[94] As one article in *The Improvement Era* pointed out, "the discovery by some that 'God is dead' marks the dead-end, logical result of . . . 'the great apostasy.'"[95] N. Eldon Tanner, a member of the church's First Presidency, used his 1967 Easter address to accuse the "God is dead" theory as having "originat[ed] within Christendom and . . . being argued by . . . theologians, teachers of the seminaries . . . ministers, and bishops who preach it from the pulpit."[96] Yet such a result was hardly surprising to Mormons who understood Christians as having "lost touch with God and . . . [being] led by blind guides."[97]

As it had for evangelicals and Catholics, the "death of God" controversy for the LDS Church ultimately occasioned not a worry for the spiritual health of Americans, or a spirited attack on atheism, and certainly not a call for Christian unity. Instead, it permitted LDS leaders to assert Mormonism's exclusive truth against the erroneous Christian churches that had given rise to such unorthodoxy. Led by "false prophets" and "worshipping an unknown God," Christians who did not understand the LDS Church's restored gospel of Jesus Christ couldn't help but eventually conclude that God no longer existed, President Tanner contended.[98] A leading Mormon thinker explained it was unsurprising that so many who sought God through "the accumulated superstitions and myths that have encrusted revelation" have concluded that God is dead.[99] In fact, Mormon leaders countered, it was a good thing they had been led to such a result. "It represents and marks opportunity for continuing the search for truth," one argued.[100] Further, this LDS intellectual explained, those who concluded the Christian God was dead had at last come to a fundamental Mormon truth. "This does not mean that the true and living eternal God is dead," the Mormon advocate explained. "It only means that the God they were taught about in childhood, and in some traditional doctrinal statements, is dead, as Joseph Smith's revelation also indicated."[101]

For LDS theologians and leaders, the "God is dead" theology affirmed Mormonism's basic principles and historic origins. As a young Joseph Smith had discovered, the God of Christian lore and superstition had passed away. Those who advocated the "God is dead" theology were acknowledging that "the concept of God in historic Christianity . . . has been one that defies common sense and scientific thought."[102] "A god that cannot talk, be seen, nor exist in space, who is everywhere and nowhere, certainly cannot exist in the rational mind. Therefore such a 'god' is dead and warrants replacement," one Mormon leader contended.[103] Just as the "God is dead" theologians hoped their ideas would bring about a new conception of the divine, so too did LDS leaders imagine the "death of God" controversy might redirect some Americans away from false Christian notions of God to the restored truth of the Mormon gospel. The Christian God whom Mormons saw as imprisoned in ancient scripture might be replaced, LDS leaders hoped, by the active and vibrant God of Mormonism who spoke continuous revelation through his chosen prophets. Those prophets not only reflected God's will, LDS theologians reminded, but their prophecies revealed God's everlasting existence—a rebuke to his purported demise. "All down through the ages the prophets have borne testimony that they have talked with God," President Tanner noted in his Easter sermon, affirming his own prophetic status.[104]

The "God is dead" controversy had excited many passions, particularly among religious conservatives. While some religious conservatives believed the moment required a broad defense from the religious front, evangelical, Catholic, and Mormon leaders retreated to their corners to defend and promote their particular faiths. In the end, the "God is dead" moment elicited not an occasion for conservative ecumenism to defend the Judeo-Christian God, but rather a call to arms for their own truths. Evangelical and Catholic leaders did not squabble about the nature of God, but they did launch very different arguments of how God revealed himself and his will. For evangelicals, God was the god of scripture, everlasting and unchanging, unbound by earthly institutions. For Catholics, God was the god of scripture and tradition, who had established his church and sanctioned its authority. Mormons also believed they were God's "one true church," but who God was had been revealed by his prophets. As Mormons were reminded, Joseph Smith had revealed that God was a "distinct personage" "separate and distinct from" Jesus Christ and also the Holy Spirit: "three distinct personages and three Gods"—what Mormons called tritheism rather than the trinitarianism of traditional Christianity.[105] That unique theology defined Mormonism, of course, but it also constrained any ecumenical initiatives from within the LDS Church and enlivened attacks on Mormonism, especially from evangelicals, that accelerated in the late 1960s, even as evangelicals worried that few other Americans shared their political and cultural conservatism.

The Mormon Menace

Thanks largely to President David O. McKay's proselytizing push, the LDS Church prodigiously grew during the 1960s. When McKay became president in 1951, the church counted 1.1 million members. At his death in 1970, nearly 3 million called themselves Mormons—a near-tripled growth.[106] Thirty percent of that growth had come from missionary work, with the increase particularly taking place outside the church's Intermountain West base and on the international front.[107] The LDS Church's expansion drew concerned responses from evangelical and Catholic leaders, but Catholic and evangelical fears about Mormonism's growth in the 1960s grew out of long-standing critiques both faiths had made since Joseph Smith's days.

In the mid-1960s, relations between the Catholic and LDS churches had cooled a bit after a recent series of skirmishes. Catholic attitudes toward Mormonism understandably were shaped by a defensive response to what was generally seen as the Book of Mormon's anti-Catholic theology. Mormon theology maintained that the truth held by the first Christian church had been corrupted through the years by developments in doctrine, liturgy, and religious practices organized by the Catholic Church. So much did the Catholic Church depart from the truth of Christ's first church, Mormon doctrine taught, that that early primitive church eventually disappeared entirely, replaced by a heretical institution that would further fall away from Christ's intents for his church as it eventually splintered into thousands of different sects. So, Mormonism had always been anti-Catholic in the sense that it saw the Catholic Church as the source of Christianity's apostasy.[108]

LDS scripture sanctified such views. Early in the Book of Mormon, the prophet Nephi has a vision that unleashes a vicious attack on the Catholic Church. Nephi foresaw the United States in its last days, the blight of which would be the Catholic Church.[109] Verse after verse excoriates the "great and abominable church."[110] Though the Catholic Church is never named, the descriptions of the "great and abominable church" make clear the target of Nephi's wrathful vision. Nephi described seeing priests draped in "gold, and silver, and silks, and the scarlets, and fine-twined linen, and all manner of precious clothing." He also saw "many harlots" surrounding the priests.[111] "Founded by the devil and his children," the Catholic Church was also "the whore of all the earth."[112] Nephi attacked the proliferation of sects and further schisms within Christianity—the foundational critique of Mormonism. Still, among all the churches of Christianity, the Catholic Church stood out, "most abominable above all other churches."[113]

Given this scriptural basis, most Mormons were unsurprised to see the Catholic Church's treatment in *Mormon Doctrine*, an unofficial encyclopedia of Mormonism published in 1958 that, although not church-sanctioned, still became a de facto reference tool for thousands of lay Mormons. The entry for "Catholicism" directed readers to "*See* Church of the Devil." Turning to that entry, one read: "The *Roman Catholic Church* specifically – singled out, set apart, described and designated as being 'most abominable above all other churches,'" with a citation to the verse from Nephi.[114] Though President McKay certainly bore his share of anti-Catholic views, he was incensed by the explicit statement of such theology in a book that LDS officials had not known about prior to publication. An audit by two high-ranking Mormons, Mark E. Petersen and Marion G. Romney, found the encyclopedia contained over a thousand errors.[115] Subsequent editions of *Mormon Doctrine* removed the "Catholicism" entry, and LDS officials stressed to Mormons that the volume was not church-approved, but the 1958 edition had only made visible what most Mormons, including its leaders, already believed about the Catholic Church.

While LDS officials wanted to ignore the Catholic controversy in *Mormon Doctrine*, Duane Hunt, Salt Lake City's Catholic bishop, understandably could not overlook the swipe. In response, Hunt authored a spirited defense of *The Unbroken Chain*, as the title of his book declared, of the Catholic Church. Later retitled *The Continuity of the Catholic Church*, Hunt's book argued that "any break" in the church's succession or "in the teaching of the gospel would have been and has been proved to be impossible"—a direct refutation of Mormonism's charge against Catholicism and all of Christianity. Still, Hunt confessed a general indifference to Mormonism shared by most other Catholic leaders through the 1960s. "I am not in the least interested in any Mormon doctrine except in so far as it is unfavorable to the Catholic Church. Then, to the best of my ability, I shall reply," Hunt contended.[116]

Overall, the Catholic Church tended to take this response to Mormonism through the 1960s, defending against LDS challenges of Catholicism but not launching its own attacks on Mormonism like evangelicals regularly did. When George Romney, Michigan's Republican governor and a devout Mormon, ran for president in 1968, Catholics saw it as an opportunity to learn more about, as one Catholic magazine headline described, "Those Mystifying Mormons."[117] The article acknowledged Romney faced some of the same questions about his faith and its relationship to politics that John F. Kennedy had endured eight years ago, but believed Romney's candidacy provided a chance to investigate the LDS faith and the "doctrines [that] are unheard of in other Christian religions."[118] These included what it characterized as the faith's "anthropomorphic concept of God the Father as an exalted man," its denial of the trinitarian nature of God for a Godhead of three completely separate Divine Persons, and its belief that the Bible was the word of God only so long as it was translated correctly—all beliefs the LDS Church had emphasized during the recent school prayer debate.[119] Lastly, the article detailed Mormonism's theology of history that outlined the continual cycle by which God gave the gospel to people only to take it back when they proved they could not live up to it. Jesus had come to earth to restore the gospel and entrusted it to his apostles, but after their deaths it became corrupted again and taken away by God until Joseph Smith, the article explained, "would accomplish what Jesus Christ had failed to do."[120] Such an accounting of Mormon theology depicted a faith that elevated Smith's actions over Jesus' saving mission while also minimizing the divine omnipotence of God. In outlining the LDS Church's history of the gospel on earth, the article pointed out, just as Bishop Hunt's earlier book had, the discrepancy between a Catholic Church that traced its own history directly back to those apostles and an LDS Church that insinuated Catholicism's early years had required God remove the gospel from humankind for nearly two thousand years.

These intermittent responses to Mormonism from Catholic voices paled in light of the constant and increased attention evangelicals showed through the 1960s, fueled by fears of Mormonism's expansion. As Mormonism moved out of its historic base in the Intermountain West into new regions, particularly the Southern Bible Belt, evangelicals developed educational tools to ward off the dangerous new faith. Like their older fear of unbounded Catholic growth, evangelicals made frequent references to Mormonism's accelerating expansion in the 1960s. An advertisement in *Christianity Today*, which routinely ran ads for books about Catholicism, Mormonism, and other "cults," worried that the "growth of the combined non-Christian cults"—including the LDS Church—"is estimated to be ten times that of evangelical Christianity."[121] More specifically, a *Christianity Today* report on "the bizarre Mormon religious system" in 1964 expressed concern that the LDS Church had grown by one hundred and fifty thousand members in just one year and that, more worryingly, two-thirds of that increase had come from conversions to the faith. Now with 2 million members, the LDS Church, the magazine pointed out, had almost as many members as the American Lutheran Church, "currently the ninth-largest American Protestant denomination."[122] "Since many of the additions to the Mormon church [*sic*] come out of Protestant denominations," another article explained, "it is imperative that Protestants understand the nature and dangers of Mormonism."[123] Evangelicals were also warned that though the LDS Church, like evangelical churches, had little regard for the ecumenical movement of the day, Mormons were being encouraged by their church to develop "a more understanding attitude" toward outsiders in order to enhance their conversion efforts, especially among Protestants.[124]

As the LDS Church continued growing through the 1960s, evangelicals watched nervously. By the late 1960s, a Southern Baptist pamphlet noted that the 2.5 million Mormons in America "can hardly be ignored."[125] The Convention worried about the LDS Church's successful proselytizing, a chilling prospect in light of the SBC's own evangelistic aims. "There are ample reasons," the pamphlet noted, "for their rapid spread despite largely unbiblical doctrine." These included Mormons' earnest commitment to spreading their faith, best shown through their thirteen thousand missionaries, who visited over 3 million American homes each year. In contrast, 11 million Southern Baptists had only six thousand missionaries at their service.[126] One frequent evangelical watcher of Mormonism credited the LDS Church's growth to its church members who "believe their story and tell it with all the salesmanship of Avon."[127]

Evangelicals also pinpointed the LDS Church's emphasis on strong families for its successful proselytizing efforts in the tumultuous 1960s. To some extent, evangelicals appreciated how deeply Mormons cared about the institution of the family. One *Christianity Today* piece cited the "strong practical emphasis on home and family solidarity" the LDS Church promoted.[128] Another noted Mormons' "high standards of morality and ideal concept of family life."[129] Given the assault evangelicals believed the traditional family faced in the 1960s, Mormons' commitment to strong families and their concomitant devotion to the values and practices that supported the traditional family structure—sexual monogamy, conservative gender roles, and unchallenged parental authority—had to be applauded by evangelical observers. Yet because evangelicals believed Mormonism posed as great a threat to the authentic Christian message as secular culture did to the traditional American family, evangelicals ultimately interpreted Mormon family values as part of the LDS Church's deceptive ploy to hoodwink potential converts into the lie of Mormonism. This was the real danger of living in a culture that showed decreasing respect for the traditional family, evangelicals argued. Surrounded by its decline and disregard, those Americans who still believed in strong, conventional families would be lured into heresies like Mormonism that showcased their traditional cultures in order to cover their deceptions. After the LDS Church in 1969 reaffirmed its long-standing policy that African-American members could not hold the priesthood, *Christianity Today* responded that blacks should feel fortunate to be denied this since the LDS Church was "tragically misguided."[130]

Because evangelicals feared the LDS Church's emphasis on the family made it attractive to converts, they emphasized the darker historical practices of the Mormon family in their treatments. *Christianity Today* seemed delighted in reminding its readers of Mormonism's polygamous past. The magazine contended the LDS Church had abandoned polygamy only because the government had forced it to, "but the principle of polygamy remains on their books as divinely approved."[131] Another article argued that polygamy "remains an essential point of [Mormon] doctrine," lest evangelicals be seduced by the images the LDS Church presented of its nuclear, monogamous families.[132] The magazine also depicted Mormon teachings as especially lurid. *Christianity Today* observed that the Mormon theology of salvation depended on the sexual relationship of husband and wife on earth, who reached exaltation in the afterlife through "physical relationships and ceremonious activities" and looked forward to a "sex relationship [that] continues in the eternal state."[133] The Mormon family, in evangelical descriptions, perverted the Christian gospel from its message of free grace to a sexualized works-based notion of salvation.

Evangelical depictions of Mormonism at mid-century resembled much of the Cold War propaganda of the time. Like Communism, Mormonism was described as a system of lies that appealed to Americans' sensualist proclivities through coded language and ensnared them in a trap they could not escape. In 1954, the Southern Baptist Convention's Sunday School Board published a pamphlet entitled "The Menace of Mormonism" that they hoped SBC Sunday school classes would use to warn Southern Baptists about the blasphemous cult. The pamphlet provided an overview of Mormon history and theology, but more often veered into inflammatory barbs. "'Mormon' is a Greek word literally meaning a hideous, female monster," the pamphlet charged. "Wholly materialistic, Mormonism is the concept of the flesh. Therein lies its strength and appeal. It is the antithesis of everything Jesus Christ stands for." Mormon doctrine, according to the Southern Baptist document, exhibited "unbelievable crudeness—sometimes repulsiveness," and demonstrated "unmitigated blasphemy." "Mormonism has deliberately distorted, misinterpreted, and misused the holy Scriptures, the Word of God," the pamphlet concluded, "It has flagrantly blasphemed against God. It is wholly sensual and materialistic. It is based upon superstition and ignorance."[134]

Christianity Today also described Mormonism as "materialistic in emphasis" because the faith encouraged Mormons to attain higher educations and work hard for professional success.[135] A "cult expert" writing in the magazine in 1964 wondered how a people with such high rates of college education could also be known for their "simultaneous insistence upon the impossible myths that underlie the system" of Mormonism.[136] That same year, the evangelical writer Harold Lindsell characterized Mormonism as one of the "Four Major Cults" along with Christian Science, Jehovah's Witnesses, and Seventh-Day Adventism.[137] Elsewhere, the magazine attacked Mormon concepts of sin, salvation, and the Savior, warning that Mormons used "standard Christian terms . . . but they put them into a meaning radically different from that found in the Bible."[138] Another article warned of the deviousness of Mormons who "are careful to make certain that they do not use language which might reveal the true nature of their theological deviations" and of the "Mormon religion [that] utilizes biblical terms and phrases and even adopts Christian doctrines in order to claim allegiance to the Christian faith." The piece recommended evangelicals looking to combat "the propaganda of Mormonism" should read Walter Martin's *The Maze of Mormonism,* which the magazine praised for exposing "the great gulf that exists between Christianity and the religion of Joseph Smith and Brigham Young."[139] Similarly, a "Protestant layman" from Salt Lake City reported to *Christianity Today* that the LDS Church calculatingly emphasized the Bible in order to "establish itself as Christian."[140]

Mormon salvation was a "matter of striving" rather than the "free gift of God's grace" evangelicalism presented. "To those enmeshed" in Mormonism, the magazine exhorted, "evangelical Christians must hold out an all-sufficient Saviour [*sic*] who saves, sanctifies, *and glorifies* unworthy sinners who place all their confidence in Him alone."[141] Other evangelical groups like the Southern Baptist Convention and the National Association of Evangelicals urged their members to present the Christian gospel to Mormons. In 1966, the NAE listed "Ministering to Mormons" as one of its areas of emphasis for the year.[142] Evangelical seminaries also included courses on Mormonism in their offerings to educate their students about the Mormon "cult" and how evangelicals could, as one syllabus explained, "approach adherents . . . so as to most effectively present biblical truth."[143] Evangelical fears of cults abounded in the 1960s, and books like Walter Martin's *The Kingdom of the Cults* (1965) became huge evangelical bestsellers. While most Americans in the 1960s were more likely to think of Hare Krishna and other Eastern-based religious groups when they heard the word cult, for evangelicals Mormonism remained the dominant focus of their anti-cult literature. In response, evangelicals encouraged each other to take the truth of the gospel to the Mormons. Not unlike Mormon doctrine, which pointed to the splintered sects and denominations of Christianity in contrast to its unique position as God's one restored church, in the 1960s evangelical theologians and thinkers used the presence and strength of Mormonism and other so-called cults to highlight their own sole possession of truth. "Truth by its nature is singular and unitary," the Dallas Theological Seminary journal explained, "while error is multifarious and multitudinous . . . This is the truth about error."[144]

Conclusion

"American churches, identified no longer by their religious beliefs, are in the throes of a realignment based on how they view events outside the church walls. . . . Conservatives of most Christian denominations, regardless of their once bitter debates over Bible interpretations and church history, are looking to one another for support against what they see as destructive forces in the ranks of organized religion."[145] So read an article in the *Los Angeles Times* at the end of the 1960s. This wasn't a totally accurate reading of the realignment remaking the American religious landscape, but it wouldn't be the first time a secular media outlet misinterpreted events in conservative Christendom. Despite the conclusions of the *Los Angeles Times*, religious beliefs had been the basis of that realignment, particularly within American Protestantism. While mainline and evangelical churches and denominations alike grew during the upsurge of religiosity from World War II until the 1960s, they both thrived in a vibrant religious marketplace where they offered competing interpretive views of scripture and salvation.[146] Evangelical churches, aided by a robust network of parachurch organizations like the National Association of Evangelicals, *Christianity Today*, the Billy Graham Evangelistic Association, Youth for Christ, and Bill Bright's Campus Crusade for Christ, presented a clear and exclusivist message that rejected the ecumenical tide in mainline Protestantism while also softening the boundaries of denominationalism and remaking the basis of religious identity. Many of their adherents recognized themselves as evangelicals or "born-agains," but more of them simply identified as Christians, an expansive yet also orthodox self-conception—from Pentecostals to conservative Anglicans—that stood in stark contrast to what they saw as the permissive vagueness of mainline ecumenical belief.[147] Because of this, they were less devoted to the denominations they might have been raised in and more committed to the evangelical message they found in various churches and organizations. This theological commonality helped gather together a loose but powerful interdenominational alliance of conservative Protestants who were linked by religious belief, but who were also, in the context of both mid-century American Protestantism's shifting terrain and the nation's social and political upheavals, open to other conservative allies, as the *Los Angeles Times* had concluded. Still, strong denominational identity among some evangelical groups, like the Southern Baptist Convention, persisted and strengthened anti-ecumenical sentiments in conservative Protestant corners. As W. A. Criswell, pastor of the SBC's preeminent congregation, First Baptist Dallas, would write in his 1970 book, *Look Up, Brother!*, "Ecumenicity is another name for death to our Baptist faith."[148]

The 1960s had presented a turning point in the relations among Mormons, Catholics, and evangelicals as the three faiths began to recognize each other as sympathetic allies opposed to a secularizing culture and the increasing liberalization of mainline Protestantism. But that recognition just as often helped highlight the substantive theological disagreements that remained. Catholics, Mormons, and evangelicals shared a belief in an active and engaged God and the conviction that the United States was singularly blessed because of its status as a Christian nation. All three believed in scriptural authority, though that, of course, meant different things to each of them, as had been revealed by both Vatican II and the school prayer debate. Mormons, Catholics, and evangelicals shared the Bible, but there were important differences in translations and what was included in their own versions of the text. Catholics had extra books in their Bible, and the LDS Church had additional scriptures, like the Book of Mormon, the Doctrine and Covenants, and the Pearl of Great Price. What scriptural authority meant also varied among them. For evangelicals, *sola scriptura* ("by scripture alone") was a foundational precept of Christian belief—only the message of the Bible, not a pastor, not a church, possessed ultimate authority. *Sola scriptura* had also been a central charge of the Protestant Reformation against the Catholic Church. For Catholics and Mormons, scriptural authority was bound up in the institutional authority of the church. Their churches had the power to interpret, control, revise, and update scripture, whereas evangelicals insisted on the authority of the individual believer to interpret an unchanging and infallible scripture.

Between Catholics and evangelicals there had been a growing respect, if not affinity, especially after the Second Vatican Council, as evangelicals appreciated the Catholic Church's increased emphasis on the Bible and conservative Catholics' defense of orthodoxy in contrast to mainline Protestant liberalism. As the decade drew to a close, the theologian Harold O. J. Brown writing in the pages of *Christianity Today* advised that his fellow evangelicals "must recognize that now the God-fearing, Christ-honoring Catholic and the evangelical Protestant are in the same situation." He also hoped that Catholics and evangelicals "will learn to co-operate" and stop the "headlong rush" of liberals in the churches.[149] Given *Christianity*

Today's consistent critique of Catholicism, Brown's comments represented a remarkable development in evangelical attitudes and an important advance in evangelical-Catholic relations. Catholic reforms through Vatican II along with cultural and political changes in the nation and theological developments within mainline Protestantism together encouraged such developments. But the presence and expansion of Mormonism and other competing "cults" in the 1960s also shaped evangelical assessments of Catholicism. Combined with appreciation for the Vatican's increasing orthodoxy, evangelical evaluations of Mormonism's false claims to Christianity highlighted that evangelicals shared a true history and values system with Catholics.

Still, this did not change the larger question of ecumenism or Christian unity. For evangelicals, Christian unity meant the coming together of only those denominations and churches who believed in the narrow theology of the evangelical message. This union, emphasized by bodies like the National Association of Evangelicals and *Christianity Today*, developed in part as a reaction to the ecumenical movement itself and in spite of improving attitudes about Catholicism. Believing that false Christians were being pulled into unbiblical associations, evangelicals joined together as a defense of the faith against the heretical unions that diluted the gospel message. While evangelicals hoped aligning themselves would both enhance their proselytizing efforts and form a stronger bulwark against the liberal ecumenical associations, they also undercut most efforts among them to partner with non-evangelicals. In 1966, for example, the Golden Gate Baptist Theological Seminary, a Southern Baptist institution in California, fired one of its professors for his "ecumenical proclivities."[150] In another example, *Christianity Today* recommitted to opposing unbiblical ecumenism in its pages. In 1967, Carl Henry warned fellow staffers at the magazine that evangelical Christianity stood "at the brink of a crisis" and that the next ten years would determine "whether it survives as a virile force in the modern world or whether it will be dismissed as a solitary wilderness cult. This crisis is theological, evangelistic, social, and ecumenical. The battle will need to be waged on all four fronts."[151] Through *Christianity Today* editorials, NAE resolutions, seminary courses, and Sunday sermons, evangelicals heard repeated warnings against ecumenism. Those admonitions would continue, but political and cultural developments would influence how conservative religious faiths thought about and acted with one another. As religious conservatives from various denominations increasingly believed their nation was departing from its religious foundations and traditional values, they began to fear the agents of secular humanism that they believed controlled the nation as much as they worried about the theological disagreements and historic hostilities among their cultural and political allies.

Conservative Catholics, evangelicals, and Mormons also recognized each other as defenders of traditions that seemed increasingly under attack throughout the 1960s—most principally, the traditional monogamous, heterosexual family. All three lamented the rising divorce rates, the increase in sexual openness and freedom, and the growth of a visible homosexual community the decade witnessed. All three championed conservative gender relations, the primacy of the male breadwinner, and opposed any threats to total parental authority they thought institutions like the public schools and the federal government often posed. And all three believed the family unit itself, rather than the individual or the democratic tradition, stood as the bedrock of the American experiment. The perceived threat to the traditional family by secular culture, Supreme Court decisions, federal policies, and the liberal churches that supported so many of these trends brought Mormons, evangelicals, and Catholics closer together. Moving into the 1970s and beyond, they found themselves even more closely aligned on positions regarding abortion, the Equal Rights Amendment, sex education, gay rights, and pornography. But they also quickly found that aligned positions did not always produce closer connections.

4

This Is My Body

ON JANUARY 22, 1973, the Supreme Court of the United States issued two decisions that would profoundly influence the nation's social and political course, although the rulings sparked little controversy at the time. In *Roe v. Wade* and its less-remembered companion, *Doe v. Bolton*, the Supreme Court abolished all state abortion laws and declared a woman and her doctor alone could decide to have an abortion during the first trimester.[1] These rulings struck down laws prohibiting abortion dating back to the nineteenth century and also overturned recent state laws that had liberalized the practice. Sixteen states had done so, but the conflicting and confusing laws in each of these states had created a complicated situation that the Supreme Court's ruling clarified. Now all fifty states would share a uniform law similar to those already in place in New York, Alaska, Hawaii, and Washington, which permitted abortion in the first months of pregnancy.[2] Even pro-choice advocates were surprised by the court's permissive decision. "We neither asked for nor expected this much," one supporter declared.[3]

Following the court's ruling, most Americans appeared supportive. Indeed, part of the court's decision to rule in favor of abortion rights had been based on its understanding that abortion was supported by a nationwide social movement and by national medical organizations.[4] A poll taken shortly after the court's decision found that 58 percent of voters questioned, including 46 percent of Catholics, supported laws allowing abortion in the first trimester.[5] Three years later, two-thirds of Americans polled in 1976 said abortion should be a matter between a woman and her doctor. Sixty percent of Catholics agreed. Various studies of abortion opinion polls, however, also showed that the deeper one's commitment to one's religious faith, the more likely one was to oppose abortion, especially beginning in the late 1970s and after.[6]

But in 1973, most religious conservatives did not oppose abortion. The literature of the Religious Right and of modern conservatism, however, has contended the anti-abortion movement provided the opportunity for those of conservative religious faiths to bury their theological divisions and historical tensions and unite in a political cause.[7] As the political scientist Kerry N. Jacoby has argued, the pro-life movement "fused Catholic and Protestant, fundamentalist and Pentecostal. In the name of the unborn, [abortion] abolitionists have been able . . . to overcome divisions that once seemed unbridgeable."[8] But those divisions actually remained alive during the early years of the pro-life movement and shaped the development of anti-abortion organizations and the pro-life network. This is not to say that there were no attempts at ecumenism, but they remained feeble efforts usually more symbolic than actual. The Catholic Church routinely characterized abortion as a moral issue concerning all Christians, yet church bishops remained unwilling to relinquish their position at the forefront of the pro-life movement and undermined lay Catholic attempts to organize an ecumenical grassroots activism. Mormon leaders lamented that the nation's embrace of social ills like abortion demeaned its Christian heritage and overturned its biblical basis. Still, the LDS Church maintained its isolationist ways, turning down invitations to participate in an anti-abortion cause beyond its borders. *Christianity Today* urged evangelicals that abortion was not a Catholic issue, but one they as Bible-believing Christians needed to engage. The magazine's readers, however, ignored and even resisted the call to actively oppose abortion, often employing explicitly anti-Catholic arguments for doing so. The Southern Baptist Convention revealed the decade's diverse evangelical responses to abortion as Baptist leaders initially offered mild support for abortion law reform. Some Baptists even scoffed at Catholic involvement in the issue before eventually taking an absolutist stand against abortion. The National Right to Life Committee (NRLC), the nation's most important grassroots pro-life organization, made constant talk and occasional efforts on the question of ecumenism in the movement but remained closely tied to the Catholic Church that had founded it for most of the group's early history. The strategies the NRLC ultimately employed in recruiting Protestants, particularly evangelicals and fundamentalists, into what was perceived as a Catholic movement appreciated the historic tensions and theological disagreements among the various faiths. In their plans to navigate those divisions, the NRLC failed to challenge them but instead maintained their very existence, thereby replicating denominational and theological divisions as an organizing principle of the pro-life movement and casting a blow to hopes for a truly ecumenical political effort against abortion.

Churches and Abortion before Roe

From its earliest days, the Catholic Church had objected to the practice of abortion.[9] Around 100 AD, the *Didache*, an important document of early Christianity, denounced the procedure.[10] Through the twentieth century, various formal church statements reaffirmed church laws banning abortion and promised excommunication for any woman or doctor involved in the practice.[11] Though the Second Vatican Council had overturned many of the church's long-held traditions and practices, it underscored the church's continual opposition to abortion by listing it along with infanticide as "from the moment of conception . . . abominable crimes" in the "Pastoral Constitution on the Church in the Modern World."[12] Written in 1965, the "Pastoral Constitution" predated *Roe v. Wade* by nearly a decade. A rubella outbreak in California in 1964 and 1965, however, made the typically private discussion of abortion into an urgent public conversation when thousands of women sought abortions to avoid giving birth to babies who may have endured serious prenatal injuries from the disease.[13] Across the country, state legislatures had debated liberalizing their abortion laws, most notably the Beilenson Bill that had bounced around the California legislature since 1961 before finally being signed into law by Governor Ronald Reagan in 1967.[14] In reiterating a strong and solid opposition to abortion amid this liberalizing national trend, the Catholic Church made clear that progressive reforms were not the Second Vatican Council's only legacy.

Far more remarkable than reaffirming its anti-abortion position, the "Pastoral Constitution" in keeping with the Council's larger ecumenical ethos authorized its bishops to involve themselves in politics to oppose the liberalization of abortion laws and also called on other Christians "who are not yet living in full communion with us; yet we are united by our worship of the Father, the Son, and the holy Spirit and the bonds of love," to work with the church to achieve results.[15] This ecumenical vision of the church's religious mission to oppose abortion, among other social and political issues, would be challenged both internally and externally by theological differences and historical tensions. But the willingness to engage and work with other groups was significant, even if the limitations of that possibility remained unrealized at the moment.

Still, in 1965 there were few encouraging signs that other Christian groups would join in what many deemed a "Catholic cause." Given how closely they had been following Vatican II's proceedings, evangelical silence on the Council's abortion language revealed how small an issue abortion remained for most evangelicals in the mid-1960s. In fact, on matters of reproduction and the Second Vatican Council, evangelicals had devoted considerable attention to attacking the church's intransigence on reforming its birth control laws.[16] Yet as states began liberalizing their own abortion laws—between 1967 and 1969 fourteen states passed legislation allowing for abortions under certain circumstances, including rape, incest, fetal deformity, and the health of the mother—some evangelicals and Mormons also began developing and publicizing their own anti-abortion objections.[17]

With its population base concentrated in the American West, the LDS Church watched the liberalizing laws on abortion coming out of California and Colorado closely. By that time, the LDS Church had opposed abortion for more than one hundred years. In 1855, church President John Taylor issued a statement warning Mormons "against those . . . practices of foeticide [*sic*] and infanticide."[18] President Taylor later decreed in 1884 that no one who participated in an abortion could enter the temple, that any woman who had an abortion would be "sever[ed] from the church," and that anyone involved in an abortion would "never inherit the Kingdom of God."[19] Now, as Nevada, a state with more than a quarter of its population belonging to the LDS Church, took up a bill liberalizing its abortion law in 1969, the church's First Presidency publicized its opposition. "We have given careful consideration to the question of proposed laws on abortion and sterilization," the statement read. "We are opposed to any modification, expansion or liberalization of laws on these vital interests."[20] Two years before, seven out of fourteen LDS state legislators in Nevada had voted for abortion reform on a measure that ultimately was defeated. But after the release of the church's 1969 statement—an action that church officials made sure Nevada's LDS legislators were aware of before they voted on the new bill—only two of the eleven LDS legislators in Nevada's lower house voted to liberalize the state's abortion law. Lacking enough votes for passage by the lower house, Nevada's 1969 attempt at abortion reform died before it could reach the legislature's upper house for consideration.[21]

In 1971, the LDS Church made its position on abortion clear to all church members, rather than just selected LDS politicians, through a statement in its *Priesthood Manual*, a publication that communicated official church policy to every LDS ward or congregation. The prohibition declared abortion as "one of the most revolting and sinful practices of this day." All Mormons were to avoid procuring or administering abortions except in the rare cases of rape or to save the life of the mother. Even in these situations, however, church members should only seek an abortion after they had been counseled by "the local presiding priesthood authority and after receiving divine confirmation through prayer," the manual advised.[22] The church reprinted its statement in the *Priesthood Bulletin* a year later, and published it for a larger audience in the *Church News* section of its *Deseret News* daily newspaper just days after the January 1973 court ruling.[23]

The LDS Church's failure to equate abortion with murder likely stemmed from its unsettled theological position on when life began. Brigham Young had argued that the spirit entered the body at the time of quickening, and most church leaders through the years had agreed. Some church presidents, like David O. McKay during the 1950s and 1960s, however, contended the moment came as late as birth itself. The church certainly presented abortion as an interference with procreation—an act Mormons had long been encouraged to heartily engage in.[24] But Mormon prohibition against abortion lacked the common Catholic characterization of the act as murder, instead emphasizing it as a societal example of "the frightening evidence of permissiveness leading to sexual immorality."[25]

Several mainline Protestant denominations, including the United Church of Christ, the United Methodist Church, and the Lutheran Church in America, along with organizations like the National Council of Churches, supported and sometimes worked for abortion law reform in the 1960s, lending a movement based largely on arguments about medical authority and women's rights a sort of moral dimension.[26] But several evangelical denominations and outlets went on record against abortion as states liberalized their laws, demonstrating another divergence emerging within American Protestantism. The Lutheran Church—Missouri Synod issued a statement in 1971 maintaining abortion, outside of certain rare exceptions, was contrary to God's will.[27] The following year, the Christian Reformed Church and the Evangelical Free Church of America both passed resolutions against abortion.[28] At first, *Christianity Today* seemed hardly concerned by the legal reforms, reporting on the state-by-state developments with little passion.[29] "No doubt most state abortion laws need revision," an editorial in 1969 admitted.[30] But after New York passed its liberal abortion law in April 1970 and the calls for federal legislation matching the New York law mounted, *Christianity Today* began turning from its moderate stance on therapeutic abortion to a growing attack on abortion on demand. "The War on the Womb" had begun, a magazine editorial declared after the New York law passed, and *Christianity Today* launched its campaign against further abortion reform.[31]

In part, the magazine recommended evangelicals engage in politics in order to turn back abortion legislation. "At a time when Christians are becoming involved, on all levels, in political and social efforts," one *Christianity Today* editorial commented in 1971, "to ignore the question of abortion is a serious mistake."[32] The magazine also attacked denominations, religious organizations, and churches that supported abortion law reform.[33] Such a move was part and parcel of the publication's larger project of critiquing liberal Protestantism, but in condemning groups that supported abortion reform the influential magazine made clear to its readership that adherence to the evangelical gospel required firm opposition to abortion—a novel idea at the time but also a consequential addition to the litmus test of evangelical orthodoxy when other evangelical leaders and institutions remained equivocal over abortion.

Still, *Christianity Today* recognized mobilizing a vast evangelical army against abortion posed challenges considering how few evangelicals seemed concerned by the liberalization of abortion laws. Recognizing this, the magazine recommended that those evangelicals who wanted to oppose abortion reform work with Catholics. "A broad alliance is more likely to accomplish change than a group restricted to people who agree on a broad range of issues," the magazine reasoned. For those evangelicals, *Christianity Today* recommended they consult "a very practical manual for social action" put out by the Catholic organization New Jersey Right to Life Committee called *In Defense of Life*.[34] In another issue, the magazine favorably reviewed two anti-abortion books produced by Catholic authors, including *Handbook on Abortion* by J. C. Willke and his wife, Barbara, both heavily involved in the newly organized NRLC. The review praised the books for showing that "opposition to abortion . . . ought to be characteristic of all Christians . . . who take human life and moral responsibility seriously, not merely of Catholics."[35]

The evangelical magazine had hardly abandoned its consistent critique of Catholicism, but in recommending pro-life evangelicals seek partnership with Catholics to fight the liberalization of abortion laws, *Christianity Today* suggested theological differences might be set aside momentarily to attack shared ills. More likely, it also acknowledged that evangelicals scarcely had the numbers in the early 1970s to mount much of a significant effort against abortion reform alone. Still, the magazine had to admit that politics didn't stand completely apart from theology and this might pose problems for a Catholic-evangelical anti-abortion alliance. For example, Catholics were wrong to link abortion and birth control, one article contended: "Responsible Protestant thinkers have for several decades insisted that contraception stands upon a wholly different moral ground than abortion. It would seem that churchmen would do well to maintain this distinction with clarity."[36] Yet despite its objection to abortion, *Christianity Today* had spent little column space on the issue before the *Roe v. Wade* decision. Less than twenty editorials or articles directly addressing abortion appeared in the magazine's pages prior to 1973.[37] While the magazine clearly opposed abortion and believed that evangelicals needed to become convinced of its wrongness, it had given much greater attention to other political issues like Communism, race relations, and even school prayer. In contrast, Catholic periodicals during the same time period had made abortion their number one issue.[38]

Even the handful of articles on abortion *Christianity Today* published before 1973 lacked any real substantive biblical basis for its anti-abortion position and represented the magazine's most underdeveloped theological reasoning—a remarkable failure given the magazine's attention to outlining a comprehensive evangelical theology for its readership. Some articles contended the Bible mandated Christians protect all life, and since abortion meant the ending of a life Christians should oppose it, but this was as theologically deep as most of the articles ventured. One article admitted "the Bible does not comment directly on abortion," so instead noted Catholic writings that denounced the procedure through the centuries—probably an uncomfortable choice for a publication that usually criticized extra-biblical Catholic texts.[39] Another piece authored by a Fuller Theological Seminary theologian confessed of the "paucity of biblical references to pre-natal life."[40] A 1967 article in the evangelical magazine *Eternity* concurred, remarking the Bible fell "strangely silent" on the question of whether the "unborn fetus [is] to be considered a living person with all the rights of life."[41] One *Christianity Today* reader from Iowa wrote to the magazine that not only did the scriptures not address abortion; ancient Israel had been surrounded by cultures that practiced abortion. "Since the biblical writers could not have been unaware of the practice of abortion among the surrounding nations," he concluded, "their silence would seem to suggest that they did not consider abortion wrong. If this be the case, our concern for biblical fidelity should lead us to support liberalized abortion laws."[42]

Christianity Today's other readers, by indication of letters to the editor, seemed far less concerned about abortion than the magazine's editors. Most abortion articles generated no letters that the magazine published. The few pieces that did elicit responses drew mostly negative reactions. Considering how much the magazine hoped to engender an evangelical movement against abortion, it is probable that the editors would have printed almost all supportive letters they received, but the few readers' responses were generally critical of the magazine's position. A Presbyterian pastor from Tacoma, Washington, remained unconvinced that abortion posed a real threat to the nation. "I felt that Christianity Today's [*sic*] writer . . . tried to rally support by, in effect, yelling 'Wolf!'" A writer in Minnesota believed the magazine had done a "disservice" in how it portrayed abortion. "There is a greater need from evangelical circles for a serious and rational discussion of the issues," the reader wrote.[43]

Perhaps because of *Christianity Today*'s weak theology on abortion, readers seemed unmoved—and even resistant to—its call for evangelicals to oppose abortion. One reader from Columbus, Ohio, chastised the magazine for urging Christians to become politically involved so that they could oppose things like abortion. This "only reinforces the opinion that most unsaved persons have of Christ's religion – that it is a religion that only tells them what they cannot do," he complained. More importantly, the Ohioan insisted the magazine was wrong to denounce abortion, finding instead "it incomprehensible that a person who takes his Bible seriously could pontificate against something like abortion. It would take a totally perverted hermeneutic to say abortion is always wrong—no questions."[44] As Kerry Jacoby has observed, evangelical Protestants lacked many of the conditions and beliefs that required Catholics to oppose abortion. They did not believe in the infallible directives of a leader—a pope—who had declared abortion as morally evil. They lacked reverence for the example of the Virgin Mary and the belief that every abortion grieved the Holy Mother directly, as Catholic theology taught. Lastly, the Catholic Church's prohibitions against all forms of birth control, including abortion, had no purchase with most Protestant pastors and their faithful, who shared no objections to contraceptives.[45] Providing little theological basis for its opposition to abortion, *Christianity Today* hardly succeeded in convincing its evangelical readers of abortion's sinfulness in the years before *Roe*. Even after the Court's decision, the magazine and other evangelical sources opposed to abortion would struggle for several years to convince fellow evangelicals that abortion was something they should denounce and work against politically.[46]

But before *Roe*, conservative Protestants held diverse views on abortion. Daniel Williams has noted the regional division among evangelicals over the question of abortion at the time, with northern evangelicals, represented by organizations like *Christianity Today* and the National Association of Evangelicals, having much stronger anti-abortion convictions than their southern counterparts, such as the Southern Baptist Conviction.[47] As a leading evangelical voice and the nation's largest non-Catholic denomination, the SBC's positions on abortion posed a powerful, if surprising, counterweight to the evangelical outlets expressing opposition. At first, that voice remained largely silent, as Southern Baptists barely responded to abortion law reform in the 1960s. As Paul Sadler has shown, Southern Baptists before 1969 rarely addressed abortion; even the case of Sherri Finkbine, an Arizona woman who garnered major national media attention after her doctor recommended a therapeutic abortion for her potentially deformed fetus from thalidomide she had taken during her pregnancy, received no mention in the state Baptist paper while the Catholic Church denounced her over the Vatican Radio.[48] When Southern Baptists did discuss abortion, especially after 1970, they often did so in surprising ways. In fact, resolutions passed at the SBC's annual meetings may have aided abortion reform. In 1967, the "Resolution on Population Explosion" worried about "overpopulation and the threat of mass starvation" and recommended that married couples make "judicious use of medically approved methods of planned parenthood and the dissemination of planned parenthood information."[49] A few years later, another resolution more directly addressed one of those potential methods. The 1971 "Resolution on Abortion" called for Southern Baptists to "work for legislation that will allow the possibility of abortion under such conditions as rape, incest, clear evidence of severe fetal deformity, and carefully ascertained evidence of the likelihood of damage to the emotional, mental, and physical health of the mother."[50] This statement would later be cited in appeals to the Supreme Court to legalize abortion with *Roe v. Wade*.[51]

While the denomination supported the right of abortion for certain medical scenarios, some members and pastors were displeased with the SBC's stand. About a half-dozen Baptists wrote to Carl Bates, the Convention's president from 1970 to 1972, expressing dismay at the 1971 resolution's passage.[52] Bates responded to one letter with an uncertainty that would not characterize future Southern Baptist positions on abortion by noting that the unanswered question of when life began was at the heart of the matter of abortion. "As you know, many doctors, as well as a host of theologians, believe that the person does not begin to live until he breathes on his own," Bates wrote, "While I do not necessarily agree with this position, I thought I might share it with you for your own thinking."[53] Such a letter points to the ambiguity, especially before *Roe*, among Southern Baptists, and evangelicals more generally, regarding abortion. But that indecision would not survive for long. One Southern Baptist minister forwarded an article he had written to Bates entitled "When Is Murder Not Murder?" that condemned abortion. Bates wrote back to express his belief that "much of the greatness of our Convention may be attributed to the unity that still exists in diversity."[54]

Diverse Baptist views on abortion would not continue much longer, but for a time strong anti-abortion voices within the Southern Baptist Convention represented a minority. In 1970, a survey conducted by the Baptist organization VIEWpoll asked the denomination's ministers and Sunday School teachers if they would favor or oppose laws legalizing abortion. Nearly 70 percent of the pastors and almost 80 percent of the Sunday School teachers supported the right to abortion for women whose pregnancy threatened their mental or physical health. In pregnancies produced by rape or incest, 70 percent of the pastors and 77 percent of the teachers approved of abortion. Even in cases of deformity of the unborn, 64 percent of the pastors and 76 percent of the teachers thought abortion should be allowed. When asked in the same poll, however, if the use of marijuana should be legalized, 98 percent of both ministers and Sunday school teachers said it should not.[55] Before *Roe*, Southern Baptists clearly understood abortion as a rare, private, and difficult medical situation that families would make in consultation with health professionals.

The question of personhood remained ambiguous for many Southern Baptist ministers and theologians, contributing to the restrained acceptance of abortion rights within the Convention. In 1971, Andrew D. Lester, the director of pastoral care and counseling at the North Carolina Baptist Hospital, contributed an article to *Review & Expositor*, a Baptist theological journal, that challenged Catholic opposition to abortion for several reasons, including the Southern Baptist belief that not "every conception which occurs is the result of God's action or in keeping with God's will" and that not "every conceptus should be granted an equal status or given equal value with actualized human persons, even though the conceptus is potentially a human person and has rights that must be protected."[56] Thirteen percent of Southern Baptist ministers and nearly 20 percent of Sunday School teachers questioned in the 1970 poll agreed, answering they would support the right to abortion for any reason within the first trimester.[57] Such a view was clearly in the minority and likely came from the moderate and progressive wing of the Convention that would be pushed out by fundamentalists a decade later. But it demonstrates how far the Southern Baptist Convention was in the early 1970s from the ardent, hard-line, pro-life denomination it would soon become.[58]

Going Alone: The Catholic Church Fights Abortion

While the Catholic Church had championed an ecumenical vision for opposing abortion, its actions in establishing its anti-abortion efforts in the United States belied that claim. Considerable work went to building up the church's internal pro-life operations. This was hardly a surprising move, but it served to deepen its attentions inward rather than looking outward to interreligious efforts. As states tried to liberalize their abortion laws, the Catholic Church created pro-life groups to fight back at the local level. As early as 1963, these groups used the "right to life" phrase in their names.[59] For example, during California's debate over the Beilenson Bill, Cardinal McIntyre of Los Angeles organized a Right to Life League. From San Francisco, the archdiocese encouraged parishioners to let legislators know they wanted the bill defeated.[60] In Illinois, the Chicago Archdiocesan Office for Pro Life Activities worked closely with the church-created Illinois Right to Life to keep abortion illegal in the state despite several bills in the legislature pushing for reform.[61] And in New York, after the Catholic Church issued a pastoral letter against a 1967 state abortion reform bill, the Protestant Council of the City of New York along with three Jewish organizations responded asking whether "the cause of ecumenism is best served by attributing to us the advocacy of murder and genocide."[62] Just as the Catholic Church was emerging from Vatican II, the issue of abortion struck at the church's budding ecumenical spirit since the denominations and churches most open to ecumenism usually supported abortion reform. Additionally, through pastoral letters on abortion and the 1968 papal encyclical *Humanae Vitae* that maintained the church's prohibition against contraception and abortion, the bishops increasingly characterized opposing abortion as a fundamental aspect of Catholic belief and identity in contrast to a liberal ecumenical identity generally comfortable with abortion reform.[63]

At the same time that parishes and dioceses created anti-abortion groups to tackle legal reform at the local level, the church's hierarchy organized to monitor and combat abortion liberalization on a church-wide scale. In 1965, in response to *Griswold v. Connecticut*, the Supreme Court decision overturning a state law ban on the sale of contraceptive devices, the United States Catholic Conference allocated $50,000 to create the Family Life Division within the National Conference of Catholic Bishops (NCCB). (At the National Association of Evangelicals' annual meeting in 1963, one speaker noted the Catholic Church's growing involvement in *Griswold* threatened First Amendment principles. "Church-State relations are definitely involved," he argued.)[64] From this anti-contraception effort grew the Catholic Church's anti-abortion movement. At a meeting of its administrative board in 1967, the NCCB asked the Family Life Division's Director, Monsignor James McHugh, to closely watch abortion law reform across the nation.[65]

McHugh then created an advisory group that he coined the National Right to Life Committee, and the group began linking with small anti-abortion groups across the nation that had sprouted up in parishes and dioceses. The NCCB provided McHugh's group with $50,000 to spearhead the efforts against abortion law reform in the states. The NRLC would officially separate from the Catholic Church shortly after the Supreme Court issued *Roe*, but a few months before the court decision, the church established the Bishops' Committee for Pro-Life Activities to coordinate its efforts against abortion throughout the nation. Groups outside of the Catholic Church, though still containing mostly Catholic members, also arose to oppose abortion before the *Roe* decision, like Birthright (1968), Feminists for Life of America (1972), and the U.S. Coalition for Life (1972).[66] The early pro-life movement remained concentrated in states, mostly in the north, that had large urban centers and high Catholic populations. Perhaps surprisingly, virtually no pro-life movement existed in the South before *Roe* despite at least seven southern states having liberalized their abortion laws prior to 1973.[67]

As states continued liberalizing their abortion laws, Catholic leaders took pains to ensure church members understood abortion was not simply a "Catholic issue," as press and politicians alike often claimed. *The Pilot*, the Boston archdiocese's official publication and the nation's oldest Catholic newspaper, editorialized in 1971 about the "charade" perpetuated by abortion reformers that depicted only Catholics as opposed to abortion. Citing a recent *Time* magazine article that pointed to a diverse pro-life constituency including Mormons and "hard-shelled fundamentalists," the Boston archdiocese explained that "most of the anti-abortion strength comes from those who object on religious and moral grounds."[68]

Given messages like this, one new group not surprisingly attempted to unite Catholics with non-Catholic abortion opponents. Calling itself the National Right to Life Congress, the group had been founded by conservative Catholics who believed their church hadn't been doing enough to stop abortion reform.[69] Still, the Congress realized that in order to establish any sort of significant anti-abortion organization, it would need the resources—financial and organizational—of the Catholic Church. Reaching out to Monsignor McHugh, the group's founders received a cool response. For one, McHugh didn't appreciate that the Congress's name so closely approximated the organization he had founded within the church. Second, McHugh worried that some of the Congress's backers advocated violence as a means of stopping abortion reforms, something the church could never condone. Lastly, McHugh expressed reservations about giving church endorsement to the Congress's ecumenical aims. In a confidential letter to all of the U.S. bishops, McHugh asked them to ignore any of the Congress's requests for financial or organizational assistance, but instead to "direct all support toward the local groups, and toward those agencies that are directly helping our people."[70] Catholic money and resources should only go to Catholic Church–run efforts, McHugh argued, in keeping with general prohibitions coming from the church about Catholic lay-led ecumenical activities after Vatican II's reforms. Charles Rice, one of the Congress's organizers, then sent his own letter to the U.S. bishops, lamenting that "if the Catholic boycott of the Congress, which Father McHugh is attempting to arrange, does in fact take place—there can be no Congress. There can hardly be an effective national effort to stop abortion . . . with participation limited to Protestants and Jews."[71] Unable to garner the Catholic hierarchy's support, the Congress's organizers folded their attempts to develop an ecumenical pro-life group despite the church's insistence, expressed explicitly in Vatican II's "Pastoral Constitution on the Church in the Modern World," that stopping abortion reform required an ecumenical attack.

In addition to Vatican II's political conception of an ecumenical fight against social ills like abortion, Catholic philosophical arguments against abortion often displayed a more ecumenical outlook than the church's organizational efforts did. Various writings even before *Roe* tried to portray a common anti-abortion Christian basis among Catholics and Protestants, but even still they usually could not avoid using heavily Catholic reasoning and teachings. One pamphlet produced by the Catholic publishing group, *Our Sunday Visitor*, stressed "'Thou shalt not kill' is a heritage of Protestant, Catholic and Jew." "Americans who have the common Judaeo-Christian heritage of morality" understood abortion was murder, the pamphlet argued. Still, the pamphlet admitted there were "Specifically Catholic Principles," including infant baptism and adherence to church teaching, that made Catholics "even more opposed to abortion." Therefore, "As Catholics, we cannot accept abortion, without, in effect, ceasing to be Catholic."[72] An early National Right to Life Committee pamphlet spoke of a common "Christian tradition" that defended life by opposing abortion and credited "Protestant moral thinking" for the nineteenth-century laws that had outlawed the practice across the nation. But given its close association with the Catholic Church, the National Right to Life Committee couldn't avoid giving the bulk of the pamphlet's space to elucidating the "Catholic moral teaching" that continued to condemn abortion.[73] Catholic imagery and iconography often appeared throughout anti-abortion literature with rosaries, crucifixes, and the Virgin Mary—all figures repellent to Mormons and Protestants, particularly conservative evangelicals—depicted alongside renderings of innocent human life in the womb. Priests and nuns populated pro-life meetings that opened and closed with Catholic prayers and readings from church teachings. All of this worked against ecumenical cooperation, alienating non-Catholics from what all too often looked and sounded like a Catholic project rather than a Judeo-Christian mission to defend life.

But the Supreme Court's ruling in 1973 complicated some of these feelings and strengthened the suspicion that Christians needed to band together against a nation now sanctioning the murder of innocent life. One organization, the National Right to Life Committee, rose up to provide this response. And though a thoroughly Catholic-originated organization, some of the NRLC's leaders began to think that non-Catholics had to be brought into the pro-life movement if any ground could be made in overturning the court's ruling. Their attempts to do so would reveal both the limits of the Catholic Church's ecumenical vision and the persistent anti-Catholic prejudices that remained simmering below the surface for many American religious conservatives.

Responding to Roe

A year before *Roe v. Wade*, Pope Paul VI declared in a papal pronouncement, "Every human being, even the infant in its mother's womb, has the right to life immediately from God, not from the parents or any human society or authority."[74] Upon the issuance of *Roe*, Catholic Church leaders immediately announced opposition to the ruling. From Rome, the Vatican criticized the court's action via a radio broadcast.[75] In the States, Cardinal Terence Cooke of New York issued a statement labeling the decision as "shocking" and "horrifying." And Philadelphia's Cardinal John Krol, who also served as the National Conference of Catholic Bishops' president, declared the ruling "an unspeakable tragedy for this nation." "No court and no legislature in the land can make something evil become something good," Cardinal Krol added, "Abortion at any stage of pregnancy is evil."[76]

Other cardinals immediately began working against the ruling. Cardinal John Cody, the chairman of the Committee for Pro-Life Affairs of the NCCB, declared the Catholic Church would use "all means possible" to oppose the court's ruling.[77] The Committee also issued a statement declaring the decision "bad morality, bad medicine and bad public policy, and it cannot be harmonized with basic moral principles."[78] In Washington, the archbishop Cardinal Patrick O'Boyle sent out a letter to his 126 parishes the day after the court's decision asking them to use the following Sunday to deliver a homily "reminding the people that abortion is morally evil." Cardinal O'Boyle worried some Catholics might be confused about the immorality of abortion, despite the church's nearly decade-long fight against it. Especially for those Catholics living in states where there hadn't been a fight over abortion reform, the church's unyielding position on abortion had to be clarified now that the court had acted. "I do not think we can relax our stance on such a widespread evil," Cardinal O'Boyle wrote his pastors, "lest our people think that because of the Supreme Court's decision, abortion no longer is murder."[79] In Chicago—just as in other dioceses across the country—Cardinal John Cody asked the same of his priests.[80]

The varied responses religious groups had shown to states liberalizing their abortion laws continued after the Supreme Court ruling. "Churches Not

United on Question of Abortions," one newspaper headline rightly read shortly after the decision.[81] The fundamentalist pastor Carl McIntire blasted *Roe* as "a mammoth sin against God and the people."[82] Just days after the court's ruling, the LDS Church reprinted its 1971 denunciation of abortion in the *Church News* section of its *Deseret News*.[83] The Lutheran Church in America stood by its 1970 pro-choice statement, while the conservative evangelical Lutheran Church—Missouri Synod reiterated its 1971 opposition.[84] The National Association of Evangelicals passed a resolution at its annual meeting in Portland, Oregon, that year that "deplore[d] in the strongest possible terms the decision . . . which has made it legal to terminate a pregnancy for no better reason than personal convenience or sociological considerations." Still, the NAE acknowledged that abortions for rape, incest, or therapeutic abortions "to safeguard the health or the life of the mother" should remain available.[85] A spokesman for the United Church of Christ—a leading supporter of abortion reform—declared the decision as "historic not only in terms of women's individual rights but also in terms of the relationships of church and state."[86] When the national Baptist news service sent all its state papers an analysis of the *Roe* decision that began by declaring the Supreme Court had "advanced the cause of religious liberty, human equality, and justice," some guessed that this was a thinly veiled jab at the Catholic Church.[87]

The summer following the *Roe* decision, the SBC's newly elected president, Owen Cooper, criticized two recent Supreme Court decisions: *Roe* and the ruling banning capital punishment. Cooper charged that the court's decision to allow abortion on demand in the first three months went too far, but he added that the denomination would continue to support abortions "where it clearly serves the best interests of society."[88] The next summer, the SBC reaffirmed its 1971 resolution and pledged to seek "solutions to continuing abortion problems in our society."[89] Such decisions demonstrated the Southern Baptist Convention's general understanding of abortion at the time as a rare and difficult medical decision for a woman to make with her doctor rather than something symptomatic of a sexualized culture.

This Southern Baptist perception continued for a few years after *Roe*. The summer following the Supreme Court's decision, the Christian Life Commission (CLC) of the Baptist General Convention of Texas devoted the July 1973 issue of its "Christian Faith in Action" newsletter to the topic of abortion. The newsletter granted that there were "extremist positions" on both sides of the issues and that Christians could likely see "points of validity" in both opposing arguments. Because of this, the CLC explained, it had developed a newsletter to guide pastors counseling members confronting the difficult question of whether or not to procure an abortion. Included in the newsletter was a copy of a sermon recently delivered by the president of the Baptist General Convention of Texas. In the talk, Dr. Landrum P. Leavell blamed abortion on a liberalized culture that commodified sex and cheapened its consequences. Yet, Rev. Leavell admitted, "I can find no clear, biblical command dealing with this problem in a specific way." Leavell's sermon wrestled with the notion of when life began, agreeing with the Supreme Court that such a moment remained unclear and best "left up to your personal lifestyle, your philosophy, your belief." Because of this, the pastor concluded, "no clearcut [*sic*], final solution" existed on how Christians should regard abortion.[90]

In Dallas, First Baptist's arch-conservative W. A. Criswell, pastor of the Southern Baptist Convention's largest congregation, expressed surprising views regarding personhood and the right to abortion. "I have always felt," Criswell said to *Christianity Today* just after the *Roe* ruling, remarks later reprinted in the Baptist General Convention of Texas's abortion newsletter, "that it was only after a child was born and had life separate from its mother that it became an individual person, and it has always, therefore, seemed to me that what is best for the mother and for the future should be allowed." But Criswell's mild acceptance of abortion may have also been influenced by his rather notorious anti-Catholic prejudices—views that had been particularly public during John F. Kennedy's bid for the White House.[91] "I think the Catholics have it in their heads . . . that they're going to outbreed the rest of us," Criswell jeered about the pro-life movement, "I just think that's their way of survival and it's working pretty good."[92] Criswell's comments strangely resembled feminist arguments that abortion opponents sought to force women into a lifetime of baby production, but they also borrowed from a long history of Protestant fears that Catholics would use unbridled reproduction to overtake the nation. These suspicions had appeared during earlier debates over contraception and throughout Kennedy's 1960 campaign. They resurfaced as Catholics emerged as the near sole opponents of abortion. Rightly observing the situation, the liberal *Christian Century* commented "we are in danger of a return to Catholic-vs.-Protestant enmities of pre-Vatican II days because of the emotionalizing of the abortion debate."[93]

One leading evangelical concluded that anti-Catholic sentiments among evangelicals had shaped conservative Protestants' abortion views. "If the Catholics are for it, we should be against it," Harold O. J. Brown, the Harvard-educated associate editor of *Christianity Today* mockingly paraphrased the thinking among many evangelicals. "The fact that Catholics were out in front caused many Protestants to keep a low profile," he later remembered.[94]

Brown continued the magazine's efforts to convince evangelicals of the need to fight abortion. In an editorial a month after the court's ruling, Brown blasted the decision as rooted in pagan ethics rather than the Christian morality the nation and its Constitution had been based on. "We would not normally expect the Court to consider the teachings of Christianity and paganism before rendering a decision on the *constitutionality* of a law," Brown wrote, "but in this case it has chosen to do so, and the results are enlightening: it has clearly decided for paganism, and against Christianity."[95] Another article in the magazine continued the theme, lamenting "the anti-Christian militancy underlying the court's rejection of our once dominant Judaeo-Christian ethical tradition in favor of [the] 'ancient religion'" of paganism. The magazine accused the court for its "massive substitution of principles from pre-Christian paganism and post-Christian utilitarianism for those of the biblical heritage."[96]

Catholic pro-lifers had also seen the most sinister hands at work in the abortion decision. Writing in the Catholic clergy magazine, *Homiletic & Pastoral Review,* one pro-life crusader contended that "the legalization of abortion . . . came about when the court accepted and interpreted the Constitution in light of a received pagan morality accepted and promoted by an elite minority in our society."[97] Brown's original editorial in *Christianity Today* echoed such thoughts, predicting dark days ahead for America's Christians. The last sentence of his editorial connected the abortion decision to this larger threat: "Christians should accustom themselves to the thought that the American state no longer supports, in any meaningful sense, the laws of God, and prepare themselves spiritually for the prospects that it may one day formally repudiate them and turn against those who seek to live by them."[98]

One *Christianity Today* reader shot back at the magazine's diagnosis and reflected the persistent evangelical sentiment that politics was something the Christian should probably avoid. "We in America have lived under the illusion that this is a Christian nation, and that our laws will always reflect the highest morality," the man wrote. "If for no other reason, the Court's decision should awaken Christians to the fact that legality for the American and morality for the Christian are two different things. . . . If we Christians would get over the idea of political power and influence and concentrate our efforts of persuasion toward setting forth the higher morality of the Christian, much of our labor would no longer be wasted as it is now." The writer also took issue with the magazine's version of both American history and the biblical example: "I question whether the American state has ever supported the laws of God, but in any case, first-century Christians must indeed be amused . . . at your concern over lack of support from the 'state.' As I understand it, the world, including our own country, is and has been from the beginning at enmity with Christ and those who are determined to follow him."[99] The evangelical feminist and author Nancy Hardesty, who had written the 1967 *Eternity* article noting the Bible's silence regarding abortion, rejected *Christianity Today*'s portrayal of abortion as a clear wrong that evangelicals should oppose. "I would like to point out," she wrote the magazine, "that there are many . . . evangelicals like myself . . . who feel that abortion is a question of Christian liberty. I resent your constant equation of your personal position on the issues with 'the moral teachings of Christianity through the ages.'"[100]

Despite the continued indifference or opposition its readers seemed to show to its attempts to arouse an anti-abortion evangelical ethic, *Christianity Today* maintained a steady, if infrequent, campaign in its pages against abortion. Since so many evangelicals remained unmoved by this cause in the early years after *Roe, Christianity Today* often found itself in the odd position of attacking fellow evangelical outlets while positively highlighting the non-evangelical churches it elsewhere subjected to theological scrutiny. One early article, for example, blasted the Baptist news service for its statement that the abortion decision had advanced "religious liberty, human equality, and justice." "Advanced for whom?" the magazine demanded. "Certainly not the fetus!" Instead, the magazine cited the Catholic and LDS churches for their opposition to the ruling.[101] Still, the magazine continued its attack on the LDS faith—two recent book reviews had praised books classifying Mormonism as a cult, crediting one as particularly valuable for "those who want to understand this growing religion and reach some of its adherents with the first-century Gospel."[102] Another article appearing not long after the magazine commended the LDS Church for its opposition to *Roe* sought to explain "Why Your Neighbor Joined the Mormon Church." Noting the LDS Church had added one million members since just 1967, *Christianity Today* contended "No other cult confronts the true Church with a more serious challenge." In contrast to evangelical Christianity's free gift of salvation, the magazine characterized Mormonism as "a complicated works-righteousness system in which the faithful are always moving up the ladder into a better and better life."[103]

Even more than an occasional nod to Mormonism's pro-life commitment, *Christianity Today* showed a growing appreciation for the Catholic Church's strong stance against abortion rights and other social ills. One article extensively outlined Catholic reaction to the Supreme Court ruling—a large space probably made all the more available by the near silence at the time from evangelicals on the issue.[104] For those Catholics and evangelicals who shared concerns about abortion's legalization, the increasing liberalization of American culture, particularly in regard to its sexual mores, and growing intolerance for religion in the nation's public life, the magazine observed the "feeling may also be growing . . . that the issues separating them are becoming less important than their common perils in an increasingly secular and atheistically dominated world."[105] An advertisement in *Christianity Today* for the book *A Prejudiced Protestant Takes a New Look at the Catholic Church* described the work as an "account of the growing fellowship and understanding between evangelicals and Catholics around the world," though in its review of the book, the magazine regretted "as a personal testimony, his account is not interested in theological precision."[106] Still the pages of *Christianity Today* in the early 1970s displayed a small but growing rapprochement between evangelicals and Catholics based almost entirely on common reactions to changing cultural and political trends in the nation.

But even as *Christianity Today* praised the Catholic Church for its outspoken attack on abortion legalization, it could not depart from its history of theological critiques against the church, as it also treated pro-life Mormonism. Tellingly, Mormon and Catholic outlets rarely tracked evangelical responses to abortion's legalization—likely because of both the general evangelical apathy to the issue but also their own respective disinterest in engaging with an evangelical community frequently combative with them. One *Christianity Today* article noted rather opportunely that the Catholic Church's having "accustomed its adherents to think in terms of absolute truth and binding principles" made Catholics ripe for conversion to the absolute truth of evangelical Christianity. That orthodoxy guaranteed Catholic commitment to opposing abortion and defending other biblical cultural positions, but it also primed them to receive the evangelical message. This unique circumstance allowed evangelicals in the 1970s to view conservative Catholics as both politically useful and religiously susceptible—unlike Mormons, who shared many evangelical cultural concerns but were trapped in a web of lies that turned them away from rather than toward the evangelical gospel. "Roman Catholicism in the past may not have given them a confidence-inspiring, satisfying personal faith, but it has conditioned them to look for one," the magazine explained. The Catholic Church had set their followers up for something it couldn't actually deliver—true salvation—but that expectation could be met by evangelicals "proclaim[ing] the Gospel of Jesus Christ to them in simplicity and in power." "Whether a world-wide breakdown of Roman Catholicism is imminent" was unclear however, the magazine admitted.[107] In the same issue, another article praised those Catholics who had recently supported a Billy Graham crusade in St. Louis—a far cry from the magazine's response to the Catholic hostility that had greeted Graham's 1957 revival in New York. But again the magazine saw such developments not as a reason to lay aside theological difference but instead as an opportunity to convert those Catholics who in their "new appreciation for basic Christian virtues" were clearly hungering for the evangelical message. "Pope John and the Second Vatican Council caused such an upheaval," the magazine explained, "that many Catholics no longer are sure what they are supposed to believe." In that confusion, evangelicals could offer a lifeline of truth to those looking for a path out of the darkness of Catholicism.[108] "A new kind of ecumenism is emerging," the magazine concluded. But what it meant by that was not a joint partnership of evangelicals and Catholics so much as it described the magazine's hope that some Catholics were becoming a little more evangelical.[109] It also signaled an evangelical appropriation of the "ecumenical" nomenclature, depicting it not as a heresy of liberal Protestantism or the threat of ravenous Catholicism but instead as an evangelical opportunity to capitalize on shared cultural affinities for the purposes of advancing the evangelical gospel. Yet in light of a readership that seemed largely unmoved by its calls for anti-abortion commitments and activism, *Christianity Today*'s persistent critique of Catholicism may have inadvertently continued to shape that evangelical ambivalence toward abortion more than any occasional praise it offered for the Catholic Church's leadership in the anti-abortion fight.

Southern Baptists, on the other hand, stood squarely within the evangelical orthodoxy *Christianity Today* championed. While few Southern Baptists likely read the magazine at the time—there were plenty of denominational magazines and newspapers for a Southern Baptist to choose from—*Christianity Today* often chronicled the goings-on of the nation's largest Protestant group. Throughout the ecumenical craze of the 1950s, the magazine repeatedly praised the SBC for avoiding the liberal National Council of Churches, though given the close relationship between *Christianity Today* and the National Association of Evangelicals, the magazine's editors probably shared the NAE's disappointment that the SBC's extreme anti-ecumenism also kept it from joining the evangelical organization.[110] In 1972, the magazine commended Southern Baptist efforts the previous year in baptizing over four hundred thousand new Christians—a number that dwarfed the entire membership of many other denominations.[111] But given the SBC's size and its consistent evangelical message, *Christianity Today* had to be frustrated with the Southern Baptist Convention's failure to stand firmly against abortion.

A small controversy erupted between the magazine and Foy Valentine of the SBC's Christian Life Commission after *Christianity Today* published an editorial in the summer of 1974 warning that abortion's legalization would, in a country concerned about unfettered population growth, lead to the adoption of euthanasia and infanticide under the guise of family planning and "population 'experts.'"[112] In the piece, the magazine contended the SBC's Christian Life Commission had endorsed one family planning expert's proposal that the nation pass tax disincentives for parents who had more than two children. Southern Baptists needed to realize their denomination was supporting a proposal that had darker consequences than simply tax penalties for parents with more than two babies, *Christianity Today* contended. The expert had also argued that parents who bore three children would have to be sterilized. If one or both of the parents failed to show up for this forced sterilization, the expert continued, then the new baby could be sterilized in place of the absent mother or father.

Foy Valentine was infuriated the editorial insinuated the Southern Baptist Convention endorsed coerced sterilization, euthanasia, and infanticide. He wrote *Christianity Today*, accusing the magazine of spreading falsehoods about the Christian Life Commission. Harold Brown wrote back, explaining he held in his possession the pamphlet "Issues and Answers: Population Explosion" produced by the Christian Life Commission that contained the same recommendation the population expert had made regarding tax disincentives. "If you and your commission members really do reject and oppose the line taken by . . . the Zero and Negative Population Growth people, with all its implications for coercion and totally mechanistic, utilitarian views of man," Brown continued, "then why in heaven's name don't you distinguish yourselves from them in your published material, instead of repeating in substance so much of their program and spirit?"[113] Valentine responded that the CLC had developed that brochure in 1969 and so couldn't have borrowed the ideas from the population expert who had made her statements in 1971.[114] *Christianity Today* published a separate letter from Valentine characterizing the magazine's editorial as "utterly false," but the magazine followed Valentine's letter with its own editorial comment that the SBC's pamphlet under discussion indeed contained "the recommendations to which we drew attention."[115] Elsewhere in its pages, *Christianity Today* continued pressuring the SBC and other evangelical denominations to adopt a more thoroughly pro-life commitment. As Brown had written to Valentine, "I really would like to believe that you have an independent, biblical approach to these issues that are so important for Christian people."[116] But developments at the SBC annual meeting earlier that summer indicated the Convention still did not share *Christianity Today*'s convictions about abortion. Robert Holbrook, a pastor from Texas, proposed amending the SBC's 1971 resolution supporting abortion law reform to now only condone abortions conducted to save the life of the mother, but his amendment failed.[117] Instead, messengers at the 1974 meeting passed a resolution that reaffirmed the 1971 statement and described it as reflecting "a middle ground between the extreme of abortion on demand and the opposite extreme of all abortion as murder."[118] Far from an evangelical consensus—let alone Southern Baptist unity—existed on the abortion question in the immediate wake of *Roe*.[119]

The Catholic Church and the National Right to Life Committee

Without the Catholic Church, there would have been no pro-life movement. Though the NRLC owed its creation, organizational structure, and some of its financial backing to the Catholic Church, not all of its leaders and members were Catholic, however. Shortly after the *Roe* decision, Marjory Mecklenburg, a key Methodist pro-life leader in Minnesota, called Carolyn Gerster, an Episcopalian doctor who directed the movement in Arizona, and said the NRLC needed to be changed. It was entirely "too Catholic," she worried, it was run by a priest from inside a church division, and it held its regional meetings on Catholic campuses. "We need a national nonsectarian organization," Mecklenburg said to Gerster.[120] In Pennsylvania, Judy Fink, a Baptist woman and prominent pro-life activist since the 1960s, coordinated with Mecklenburg, Gerster, and other Protestant pro-life leaders throughout the country to work on limiting what they saw as Monsignor James McHugh's stranglehold on the NRLC.[121] Even some Catholics inside the organization felt uncertain about the relationship the NRLC should maintain with the church and agreed with their Protestant colleagues that McHugh too tightly controlled the organization. William C. Hunt, a Catholic theology professor active in the Minnesota pro-life movement, remembered McHugh ran the NRLC as a "front organization for the Catholic Conference" and often stoked clashes with Protestant leaders who wanted more independence from the Catholic Church.[122]

These two competing visions of how the NRLC should be run became a dominant issue for the organization. In creating the NRLC within the Committee on Family Life, McHugh had envisioned an organization mirroring the church itself: highly centralized with a powerful leadership that although ecumenical still followed Vatican II's directives that it be a Catholic Church–led project. But state leaders preferred a federated model, believing strong, autonomous chapters would best activate a grassroots movement of diverse Americans. In the summer of 1972, Mecklenburg and Joseph Lampe had written to McHugh and the National Right to Life Committee arguing for a "more independent . . . national pro-life organization."[123] Although McHugh seemed at first to suppress that bid, the state leaders continued to strategize breaking from the Catholic Church and diminishing McHugh's role in the organization, a plan ultimately embraced by NRLC board members and written into the group's constitution, thereby securing the NRLC's independence. Though the church and its organization had officially separated not long after the *Roe* decision, the two would continue close ties.[124]

The NRLC needed money, and the Catholic Church provided most of it in the early years in various ways. The National Conference of Catholic Bishops regularly extended critical dollars to the national organization, calling on dioceses to fund local right-to-life groups. In New York, for example, the Catholic Conference collected special offerings in churches throughout the state on "Respect Life" Sundays, dividing the collection between the national and state chapters. Also, the church's loaning of its institutional infrastructure to the NRLC and its state chapters provided the movement with critical financial savings. The Catholic Church provided space and supplies through its churches, parish and diocesan offices, and schools. It paid for advertising and offered transportation services for various events. Catholic newspapers also covered no issue more than abortion, providing enviable free publicity for the movement.[125] "We feel we've editorialized the issue to death—no pun intended," the editor of the Boston archdiocese's weekly newspaper remarked during the 1976 campaign season.[126] The pro-life movement remained afloat in its early years because of the Catholic Church's investments, but this also perpetuated the sense among many non-Catholics, both inside and out of the pro-life movement, that abortion remained a Catholic concern.

Because of this, Catholics comprised the majority of the pro-life movement and remained the overwhelming membership of the National Right to Life Committee throughout the 1970s. In her study of anti-abortion activists in California in the 1960s, Kristin Luker located only eleven volunteers who had been active in the pro-life movement before the state's passage of the Beilenson Bill in 1967. Ten of the eleven were Catholic. The number of anti-abortion activists would skyrocket in California after the bill passed, but the growing movement remained nearly completely Catholic in the state.[127] Other states showed similar trends. Catholics represented 85 percent of the membership in New York's Right to Life organization in 1972, according to the group's founder, Ed Golden.[128] At the time of the Supreme Court ruling, Catholics comprised almost the entirety of pro-life activists nationwide. An official with the NRLC estimated in 1974 that only 15 percent of its membership was non-Catholic.[129] Though more non-Catholics joined the cause in the following years, a 1980 survey found the NRLC's membership still reflected the movement's initial demographic with more than 70 percent identifying as Catholic.[130] Luker found that over 80 percent of women anti-abortion activists in the early 1980s belonged to the Catholic Church.[131] Protestant evangelicals had become involved in larger numbers in the pro-life cause by the late 1970s, but they remained a shadow of the Catholic presence in the movement. And these evangelical pro-lifers had largely founded their own organizations rather than joining the NRLC in any significant numbers. The NRLC remained the poster organization of the movement, and Catholics dominated its membership.

Because of this Catholic dominance, the media, not surprisingly, characterized the pro-life movement as a Catholic issue, much to the chagrin of various pro-life leaders hoping to broaden the movement (and to some leaders of the Catholic Church). A communications official with the United States Catholic Conference sent a letter shortly after the *Roe* ruling to various newspaper editors and news directors throughout the country enclosing clips from both Catholic and non-Catholic writers opposing the decision. "I think they illustrate," he wrote, "that abortion is not a 'Catholic' issue but a 'catholic' issue."[132] Still, most media outlets remained unconvinced, and some of their depictions of the pro-life cause bordered on the inflammatory, like a 1974 *Harper's* article that described the movement as "passionately concerned with the rights of unborn embryos which, in accordance with Catholic tradition, has minimum concern for the rights of women."[133] Pro-life activists regularly complained about such treatment in the media. But they also realized that some of the charges, specifically those regarding the preponderance of Catholics in the movement, were true and therefore shaped public perception of the right-to-life cause.

Desiring to present their movement as more than a Catholic preoccupation, once it had officially separated from the Catholic Church, members of the NRLC consciously placed Protestants at the organization's highest levels. The NRLC's first executive committee of the board of directors after the separation included four Protestants among its nine members.[134] The organization also chose a series of Protestant leaders who might lessen the group's Catholic image and constantly publicized its Protestant leadership. From 1973 through 1980, three Protestant women led the organization. The first, Marjory Mecklenburg, had been one of the few Protestants working against abortion before *Roe*. A Methodist, Mecklenburg was married to Dr. Fred Mecklenburg, an obstetrician-gynecologist who also held an officer position with the NRLC. Before joining the NRLC, the Mecklenburgs had established their pro-life credentials by creating the most powerful state anti-abortion group existing prior to the Court's decision, the Minnesota Citizens Concerned for Life (MCCL). By 1973, the group boasted ten thousand members.[135]

As NRLC chair, Mecklenburg headed the organizational structure created when the organization broke from the Catholic Church. Mecklenburg had been one of the leading advocates for the winning federalist model when the break with the church was up for vote. It was decided then that a board of directors made up of fifty-one representatives from every state and the District of Columbia would preside over the organization. The chair would operate as chief executive officer and lead the organization while a president would enact the board's will. All decisions would be reached through a majority vote of the board. Any state chapter could withdraw from the national organization at its discretion or oppose any of its policies.[136]

Now that the NRLC had officially separated itself from the Catholic Church, some of its leaders thought the group should work on diversifying its membership. While a few Catholics in the organization, like William Hunt, were sympathetic to opening up the organization, most of the ecumenical push came from the NRLC's small group of Protestant leaders. In addition to the Mecklenburgs, other important Protestants in the organization included Episcopalians Carolyn Gerster and Warren Schaller; the Presbyterian Gloria Klein from Michigan; Jean Garton, a member of the Lutheran Church—Missouri Synod; Judy Fink, an Independent Baptist; and Robert Holbrook, a Southern Baptist. Importantly, these Protestants were a diverse group in themselves, from mainline and evangelical denominations alike, and they ranged across the political spectrum since abortion had yet to become an issue strongly identified with either political party. (The Mecklenburgs were political liberals, for instance.)[137] That diversity, for the Protestant members at least, offered a powerful counterpoint to the seemingly church-bound justifications against abortion that Catholic pro-lifers so often offered, and it shaped Protestant conceptions about what the NRLC, and the pro-life movement more broadly, could become: a diverse grassroots constituency mobilized by the simple cause of defending innocent human life no matter the doctrine or denomination that undergirded such convictions.

In light of these views, Judy Fink, a member on the Executive Committee of the NRLC's Board of Directors, authored a proposal shortly after the NRLC's separation from the Catholic Church that advocated the organization appeal to Protestants to join the cause. Fink noted there were some Protestants out there who objected to the Supreme Court's decision "on scriptural grounds," but hesitated involving themselves in the pro-life cause because "they tend to see the public battle as Roman Catholic originated and Roman Catholic dominated." The Catholic Church and the NRLC had wrongly assumed Protestants could not be brought into the pro-life movement, Fink explained, because some Protestant denominations had supported abortion rights. These developments, Fink argued, had been craftily engineered by "proabortionists" who had targeted susceptible clergy. "What is little known by Catholics . . . ," Fink countered, "is that these resolutions have met with increasing resistance by members of these denominations, once they are made aware of how they were enacted and what they mean." In light of this, Fink proposed the NRLC establish a committee that would work to further develop a pro-life movement among Protestants "in their own communities." Fink recognized that suspicions of the pro-life movement's association with the Catholic Church coupled with the general resistance to political engagement that many evangelicals felt could stymie their involvement in the right-to-life cause. Because of this, Protestants would have to be approached on their own turf, "in their own congregations," and by their fellow denominationalists. Protestant politicians needed to be asked, as well, to deliver pro-life statements along with their Catholic colleagues to convey a broader ecumenical picture of political opposition to abortion rights. And relations with Protestant denominations and organizations, like Billy Graham's evangelistic group and the editorial staff of *Christianity Today*, needed to be cultivated. Also, Fink explained that Protestants had no interest in debates over contraception. "It is accepted almost exclusively," she explained, and should never be included in conversations with Protestants.[138]

Many Catholic members of the NRLC, however, felt the organization should issue a statement opposing artificial birth control devices, particularly oral contraceptives and IUDs. The Catholic Church—still closely involved in the organization even if the official ties had been severed—pressured the organization to do so as well. But Fink and other Protestants in the NRLC knew that position would alienate potential non-Catholics from joining the cause and further substantiate feelings that the anti-abortion movement was only a Catholic concern.[139] Fink drew up a separate memo addressing the potential birth control statement, marked it "Strictly Confidential," and delivered it to NRLC's leadership in May 1973. The memo recommended the NRLC avoid any public pronouncements on contraception. To renounce contraception, Fink warned, would "count out the participation of the 12 million Southern Baptists in the nation . . . the huge (and uncounted) rapidly growing Independent, Fundamentalist, and Pentecostal Protestant groups; the 11 million Methodists; the 8 million Presbyterians; untold numbers of Catholics; and—need I go on?"[140] The NRLC eventually sidestepped the issue by declaring itself completely neutral in regard to contraception, a decision that ultimately pleased hardly anyone in the organization.[141] But the disagreement highlighted the different context in which pro-life Catholics and Protestants understood their opposition to abortion and revealed the practical challenges of developing conservative ecumenism. Catholics situated abortion within a sanctity-of-life continuum, leading them to fight any threats to life—or the possibility of it—from birth control to the death penalty. What pro-life Protestants there were at the time, on the other hand, saw abortion in a more isolated context—its own singular horror.[142] Such differences would shape the movement as it went forward.

Some leaders in the NRLC, especially other Protestants like Mecklenburg, appreciated Fink's proposal to reach out to Protestants. In the summer of 1973, the Executive Committee created a six-member Intergroup Liaison Committee (ILC) to work to establish relations that would help develop a broad-based support for the NRLC's aims. Of the six members, at least four were Protestant, in addition to Rev. William Hunt, the Catholic theologian critical of the Catholic Church's dominance of the NRLC.[143] The ILC established as its "first priority [a] program of building bridges to certain Protestant religious groups."[144] Leaders of the NRLC recognized they needed to expand the pro-life movement beyond its traditional Catholic base, and they looked to the Intergroup Liaison Committee to carry out that work. But Fink, the ILC's chair, understood, as she wrote in her introductory letter to the other five ILC members, "developing a broad populist movement is obviously fraught with complexities." Fink noted that many of the groups they hoped to work with "will prefer to speak to their people as Baptists, Lutherans, Mormons, blacks, etc. rather than echoing an 'outside' voice; wherever possible, direct cooperation with NRLC in developing educational materials is most desirable, but when required we may have to be satisfied with merely providing the impetus for these groups to develop their own teaching materials for distribution to their congregations as they see fit." Working with groups that often tended to be isolationist would pose its challenges, but it could also be very fruitful for the pro-life movement. "Far more of us exist than we realize," Fink contended.[145]

A few months later, the ILC presented the NRLC's leadership with its recommendations for establishing stronger ecumenical ties. "There is a large and mostly silent prolife untapped constituency in the United States," Fink wrote in her introduction to the report delivered at the end of 1973, "and they are ours to teach." The ILC's members had discovered in their initial meetings with one another that the Protestant absence from the pro-life movement was "due more to the lack of a 'sparking' mechanism than to lack of interest or willingness to respond." This spark, however, needed to come from within the denominations themselves, the ILC members concluded, because many pastors and members lacked clarity on how to regard abortion in light of their denominations' silence or mixed messages. The ILC realized quickly its whole associational purpose could not be achieved as long as Protestant churches failed to develop a pro-life message and create their own pro-life organizations.[146] The ILC then decided it would have to do this work and disseminate its pro-life message among receptive denominations. Rather than developing a broad moral argument emphasizing a generic Christian identity or a "family values" politics that would gain purchase in later decades, early pro-life activists believed their cause's viability had to navigate the divisions within Christianity and tailor the message and movement to individual theologies and institutional practices.

The LDS Church, despite its ardent pro-life position, would have to be left alone. This was the ILC's conclusion after NRLC executive Dr. J. C. Willke and his wife, Barbara—authors of the groundbreaking pro-life book *Handbook on Abortion*—met with the LDS First Presidency in the fall of 1973. The Willkes had come to Utah for a speaking tour, addressing Mormon audiences at Brigham Young University and other spots while also taping two television programs at the BYU television station. The First Presidency of the LDS Church endorsed the Willkes' talks and said that Mormons stood "shoulder to shoulder" with the Willkes on the pro-life issue.[147] But later in a private meeting with the Willkes, the LDS Church hierarchy "had made it understood that the program will be done within its own confines by its own people," Fink reported, though LDS officials were willing to use some NRLC materials in developing a Mormon educational pro-life packet for church members.[148]

Protestant denominations and churches, however, might be infiltrated by the National Right to Life Committee's message and projects, but only via methods that worked within each denominational structure. In other words, the ILC recommended the NRLC target various Protestant denominations through their own institutional networks by placing ads in denominational magazines and newspapers, developing denominationally specific pamphlets and tracts, creating specialized mailings to clergy, monitoring denominational meetings and introducing pro-life resolutions at the conventions, and making presentations at seminaries and Bible colleges in order to reach the next generation of religious leaders. All of this would be accomplished within the particular denominations themselves in the hopes that a Baptist or a Lutheran or a Methodist pro-life movement would spring up from its own churches and then connect to the NRLC's larger vision of an ecumenical, broad-based anti-abortion network. But that very word—"ecumenical"—was to be avoided when reaching out to these possible allies, the ILC advised. Instead, phrases like "common Christian witness" or "common prolife concern" ought to be used. "Quite a few evangelical protestant [*sic*], Baptist and Lutheran groups and churches do not fellowship with one another," the ILC instructed, "and their separatism must be recognized and respected."[149] That separatist instinct would be at the heart of how the NRLC navigated its relationship with potential associates and would characterize the general shape of the anti-abortion network that would develop over the coming decade.

Given the ILC's recommendations, one might wonder as to how the ILC's plans to develop a pro-life movement from within various Protestant denominations varied from its decision to let the LDS Church work on its own in developing Mormon opposition to abortion rights. For one, LDS leaders had made clear in their meeting with NRLC executives that their church would act independently with little outside consultation. But, perhaps more importantly, the lack of a Mormon presence in the NRLC's national leadership or in its state chapters prevented the organization from making the inroads within Mormonism that they hoped to achieve with various Protestant churches. Several Protestants worked throughout the NRLC's hierarchy. Even more were represented in various state organizations under the NRLC umbrella. So, the NRLC could utilize these members to reach out to their particular faith communities and present a pro-life message divorced from the Catholic undertones and associations that characterized so much of the National Right to Life Committee's message and image, providing instead one rooted in the theology, language, and culture of each specific denomination.

Ironically, those churches most receptive to a pro-life message were often those most opposed to any sort of ecumenical activism, particularly if it involved work with Catholics. "Separatists tend to be theological conservatives," Judy Fink explained, "and such a posture allows no room for abortion." This was the conundrum of developing a broad-based anti-abortion movement. The very theology supporting the most ardent opposition to abortion among fundamentalist Protestants also advocated the strictest separatist impulses, condemned associational ties, and had been the most vocally anti-ecumenical for more than two decades. Oftentimes, that theology was also avowedly anti-Catholic. Fink, herself a member of an Independent Baptist church in Pittsburgh, understood the difficulty of forming alliances with the very churches that might most support pro-life activism. For one, they could only be reached internally. "It would be no more acceptable to send a Methodist to make the approach than to send a Roman Catholic," Fink noted.[150] She also pointed out that Independent Baptists and other fundamentalists would only trust materials produced and distributed by their own pastors and churches—a habit reaching back to fundamentalism's origins and underscoring the persistent anti-ecumenical convictions among Protestantism's most conservative churches.

Robert Holbrook, one of the Intergroup Liaison Committee's six members and the Southern Baptist pastor from Hallettsville, Texas, who had tried to pass an anti-abortion resolution at the SBC's 1974 meeting, echoed Fink's comments about the challenges of reaching Baptist audiences with the pro-life message in a paper he contributed to the ILC report. Holbrook observed that the National Right to Life Committee's typical method of working directly with Catholic bishops and priests to disseminate a pro-life message and objective throughout the church would not work in the non-hierarchical, anti-institutional settings of many Protestant faiths, especially Baptists and other fundamentalist groups. Instead of the hierarchical power of the Catholic Church, the NRLC needed to appreciate the congregational model when dealing with many potential evangelical allies. In these settings, Holbrook explained, the pastor "is a follower not a leader. Especially on social issues it is true that he will usually wait to see which direction the congregation is pointing and then he will step out and assume the stance of 'a leader of men.'" This is why NRLC mailings to Baptist and other denominational pastors in Texas had produced few replies of interest. "The apathetic pastor," Holbrook added, "needs to be 'bypassed' and his congregation sensitized." In other words, lay Baptists themselves needed to be directly engaged. They would then take their activated pro-life consciences to their pastors who, with the backing of their congregations, would press upon the denomination to develop a pro-life position and mission that would then reflect back on the pastors and churches not yet engaged in the movement. With Baptists and other fundamentalists groups, Holbrook explained, the movement would have to be truly grassroots if it was to succeed. Stirred from below, rather than directed from above, fundamentalist Protestants would rally to the pro-life cause in ways directly opposed to typical Catholic mobilization.[151]

Holbrook suggested the NRLC reach Baptists directly through the twenty-three state Baptist newspapers, one or more of which nearly every Southern Baptist member received in his or her home. To that end, Holbrook authored an article in the influential *Baptist Standard* imploring Southern Baptists to become active against abortion.[152] For the NRLC, Holbrook recommended placing advertisements in Southern Baptist newspapers that spoke to the concern of the "trauma of an un-wanted pregnancy, etc., etc.," and provided an address for more information, but concealed any reference to both abortion and the NRLC. Only after a person had written to the address would they be sent information "which is written by a 'fellow Baptist'" specifically about the abortion issue. The names of those who wrote in would then be added to a file for use in developing "a concerned network of Baptists who can be brought to bear on denominational 'pressure points.'" As a pilot test, Holbrook suggested placing the ads in the five states with the largest Southern Baptist newspaper circulations, totaling nearly one million readers: Alabama, Florida, Georgia, Mississippi, and Texas.[153]

In late 1973, at the same time the Intergroup Liaison Committee submitted its report to the NRLC's leadership, Holbrook created Baptists for Life, Inc. Holbrook gave the organization space in his Texas church, though it soon relocated to Dalton, Georgia, when he moved to pastor a congregation there. Baptists for Life shared the NRLC's educational and political goals, but it also worked to develop a Baptist-led anti-abortion movement that would expand the pro-life cause and transform the Southern Baptist Convention into an adamantly pro-life member of the coalition. Holbrook distributed a pamphlet he had authored to potential members, "A Baptist Preacher Looks at the Catholic Issue of Abortion"—a title that confronted head-on the prevailing Baptist conception of abortion as a Catholic preoccupation. The organization also encouraged the development of other denominationally specific pro-life groups, at times even providing funds to initiate their formation.[154] Baptists for Life would eventually play a key role in the Southern Baptist Convention's transformation into an aggressive anti-abortion denomination, but for most of the 1970s it struggled for support from Baptists.[155] Still, Baptists for Life's eventual success in expanding the pro-life movement to Southern Baptists depended on a key member of the National Right to Life Committee creating an organization void of outward associations with the NRLC and based solely in the Baptist world.

Paulette Standefer, chair of the Oklahoma Right to Life board of directors, also contributed a paper to the Intergroup Liaison Committee's report, though she was not one of the ILC's six members. Standefer's expertise, however, had been requested to demonstrate how she navigated the challenges of building a pro-life movement in a state with a Catholic population of only 3 percent. Her strategy, Standefer revealed, depended on careful subterfuge: "I never bring up the fact that I am a Catholic," she confessed of her meetings with potential pro-life allies in the state. But the biases could run both ways, and Standefer reminded her largely Catholic readers at the NRLC to respect the values of other religious faiths, particularly the shared pro-life conviction that would be the basis of any associational ties. "Try to transmit this bond," Standefer encouraged, "though try not to make reference to your different denomination."[156]

Standefer also encouraged fellow Catholics to learn the language and culture of their Protestant friends before approaching them. "Sit down and examine your terminology," Standefer suggested, "Does it smack of Romanism?" Protestant phrases like, "I would like to share this with you," and, "I have a burden," could be useful in conversations with them, she explained. Such expressions "are so simple and yet so foreign to Catholics," Standefer noted, but they could greatly help in establishing a friendly rapport with Protestant sympathizers.[157]

In Oklahoma, Standefer explained, the workers in the pro-life movement were Catholic. However, she had brought a few key Protestants into her work, and she used these to help present a public image to her audiences of "a diversified group working for one goal"—a move she recommended to other Catholic pro-lifers working in heavily Protestant areas. In always appearing with one or two of her Protestant recruits, Standefer demonstrated to her audiences that abortion should be a Protestant concern. She could also use their Protestant presence to distract from her own Catholicism. "Work with another person, a speaking partner, who is not Catholic," Standefer advised, "Then if you are asked your religion and wish to dodge the question you can put the spotlight on your partner, but if you do get cornered you have two choices. 1. 'Fess up' I happen to be a Catholic but this is not a denominational issue. It is a moral issue, that is why the Right to Life Committee is made up of persons from varying backgrounds such as my partner and I, etc. etc. 2. If you happen to be alone you will have to 'wing it.'"[158]

Such was the challenge of working in explicitly religious contexts for pro-life leaders. The religious milieu of anti-abortion politics—the social location of pro-life presentations held in worship sanctuaries, Sunday school classrooms, and church basements—automatically raised questions about the presenters' religious identities. That religious identity could provide critical legitimacy among a group of potential pro-life converts, still formulating their personal positions on abortion in light of many denominations' silence. Baptists would be reassured, for example, to learn their guest speaker on pro-life issues belonged to a fellow church in the Convention. Marjory Mecklenburg would later describe this as "'inside' work," where people from various denominations would "work as 'life activists' identified with their denominations, i.e., the Baptists for Life concept." Otherwise any legitimacy of the pro-life movement could be undermined for many of the most promising Protestant converts to the cause—evangelicals and fundamentalists—if they were met by only a Catholic representative. Instead, they needed to be approached by pro-life activists wearing "their religious group's hat." These separate denominational groups and their leaders could still work with the NRLC privately, Mecklenburg explained, but "at least for the time being, more will be accomplished if NRLC operates one step removed from the activity."[159]

No records exist to indicate how the NRLC's Executive Committee responded to the Intergroup Liaison Committee's report. It is unclear whether the Executive Committee ignored the push to develop an ecumenical movement, rejected outright the recommendations, or pursued them with ineffective or halfhearted efforts. What is clear, however, is the increasing frustration Protestant leaders in the NRLC felt about the organization's direction, particularly as related to the question of broadening the movement beyond its Catholic base. Some Protestant leaders, like Robert Holbrook who had founded Baptists for Life and Jean Garton who founded Lutherans for Life, would throw their attention to the denominationally specific organizations they had created, building up those groups as formidable players in the antiabortion coalition, even if the NRLC failed to provide much support for those efforts. (When Holbrook addressed the NRLC's 1974 convention, *Christianity Today* heralded his speech as evidence of "the latest indications of growing interest in the right-to-life issue among evangelicals.")[160] Others, like Mecklenburg and Fink, for a time continued battling other NRLC leaders to reshape the organization and its direction. But they found that fight increasingly difficult in light of the influence they felt the Catholic Church maintained over the NRLC, its leaders, and its political goals.

A few months after the ILC submitted its report, Mecklenburg, Fink, and other NRLC Protestants became incensed when four cardinals from the Catholic Church testified before a Senate Judiciary Committee subcommittee hearing on abortion. The bishops' testimony before Congress was unprecedented, and the four made it clear their presence signaled the importance the Catholic Church had given to the issue. Chaired by Senator Birch Bayh of Indiana, the subcommittee had convened to consider two proposed amendments that would extend constitutional protections to the unborn fetus. One amendment, offered by Conservative Party Senator James Buckley of New York, would ban all abortions except in cases where pregnancy threatened the life of the mother. It also posed an ambiguous definition of when life began, calling for protection of the fetus "from the time a biologically identifiable human being comes into existence."[161] This definition would not pass muster with the most ardent right-to-lifers, particularly the Catholic Church.

The other amendment, written by North Carolina's Republican Senator Jesse Helms, sought to go beyond merely overturning *Roe* by banning abortions without exceptions. Even many states that had not allowed abortions before *Roe* had made allowances for cases where the procedure would save the life of the mother, but Helms's proposed amendment made abortion for any reason illegal. The four cardinals did not endorse either of the amendments, but they made it clear the church would only accept an amendment that granted legal personhood to the fetus from the moment of conception and banned abortion for all reasons. "We cannot support any exceptions," Cardinal John Krol, the archbishop of Philadelphia and the president of the NCCB, testified.[162]

Though representatives from the LDS Church and the Lutheran Church—Missouri Synod along with Robert Holbrook, speaking on behalf of his Baptists for Life organization, were also on hand to testify in support of the more lenient Buckley amendment, the media concentrated on the four bishops and the Catholic Church's role in opposing abortion.[163] In contrast, the media noted several Protestant and Jewish groups had journeyed to Washington to testify in support of abortion rights. Various articles detailed the presence of these progressive faiths in contrast to the rigidity of the Catholic bishops, who would accept no amendment but their own. Such a depiction, barely a year after *Roe*, added to the public perception that abortion was little more than a Catholic preoccupation dominated by authoritarian church leaders forcing their personal theological convictions on all Americans. This was the very characterization of their movement pro-life activists had consciously sought to dispel, and Protestant leaders in the NRLC, particularly Mecklenburg and Fink, were infuriated the bishops had spoken before Congress with seemingly little regard for the impact their testimony might make on the burgeoning movement.[164]

The Jesuit magazine *America* shared Mecklenburg and Fink's frustrations with the Catholic hierarchy. Given its Jesuit provenance, *America* was a fairly progressive publication that often saw its duty as critiquing the Catholic Church's more orthodox corners. *America* blasted the bishops and the NRLC as "rigoristic Catholics [who] are defending what they believe to be their faith's basic propositions" by supporting the pure but politically unviable Helms amendment. Protestant pro-lifers, on the other hand, "have a more cerebral sense than do rigorists of the civil order within which public moral issues must come to rest," the magazine argued, because they were willing to support an anti-abortion amendment that allowed for abortions under certain exceptions since this would still drastically reduce the number of abortions. Unlike rigoristic Catholics, who could not separate their absolutist theology from their political strategies, *America* praised these non-Catholic pro-lifers, who were willing to bend a little to achieve an overall good. "They are not Baptists defending the Baptist faith, Mormons defending Mormonism, Lutherans defending the Reformation or Protestants defending justification by faith." "It is ironic and a little dismaying," the piece concluded, "to observe . . . it is the Protestants who seem more aware that 'Thou shalt not kill' is not the only commandment; there is another which goes: 'Love one another.' Given the rough road lying before any amendment, it is clear that unborn children will not be protected by law and love until all pro-lifers learn the law of love."[165]

Within the NRLC, an internal memo captured the frustration the group's non-Catholics felt over the bishops' testimony before Congress and in light of the ongoing power struggle for control of the NRLC. Though the memo is undated, its content suggests it was written right after the Bayh subcommittee hearings. The memo also lacks an author, though one study suggests it was written by Warren Schaller, an Episcopal priest active in the pro-life movement in Minnesota, and it seems written for a Catholic leader in the NRLC sympathetic to the author's concerns about Catholic domination of the organization.[166] "It is a Protestant thing, you see," the memo began, "that authority rests in the people of God." This, the author wrote, contrasted with Catholic perceptions of proper leadership: "It is hard for the RC hierarchy, or those who related well to them, to be comfortable w/ such a system. . . . To them it seems better to depend on recognized authority." The author then erupted at an unspecified event, likely the bishops' testimony before Congress: "If you don't understand why I say that it is now just about irreversible that the RTL movement is a RC movement, & why it will . . . be impossible for Protestants to participate in any meaningful way in NRLC, then just believe me when I say that I don't see how you don't see. I don't think the RC church knows how not to lose the human right amendment. Because to win it will have to look & act different than it knows how to do." "For that reason," the memo concluded, " . . . you won't be able to establish real cooperation of Protestant groups or where only 3% of the people are RC, you'll never arouse more than 3% of the people. . . . next year, the press and politicians will very quickly recognize that even though concern for life crosses denominational boundaries, the NRLC is a RC movement w/ some Protestant 'fronts.'"[167] Mecklenburg and Fink didn't keep their frustrations private either. "Catholics are trying to control the pro-life movement," they complained publicly to one newspaper around the same time.[168]

Almost a year earlier, one day after the Intergroup Liaison Committee's creation, the ILC's chair, Judy Fink, perhaps newly emboldened by her new position and charge, fired off a memo to an Executive Committee member criticizing the Policy Committee's composition. Noting that only men were represented on the Policy Committee, Fink also challenged its all-Catholic membership. "Since the prolife movement must be broad-based and pluralistic if it is to grow and remain healthy," Fink wrote, "I feel that it is a serious mistake for a Committee of this importance to not seat any individuals except male Roman Catholics, and I respectfully urge that you, and the Executive

Committee, consider placing at least two persons on the Policy Committee, in addition to those already chosen, who will give it a broader spectrum of input."[169] That the Policy Committee remained in the hands of Catholics greatly impacted the NRLC's political direction. Sensitive to the political mission of the Catholic Church, the NRLC's Policy Committee pursued a political course of hard-line anti-abortion opposition that exacerbated interdenominational tension within the NRLC's leadership and worked against a broadening of the movement from within the organization. Two months after Fink's memo, Marjory Mecklenburg learned that an ally of Father McHugh had asked another Protestant member of the NRLC's Executive Committee—perhaps Fink—that if the Catholic Church gave the organization $20 million "would the Protestants be willing to be window dressing – no rocking the boat?"[170]

After more than a year of challenging that Protestant marginalization within the NRLC, Mecklenburg and Fink could endure it no longer. On August 21, 1974, both Fink and Mecklenburg submitted their resignations. That same day both women became directors of the American Citizens Concerned for Life, an anti-abortion organization based in Mecklenburg's home state of Minnesota and run by several volunteers who had also left the NRLC. Fink and Mecklenburg explained their departure from the NRLC as due to frustration with the Catholic hierarchy's continued control of the organization. "The overbearing and separatist attitudes of the Catholic hierarchy," Fink declared to reporters, "can only serve the purpose of abortion groups who want to prove once and for all that abortion is truly a Catholic issue." Fink and Mecklenburg charged that certain factions within the organization were working with the United States Catholic Conference to take over the NRLC and redirect it to absolutist positions on the constitutional amendment and on contraception. The disagreements inside the NRLC largely fell along religious lines, as Catholic leaders in the NRLC advocated their church's objectives and non-Catholics resisted taking such hard-line directives. Various state directors of NRLC's chapter organizations shared Fink and Mecklenburg's feelings about the Catholic Church's interference. Nearly a dozen of these state directors stepped down from their NRLC positions as well and assumed roles as area representatives with the ACCL.[171]

Two months before her departure, Mecklenburg had been ousted from her position as NRLC chair, likely contributing to her decision to leave the organization completely. Mecklenburg's resistance to the most stringent objectives of the Catholic Church and its friends in the NRLC had made her a target. Her advocacy of liberal positions in direct opposition of Catholic teachings, however, like supporting the distribution of contraception to teenagers to help cut abortion rates, may have been her real undoing as the NRLC's chair.[172] But if NRLC's leaders wanted to hew a closer line to the Catholic Church's objectives, they still did not feel they had to elect only Catholics to the organization's highest leadership. A year after Mecklenburg's ousting, the NRLC chose another Protestant woman, Dr. Mildred Jefferson, to lead the organization, allowing the group to continue to present a diverse religious image to outsiders. And in the headquarters' offices in Washington, D.C., Ray White, a Mormon, had recently taken the paid position of executive director for the voluntary organization.

But these were token moves within an organization (and movement) that remained decidedly Catholic. While both the NRLC and the Catholic Church frequently challenged any characterization of the pro-life movement as a Catholic issue, these objections seemed like merely lip service given the actual actions of both. The NRLC had allowed some of its most prominent Protestant leaders to slip away over frustrations about opening up the organization to non-Catholics and developing a concerted evangelical group and identity. At the same time, the Catholic Church continually pressured the NRLC to hew to its most unbending positions despite repeated warnings that its inability to compromise threatened ecumenical cooperation on abortion and heightened public perception of it as only a Catholic preoccupation. Some within the NRLC even believed its inability to develop a truly ecumenical membership benefited the larger anti-abortion movement overall because those non-Catholics that were willing to fight against abortion were creating their own organizations that expanded the pro-life network. Mary Ann Henry, the Catholic coordinator of the Ocean County Right to Life Committee in New Jersey, had authored a paper included in the Intergroup Liaison Committee's 1973 report about the challenges she faced in dealing with non-Catholics in the movement. In New Jersey, like so many other states, Henry had found that those Protestants who wanted to work against abortion rights preferred to create their own organizations rather than join a local chapter of the NRLC because they perceived it was a Catholic organization. Henry still worked to coordinate the small, independent groups in her county, but she admitted that task was often difficult. Still, she recognized that her personal challenges actually had benefits for the larger pro-life movement. When Henry spoke to the local press about an upcoming event or certain pro-life work in Ocean County, she could mention that such efforts were "supported by a half-dozen other pro-life groups in the area. It impresses them that there are so many of us who are now active."[173]

A decade before, the Second Vatican Council had emphasized the Catholic Church's new commitment to ecumenism and to working with other religious groups on causes of mutual concern. Yet when an opportunity for actualizing this came in the burgeoning pro-life movement, the Catholic Church seemed to reject prospects for ecumenical cooperation in favor of maintaining its authority and dominance of the anti-abortion fight. In an address to the Archdiocese Council of Catholic Women in Chicago the summer after the *Roe* decision, Cardinal Cody, the church's leading figure in its anti-abortion work, warned against disunity among his church's pro-life efforts and called for Catholic adherence to the church's work. Praising the church's leadership, Cody boasted to the women, "When our history is being written, the Catholic Church will find in golden letters its account of fighting for the integrity of our nation." "What I would like to leave you with," Cody concluded his talk, "is that we must stick together." He continued:

> We must have unity; organization will depend on the unity that we have. Already in the fight on abortion we have lost that unity. We have numbers of organizations, individuals, some not always with an unselfish interest, who are coming out and saying 'we know how to do it best.' Well, as one of the successors of the apostles, as one of the three hundred and three bishops now in the United States, I must tell you that we need your backing. We have qualified expert people who are advising from a political standpoint. We must not let ourselves be divided and there are many out to do just this. We must stay together so that the approximately forty-eight million people in our country will be speaking with one voice. I am sure that if we can maintain that unity and if we will work together . . . that we can handle this thing very well.[174]

Cody's words reflected the Catholic hierarchy's sentiments in fighting abortion rights. Instead of championing an ecumenical—or even "moral"—cause shared by Americans across denominations, Cody presented the abortion fight as a Catholic responsibility that Catholics should engage through church-led means. This was hardly an invitation to interfaith cooperation. But given the anti-Catholicism that had flared up from some corners—like Rev. Criswell in Dallas—in response to the Catholic Church's reaction to *Roe*, it was hardly surprising that Catholic leaders believed they might have to go it alone in the abortion fight, even if some encouraging signs of ecumenical possibilities had come from places like *Christianity Today*.

Closer to home, an experience within the pro-life movement in Illinois had also likely colored Cody's attitude about ecumenical activism. Earlier that summer, pro-life leaders across the state had begun discussing the possibility of forming a state-wide coalition. Cautiously, the Chicago Archdiocesan Office for Pro Life Activities let its parishioners know about the discussions, but stressed that Chicago's Catholic churches look to the archdiocese for any instructions about moving forward. "If a coalition is formed," the Office's newsletter explained, "I will notify all the parishes as to which Pro Life groups belong to the Coalition, and at the same time, I will specifically request that all Pro Life groups not in the Coalition, be excluded from parishes, schools, and agencies in the Archdiocese of Chicago."[175] A month later, the Office let its churches know that attempts at a coalition had fallen apart because one anti-abortion group, the small, mostly Protestant organization Illinois Citizens Concerned for Life, had created "a disaster" with their demands that the Catholic Church loosen its control of the pro-life movement in the state. "The ICCL has clearly demonstrated that they wish to separate themselves from any group which includes the Roman Catholic Church," the newsletter reported, "We respect their wishes. We will not trouble them in the future and trust that they will be consistent and not request the assistance of the Church or use of its facilities."[176] While the Chicago archdiocese presented the failure to organize an ecumenical pro-life coalition in the state as the work of anti-Catholic forces, it was unable to see that the Catholic Church's own intransigence that the ICCL objected to played a role too. While the truth likely remained somewhere between the two sides' accounts of the situation in Illinois, the inability to broker an ecumenical pro-life movement in the state depended as much on the Catholic hierarchy's unwillingness to yield leadership and control as it did on any anti-Catholic bigotries from ICCL or other non-Catholic groups.

Conclusion

Inside the Catholic Church, leaders continued to develop the church-wide pro-life cause it had been building since the mid-1960s, now with even more haste in light of the federal extension of abortion rights and now that the church and the NRLC had separated themselves—at least officially—following the court's decision. The United States Catholic Conference began developing reference and educational materials to distribute throughout the church's parishes and schools "that will present the case for the sanctity of the child's life from conception to birth." The conference also suggested there where many issues already addressed in church liturgy and educational programs where "an abortion component" could be added on. "Given the extensive nature of the abortion question itself and the already widespread ramifications of the Supreme Court decision," the Conference wrote in an internal planning memorandum, "it seems fairly clear that such a logical tie-in is likely to exist in many instances (e.g., programs relating to various aspects of human rights and human dignity, conferences on social justice, general catechetical programs)."[177]

At the local level, dioceses and parishes used these materials to educate their members on abortion's immorality and the church's political efforts against it. Respect Life Week became a regular commitment on church calendars, but abortion received consistent attention in most parishes throughout the year. Catholics attending Mass regularly heard pro-life homilies, anti-abortion pastoral letters, and exhortations to keep the abortion issue at the forefront of their voting decisions during an election. Dioceses also continued to build up their pro-life activities, creating anti-abortion newsletters, parish pro-life groups, and letter writing committees to inundate the media and lawmakers with anti-abortion messages. In Illinois, six diocesan pro-life directors oversaw over one thousand parish coordinators who led more than one hundred thousand members who had joined their parish's pro-life group.[178]

One homily prepared by the Archdiocese of Chicago for its priests to mark the first anniversary of *Roe v. Wade* reminded congregants, "Abortion is not a 'Catholic' issue; it involves principles which cut across religious lines. The life of every human being is sacred from conception to death. This is so because God has created each of us, and because each of us shares in the redemption of Christ our Lord."[179] But those principles often remained hampered by religious lines rather than being transcendent of them. Some of that, especially from the evangelical and fundamentalist wings of Protestantism, owed to lingering anti-Catholic suspicions, though some conservative Protestants were developing pro-life convictions in spite of Catholic associations with the cause. Other pro-life advocates, notably the LDS Church, preferred to wage their campaign against abortion on their own not so much out of anti-Catholic animosity—though some of that would eventually surface too—but more from the persistent Mormon tradition of institutional independence and self-direction. The Catholic Church too undercut opportunities to build an ecumenical pro-life movement even as it insisted the church was not alone in opposing abortion. While the Catholic Church clearly wanted to remove the target the media and pro-choice advocates had placed on it as the sole source of the anti-abortion cause, it did not seem as willing to share with non-Catholic pro-lifers leadership and control of the movement. Its efforts both in the National Right to Life Committee and within its church-wide anti-abortion network worked against broaching a true ecumenical movement in the early moments after *Roe*. But a firestorm against a liberalizing culture—especially in regard to its sexual ethics—was slowly growing within the various corners of conservative religion. That outrage would eventually erupt with passion, generating new political activism and suggesting new alliances.

5

We Gather Together

THROUGH THE 1970S, evangelical, Mormon, and Catholic leaders still largely resisted the calls to ecumenism. LDS membership continued its steady climb upward and evangelical churches were also enjoying a boom; bolstered by their increases and strengthened by their exclusivist theologies, they largely shunned associational ties. After the ecumenical push coming out of the Second Vatican Council, the Catholic Church had tempered some of those impulses with warnings about non-Catholic-led ecumenism and an emphasis on one-on-one dialogue with particular religious groups over a general ecumenism. Evangelical denominations and the LDS Church also seemed more amenable to this structured relationship with others, seeing "interfaith" discussions as distinct from and in some ways oppositional to the goals of ecumenism. (Indeed, evangelicals and Mormons, in particular, often saw it as a strategic avenue to proselytizing.) In interfaith dialogue, religious distinction and denominational separation would structure and animate the relationship rather than pose the obstacles to be overcome. This was the focus of a selection of interfaith meetings, for example, between regional leaders of the Southern Baptist Convention and the Catholic Church.[1] Additionally, the LDS Church created a professorship for "Religious Understanding" at its Brigham Young University. As part of the job, the professor traveled to mostly Protestant seminaries to present the Mormon view on religious questions. These efforts pointedly contrasted from the principal aims of the liberal ecumenical movement, but they also helped structure the burgeoning relationships between—if not among—the Mormon, Catholic, and evangelical faiths.

Politics too provided more moments to recognize commonality. Abortion became a pressing concern of Mormons and evangelicals as the decade continued. The Equal Rights Amendment (ERA) also met opposition from conservative Catholic, evangelical, and Mormon circles. Despite these shared political concerns, Mormons, Catholics, and evangelicals tended to remain isolated in their political engagement, at times citing interfaith tensions and historical grievances as the reason for this. There were moments of collaboration to be sure, such as some coordination among evangelical and Catholic anti-abortion groups, but the larger political scene revealed religious conservatives acting separately more often than together. As the decade closed, the presidential candidacy of Ronald Reagan and the work of New Right political strategists overlooked this trend and championed a "Religious Right" coalition that could stoke the nation's moral rejuvenation and attain the desired political results that often seemed elusive. But the events of the 1970s would foreshadow how difficult that unity would be to achieve.

Growth of Conservative Churches

In 1972, Dean M. Kelley, a liberal Methodist preacher associated with the National Council of Churches, issued a book that closely examined a largely ignored trend that was about to remake the American social and political landscape in the coming decade.[2] The book's title, *Why Conservative Churches Are Growing*, flew in the face of those who thought religion was on its way out of American life. After decades of impressive increases, most mainline Protestant denominations were now hurting. Until the 1960s, all major denominations in the United States had continued growing. But by 1965, that trend had reversed itself for nearly all major religious groups.[3] "Are the Churches Dying?," Kelley's first chapter asked. Looking at five major Protestant bodies—what Kelley called the "five 'wheel-horses' of the ecumenical movement"—it appeared so, as all were undergoing "significant decline."[4]

Conservative churches and denominations revealed a much different picture, Kelley found, showcasing sustained and enviable growth. The Southern Baptist Convention had surpassed the United Methodist Church in 1967 as the nation's largest Protestant denomination, growing at more than a 2 percent clip each year while the Methodist Church began losing members. Between 1960 and 1970, the SBC had expanded by nearly two million.[5] Within the next ten years, another two million more would call themselves Southern Baptists, enlarging the rolls to nearly fourteen million.[6] That growth depended in part on the SBC's steady expansion outside of the American South. In one example, three hundred and twenty thousand Southern Baptists in California now made it the state's second largest Protestant denomination, with particular dominance in Southern California's Orange, Riverside, San Bernadino, and San Diego counties.[7] Other smaller evangelical denominations like the Lutheran Church—Missouri Synod and the Church of the

Nazarene continued to balloon while liberal groups like the Episcopal Church and the United Church of Christ entered their steep declines.

Some of the most interesting pages of Kelley's book featured graphs that juxtaposed the upward growth lines of conservative branches of a denomination against the downward lines of the liberal branch, like the ascending Wesleyan branch of Methodism versus the flat-lining establishment United Methodist Church or the skyrocketing Christian Reformed Church against the ebbing Reformed Church in America.[8] *Christianity Today* praised Kelley's work as "a well documented, statistically grounded, sociological analysis of denominational membership trends. His prognosis is not good for the liberal, ecumenical denominations in America: he thinks the foreseeable future belongs to the conservative evangelicals."[9] *Christian Century*, the magazine that spoke for many of those declining ecumenical denominations, took issue with the book's methodology, but admitted the book's flaws weren't enough "to get liberal churchmen completely off the hook."[10]

Kelley argued conservative church groups continued to grow because they offered a way for "vigorously and effectively making sense of life" for their members.[11] While liberal and moderate denominations entertained complicated speculations about the nature of life that drew from scientific discoveries, psychological theory, and literary criticism, conservative churches offered definitive answers about life's meaning rooted in close readings of the Bible. Conservative churches, Kelley argued, provided a clear and constant alternative to a world made uncertain by rapid cultural transformations, a brutal (and seemingly endless) war, and massive social unrest.

In demanding firm adherence to strict personal regulations, like abstaining from alcohol or delaying sexual activity until marriage—the various requirements of what Kelley called a "high-demand movement"—and fiercely defending their borders against the enticements of ecumenical associations and modernizing trends, conservative churches walked against the tide of a permissive society.[12] In fact, it was the churches that were most open to outsiders that suffered some of the worst setbacks in membership. Some declining denominations tried to prevent their falls by merging with other shrinking denominations, but those fusions often only hastened their marginalization and strengthened evangelical critiques about ecumenism's deadly impact. Meanwhile, highly separatist denominations, like the Baptist Bible Fellowship, continued to flourish. The religious scholar Elmer Towns had shown in his 1972 book, *America's Fastest Growing Churches*, that eight of the ten fastest-growing churches in the nation belonged to the Baptist Bible Fellowship.[13] Kelley's book set that growth against mainline Protestantism's decline, highlighting the winners and losers in the independent-ecumenical debate. Evangelical leaders passed Kelley's book back and forth gleefully, cherishing the statistical validation of their theological convictions.[14]

The Decade of the Evangelical

Celebrating its bicentennial in 1976, America was awash in patriotic tributes filled with fireworks, marching bands, and waving flags. Bunting seemed to hang from every spot. The tiny outpost of democracy on the edge of the world had become its center—strong, proud, and, at times, a little defiant. But while the nation commemorated two hundred years of its radical experiment, a presidential race divided the country into competing political camps. Gerald Ford and Jimmy Carter faced off against each other in the first campaign since the Watergate affair, a scandal many Americans saw as symptomatic of the spiritual crisis plaguing the nation. Both candidates sought to heal the nation from that trauma, and the race largely reflected the nation's desire to restore civility and honor to the White House. But the 1976 election also revealed another significant development in the United States: the rising prominence and diversity of evangelical Christians.

Before Jimmy Carter had won his party's nomination for the presidency, he faced a crowded field in the Democratic primaries. Early in the primary season, Carter offhandedly dropped that he was a "born again" Christian. While all the candidates in the Democratic race were trying to distinguish themselves to voters, Carter hadn't thought this simple biographical fact was particularly controversial or confusing. The media begged to differ. The *New York Times'* religion writer Kenneth Briggs would later recall how Carter's words perplexed the mainstream media. What did he mean that he had been born again? And what exactly was an evangelical? Hadn't they disappeared after the Scopes Trail?[15] Briggs sought to clear up the confusion about Carter's religious faith by penning a lengthy article on evangelicalism for the *Times*. In the piece, Briggs suggested that it was the press's—and maybe more than a few readers of the *New York Times'*—ignorance rather than Jimmy Carter's faith that was the rarity of 1976, remarking that Carter's "stance of evangelical theology is not only widely shared but is also growing more rapidly than any other Christian perspective."[16]

Another expert tried to combat the uncertainty about Carter's faith among the nation's media elite and cultural intelligentsia. The pollster George Gallup, Jr., had just surveyed Americans' religious convictions and released his results that summer. Gallup found that 34 percent claimed to have undergone a "born again" experience, a designation that sidestepped denominational affiliation while grouping fundamentalists, evangelicals, charismatics, and Pentecostals together. This represented some fifty million adult Americans, Gallup explained, and because of those numbers—and Carter's campaign—Gallup christened 1976 "The Year of the Evangelical."[17] Anyone who had kept an eye on the nation's churches for the last twenty years realized that there had been a great evangelical stirring across the country. But it had taken Carter's campaign and Gallup's polling results for most of the ruling class in New York and Washington, D.C., to recognize the religious revival transforming the country.[18] In the scramble to understand this overlooked, but apparently sizeable, slice of the American public, media outlets now published extensive investigations of the American evangelical, like *Newsweek*'s six-page cover story that ran in the fall of 1976.[19] Politicians aside from Jimmy Carter eagerly seized on any noticeable demographic of the electorate, and they made extensive overtures toward American evangelicals for their votes. The year 1976 demonstrated how far evangelicals had come in asserting themselves as a social and political force in the nation. While evangelicals would flex their political muscles throughout the year, there were also signs of dissension and infighting among the evangelical ranks. As the *Newsweek* reporter concluded his investigation, "1976 may yet turn out to be the year that the evangelicals won the White House but lost cohesiveness as a distinct force in American religion and culture."[20]

While the news media needed George Gallup to alert them to the phenomenon, there had been plenty of signs that an evangelical revival was sweeping the nation aside from Dean Kelley's predictive book published in 1972. That same year, eighty-five thousand college students had journeyed to Dallas for a weeklong revival sponsored by the evangelical ministry, Campus Crusade for Christ. "Explo '72"—called "Godstock" by some as a spoof on the far-less-godly Woodstock festival held three years before—brought evangelical young people together for discipleship sessions and workshops on Christian ministry, missions, and political engagement. At night, a packed Cotton Bowl hosted revival sessions that jammed to the hot sounds of a burgeoning Christian rock industry before quieting for sermons led by American evangelicalism's biggest stars, including Billy Graham. John Lennon may have recently quipped that the Beatles were "more popular than Jesus," but he wasn't the only one oblivious to the religious revival taking place among America's youth. While the nation seemed fixated on the kids who were turning on, tuning in, and dropping out, millions of other American youths were tapping into the evangelical faith. By the early 1970s, Campus Crusade for Christ had become one of the country's largest college organizations.[21]

There were other signs—many found right there on the nation's televisions—about the booming evangelical movement of the 1970s. Jerry

Falwell, an independent Baptist minister who presided over the enormous Thomas Road Baptist Church in Lynchburg, Virginia, hosted a television program that in the mid-1970s aired on more than two hundred stations and was watched by more than a million Americans each week.[22] Other televangelists like Jimmy Swaggart, Pat Robertson, James Robison, and Jim Bakker enjoyed similar successes.[23] By 1972, the evangelical National Religious Broadcasters, an affiliate of the National Association of Evangelicals that aided the exploding television ministry industry, had quadrupled its membership from just five years before.[24]

These television programs belonged to a larger evangelical cultural industry that turned out popular Christian albums, magazines, and bestselling books. Evangelical books represented yet another clue the mainstream media might have noticed about the growing evangelical presence. In fact, the bestselling book of 1976 (more than two million copies sold) was Billy Graham's *Angels*, which promised to tell its readers everything they wanted to know about the cherubim.[25] Not one secular book came anywhere as close to *Angels*' sales numbers. But most media outlets, like the *New York Times Book Review*, did not track book sales from religious bookstores, so even though many evangelical books were far outselling the *Times*' official bestsellers, popular books by authors like Harold Lindsell, Chuck Colson, Francis Schaeffer, and Tim and Beverly LaHaye remained off the radar for the country's cultural arbiters.[26]

Still, as the *Newsweek* article had noted, the boom of American evangelicalism revealed not just the movement's size but also its scope and sometimes strife. "The age of monolithic unity" in American evangelicalism, the evangelical theologian Donald Bloesch wrote at the time, was as much a fiction as the notion that evangelicals were some "obscure group of religious fanatics" irrelevant to American life.[27] One of the fault lines wrinkling the pretense of evangelical unity in the 1970s concerned the rise of charismatics, sometimes also called neo-Pentecostals to distinguish them from the first wave of Pentecostalism that arose from the 1906 Los Angeles Azusa Street revivals. Starting in the 1950s and accelerating in the 1960s, the "charismatic renewal movement" touched off revival and Spirit-filled church services that included speaking in tongues, faith healings, and ecstatic worship in nearly every denomination, with surprising appearances even in mainline Lutheran and Episcopalian churches. By the 1970s, the charismatic movement was booming, claiming some of the nation's fastest-growing churches and denominations, like Calvary Chapel and the Vineyard Churches; enjoying huge public visibility through the emotional broadcasts of televangelists, like Jimmy Swaggart and Jim Bakker; and finding particular purchase among a generation of unchurched young people, like the Jesus People, who turned from the secular counterculture to embrace the gospel while also spurning the trappings of the traditional church.

Evangelicals had to respect the neo-Pentecostal phenomenon, particularly its enviable conversion rates—over five million Americans participated in charismatic Christianity by 1975—but they also questioned the charismatic emphasis that believers experience the gifts of the Holy Spirit.[28] As one Pentecostal noted in the evangelical *Trinity Journal*, "the present church climate of dialogue allows serious consideration of theological items generally rather than reactionary dismissal, except among Fundamentalists," permitting evangelicals to reckon more thoughtfully with the charismatic movement in the 1970s, but they still worried about the basic theological and worship-style divergences revealed in charismatics' Spirit-filled enthusiasms.[29] Evangelicals believed God had only allowed these gifts to flourish during New Testament times. Disagreements over worship styles and the work of the Holy Spirit tore some evangelical churches apart, as the church members touched by charismatic fervor left to form their own Spirit-filled congregations.[30] Some evangelical denominations attempted to quell the charismatic movement from taking hold within, such as the Lutheran Church—Missouri Synod's 1977 resolution that characterized some charismatic doctrines as "mere human opinion not clearly taught in Holy Scripture and therefore contrary to the Holy Scriptures," but charismatic streams still continued to rise within evangelical bodies, including the Missouri Synod.[31] As Stephen Miller has pointed out, taking shape amid the fervent religious ground of 1970s conservative Protestantism were "the porous boundaries between the three great traditions in postwar American evangelicalism: hard-line fundamentalism, spirit-filled Pentecostalism, and comparatively moderate 'neo-evangelicalism.'"[32] But that porousness, especially from charismatics, troubled many evangelicals. Spread across denominations and even to some corners of the Catholic Church, the charismatic movement displayed a loose ecumenism that connected its followers through the shared experience of miraculous encounters and ecstatic worship rather than the orthodoxies of theology.[33] Evangelicals were suspicious enough of experience as a source of a believer's testimony, but experience rather than theological conviction rooted in authoritative scripture as the basis of Christian unity led many conservative evangelicals, particularly fundamentalists, to dismiss charismatics as misguided worshipers more interested in fanning the flames of spiritual enthusiasm than in genuine revival.

The Battle for the Bible

Evangelical theology was not without its own controversies. During the 1960s, internal tensions over matters of theology began appearing in the evangelical movement. *Christianity Today* had documented many of these skirmishes, such as within the Southern Baptist Convention and the Lutheran Church—Missouri Synod. Those articles, while typically siding with the most orthodox advocates in the fights, generally reflected the measured and sober tone the magazine had historically shown toward most matters. But with the change to a new editor, Harold Lindsell, in the late 1960s, the magazine turned in a more aggressive and sometimes militant direction. Outside of *Christianity Today*'s pages, Lindsell launched an even fiercer attack for the faith with the 1976 publication of his book, *The Battle for the Bible*.

Lindsell had risen to the top of the evangelical ranks long before he assumed the editorship of *Christianity Today*. Though a Southern Baptist, Lindsell traveled generally in the circles of northern evangelicalism. Born in New York City in 1913, Lindsell attended Wheaton College, where he was close friends with Carl Henry and Billy and Ruth Graham. After earning his Ph.D. from New York University, Lindsell joined Henry on the faculty at Northern Baptist Theological Seminary in Chicago. The two then worked with other evangelicals to launch Fuller Theological Seminary in Pasadena in 1947, where he taught before serving as dean and then vice president. In 1964 Lindsell left Fuller to become associate editor of *Christianity Today*.[34] Lindsell arrived at a difficult time for the magazine. J. Howard Pew, *Christianity Today*'s wealthy backer, had grown increasingly frustrated with Henry's leadership. Pew wanted the magazine to adopt an even more aggressive stance against the liberal theology and politics of ecumenical churches and to more forcefully advocate for political conservatism. Although Henry was a diehard Republican, Pew resented Henry's resistance to full-scale militancy. Nelson Bell shared Pew's concerns about Henry. Not wanting to lose the substantive investments from Pew, the magazine's board offered no support for Henry. Knowing what was coming, Henry resigned in 1968 and Lindsell assumed the top spot at the publication. Lindsell was particularly attractive to Pew and other supporters of the magazine because they knew he would assertively move *Christianity Today* in an even more conservative direction theologically and politically.[35]

From his perch at the magazine, Lindsell did exactly that. *Christianity Today*'s anti-abortion advocacy in the years around *Roe* provided one example of the conservative politics the magazine pushed, but the publication also spoke out strongly against issues like sex education in public schools, the Equal Rights Amendment, and the gay rights movement.[36] On theological matters, Lindsell kept a close eye on the scriptural inerrancy debate roiling the evangelical community. Two of his associations made Lindsell especially attuned to the controversy. His former haunt, Fuller Seminary, began to veer from its history of conservative evangelicalism to a more progressive outlook with leadership, faculty, and an increasing percentage of its student body amenable to less-than-orthodox views on biblical inerrancy, positioning Fuller on the more moderate end of evangelicalism. Lindsell was infuriated that Fuller was in the process of developing a new statement of faith, a move Lindsell interpreted as a departure for Fuller from its historic defense of inerrancy.[37] And in Lindsell's denomination, Southern Baptists continued their spar over biblical inerrancy that W. A. Criswell had been highlighting in sermons and writings for more than a decade.

Lindsell launched his defense of biblical inerrancy in *The Battle for the Bible*. The Bible contained no errors, Lindsell argued, and served as a perfect source for all its historical, scientific, and cosmological assertions, not just its spiritual claims. Moreover, Lindsell contended there was no middle ground or even moderate position when it came to the question of the Bible's perfect truth. Instead, he argued, "every deviation away from inerrancy ends up by casting a vote in favor of limited inerrancy. Once limited inerrancy is accepted, it places the Bible in the same category with every other book that has ever been written."[38] For Lindsell, inerrancy, rather than the born-again experience, became the litmus test that separated true evangelicals from those who wrongly claimed the name. Although neo-evangelicals had once sought to elevate the faith above the separatist impulses and internecine wars of fundamentalist Christianity, as the father of neo-evangelicalism, Harold Ockenga, pointed out in his supportive foreword to *Battle for the Bible*, evangelical inerrantists like Lindsell now seemed determined to divide the evangelical movement over the question of inerrancy. Lindsell, as other inerrantists like Criswell had argued, likened tolerance of anything less than complete orthodoxy on the matter of biblical inerrancy as a virus that would spread within a church or denomination, spelling its eventual demise. In a scathing series of chapters, Lindsell attacked the Lutheran Church—Missouri Synod, the Southern Baptist Convention, and Fuller Theological Seminary as evangelical bodies where the rot of biblical unorthodoxy festered. Unless these groups rooted out this deviancy, they would fall into decline, becoming yet another marginal example of liberal Christianity. The battle to which the title referred was necessary because inerrancy and anything less than that position could not coexist within a denomination or the evangelical movement in general.

The presence of both necessitated war. While evangelicals had overlooked many differences among them in order to establish a forceful unity, Lindsell argued the matter of the Bible's inerrancy allowed for no disagreements. To posit that the Bible might be anything less than God's infallible word was to deviate from the foundational truth the evangelical message rested upon, and the evangelical movement could not contain within it a disagreement that struck at its very basis.

Lindsell's controversial book received mixed reactions from the evangelical community, an unsurprising response given its diversity but one that also revealed the fault lines in American evangelicalism. Billy Graham called it "one of the most important of our generation."[39] The National Association of Evangelicals enthusiastically endorsed *The Battle for the Bible* in its magazine. Speaking at the NAE's annual meeting that year, Francis Schaeffer named inerrancy the "watershed event of the evangelical world," and the NAE made plans for its next convention to focus on the theme "God's Word: Our Infallible Guide."[40] *Christianity Today*, not surprisingly given Lindsell served as its editor, called the book "clear, cogent, and convincing." "It is a timely book," the review explained, "since it seems that evangelicals who do not accept biblical inerrancy are not aware of the seriousness and danger of their decision, and also many evangelicals who believe in inerrant Scriptures are not sufficiently aware of the threat to biblical Christianity that denying this doctrine presents."[41]

Other evangelicals pushed back at the book, unwilling to let Lindsell's absolutism become the standard for the faith. *Eternity* magazine warned against the book's "spirit of suspicion and hostility which ought not to characterize our intra-evangelical discussions about inspiration. It certainly will not help to bring about reconciliation amongst the evangelical brethren, or do much to change anybody's opinion who is not yet convinced."[42] (Despite the magazine's hesitations about the book, later that year *The Battle for the Bible* placed third in its annual "most-significant-evangelical-book" poll.)[43] Fuller's president, David Hubbard, was understandably outraged at Lindsell's book given its assault on his seminary. Hubbard deplored Lindsell's insistence that only inerrantists could claim the evangelical mantle. "This large and cherished word must never be given a sectarian meaning," Hubbard contended.[44] Carl Henry charged Lindsell was "relying on theological atom bombing. As many Evangelical friends as foes end up as casualties."[45] In a series of essays and interviews, Henry fretted about the temperament of his former magazine now that a hotheaded absolutist like Lindsell helmed the publication. While Henry acknowledged that *Christianity Today* had always been editorially committed to biblical inerrancy, he also argued the magazine had never meant for that doctrine to serve as the lone qualifier of true evangelicalism, as Lindsell now argued. Henry also criticized the mean-spirited tone Lindsell seemed to so easily take—an attitude the neo-evangelical movement had determinedly sought to reject as it distinguished itself from fundamentalism.[46] Such critiques may have only emboldened Lindsell's rigid theology. By 1979, he had switched his self-identification from "evangelical" to "fundamentalist."[47]

Though the evangelical movement had long struggled with internal scuffles over some of the faith's most fundamental theological claims, *The Battle for the Bible* gave the fight over biblical inerrancy its widest public exposure. Less than two months after publication, the book had already entered its third printing and continued to sell swiftly in the coming years.[48] Hotly debated in evangelical publications, churches, and seminaries, Lindsell's book opened up a conversation that had largely been confined within the most conservative wings of American evangelicalism. Now nearly all evangelicals seemed engaged in the question of biblical inerrancy. That controversy would only grow in the years ahead as some of the most important evangelical denominations, the Southern Baptist Convention and the Lutheran Church—Missouri Synod, wrestled over and won the fight for biblical inerrancy. While that battle might have seemed an obscure theological brouhaha to outsiders, the fight over biblical inerrancy within the evangelical movement would have far larger political implications. Inerrancy's backers typically came from the most conservative corners of evangelicalism, and that conservatism remained consistent across their spiritual and political convictions. Emboldened to fight for absolute orthodoxy on biblical inerrancy in their churches, seminaries, and denominations, inerrantists also committed to rooting out any traces of moderation. Indeed, for inerrantists, the failure of evangelical churches and denominations to fully commit themselves to hardline biblical inerrancy had created the conditions that allowed for evangelicals to tolerate and even endorse some of the worst political and cultural transformations of their age. As biblical inerrantists won the battle for the Bible erupting across evangelical institutions through the 1970s they also secured the victory for ardent political conservatism, particularly in terms of pro-life, anti-ERA, and anti-gay politics, throughout the evangelical movement. There would be some internal resistance to that assertive political conservatism, of course, but the bulk of evangelical Americans had aligned themselves with the inerrant position and its spiritual and political consequences. The nation at large would soon feel the political effects from an insider theological debate about the nature of the Bible.[49]

Maintaining Mormon Anti-Ecumenism

Outside of the ardently separatist evangelical denominations, Dean Kelley had noted in *Why Conservative Churches Are Growing* that the equally isolationist LDS Church also enjoyed one of the best growth rates in the country.[50] Leaders of the LDS Church encouraged Mormons to keep expanding the church in the 1970s. As President Spencer W. Kimball noted in a 1976 church address, it had taken nearly 120 years for the church to gain its first million members. But only sixteen years later, membership was at two million, and another nine years after that, church membership had grown to three million. "It will probably take about four or five years to move up to the four million mark, and then we can guess what the future holds," Kimball proclaimed.[51] Accompanying and fueling those gains, LDS leaders emphasized the church's exclusive truth as the Lord's one true church while spurning an ecumenical movement that, by the 1970s, was waning in Protestant and Catholic circles. Yet the LDS Church's mounting critique of ecumenism reflected not only a delayed historical reaction to a movement that had peaked a decade before but also a real reflection of the church's increasing visibility and prominence on the national stage through the 1970s.

The explosive growth of the LDS Church heightened and, in Mormon logic, owed itself to Mormonism's exclusive notion of salvation, providing a rebuke to the ecumenical movement that, in one LDS leader's description, required Christians to "give up their basic principles and be united in a nebulous organization." LDS officials predicted ecumenism would bring about nothing but a weak "universal organization."[52] This differed from the evangelical fear that ecumenism would ultimately result in a powerful and monopolistic Catholic Church, but it did resemble another frequent, if somewhat contradictory, evangelical prediction that the ecumenical movement would produce a watered-down, unorthodox conglomerate of Social Gospelers more concerned with "unity" than the hard truth. Mormonism offered that sole truth, LDS leaders reminded the faithful, and that singular saving truth was attracting millions of new believers to the faith. "It may sound exclusive, or snobbish, or even fanatical," the LDS Church editorialized of its claim as God's chosen church to grant salvation, "but it is in fact the motivating belief of upwards of three million people throughout the world."[53] Ecumenism, then, was both a boon and a challenge for Mormonism's unique message, according to church leaders. While the LDS Church stood as a firm and resolute beacon proclaiming an unmistaken gospel message against the vague theology of ecumenical Christianity, ecumenism along with atheism, one LDS leader explained, had actively weakened the "visibility" of Christianity and its status as the "foundation of conventional wisdom" for a generation of Americans.[54] In a religious landscape where both atheism and indifferentism seemed dominant, LDS leaders warned their followers to expect persecution for "the idea that there is but one true church . . . one narrow path to salvation, one chosen people." Such a claim "does not fit with this permissive, egalitarian, ecumenical age."[55]

The LDS Church continued to reject ecumenism and assert its exclusive message through the 1970s, but it also began to dialogue with other faiths, particularly Christian denominations. In 1973, the church established the Richard L. Evans Chair of Religious Understanding at Brigham Young University and appointed Truman Madsen, a religion professor at BYU, to the position. Given the task to "promote understanding among people of differing religions through teaching and other activities centered in Jesus Christ," Madsen traveled to other universities and seminaries as a representative of Mormonism and brought speakers from other faiths to BYU's campus to engage in dialogue.[56] Still, "religious understanding" and dialogue were pointedly not exercises in ecumenism. Though Jesus Christ provided the common ground among participants, the task of understanding and dialogue centered on clarifying points of difference, such as the Mormon belief in tritheism over trinitarianism and differing notions of salvation. Madsen's work focused on clarifying those Mormon beliefs vis-à-vis other religious philosophies for young Mormons at BYU as much as it did for the non-Mormon audiences he visited across the country. In a 1974 address at BYU, for example, Madsen recounted a recent trip to a "widely known theological seminary in the East" where he defended Mormonism's belief that God had once been a man and that Mormons would become divine too. Contrasting Mormon theology to the salvation theology that had been presented at the East Coast seminary, Madsen instructed his BYU listeners, "We could answer that the work of salvation is the glorious work of Jesus Christ. But it is also the glorious work of the uncovering and recovering of your own latent divinity. I know that idea is offensive to persons whom I would not wish to offend."[57]

Remarkably, Madsen reflected a new public face of Mormonism that diverged from not only the church's history but also its own internal messages. When asked why the LDS Church had never joined any ecumenical organization, Madsen coyly responded it was because the church had never been invited. "I believe there would be some efforts to accept the invitation," Madsen ventured.[58] Madsen's comments reflected a public relations strategy to convey a more open and engaged LDS Church to the American public, but in church publications, sermons, and conference talks throughout the 1970s, LDS leaders' rejection of ecumenism couldn't be any clearer. Still, the church's desire for sustained membership growth, national prominence, and political influence necessitated alterations of its public image. Presenting the church as one that had been overlooked by ecumenism rather than consistently antagonistic to it tied into the church's longer experience with persecution and marginalization, especially from other religious groups, and positioned the LDS Church as desiring deeper relationships with others even while excusing the church from pursuing such associations. That rhetorical conceit would be especially critical as the church engaged political issues, namely the Equal Rights Amendment and abortion, while largely spurning alliances with fellow religious conservatives who shared those political convictions.

Secular Humanism

Through the 1970s, religious conservatives increasingly worried that "secular humanism" had gained a foothold in the nation's laws and culture, and particularly in public schools where they argued the secular state imposed its values on their children. Mormon, evangelical, and Catholic leaders had warned in the 1960s that federal legislation and Supreme Court rulings, especially the school prayer and Bible-reading cases, promoted secular humanism at the expense of religious traditionalism and the nation's Judeo-Christian heritage. Events in the 1970s, these same religious leaders argued, demonstrated their conviction that, if given an opening, secular humanism would overtake the nation and uproot its Christian foundations.[59]

Although Mormon and Catholic officials regularly decried secular humanism, evangelicals were particularly concerned with the threatening philosophy, in large part because of the efforts of Francis Schaeffer, an evangelical intellectual and theologian from Pennsylvania who ran a religious retreat center in the Swiss Alps.[60] Schaeffer's 1976 book, *How Should We Then Live?*, explained, as the subtitle said, *The Rise and Decline of Western Thought and Culture*, as the result of the West's move from a Christian worldview to a secular humanist outlook. Despite its dense and often plodding history of Western civilization, *How Should We Then Live?* became an instant best seller and evangelical classic, still near the top of the *New York Times'* newly created religious bestsellers' list two years after its publication.[61] In evangelical seminaries and universities, the book became a curricular staple, and churches and Sunday schools across the nation led their own workshops on Schaeffer's opus.

Schaeffer traced the decline of Western civilization from ancient Rome to the modern age and argued that societies reflected the "presuppositions" of its peoples. "By *presuppositions*," Schaeffer explained, "we mean the basic way an individual looks at life, his basic worldview, the grid through which he sees the world. Presuppositions rest upon that which a person considers to be the truth of what exists. People's presuppositions lay a grid for all they bring forth into the external world. Their presuppositions also provide the basis for their values and therefore the basis for their decisions."[62] Christians needed to purposely form a biblical worldview supported by Christian presuppositions as a defense against those who operated from a secular humanist perspective. In Rome, Schaeffer argued, the strength of their worldview allowed Christians "to resist religious mixtures, syncretism, and the effects of the weaknesses of Roman culture." Christianity gave the Roman Christians "absolute, universal values by which to live and by which to judge the society and the political state in which they lived."[63]

"Nevertheless," Schaeffer continued, "the pristine Christianity set forth in the New Testament gradually became distorted. A humanistic element was added: Increasingly, the authority of the church took precedence over the teaching of the Bible."[64] This, of course, was an attack on the Roman Catholic Church—an assault Schaeffer frequently made. The Reformation corrected the increasingly human-centered presuppositions of the Catholic Church by reorienting real Christianity to its biblical basis. Whereas the Catholic Church had, in Schaeffer's estimation, helped generate the humanist Renaissance, the Reformation led to many of history's best moments, including the American Revolution and the creation of the U.S. Constitution. While Schaeffer acknowledged that many of the founding fathers were not Christian, he contended that they all worked from a "Christian base" inherited from the intellectual thought that had grown out of the Reformation, especially the writings of the Scottish intellectual Samuel Rutherford. The Reformation, Schaeffer contended, had produced American democracy.

The Reformation kept secular humanism at bay in northern Europe and the United States until the twentieth century, when the "false values of personal peace and affluence" derived from humanism "destroyed the old basis of values."[65] Modernism had destroyed absolutes, replacing them with subjectivity and "experience." Now the law was at risk because it was guided by "what the courts of the present want it to say—based on a court's decision as to what the court feels is sociologically helpful at the moment."[66] This is where Schaeffer transitioned the last pages of his book into a political critique of the United States, a move he had hesitated making in previous works but one that by the mid-1970s he felt necessary given the country's direction. While the modern age revered technocratic and bureaucratic experts, Schaeffer feared these very people the most because he believed they sought to change laws and other societal foundations, like the family, based on personal whims they disguised in the language of science, reason, and professional expertise. This critique of the intellectual and ruling elite appealed to Schaeffer's evangelical audience who worried a secular class threatened their simple lives and biblical traditions. As Barry Hankins has pointed out, Schaeffer had long attacked secular humanism as an abstract philosophy promoting a "dangerous worldview." But in *How Should We Then Live?*, Schaeffer now wrote about "humanists" as real people, such as federal judges and politicians, who actively worked to uproot the Christian foundation of society, replacing it with their own arbitrary absolutes.[67] Christians had to become politically involved to fight against secular humanism's advocates and public apathy that aided their rise. In short, history demonstrated the universe contained a battle between Christianity and secular humanism, but that war was waged not in a mystical realm of ideological abstraction but in the real world by Christians and secular humanists. No less than the very basis of the American nation was at stake in this fight.

A film version of *How Should We Then Live?* reached even more evangelicals than the book, introducing an entire generation to Schaeffer and his political philosophy. Produced by his son, Franky, the movie included a stronger emphasis on abortion, an important issue to Franky. Franky had led an often-wild life as a youngster, impregnating his girlfriend when they were teenagers. That experience had chastened Franky in many ways—Franky and his girlfriend married, for one—but he became especially incensed by the talk of "unwanted pregnancy" so often accompanying the debate over abortion reform. Franky pressed Schaeffer to include an attack on abortion in his book and film, but the father resisted. "I don't want to be identified with some Catholic issue," Schaeffer objected, "I'm not putting my reputation on the line for them!"[68] Schaeffer finally relented, however, after Franky convinced his father that his intellectual argument about Christianity's defense of the uniqueness of each created human would mean nothing if he didn't denounce abortion.[69]

In 1977, Schaeffer and Franky embarked on a fifteen-city, eighteen-week national tour. Audiences came for the all-day event, watching the ten half-hour episodes—the last two completely devoted to abortion—and listening to Schaeffer speak between each one. In New York, the crowd filled Madison Square Garden. In Dallas, some six thousand people, including half of the Cowboys football team, turned out.[70] In Anaheim, seven thousand people, "mostly white and many young," as the *Los Angeles Times* described the audience, watched the film series.[71] By the tour's end, more than forty thousand people had attended the seminar series, easily making Schaeffer one of the country's most famous evangelical leaders. Many more Americans encountered the film outside the seminar tour, watching it in their churches. In Chicago, the fundamentalist mega-church Moody Church showed the film series to its members.[72] Across the nation, evangelical churches, like Church of Northern Virginia; Central Baptist Church of Ewing Township, New Jersey; and Casa Linda Presbyterian Church in Dallas, screened the ten-part series on successive Sunday evenings.[73] Thanks to Schaeffer, evangelicals now spoke in dark tones about the scourge of secular humanism spreading throughout the nation.

For Schaeffer, the Supreme Court's legalization of abortion exhibited the worst overreaches of secular humanism. Other trends of the decade also portended secular humanism's ascendancy, including the rising divorce rate, increasing sexual permissiveness, and a burgeoning gay rights movement. Through it all, Schaeffer, evangelicals, and other religious conservatives contended that secular humanism sought to destroy God's first institution he had created even before his church: the family. Interchangeably, secular humanism and feminism were cited as Satan's attack on the traditional family, and the Equal Rights Amendment as the devil's route to victory.

The Equal Rights Amendment

"Equality of rights under the law shall not be denied or abridged by the United States or by any state on account of sex," read the proposed ERA to the Constitution, passed by Congress in 1972. Less than two years later, thirty-three states had passed the amendment, just five less than the number required for ratification.[74] Though victory seemed imminent, religious conservatives opposed the ERA believing it was an attack on traditional marriage and the divinely ordained and interdependent roles of men and women. Christian conservatives worried about the state of the family as the 1970s began. They translated these fears into defeating the ERA.

The American family was changing in the 1970s, in almost every way. The decade's economic transformations, including deindustrialization and shifts in the labor market to a service-based economy, profoundly influenced individual families. The end of post–World War II American prosperity was felt first and most acutely in the American home, where stagnating wages imperiled the ideal of the male-breadwinner home, a particularly revered economic system and social order for religious conservatives. Still, for all the economic shifts bringing changes to American family life, religious conservatives narrowed their focus to the cultural forces, especially the women's movement, they believed weakened their families' vitality and moral well-being. An American culture that once seemed so hospitable to traditional conceptions of marriage, family life, and sexuality now struck many social conservatives as openly antagonistic to those values. Both the divorce rate and out-of-wedlock birth numbers had escalated coming out of the 1960s, and Christian conservatives contended feminism's calls for female independence and autonomy were to blame. While its advocates argued the Equal Rights Amendment provided a simple constitutional protection of equality for the sexes that would elevate women's legal and social standing, its opponents, particularly conservative Christian women, believed the ERA was a nefarious feminist plot to destroy women's special status as the protected helpmates of their provider husbands and the moral guardians of their home and children. Citing their belief in God-given gender and sex roles, these women charged the ERA would eradicate sexual difference and femininity, the very basis of their power and purpose. In the march to women's equality, they argued, the American family—the backbone of the nation—would be destroyed.[75]

Phyllis Schlafly, a Catholic conservative from Illinois who had authored the best-selling *A Choice Not an Echo* for Barry Goldwater's 1964 presidential campaign, seized on the ERA as a political cause to unite religious conservatives, particularly women. Her organization, STOP ERA, launched in 1972, soon operated out of twenty-six battleground states, creating a broad antifeminist network to prevent the amendment's ratification.[76] Schlafly recognized the untapped political resource in conservative religious churches and their members, and she reached out to women of faith to take up her political movement.[77] In doing so, she wrapped her anti-ERA arguments in language that they would understand and support, speaking of the divine origins of life and sexual difference, the Judeo-Christian morality of the nation, and the embattled, but honorable, role as defender of the faith. Every victory that Schlafly's forces earned—every defeat of the ERA in a state legislature or on a ballot initiative—afforded an opportunity for Schlafly to link her cause to a higher source. The forces arrayed against "us were so formidable that there is simply no way we could have accomplished what we did without help from God. If we continue doing His will," one *Eagle Forum Newsletter* noted, anything was possible.[78] One popular pamphlet widely circulated among evangelical women recruited by STOP ERA was "A Christian View of the Equal Rights Amendment." "As Christians," the leaflet stated, "we ought to support laws that provide equal opportunity for women, but we must oppose a sweeping Constitutional change that would take away their individual choice and alter Americans' lifestyle. Jesus cautioned us about wolves in sheep's clothing."[79]

Schlafly achieved unparalleled success in making the anti-ERA movement an ecumenical effort. Other political leaders would look to Schlafly's success and envision further possibilities for conservatism based on this ecumenical model, but the anti-ERA battle provided a false vision. Conservative Catholics, Mormons, Southern Baptists, and other evangelicals and fundamentalists all joined STOP ERA and her later organization, Eagle Forum. But in many ways that ecumenical diversity played out mostly from a national vantage point, obscuring the divisions that remained among the grassroots.[80] At the local level—where Schlafly's organizations did the work of pressuring state legislatures and building anti-ERA activism—her state chapters largely reflected the local religious demographics. In her home state of Illinois, for example, Roman Catholics dominated the organization. Out west, in states like Utah, Arizona, and Nevada, Mormons made up the membership. In Oklahoma, Church of Christ women predominated, whereas Southern Baptists and those from independent fundamentalist churches comprised the membership for most of the Southern states.[81]

Perhaps most importantly, however, Schlafly made a conscious effort to overcome the challenges of religious diversity in her organization. Likely, Schlafly had been shaped by the religious bigotry she had endured at an earlier moment in her political career. In the late 1950s, Schlafly and her husband wanted to create an organization to bring Catholics into the anticommunist movement. The Schlaflys reached out to Dr. Fred Schwarz, the founder of the Christian Anti-Communism Crusade, suggesting they create a Protestant-Catholic anticommunist organization. Schwarz's conversion from Judaism to Christianity had coincided with his political turn into a fierce anticommunist, but his own religious history did not make him receptive to the possibilities of interfaith cooperation. "No," he adamantly responded to the Schlaflys' proposal. His organization received most of its support from evangelicals, he explained to the Schlaflys, and he worried that an alliance with Catholics "would be suspect in certain circles." Rather, he advised, the Schlaflys should create a group just for Catholics, which they did by organizing the Cardinal Mindszenty Foundation in 1958.[82]

When Schlafly created STOP ERA and Eagle Forum, she strived to make both seem open and receptive to all people, no matter their religious faith. Her newsletters frequently referenced Catholic, Mormon, and various Protestant denominations and the efforts their members supplied in fighting the ERA. She also created literature directed at specific religious groups, like a flier for distribution to Catholics advertised in the *Eagle Forum Newsletter*.[83] At national meetings for her organizations, Schlafly made sure that the major religious groups represented had their own religious services to attend. For example, the 1980 schedule for the Eagle Forum convention in St. Louis, listed Sunday church services for "Protestant," "Church of Christ," "Mormon," and "Catholic" groups held in different conference rooms at the Marriott.[84] Schlafly believed that conservative Christian women, despite their different denominational ties and theological disagreements, could be brought together by their shared concerns and their general beliefs in, as one Eagle Forum pamphlet declared, "God, Home, and Country,"—those who "are determined to defend the values that have made America the greatest nation in the world," and who "support the Holy Scriptures as providing the best code of moral conduct yet devised."[85]

But though Schlafly largely succeeded at uniting religious conservatives in opposing the ERA, she still faced challenges that demonstrated the difficulties interfaith politics faced. Schlafly's greatest struggle was attracting fundamentalist Protestant women to her organizations. While the vision Schlafly painted of the ERA destroying the traditional American family alarmed fundamentalist women especially, many of these women resisted joining STOP ERA and Eagle Forum because they viewed them as Catholic organizations. No official affiliation existed between Schlafly's groups and the Catholic Church, and she routinely described her organizations in terms of an entirely generic Judeo-Christian defense of tradition. Still, Schlafly's Catholicism was well-known, and fundamentalist women, especially in the South, expressed discomfort aligning themselves with her organizations because of it. Rather than taking offense, Schlafly encouraged the development of denominationally centered anti-ERA organizations, such as Women Who Want to be Women (later renamed Pro Family Forum), created by two Church of Christ women from Texas, with robust chapters there and in Florida where Southern Baptist and fundamentalist women joined the group.[86] Women Aware, another group for Southern Baptist and fundamentalist women, had strength in the Southwest, particularly New Mexico.[87] Similar quasi-denominational anti-ERA organizations abounded in the battleground states of the Equal Rights Amendment, providing alternatives to Schlafly's organizations and working around—and perhaps helping to maintain—the historic tensions between fundamentalists and Catholics. Many of these women had, for several years now, listened to encouragements from the pulpit and religious publications to engage political life. Now that their very way of living—the lifestyle they believed was based in biblical values—was under attack, these women understood why their pastors had been prodding them with mounting fervor to observe what was happening around them and to do something about it. For those women who belonged to the most conservative wings of Protestantism, though, messages about separatism, about exclusive truth, and even lingering messages of anti-Catholicism continued apace. At home in orthodox denominations or independent churches that could easily split apart over minute disagreements regarding scripture or worship styles, these women were hardly prime candidates for ecumenical political work. Instead, they created their own anti-ERA organizations, filled them with fellow members from their churches or Bible studies, and prepared to stop the ERA from passing in their states.

Similarly, Mormon grassroots anti-ERA organizations arose for LDS women who felt most comfortable working alongside their fellow Saints. Happiness of Womanhood, an anti-ERA organization founded by the anti-feminist Mormon Jaquie Davison, author of *I Am a Housewife!*, soon claimed ten thousand members.[88] Davison liked to point out that HOW had been around longer than the better-known Schlafly organization. "I was in on it two years before Phyllis Schlafly and her 'Stop ERA,'" she bragged to a reporter.[89] In Utah, a group called HOTDOG, which stood for "Humanitarians Opposed to Degrading Our Girls," became active even before the LDS Church moved into its full-scale war against the ERA. But once it did, the LDS Church directed its members into its own anti-ERA organizations, deepening Mormons' political engagement through the auspices of their church rather than the conservative ecumenical organizations beginning to emerge.

Mormons and the Equal Rights Amendment

For some time after Congress's passage of the ERA, the LDS Church issued no position statement about the amendment.[90] However, throughout the 1970s, Mormon publications and conference speeches continually touted the divinely created difference between men and women. "The Lord defined some very basic differences between men and women," one article in the church's *Ensign* magazine explained, ". . . . He did not intend either of the sexes to adopt the other's traits. . . . When these differences are ignored, an unwholesome relationship develops, which, if not checked, can lead to the reprehensible, tragic sin of homosexuality."[91] For much of the church's early history, Mormon women had enjoyed unique prominence and visibility as near-equal partners to men in building Zion, but LDS teachings in the 1970s responded to the nation's liberalizing trends by routinely instructing Mormon women to, as one *Ensign* article was entitled, "Maintain Your Place As a Woman." In doing this, Mormon women were to reject the worldly lures of career, self-fulfillment, and independence in favor of the "eternal" womanly responsibilities of marriage, motherhood, and submissiveness. Most pointedly, church teachings in the 1970s constantly warned Mormon women to spurn the popular calls to liberation that feminism and its projects, like the ERA, advocated. Liberation was a guise, church leaders contended, that promised fulfillment but would destroy the timeless and divinely created distinctions between man and woman that ordered life.[92]

Teachings like these laid the theological groundwork for the LDS Church's eventual attack on the Equal Rights Amendment. Entering the national political stage for the first time, the LDS Church continually justified its involvement by arguing the "ERA is a moral issue."[93] "Moral issues" had become the justification for LDS political involvement since the presidency of David O. McKay. Now the ERA's bid for a constitutionally protected equality of the sexes struck at the very core of Mormonism's deepest beliefs about the gender-specific functions for men and women in life. Because the question of the amendment concerned key Mormon beliefs about life's most fundamental aspects, the LDS Church entered the fight over the Equal Rights Amendment to defend its most important teachings about the proper place and responsibilities of women. On October 22, 1976, the *Deseret News* published an official statement from the First Presidency opposing the amendment, warning it could bring women "far more restraints and repressions. We fear it will even stifle many God-given feminine instincts. . . . We recognize men and women as equally important before the Lord, but with differences biologically, emotionally, and in other ways. ERA, we believe, does not recognize these differences."[94] Church stake and mission presidents received a memo later that year from Ezra Taft Benson, president of the Quorum of the Twelve Apostles at the time (and future church president), instructing them to "urge members of the Church, *as citizens* of this great nation, to join others in efforts to defeat the ERA."[95]

More than merely encouraging its members, the LDS Church organized Mormons into a church-wide campaign against the Equal Rights Amendment. Though church officials might have directed Mormons to join STOP ERA or other smaller grassroots organizations, it instead created its own groups to battle the amendment in key states. This decision owed to Mormonism's long-standing autonomy and self-reliance while also demonstrating the church's reluctance toward association even with like-minded allies. The church did occasionally tap into the larger anti-ERA network, particularly Phyllis Schlafly's resources, to support its own endeavors. In LDS wards across the country, church organizers stocked Schlafly's STOP ERA literature in their foyers alongside church-produced materials against the ERA.[96] Schlafly also delivered an anti-ERA address at BYU.[97] And the church occasionally coordinated with other religious groups, such as a successful partnering with Catholic bishops in Nevada.[98]

But the bulk of LDS anti-ERA energy focused on building, coordinating, and directing an internal movement against the amendment through its grassroots organizations. The LDS Church created and financed these groups, providing constant direction. Mormon laypersons joined the anti-ERA organizations largely because church leaders insinuated and often insisted that participation was a religious obligation. The LDS Church named the organizations so as to purposefully hide any Mormon connection, instructing LDS volunteers to never mention their religious faith when working against the amendment but instead to describe themselves as "concerned citizens." The LDS anti-ERA groups included Arizona Home and Family Rally Committee, Citizen's Quest for Quality Government (Nevada), Families Are Concerned Today (Florida), Illinois Citizens For Family Life, Pro-Family Coalition (California), Save Our Families Today (Tennessee), Missouri Citizens Council, and Virginia Citizens Coalition.[99] These organizations besieged their state legislators with phone calls, letters, and visits, demanding they vote against the ERA's ratification.

The LDS efforts significantly contributed to the ERA's defeat. In Nevada, nine thousand Mormons canvassed greater Las Vegas on the eve of a state referendum on the ERA. The day of the election, 95 percent of all eligible Mormons in Nevada showed up to vote. Having rallied its members and widely disseminated through its women its anti-ERA message, the LDS Church brought about a rousing two-to-one defeat for the Nevada referendum.[100] In Virginia, the church's anti-ERA organization grew to sixteen thousand members. Though accounting for less than 1 percent of Virginia's population, Mormons wrote approximately 85 percent of the anti-ERA letters Virginia state legislators received.[101] Virginia never ratified the amendment. Mormons in other states, including Idaho, Arizona, Florida, Tennessee, Missouri, and Illinois, helped prevent the ERA's ratification or support its rescinding, ultimately dooming the amendment.

Evangelicals and Abortion

Despite the work of some leading evangelical theologians and thinkers, many lay evangelicals—and even ministers—displayed ambivalence toward the legalization of abortion. Many had believed abortion would be used as a rare medical procedure, a difficult decision made by married couples in consultation with their doctors and, hopefully, a spiritual adviser. Abortion rates, however, quickly overturned evangelical conceptions about how abortion would be used. By 1975, 3.5 million women, representing one in fourteen women of reproductive age, had procured an abortion.[102] *Christianity Today* reported in 1976 that more than one million teenage girls alone were becoming pregnant each year with a third of those pregnancies ending in abortion.[103] By 1980, records indicated 8 million legal abortions—or over 1 million per year—had been performed.[104] Clearly, evangelicals recognized, abortion was not a rare medical procedure.[105]

These numbers coupled with the insistent and increasing anti-abortion message from leading evangelical publications and leaders convinced millions of evangelicals to embrace the pro-life position by the decade's end. The creation of the Christian Action Council (CAC) represented an important development in evangelical participation in the pro-life movement. In 1975, Harold O. J. Brown, the *Christianity Today* editor who had tried to stir up an evangelical pro-life movement from the pages of his magazine, met the prominent pediatric surgeon, C. Everett Koop, at a conference for Christian men. Brown knew that Koop had stridently condemned abortion in a 1973 commencement speech at Wheaton College, and he discussed with Koop how they might develop an evangelical anti-abortion movement that could rival Catholic involvement. When Billy Graham announced he would attach his name to their efforts, Brown and Koop traveled to Graham's North Carolina home for a two-day organizational meeting, which led to the creation of their new organization.[106] At the announcement of the CAC's formation in Washington, D.C., in 1975, Brown declared that "its immediate purpose is to stress that the defense of the unborn . . . is a common concern of all Christians, and not one limited to the Roman Catholic Church."[107] Three years later, CAC boasted to its members that it was well known as "the largest Protestant pro-life organization in America." It also billed itself as "the only one specifically speaking out in the name of Christ, as professing Biblical Christians," perhaps a slight at the Catholicism of the National Right to Life Committee since most evangelicals believed that Catholics had little knowledge or reverence for the Holy Scriptures.[108] Either way, it reflected a self-conscious and explicit evangelical identity as the basis for its operations. Rather than pointing to its anti-abortion position to attract members, CAC highlighted and promoted its evangelical identity to bring evangelicals to a cause many still saw as Catholic.

Francis Schaeffer also proved critical in bringing evangelicals into the pro-life cause. His book and five-part film series, *Whatever Happened to the Human Race?*, released in 1979, electrified evangelical audiences with the anti-abortion message, tying the atrocity back to Schaeffer's consistent culprit of secular humanism, an argument he first launched three years earlier in *How Should We Then Live?*[109] "Why has our society changed?" Schaeffer asked. "The answer is clear. The consensus of our society no longer rests upon a Christian base, but upon a humanistic one."[110]

Though abortion was the law, it was not settled law, Schaeffer argued in the book companion to the film series he coauthored with Koop. The Supreme Court had thought its ruling on abortion would end the debate, but instead "abortion remains the hottest moral issue of our time." For this, Koop and Schaeffer credited the "concerned group of citizens [who] took the time and energy to band together to oppose the Supreme Court's decision."[111] When the Supreme Court's ruling had at first appeared decisive, this small group had refused to accept the decision, instead mounting the movement that grew into the national pro-life cause. Schaeffer and Koop did not identify these early anti-abortion activists as mostly Catholic, but elsewhere the authors reminded that "abortion is not a 'Roman Catholic issue.' This must be emphasized." The authors acknowledged, "We must indeed be glad for the Roman Catholics who have spoken out, but we must not allow the position to be minimized as though it is a 'religious' issue. It is not a religious issue."[112] This was an odd argument for the authors to make in a book that characterized abortion as the product of a society that had abandoned Judeo-Christian teaching for a secular humanist worldview. Koop and Schaeffer had hardly championed human rights arguments or even constitutional theory as the basis of their objections to abortion. Rather, their argument depended almost entirely on strict biblical teachings of the divine basis of creation and the scriptural mandate for Christians to protect life. When Koop and Schaeffer argued that abortion was not a "religious issue" they meant that objections to abortion did not derive from particular sectarian teaching—namely, Catholic theology—but rather reflected ancient and unchanging Judeo-Christian tradition. That Koop, Schaeffer, and much of their evangelical audience believed this tradition also formed the basis of American history and its constitutional principles only added to their sense of how far the nation had departed from its foundation in legalizing abortion.

That *Whatever Happened to the Human Race?* acknowledged, though only briefly, Catholics' work against abortion was hardly revolutionary. One could not speak accurately of the pro-life movement without crediting the Catholic Church. But like many conservative evangelicals, Schaeffer had a strained relationship with Catholicism. In 1957, Schaeffer joined other fundamentalists in denouncing Billy Graham for including a Catholic bishop with him on stage during his New York crusade. In Switzerland, the experience of being driven out of a Roman Catholic canton for preaching Protestant heresy added to Schaeffer's convictions that Catholicism opposed the Christian gospel.[113] Many of Schaeffer's writings, as his biographer Barry Hankins has pointed out, contained an anti-Catholicism "just below the surface."[114] Yet at other times, Schaeffer expressed growing tolerance for the Catholic Church, mirroring a similar transformation within American evangelicalism. In 1964, near the close of the Second Vatican Council, Schaeffer noted the "Roman Catholic Church [had] changed more between 1950 and 1963 than it did between 1600 and 1950."[115] And Schaeffer appreciated the respect that Catholic Bishop Fulton J. Sheen had shown for his writings. Sheen, in an interview with *Christianity Today*, praised Schaeffer's works on philosophy as "one of the best I have ever read."[116] But it had been the abortion episode from *How Should We Then Live?* that brought the Catholic bishop and the evangelical activist into contact. When Sheen learned Schaeffer was working on a new pro-life project, he invited Schaeffer's son, Franky, to his New York apartment to discuss strategy for expanding the pro-life movement. Sheen worried to Franky that abortion continued to be perceived as a Catholic issue, but hoped the Schaeffers could change that. "The unborn need more friends," Sheen told Franky as he pledged the Catholic Church's support for the Schaeffers' efforts. The Knights of Columbus would raise money to help fund the production of *Whatever Happened to the Human Race?*, and Sheen made sure the Schaeffers could film one scene for the movie in a Catholic cemetery in Brooklyn.[117]

Evangelical churches across the country hosted their own screenings of the film, allowing its message to occupy a Sunday morning service or Wednesday night prayer meeting. The movie also became a staple in the classrooms of evangelical seminaries, universities, and Bible colleges, helping shape the pro-life consciences of a new generation of conservative Christians, many training for the ministry. A few churches were less supportive of the film, with pastors cautioning their church members from viewing what they worried would get them caught up in a movement many still perceived as Catholic.[118] But far more were mobilized by the movie, forever changed by what they had seen. Both the film and book graphically described various abortion procedures—Schaeffer believed evangelicals unmoved by biblical arguments about abortion had to be shocked into understanding abortion's atrocity through grotesque images and details. One particularly memorable scene in the film—one repeatedly cited by viewers as the moment where they had come to understand the vastness of abortion's horror—showed thousands of plastic baby dolls bobbing face down in the Dead Sea while Koop stood perched on a rock. Koop explained he was standing where the Old Testament city of Sodom had once existed, "the most humanly corrupt city on earth," as Schaeffer described it. The linkage was obvious. As God had destroyed Sodom for its wickedness, so too might he bring down his judgment on an American nation now permitting abortion.[119]

Southern Baptist churches were particularly active in showing the film to their congregations throughout 1979, perhaps influencing the SBC's first wholly pro-life resolution passed by the Convention the next year.[120] The 1980 resolution opposed the ethos of "abortion on demand" in the nation's policies and culture, condemning the use of public money and tax-supported medical facilities "for selfish, non-therapeutic abortion," and supported the efforts for a legislative "and/or" constitutional amendment prohibiting abortion in all cases but to save the life of the mother.[121] One influential Baptist activist mailed the resolution to every senator and congressperson so they would know the large Southern Baptist Convention now stood against abortion. The Ohio congressman John Ashbrook had the resolution read into the *Congressional Record* after he introduced it by remarking, "Once again, the absurdity of the pro-abortion movement as a Catholic bishop's plot is revealed. The influence of Catholic bishops at a Southern Baptist convention is generally agreed to be minimal."[122] Elsewhere, anti-abortion organizations thrilled at the SBC's strong condemnation of abortion rights and its support for a constitutional remedy. "I thank God for the Southern Baptist decision and await the other major Christian bodies," the Rev. Edward Bryce, director of the Catholic Bishops' Committee for Pro-Life Activities said, "I see many Protestant people in agreement with the Catholic Church that abortion on demand is immoral and not a sound basis for public policy." As the nation's largest Protestant body, the Southern Baptist Convention's decision would influence other evangelical bodies to commit themselves against abortion rights, pro-life leaders hoped. "There's an awakening on the abortion issue going on among evangelical Protestants," the National Right to Life Committee's president, Dr. Carolyn Gerster, proclaimed, "The Southern Baptists' decision will have a very profound affect [*sic*]."[123]

Other results demonstrated evangelical commitment to the pro-life cause and sometimes working with Catholic groups to oppose abortion rights. Both the National Right to Life Committee and the Christian Action Council targeted the 1978 mid-term elections as a key moment to exert the growing pro-life movement's political muscle and lay the foundation for bigger results in 1980. Both the NRLC and CAC worked within their respective religious communities, Catholic and evangelical, to mobilize pro-life voters. The lit drop, where pro-life groups blanketed church parking lots with political pamphlets and voter guides on the eve of an election, helped energize voters. Anti-abortion groups divided the work largely along denominational lines. The National Right to Life Committee, for instance, mainly concentrated on the parking lots of area Catholic churches, while the Christian Action Council and other evangelical organizations visited the Protestant congregations they knew to be most supportive of electing pro-life candidates. In Senate and House of Representatives races in Iowa, New Hampshire, Massachusetts, New Jersey, and Colorado, pro-life voters helped defeat incumbent Democratic and Republican pro-choice officeholders, replacing them with Republican pro-life candidates. Many of the victories were of the slimmest margins with pro-life voters contributing the critical difference, such as in Iowa where the pro-life Republican Roger Jepsen defeated the pro-choice Democratic incumbent Senator Dick Clark by just twenty-six thousand votes. Twenty-five thousand voters indicated they had supported Clark because of his pro-life stance alone.[124] In Minnesota, pro-choice Congressman Don Fraser lost his reelection bid by less than 1 percent of the vote.[125] In New Hampshire, the pro-life Gordon Humphrey knocked off Democratic Senator Thomas McIntyre by just four thousand votes.[126] Political observers at the time remarked on the rise of a new "single-issue" voter who determined their political support based only on abortion. As Robert Self has argued, by the late 1970s many Americans on both sides of the political fence felt that abortion provided a means to determine and defend a larger political universe.[127] For religious conservatives especially, abortion encapsulated and made real their deepest anxieties about the traditional family, shifting gender roles, and loosening sexual norms while augmenting their self-conception as the nation's moral guardians and biblical defenders against the excesses of permissive liberalism.

Mormons and Abortion

In Utah, however, the results of 1978 showed denominational divisions and inter-religious suspicions could still set back religious conservatives' political goals. There, pro-life activists hoped to use that year's election to limit abortion rights in the state. The prospects of working with a heavily Mormon state legislature encouraged many pro-life workers in Utah. The LDS Church's anti-abortion position had greatly influenced votes on abortion in Utah's state legislature through the years. Five of six Utah legislators who had supported abortion reforms in 1967 switched their votes in 1969 after the church started publicizing its opposition. In the next election Utahns booted from office the one legislator who maintained a "yes" vote in 1969.[128] The 1973 state legislature had quickly demonstrated its disapproval of *Roe*, voting 66 to 1 to condemn the Supreme Court's decision.[129] Many hoped the Utah legislature, as other state legislatures had, would start passing laws curtailing the right to abortion in the state.

In the spring of 1977, Myrna Tulloch, the Catholic public relations director of the Utah Right to Life, asked the LDS Church to help restore Utah's anti-abortion law. The Utah NRLC hoped to place an initiative on the 1978 ballot, but needed to collect fifty-four thousand signatures from ten Utah counties by September 1977 in order to do so. Utah anti-abortion activists, likely aware of the church's work against the ERA, knew there was no better way to gather those signatures than through the LDS Church network. Though the church had voiced its opposition to abortion for several years, it had never asked its members to engage the anti-abortion movement as it had the fight against the ERA. The results of that silence were obvious within Utah's small right-to-life movement. The state Right to Life chapter hoped to hold rallies throughout Utah in support of its ballot initiative drive, but it estimated these would only attract a few hundred attendees at best if the LDS Church did not encourage its members to go. Tulloch hoped the church would at last initiate pro-life activism among Latter-day Saints.[130]

Church bureaucrats were stumped over how best to handle the request. For one, they knew that while the church philosophically opposed abortion, its leadership had still hesitated to get involved in the drive to overturn the court's decision in the way the Catholic Church had. On the other hand, Mormon leaders worried about increasing abortion rates, particularly in Utah. Later that summer, the church's newspaper would print an article lamenting the 15 percent increase in abortions in the state from 1975 to 1976 alone, although Utah's numbers actually remained among the lowest in the nation.[131] Still, the prospect of working with the Utah Right to Life organization troubled church workers given the difficult relationship the group had had with the church in prior years. Higher-ups in the church told the Public Communications office worker handling the Utah Right to Life's request that the church had no qualms supporting the ballot initiative, but they cautioned "against affiliating with the 'Right to Life' group because of their past attacks on the Church by some members of the organization."[132]

Tulloch understood the caution, and she assured L. Darrel Welling, her contact in the church's Public Communications department, that the Utah Right to Life's difficult relationship with the church owed itself to one member having written several anti-Mormon letters to the local newspapers. This person no longer belonged to the organization, she explained, and the anti-Mormon letters represented his personal convictions rather than the NRLC's organizational stance despite its Catholic affiliation. The chapter's officers deeply regretted the action, Tulloch added, as some of them were active Mormons. Welling seemed assured by Tulloch's apology and he met with Representative P. Lloyd Selleneit, author of the ballot initiative, to discuss strategies for procuring the necessary signatures from church members. Welling then recommended to Wendell J. Ashton, the director of the church's Public

Communications department, that Ashton seek approval from church leaders to authorize a meeting of twenty-five stake presidents in the Salt Lake area for discussing how the church could support the signature drive. In a pattern similar to the church's anti-ERA efforts, Welling proposed that each of those twenty-five stake presidents would be charged with enlisting five other stake presidents for the petition drive, ensuring the participation of more than 100 church stakes encompassing at least fifteen Utah counties. Welling recommended the "priesthood activity should be a cooperative but independent action, not tieing [*sic*] in with the 'Right to Life' group."[133] Whether lingering concerns of anti-Mormonism from the Utah Right to Life chapter or the church's tradition of isolated, independent action guided this decision is unclear. But the LDS Church's decision to join the anti-abortion movement in Utah unattached to the efforts of the NLRC demonstrates the way in which religious tensions, perceived prejudices, and anti-ecumenical traditions could shape the anti-abortion movement at the local level.

However, that decision would be short-lived. The church's highest leaders decided in a Salt Lake City temple meeting that the proposed ballot initiative was something the church should not engage publicly. Legal counsel for the church had determined the proposed initiative was likely unconstitutional, and the church presidency did not want to attach itself to such a measure. "It would be inappropriate to use priesthood channels in securing these signatures," Welling wrote Ashton in a memo. "By the same token, it would appear equally inappropriate for Church members to participate in a program not endorsed by the Brethren." Yet Welling and other church bureaucrats knew the ballot petitions would still be placed in Mormons' hands, even if not done officially through the church's networks. They worried about how to handle the situation. "In spite of our enthusiasm to support the anti-abortion movement," Welling wrote, "there are many members that would feel as I do that they would not do it in opposition to a policy not endorsed by the Church. What do you suggest?"[134]

The LDS Church's silence on the proposed ballot initiative for the 1978 election provided the answer. The petition did not appear on the ballot the following year, likely a result of the church failing to encourage its members to sign the ballot initiative petition.[135] Some Mormons criticized their church for not activating members to oppose abortion rights at the same time it was mobilizing them to fight against the ERA. While Mormons in Utah, of course, could have signed the petition on their own initiative, the failure of the church to provide a directive to do so, especially in light of the specific instructions it gave on ways to battle against the ERA, suggested that Mormons should avoid the issue altogether. Indeed, this was the result that church bureaucrats had hoped for. But Mormon pro-life activists regretted their church's silence and the absence of a significant LDS pro-life movement. As one Mormon pro-life activist wrote a few years later, "Church members are so often involved in the Church that they have no time left for other commitments. . . . Our failure to become involved looses an evil that sooner or later infects us all."[136]

Political Responsibility

By the late 1970s, evangelical, Mormon, and Catholic leaders had encouraged political involvement from their members for more than a decade. For Catholics, Vatican II's call to civic engagement and political involvement became a powerful justification for the church's increased visibility in matters beyond the parish walls. Building on that legacy and responding to events at home, particularly the legalization of abortion, the U.S. bishops released a statement in 1976, "Political Responsibility: Reflections on an Election Year."[137] More than just a voting guide for that election cycle, "Political Responsibility" justified the church's participation in civic matters as "not a threat to the political process or to genuine pluralism, but an affirmation of their importance."[138] Spencer W. Kimball's leadership as LDS president witnessed the church's vast expansion, which strengthened Mormonism's call to politics. Now in every corner of the nation, Mormons frequently heard from church leaders about their obligation to be a "moral" force in stopping the nation's slide into secularism and moral depravity. Though many evangelicals had traditionally abstained from politics for theological reasons, since mid-century evangelical leaders and theologians had increasingly emphasized the religious obligation of civic participation and political involvement. The evangelicals of *Christianity Today* and the National Association of Evangelicals had been instrumental in developing and disseminating this position in part as a way to distinguish evangelicals from fundamentalists, whom they accused of the unbiblical decision to abandon the public square. Supreme Court decisions and a radically changing American culture only enhanced the convictions among these religious conservatives that they had to play a larger and more self-conscious part in the nation's politics, but for evangelicals, their theological debates regarding scriptural inerrancy and authority had also compelled their public turn. School prayer, abortion, and the Equal Rights Amendment had unified a diverse group of religious conservatives, but other issues like tuition tax credits for religious schools, sex education in public schools, and gay rights helped evangelicals, Catholics, and Mormons recognize each other as political and cultural allies in what they saw as a radically secularizing culture.

Internal theological developments regarding the political responsibility of Mormons, Catholics, and evangelicals soon met up with the shifting political terrain of the 1970s and the tactical strategies of key political operatives, such as Paul Weyrich and Howard Phillips. Weyrich had been handpicked by the brewing magnate, Joseph Coors, to run the conservative think tank, the Heritage Foundation, in the early 1970s. A few years later, Weyrich created the political action committee, the Committee for the Survival of a Free Congress, to elect conservatives to Congress. Howard Phillips, a good friend of Weyrich's and a former member of the Nixon administration, founded his own conservative political organization, the Conservative Caucus, at the same time. Phillips was a Jewish convert to evangelical Christianity and Weyrich was a conservative Catholic who worried that Vatican II had pushed the Catholic Church in too liberal a direction. Both men believed mobilizing Christian conservatives around a few key "family" issues could produce a political realignment and remake the Republican Party.[139]

As leaders of the "New Right" movement they had named themselves, Phillips and Weyrich intentionally distinguished themselves from both the "Old Right" of Sen. Robert Taft's era and the establishment elite that dominated the present GOP. The New Right championed vigilant national defense, aggressive tax cuts and deregulation, and legislation to secure and protect "family values." It promised to protect what it contended were traditional American ideals, like the husband-led nuclear family, Judeo-Christian morality, law and order vigilance, and the free enterprise system, an appealing message to a broad swath of cultural conservatives from rural America, the burgeoning Sunbelt suburbs, urban Catholic centers of the Northeast and Midwest, and the Mormon Intermountain West. Disappointed by a party they believed far too often compromised its mission to reduce government, these New Right activists worked outside of the establishment's traditional channels, creating their own grassroots organizations perfectly suited for activating newly engaged evangelical and fundamentalist voters while also appealing to traditionalist Catholics who remained in the Democratic Party. The New Right combined its radically free market impulses with a strident cultural conservatism, most visible through rabid opposition to abortion, gay rights, and the ERA, to create a potent political force with roots reaching back to the campaigns for Barry Goldwater, Richard Nixon, and George Wallace. Now brought together as much out of frustration with the Republican Party establishment as it was in opposition to the Democratic Party and the advance of secular culture, the New Right drew its most spirited energy from its emboldened and determined Religious Right faction.[140]

Weyrich and Phillips reached out to Jerry Falwell. As a typical fundamentalist, Falwell had famously attacked religious leaders for their political involvement in the civil rights movement, a position that was political in itself for it helped prop up the South's legal system of racial oppression and discrimination.[141] But by the early 1970s Falwell recognized he could no longer remain silent on political matters, especially when so many other conservative ministers were speaking out. Falwell had a huge following—more than twenty thousand members now belonged to Thomas Road and millions more tuned in to his television program—and they clamored for direction from him on all matters of their lives.[142] Viewers of "The Old-Time Gospel Hour" especially responded to any casual mentions Falwell made of politics, sending the minister letters with questions about various issues. But Falwell felt nervous about fully embracing politics at first. What did he know about national defense or tax policy or the Panama Canal? Those issues remained obscure to him, but fortunately his audiences at Thomas Road and "The Old-Time Gospel Hour" indicated far more interest in topics concerning the family. Since the 1960s, evangelicals had given almost obsessive attention to the family. *Moody Monthly*, the fundamentalist magazine, changed its subtitle from "The Christian Service Magazine" to "The Christian Magazine for All the Family," in 1960, only to change the subtitle again to "The Christian Family Magazine," in 1975, underscoring how central the family had become to both conservative Christian identity and theology.[143] Knowing this, Falwell realized he could easily connect fundamentalist theology to issues of the day affecting the family—the Equal Rights Amendment, the rise in divorce, the threat of homosexuality, secularism in the classroom, and abortion—which he threaded through his sermons and telecasts. In 1976, Falwell took his show on the road, holding "I Love America" rallies across the country, often staged on the steps of a state capitol building. More than 100 rallies took place, and Falwell used them to inveigh against the country's ills and to preach his message that Christian citizens had to become involved in politics in order to protect their beloved homeland from descending into godlessness.[144] In his stump speech, "America Back to God," Falwell argued, "This idea of 'religion and politics don't mix' was invented by the devil to keep Christians from running their own country."[145] Ignoring both history and a long theological legacy, Falwell now presented conservative Christians' disengagement with public life as Satan's ploy. In order to defeat the devil, Christians needed to not only spread the gospel, but take back their country too. "What has gone wrong?" Falwell asked in his speech, "What has happened to this great republic? We have forsaken the God of our fathers. . . . Our country needs healing. Will you be one of a consecrated few who will bear the burden for revival and pray . . . ? The destiny of our nation awaits your answer."[146]

Weyrich and Phillips had approached Falwell in 1976 with the idea of creating a political organization to recruit evangelicals and fundamentalists, but he turned them down.[147] When the two revisited the invitation on the eve of the 1980 election, Falwell jumped at the offer. Between the two presidential elections, Falwell had become active in local and state political battles across the nation on moral issues, such as anti-gay ballot initiatives in California and Florida.[148] By 1979, Falwell was ready to extend that involvement to the national stage. Meeting with Falwell in Lynchburg, Weyrich noted, "Out there is what one might call a moral majority." Weyrich explained that these were people who believed in the Ten Commandments and shared traditional social views, but were separated from each other by geography and denomination. Falwell, they hoped, would lead an organization that would bring these people together by helping them see their common political interests. Falwell seized on Weyrich's words about a moral majority. "That's the name of the organization," he cried, and the group was born.[149]

Moral Majority

From the beginning, Falwell hoped to make his organization ecumenical. Weyrich and Phillips had stressed to Falwell that millions of conservative Christians divided by their denominations could be brought together out of shared political concerns, and Falwell made constant reference to this ecumenical goal. Weyrich saw the coalitional advantages, not surprisingly, in strategic terms. Evangelicals would bring their knowledge and unshakeable adherence to biblical precepts to the table, strengthening the group's political commitments; Catholics would leaven this with their "philosophical underpinnings," buttressing the intellectual foundation against outside attacks; and Mormons would lend their lauded organizational and missionizing skills, giving coherence and efficiency to the movement.[150] Falwell, on the other hand, understood the theological hurdle his organization had to overcome, especially with fellow fundamentalists who resisted working with outsiders. To these, Falwell reached out. "I know that some object that we are compromising in our involvement with people of different doctrinal and theological beliefs," Falwell wrote, "As a fundamental, independent, separatist Baptist, I am well aware of the crucial issues of personal and ecclesiastical separation that divide fundamentalists philosophically from evangelicals and liberals."[151] But there were many Americans, Falwell explained, "who do not share our theological beliefs but who do share our moral concerns," and this dwindling number of people—even if named the Moral Majority—needed to band together on behalf of shared moral issues. "I would not for a moment encourage anyone to water down his distinctive beliefs," Falwell continued. "But we must face realistically the fact that there are Christians in the world today who have lost the luxury of disengagement. When the entire issue of Christian survival is at stake, we must be willing to band together on at least the major moral issues of the day."[152] "Our ministry is committed as it ever has been to the basic truths of Scripture . . . . ," Falwell assured his readers, "But we are not willing to isolate ourselves in seclusion while we sit back and watch this nation plunge headlong toward hell."[153]

From its inception, Falwell touted the Moral Majority's ecumenical aims. This may have been as much for publicity's sake as it was a recruiting mechanism, since Falwell was skillful with public relations and wanted to gather a vast movement of Americans behind his cause. To do so, Falwell targeted groups he believed most receptive to the anti-abortion aims and cultural traditionalism of the Moral Majority: evangelical and fundamentalist Christians, Catholics, Mormons, and conservative Jews, whom he hoped to attract with his ardent Zionism and pro-Israel positions. Falwell's ideas about political engagement and his surprising openness to ecumenism for the sake of politics, especially given his ardent separatist theological convictions, owed largely to the works of Francis Schaeffer.[154]

Schaeffer's concept of "cobelligerency" had profoundly influenced Falwell. By this, Schaeffer meant that evangelicals and fundamentalists should align themselves with people who might hold different doctrines but who would work with them on achieving certain political goals, what Schaeffer's son Franky would soon describe as an "ecumenism of orthodoxy."[155] As William Martin points out, this was an idea with a long history in politics, but for evangelicals and fundamentalists who rarely agreed even among themselves, the concept was ground-breaking.[156] Schaeffer had urged Falwell to use "The Old-Time Gospel Hour" to push its viewers into political action, and he stressed the need to adopt cobelligerency as a way of tackling the most pressing issues. Falwell resisted, doubting that such alignments could ever work. "Listen," Schaeffer countered, "God used pagans to do his work in the Old Testament, so why don't you use pagans to do your work now?"[157] By the time that Falwell was leading the Moral Majority, he had become convinced that the organization's success depended on its ability to create an ecumenical coalition tackling the nation's ills. Paul Weyrich and Howard Phillips agreed. Weyrich would later describe the Moral Majority's work to the *New York Times* as "reverse ecumenism." The original ecumenical movement, Weyrich explained, had been a liberal movement of the progressive churches. The Moral

Majority was bringing about cooperation among "all kinds of other people who frankly didn't speak to each other."[158]

While Schaeffer had provided Falwell with a quasi-theological basis for ecumenical political action, Falwell likely needed little convincing that other conservative Christians offered prime resources for a political movement based on traditional moral convictions. Falwell was a shrewd and brilliant leader—he had built his Thomas Road Baptist Church from a tiny congregation into one of the nation's largest mega-churches with a booming television ministry and a growing fundamentalist university attached—and through the 1970s he closely observed and increasingly engaged the political scene he had once preached fundamentalists ought to ignore. Anyone who had kept watch over the most vibrant political movements of the 1970s surely understood that Catholics and Mormons represented the brightest lights of conservative Christian political activism. The Catholic Church had almost single-handedly launched the anti-abortion movement, now drawing millions of non-Catholics into it; the LDS Church and its faithful members had emerged from their regional corner and historic inward focus to play a critical national role in turning back the Equal Rights Amendment and, with that impending defeat, ushering a crushing blow to the aims of equality feminism. The Catholic Church, while not using the language of cobelligerency, was beginning to reflect its values, even if acting on them sometimes proved challenging. The U.S. bishops' statement on "Political Responsibility," for example, had explicitly called on Catholics to work "with other concerned parties" on shared concerns, particularly abortion.[159] The LDS Church, however, continued insisting its distinctiveness and independence. A 1980 General Conference talk reminded the Saints, "Our position among the Christian denominations of the world is unique. We are not affiliated, either directly or indirectly, with any other so-called Christian or non-Christian church. The Church of Jesus Christ of Latter-day Saints does not have, nor has it ever had, any connection or relation with any other church or religious group."[160]

Since the concept was revolutionary, and possibly heretical, in fundamentalist circles, the Moral Majority had its critics.[161] No Christian conservative protested the Moral Majority's ecumenical aims more than Bob Jones III, the president of the ultra-fundamentalist Bob Jones University in Greenville, South Carolina. After the Moral Majority's formation, Jones wrote a book denouncing the organization for its promise to transcend theological divisions for political gain. "The aim of the Moral Majority," Jones began his book,

> is to join Catholics, Jews, Protestants of every stripe, Mormons, etc., in a common religious cause. Christians can fight on the battlefield

> alongside these people, can vote with them for a common candidate, but they cannot be unequally yoked with them in a religious army or organization. Morality is a matter of religion: a man's morality is based upon his religious beliefs. . . . Alliances we would avoid at the local level are not made acceptable or less ecumenical due to the national level on which they operate. . . . A close, analytical, biblical look at the Moral Majority . . . reveals a movement that holds more potential for hastening the church of Antichrist and building the ecumenical church than anything to come down the pike in a long time, including the charismatic movement.[162]

Though Jones represented the most radical fringe of fundamentalism, his gripe with the Moral Majority came from fundamentalism's most basic doctrines of separatism and exclusive salvation. Yet those sentiments would shape the Moral Majority, even as its founder tried to distance it from such traditions.

Conclusion

Evangelicals, Catholics, and Mormons rallied around the 1980 presidential campaign of Ronald Reagan, a candidate who touted the Bible as the answer to all the nation's problems and made bold promises on their cherished issues. Convinced that they alone stood between the nation and its decline into godless amorality, Mormons, Catholics, evangelicals, and fundamentalists united around Reagan, believing his election would turn the nation back from secularism and protect political and cultural assaults on the family. They also believed that a Reagan victory would restore religious conservatives to their proper position as the nation's guardians and moral authorities. In supporting Reagan, religious conservatives championed their newfound unity as nearly as vociferously as they promoted their savior candidate. Doing so signaled a new stage in the nearly three-decade discussion many of them had been engaging in about both political activism and ecumenism.

In his landslide win in 1980, Reagan benefited from the support of religious conservatives. Reagan's win among Catholics represented one of only three times, including 1952 and 1976, when a Republican presidential candidate had won a majority of Catholic voters.[163] Sixty-one percent of white evangelicals sided with Reagan.[164] Such a showing was especially significant considering half of evangelicals still were registered as Democrats, with only 25 percent belonging to the GOP. Despite the efforts of Falwell and others, an estimated 30 percent of evangelicals remained unregistered voters.[165] No religious group gave more support, however, than Mormon voters who provided Reagan with 80 percent of their votes, 15 percent more than they had given Gerald Ford in 1976.[166]

After having worked so hard for Reagan and other victorious conservative Republican candidates in 1980, Religious Right activists and conservative Christian voters faced the harsh reality of American politics once Reagan took office. Yet mostly they remained hopeful that a Reagan administration would deliver on the goals they had outlined in their mobilization efforts, so many of which Reagan himself had echoed in his campaign run. These included chipping away at federal laws that limited the influence of religion in American public life; reinstituting school prayer and removing secular humanist influences in the public schoolroom, including the teaching of evolution and sex education; cracking down on pornography and curtailing gay rights; and, most centrally, overturning the federal right to abortion. These were ambitious, perhaps even impossible aims, but the belief that the right president along with a growing army in Congress might achieve these ends had galvanized millions of Americans to vote in 1980. The Religious Right's architects understood the difficulty of realizing the changes they sought, but they also believed they had a powerful cudgel in millions of voters to threaten the White House with should it fail to prioritize and deliver on their wish list.

But for the Religious Right to be as effective a force in the day-to-day battle of national politics as they had on one election day, they would need to remain a united force in the trenches. Jerry Falwell understood the need for unity among religious conservatives if they hoped to achieve any of their goals, even as he acknowledged how impossible that still might seem given the history. "When Mormons, Catholics, Jews and Protestants come together you'd have a blood bath if it weren't political," he joked to a reporter near the election. "We're willing to fight now for a common cause, so we can fight with each other later."[167] But the 1980s would hardly witness the détente among the factions of the Religious Right as Falwell hoped, and the political consequences of that failure would be many. Rather than bringing about a moment of political unity among religious conservatives that would achieve important legislative results, the 1980s witnessed a flourishing of anti-ecumenical impulses among these religious bodies, particularly from evangelicals. In the end, Catholic, Mormon, and evangelical leaders used the Reagan years as much to attack each other religiously as they did to promote and advance a political consensus of religious conservatives.

6

A Moral Majority

IN MARCH 1983, a Catholic businessman in Phoenix reached for his phone after reading an alarming article in the Mesa *Tribune.* Sitting in his office where he served as the Arizona Regional Director of the National Conference of Christians and Jews (NCCJ), Donald Alvin Eagle, a former minister in the liberal Disciples of Christ, answered the call. Eagle listened as the businessman explained the article that had prompted his call: a vicious anti-Mormon film, *The God Makers,* was making the rounds in evangelical circles and had just played before a packed audience of 1,500 in Mesa, sponsored by a group calling itself Concerned Christians. These Christians were concerned for the eternal fate of LDS members; the group proclaimed its purpose was "to reach out in love to those lost in Mormonism." The NCCJ quickly mobilized against the film, recruiting local ministers to write disapproving letters to the press about the movie and assembling an ad hoc committee of Protestant, Catholic, Jewish, and Mormon clergy and laypersons to study the film and propose a response. A professor of religion from Brigham Young University traveled to Phoenix to explain basic Mormon beliefs to the NCCJ committee and outline the film's many errors. It was unusual enough for Mormons to work with people of other faiths, and all the more so to partner with a liberal ecumenical organization like the NCCJ, but the movie's popularity with evangelicals alarmed Mormons, making them grateful for the sympathetic backing the NCCJ offered.[1]

Not long after the incidents in Phoenix, the Catholic Church's Cincinnati diocese published a study guide to help its members defend themselves against conversion efforts from evangelical and fundamentalist Christians. Many Catholics had experienced an occasional evangelistic overture from conservative Protestants at some point in their lives, but in the early 1980s Catholics in the anti-abortion movement complained they were enduring constant proselytizing from evangelical Christians they were meeting in their pro-life activities.[2] Mobilized to save the lives of the unborn, these

Catholics kept meeting pro-life evangelical Christians who seemed more interested in saving their souls.

Evangelicals have always been concerned with soul-winning, of course, but in the 1980s, much of that evangelistic fervor was directed at members of those religious groups they were most often linked with politically. Brought closer together by shared politics and a Religious Right movement that asserted their unity, evangelical, Catholic, and Mormon leaders asserted their distinctions and drew boundaries between each other. That boundary drawing also involved proselytizing each other and defending against proselytization, for the act of evangelism pointed to the boundary that had to be crossed (or defended) to achieve true salvation. But these religious boundaries also shifted in relation to each other. For evangelicals, the Catholic Church still offered a false conception of the Christian faith. But the distance between evangelicals and some individual Catholics had shortened thanks to increasing emphasis on the Bible and a personal relationship with Jesus among many Catholics and also in contrast to the remove evangelicals felt from mainline Protestantism. That softening boundary between evangelicals and some Catholics stood in contrast to the hardening border dividing evangelicals and the LDS Church, strengthened by both sides. Unlike Catholics, whom they had come to appreciate as separate from their mother church, evangelicals drew no distinction between lay Mormons and their institutional church. They coupled a full-scale attack on Mormonism with a robust evangelistic outreach to Mormons. The LDS Church responded with a spirited defense of itself as God's only true church, a condemnation of associational ties, and its own religious mission that especially targeted evangelicals for conversion. With Reagan in the White House and a conservative resurgence realigning American politics and culture, conservative religious leaders might have exulted in the moment as a return to the nation's Judeo-Christian foundations and a triumph of conservative ecumenism. Instead, many of them saw it as a time of religious crisis that demanded clear messages that distinguished and promoted their particular faiths. That interpretation would have political consequences for the Religious Right and the Reagan administration, as Chapter 7 will elaborate, but it also complicated relations among the "moral majority" who had helped bring about Reagan's win.

Brokering an Evangelical-Fundamentalist Truce

Although evangelicals delineated their boundaries between Catholics and Mormons, the relationship between evangelicals and fundamentalists received new attention from both quarters in the early years of the 1980s, as many felt the political and cultural climate of the time needed a strong alliance among conservative Protestants in order to deliver on the opportunity of the recent election and to meet the religious challenges from other Christian faiths. Buoyed by his political achievements and his high public visibility, Jerry Falwell led the efforts from the fundamentalist wings to broker a rapprochement with evangelical forces. While Falwell's pronouncements of a broad ecumenical alliance spanning conservative Christendom remained as yet more wishful thinking than actual reality, a linking of forces between the evangelical and fundamentalist camps of Protestantism had always been the most likely alliance among the options. As Falwell pointed out in his 1981 book, *The Fundamentalist Phenomenon*, "there is little difference theologically between Fundamentalists and Evangelicals."[3] Falwell beseeched both sides to put aside their small disagreements and recognize, especially compared to all other choices, their extensive points of agreement on foundational matters. "I say it is time we denied the 'lunatic fringe' of our movements and worked for a great conservative crusade to turn America back to God," Falwell wrote.[4]

Leading evangelicals signaled they were ready to talk. Robert Dugan, head of the National Association of Evangelicals' Washington office, wrote Falwell a fawning letter, gushing that he'd devoured *The Fundamentalist Phenomenon* in one day. Dugan lauded Falwell for seeking rapprochement with evangelicals, "the first such call that I have ever heard emanating from Fundamentalist circles," he noted, and appreciated that Falwell had admitted to fundamentalism's shortcomings. "This is a praiseworthy example for us Evangelicals," Dugan acknowledged.[5] For evangelicals accustomed to only seeing fundamentalism's strident separatism and legalistic imperiousness, Falwell's book offered a welcome note of humility, grace, and Christian comity.

Six months later, in February 1982, Carl Henry, whose writings and particularly his editorship of *Christianity Today* had helped define the lines separating evangelicalism and fundamentalism, invited a roster of evangelical and fundamentalist leaders to his Arlington home to discuss Falwell's proposal. Joining Henry and Falwell at the historic gathering were important evangelicals like Wheaton College president and former NAE head Hudson Armerding, and Dugan. Leading fundamentalists at the meeting included Francis Schaeffer and John Walvoord, president of Dallas Theological Seminary. Kenneth Kantzer, then editor of *Christianity Today*, took unofficial notes that he later distributed to the attendees.

Francis Schaeffer had recently authored another book, *A Christian Manifesto* (1981), that had electrified the conservative Protestant wing of the Religious Right. *A Christian Manifesto* reiterated Schaeffer's prior contentions that the American nation and its founding documents arose from a Christian base. From that Christian origin, two major developments hastened the nation's departure from this tradition. First, the great waves of non-Protestant immigrants who arrived in the second half of the nineteenth century yielded a "sharp increase in viewpoints not shaped by Reformation Christianity."[6] A *Newsweek* writer at the time noted Schaeffer's book unintentionally exposed what the Religious Right's promoters hoped to obscure. "Schaeffer's note of rankled Protestant nativism," Kenneth Woodward wrote, "reveals more about the emotional underpinnings of the modern fundamentalist movement than do any of the more polished position papers of the new religious right."[7] Second, the rise of secular humanism that Schaeffer characterized as a religion "the government and courts in the United States favor over all others" meant humanism had replaced Christianity as the religion of the American state.[8]

Because of these developments, Schaeffer advocated increased Christian political action to stand against the nation's humanist forces. Famously, Schaeffer contended that for some of the state's most vile ills, civil disobedience would be a useful way to respond. This became a cherished tactic of the extreme fringe of the anti-abortion movement, but the broader message of Schaeffer's book endorsed an active and engaged Christian political movement. Citing the recent 1980 election and the country's "conservative swing," Schaeffer depicted the moment as "a unique window open in the United States. It is unique because it is a long, long time since that window has been open as it is now."[9] While the window remained open, Christians needed to do all they could to beat back secular humanism and its consequences, replacing it with the Christian worldview the nation had once looked to as the basis for its constitutional system.

For all its readers—twice as many Americans had purchased *A Christian Manifesto* as they had *Jane Fonda's Workout Book*, the number one best seller on the *New York Times'* list in 1982—Schaeffer's book drew mixed responses from the diverse evangelical world. Moral Majority president Cal Thomas called it his organization's "battle plan." Pat Robertson, the nation's most important Pentecostal, who ministered to millions on his *700 Club* television program, drew heavily from *A Christian Manifesto* in his own jeremiads against the nation's secular path and as he plotted his political ascendancy. Evangelicals, especially scholars like Mark Noll and George Marsden, however, were less impressed with Schaeffer's interpretations of American history, unwilling to sacrifice historical accuracy at the altar of political expediency as Schaeffer often seemed all too game to do.[10] Like so many other missives launched into the evangelical world, *A Christian Manifesto* was as notable for the varied responses it elicited as it was for its own contribution, highlighting again the diverse camps and boundaries within conservative

Protestantism. Back at Carl Henry's house, those divisions had brought the participants together. Following the 1980 election, it could seem that evangelicals, fundamentalists, and charismatics had patched together a formidable unity. The secular media and the Democratic Party certainly seemed to think so, although, particularly for the Democrats, this was a useful myth cultivated to stir up its own base.[11] But the ballot box was hardly the place to take an account of evangelical-fundamentalist relations or answer the question of evangelical unity.[12]

At Henry's house, the meeting began with a scripture reading from John 17, a passage where Jesus spoke of Christian unity, followed by prayers led by several of those in attendance. Speaking first, Falwell shared his testimony of Christian conversion and his experience as a fundamentalist pastor. Falwell identified two divisions within fundamentalism—the camp of Bob Jones, Jr., who advocated extreme separatism, and the rest of fundamentalists, including himself, whom Falwell estimated accounted for as much as 85 percent of the movement. Falwell would come to call his camp "New Fundamentalism," for those who desired closer spiritual unity with moderate evangelicals.[13] Falwell wanted, as Kantzer recorded in his notes, "to recognize Evangelicals as brothers, to work together with them when he can, and to show respect for them before the world." "Five years ago Fundamentalists risked the most in such cooperation," Falwell observed. "Today Evangelicals risk the most in such cooperation."[14]

Of all those who spoke that afternoon, Francis Schaeffer appeared the most heated in his comments. Given the tide of secularism and the responsibility they all bore to the Great Commission, evangelicals and fundamentalists needed to stop their attacks on each other, which weakened their witness to the nation, he argued. "Fundamentalists and Evangelicals must mutually confront opponents of Biblical positions" rather than each other, Schaeffer implored. They could all do so much more for the Kingdom, Schaeffer continued, if they directed their energies "more carefully against those who are opponents of basic Biblical truth. We are one as brothers of Christ. If someone attacks my brother, he attacks me."[15]

Schaeffer had demonstrated this commitment in his recent book. In *A Christian Manifesto*, Schaeffer publicly praised the Moral Majority for using "the freedom we still have in the political arena to stand against the other total entity" of secular humanism. "And if you personally do not like some of the details of what they have done, do it better," Schaeffer chastised the Moral Majority's Christian critics.[16] Privately, as Schaeffer's biographer Barry Hankins has shown, Schaeffer harbored concerns about Falwell's rising power, even though he had once encouraged it. Falwell's often-abrasive public persona troubled Schaeffer, who worried that Falwell would alienate potential allies and unnecessarily antagonize foes. Though Schaeffer appreciated Falwell's devotion to fighting abortion and opposing state regulation of churches and Christian schools, he feared Falwell risked undermining the conservative Christian movement by taking on issues, like nuclear armament and gun control, that good Christians could disagree on.[17] But for the cause of Christian unity he believed essential for achieving political goals, Schaeffer kept his disagreements with Falwell out of his writings and his comments at Henry's home.

Carl Henry, though host of the event, still harbored reservations about the meeting.[18] Henry characterized the fundamentalists' willingness to now meet with evangelicals as "too slow," and he worried that other major evangelical bodies, like the Southern Baptist Convention and the Lutheran Church—Missouri Synod, were noticeably missing from the proceedings (although Bellevue Baptist's Adrian Rogers had been invited), along with charismatics. Still, Henry was willing to listen to what people had to say, especially thoughts on "how to plan a better strategy" for the future. Schaeffer contended that going forward, "Confrontation is necessary." Within religious circles, evangelicals and fundamentalists needed to unite to battle any threats to biblical inerrancy. On the civil front, the two "must stand against and confront" the horror of abortion. As the meeting neared its end, Hudson Armerding recounted the four issues the attendees had all agreed they needed to show a "united stand" on: working together to better distribute the Bible, cooperating on relief to the poor and destitute, defending biblical inerrancy, and presenting an anti-abortion position to the nation.[19]

Though the conversation that February afternoon had demonstrated some lingering suspicions between evangelicals and fundamentalists, not to mention the uninvited charismatics, and had also lacked the full participation of the conservative Protestant community, much had been done to broker a truce between the major evangelical and fundamentalist leaders of the day—a truce, as Susan Harding notes, "essential to the formation of the core constituency of the New Christian Right."[20] As Kantzer recorded in his notes, the meeting concluded with everyone's agreement "to cultivate personal friendship among Evangelical and Fundamentalist leaders. They will promise to be responsible to defend each other." And in perhaps the most notable sign of their openness to working with fundamentalists, the evangelicals at the meeting promised "to present Falwell fairly and favorably."[21] Out of the shadows of separatist fundamentalism and political and cultural abstention, Falwell had now taken his place front and center in conservative Protestantism's confrontation with the nation.

The Third Wave

Beyond fundamentalist-evangelical relations, other divisions emerged in the Arlington discussion at Carl Henry's home. When one participant asked if Pentecostals ought to be included or if this was "too much to expect," Falwell responded, "My problem is not with the Pentecostals but with Charismatics."[22] (Other comments Falwell made elsewhere showed he had problems with both groups.) But the question of charismatics had become a particularly vexing one for fundamentalists and evangelicals in the 1980s, as a "Third Wave" revival brought a vibrant neo-charismatic movement to the forefront of American evangelicalism.[23] For independent separatists like Falwell, charismatic Christianity stood too far from the fundamentalist fold. But some evangelicals were softening their views in response to reforms within charismatic Christianity, including downplaying glossolalia, faith-healing, and other "Spirit-filled" worship practices that had once attracted evangelical reproach. Charismatics now focused more on evangelism and prioritized scripture's ultimate authority, even above the Holy Spirit's stirrings.[24] Jim and Tammy Faye Bakker, for instance, made sure to keep speaking in tongues and faith-healing services off of their popular television program, *The PTL Club*, even as their South Carolina headquarters was awash in such charismatic fervor behind the cameras.[25] "From almost every point of view, in doctrine and practice they are part of the warp and woof of evangelicalism," Kenneth Kantzer allowed of charismatics in 1980.[26]

The Third Wave, a term coined by Fuller Theological Seminary professor C. Peter Wagner, represented "an opening of the straight-line evangelicals . . . to the supernatural work of the Holy Spirit that the Pentecostals and charismatics have experienced, but without becoming either charismatic or Pentecostal," a description that represented his own spiritual path.[27] Wagner, who described himself as "neither a charismatic nor a Pentecostal" but rather a "Scofield Bible dispensational evangelical," attended Pasadena's Lake Avenue Congregational Church, near Fuller's campus.[28] Wagner had started questioning his opposition to Pentecostalism while serving as a missionary in Bolivia for sixteen years. Like other evangelicals working in South America, Wagner envied the inroads Pentecostal churches were making with Catholics and non-Christians. Evangelicals, with their cool, logical gospel message, found they couldn't compete with the Spirit-filled Pentecostal expression of tongues, prophecies, and healings, a religious experience that seemed perfectly attuned to the sizeable South American population that practiced spiritism or animism.[29] Back in California, Wagner joined the Fuller faculty and became a pioneer of the Church Growth movement, a burgeoning missionizing program that utilized social science tools from anthropology and sociology to win cultural groups, rather than individuals, to Christ (though individual regeneration was seen as the next step of successful ministry and discipleship).[30]

John Wimber attended Wagner's class while a student at Fuller in the 1970s. Wimber, a rock musician some credited with founding the Righteous Brothers because he had introduced Bobby Hatfield and Bill Medley, had left his drug-filled rock-and-roll days to become an evangelical Quaker. After graduating Fuller, Wimber became director of its recently created Department of Church Growth while also leading a home church that quickly grew to 100 members. When Wimber's home church began focusing on worship with extended praise singing and speaking in tongues, the Quakers asked Wimber to leave their fold. Wimber then linked his growing church to Chuck Smith's Calvary Chapel network out of Costa Mesa, the locus of the Jesus People movement and a vibrant charismatic association in Southern California. Smith and Wimber soon parted ways as well when Wimber started conducting demonic exorcisms during his services, a step too far for the reserved Smith. Wimber switched his church's affiliation from Calvary Chapel to the Vineyard, a fledgling neo-charismatic association not all that different from the Calvary Chapel. Wimber's group, now called the Anaheim Vineyard Christian Fellowship, quickly grew to thousands of members, making Wimber the de facto leader of the Vineyard Movement as it ballooned to hundreds of churches in the 1980s.[31]

As the Vineyard prospered, Wimber returned to Fuller to co-teach a class with Peter Wagner called "Signs, Wonders, and Church Growth," a course the professors billed as suited for those "who want to be helped beyond their own littleness of faith."[32] When Wimber and Wagner started their course in 1982, 44 percent of Fuller's students identified themselves as a Pentecostal or charismatic Christian, a remarkable constituency for neo-evangelicalism's most important seminary, but beyond even those numbers were many evangelicals, like the two professors, who were interested in developing a more Spirit-filled religious life.[33] Given this, the course proved hugely popular with students. Fuller's administrators, however, grew nervous as they learned it involved "practical sessions" where students experimented with signs and wonders, including faith healings, during class time, leading to the course's cancellation in 1985. While Fuller, in keeping with its neo-evangelical temperament, had been remarkably open to Pentecostals and charismatics—going so far as to establish a prominent research center for Pentecostal studies in 1958—the Signs and Wonders course pushed the limits of neo-evangelical tolerance at a seminary used to being at the center of theological squabbles.[34]

Wimber drew more raised eyebrows from traditional evangelicals over his "power evangelism" strategy that used miracles and wonders to convert non-believers in place of a rational articulation of the gospel message most evangelicals preferred, such as Bill Bright's Four Spiritual Laws method.[35] Many evangelicals worried that believers converted through power evangelism had been seduced by miraculous manifestations rather than persuaded of their need for personal holiness and regeneration.[36]

Caution and concern would continue to characterize evangelical assessments of the charismatic renewal movement, heightened by the financial and sexual scandals of several leading Pentecostal televangelists including Oral Roberts, Jimmy Swaggart, and Jim and Tammy Bakker, whose PTL Ministries people now snickered was an acronym for "Pass the Loot" rather than "Praise the Lord."[37] Instead of defending them, most evangelicals distanced themselves from the fallen Pentecostal stars, worried how their own witness had suffered from being grouped together in the public's imagination. But the mainstreaming of charismatic worship and the careful welcome granted by evangelical bodies, like *Christianity Today* and Fuller Seminary, strengthened the Third Wave movement as a religious force transforming and broadening evangelical identity, beliefs, and practices in the 1980s. Some parachurch evangelical organizations, like Campus Crusade for Christ, began allowing charismatics and Pentecostals on their staffs, reversing previous organizational policies.[38] Still, powerful evangelical denominations, like the Lutheran Church—Missouri Synod and the Southern Baptist Convention, resisted the charismatic upsurge, not only over theological objections to charismatic biblical hermeneutics and worship styles, but also as a defense against the slippery ecumenism they believed the charismatic movement had advanced, not least its close association with Spirit-filled Catholics. The Missouri Synod enacted policies against the charismatic movement in its churches and seminaries, including preventing charismatically inclined pastors from joining the denomination.[39] In the SBC, the charismatic movement had taken hold among some individual believers and churches, causing wide debate throughout the Convention. "Some interpret the charismatic movement as a response to spiritual hunger among Baptists," the SBC journal *Review & Expositor* commented in 1982, "while others see it as either a form of doctrinal divergence or the result of emotional instability among its adherents."[40] SBC leaders, especially the denomination's most powerful fundamentalist preachers, tended to take the latter view, leading the Convention's trustees in 1987 to prevent those "actively participating in or promoting glossolalia" from working as missionaries or SBC chaplains, while signaling strong disapproval even for non-glossolalic charismatic Baptists.[41] When

James Robison, a Baptist televangelist from Fort Worth, took a charismatic turn in the 1980s by emphasizing demonology and supernatural healings and cozying up to questionable (for Southern Baptists) Pentecostals like Roberts and Bakker, he drew strong rebuke from Southern Baptist leaders even though he never spoke in tongues.[42]

A strong denominational identity and devotion to scriptural authority had always marked both Southern Baptists and the evangelical Lutherans of the Missouri Synod, emboldened their anti-ecumenism, and now shaped their views of the charismatic movement, providing some of the toughest resistance from evangelical voices. Echoing mid-century evangelical assessments of liberal Protestantism, evangelical critics, like the Missouri Synod theologian David Scaer, warned the "final result of the [charismatic] movement is a doctrinally unrestricted ecumenism where doctrinal boundaries are no longer enforced, simply because they are no longer recognized as important." Importantly, for the most conservative evangelicals, charismatic ecumenism now represented a greater threat to evangelical orthodoxy and the gospel message than the traditional ecumenical movement of mainline Protestantism, a rather weakened cause by the 1980s. Seeing charismatics as willing to unite across (and outside of) denominations through their Spirit-filled religious experiences rather than doctrinal soundness, Lutheran evangelicals like Scaer countered that true Christian fellowship was "possible only among those who share, not a common emotional experience allegedly identified as originating with the Holy Spirit, but a common commitment to what God has revealed through the Spirit-inspired Scriptures."[43] Jim Bakker had defended James Robison as "totally committed to bringing the body of Christ together," but Southern Baptist leaders charged charismatics sought that goal through an anti-denominational theology that undermined the authority of the local church and pastor in a believer's life.[44] The Third Wave movement had washed over every inch of American evangelicalism—it was hard to find a congregation that hadn't enlivened its worship with contemporary Christian music praise songs made popular by the Vineyard churches—but many evangelicals pushed back against the larger tide. The resistance of some evangelicals to neo-charismatics' beliefs and practices exhibited familiar patterns, drawing sustenance from while also reshaping older anti-ecumenical impulses that always arose in moments of religiosity and revival.[45]

"What Separates Evangelicals and Catholics?"

In the years since Vatican II, evangelicals had shown increasing willingness to differentiate individual Catholics from the institutional church, a result largely due to what evangelicals saw as the church's more "biblical" direction following the Council. By encouraging its members to study and read their Bibles more faithfully, the Catholic Church had awakened evangelical sympathies to the image of lay Catholics wrestling with scriptural truth not unlike Martin Luther. Evangelicals had to see Catholics as separate and distinct from their mother church so that they might minister to their spiritual needs, including the possibility of conversion, and not merely as an undifferentiated mass unquestioningly attached to the church. Though few, evangelical-Catholic Bible studies had augmented this new understanding among evangelicals of their Catholic friends; the presence of committed and engaged Catholics on the frontlines of anti-abortion politics, leading a battle long before evangelicals joined the ranks, certainly heightened evangelical appreciation and admiration for the Catholic individual. By the late 1970s, when evangelicals thought of Catholics in the pro-life movement, they imagined a pious and selfless servant stirred by personal conviction rather than admonished to action by a controlling magisterium. This was quite different from how evangelicals of prior decades had envisioned Catholic public actors, including John F. Kennedy, as puppets of the papacy.

As the 1980s opened, evangelicals found further encouragement in the example of Catholic charismatics, members of a small but vibrant movement in the church that stressed the gifts of the Holy Spirit in their worship experiences and a personal relationship with Jesus Christ, not unlike their Protestant charismatic counterparts. While neo-Pentecostalism required all sorts of soul searching for evangelicals, the example of charismatic Catholics proved less troubling and aided evangelicals' re-imagining of Catholics as agents of their own spiritual lives rather than as captives of a hierarchical church, seeing them as fellow Christians who had found the saving grace of Jesus.[46] "Nothing separated us from our Roman Catholic charismatic brothers as we sat together sharing the good things of Christ," one *Christianity Today* editorial enthused, praising these Catholics for their adherence to the Bible and their claim that faith in Jesus Christ provided their salvation.[47] With these "Roman Catholic believers in Christ," evangelicals experienced the same unity they had with other true Christians.[48] "Unity in the gospel surmounts all other problems," *Christianity Today* explained, echoing arguments it had made during the heyday of mid-century ecumenism, "and is basic for a truly ecumenical fellowship."[49] "Roman Catholics are not all alike," the magazine admitted. "Clearly everything depends on which Roman Catholic one is relating to."[50]

That evangelicals might relate to the 25 percent of Catholics who claimed to be "born again" in 1981 was hardly surprising, nor was it difficult for evangelicals to feel close to the one quarter of Catholics who had cited the Bible, rather than the church, as their first source for answering their religious questions.[51] But admiration for Pope John Paul II and Mother Teresa demonstrated how far evangelicals had come in understanding individual Catholics, even the highest-ranking one, as distinct from the Catholic Church. Mother Teresa's selfless service in the slums of Calcutta was hard to dismiss; only the most heartless—or impolitic—evangelical would view such a life as a works-based bid for salvation, as evangelicals had often characterized Christian social reformers. Instead, evangelicals routinely cited Mother Teresa as a model for the Christian life and a living embodiment of the scriptural injunction that "faith without works is dead."[52] But evangelicals especially praised Mother Teresa for her unflinching voice against abortion to the world's secular elites who honored her charitable endeavors, such as when she used her 1979 Nobel Peace Prize address to condemn abortion as the world's "greatest destroyer of peace" to a flummoxed audience in Stockholm.[53] (To this day, evangelicals still fondly remember Mother Teresa's speaking "truth to power" moment when at the 1994 National Prayer Breakfast, with President Bill Clinton and Vice President Al Gore sitting nearby, she focused the entirety of her speech on defending the unborn.)[54] In 1985, *Christianity Today* approvingly published Mother Teresa's address to the National Right to Life Committee's convention during a trip to the United States.[55]

Evangelicals found much to admire in the biography of Pope John Paul II, particularly his anti-Communist efforts as a bishop in his native Poland, which he continued from Rome. As pope, John Paul spoke forcefully against abortion and the liberalization of sexual mores in the West. His theological and political conservatism encouraged evangelicals, especially when those leanings inspired pointed challenges to liberal political and cultural developments in the United States. Evangelicals lauded the pope's visits to the States in 1979 and 1987 for inspiring religious revival and for his consistent promotion of religious freedom, his defense of the sanctity of life, and his rebukes of materialism, sexual permissiveness, and secular humanism.[56] John Paul's conservative movements within the Catholic Church, however, drew more complicated responses from evangelical observers. On the one hand, conservative evangelicals appreciated John Paul's crackdown on supporters of liberation theology and Marxism within the church and his resistance to liberalizing Catholic teachings regarding sexuality and gender.[57] In opposing women's ordination and other liberal reform movements within the Catholic Church, Pope John Paul II reminded many evangelicals of their own battles over orthodoxy and struck them as far more akin to themselves than leaders of liberal Protestantism. Lastly, evangelicals appreciated that

John Paul's conservatism "has slowed down the ecumenical movement," as he shifted the church's "ecumenical interests primarily to the Eastern Orthodox churches."[58] On the other hand, John Paul's conservatism also hampered many of the post–Vatican II reform trends evangelicals had interpreted as moving Catholicism in a more Protestant and "biblically based" direction. As John Paul curbed the liberalizing, democratizing, and sometimes radicalizing movements within the church, he reasserted church traditions and practices, including the veneration of Mary, a return to relic-filled processions and other formal rituals, and renewed emphasis on papal authority—all roadblocks for a closer evangelical-Catholic relationship and, as far as evangelicals were concerned, significant barriers for Catholics to come to a saving knowledge of the gospel. "His Roman Catholic concerns do not complement, but rather undercut, his universal concerns," a writer for *The Reformed Journal* concluded.[59] "True, Rome has changed," a leading evangelical agreed, "and Pope John Paul II has moved many things in it toward the good. But on many other vital matters that affect the souls of men and their relationship to God, Rome is still Rome, and Pope John Paul II is simply its most effective voice."[60]

Still, most evangelical evaluations of Pope John Paul II leaned to the positive, a remarkable shift from the general treatment all prior popes had received. Both coinciding with and reinforcing the era's wider rapprochement of the two faiths, John Paul's papacy smoothed and deepened evangelical-Catholic relations. Admiration and respect so characterized evangelical regards for John Paul and so thoroughly transformed sentiments of the Catholic Church that one evangelical professor in 1981 could suggest that "the time may have come to admit that the doctrine of the pope as the antichrist was valid for the Reformers but inapplicable now."[61] (Similarly, a Mormon leader in 1988 clarified that the Catholic Church was not the "abominable church" in the Book of Mormon, a view that had never had official LDS sanction but still enjoyed considerable currency among lay Mormons.)[62] In recognizing Catholics as individuals distinct from their church, evangelicals could present no more significant example of such logic than the pope himself. But a pope and the papacy were not the same, and "the modern papacy," the evangelical professor reminded, "still presents at least some of the Reformers' problems. Beneath the robes of the congenial churchman is a secular ruler. No ecclesiastical leader can be Christ's sole spokesman."[63] Upon John Paul's 1987 visit to the States, an NAE statement reminded that the "papacy, with its claim of infallible doctrine, poses for Evangelicals a continuing obstacle to Christian unity. Evangelicals seek unity, but the only valid unity is one based on biblical truth."[64]

Though bolder than the rather mild critiques of John Paul II, evangelicals offered fairly muted and infrequent evaluations of the papacy and the institutional church in the 1980s compared to the inflamed tirades they had persistently launched in previous decades, but they still tore at the ecumenical fabric some evangelicals were knitting with Catholics. While evangelicals had not revised their basic assessment of Catholicism's theological errors and the church's unbiblical practices, they lacked a sense of urgency or dread in their discussions, striking a more perfunctory than paranoid tone.[65] Instead, evangelical leaders seemed far more prone to praising the Catholic Church's "biblical" developments, highlighting its conservative causes, and encouraging deeper affinities between evangelicals and Catholic laypersons. Even in evangelicals' critical assessments of the Catholic Church through the 1980s, the greater focus remained on finding kinship with Catholics. As the influential evangelical theologian J. I. Packer contended in 1985, "Catholics are among the most loyal and [spiritually] virile brothers evangelicals can find these days." Although Packer commented that the Catholic Church remained "simply wrong on some key issues," he echoed other leading evangelical voices of the decade in insisting evangelicals differentiate individual Catholics from their church.[66] Mormons, however, received no such judicious treatment.

The "Cult" of Mormonism

As the 1980s opened, evangelical anti-Mormonism spiked, further damaging evangelical-Mormon relations and undermining attempts at any ecumenical coalition-building Religious Right leaders hoped to carry out. While anti-Catholicism had taken on a subtle and often restrained tone by the 1980s, anti-Mormon sentiment reached some of its fullest expression. Evangelicals had always been generally aware of Mormonism, particularly as a competitor in the foreign mission field, but the explosion of the LDS Church's domestic missionary efforts in the 1970s and the early 1980s brought concerns about the Mormon faith to the fore on the home front.[67] In 1952, only 3 percent of Mormons had lived outside of the American West.[68] By 1980, half of the LDS Church's approximately 2.7 million American members resided beyond its traditional base of Utah, Nevada, and Idaho, with some of the strongest concentrations in the South, particularly Florida and Virginia.[69] Evangelical leaders increasingly worried that all sorts of Americans—from new refugee immigrants to Boy Scouts who found themselves in one of the LDS Church's seventeen thousand sponsored Scout units—were falling prey to Mormonism's missionary zeal.[70] When the noted sociologist Rodney Stark concluded in 1984 that Mormonism was the world's fastest-growing religion and would count as many as 265 million members by the year 2080, it only confirmed evangelical fears that Mormonism posed the greatest threat to orthodox Christianity.[71] Nothing troubled evangelical leaders more than reports that LDS growth came mainly from Christian converts. A survey of evangelical "cult experts" in 1985 named Mormonism as the "most dangerous" to Christian churches of the "pre-1960s cults."[72]

Southern Baptists, in particular, grew concerned about Mormonism's growth in the Convention's backyard of the American South. As the decade began, the LDS Church announced its physical presence in the South by beginning construction on temples in Atlanta and Dallas, two of the most important centers of Southern Baptism. The temples were necessary for the increasing number of Southern Saints, many of them converts to the church. A 1982 article in a Southern Baptist magazine worried that 40 percent of the LDS Church's 217,000 converts in 1980 came from Baptist backgrounds and cited the more than 150 Mormon missionaries proselytizing in northern Georgia alone, leading a director in the SBC's Interfaith Witnessing Department to name Mormons along with Jehovah's Witnesses and the Moonies as "the most aggressive religions" in the nation.[73] (Notably, the LDS Church had often touted stories of Southern Baptist converts to Mormonism in its publications.)[74] Continued Mormon growth across the Southern Bible Belt through the 1980s elicited further panic. "They're moving across the Southland," an SBC official in Nashville told *Newsweek* in 1985. A Texas pastor claimed Mormons were capturing Baptist converts at a rate of "231 every single day." The feeling that Mormons were "penetrating" the South, in the words of the SBC official, generated a full-scale response from the Convention.[75] Notably, the SBC was experiencing its own expansion boom at the same time, growing by two million members from 1970 to 1985, making it the fastest growing of the large denominations.[76] But such success may have only fueled fears about any competition to that growth.

Ignorance about the "cult" of Mormonism among lay Southern Baptists especially concerned SBC leaders. A nationwide survey had revealed Southern Baptists regarded Mormons more positively than they did members of the Unification Church, "this despite the fact," one Southern Baptist magazine article commented, "that Mormon theology is as strange and non-Christian as 'Moonie' theology." In response to this and the loss of so many Southern Baptists to Mormonism, the SBC charged its Home Mission Board with developing programs to teach Southern Baptists about the dangerous faith. The Board created training sessions and held Mormonism awareness conferences; fifty pastors and laypersons became SBC "certified" experts in

Mormonism who traveled to churches and meetings to instruct fellow Southern Baptists on Mormonism's dangers. Because of challenges overseas, the Foreign Mission Board added courses on Mormonism to its orientation program for new missionaries who were likely to encounter LDS missionaries in the field. The SBC frequently ran articles on Mormonism in its state newspapers and women's and youth magazines.[77] And Southern Baptist seminarians began writing theses on how they could respond to the growth of Mormonism.[78]

To equip churches in educating Southern Baptists on Mormonism, the Sunday School Board developed an instruction kit, *The Christian Confronting the Cults*. The booklet addressed five religious groups the SBC characterized as cults, with a handful of pages on the Jehovah's Witnesses, the Worldwide Church of God, the Unification Church, and Christian Science. The LDS Church, however, garnered seventeen pages of scrutiny, representing how much Mormonism occupied the SBC's imagination of its biggest threat. "No Christian should be unaware of the history and distinctive doctrines of the Latter-day Saints, unwilling to learn from Mormon strengths and weaknesses or unable to point out clearly their basic weaknesses. Christians must not be too ill-equipped to relate their understanding of the Christian gospel to their Mormon friends," the section started before giving an overview of Mormonism's history, doctrine, church organization, and strict moral standards.[79] A closing section on "How to Witness to a Latter-Day [*sic*] Saint" warned Baptists of the difficulty of proselytizing Mormons. "One is to be aware that the typical Mormon is not a 'hot prospect,'" the booklet noted, but it encouraged those Baptists who did evangelize Mormons to avoid discussions of Christian denominations and instead speak about their own personal conversion experience.[80] The book quickly became the Sunday School Board's top-selling item.[81]

Even two films produced by Brigham Young University were purged from the distribution lists of the Baptist Film Center. Though neither film addressed doctrinal issues, the Southern Baptist Convention still dropped the titles fearful of their "potential damage to the ministries of Southern Baptist churches," a press release announced. Convention pastors had also expressed concern in letters to the SBC that by distributing the two films, the Convention appeared to approve of Mormon-produced messages, even if neither of the films touched on theological issues.[82] All of these efforts, an SBC magazine explained, were "to help Baptists witness to Mormons without becoming 'Mormonized' themselves."[83]

This work mirrored a larger evangelical trend in the 1980s. *Christianity Today* regularly ran articles criticizing Mormon theology and, in response to worries of the LDS Church's increasing mainstreaming, continuing to describe it as a cult.[84] A review of John Heinerman and Anson Shupe's new book, *The Mormon Corporate Empire* (1986), worried about the LDS Church's political ambitions, describing the church's "crusade to undermine religious pluralism, influence the contours of economic power, and reshape the status quo of the American political system." "For what it's worth," the review continued, "the authors point out that the Reagan administration has employed more Mormons than any other administration. And they remind us that the eschatological theme of the annihilation of America and its eventual dependence on the LDS Church is still popular among contemporary Mormons."[85] In reviews like this and elsewhere, evangelicals characterized the LDS Church as pursuing its own political course to obtain ultimate domination. "What is the Coming Theocracy?" an advertisement for an evangelical ministry's informational materials and cassette tape on Mormonism ominously asked.[86] If such prognostications resembled earlier charges against the Catholic Church the similarity was hardly coincidental, for they occurred in the very outlets and from the very leaders that had promoted anti-Catholic accusations in an earlier age. Rather than recognizing shared political convictions and alliances in this moment of the Religious Right's political prominence, evangelical critics depicted the LDS Church as a self-seeking political force outside of the circle of religious conservatives working to redeem the nation.

Evangelical publishing houses exploded with offerings warning about Mormonism in the 1980s, many boasting sinister titles like *The Maze of Mormonism*.[87] This work, by the well-known evangelical author of another popular book, *The Kingdom of the Cults*, suggested the LDS Church's growth rate was owed in part to the failure of Protestant churches, especially the liberal-leaning ones, which had become cold and distant, though this didn't explain why conservative Southern Baptist churches were losing so many members to Mormonism. But no book could compare to the arrival of a little film that would rock the evangelical world.

"*The God Makers*"

On December 31, 1982, four thousand evangelical Christians gathered in Southern California for an unusual New Year's Eve celebration. Assembled in the large worship hall at Grace Community Church, a nondenominational mega-church in the Los Angeles suburb of Sun Valley, the audience watched the premiere of a new movie that would soon electrify evangelicals around the country and attract the worried attention of Mormons and their sympathizers: *The God Makers*.[88] The latest iteration in a long history of anti-Mormon tracts, *The God Makers* had two noteworthy characteristics. One, the film's creators, Ed Decker and Richard Baer, were both former Mormons who had converted to evangelical Christianity. Decker ran a ministry called Saints Alive/Ex-Mormons for Jesus and had devoted his life to helping other Mormons find the evangelical gospel by leaving the LDS Church. Saints Alive held an annual meeting each summer near Temple Square in Salt Lake City where former Mormons would spend several days sharing with each other their testimonies of escaping Mormonism and encountering the real Jesus of evangelical Christianity.[89] But as Sara M. Patterson has pointed out, Saints Alive soon became focused more on educating evangelicals about the threat of Mormonism. *The God Makers* played the largest role in that education.[90] Decker and Baer's status as ex-Mormons lent the production added credibility for its evangelical audiences who trusted the filmmakers as reliable authorities on their former faith. Second, as a movie *The God Makers* stood apart from the dozens, perhaps even hundreds, of anti-Mormon books and pamphlets evangelicals had produced through the years. The movie allowed very large groups of evangelicals to experience together an entertaining dramatization of the threat posed by Mormonism and its unbiblical theology. Often, representatives from anti-Mormon evangelical organizations, such as "cult expert" Walter Martin's Christian Research Institute, led discussion sessions after churches watched the film.[91] Gathered in sanctuaries, worship centers, and church basements, these moviegoers participated in an unprecedented collective education in evangelical anti-Mormonism—an immersive experience that both cemented a particular knowledge, awareness, and attitude of Mormonism for millions of evangelicals in the 1980s and reasserted the exclusive boundaries of authentic Christianity.[92]

The God Makers used its fifty-eight minutes to depict the LDS Church as "one of the most deceptive and most dangerous groups in the entire world," a cult bent on carrying out a subversive plot. "It looks beautiful from the outside," a narrator darkly spoke as a camera soared above the grounds of an LDS temple, "but when you peel off the mask and talk to the victims you uncover another part of the story."[93] An advertisement for the movie claimed the film "peels back the mask of lies to expose today's most respectable yet deceitful and fastest growing cult."[94]

That Mormonism needed to be "peeled back" reflected the evangelical conviction that the LDS Church's pleasing exterior of smiling missionaries, beautiful church buildings, all-American patriotism, and what *The God Makers* called "a carefully-groomed Osmond Family image" had been cleverly constructed for the purpose of covering its dark secrets and cultic practices. In one scene, Decker and Baer consulted with a fictional Los Angeles law firm about the possibility of waging a class action lawsuit against the church because of its ties to the occult and its pattern of destroying lives and families. One of the lawyers, played by an actor, protested, "I find this very hard to believe. I mean, these people pride themselves in a sense of family togetherness and a very conspicuous form of moral rectitude." "That's part of the incredible deception," Decker responded, "and that's what we have to dig into and we need to expose it and open it up to the truth."[95]

As evangelical anti-Mormon literature had done in earlier decades, *The God Makers* presented Mormonism's focus on the family as both a hollow public relations act and as a cultic mechanism of control. Footage of Mormon families singing songs and playing games together were depicted as sinister activities directed by the LDS Church to increase its domination over members. Mormon families spent time together not because they wanted to, the film alleged, but because their church had told them to as a way of insinuating itself into every aspect of their lives. Clean-cut, wholesome families engaged in pagan rituals in Mormon temples, the film charged, and they shunned relatives who turned from the church. Former Mormons provided wrenching testimonials of having their brainwashed families turn against them when they questioned the LDS faith. Another scene dramatically told the story of a teenage Mormon boy who had committed suicide because he didn't feel he could live up to Mormonism's exacting standards of sexual chasteness—a strange example for the film to highlight given evangelicalism's own sexual conservatism—and suggested that many Mormon teenagers killed themselves because of their faith's overwhelming pressures. According to the movie, Mormon women suffered from unusually high rates of depression. Mormons felt incapable of meeting the faith's standard of perfection, unlike Christianity's gospel of grace. "Where is the love?" one former Mormon woman asked about her time in the church.[96] Given the era's political context and how evangelicals and Mormons found themselves aligned on political questions regarding the family, particularly abortion and the ERA, *The God Makers* worked to replace any feelings of cultural sympathy or like-mindedness with a stronger theological conviction of Mormonism's erroneous and dangerous beliefs and evangelicalism's exceptionalism. As the *New Republic* commented in the 1980s, Mormonism "upholds other values cherished by the vast majority of ordinary Americans, which they feel have been seriously threatened in recent years—not least the strength, stability, and attractive numerousness of the characteristic Mormon family."[97] But *The God Makers* disputed that depiction. Rather than admiring and elevating the Mormon family as a model for a wayward nation, the film urged evangelicals to see it for what it was—a corrupt agent of deception for a cultic religion.

Amid the heyday of pro-family politics and evangelical worries of the disintegration of the American family, *The God Makers* presented the Mormon family as a cultic monster that could lure people into its deception and away from the gospel truth. An interview with husband and wife converts to the LDS Church confirmed how easily good Christians could be duped by Mormonism if not properly aware of its errors. The woman, speaking in a thick Southern accent—perhaps a former Southern Baptist, a viewer could wonder—explained that she and her husband "came from very strong Christian families." They had joined the LDS Church because the Mormons who had proselytized them "seemed to be Christian. . . . just kind, good, loving people, family oriented." Other scenes focused on the "tens of thousands of missionaries"—a virtual army—"whose goals are to spread Mormonism around the world."[98] "Why do concerned pastors find this shocking exposé essential viewing for their congregations?" asked an advertisement for the film. "Because 30,000 door-to-door Mormon missionaries lure over half their converts from Christian churches!"[99] Saints Alive literature, often packaged as educational material with *The God Makers* for churches showing the film, promoted this concern. "Mormon missionaries are not going into the poorest regions of India," one pamphlet observed. Instead, they were descending on suburban America, picking off converts, "some 80 percent . . . from the traditional Christian churches." "They are out to gather your people," the materials warned pastors showing the film.[100] Converting Christians to Mormonism depended in part on representing the LDS Church as belonging to mainstream Christianity, the group noted, but Saints Alive and *The God Makers* served to educate evangelicals that Mormonism stood outside of Christianity, only using its elements as a deceitful lure. "Mormons are instructed to use Christian terminology when talking to potential converts," the movie alleged.[101] A Saints Alive newsletter revealed the LDS Church's latest strategy was to "buddy up" with local Protestant churches, garnering Christian authenticity and credibility by doing so with the purpose of yielding converts. "With Mormonism's latest ploy to look, act and talk like Christians," the newsletter asserted, "many more-than-usual unsuspecting souls are being taken in by their ever evolving deception."[102]

While they attributed only sinister motives to it, evangelicals were right that the LDS Church was increasingly asserting its identity as a Christian faith. This represented a break from the church's prior emphasis that often sidestepped the question of whether or not Mormonism was Christian by focusing instead on the faith's distinctiveness and separateness. As both Jan

Shipps and J. B. Haws have shown, beginning in the 1970s and amplifying in the 1980s, LDS leaders, conference talks, publications, and public relations campaigns increasingly showcased Christian terminology and themes while Mormons began to call themselves Christians with growing frequency and ease. This transformation was both cosmetic—replacing the commonly used name of the "Mormon Church" with the official Church of Jesus Christ of Latter-day Saints and a logo that displayed the words "Jesus Christ" in a larger font than the rest of the name—and, notably, theological, giving increasing attention to the example of Jesus Christ over Joseph Smith and the church's living prophets.[103] The church's decision in 1982 to add "Another Testament of Jesus Christ" to the title of the Book of Mormon brought cosmetic and theological changes together. As a church spokesman explained, "We simply want to educate those who think the Mormon church [*sic*] is not Christian, to clarify that Jesus is a central figure in the *Book of Mormon*." Predictably, *Christianity Today* reported on the development disapprovingly.[104] Rather than its historic self-representation as an alternative to Christianity, the LDS Church in the 1970s and 1980s sought to include itself in the pantheon of Christian denominations and minimize its historic outsider status as part of the church's overall strategy for playing a more prominent role in the nation's political and social life. This, of course, did not mean from the church's perspective that Mormonism was interchangeable with Christianity (or, more importantly, vice versa), but it did mark a significant shift in how the church characterized itself while at the same time maintaining its self-image as the one, true Christian church. In light of such developments, *The God Makers* and its anti-Mormon counterparts pushed back at Mormonism as "counterfeit Christianity" fraudulently claiming its place in the lineage of the historic church.

The film also charged the LDS Church truly operated as a multi-billion-dollar "corporate empire," and provided glimpses of Mormon sacred garments and reenactments of the highly secretive temple ritual it described as "reserved for an elite few."[105] Its often-inaccurate explications of Mormon theology included an argument that the faith was linked to the occult and Satanism, a significant departure from previous evangelical arguments about Mormonism. While the film repeated long-standing challenges to the historical evidence of Joseph Smith's claims, *The God Makers* alleged a darker inspiration for the faith than few had dared to voice before. In the early Cold War years, evangelical publications had described Mormonism as a man-made "system," an invented religion that churned on its own lies. But *The God Makers* cast Mormonism in a larger cosmic struggle—or "spiritual warfare" in the parlance of 1980s evangelicalism—claiming Satan had created the

LDS Church as one of his earthly agents.[106] Still, the filmmakers provided just two bizarre pieces of evidence for their grand claims. They pointed out that the Chinese word for "gates of hell" sounded similar to "Mormon," and they showed a satanic bible that used the word "Mormo" to describe a god who was "king of the ghouls."[107] Given the heightened attention to the Devil in the early 1980s (thanks in part to Reagan's frequent mentioning of Armageddon but also to the constant apocalyptic talk in evangelical and fundamentalist circles of Satan's aims to destroy America through secularism, abortion, homosexuality, and feminism), the film's inclusion of the LDS Church among Satan's arsenal brought the urgency of "spiritual warfare" to the center of Mormon-evangelical relations.[108] While some Religious Right leaders might talk of the shared moral concerns of evangelicals and Mormons, the louder message of anti-Mormonism reverberating throughout American evangelicalism at the time revealed that the Religious Right's supposed ecumenism paled in comparison to the heated theological debates occurring within conservative Christianity. The ecumenical political organizing of the 1980s raised challenges to evangelical self-identity as it promoted "Judeo-Christian values" and "traditional Christianity" as a unifying conceit for millions of Americans. *The God Makers*, and the larger anti-Mormon industry of the 1980s, pushed back at this ecumenical lumping by reasserting denominational difference and evangelical distinctiveness. Critical to navigating political alliances and cultural affinities after a committed history of anti-ecumenism, evangelicals used anti-Mormonism to draw the limits of conservative political ecumenism and prioritize religious mission over political objectives.

To augment his popular movie, Decker coauthored a companion book to the film published in 1984 with Dave Hunt, an evangelical writer of several "anti-cult" books.[109] Despite Decker and Baer's prior Mormonism and Hunt's supposed expertise in alternative religions, the film and book were both riddled with errors about the faith and the church's history. But this was no matter to their audiences. Though Decker had claimed that the film's purpose was to "bring Jesus of Calvary to the Mormon people," its audience was primarily evangelical Christians, and the film became an instant hit among them.[110] The film included the accounts of former Mormons who had become evangelical Christians, but these testimonies served to authenticate the unchristian nature of Mormonism to evangelical audiences as much as they offered any proselytizing message to Mormons. Aside from seeking to educate evangelicals about Mormonism, *The God Makers* also clarified and affirmed evangelical beliefs and identity, an important aspect of the film's popularity among evangelical leaders and churches given how many of their members were new Christians converted in the previous decade's flurry of religious revival. The question and answer sessions that generally followed viewings of the film served as a critical component of the evangelical experience of *The God Makers*. Taking place in church sanctuaries and fellowship halls, the post-movie discussions lent the proceedings a worship service feel, often including an altar call for conversion or recommitment to the evangelical faith. Audiences were implored to not only understand Mormonism but to ensure their own salvation. In contrast to the heretical religion they had just watched on the movie screen, evangelical viewers could have assurance of their right standing with the one true God.

At the same time, LDS leaders watched developments within evangelical Christianity closely, dismissing the televangelists and arena-filled worship services for "millions of devout but deluded people," in the words of one LDS official, as fleeting emotional fervor rather than true religious commitment. As *The God Makers* and other evangelistic outreaches to Mormons in the 1980s presented a gospel of free salvation through faith alone, the LDS Church countered that the message required merely a cheap and simple faith that allowed one to "continue to live in our sins." The "delusion and mania that prevails to this day in the great evangelical body of Protestantism," the leading LDS theologian Bruce McConkie told a group of Brigham Young University students in 1984, was a belief in salvation by faith alone. This was the "heresy" at the heart of the great apostasy of the Christian churches. Shunning the temptation of an easy "born again" experience offered by evangelicals, McConkie reminded the Saints that true salvation came only through the LDS Church and a life of righteous living. "Man cannot be saved by grace alone," McConkie concluded, " . . . he must keep the commandments; he must work the works of righteousness; he must work out his salvation."[111]

Originally, *The God Makers* played predominately in Western states with large Mormon populations. One newspaper ad, for example, in the *Sacramento Union* listed showings of *The God Makers* in six area churches during one month alone of spring 1983. The advertisement, clipped by an LDS communications officer in California, provided show times for the film at Sunrise Baptist Church, Hillsdale Baptist Church, and other evangelical and fundamentalist congregations in the Sacramento area.[112] But the film quickly spread through evangelical churches across the country. The Baptist State Convention of North Carolina, for example, circulated the film to its congregations.[113] Several Christian cable stations also broadcast the film. Decker boasted that as many as two hundred thousand people a month viewed the film at its height in the mid-1980s.[114] For evangelicals who missed seeing the film at a church screening, video cassette recordings of the movie passed from one interested viewer to another. A 1986 *New York Times* article about the increasing popularity of VCRs cited as an example the fact that "thousands of people each month" from "Christian fundamentalist churches in the South" could watch and pass along copies of *The God Makers*, "a video that is highly critical" of Mormonism, thanks to the device found in more and more homes.[115]

In November 1983, nearly a year after the film's premiere, the LDS Church responded to *The God Makers*. "In a country which prides itself on religious freedom and religious plurality," the statement read, "fairness and mutual regard should not let that happen. Simple courtesy would dictate a decent respect for that which is sacred to others."[116] A month before, Gordon B. Hinckley, Second Counselor in the church's First Presidency, did not directly name *The God Makers* in his General Conference talk, but deplored those "who have taken it upon themselves as their mission to belittle and demean and destroy the faith of the weak, with a badly flawed argument that we are not Christians."[117] Importantly, Hinckley's talk suggested that Mormons who fell prey to *The God Makers* and other challenges to the faith had a feeble commitment to their beliefs; true Saints would resist and ignore such appeals. Conversely, Saints Alive literature routinely suggested that less committed Christians, particularly those not grounded in proper Biblical understanding and knowledge, were most vulnerable to Mormonism, easily seduced by its faux-Christian pretenses. For both Mormons and evangelicals, *The God Makers* demanded the faithful commit more deeply to knowing their own faith as a guard against the other.

Aside from the November statement, the church tended to avoid engaging *The God Makers* at the national level, perhaps not wanting to draw greater attention to a movie that mostly had found only an evangelical audience. Instead, the church directed local and regional branches to deal with the film as it came up at the community level.[118] In a message to local leaders, the church's First Presidency reasoned the film's controversy might drive further interest in the church rather than rejection. "We have evidence to indicate that in areas where opposition has been particularly intense," the letter explained, "the growth of the Church has actually been hastened rather than retarded."[119] Occasionally in the years ahead, the church would address *The God Makers*, typically using it as an example of the persecution and slander Mormons faced for their faith.[120] As late as 1998, an LDS official highlighted a Norwegian Mormon who had gotten *The God Makers* removed from all Christian bookstores in her country as an example of a righteous Saint other Mormons should emulate.[121]

At the local level, church leaders attacked the film, in large part to equip their members with how to respond should their evangelical neighbors bring it up to them. Robert Starling, a president of the LDS stake in Van Nuys, California, authored a pamphlet, "Errors, Distortions and Untruths in the Movie 'The Godmakers' [*sic*]," and distributed it among fellow church members.[122] *Dialogue*, an unofficial LDS publication, ran a series of articles in 1985 critiquing the film and its errors.[123] And Truman G. Madsen, the BYU professor of "Religious Understanding," traveled to Arizona to work with the interfaith committee organized by the National Conference of Christians and Jews' regional chapter that had protested the showing of *The God Makers* in Mesa.

The seventeen members of the NCCJ's ad hoc committee soon drafted a letter to Concerned Christians, the evangelical organization sponsoring the movie in Arizona. The letter charged, among other things, "the wisdom of mass public meetings which had as their primary intent attacking Mormon beliefs" and warned that the film was a "danger to community harmony." Citing the film's many errors that Madsen had pointed out to them, the NCCJ admonished Concerned Christians to cease their support for a film that used sensationalism, innuendos, and half-truths to depict Mormonism, and they chastised the group for the film's "emphasis that Mormonism is some sort of subversive plot—a danger to the community."[124]

"Mormonism *is* a subversive plot and a danger to the community," Concerned Christians responded in their letter to the NCCJ's comments. "We are not attacking people," the group insisted, "but we are attacking doctrines."[125] Other letters from evangelicals poured into the NCCJ's offices in response to the public campaign against the film they launched in cooperation with the Arizona Ecumenical Council.[126] While the NCCJ advocated tolerance, pluralism, and harmony as the justification for banning *The God Makers*, the movie's evangelical supporters countered that ultimate truth and Christian concern for the unsaved trumped the NCCJ's ecumenical values. "I happen to care about the Mormons too much," a typical letter to the NCCJ contended, "to allow them to go on in their deception. They need to be saved."[127]

Political operatives and Religious Right leaders kept insisting evangelical Christians and Mormons were political allies in the 1980s, but evangelical leaders worried far more about the theological threat Mormonism posed to traditional Christianity than they promoted possible political partnerships. *The God Makers* enacted and disseminated that fear, equipping a generation of evangelicals with an understanding of the LDS Church as a dangerous cult. Above a crowded field of anti-Mormon literature, *The God Makers* emerged as the leading educational and organizational tool for evangelicals against the perceived Mormon menace. While *The God Makers* advanced a theological argument about the exclusive saving nature of the evangelical gospel, its critics responded with largely political objections to the film's attack on Mormons' freedom of conscience and religious liberty. Mainline and liberal Protestants, generally no sympathizers to Mormon political causes, rallied to defend the LDS Church against the movie, objecting to its disrespect for Mormons' religious beliefs and seeing it as an attack on America's tradition of pluralism and its values of tolerance and diversity. In doing so, they believed they were not merely defending Mormonism, but instead living out the values of a liberal democracy. As a leader in the Jewish organization, the Anti-Defamation League, explained, *The God Makers* was "a challenge to the religious liberty of all."[128] Sensitive to their own history of religious persecution, Catholics too joined that cause, protesting the film's inaccuracies and its conspiratorial assertion that the LDS Church intended to take over the nation, something Catholics had heard far too often about their own church. While evangelical political activists were busy in the 1980s asserting their ecumenical political alliance with other conservative Christians fighting against America's liberalization and secularization on the basis of a shared moral code, privately evangelical leaders and theologians drew important distinctions between their political and theological sympathies for their culture war allies. Concerned about the rapid growth of Mormonism and, particularly, its inroads among conservative Christian faiths, evangelical leaders used *The God Makers* to ensure that lay evangelicals understood the LDS Church not as a like-minded political partner, but rather as a dangerous cult peddling a heretical and unbiblical Christianity.

Moral Homogeneity

Jerry Falwell's aspirations extended far beyond the evangelical-fundamentalist corner he had sought to unify in the meeting at Carl Henry's home. In leading his Moral Majority political organization, Falwell routinely promoted its ecumenical nature as a means to justify his position at the forefront of the Religious Right.[129] A brochure published by the organization in 1983 claimed, "Moral Majority is made up of millions of Americans, including ministers, priests and rabbis, who are deeply concerned about the moral decline of our nation."[130] Despite Falwell's claims, the Moral Majority included virtually no religious diversity in its membership. Rather, religious particularism remained at the heart of Moral Majority's organizational development, shaping and influencing the organization itself and the opportunities and possibilities of the Religious Right during the Reagan years.

Overwhelmingly and almost exclusively, the Moral Majority drew its support from evangelical and, especially, fundamentalist Protestants.[131] The vast majority—90 percent by one account—of Moral Majority members were

Baptist, mostly from independent churches and from the Baptist Bible Fellowship, a loose federation of independent fundamentalist Baptist churches that included Falwell's Thomas Road Baptist Church. Among the major denominations, the Southern Baptist Convention had the largest representation in the organization, but they still only accounted for 3 percent of Moral Majority's members.[132] Pentecostals and charismatics, on the other hand, were noticeably absent from the Moral Majority, despite their similar politics. Falwell's consistent theological assault on charismatic and Pentecostal Christianity—he had once famously scoffed that those who spoke in tongues must have eaten too much pizza the night before—was well known. When organizing his roster of prominent pastors to serve as Moral Majority's advisors, Falwell had pointedly omitted Pat Robertson.[133]

Mormons, too, passed on joining the Moral Majority. While Falwell often praised the pro-life activism of the Catholic Church, the public record reveals no similar expressions for the LDS Church, especially surprising given the anti-ERA efforts it had so vigorously engaged. Falwell promised to *Christianity Today* that he would not preach against the beliefs of the Mormon members of Moral Majority, although his interviewer worried about the religious price for such a détente. "I'm concerned that we could get the country morally straight and people would still go to hell," the magazine's reporter responded, echoing a growing concern among many evangelicals that political ambitions could soften evangelical convictions and soul-saving commitments.[134] Other comments from Falwell may not have struck Mormon listeners as exactly positive and discouraged LDS involvement in the Moral Majority. "I would literally fight to the death for the right of a Madalyn O'Hair to say what she believes, for the Mormon church [*sic*] to preach what it preaches," Falwell said in an interview with the *Washington Post* about American pluralism.[135] Equating his willingness to defend Mormon beliefs with those of America's most famous atheist likely only demonstrated how repugnant both were to him. Beyond Falwell, conservative Protestants continually made it clear that they did not want a Mormon-evangelical alliance. After Anson Shupe, a noted sociologist and expert on Mormonism, wrote a column in a Texas newspaper in 1984 suggesting that Mormons and evangelicals, given their vast range of political sympathies, would do well to work together in an organization like the Moral Majority, letters to the editor poured in from conservative Christians declaring the suggestion "preposterous."[136] In an advertisement for its information materials about the LDS Church, Ex-Mormons for Jesus provocatively asked "What is their connection with the Moral Majority?"[137] Although there was little connection in reality, the ad's question suggested evangelicals worried more about the LDS Church's possible involvement with the Religious Right than they saw the church as a political ally.

At the same time, LDS teachings through the 1980s continued to warn against Mormon associations with other groups for fear "we will be required to compromise principles," as one LDS official explained.[138] In a 1985 General Conference talk titled "The Only True Church," Boyd K. Packer, a member of the church's Quorum of the Twelve Apostles, reminded the Saints, "We do not join associations of clergy or councils of churches. We keep our distance from the ecumenical movements. The restored gospel is the means by which Christians must ultimately be united."[139] Importantly, having secured the ERA's defeat by the early 1980s, LDS leaders redirected their church members' energies away from the political arena. President Spencer W. Kimball told the LDS faithful in 1982 that they were now to avoid general political activism as "the result would be to divert the Church from its basic mission of teaching the restored gospel of the Lord to the world."[140] Some evangelical leaders began to worry too about the price political activism was exacting on their missionizing goals, but they seemed unable or unwilling to challenge the political zeal emanating from other evangelical corners.

Though Falwell boasted often of an ecumenical leadership as well, the Moral Majority expressed homogeneity as much among its leaders as its members. Indeed, the uniformity of its leadership likely bore responsibility for the same among the grassroots. A survey of Moral Majority's state chairs (all men) in the early 1980s identified the denominational affiliations of forty-five leaders. All forty-five chairmen worked as pastors for Baptist churches. Twenty-eight of the pastors led churches belonging to the Baptist Bible Fellowship, while the rest ministered to Southern Baptist or independent Baptist congregations.[141] In quickly creating a national organization, Falwell had tapped into the network that he knew best, seeking out pastors of like-minded and often affiliated congregations. If Falwell's publicized vision was ecumenical, his execution was entirely denominational. While such a move meant instant reliability—Falwell knew these leaders, trusted their theological views, and shared their political concerns—it also had organizational consequences. State chairmen recruited their church members; coordinated with similar, if not associated, churches; and forgot to include, and often purposefully ignored, churches and congregants outside the evangelical and, especially, fundamentalist community, generating a mostly homogenous membership. Furthermore, the fact that all of Moral Majority's chairmen were pastors gave the organization an even closer identification with Protestant fundamentalism than would have likely existed had regular laymen and women composed more of its leadership.

Despite this, Falwell's biographer, Dinesh D'Souza, asserted in 1984 that the Moral Majority included a Catholic membership of 30 percent, a number he'd likely gotten from Falwell himself, who had made the same claim about Moral Majority's Catholic rates at Carl Henry's home in 1982.[142] No other study of the organization, however, found numbers anywhere as close, but it was important for Falwell's own political ambitions—and particularly for his prominence in the expansive coalition of the modern conservative movement—to depict his political army as enormous and broad-based as possible. In fact, in many places, like Indiana and Arkansas, the state chapters claimed zero Catholic members, though 8 percent of the members in these two states had once belonged to the Catholic Church before converting to fundamentalist or evangelical Protestantism.[143]

For one, most Catholics would not have supported the broad range of conservative issues that the Moral Majority supported. While Moral Majority's pro-life stance obviously pleased conservative Catholics, the National Right to Life Committee already provided a well-established and comfortably Catholic organization to carry out such work, not to mention the robust pro-life efforts within the Catholic Church. Other Moral Majority concerns, however, such as ardent opposition to the ERA and vigorous defense of free market capitalism and strong national defense, had varying levels of low support among American Catholics. In seeking to establish an ecumenical organization, Falwell had developed a particularly narrow political vision that reflected Southern conservatism more than Judeo-Christian religious traditionalism.

More importantly, however, Catholics refused to join an organization they perceived as ultimately anti-Catholic. Falwell's fiery Southern televangelist persona repelled many Catholics, who had historically feared such characters. And his association with the most ardently and aggressively anti-Catholic strands of Protestantism certainly belied any charitable words Falwell might have had to offer publicly about the Catholic Church. Catholics, noting this history, responded to the Moral Majority in kind. A survey in 1981 found that less than 10 percent of Catholics expressed support for the Moral Majority. Falwell sought to combat these sentiments by inviting priests to appear with him at Moral Majority rallies, particularly in heavily Catholic states, and inserting himself in Catholic-led pro-life events.[144] He routinely praised the Catholic Church's leadership in the anti-abortion movement, once saying, "For years they stood alone and fought the abortion issue. We, the Protestant ministers, were negligent. It is their moment of glory and our moment of shame."[145] But new overtures to Catholics could not erase memories of the long-standing anti-Catholicism among the most conservative branches of American Protestantism.

Memories aside, anti-Catholicism remained alive at the grassroots level of the Moral Majority. When a reporter asked Rev. Daniel Fore, the state chairmen of Moral Majority New York and pastor of Staten Island Baptist Church, how he justified Christian political action when Christians had so violently persecuted others during the Inquisition, he responded, "Oh, those weren't Christians, those were Roman Catholics." Fore soon was forced to resign from his position.[146] (Fore had already drawn negative attention to himself when he declared that Jews controlled the media.)[147] When Falwell visited Ohio, the pastor of Toledo Baptist Church complained of the difficultly in mobilizing a political force in the city. "Toledo is largely Catholic," Ed Holland explained to Falwell and then launched into an attack on the Catholic bishops. Falwell cut off the anti-Catholic diatribe, responding, "I bet I could get a big crowd of Catholics and Jews out here. Hey, those people have a common cause with us on the moral issues."[148]

But what Falwell failed to realize was that these shared moral issues could not erase the historic and persistent prejudices mitigating full ecumenism in the Moral Majority. Also in Ohio, one county coordinator, an evangelical, lamented that fundamentalists drove away other potential members by regularly expressing anti-Catholic sentiments during monthly meetings. At one of the Ohio Moral Majority's state meetings, the proceedings opened with a sermon, "Roman Catholic Church: Harlot of Rome."[149] Meanwhile, Falwell's own ministry continued to fan the flames of fundamentalist anti-Catholicism even if he repudiated such sentiments in public. Around the time that President Reagan began discussing the possibility of establishing full diplomatic relations between the United States and the Vatican, one Alaskan viewer of Falwell's "The Old-Time Gospel Hour" sent the television ministry a long, rambling hate-filled letter about the Catholic Church. Citing nearly two dozen verses from Revelation that he argued clearly pointed to the Catholic Church as the "great whore," the man also predicted that John F. Kennedy would "publicly reappear, amaze the world, take world power" and prove to be "in fact the 'beast' of the Revelation." Perhaps the letter writer had heard Falwell's praise of the Catholic Church's leadership in the abortion fight and worried the minister had lost his way on the matter of Catholicism's errors. "It is very much to your advantage," he closed his letter, "to know how to identify the 'beast' and 'great whore' according to scripture."[150] But a staffer in the Correspondent Department of Falwell's television ministry assured the writer that "The Old-Time Gospel Hour" still knew what Revelation meant. "We believe that the 'great whore' described in the book of Revelation refers to the Roman Catholic Church. . . . However, we do not believe that John F.

Kennedy is alive or that he will be revealed as the Antichrist. Please write again if we may be of service to you," he responded.[151]

These were the associations that made the Moral Majority an unattractive option for conservative Catholics interested in joining a political organization. If Catholics had ignored the various anti-Catholic comments that Moral Majority leaders publicly expressed, if they had overcome their own fears of fundamentalist anti-Catholicism, and if they had found their way to a Moral Majority meeting they had never been recruited to, they would often have faced a situation still unwelcome, and often antagonistic to, their very presence, no matter what Falwell claimed to the national media. In light of this, it was easier to leave the Moral Majority to the evangelicals and fundamentalists. If Catholics wanted to oppose abortion rights, a much more hospitable home awaited them in the right-to-life groups sprung from their own church.

While some Catholic leaders warmly welcomed Falwell and the Moral Majority, still more of them worried about the rise of fundamentalist Christianity and its enhanced visibility at the height of the Religious Right's moment. Aside from many shared political concerns, Catholic leaders worried more about the revived anti-Catholicism that seemed to coexist with fundamentalists' newfound political engagement. Many Catholic leaders interpreted evangelical and fundamentalist political activism with emboldening anti-Catholicism rather than enhancing closer relations with Catholics, as Falwell and other conservative Protestant political operatives claimed. "I think groups like the Moral Majority feel their kind of thinking is 'in' right now," the editor of one diocesan newspaper explained, suggesting that fundamentalists' anti-Catholic bias still surmounted any shared political objectives.[152] In Cincinnati, the Catholic Church published a study guide for its members facing proselytizing pressure from evangelical and fundamentalist colleagues in anti-abortion organizations and other Religious Right groups entitled *Fundamentalism—What Every Catholic Needs to Know*.[153] Written by Anthony Gilles, a Catholic writer who had grown up in the Baptist citadel of Nashville, the book provided Catholics with advice on how to respond to fundamentalists' questions about the Virgin Mary, the papacy, transubstantiation, and Catholic theology regarding salvation. Gilles acknowledged that Catholics and fundamentalists shared many basic doctrines, but fundamentalists, he explained, had gone awry in their "distortion—a hyperextension, one might say—of the fundamentals."[154] Unlike most evangelical books about Catholics, Gilles's work contained no emphasis on or strategy for converting fundamentalists to Catholicism. Instead, it contended that Catholics should seek deeper knowledge and greater confidence in their own faith so they could withstand fundamentalist efforts to sway them from the church. "The ultimate solution to fundamentalism," Gilles wrote near the book's end, "lies not in improving fundamentalists, but in improving ourselves."[155]

Catholics in the pro-life movement had now been given a defense of the faith to use in pushing back against the claims of Protestant fundamentalism that seemed ever-present in their fight to defend the unborn. In San Diego, Catholic officials worked closely with the city's Ecumenical Conference to denounce anti-Catholic literature circulating among Moral Majority and other fundamentalist groups in the area. The group deplored the "insidious, cancerous growth" of anti-Catholicism among San Diego's fundamentalists, and, along with the ecumenical efforts in Arizona against *The God Makers*, suggested that ecumenical work in the 1980s consisted more of defending religious groups against attacks from one another than in bringing churches together into a Christian union.

Conclusion

The Religious Right's most visible leaders, like Jerry Falwell and Phyllis Schlafly, promoted their ecumenism, strategically planning public events that suggested broad cross-denominational ties. Schlafly became the first Catholic to speak from Falwell's pulpit at Thomas Road Baptist Church when she delivered a talk on the ERA, a move that incensed Bob Jones, Jr.[156] Brigham Young University also invited Schlafly to share a similar address with its students—a rare appearance of a Catholic at the Mormon institution.[157] Scholars have pointed to these moments and the coordination of figures like Falwell and Schlafly, who spoke at each other's meetings and shared materials with each other, as proof of the disappearance of religious tensions and animosities as a distinguishing trait of the modern Religious Right political movement. Yet such a view fails to consider the very nature of Religious Right organizations and to understand why these groups represented the persistent sectarianism, rather than ecumenism, of American Christianity. Events like these and others were largely symbolic public relations efforts that obscured the chiefly divided workings of the Religious Right network. These moments gave Religious Right figureheads the opportunity to boast to a credulous press about their interconnected ecumenical movement that had brought together people of faith from various theologies united by shared moral values and political concerns. In truth, that unity existed largely in the imaginative realm where religious conservative activists envisioned a cross-denominational community of God-fearing moral traditionalists and at the ballot boxes where the Republican Party reaped the benefits of an awakened and enraged electorate, ready to vote for candidates based on a handful of social issues. But throughout the Religious Right, real theological disagreements, religious tensions, and historical animosities shaped and influenced the network.

If leaders of Religious Right organizations and some prominent ministers talked publicly of the need to work with others outside of their faith for the good of common political goals, far more separatist and suspicious messages circulated throughout church sermons, religious publications, and evangelistic outreaches. Repeatedly instructed in theologies that maintained their faith possessed exclusive truth, Catholics, Mormons, and evangelicals also routinely encountered each other through the teachings of their own faith communities as heretics, apostates, cultists, and worse. Such prejudices did not bode well for interdenominational efforts, even if some religious leaders publicly condoned and encouraged such work. Wary of each other, Catholics, Mormons, and evangelicals largely chose to stick to denominationally based or theologically specific political organizations, rather than come together in ecumenical groups that brought them too closely in contact with one another. As the scholars Anson Shupe and John Heinerman have argued, "one does not maintain an ongoing working relationship with a religious ally while simultaneously denouncing him as a 'cult.'"[158] As evangelicals, Catholics, and Mormons launched new theological critiques and new proselytizing efforts at each other in the years ahead, they also tore at the thin fabric of their political unity. And as disagreements broke out within different wings of the Religious Right about questions of politics, the unity of the Religious Right and its ability to achieve their ambitious political goals became just another wishful prayer.

7

The Promised Land?

"REAGAN WINS!" EXCLAIMED the headlines across the media outlets of the Religious Right in 1980. It was hard to show humility—or patience—after such a huge election they had helped bring about, but religious conservatives quickly learned their agenda wouldn't be the first priority of the Reagan White House. Instead, the White House explained Reagan first had to address the nation's poor economy and tackle the tax burden. But once the president's tax package passed, it became clear the Reagan administration would give little attention to the conservative moral issues the Religious Right had expected the new president to address. The journalist Lou Cannon, working on a biography of Reagan during his first administration, asked a presidential adviser what the White House planned to give the Religious Right. "Symbolism," the staffer responded. Pointing to the blockbuster film, *The Godfather*, the adviser explained the Reagan White House intended to follow the mafia don's philosophy, "Hold your friends close, hold your enemies closer." He elaborated, "We want to keep the Moral Majority types so close to us they can't move their arms."[1] The *Washington Post* quoted a more high-ranking Reagan staffer, Deputy Chief of Staff Michael Deaver, who said the only way any Religious Right leaders could enter the White House would be through "the back door."[2]

Another journalist covering the Reagan White House, Sidney Blumenthal, found the president's team practiced a tacit "containment strategy" whereby key Senate leaders and White House staffers were encouraged to meet regularly with Religious Right operatives to discuss pressing concerns so to give the appearance that work was being done on the issues without actually delivering on them in any substantive way. This would keep the Religious Right happy—or at least, distractedly busy—while not eliciting the concern of Reagan's larger, more secular support. Small gestures could be extended, like proposing a bill on a tiny aspect of a larger social concern or delivering a speech to a key Religious Right organization, but less effort would be done to see that such a bill—let alone one with more political substance—would pass or that a speech's promises would actually be carried out. Morton Blackwell, a presidential assistant, was responsible for looking after the Religious Right constituency and given the charge to keep them, as Blumenthal explains, "in a state of perpetual mobilization." "The flaw in that strategy," Blumenthal notes, "was that the White House served as an incubator for the movement it was trying to contain."[3] Of course, with Religious Right operatives, Blackwell presented a different explanation of the White House's strategy. In a letter to a Moral Majority leader, Blackwell explained that the White House would approach the Religious Right's agenda through a tactic of "incrementalism." "The fact is that it works," Blackwell contended. "It is unrealistic to expect to undo fifty years of bad increments in one year or even in one presidential term. . . . A foolish belief in the possibility of total, instant victory is a prescription for unrealistic hopes and early disillusionment at the grassroots."[4]

The first disappointment the president's evangelical supporters admitted concerned the administration's lack of a sizeable evangelical presence, particularly since Reagan had made campaign promises that he would staff evangelicals within his administration in proportion to their representation in the American public.[5] The idea that some 40 percent of the Reagan administration would be made up of evangelicals was preposterous, of course, but the paltry numbers of evangelicals who actually made it into the administration must have seemed even more ridiculous to those watching closely. Two scholars later counted only four evangelicals among Reagan's thirty-one cabinet appointees, with Secretary of the Interior James Watt being the only evangelical appointed in Reagan's first cabinet.[6] Reagan did appoint Moral Majority executive director Robert Billings as his assistant secretary of education for non-public schools, but he was soon removed from the position because of protests from Catholic educators worried about a fundamentalist Protestant having so much power over the federal government's relationship with parochial schools.[7] While more evangelicals were scattered throughout the lower ranks of the White House and administration, it was no presence of note. But this hardly tempered evangelical expectations. One frustrated evangelical in the White House attracted controversy when she told a reporter Reagan's close advisers should either "get saved or get out."[8]

Evangelicals' next disappointment came when Reagan nominated Sandra Day O'Connor to the Supreme Court in his first year in office. In running for the presidency, Reagan had courted key Religious Right operatives by vowing to nominate only committed pro-life jurists to the nation's highest court. His winning of the National Right to Life Committee's endorsement, in fact, had been secured in two private meetings with NRLC president Carolyn Gerster where he had promised her just that. O'Connor, then, was a startling choice. Pro-lifers dug up O'Connor's voting records from her time as an Arizona state legislator and found a worrisome history of pro-choice votes.[9] Reagan's "shocking intention," in the words of a Christian Action Council fundraising letter, to nominate O'Connor seemed an especially insulting move to pro-life activists, and anti-abortion newspapers and magazines decried the president's move.[10] At the White House, fifty leaders from various Religious Right organizations complained to Morton Blackwell of their growing sense that, given his actions, the president didn't "think this coalition contributed significantly to his election."[11]

Internally, the Religious Right faced challenges of its own making. Importantly, for all the talk of an ecumenical movement on behalf of conservative social issues, the Religious Right operated largely along denominational lines in its dealings with the Reagan White House. At the leadership ranks, Religious Right organizations sometimes coordinated with each other, but more often worked alone or in partnership, especially evangelical and fundamentalist groups, with like-minded believers. This had been the case in the run-up to the 1980 election, but divided operations in a campaign season seemed the most logical way to mobilize diverse constituencies. The conviction among conservative Catholics, Mormons, and evangelicals that Ronald Reagan was the man they needed in the White House to deliver on their goals had united their divided efforts. Once Reagan assumed the presidency, these disparate strands of conservative Christianity would come together as the bloc representing traditionalism and religious values—a moral majority, one might describe it—to make sure the president turned the nation back to God and delivered on their agenda.

While there were moments of cooperation and common cause within the Religious Right during the Reagan years, far more often the various components of the network worked in isolation, opening up divisions even within shared issues and working in direct opposition on other issues they had never really discussed. The Religious Right foundered at what could have been its best moment, riven by theological disagreements that yielded political consequences and often divided by different political objectives reflecting their unique theological convictions. What emerged during the Reagan years was at best a loose coalition of religious conservatives, frequently fraught with dissension, disagreement, and the possibility of dispersion. For a White House that hesitated over aligning itself too closely with what often appeared a radioactive Religious Right, the divisions within the network proved a useful scapegoat. Rather than working to smooth over disagreements and broker compromises, Reagan officials largely sat back and allowed the infighting and disunity to continue, then pointed to the chaos as a way to avoid the responsibility of leadership or to explain away disappointing legislative setbacks. On the Religious Right's two major objectives for the Reagan presidency—school prayer and abortion—the network's fractured nature helped doom policy objectives that had always been a formidable prospect. And on other issues of national concern, including welfare reform and the nuclear arms race, evangelicals, Catholics, and Mormons took differing positions that demonstrated their political divergence and challenged the notion of a conservative ecumenism.

Abortion and the Reagan Administration

The White House quickly frustrated pro-life activists. Since *Roe v. Wade*, pro-life activists had worked to pass a right-to-life amendment to the Constitution. Two bills in the Senate in 1981 addressed this goal, one directly. The Hatch Amendment, a constitutional amendment proposed by the conservative Mormon and Utah Republican Senator Orrin Hatch, gave Congress and individual states the right to pass their own abortion laws. Hatch's backers liked his amendment because they saw it as a good route to a quick victory at the state level and believed it could survive any court challenges. Others appreciated it as a defense of federalism and a reproach to what they believed was *Roe*'s overreaching power. But the amendment's biggest drawback made it unworkable. Even Senator Hatch admitted his amendment could never receive the needed two-thirds support from Congress.

Jesse Helms, the arch-conservative Southern Baptist Republican Senator from North Carolina, offered an alternative to the Hatch Amendment. Helms's bill sidestepped the issue of congressional support by offering a statute rather than a constitutional amendment. The Human Life Bill, as Helms's proposal became known, also directly addressed the important philosophical point that Hatch's amendment had ignored by declaring life began at conception, thus equating abortion to murder. "This measure," the Christian Action Council declared, "is centered upon the very principles that have drawn us together as a movement."[12] Helms's bill also prohibited any federal dollars going to abortion and sought to avoid legal challenges by asserting that courts had no jurisdiction over the matter of abortion.

Faced with two options, the pro-life community divided over which to support. As *Congressional Quarterly* pointed out, "translating the general rhetoric about abortion into stark legislative language" exposed the divisions in a movement that seemed united when the issue at hand merely involved voicing opposition to the horror of abortion.[13] Evangelical groups and New Right leaders supported the Helms bill. Several major Catholic anti-abortion groups, like the National Pro-Life Political Action Committee led by Father Charles Fiore, backed the Hatch bill.[14] The National Right to Life Committee, after pressure from the National Conference of Catholic Bishops (NCCB), threw its support to the Hatch Amendment. The NCCB had testified before Congress in support of the Hatch Amendment, declaring it an "achievable solution to the present situation of abortion on demand."[15] But many Catholics, including some inside the NRLC, criticized the bishops for choosing political expediency over principle and noted that their endorsement of the Hatch Amendment departed from their prior insistence on a constitutional amendment guaranteeing full personhood to the unborn child. This turnaround, one conservative Catholic publication noted, "lacks any proper moral foundation, and indeed exists in a metaphysical and moral vacuum."[16]

But the bishops continued on with their efforts. As they had before, the bishops pushed the church to give its full support to the Hatch Amendment, directing priests in various archdioceses across the country to deliver messages supporting the Hatch Amendment at Mass and to ask parishioners to sign petitions in support of the amendment.[17]

Even those supportive of the bishops' move recognized its play for power.[18] The Catholic Church had created the pro-life movement and its most important organization in the National Right to Life Committee. Yet by 1981, evangelical anti-abortion organizations had begun to eclipse the Catholic Church's hold on the movement, especially after the political victories they had helped secure for pro-life candidates in the 1980 election. Those evangelical organizations had been largely courted by the New Right that, apart from the abortion issue, supported political positions in contradiction to many of the Catholic Church's concerns. Supporting the Hatch Amendment, then, when the majority of the pro-life community and the New Right supported Helms's bill, allowed the Catholic Church and its affiliate organizations to stand outside the anti-abortion consensus and New Right coalition and reassert its independence. In pressuring the NRLC to support the Hatch Amendment while evangelical groups backed the Helms bill, the Catholic Church also revived the theological divisions in the pro-life movement.

"Protestants are dismayed by the United States Catholic Conference approval of the Hatch amendment," the executive director of the evangelical Christian Action Council stated after the bishops testified before Congress on behalf of the Hatch Amendment.[19] Even Phyllis Schlafly displayed her greater allegiance to the New Right political agenda than the spiritual directives of her own church when she urged her *Eagle Forum Newsletter* readers to support the Helms bill, noting, "Catholics are not bound by any political statements made by a Bishops conference."[20] And the news media jumped on the chance to cover the widening divisions in the pro-life community.[21] "Political reality has come home to the prolife movement," one prominent activist commented, "and it has been totally unpleasant."[22] The division, of course, only doomed both bills, allowing Reagan to remain above the fray. Falwell said in the summer of 1982 that though he retained "personal confidence" in Reagan's commitment to ending abortion, he was also "a little anxious that we haven't had some aggressive support."[23]

For quite some time, Reagan refused to endorse either bill, insisting instead that the pro-life movement agree on which bill they wanted to get behind.[24] Recognizing the Helms bill had vociferous support from the evangelical pro-life wing, the National Right to Life Committee and other pro-Hatch organizations finally announced their support for the Helms bill as a vote approached, but they intended to continue supporting the Hatch Amendment also.[25] Still, pro-life forces expressed ongoing frustration with the paltry efforts the White House expended on either bill.[26] Reagan eventually decided to back each bill as it came up for a vote, a move calculated in part to keep all the factions of the pro-life movement happy but also a strategy that ultimately communicated the White House's indifference to either measure.[27] Reagan endorsed the Helms bill that came up first and lobbied for its passage at the last minute, but he did little to bring about consensus on the measure from the Religious Right.[28] Now up for a vote in the Senate before the close of the 1982 congressional session, the Helms bill had been altered to also include language restoring school prayer. It failed to pass the Senate.

After the Hatch bill also failed early in 1983, pro-life activists fell into infighting, convinced the Helms-Hatch battle had weakened the effectiveness of a pro-life movement and distrustful they could ever act as a truly united force. Many shared *Christianity Today*'s fear that the president had hesitated to "endorse any particular initiative because prolife groups failed to patch up their intramural differences."[29] Bickering inside the pro-life community reflected the tensions of a movement struggling to remain relevant. Polls showed an increasing numbers of Americans supported abortion rights, and the threat of a human life amendment had boosted the pro-choice movement. The National Abortion Rights Action League, for instance, reported membership grew by over 50 percent in just one year since the 1980 election, though its 125,000 members still paled in comparison to the millions who belonged to the NRLC and other pro-life groups.[30] But the pro-life movement's size provided room for the many disagreements that would challenge its success.

"Jerry Falwell couldn't spell abortion five years ago," Paul Brown took to saying.[31] Brown and his wife, Judie, had been high-ranking officers in the National Right to Life Committee, but exited the NRLC in the late 1970s to form their own American Life League (ALL) when they grew disgruntled over various decisions by the NRLC's board, including the removal of Mildred Jefferson from the presidency.[32] The Browns, though deeply Catholic, had attempted to use ALL to engage Protestant fundamentalists in the pro-life cause. But Brown's comments represented growing Catholic frustration with the results of fundamentalist and evangelical Protestants' increasing presence in the right-to-life movement in the 1980s. Though anti-abortion organizations remained largely denominationally divided, some crossover occurred in the groups. Catholic pro-life activists especially voiced discomfort over frequent proselytization of them by evangelicals who joined largely Catholic anti-abortion organizations.[33] Such gestures, of course, only heightened the divisions within the pro-life community and challenged its ecumenical aspirations. "We are a movement in disarray," commented Brown.[34]

School Prayer

The twentieth anniversary of the Supreme Court's school prayer decision provided an opportunity for religious conservatives to renew their demand for a voluntary school prayer amendment. Ed McAteer of the Religious Roundtable declared, "The issue of PRAYER is the issue of liberty. LIBERTY from our physical, as well as our spiritual selves." McAteer, like many other religious conservatives, believed that the removal of prayer from public classrooms had hastened other disasters. "When in 1962," McAteer wrote, "the courts of our land declared God UNWELCOME IN OUR CLASSROOMS, the stage was set for the ushering in of that dark and infamous day commonly called Roe vs. Wade but more correctly termed the day of the SLAUGHTER OF THE INNOCENTS. There is UNMISTAKENLY a direct connection between the two."[35] Vonette Bright, the wife of Campus Crusade for Christ's founder Bill Bright, claimed "venereal disease, abortion, alcoholism, teen-age pregnancies, delinquency and drugs . . . are directly traceable to the removal of prayer from the public schools."[36] Reagan, at least publicly, agreed that the Supreme Court's decisions had yielded disastrous social consequences and possibly foretold the nation's eventual decline. Speaking to a group of California high school students, Reagan explained the "collapse of great civilizations, like the Greek and Roman" came about when "they began to desert and abandon their gods."[37]

One million letters, mobilized by Religious Right organizations, flooded the White House in the spring of 1982 urging Reagan to push for a prayer amendment.[38] Reagan had declared May 6 a National Day of Prayer, and Gary Bauer, a presidential assistant, suggested using a planned Rose Garden ceremony to announce the president's support for a constitutional amendment. Bauer noted the ceremony "will be one of the most publicized religious events of the year. The 'ripple' effect could be tremendous. For example, under the auspices of Religious Heritage of America, there are already 1,000,000 women meeting each week around the country in small prayer groups. This is not a small, fly-by-night undertaking."[39]

Bauer had convinced the White House. Reagan staffers drew up lists of organizations "expected to be supportive" of a school prayer amendment and dabbled with possible language, but doing so revealed the numerous challenges in crafting an amendment that would both satisfy the legal requirements and the American public.[40] Instead, the White House eventually decided, as a Reagan staffer explained, to develop a statement for the ceremony "embracing the Amendment in concept . . . yet avoid[ing] the numerous problems to which a premature proposal of exact language might give rise."[41]

"No one will ever convince me that a moment of voluntary prayer will harm a child or threaten a school or state," Reagan told the crowd of more than 150 clergy, Moral Majority leaders, and congresspersons assembled in the Rose Garden as he announced his endorsement of a school prayer amendment. Following the president's speech, Jerry Falwell told those gathered, "after 20 years of the expulsion of almighty God from the public schools of our nation, I think this is the light at the end of the tunnel that we have all hoped and worked and prayed for."[42] A handout of questions and answers provided by the White House to the press covering the event explained the amendment would forbid required participation by any student in a school prayer and would respect the diverse religious traditions of the nation. Yet it also noted, "The Lord's Prayer and the Ten Commandments are reflections of our Judaeo-Christian heritage that could not fairly be described as instruments for the imposition of narrow sectarian dogmas on school children."[43]

Less than two weeks later, Reagan proposed the language his administration had hammered out for the amendment. It read: "Nothing in this Constitution shall be construed to prohibit individual or group prayer in public schools or other public institutions. No person shall be required by the United States or by any state to participate in prayer."[44] As the *New York Times* noted, the proposed language displeased many school prayer supporters by providing "something less than the 'affirmative right to prayer' that some of the most militant conservatives advocated."[45]

The Catholic Church indicated it might support the president's amendment if it included an important change. In a letter to the White House, the

United States Catholic Conference explained it would stand by its 1973 statement supporting a school prayer amendment only if it included means to permit religious instruction in the schools—a position opposed vehemently by most evangelicals.[46] Writing in the *National Catholic Reporter*, the liberal Jesuit priest Robert F. Drinan warned that if Catholics supported the amendment "they would stir up the interdenominational tensions and conflicts already present as the result of official Catholic support of pro-life constitutional action and tax credits for private and church-related schools. There is, however, no clear Catholic tradition or teaching on prayer in public schools as there is on abortion and the role of parents in the operation of Catholic schools." "Predictably," Father Drinan almost scoffed, "evangelicals and fundamentalists" would give the most support to the prayer amendment.[47]

After the Rose Garden ceremony, various mainline Protestant churches and groups along with several Jewish organizations voiced their disagreement. But perhaps no objection received more attention from the media than that from the Baptists. Rev. James Dunn, executive director of the Baptist Joint Committee on Public Affairs, declared after the president's speech, "It is despicable demagoguery for the president to play petty politics with prayer. He knows that the Supreme Court had never banned prayer in the public schools. It can't. Real prayer is always free. . . . What the court has done is protect religious liberty."[48] One man wrote the *Washington Post*: "If my good Southern Baptist upbringing taught me anything, it is that the prayer God hears is the cry from the individual human heart, and any prayer concocted by a committee presided over by a government bureaucrat couldn't get through the schoolhouse roof. The prayer amendment is bad business, even if the liberals don't like it."[49] But these were the voices of moderate Baptists, a dying breed in the Southern Baptist Convention (SBC) after fundamentalists took leadership of the denomination in 1979. In opposing school prayer legislation, moderate Baptists represented the faith's historic defense of the separation of church and state, but conservative Southern Baptists believed secular humanism posed a far greater danger, particularly its insidious reach into the nation's public classrooms.[50]

A month later, conservative Baptists showed their strength when messengers to the SBC's annual convention voted to support a school prayer constitutional amendment by a 3 to 1 margin.[51] Just two years earlier moderates had won one of their last victories when the Convention passed a resolution opposing any efforts "to circumvent the Supreme Court's decision forbidding government authored or sponsored religious exercises in public schools," but by 1982, the fundamentalist takeover demonstrated politics now trumped denominational tradition.[52] One Texas pastor indicated that the composition of school prayer's opponents may have influenced the Baptist reversal. "The atheists, humanists and secularists are against prayer in schools," Rev. Morris Chapman explained, "and that's not the company we need to be keeping."[53] School prayer and other issues suggested the opportunity for new alliances, most notably between evangelicals and Catholics. But other actions often undercut that possibility. As the SBC passed resolutions supporting the teaching of scientific creationism and opposing abortion rights at the 1982 meeting, the Convention also passed a resolution opposing tuition tax credits legislation, one of the Catholic Church's most important issues, expressing its "concern over such legislation's threat to the First Amendment guarantees of non-establishment of religion and the free exercise of religion."[54]

Gary Bauer was thrilled with the SBC's reversal on school prayer, noting in a White House memo that the support of nearly 14 million Southern Baptists "could be a major factor in the eventual passage of the proposal."[55] Adrian Rogers, pastor of the influential Bellevue Baptist in Memphis, assured the White House that Baptists who spoke out against the SBC's resolution were "poor losers." "Believe me . . . ," Rogers closed his letter, "the rank and file of Southern Baptists are solidly behind the Prayer Amendment proposed by the President."[56]

Winning Southern Baptist support for school prayer may have led the Reagan administration to adopt a strategy increasingly focused on and directed by evangelicals. If the White House had ever hoped to use an ecumenical coalition to restore school prayer, their efforts fell far short. For one, the White House gave no attention to the Catholic Church's request the bill authorize religious instruction in the schools, likely realizing the proposal would bring strong evangelical rebellion. Also, an invitation list for a July 1982 strategy meeting is indicative. Twenty-one names appear on the list; only two did not come from an evangelical church or organization. One professor from the Jewish Theological Seminary and a representative from the Knights of Columbus stood out among luminaries of the evangelical-fundamentalist world: Pat Robertson, Adrian Rogers, Jim Bakker, James Robison, and Tim LaHaye. Evangelical organizations like Christian Voice, Religious Roundtable, Moral Majority, and the National Association of Evangelicals rounded out the list.[57]

Whether the White House created the list or received it from a pro-school prayer organization remains unknown, but Reagan administration records reveal evangelical leaders and organizations almost entirely orchestrated the White House's school prayer campaign. Though many evangelical activists had spoken during the 1980 campaign of their plans to work with others in a broad coalition of like-minded religious conservatives and though many continued making such claims to the media throughout the Reagan years, once Reagan assumed the presidency the records indicate evangelicals operated almost exclusively without the Catholic and Mormon allies they had claimed. When Bob Dugan of the NAE compiled his annual report to the organization's executive board in 1983, he noted, "We are drawing together the beginnings of an evangelical coalition in Washington. . . . Never has there been a more opportune time for evangelical influence in Washington, D.C."[58] Granted, the NAE had never entertained any pretense of ecumenism beyond evangelical circles. Indeed, it had consistently spoken against watering down the evangelical message by associating with any other form of Christianity. But Dugan's comment reflected the prevailing sentiment among evangelicals who had found their way to the center of political power during the Reagan years and marveled at the unique opportunity the moment provided them. Emboldened by their unprecedented access to the White House and the size of their force, not to mention shaped by their theology of exclusive truth and influenced by the heightened sense of religious competition from their churches, evangelicals almost always worked alone to accomplish political goals during the Reagan years.

The fundamentalist Christian Voice emerged as the most forceful pro-prayer group lobbying the White House. The California group had only existed for a few years, and it had a reputation for antagonizing potential allies. In fighting for school prayer, however, Christian Voice appeared to have abandoned some of its exclusivist militancy in creating Project Prayer, a coalition of school prayer amendment supporting organizations. Still, Project Prayer's ecumenism was minimal. Despite the more than fifty groups represented on its letterhead, Project Prayer included only a small handful of Catholic organizations. And when Gary Jarmin, the executive director of both Christian Voice and Project Prayer, proposed a meeting with White House officials at a critical moment in 1983 his list of suggested attendees included only evangelical figures.[59]

The year 1983 proved challenging for the supporters of school prayer as their hopes met the challenges of the political process. In March, Reagan sent his proposed constitutional amendment to Congress. Another amendment from Senator Orrin Hatch proposed a silent prayer amendment, infuriating evangelical activists. Many worried that Hatch's bill would bring together a moderate coalition of senators who did not want to be on record for voting against school prayer and those who were willing to support any type of constitutionally protected prayer. But as Dick Dingman, legislative director of the Moral Majority, explained: "We haven't fought all these years for the right to remain silent."[60] Pat Robertson informed the White

House he would use his hugely popular Christian Broadcasting Network to oppose the silent prayer amendment.[61]

Evangelical supporters became more infuriated when they realized the White House—so inattentive to its own amendment's life in Congress—was unaware of Hatch's alternative proposal. Gary Jarmin repeatedly reminded the White House he had been the one to alert them of the competing amendment and pushed the White House to tweak its own language. The Moral Majority and other organizations backed the president's language, but Christian Voice now wanted additional protections. In a series of memos to the White House, Christian Voice demanded that additional language to the president's amendment ensure that only "nondenominational" or "nonsectarian" prayer be allowed. While this request might have seemed especially pluralist, its explanation revealed the hard reality of religious intolerance that school prayer could expose and evoked memories of the same concerns that doomed a school prayer amendment in the 1960s. "Jewish parents . . . may be very supportive of their child reciting a prayer," Christian Voice explained, "but could be offended if the prayer was the Lord's Prayer or concluded with 'in Jesus' name, Amen'. Likewise, Protestants would object if the prayer offered was Mormon or Catholic."[62]

Christian Voice argued local communities would best determine the appropriate prayer for their classrooms, but this would mean the local religious majority would likely put in place the sectarian prayers Christian Voice ostensibly hoped to guard against. Yet their move showed political savvy, hoping to bypass the potential divisions at the national level under the guise of ecumenism while realizing that ecumenical spirit would likely break apart at the local level. The White House, however, refused to add "nondenominational" to its amendment despite Christian Voice's predicting "a bloody internal split amongst our forces" should their proposals not be adopted.[63] While Christian Voice had been a powerful force in the 1980 election, especially in Western states, the Moral Majority had played a much larger role in mobilizing millions of new voters to turn out for Reagan, and it enjoyed far greater access to the White House. Now the Moral Majority was backing the president's amendment and had launched an enormous campaign in key states to stir up support for Reagan's proposal.[64] Given that, the particular demand from Christian Voice found no charity from the White House. "We had expected you to become part of the large coalition committed to fighting off all attempted changes," Blackwell wrote Christian Voice's Jarmin. "You are, of course, free to chart an independent course."[65]

Christian Voice fared better with its request that language be added barring the government from writing the prescribed prayer, as such a demand found increasing support throughout 1983. The SBC, perhaps realizing the consequences of its historic reversal the previous year to supporting school prayer, pulled back on its endorsement. James Draper, Jr., the SBC's president, wrote President Reagan that he was a strong proponent of voluntary school prayer. "We are a theistic country," he explained. But he wrote to Reagan to voice his concerns with the proposed amendment and to "urgently request that distinct language be employed by the proposed amendment" banning any state authority from determining the prayer's content. "If such changes are made," Draper wrote, "I would strongly support it."[66] Nearly a year earlier, *Christianity Today* had made the same point and provided its own revised version of Reagan's amendment.[67]

At first, the White House resisted adding such language, arguing that it would make "it possible for government to become more intrusive rather than less intrusive in matters relating to prayer" by possibly threatening to prevent chaplains in the military or Senate or even a school teacher—all government workers—from leading prayers.[68] But with the pressure from Christian Voice and the tenuous support from, as Draper reminded the White House, "14 million Southern Baptists," the Reagan administration reconsidered its amendment. "It is clear that many in the protestant [*sic*] community who support voluntary prayer are concerned with the idea of 'state written' prayers," Morton Blackwell wrote Grover Rees, the University of Texas law professor who helped draft the president's amendment. "We may not be able to get together a broad enough coalition, therefore, to pass the President's amendment."[69] By summer's end the Reagan administration had acceded to the language, adding to the amendment: "Nor shall the U.S or any State compose the words of any prayer to be said in public schools."

But once the Reagan administration sent its new language to Congress, it failed to give much effort pushing the bill through Congress. *Christianity Today* observed Reagan had "expended very little political capital on the prayer issue. . . . There was no evidence of congressional jawboning by the President that often accompanies priority legislation."[70] Reagan had begun the year outlining four education goals in his State of the Union address: increasing math and science block grants to the states, establishing education savings accounts, passing tuition tax credits, and securing a constitutional amendment permitting voluntary school prayer. "God never should have been expelled from America's classrooms," he told Congress.[71] But the absence of strong presidential leadership on his amendment allowed congressional backers of school prayer to remain splintered among their choices which now included an additional proposal from Senate Majority Leader Howard Baker.[72] The *New York Times* noted in the school prayer battle a familiar trend for social issues: "Conservatives have not been able to agree on a proposal, and as in the recent Senate debate over abortion, the fragmentation has damaged their effectiveness."[73] Though school prayer lacked the rancor that the roiling fight over banning abortion was creating at the same moment, the inability to unite behind a bill exposed the ease with which factions could emerge within the Religious Right once the abstract fight against secularism in public life gave way to the pesky mechanics of political change. The school prayer amendment battle also did not show the level of interdenominational hostility that helped destroy the movement for a human life amendment during the Reagan years. Indeed, much of the division within the school prayer coalition fell along the evangelical-fundamentalist line within conservative Protestantism as potential Catholic allies of school prayer were largely ignored and Mormons remained uninvolved. But it did make clearer the tenuous unity of the Religious Right coalition.

As the school prayer amendments moved into 1984, debate on the floor of Congress alternated between heated and humorous. After Republican Representative Marjorie Holt justified her support for school prayer by declaring, "This is a Christian nation," Barney Frank, who had chaired an all-hours debate at the request of the House leadership, quipped, "If this is a Christian nation, how come some poor Jew has to get up at 5:30 in the morning to preside over the House of Representatives?"[74] No answer came for Frank, of course, but Holt's hopes too were dashed when no school prayer amendment gained sufficient support for passage.

Four years had passed since Reagan's momentous election, and little of the Religious Right's agenda had been accomplished. A new bill in the Senate, however, would please many religious conservatives. The Equal Access Bill guaranteed public school students the right to meet on campus for religious purposes. Jerry Falwell quickly endorsed the bill. "This is the ultimate in freedom of choice," Falwell explained, "and could be better than the prayer amendment."[75] Later passed overwhelmingly by the House and Senate, the equal access provision seemed to take much of the impetus away from the push for a school prayer amendment during Reagan's second administration and beyond.[76]

The Year of the Bible

As his bid for reelection approached, Reagan backed a plan to honor the Bible in American public life. At a meeting of the National Religious Broadcasters, Reagan announced he would sign a presidential proclamation making 1983 the "Year of the Bible." In doing so, he argued the Bible held the solution for all the nation's challenges, even the federal budget. "We might come close to balancing the budget if all of us lived up to the Ten Commandments and the Golden Rule," Reagan told the audience. At the National Prayer Breakfast a few days later, Reagan signed the proclamation and agreed to serve as the Year of the Bible's honorary chairman. At the prayer breakfast, Reagan implored that "we resolve to read, learn, and try to heed, the greatest message ever written—God's word in the Holy Bible. Inside its pages lie all the answers to all the problems man has ever known."[77]

Bill Bright had been the mastermind behind a national Year of the Bible. Bright had spoken with Reagan about the idea shortly after his inauguration. Now that the reelection campaign was nearing and Reagan's campaign team sensed the need to reconnect with conservative religious voters, they jumped on Bright's suggestion and encouraged him to head up the preparations.[78] Near the end of 1982, Bright organized the executive committee. Since the Year of the Bible had governmental backing, it needed to be an ecumenical affair, so one of Bright's first objectives was to select Protestant, Catholic, and Jewish vice-chairmen.[79] In his invitation letters to these men, Bright explained the Committee for the Year of the Bible held two goals: to encourage Americans to read the Bible regularly and "to call to the attention of the American public the role of the Bible in the nation's heritage."[80]

Dr. Thomas Zimmerman, the executive director of the Assemblies of God who had once coordinated his denomination's efforts with other evangelicals against Kennedy's bid for the White House in 1960, now found himself joining the ecumenical effort to honor the Bible. He accepted the Protestant vice-chairmanship. Cardinal John Krol of the Archdiocese of Philadelphia agreed to be the Roman Catholic representative, and, after several Jewish candidates turned down the invitation, Dr. Gershon Cohen, chancellor of the Jewish Theological Seminary of America, accepted the role. (No consideration for a Mormon representative appears in any records for the Year of the Bible.) "It is . . . ," Bright wrote to Zimmerman about Cohen, "a somewhat complicated and sensitive matter from his perspective because of the quite different meaning that Judaism and Christianity attach to the term, 'Bible.'" But as Bright explained to each of the vice-chairmen, their job was to put aside potentially divisive issues of biblical interpretation and theology and find common ground in their "unequivocal faith in the God of the Bible and reverence for the Scriptures themselves as His unique and inspired written Word to mankind." "Primary emphasis," Bright wrote, "will be given to those areas of belief that we hold in common."[81]

In addition to the three vice-chairmen, Bright invited several dozen members of the three faiths to serve on the national advisory board. Still, evangelicals dominated the more than sixty-member committee, including Carl Henry; televangelists Jim Bakker and Pat Robertson; Adrian Rogers; and James Draper.[82] While most invitees accepted the honor, John MacArthur, the fundamentalist pastor of Grace Community Church in California, rejected Bright's invitation with a withering rebuke of its ecumenical aims. Grace Community was the church where *The God Makers* would premiere later that year, and its pastor had a long history of interlacing anti-Catholic diatribes in his sermons. "Frankly, I am shocked at such an obvious acquiescence to unbelief," MacArthur wrote Bright. "To have Roman Catholics who give tradition equal weight with Scripture (this adding to the Bible) and to have Jews who believe only in the Old Testament (which is taking away from the Bible) clearly violates Revelation 22:18, 19. By making it appear to all the nation that these groups affirm the glory of the Word of God without addition or deletion is ludicrous." MacArthur objected to compromising biblical truth for political advantage and scolded Bright for associating with nonbelievers. God did not need such couplings, MacArthur wrote. "He will do His Holy work . . . without unholy alliances. It is inconceivable that we could link such elements as you suggest and hope to glorify the Word of God! . . . The inerrancy of the Bible demands that such an effort as yours be thwarted, and I would be more willing to work on a committee to stop it." Instead, MacArthur informed Bright that he would be speaking out against the Year of the Bible to other pastors and religious leaders, and he enclosed with his letter a recent policy statement his church had adopted that promised to "refuse to associate with non-Christian groups in any defense of 'religious freedom' because to be associated in any way with false religionists will render our message or ministry misunderstood by the lost world."[83]

Those who joined the national board, however, believed the project's great strength came from its unifying mission for Judeo-Christian Americans. The purpose statement for the Year of the Bible's media committee committed "to demonstrate to a splintered society . . . that we all share a fundamental hope: that we will find meaning . . . in the Bible's timeless message." At a national committee meeting in the summer of 1983, Cardinal Krol emphasized the need for believers to unite against the forces of disbelief. "We are witnessing, regrettably, a drift towards human secularism," Krol told the group, "and the problems that face us arise less from our religious differences than from religious indifference." The nation's problems, Krol explained, resulted from "a drift away from the Bible and the principle of the Bible from our Judeo-Christian tradition. . . . we need jointly to be concerned about bringing the Word of God before the people helping and inspiring them to live according to it."[84]

Not surprisingly, the Year of the Bible faced some challenges. The ACLU filed a suit to overturn the government's declaration of 1983 as the Year of the Bible, arguing it violated the First Amendment.[85] A group of fundamentalist Californians, including Tim and Beverly LaHaye, a handful of pastors, and a representative from the group Californians for Biblical Morality, banded together to serve as the defendants in the case filed with a Los Angeles federal district court. Recognizing their own insularity would pose a challenge for countering the ACLU's claim that the Year of the Bible represented an establishment of religion, the group's lawyer advised they should bring in "the wide cross-section" of religious faiths from the Year of the Bible's committee to demonstrate it reflected no one particular faith.[86] Before the ecumenical defense team could be assembled, though, a federal district judge dismissed the suit.[87]

As 1983 drew to a close, the Year of the Bible's planners celebrated its successes. Millions of pieces of scripture had been distributed to American homes; more than six million pieces of publicity material had blanketed the nation in the form of bumper stickers, posters, bulletins, advertisements, billboards, and TV and radio spots proclaiming 1983's biblical status. The Year's organizers had no doubt that the heightened attention on Holy Scripture had produced far-ranging benefits for the nation, including the national crime rate's first decline since 1977 and the greatest increase in productivity for one quarter reported by the Department of Labor since 1975.[88] Bill Bright had no intention of letting this momentum abate, but he hoped that as the official government-backed period drew to an end, evangelicals might redirect the Year of the Bible from a celebration of the nation's Judeo-Christian heritage into an evangelistic outreach to win unsaved Americans to the gospel.[89] As a *Christianity Today* headline had lamented at the start of the decade, the Bible in America was "Highly Revered but Seldom Read." Evangelicals hoped to build from the Year of the Bible's momentum.[90] Now fully privatized with nearly $20 million in funding from the DeMoss Foundation, a frequent backer of evangelical causes, the Year of the Bible Foundation dropped its Catholic and Jewish committee members and assembled an entirely evangelical Board of Directors.[91] At its first meeting, the reconfigured board amended the Year of the Bible's purpose statement to include language about its "evangelical outreach through all available media opportunities," reflecting its new proselytizing mission.[92] Conceived as an interdenominational effort to restore the Bible's place in American public life, the Year of the Bible ultimately returned to its evangelical origins. Though evangelical members of the Religious Right spoke often of the nation's Judeo-Christian heritage and the shared moral values of their ecumenical community, events like the Year of the Bible revealed the particularity of evangelicalism's larger agenda for the nation. The Year of the Bible's ecumenical makeup had been necessary as a government-backed initiative that also facilitated a president's reelection efforts. Having cooperated with that purpose—and benefiting from a year of enormous publicity—evangelicals now reclaimed the ecumenical Year of the Bible and redirected it toward their own purposes.

Diplomatic Relations with the Vatican

In the run-up to the 1984 reelection campaign, the Reagan White House again enthusiastically courted the religious conservatives who had aided Reagan's first victory, with focused targeting of the evangelical, Mormon, and Catholic communities.[93] Catholic Democrats had been an important Reagan constituency in 1980, and the reelection team worked to win them again.[94] But the White House feared backlash from Southern evangelicals for publicly courting Catholic voters. The "best way to disguise this maneuver," Morton Blackwell recommended, was to stress moral issues rather than making direct overtures to Catholics.[95] To that end, the campaign committee ran ads in various Catholic publications that showed Reagan meeting with Pope John Paul II and listed the president's support for issues like anti-pornography laws, school prayer, tuition tax credits—a particularly important issue for many Catholics—and the "rights of the unborn." Almost a dozen Catholic newspapers, however, refused to run the ads, believing they exploited the pontiff for political purposes.[96] Reagan also spoke frequently to Catholic audiences during the campaign, always referring to the pope as "one of the greatest moral leaders of our time."[97]

More controversially, Reagan restored full diplomatic relations with the Vatican for the first time in a century—a move Carter had considered but abandoned when evangelicals erupted over the idea.[98] Reagan's decision also drew ire from across the religious spectrum, from the liberal National Council of Churches to the arch-fundamentalist Bob Jones, Jr., who sent a scathing four-page letter to the president, warning his decision would "bring a curse upon our nation and make us, as a nation, the servant of Antichrist."[99] "A bad precedent is being set," Jerry Falwell said after the White House ignored his private recommendation to drop the plan to appoint an ambassador. "I wonder when Mecca will want one. I told the White House if they give one to the Pope, I may ask for one."[100] The SBC, always leading opponents of any public benefits for the Catholic Church, passed a resolution against the ambassadorship at its annual meeting that summer, deploring the move for showing "favoritism to Roman Catholicism by the United States of America."[101] The

National Association of Evangelicals organized its denominational leaders and key state activists to pressure their senators to vote against the appropriation of funds for an ambassador to the Vatican, testified twice before Congress in opposition to the appointment, and conducted a spirited campaign in its magazine *Insight* to rally evangelicals against the decision.[102] The NAE also besieged the White House with letters of opposition, citing NAE's history of resolutions against such a move and reminding Reagan's team that opposing President Truman's attempts to appoint an ambassador to the Vatican in 1951 had been what "drew NAE into the public affairs arena for the first time."[103]

Those evangelicals who opposed diplomatic relations with the Vatican clarified their position had no basis in anti-Catholicism, but instead simply reflected their abiding commitment to the First Amendment. *Christianity Today* passed on even this objection, however, contending that "on constitutional grounds the case against recognizing the Vatican and appointing a US ambassador is not very strong."[104] Despite the magazine's long history of critiquing Catholicism, *Christianity Today* had become one of Pope John Paul II's strongest voices of evangelical support since his papal election in 1978. "His excessive references to Mary notwithstanding," magazine editors wrote early in his reign, "the evidence indicates that Pope John Paul II is Christ-centered in his thinking." They routinely praised the pope for his dedicated anti-Communism and his conservative positions on abortion, homosexuality, the family, and other moral issues.[105] Though *Christianity Today* and its evangelical cohorts maintained their theological objections to the Catholic Church, admiration for Pope John Paul II himself, if certainly not for his papal status, represented a significant development in evangelical-Catholic relations. Even as groups like the NAE and the Baptist Joint Committee on Public Affairs testified before Congress against the Vatican ambassadorship, they paused to express appreciation for the pope. "Evangelicals join in applauding Pope John Paul II," the NAE's Forest Montgomery told Congress, "for his tireless efforts on behalf of human rights, in the ideological struggle between East and West."[106]

But evangelical admiration for President Reagan, even more than respect for the pope, tempered their reactions to his decision on the Vatican. Combined with his other actions, Carter's Vatican attempt had just given more proof to evangelicals that he was working in opposition to most of their political goals, but Reagan's commitment to a broad evangelical agenda softened their response to his decision. On CBS's "Face the Nation," Falwell said the decision "is not going to end my support of President Reagan."[107] "For most evangelicals it's a disappointment," conceded the NAE's Bob Dugan. "But other issues such as traditional values, national defense, and the economy will loom much more importantly" for evangelicals in the upcoming election, he explained.[108] Some felt Reagan was the only president who could have pulled off the controversial move. "There is general agreement," *Christianity Today* editorialized, "that the right President chose the right time to change a situation that had remained unresolved and uncomfortable for more than a century."[109] In the end, evangelical objections to Reagan's appointment operated more as almost ritualistic expressions of long-held convictions than real sustained efforts of political activism. Evangelicals had gone through the motions to revive their historical protests, but their hearts were no longer really in it. The possibility of a Catholic theocracy overtaking the nation now hardly seemed imaginable, and perhaps it would even be preferable to the secular humanist state many evangelicals believed now ruled over them.

Even among Catholics, the decision to restore diplomatic relations with the Vatican found mixed reactions. The U.S. Conference of Catholic Bishops expressed official support for the move, but behind the scenes many bishops opposed the decision. The American bishops had become a thorn in Reagan's side, loudly criticizing the president's policies on nuclear weapons, Central America, and the economy. Some bishops worried Reagan would use diplomatic relations with the Holy See to bypass the bishops and get the more conservative Vatican to restrain the bishops' criticisms.[110] The *National Catholic Reporter* approvingly quoted a representative from the Americans United for the Separation of Church and State who said that "many Catholics—who tend not to agree with Reagan administration foreign policy objectives—'would be concerned about the administration doing increased lobbying at the highest levels of the Vatican'."[111] The Jesuit magazine *America* suspected the decision had been made for purely political reasons and worried that diplomatic relations could mean the U.S. government would try to influence the church's internal matters. *America* recommended Reagan appoint a non-Catholic as ambassador, though the White House had already named the Catholic William Wilson as their nominee.[112] The *National Catholic Reporter* also sensed diplomatic relations really only benefited the president. "All in all, and especially in an election year, it is a good deal for President Reagan," the magazine remarked.[113] But even Catholic voters seemed unmoved by the decision. One Reagan staffer disappointedly remarked, "I must admit, I am surprised that there has not been a stronger outpouring of support."[114]

While restoring diplomatic relations with the Vatican looked to garner little enthusiasm from Catholic voters, the White House worried its campaign work with anti-Catholic fundamentalist leaders like Tim LaHaye, who had publicly called Catholicism a "false religion," could yield disastrous results. Catholics bristled too when they learned that the televangelist Jimmy Swaggart, who frequently used his television show to voice outrageous anti-Catholic attacks, had attended a White House strategy session on the school prayer amendment.[115] Letters flooded the White House from angry Catholics in response to the Swaggart connection. Father Gommar DePauw from Long Island wrote to let the president know that although conservative Catholics like him were "on most points one hundred percent supporters of your administration, an uneasiness is growing as the result of finding our national leaders' names apparently inseparably linked with . . . hate-filled anti-Catholic bigots a la Jimmy Swaggart."[116] Though Reagan and his team never publicly denounced any of Swaggart's anti-Catholic comments, the president did tell a Catholic newspaper that there was "no room in our party for religious intolerance or bigotry of any kind, and I repudiate anyone claiming to be a supporter of mine who engages in that."[117]

The Economy, Welfare, and Capitalism

Reagan's admiration for religious Americans seemed especially strong toward Latter-day Saints. Reagan had invited the Mormon Tabernacle Choir, a group he had christened as "America's Choir," to perform at his inauguration, where they sang "The Battle Hymn of the Republic" atop a parade float.[118] "If there is an America that embodies the vision that Ronald Reagan has for his country," the *New York Times* observed, "—a nation of pious, striving, self-reliant and politically conservative 'traditional' families where men work hard at their jobs and women work hard in the home raising their children—it is in Mormon country."[119] The feeling was mutual. Mormons provided a solid voting bloc for Reagan in Western states in 1980. The administration staffed its ranks with dozens of Latter-day Saints in appreciation. Reagan's first secretary of education was the Mormon Terrel H. Bell.[120] One Mormon in the administration confessed, "The LDS church has disproportionate representation under Reagan."[121]

A 1982 trip to Utah allowed Reagan to extoll the Mormon Welfare Plan, a program started by the church during the Great Depression to care for its poorest members. The LDS welfare system embodied Reagan's vision of a nation where private initiative replaced government bureaucracies, and it was well-known among conservatives who credited the church with Utah's lower welfare expenditures. Just a few years before Reagan's visit, the John Birch Society had praised the LDS system for teaching self-reliance. "Self-reliant people take care of themselves and their responsibilities," the right-wing group's magazine enthused. "They are proud and independent, not weaklings and whiners."[122] Reagan made more politic comments as he toured the church's Welfare Services Center in Ogden, with LDS President Gordon B. Hinckley and other church officials, watching volunteers and the church's welfare recipients canning tomatoes together. "This is one of the great examples in America today of what we've been talking about—about what the people could do for themselves if they hadn't been dragooned into believing that government was the only answer," Reagan beamed. "If more people had had this idea back when the Great Depression hit," he continued, "there wouldn't be any government welfare today or need for it." Reagan mentioned his own Private Initiatives Task Force included three Mormons, including Thomas S. Monson, vice chairman of the LDS Church Welfare Executive Committee, and former governor George W. Romney, who were helping his administration develop similar ideas for "ways in which the private sector, the people themselves, can meet some of these problems."[123]

The LDS Church used Reagan's Utah visit and his frequent praise of the church often in its publications and General Conference talks, a presidential endorsement that legitimated the church's national prominence and right-standing with conservative principles.[124] In touting its own welfare program, the LDS Church emphasized the virtue and effectiveness of voluntary charitable efforts over state-administered entitlements. Though the LDS Church was careful to not attack socialism too stridently—LDS Saints in Europe had complained when they felt some church leaders had too casually equated Communism and socialism—church leaders praised free market capitalism and urged the Saints to study closely the Book of Mormon "to expose and combat the falsehood in socialism."[125] The church's welfare program, LDS leaders argued, enacted the divine plan for assisting the indigent. "When we depart from the Lord's way in caring for the poor, chaos comes," one church leader admonished, reflecting a common view among many religious conservatives.[126] Despite all the sinister interpretations evangelicals had made of nearly every aspect of the LDS Church, including its tight-knit families, evangelicals generally respected and admired the Mormon Welfare Plan, perhaps suggesting in evangelical evaluations that the only thing worse than being trapped in the "Mormon maze" was to be caught in a life of government dependence.[127]

Although Religious Right operatives had complained that the president had focused first on economic issues, including passing his tax package, above social priorities like abortion and school prayer, conservative evangelicals still supported Reagan's economic agenda. Abortion, sex education, the Equal Rights Amendment, and other so-called social matters had energized evangelicals and their observers, but tax reform, deregulation, reductions in government spending, and an unrestrained defense of free market capitalism had also been central to their conservative message. For Religious Right leaders like Jerry Falwell, defending the family and the free market enterprise was an interlinked project.[128]

Outside of the political arena, evangelical pastors and publications promoted American-style capitalism and attacked the welfare state. Capitalism wasn't perfect, of course; no human-made system could be. But of all economic systems, the free market, these evangelicals argued, best reflected the biblical principles of self-reliance, diligence, work, and thrift compared to its alternatives, like socialism.[129] Evangelicals tended to blame humans' sinful heart, rather than capitalism, for materialism, corruption, and wasteful excess; they also rejected Ayn Rand's "virtue of selfishness" defense of capitalism.[130] George Gilder, an evangelical economist, delivered a robust defense of capitalism in his 1981 book *Wealth and Poverty* that found enthusiastic audiences among conservative evangelicals and Reagan administration supply-siders alike. The book's best endorsement came from the president himself who purchased several copies for friends, describing it as a "brilliant book" and "an inspiration and guide for the new administration." White House insiders began referring to it as the "bible" of the Reagan administration, a perfect fusion of the president's fiscal and religious conservatism.[131] As president, Reagan quoted no living author more than George Gilder.[132]

Gilder's opus included a chapter entitled "The Necessity of Faith" which contended capitalism could not exist without religion, preferably Christianity. Capitalism succeeded only to the extent that it reflected religious principles, including giving to others, Gilder argued, meaning that one found financial reward by giving consumers a good product at a fair price.[133] As Gilder told *Christianity Today*, "'Give and you'll be given unto' is the fundamental principle of the Christian life" and the basis of capitalist success.[134]

Gilder's great contribution both inside evangelical circles and the Reagan White House was to shift the conversation of capitalism from one of economic theory to moral ethics and theology. Because the capitalist system and governmental economic policies were ethical matters, evangelicals argued, pastors needed to be equipped to provide a biblical answer to pressing questions about capitalism, poverty, and welfare. "If the church is to be the church," the influential Reformed theologian R. C. Sproul implored, "we must press on in the debate for a thoroughgoing biblical understanding of our economic responsibilities."[135] The danger, many worried, was that a proper Christian concern for the poor could lead some to support unchristian economic policies. "What is the catalyst turning traditionally conservative and moderate Christians toward the Left?" *Christianity Today* asked.[136] Among a small but growing evangelical Left, leaders like Ron Sider, author of *Rich Christians in an Age of Hunger: A Biblical Study* (1977), and Jim Wallis of *Sojourners* magazine championed liberal economic policies to alleviate poverty.[137] Conservative evangelicals hoped to stifle the trend. "Clearly, both cannot be correct," one evangelical writer commented on the conservative-liberal economic divide in 1980s evangelicalism.[138] For conservative evangelicals at places like *Christianity Today*, Gilder provided the definitive corrective.

Christians ought to worry about poverty, Gilder acknowledged, but they shouldn't support government programs of redistribution and entitlements for three main reasons. For one, Christians were called to relieve poverty through their own voluntary charitable donations rather than by mandated taxes. Second, Gilder argued, government bureaucracy could never efficiently administer welfare relief as well as private initiatives would nor would it effectively move people from lives of dependency to self-sufficiency. Lastly, welfare reflected a spiritual crisis in the nation, rather than an economic one. Evangelical leaders especially gravitated to this last argument for it reflected their religious conviction that all of the world's problems stemmed from humans' broken relationship with God. "Their fundamental problem is spiritual," Gilder said of the poor.[139] This meant that poverty needed to be tackled with evangelizing efforts rather than government handouts. Salvation promised both an eternal reward and a spur to righteous and productive living on this earth, but government assistance drove Americans further away from God, Gilder contended. "There's . . . something about this dependence on the state that tends to erode religious belief," he argued. "People begin to orient themselves toward belief in and dependence on the state. The state can become God."[140] Aside from the government, Gilder's critique included those churches who assumed "anything that's done in the name of helping the poor is holy" and who told the poor that "the source of their difficulties lies in some conspiracy by others and in the conditions of the society rather than in their own relationship to God."[141] Gilder's economic theory thus perfectly combined 1980s individualism with evangelical theology, an intoxicating brew for his devotees, both religious and secular. For evangelicals, Gilder's condemnation of liberal churches' economic philosophy assuaged whatever guilt they may have had about backing a laissez-faire message compared to liberal churches' interventionism that struck many as more "Christian." "We're causing poverty by paying for it," Gilder countered.[142] Evangelicals had long ceded social and economic activism to the liberal churches, justifying their inaction by the prioritization of evangelism, but now a noted economist confirmed that these churches had not only abandoned their proselytizing duty but also helped worsen poverty. More importantly, Gilder's economic theory affirmed evangelicals' analysis that liberal Christianity missed the basic spiritual truth that all the problems every person faced, from economic uncertainty to eternal salvation, required confronting and finding forgiveness for sin through a personal relationship with Jesus Christ.

Conservative evangelicals found themselves on the other side of the economic arguments made by the Catholic bishops. Not long after Reagan took office, the U.S. Catholic Conference, concerned by unemployment rates and the president's economic policies, began drafting a bishops' letter on the economy. Three years in the making, the 120-page draft, "Pastoral Letter on Catholic Social Teaching and the U.S. Economy," was released by the bishops shortly after Reagan's reelection so as not to appear overly partisan, despite its sharp criticism of the president's economic agenda. A White House spokesman said Reagan "welcome[d]" the draft, but inside the administration Reagan staffers had braced for a stinging rebuke.[143] In presenting the document, Milwaukee's Archbishop Rembert G. Weakland, chair of the drafting committee, explained the bishops found "it a disgrace that 35 million Americans live below the poverty level and millions more hover just above it."[144] As the document added, "We live in one of the most affluent cultures in history where many of the values of an increasingly materialistic society stand in direct conflict with the gospel vision."[145] Such evaluations revealed the bishops' understanding of capitalism as an economic system that unfairly rewarded the few at the expense of the working poor, a noted contrast from evangelical understandings of capitalism as a fair system of work whose failings owed to humans' sinful heart rather than a capricious invisible hand.

The bishops' letter advocated stronger governmental intervention in the economy through an expanded public sector and private sector subsidies to reduce unemployment, an enhancement of welfare programs for the poor, a reduction of military spending, and federal policies that addressed the "broader social and institutional factors" shaping American poverty. The bishops made clear they were not advocating "absolute equality" in income and wealth distribution, but they argued "gross inequalities are morally unjustifiable, particularly when millions lack even the basic necessities of life. In our judgment, the distribution of income and wealth in the United States is so inequitable that it violates the minimum standard of distributive justice." The bishops' demand that "economic justice" be evaluated by how the lives of the poor were improved rather than how the middle class and wealthy fared fell largely on death ears in the White House, but enraged conservative evangelicals.[146] Jerry Falwell dismissed the bishops' plan as "socialism" to an audience of evangelical pastors.[147] *Christianity Today* highlighted the critiques of Ronald Nash, an evangelical economist in the mold of George Gilder, who warned the bishops' proposals would damage the economy and increase the welfare state rather than alleviate poverty.[148] Evangelical responses to the "Pastoral Letter" moved beyond an economic critique to a broader theological evaluation of the Catholic Church, once again characterizing Catholicism as a works-based faith seeking social justice rather than offering a message of *sola fide* salvation that confronted the problem of individual sin. "How to be free of poverty and oppression is, indeed, good news," one evangelical theologian wrote, "but it is not the gospel." Remarkably, given the enthusiasm they had shown for the bishops' leadership in fighting abortion, these same evangelicals warned "the bishops run the danger of politicizing and thus compromising their spiritual message and universal ministry" for their involvement in the American economy, as well as by getting involved in another issue that put them at odds with both the Reagan administration and conservative evangelicals: the nuclear arms race.[149]

National Defense, the Soviet Union, and Nuclear Armaments

As relations with the Soviet Union deteriorated in the early 1980s and the Reagan administration turned up its hawkish rhetoric, Americans feared nuclear war was imminent. Inside the Catholic Church, many leading bishops worried about nuclear proliferation and the threat to global peace they saw in Reagan's foreign policies and military buildup. In response, the bishops released their pastoral letter "The Challenge of Peace: God's Promise and Our Response" in 1983, a document one historian has called "the era's most influential challenge to American nuclear policy."[150] The letter outlined the church's position on war, deterrence, and the arms race in the nuclear age, contending it was "morally unjustifiable to initiate nuclear war in any form." The bishops unequivocally backed a nuclear freeze, calling for the "halt" to the "testing, production, and deployment of new nuclear weapons systems."[151] A prior draft of the document had changed "halt" to "curb," but the final version restored the "halt" language to make the letter's support for a nuclear freeze clearer and firmer.[152]

The Reagan administration had greeted the "curb" draft as more aligned with its policies, but the final version made clear the distance between the bishops and the president when it came to nuclear arms.[153] Having been unable to influence the document, the administration turned to discrediting it, helped by a small group of conservative Catholic laymen called the American Catholic Committee who opposed the bishops' nuclear policies, but the

White House couldn't overcome the power the bishops had in using church teachings to shape Catholic opinion.[154] Passed by the bishops by a vote of 238 to 9, the pastoral letter soon found strong support among lay Catholics, especially the church's most devout members.[155] At least one scholar has argued that "The Challenge of Peace" may have influenced Reagan's shift to his Strategic Defense Initiative (SDI) away from the strategic offensive doctrine of mutually assured destruction the bishops had found immoral.[156]

Apart from any effect the bishops had on Reagan's arms policies, "The Challenge of Peace" broadened the Catholic Church's political concerns in the 1980s, complicating its relationship with evangelicals and the Religious Right. As *Newsweek* had commented during the drafting phase, approval of the pastoral letter "will make opposition to nuclear war as central to the bishops' social agenda as opposition to abortion."[157] In distributing "The Challenge of Peace" along with anti-abortion materials to its diocese and churches, the Catholic Church championed a "consistent ethic of life" that defended the sanctity of life by opposing all its threats: abortion, the death penalty, euthanasia, and nuclear arms. Chicago's Archbishop Joseph Bernardin, the consistent ethic of life's originator, explained the bishops' views on nuclear arms had been shaped by their years fighting abortion, revealing to them the "direct parallel between the protection of human life in the womb and the preservation of human life in the face of the nuclear threat."[158] Some Catholic leaders acknowledged the bishops' abortion and nuclear arms positions would likely confound political observers, but they saw the church as providing a cohesive defense of life. "On right to life you called us right-wing," one bishop in California commented, "and I am sure on this [nuclear arms] you will call us left-wing. We like to see ourselves as thoroughly consistent in both instances."[159]

Though less vexing than the Catholic bishops, the LDS Church raised an unexpected roadblock to the Reagan administration's national defense agenda. In 1981, the Pentagon proposed placing an MX missile system of 210 missile-carrying nuclear warheads in a network of shelters stretching from Utah's Great Basin Desert into Nevada.[160] Since the 1950s, the LDS Church had consistently and frequently denounced Communism and the Soviet Union's military aggression as a threat to peace and religious freedom, but this did not mean the church advocated an unrestrained hawkish defense strategy. LDS President Spencer W. Kimball doomed the MX project when he issued a statement declaring the church's opposition to the missile system's deployment in Utah and Nevada.[161] Some critics accused the LDS Church of opposing the missile system only out of self-interest. Kimball's statement had worried about the environmental impact and burdens on an already meager desert water supply the project would bring along with an influx of thousands of new workers to the area; there was also concern that a concentrated missile supply would make the region a prime target in a nuclear attack. Calling it "ironic" to place a missile system where the church sought "to carry the gospel of peace to the peoples of the earth," Kimball insisted his "feelings would be the same about concentration in any part of the nation." More importantly, in objecting to the MX missile system, the church reiterated its "warnings against the terrifying arms race in which the nations of the earth are presently engaged. We deplore in particular the buildup of vast arsenals of nuclear weaponry." Instead, the church urged national leaders to find "viable alternatives" to nuclear buildup.[162] Separately, LDS leaders used the church's 1980 Christmas message and 1981 Easter address to both deplore the arms race and urge world leaders to use negotiation rather than "the unrestricted buildups of arsenals of war, including huge and threatening nuclear weaponry."[163] The liberal magazine *The Nation*, not usually an admirer of LDS politics, observed, "the left has created nothing to compare with the concentrated force of the Mormon opposition to the MX and to the American acceleration of the arms race."[164]

As they had done with the Equal Rights Amendment, the First Presidency characterized the MX missile issue as a "moral question," justifying the church's involvement.[165] The state's LDS governor, Scott M. Matheson, applauded the church's interpretation of the MX system as a moral concern: "I think it will sway public opinion more into the realm of opposition than was previously the case." Dr. Samuel Davis, the church's regional bishop for Las Vegas, echoed Matheson's comment on the connection between prophetic pronouncements and public following. "When you have a significant decision to make," Davis explained to the *New York Times*, "first you turn to the Lord with prayer and second you turn to his prophet on earth for direction and guidance. I hope the statement of the prophet will have an effect on our thinking and our plan." Davis' hopes, and those of Matheson and of church leaders, were realized as the *Deseret News* noted "MX opposition soars" among Mormons just weeks after Kimball issued his statement, a significant shift since most Utahns had indicated support for the missile program before the church announced its opposition.[166] Given that response, Reagan nixed the MX project. Many Mormons, including Utah's Senator Orrin Hatch, believed Reagan had changed his mind out of respect for the LDS Church, though the president more likely wanted to avoid the larger public fallout from an unpopular program.[167]

Conservative evangelicals generally supported the MX missile system and Reagan's other defense proposals, though some who worried about nuclear proliferation found inspiring leadership in Mark Hatfield, the evangelical Republican senator from Oregon who sponsored nuclear freeze legislation, opposed the MX missile, and advocated for reductions in military spending.[168] Still, there was probably no issue that generated more diverse responses among evangelicals in the 1980s than the question of nuclear armaments and war. While Jerry Falwell and those on the far right advocated unbridled support for Reagan's defense proposals and military budgets, other evangelicals worried about the administration's militaristic strategy for dealing with the Soviets and the possibility of an unrestrained arms race.[169] Unlike abortion, which had become an uncompromising measure of orthodoxy for evangelicals by the 1980s, the issue of nuclear armaments and national defense remained an open question in evangelical circles. In the National Association of Evangelicals, the memberships of pacifist faith traditions like the Mennonites meant the organization avoided lobbying on defense issues and instead showcased the diverse views within its organization. The March-April 1983 issue of the NAE magazine, *Action*, gave almost all of its pages to peace issues and the nuclear freeze, publishing articles that ranged across the spectrum from pacifism to just-war theory. (A year before, however, the organization had passed a resolution calling on national leaders to "rededicate their efforts to obtain a meaningful arms control agreement that will scale down the nuclear arms race.")[170] In the SBC, a series of resolutions passed at the annual meetings from 1980 to 1983 denounced Soviet aggression and supported the president's "commitment to a strong national defense" while also calling for mutually verifiable nuclear disarmament.[171]

The pages of *Christianity Today* included various positions on national defense and nuclear arms, not unlike the range of views on abortion that had appeared briefly in the magazine before *Roe v. Wade*.[172] Still, the magazine, particularly in its editorials, leaned in a measured but conservative direction, reflecting the general evangelical support evangelicals offered Reagan's arms strategy. The magazine rejected pacifism as an option, despite its respect for the evangelical "peace" churches, citing two basic Christian convictions as support: the sinful depravity of humans and the biblical obligation to protect others, especially the weak and defenseless. Pacifism, the magazine argued, ignored the biblical fact of evil's existence that throughout history and in the present example of the Soviets had taken military form. "In a wicked world we must at times use force," *Christianity Today* reasoned.[173] Yet despite the threat of Soviet Communism, which the magazine and other religious conservatives had attacked since mid-century, *Christianity Today* advocated the United States negotiate with the Soviet Union to seek an immediate freeze on nuclear weapons and a plan for future reductions along with a promise from the U.S. government that it would never use nuclear arms against the Russian territories.[174]

From a distance, it may have been hard to spot much space between the Catholic bishops' arms race position and the views of most evangelicals, especially as reflected in *Christianity Today*. Evangelicals appreciated the bishops' emphasis on Jesus' message of peace, and those at *Christianity Today* at least offered alternatives to the arms race that looked remarkably similar to the proposals found in "The Challenge of Peace." Yet the theological assumptions undergirding the bishops' positions were what troubled evangelicals and generated responses that often made it look like they were political antagonists around the question of national defense and nuclear armaments. This may have also been why President Reagan chose the National Association of Evangelicals' 1983 convention in Orlando for his "evil empire" address where he delivered a blistering attack against nuclear freeze, characterizing the arms race as a "struggle between right and wrong and good and evil." Privately, White House staffers acknowledged they had chosen the evangelical meeting in part as a rebuke to the Catholic bishops' criticisms, but the administration may not have been prepared for the mixed reactions that greeted the president in Orlando; the evangelicals gathered there refused to pass a resolution on nuclear freeze because of the divides amongst them.[175] Meanwhile, Falwell rallied the Moral Majority to support the anti-freeze position and held a "Peace Through Strength" rally on the Capitol grounds while Reagan delivered his speech in Orlando.[176]

As they had with their critique of the bishops' poverty agenda, evangelicals attacked the bishops' pastoral letter on peace for ignoring the biblical truth of humans' utter depravity. "At root," *Christianity Today* editorialized, "the good bishops have forgotten the doctrine of original sin, the inherent bent toward evil that plagues our race."[177] Tellingly, evangelicals had never quibbled with Catholic logic for opposing abortion even when it diverged from evangelical theology nor had they used it as a tool for critiquing the church, but they hammered away at Catholic teachings on poverty and peace in the 1980s because they did not consider these issues fundamental to Christian belief and identity. Instead, they provided evangelicals with yet another opportunity for their more important mission of advocating their particular message of salvation and biblical authority that often depended on contrasting it to the claims and convictions of Catholic theology. "The bishops need to go back to the drawing boards and do their homework—based on the realities of the human situation," *Christianity Today* argued. For evangelicals, the Bible clearly revealed human reality as the result of man's rebellion from God. As long as the Catholic bishops avoided this spiritual truth in their proselytizing and their politics, all of the problems of the world—abortion, poverty, and the threat of nuclear annihilation—would remain the challenge to peace that only a saving faith in Jesus could provide.

Conclusion

Despite the significant support conservative religious voters had shown Reagan, Religious Right activists demanded better attention on their issues, chiefly abortion, in Reagan's second term if the Republican Party hoped to retain their activism. "If those concerns of the coalition, particularly on abortion, are met with symbolic gestures alone," the Christian Action Council warned, "the diverse movement that brought him to power will dissolve. Much is at stake as the President orders his policy objectives for the next four years."[178] But that coalition had always been fragile. In the second Reagan administration, the pro-life community would become more divided than it had ever been, disagreeing over the intricacies of anti-abortion legislation and the methods for achieving results. In the end, Reagan's second term only achieved one pro-life victory. Sent to Congress in 1987 and finally passed near the end of his presidency, the President's Pro-Life Bill, also called the Hyde Amendment, banned the use of federal funds to pay for any abortions except to save the life of the mother—a far cry from the ban on all abortions religious conservatives had planned to achieve during the Reagan presidency. In an interview shortly before leaving office, Reagan claimed his failure to do more on behalf of the unborn had been his greatest disappointment as president, but many in the Religious Right grumbled he had never made abortion a very important priority.[179]

Outside the White House, Jerry Falwell's announcement that he would step down from the presidency of Moral Majority in 1987 seemed to signal how inconsequential the Religious Right had become during the second Reagan administration. Falwell saw things differently, of course, and he contended he merely wanted to return to his first love of preaching—"back to winning souls, back to meeting spiritual needs," as he described it.[180] But the Moral Majority's ineffectiveness in the 1986 midterm elections and the diminished sway Falwell enjoyed inside the White House played a bigger role in his decision.[181] Two years later, Falwell announced he was shuttering the Moral Majority altogether. While many observers thought Falwell's move provided further evidence of the Religious Right's insignificance by the late 1980s, Falwell claimed he had made his decision for much different reasons. "The purpose of the Moral Majority was to activate the religious right," Falwell explained to reporters. "Our mission has been accomplished."[182]

But the ambitions of the Moral Majority—and of the Religious Right—had been far more than voter mobilization and the activation of Christian conservatives. In the heady days of the 1980 campaign and Reagan's eventual win, restoring school prayer, standing up to gay rights, rolling back secularism's hold on the culture, and even ending abortion were the Religious Right's planned objectives. Eight years later, many conservative Christians wondered if they had been used. "Were Christians Courted for Their Votes or Beliefs?" a *Christianity Today* headline asked in early 1989. Looking back on the decade, many believed they knew the answer.[183]

Near the end of Reagan's presidency, Carl Henry sat down for an interview with the editors at his old stomping ground, *Christianity Today*. Henry lamented that, despite his overtures, Reagan had "given little more than lip service" to the Religious Right's concerns. "If another election confirms the Religious Right's limited impact on the national scene," Henry ventured, "its energies will then likely be focused locally on school board and regional elections. In those contests, the Religious Right may well learn some of the prudential skills it has too much neglected as a national movement."[184] In many ways, Henry foresaw correctly, as the early 1990s especially witnessed a return to the grassroots efforts of the Religious Right. Rebuilding the movement's network and tackling state and local causes became critical after the Reagan years' disappointments.[185]

Also, at the local level and outside the center of national power, religious conservatives could often avoid the ecumenical challenges that had posed such difficulties at what seemed to be the Religious Right's great political moment. Still, the dream of a national movement that could remake the country enlivened the hearts of many religious conservatives, particularly once Bill Clinton assumed the presidency. Reencountering the feelings of marginalization and desperation that had brought them together in the late 1970s, religious conservatives again began to talk of a broad-based ecumenical movement that could work together to turn the nation back to God. But some, like a political scientist from the University of Wisconsin, understood that sectarian divisions would continue to plague the Religious Right, as had been made visible not only on points of agreement among evangelicals, Mormons, and Catholics, like abortion and school prayer, but especially with other issues including poverty and the arms race. Speaking at a 1990 Heritage Foundation (a conservative think tank) conference convened to discuss why the Religious Right had achieved so little in the Reagan years, Robert Booth Fowler spoke the truth that many refused to hear. "There was a great deal of discomfort," Fowler explained, "with forming coalitions outside the evangelical/fundamentalist world and plenty of difficulty doing so within it."[186]

8

A Christian Coalition

THOUGH THE REPUBLICAN Party had retained the White House with George H. W. Bush's election in 1988, many religious conservatives worried their moment of opportunity had ended with not much to show for it. In the Republican primaries that year, Bush emerged from a crowded field, the establishment candidate who parlayed his vice-presidential stint into a position at the top of the ticket. Pat Robertson, the charismatic televangelist turned politician, challenged Bush's run for the nomination. With a strong second-place finish behind Kansas Senator Bob Dole in the Iowa caucus, Robertson looked like he might ride another wave of religious conservative activism into the White House. The snowy fields of New Hampshire, however, brought Robertson back to the cold reality of his unlikely political dream. After poor showings in the New Hampshire and "Super Tuesday" primaries, Robertson called off his campaign. Robertson's strategy to run as a conservative Christian businessman who called for a flat tax and entitlement reforms while highlighting his campaign theme to "Restore the Greatness of America Through Moral Strength," drew on the now conventional wisdom that any candidate who hoped to capture the GOP's nomination needed to appeal to its key constituencies of free-market capitalists and religious conservatives.

Despite his Yale law degree and experience running his multi-million dollar Christian media empire, Robertson failed to attract support beyond the party's most conservative Christian voters. But even Robertson's showing among the GOP's conservative religious wing proved disappointing and ultimately disastrous for his ambitions. While Robertson talked the familiar language of pro-God, pro-family, anti-abortion, anti-gay politics, he also carried the burden of his identification with charismatic Christianity, still suspect to many evangelical and fundamentalist Protestants, despite his own campaign attempts to rebrand himself as an evangelical. The NAE executive Robert Dugan gave his endorsement to Bush. So did Jerry Falwell, though this may have been due as much to Falwell's desire to undercut Robertson's ascent to the forefront of the Religious Right as to any deep theological convictions. Still, Robertson's failure with voters outside of the charismatic and Pentecostal traditions ended his run for office, highlighted the lingering evangelical-charismatic split, and demonstrated again the pesky challenges of denominationalism at the heart of the Religious Right's aspirations.[1]

Given Robertson's lackluster showing in the campaign, the dissolution of the Moral Majority shortly thereafter, and the embarrassing financial and sex scandals that embroiled some of religious broadcasting's most famous televangelists, some commentators suggested the Religious Right's moment had come and gone. Writing in the *New Republic*, historian Sean Wilentz quipped, "Rarely in modern times has a movement of such reputed potential self-destructed so suddenly. Free thinkers may want to reconsider their skepticism about divine intervention."[2] But any prayers for the disappearance of the Religious Right would go unanswered in the 1990s. Despite his electoral thumping, Pat Robertson had no intentions of leaving public life either. Instead, he created the Christian Coalition, a Moral Majority for the 1990s. Like the Moral Majority, the Christian Coalition would tout ecumenical aims, but achieve only sectarian realities.

Christian Coalition

Though Robertson had lost his bid for the GOP's nomination, he had more to show for his efforts than a distant third place finish. Hundreds of thousands of supporters, from the Midwest to New England and throughout the South, had supported Robertson's campaign. As millions of evangelicals and fundamentalists had first become politically involved in the presidential races of 1976, 1980, or 1984, Robertson's run for the White House in 1988 had activated yet another swath of conservative Protestants—Pentecostals and charismatics. And though their man would not lead the nation from 1600 Pennsylvania Avenue, they hungered for Robertson to become their political leader in a movement on behalf of their beliefs, just as he already served as the spiritual leader for so many of them who tuned into his Christian Broadcasting Network (CBN) each night. When a state coordinator from his campaign alerted Robertson of the large network that awaited his direction, Robertson sent out word for key campaign leaders and other Religious Right activists to meet with him in Atlanta in September 1989.[3]

In Atlanta, those gathered at a downtown hotel discussed where the Religious Right should go next. Many grumbled about the Republican Party, feeling it had used them for their votes to get Reagan and Bush into the White House and then ignored their pro-life, pro-family agenda once the election victories had been secured. Realizing they had spent too much time defeating the Left for the benefit of the Republican Party, the attendees now targeted the party establishment and President Bush, even if most of them had just helped Bush win the White House. Some suggested breaking off from the GOP to form a Christian third party, but others argued this would only further marginalize their movement, rendering them and, more importantly, their causes inconsequential in a system dominated by the two major parties. Instead, they decided to stick with the GOP, but rather than mobilize for its presidential and senatorial candidates, they would develop a grassroots operation from which they would work themselves into the party network, building up from the local levels to gain control of the state parties. From that position they could tailor the party platform to their agenda, choosing candidates who would best see that vision carried out. This strategy for capturing the Republican Party bore a striking resemblance to how many of them had seized their denominations from the moderate and liberal forces that threatened their churches' orthodoxy.[4] Robertson told a meeting of Christian Coalition activists in 1990 the organization planned to have elected a pro-family Republican majority to Congress by the mid-1990s and a pro-family, social conservative Republican president by 2000.[5]

At that meeting, Robertson introduced one of those in attendance, a 28-year-old doctoral candidate in American history at Emory University named Ralph Reed, as the yet-unnamed organization's first staff member, an announcement that stunned no one more than Reed himself. Reed, a GOP activist since his College Republican days at the University of Georgia, had crossed paths with Robertson several times on the campaign trail in 1988. Although a devoutly conservative Christian (he was a recent convert who had dropped his hard-partying ways for an equally zealous evangelical faith), Reed had supported Jack Kemp in the primaries, but he had been impressed with Robertson's tenacious, fighting spirit and with his message of turning the nation back to God. After the election, Robertson asked Reed to draw up a memorandum detailing how a grassroots organization could be organized. Without knowing it, Reed had submitted his job application to Robertson. Robertson announced his hiring in front of all those anxious activists in Atlanta.[6]

Reed quickly got to work steadily growing the Christian Coalition. Organized by local chapters that belonged to state affiliates, the Christian Coalition oversaw a vast network that soon stretched across the nation. By the spring of 1990, twenty-five thousand members belonged. At that year's end, membership had reached fifty-seven thousand in 125 local chapters with an annual budget of $2.8 million. Two years later, two hundred and fifty thousand members participated in one thousand local chapters now supported by an annual budget of $8.5 million. The one millionth member of the Christian Coalition signed up in 1994. One year after, affiliates in all fifty states oversaw one thousand, six hundred local chapters with a membership of 1.6 million people and a $25 million annual budget.[7] The organization had exploded in scope and size in just five years.

In Washington, an office lobbied members of Congress, tracked important legislation, monitored federal agencies, and coordinated media relations. Across the country, Christian Coalition members received newsletters that kept them abreast of political developments and voter guides to distribute in their churches and communities. They also attended Christian Coalition seminars that trained them in the basics of political activism. "Think like Jesus. Lead like Moses. Fight like David. Run like Lincoln," the seminar's slogan advised.[8] All of the organization's efforts focused on turning its members into long-term political activists who could remake the nation not in one election, but through persistent involvement in the political process. "We believe that it is God's will that those people stay involved for the long haul," Reed told *Christianity Today*, "not just for a single campaign."[9] Reed's training as a historian had given him a different vision of change that he sought to impart on the Christian Coalition's members. "Most political operatives think in two-year cycles," he explained. "I think in quarter centuries."[10]

At the local level, Christian Coalition activists worked on voter mobilization drives in their churches, distributed educational materials on upcoming elections, became active in local and state Republican Party politics, and ran for positions on school boards, city councils, and state legislatures. Surprisingly, given the Religious Right's efforts of the previous decades, Reed declared he would "exchange the Presidency for 2,000 school board seats in the United States."[11] Reed was convinced after the lessons of the 1980s that locally based activism provided the path to national transformation—a sort of trickle-up strategy for political change. "If we do that," Reed explained of Christian Coalition's local efforts, "America will continue in a more conservative, pro-family direction no matter who wins the White House."[12] "The Christian community got it backwards in the 1980s," Reed contended elsewhere. "We tried to charge Washington when we should have been focusing on the states. The real battles of concern to Christians are in neighborhoods, school boards, city councils and state legislatures."[13] The Christian Coalition waged these battles through a precinct-based structure that drew on local evangelical churches for support. As an organization training manual pointed out, "Churches are the nexus points for tens of millions of Americans who share a conservative, pro-family philosophy. No other cultural structure represents such a vast reservoir of potential help for the pro-family movement."[14] The precinct model depended on members engaging in constant recruitment to build the Coalition. Precinct captains were each charged with recruiting twenty-five new members whom they typically found from their own congregations. Each new member then was tasked with bringing in another twenty-five new members. In this way, whole congregations could be turned into Christian Coalition chapters without the pastor ever lifting a finger.[15]

This layperson-driven model represented a real departure from how its antecedent, Moral Majority, had operated. Also, unlike the Moral Majority, the Christian Coalition made no claims to represent a majority position within the nation, instead cultivating among its members and potential allies their fears that Christians were an oppressed minority in America, an especially tender soft spot in the 1990s "culture wars" landscape.[16] Moral Majority had operated from the standpoint that it reflected the bulk of American society who, thanks to their own political inactivity and the stranglehold secular elites held over the nation's public life, had watched America's Christian heritage and values marginalized from their proper prominence. The Christian Coalition, on the other hand, did not justify its political aims on the basis of representing the true (and dominant) American public; rather, it acknowledged politics as a battle of constituencies—a war won not through crushing majorities, but through close, poorly attended local elections. "We don't have to worry about convincing a majority of Americans to agree with us," the organization's national field director admitted. "Most of them are staying home watching 'Falcon Crest.'"[17] Because so few Americans participated in most elections, the Christian Coalition figured it needed only just enough voters to win each race. This would be a long, steady war of attrition rather than an overnight revolution. Reed looked to another battle tactic as his inspiration. "I want to be invisible," he explained to a reporter. "I do guerilla warfare. I paint my face and travel at night. You don't know it's over until you're in a body bag. You don't know until election night."[18]

While the Christian Coalition's strategic tactics departed from its forerunners, the organization's goal of an ecumenical grassroots movement—made clear by its very name—stood firmly in the Moral Majority's professed tradition. In fact, Jerry Falwell, despite his rivalry, had urged the new organization to include conservative Catholics in its ranks. In February 1990, at an early Christian Coalition planning meeting held at Washington, D.C.'s Mayflower Hotel, Falwell noted the "impressive . . . cross-section of leaders" in attendance. That cross-section, however, only spanned conservative Protestantism as leading evangelicals and fundamentalists, like Bill Bright of Campus Crusade, Lou Sheldon of the Traditional Values Coalition, James

Kennedy of Coral Ridge Presbyterian, Chuck Colson, and Tim LaHaye, appear to have been almost the only ones in attendance. Records of the meeting indicate only one Catholic, Keith Fournier, dean at Franciscan University and a pro-life legal activist, present that day. "We need a greater Catholic presence to add weight," Falwell told the group, noting Catholics had made up 33 percent of the Moral Majority—a number three percentage points higher than his usual contention about the group's Catholic membership. Falwell recommended the Christian Coalition aim for a similar representation. Fournier agreed. "Do not let this project become a strictly Evangelical Protestant effort with limited Catholic involvement," he urged the group.[19]

As the Christian Coalition introduced itself to potential members in the early 1990s, it explained it sought "self-identified born-again Christians and orthodox Roman Catholics who are registered to vote and are concerned about moral issues and the moral decline of America." "These voters," an early organization document continued, "attend church regularly, watch Christian television at least once per week, have a propensity to purchase or give charitably through direct mail, and hold a favorable opinion of Religious Right political activity."[20] As Clyde Wilcox has pointed out, Robertson's direct appeal to Catholics and to Baptists showed he was now aware that in order to achieve his political goals he would need to build an ecumenical movement, since his presidential campaign's failure to capture these two significant Republican constituencies had quickly ended any chance he had of winning the White House.[21] No mention, however, was ever made of recruiting Mormons to the Christian Coalition. Perhaps this owed to an awareness of the LDS Church's political retreat after the defeat of the ERA, or maybe it reflected the persistent and even growing anti-Mormon cottage industry within 1990s evangelicalism. But Christian Coalition's ecumenical vision never appears to have included the LDS faithful, though the group did try distributing its voter guides in LDS wards before elections. LDS officials, however, blocked them from doing so.[22]

By some measures, the Christian Coalition made significant steps in incorporating Catholics into the organization. The decision to have laypersons rather than pastors serve throughout the grassroots' leadership ranks helped potential Catholic members see the group as not as tied to conservative Protestant churches or denominations as they might have. It also suggested there were opportunities for them to take some of those leadership positions. Some Catholics assumed these spots. At one point, the Virginia state chapter, one of the organization's most important and influential chapters given the group's national headquarters were there, had a Catholic state chair, and in several other states Catholics worked as county chairs.[23] Also, the Christian Coalition's prioritization of abortion in its political agenda and its frequent public messages that it sought "pro-life Catholics" for its work helped attract Catholic members. The Christian Coalition gave such great attention to abortion not for recruiting aims, of course, but because it continued to represent its members' consuming political priority. A 1990 survey revealed 55 percent of Christian Coalition's donors designated abortion as "the most important issue that motivates you to political action." In a distant second, "education" only garnered 13.5 percent, and media-hyped issues like pornography (5 percent) and homosexuality (3.4 percent) ranked behind "crime/drugs" and "New Age," both with 7.4 percent, as pressing concerns.[24]

In 1995, an internal survey of the Christian Coalition found that 16 percent of its 1.7 million members were Catholics.[25] This figure—aside from Jerry Falwell's unsubstantiated claims about Moral Majority's Catholic membership—represented the largest Catholic presence in an evangelical-led political organization since the emergence of the Religious Right in the late 1970s. But Christian Coalition leaders wanted more Catholic activism, especially in light of the upcoming presidential election. Reed informed the conservative Catholic magazine, *Crisis*, that he wanted to increase Catholic membership to between 25 and 30 percent, mirroring Catholics' proportion of the American population.[26] Feeling that the Christian Coalition had met its ecumenical limits, organization leaders made plans to establish a separate Catholic group that could work under the Christian Coalition umbrella but tailor its message and identity to better attract Catholic members. On a snowy December day, Ralph Reed announced the creation of the Catholic Alliance to a crowd of four hundred gathered in a hotel ballroom in Boston, a city chosen for the event specifically for its long Catholic history. "If Catholics and evangelicals can unite," Reed spoke to the crowd, "there is no person who cannot run for any office in any city or any state in America that cannot be elected. There is no bill that cannot be passed in either house of Congress or any state legislative chamber."[27] Reed then described the new group as "the most significant flowering of ecumenical cooperation," but that blossoming represented another moment of denominational division in the Religious Right's history.[28]

Plans called for the Catholic Alliance to have its own magazine and to be led by an entirely Catholic staff sensitive to the language and issues that would most connect with their fellow believers. As Reed explained, although Catholics and evangelicals both opposed abortion, they expressed their opposition in different ways that revealed deeper theological divergences and often different political consequences. "Evangelicals,"

Reed noted, "are more likely to appeal to Scripture—Psalm 39, or John the Baptist leaping in his mother's womb—whereas Catholics are more likely to adopt a broader or more comprehensive ethic: to be a voice for the voiceless and a defender of the innocent," ranging from those on death row to the disabled and elderly. Still, Reed acknowledged there would be some positions the Christian Coalition backed, particularly on health care or economic matters like tax policy, "when the Catholic Alliance will sit out an issue" because the Christian Coalition's position differed with Catholic Church teachings or bishops' pronouncements.[29]

Without realizing it, Reed had revealed the purpose of the Catholic Alliance was not to promote conservative Catholic political activism but rather to add further support for the Christian Coalition's efforts and to stay silent when disagreements with the Coalition's broader agenda emerged. The American bishops, who had never liked taking a back seat in Catholic political efforts and who maintained a healthy suspicion of evangelical overtures, roundly dismissed the new organization. Only two American bishops bothered to endorse the new group.[30] Other Catholic leaders objected more forcefully. A Boston-area priest proclaimed there was "nothing Catholic about the Catholic Alliance," deeming it "a fraudulent group designed to fool Catholic voters and increase the political power of Pat Robertson."[31] Colorado's three bishops wrote to all of the state's priests regarding the new group. "We must say as strongly as possible: the Catholic Alliance does not represent the Catholic Church," the letter read.[32] The bishop of the Richmond diocese that included the Christian Coalition's Virginia Beach headquarters sent a pastoral letter to his parishes forbidding voter guides produced by the organization or its Catholic affiliate from being distributed at any church services.[33] Other dioceses followed suit.[34] A new bishops' statement on political responsibility released that fall spoke to the Catholic Church's larger concerns of how some church members were being used, reminding Catholics, "Our moral framework does not easily fit the categories of right or left, Republican or Democrat."[35]

But the bishops had little reason to worry about evangelical management of the Catholic Alliance. After publicizing its launch with great fanfare, the Christian Coalition virtually ignored the new group, letting it wallow in neglect before deciding to end its involvement in 1997.[36] Now independent, the Catholic Alliance sought to transform itself, removing any mention of its history with the Christian Coalition from its literature and devoting itself solely to pro-life political activism, particularly winning a ban on partial-birth abortion.[37] The group soon announced as its new leader Keith Fournier, the Catholic legal scholar who had once urged the Christian Coalition to become a true evangelical-Catholic partnership.[38]

While the ecumenical nature of the Christian Coalition never reached the goals professed by its leaders, what had developed, if only briefly, still represented an impressive partnering given the historic failures in this regard. More successfully, the Christian Coalition significantly infiltrated the apparatus of the Republican Party, reshaping and redirecting its policies and operations to its agenda.[39] At the 1992 Republican National Convention in Houston, 300 of the 2,200 delegates belonged to the Christian Coalition, and the Coalition's members may have accounted for as much as one-third of the GOP's platform committee, producing a party platform with absolutist positions against abortion and homosexuality.[40] Forty-two percent of delegates in Houston identified themselves as evangelical Christians, making the 1992 convention an especially welcome one for such a conservative platform.[41] Before Pat Robertson sat for a nationally televised interview with NBC's Tom Brokaw, Ralph Reed warned him he needed to be prepared to answer whether the Religious Right was trying to take over the Republican Party. "What is there left to take over?" Robertson laughed in response.[42]

But George Bush's loss to Bill Clinton later that fall brought with it predictions that the Religious Right's best days were in the past. Many in the GOP blamed the tent revival atmosphere of the Houston convention for dooming the party's chances with moderate and independent voters. Reed, however, refused to apologize for conservative Christian activism in the party. "If moderates complain," Reed barked, "they have to keep in mind that we're the ones licking the envelopes and burning the shoe leather. The only crime that the Christian Right has committed is the crime of democracy."[43] Rather than backing down, the Christian Coalition and other Religious Right forces kept building up their presence within the party. A 1994 study found the Religious Right had become "dominant" in eight state GOP parties and enjoyed a "substantial" presence in thirteen more. Criticisms of the Religious Right's involvement in the Republican Party abated for the moment when the sweeping Republican victories in the 1994 election gave the GOP its first House majority in fifty years, a result many credited Reed and Religious Right activists with making possible.[44] Two years later in San Diego, Christian Coalition members made up more than half of the one thousand delegates at the Republican National Convention.[45]

Earlier that year, at the Coalition's annual conference, Reed had warned his critics, "you better get used to the Christian Coalition, because we're going to be around for a long, long time."[46] But with another Republican defeat in 1996 and with declining membership and finances in the late

1990s, the Christian Coalition's influence began to decline. "I never intended to stay in this job forever," Reed declared in 1997 as he announced his resignation to start his own political consulting firm. "I believe that institutions such as the Christian Coalition . . . are energized by new blood and new ideas."[47] Robertson replaced Reed with a new president, but the Christian Coalition never recaptured the energy that propelled it in the early 1990s.

Looking back, there didn't seem to be many policy or legislative changes to boast about. Conservative Christians had grown to a sizeable force in the Republican Party's ranks, but losing presidential candidates and mixed results in congressional elections meant there was often insufficient support for the Religious Right's agenda in the 1990s. Some Christian activists began to question their political involvement in the first place. Paul Weyrich, who had spent decades helping build the movement, declared in 1999 that the culture war had been lost and recommended Christians retreat from public life and build up alternative cultural institutions to preserve and advance their values.[48] Former Moral Majority leaders Cal Thomas and Ed Dobson released a blistering book that same year that garnered enormous attention in evangelical circles. *Blinded By Might* charged that conservative Christians had grown to love political power too much and that they needed to get back to the Great Commission of saving the lost and leave politics to other people. "Twenty years of fighting has brought us nothing," they concluded.[49] The election of George W. Bush in 2000 put that retreat on hold, reviving many of the Religious Right's hopes buried since that propitious moment in 1980. By the time Bush completed his two terms as president, though, many conservative Christian activists were repeating aloud the same frustrations and expressions of disillusionment they had voiced at the end of the Reagan years.

Evangelicals and Catholics Together

Without the same access to the White House they had enjoyed for the previous dozen years, Religious Right leaders developed new ways to make their voices heard and keep their agenda alive during the Clinton presidency. As they had during Jimmy Carter's frustrating presidency, conservative Christians mounted new symbolic offenses to demonstrate their philosophical unity as traditionalist outsiders in a moment where liberalism appeared dominant. No symbolic expression signaled better the outsider status the Religious Right cultivated for its political uses during the Clinton years than "Evangelicals and Catholics Together" (ECT), but the document also revealed again how much easier it often was to develop cross-denominational efforts in times when Christian conservatives felt on the defensive. The document owed its origin to a meeting in September 1992 led by Richard John Neuhaus and Charles Colson, the two men probably best suited to head a discussion on evangelical-Catholic relations. But it also grew from more than a decade's worth of discussions among conservative evangelical and Catholic intellectuals, particularly those grouped at the University of Notre Dame, the premier Catholic university that had become an unlikely home to an impressive roster of evangelical scholars.[50] Neuhaus was a former Lutheran pastor who had recently become a priest in the Catholic Church. And as an adult convert to evangelicalism, Colson had missed growing up in the more virulently anti-Catholic days of earlier decades, an experience that had lingering effects on evangelicals raised in the faith. Colson's wife, Patty, was also a committed Catholic, and he had always admired her deep faith even during his agnostic days.

At the meeting, Neuhaus and Colson were joined by a group of Catholic and evangelical men who talked of their common concerns, their shared values, and their points of disagreement. After that first gathering, a drafting committee began crafting a joint statement. At a press conference in New York City in early 1994, Colson presented the twenty-five-page document they had produced, "Evangelicals and Catholics Together: The Christian Mission in the Third Millennium."[51] Along with Neuhaus and Colson, the document's thirty-nine signers included prominent Catholic and evangelical leaders. Catholic endorsers of ECT included priests, bishops, an archbishop, and Cardinal John O'Connor along with influential lay Catholics like the conservative writer, Michael Novak. The names of evangelicals on the document included Bill Bright, Pat Robertson, John White (a former president of the NAE), the theologian J. I. Packer, two agency heads from the Southern Baptist Convention, and the historian Mark Noll.

The signers of "Evangelicals and Catholics Together" made clear that they represented only themselves, not the churches they belonged to or even the organizations many led. ECT was not an official church statement nor was it theological doctrine. Instead, they wrote, it was meant as a simple expression of "the faith we affirm together."[52] Most shocking to many evangelicals who read the document was the declaration that Catholics should be considered "brothers and sisters in Christ."[53] Although the document acknowledged there were significant disagreements between evangelicals and Catholics, it contended that both agreed "we are justified by grace through faith because of Christ."[54] Additionally, the document called on evangelicals and Catholics to recognize their substantial places of agreement and link together in working against "what opposes Christ and His cause," including relativism, anti-intellectualism, and nihilism (a threesome William Shea rightly points out could be summed up as "post-modernism"), as well as abortion, pornography, attacks on religious freedom, the decline of the traditional family, and even "militant Islam."[55]

While by 1994 many evangelicals were happy to admit their political allegiance with conservative Catholics, especially during the hot "culture wars" of the Clinton years, a lot of evangelical critics charged ECT's creators were dangerously putting political priorities before far graver spiritual matters and theological truths. Throughout the evangelical world, televangelists, theologians, evangelical publications, and seminaries all grappled with the document's meaning and worried about its implications. Some institutions, like the National Association of Evangelicals, took pains to clarify that any signers of ECT in no way stood for the organizations they also represented.[56] Dallas Theological Seminary released a statement saying it "strongly question[ed] whether Evangelicals and Catholics can ever 'unite on the great truths of the faith.'"[57] Other churches and denominations responded to the document with clear statements distinguishing evangelicalism from Catholicism and outlining the errors of the Catholic Church. The conservative Presbyterian Church in America passed a resolution at its 1995 General Assembly affirming its beliefs were "not compatible with the teaching of the official Roman Catholic Church."[58] In California, Pastor John MacArthur of Grace Community Church, the same pastor who had rejected Bill Bright's invitation to participate in the Year of the Bible project a decade before, called Catholicism a "false religion" when a reporter asked for his response to the document.[59] MacArthur expanded his critique of ECT in a lengthy and scathing review in the pages of his seminary's theological journal. MacArthur attacked the document for prioritizing cultural and political pursuits above the gospel and contended it replaced biblical truth with shared cultural convictions. "Ecumenical unity with Roman Catholicism is not essential to the furtherance of the kingdom of God," MacArthur concluded. "Evangelism of Roman Catholics is."[60]

ECT's unclear message regarding salvation worried MacArthur and other evangelical critics the most. The document stated sinners were "justified by grace through faith," but it had not specified if this justification came through "faith alone," the crucial evangelical phraseology. That one missing word struck at the heart of evangelical's *sola fide* convictions and suggested that the Catholic teaching that salvation came by faith and works had gone unchallenged. Similarly, the document's call for both sides to stop efforts at proselytizing each other—"It is neither theologically legitimate nor a prudent use of resources for one Christian community to proselytize among active adherents of another Christian community," the document declared—suggested either evangelicals should consider Catholics as saved Christians or that they should abandon the chief mission Christ had given them to witness to the lost.[61] Evangelicals like Reformed theologian R. C. Sproul and *Christianity Today* editor Kenneth Kantzer wondered what all of this meant for the Reformation's legacy. Sproul titled his spirited attack on ECT, "After Light, Darkness," an inversion of the popular Reformation phrase, "after darkness, light," to suggest the gospel risked disappearing again should evangelicals abandon their central claim against the Catholic Church and the point of their whole historic being.[62] (Sproul expanded his response to ECT in his book, pointedly titled *Faith Alone*, released the next year.)[63] Kantzer agreed that "with the spread of moral rot" in the nation, "we evangelicals need to close ranks with our Catholic neighbors. And with Mormons, conservative Jews, and secularists who share our values." But Kantzer insisted that shared political and social values should never obscure the unbridgeable divide between evangelicals and those of other faiths nor stop evangelicals from sharing the gospel with their political allies. "Because evangelicals acknowledge Jesus Christ as Lord of their thought and life," Kantzer concluded, "they cannot do otherwise than to seek to win everyone everywhere, whether they be Catholics, Jews, Mormons, or secularists . . . to the biblical gospel that promises salvation by God's free grace through simple faith in our Lord Jesus Christ."[64]

"The Gift of Salvation," a follow-up document released in the fall of 1997, sought to continue the conversation "Evangelicals and Catholics Together" had begun and to respond to some of the criticisms the original document faced. Many of ECT's signers attached their name to "The Gift of Salvation," but there were now some noticeable absences, such as two SBC agency heads and former NAE president John White, who had also removed his endorsement of the original document. In a significant reversal, "The Gift of Salvation" restored the proselytizing mission to both its evangelical and Catholic signers, noting that both were charged with witnessing to "everyone everywhere," a phrase that may have been lifted directly from Kantzer's critique of ECT in *Christianity Today*. "Evangelicals must speak the Gospel to Catholics and Catholics to Evangelicals, always speaking the truth in love," the signers contended.[65] As to the question of justification, the signers now wrote, "We understand that what we here affirm is in agreement with what the Reformation traditions have meant by justification by faith alone (*sola fide*)."[66]

That any Catholic priests or laypersons signed on to such a view remains curious, but these signers, making no official representations of their church and certainly with no backing from Rome, may have been willing to overlook an awkward and unclear sentence for the greater purpose of public unity.[67] The reversal on the matter of evangelization and the seeming endorsement of *sola fide* salvation along with the repeating of a sizeable list of difficult doctrinal questions that divided evangelicals and Catholics meant "The Gift of Salvation" contained a clearer message that evangelical-Catholic unity consisted chiefly of political and cultural values than of religious beliefs. Still, "Evangelicals and Catholics Together" and "The Gift of Salvation" represented a significant step forward in evangelical-Catholic relations. Though the documents, and even more so the larger response they received, ultimately reaffirmed the significant divide separating evangelicalism and Catholicism, the very act of creating the documents together signified a new stage of evangelical-Catholic relations. Theological disagreements had not been entirely laid aside—or at least in the end they were acknowledged when evangelical critics worried the original signers had made too little of them—but they had not been allowed to defeat a notable moment of symbolic cooperation either.

This tension between theological incompatibility and political and cultural sympathy had been at the heart of conservative Catholic-evangelical relations for nearly twenty years. In moments like the late 1970s and again in the 1990s—eras in which conservative Christians felt especially marginalized by the political reality—such an expression of political and cultural harmony may have been particularly easy to voice. But the 1980s had shown the difficulty of translating that outsider unity into political achievements once religious conservatives had a place at the center of power. There, emboldened by their position and ever-shaped by their competing claims of exclusive truth, it had been far too easy to fall apart, drifting away in moments of policy disputes on shared concerns and forgetting each other as they pursued their own unique agendas. Now, after "Evangelicals and Catholics Together" and with the election of George W. Bush, the question remained if they could learn from their past.

Evangelicals and Mormons

Evangelical relations with Mormons did not show the progress that characterized evangelical associations with Catholics in the 1990s. That decade witnessed a new round of books and articles from evangelical authors that promised to expose readers to Mormonism's unbiblical beliefs and practices. The persistent accelerated growth of the LDS Church, more than doubling in size in twenty years from a worldwide population of 4.6 million members in 1980 to more than 10 million as the new millennium approached, continued to trouble many evangelicals. Much of that rapid expansion had taken place outside the United States in places where American evangelicals had long proselytized, but the LDS Church continued to yield bountiful harvests across the Southern Bible Belt. The construction of LDS temples in cities like Atlanta and Dallas in the 1980s and Orlando, Florida; Raleigh, North Carolina; and Columbia, South Carolina—all major Southern Baptist cities—signaled the permanent presence the church intended in the region and confirmed that, along with other demographic changes throughout the decades, Southern Baptism's days as the South's de facto religion had come to an end. "We're growing through all the Southern states," an LDS Church spokesman noted happily in 1998.[68]

Even more so than the LDS Church, the Southern Baptist Convention had become a truly national denomination by the 1990s, with impressive membership in the Midwest and California and a respectable presence in the Northeast and Pacific Northwest. The SBC's decision to hold its 1998 convention in Salt Lake City indicated not only that no corner of the nation would be ignored by Southern Baptists, but also provided an opportunity to remind Southern Baptists of the special obligation they had to share the gospel with LDS faithful. That summer in Utah, three thousand Southern Baptist volunteers fanned out through the heart of Mormonism, doing door-to-door missionary service to the lost. The denomination always conducted outreach efforts in any city where it held its annual meeting, but Salt Lake City required special preparation. To equip the volunteers, the SBC developed a video called *The Mormon Puzzle* and distributed copies of it along with a book titled *Mormonism Unmasked*. Both works promised to "lift the veil from one of the greatest deceptions in the history of religion," a blurb on the book's cover announced, repeating the popular refrain in evangelical critiques of Mormonism since the 1980s.[69] In Salt Lake City, a $600,000 budget paid for Southern Baptist radio and television spots, billboards, mass mailings, and public events to announce the Baptists' arrival and spread their message to the city's inhabitants.[70] In one television ad, Olympic-gold-medal-winning gymnast Mary Lou Retton talked about Jesus as the "only perfect 10." Jerry Falwell described the activities intended to take place that summer as an "open game for the souls of man."[71] *Christianity Today* ran an approving six-page "Special News Report" of the SBC's efforts in Utah as the meeting took place.[72]

"We are not worried," the LDS Church's president, Gordon B. Hinckley, declared before the Southern Baptists arrived in Utah that June.[73] A few months before, Dallin Oaks, a member of the LDS Church's high-ranking Quorum of the Twelve Apostles, had explained in a General Conference speech that when asked by other Christians, like Baptists, if they had been saved, Mormons should simply respond "yes," although he instructed the LDS faithful that if they were to ask it of themselves the answer was "yes, but with conditions," meaning adherence to the church and a life of good works.

"The savior taught that we must endure to the end in order to be saved," Oaks reminded.[74] By the meeting's close, the SBC could only tally one thousand conversions from their efforts, and denomination officials later acknowledged most of these had come from non-Mormons, a not-surprising finding given that Mormons now amounted to less than 50 percent of Salt Lake City's residents.[75] All accounts indicated that the doorstep interactions of Southern Baptist missionaries with potential LDS converts remained congenial. The LDS Church had instructed its members to be gracious if unyielding hosts to their guests, and many Mormons could sympathize with the missionaries' experiences having served their own two-year missions for the LDS Church. But the convention's proceedings were far more pointed. One minister opened his convention sermon by describing Salt Lake City as the "headquarters of a counterfeit Christianity." Of course, not all the pastors who addressed the Southern Baptist gathering spoke about Mormonism. In his sermon at the Pastors' Conference, Mike Huckabee—a minister and former president of the Arkansas Baptist Convention who had just recently been elected governor of Arkansas—blamed liberal religion for the problems of society that an ineffective government now tried to address. "Government knows it does not have the answer, but it's arrogant and acts as though it does," Governor Huckabee said. "Church does have the answers but will cowardly deny that it does and wonder when the world will be changed." Southern Baptists needed to translate their real convictions into public action as Huckabee had done in his race for governor. "I didn't get into politics," he explained, "because I thought government had a better answer. I got into politics because I knew government didn't have the real answers, that the real answers lie in accepting Jesus Christ into our lives."[76]

Among the resolutions passed at the 1998 meeting, many observers felt the "Resolution on the True Christian Gospel" affirming "biblical revelation as the sole source of saving truth" was a direct jab at the LDS Church's extra-biblical scriptures.[77] Journalists, however, showed far more interest in the SBC's decision to amend its 1925 Faith and Message statement of belief with a 250-word declaration on family life that acknowledged while husband and wife have "equal worth before God," a woman should "submit herself graciously" to her husband's leadership and that the husband "is to love his wife as Christ loved the church. He has the God-given responsibility to provide for, to protect, and to lead his family."[78] While the resolution arose most directly from Southern Baptists' worries about the precarious state of the traditional American family and their rejection of liberalizing cultural trends regarding women and sexuality, the amendment also grew out of long-standing evangelical suspicions and jealousies about the Mormon family, made all the more relevant in Salt Lake City that summer. One Baptist at the meetings in Utah that June confessed, "The one place that Baptists had to admit that Mormons had something was in the strength of their families." Not wanting to cede "the high ground that the Mormons have claimed" on conservative family values and issues, the Baptist acknowledged, had also helped inspire the amendment.[79] As one Southern Baptist pastor had reminded in his address before the Convention, "We're meeting in a city that, I'm afraid, has a high level of morality but a low level of salvation."[80]

While the pastor's comments revealed the unchanging evangelical position that Mormons still needed to accept the gospel of salvation, his words represented an emerging respect for Mormon morality in evangelical circles in the 1990s. For decades, evangelicals had suspiciously viewed the Mormon family and the LDS Church's teachings on traditional morality as a carefully orchestrated public image to hide its devious theology and deviant sexual practices with a cloak of wholesomeness for the sake of proselytizing non-Mormons. But with their increased worries about the coarsening culture of the 1990s, it was hard for most evangelicals to see Mormons as morally aberrant in a nation with high divorce rates, permissive abortion laws, and a growing gay and lesbian movement. Instead, Mormons looked like the pillars of decency evangelicals hoped to be.

Despite all the direct confrontations the SBC engaged with Mormonism that summer, officially the LDS Church offered the same near-silent response it gave to most evangelical efforts in the twentieth century. One church leader would only go so far as to describe the meeting, activities, and resolutions as "interesting, but not very disruptive in terms of our responsibilities."[81] But one dean at Brigham Young University lamented the larger implications of the evangelical-Mormon divide made visible by the Convention's proceedings. "There are so many things we could join hands on in spite of theological differences," he observed, "but [the differences] are big ones."[82]

Controversy erupted in evangelical circles in 2004, however, when one prominent evangelical seemed to blur the lines between the evangelical and LDS faiths. In a rare move, Brigham Young University and a Salt Lake City–based evangelical group dedicated to proselytizing Mormons called Standing Together Ministries coordinated a meeting of evangelical and LDS leaders to discuss their relationship in the Mormon Tabernacle. Many noted that not since 1871, when Brigham Young invited the fundamentalist pastor Dwight L. Moody, had an evangelical spoken to a Mormon crowd in the famed building in Temple Square. In 2004, the evangelical scholar Ravi Zacharias served as the main speaker for the event, christened "An Evening of Friendship."

Zacharias, who had also edited an encyclopedia of cults that included Mormonism, gave a pointed address on the divinity of Christ that directly rejected LDS teachings and made plainly clear the major theological differences separating evangelical Christianity and Mormonism.[83]

But evangelicals in the audience and around the country in the days following could not believe the words another evangelical spoke that night. Richard Mouw, president of Fuller Theological Seminary, walked to the pulpit and looked out at the Mormon audience. "Let me state it clearly," Mouw said. "We evangelicals have sinned against you. We've often seriously misrepresented the beliefs and practices of members of the LDS faith. It's a terrible thing to bear false witness. . . . We've told you what you believe without asking you."[84]

Though Mouw had spoken the truth—inaccuracy, exaggeration, and outright misrepresentation had characterized anti-Mormon literature since the days of Joseph Smith—his evangelical colleagues were alarmed that such a prominent evangelical figure had wasted a precious opportunity to speak the gospel to an LDS audience and instead had compromised the faith's hard-line stance against the LDS Church. The executive director of the Utah-Idaho Baptist Convention, Tim Clark, worried that Mouw was "sending a message to Mormons that they are part of mainstream Christianity"—a notion evangelical churches had consistently rejected since the 1830s. Clark also worried that Mouw's words would benefit LDS efforts to proselytize Baptists to Mormonism, something the SBC had worried about since the early 1980s. Clark cited a recent Mormon-produced movie, *Baptists At Our Barbecue,* which told the story of a Baptist pastor and his church bigotedly attacking Mormons in a small town before being won over to friendlier relations by a Mormon-hosted barbeque, as evidence that the LDS Church had specifically marked Baptists as potential converts. "The evidence is tangible," Clark proclaimed, "Why are Mormons building temples in New York City, Dallas and Atlanta? It's because they're targeting Baptists who don't know what they believe." "I did not appreciate his comments at all," one Baptist pastor in Salt Lake City said of Mouw's remarks, worrying they had just made even more difficult his task of presenting the evangelical message in Utah.[85]

Mouw's words not only made clear the overwhelming evangelical rejection of Mormonism that remained but also struck many conservative evangelicals as yet more proof of Fuller Theological Seminary's suspect leanings. Since the 1970s and Harold Lindsell's attacks in *The Battle for the Bible* that the seminary had compromised its stance on biblical inerrancy, many evangelicals began to feel that Fuller represented yet another evangelical institution that had veered from its orthodox moorings into questionable terrain. In the broad evangelical rejection of Mouw's remarks in

Temple Square, evangelicals reconfirmed that Mormonism stood outside of any acceptable definition of Christianity and also helped sketch again the tight boundaries of evangelicalism. A few decades before, debates over biblical inerrancy and textual literalism had drawn the dividing lines between true evangelicalism and those churches and denominations that risked slipping into moderate Protestantism. Now a clear, uncompromising position on the unchristian, cultic nature of Mormonism provided another litmus test for any institution's claims to authentic evangelicalism, a stance that built from the biblical literalism debates since the major evangelical charge against Mormonism was its extra-biblical scriptures.

Also, the Mormon example in evangelical circles may have helped soften responses to the Catholic Church. While Mormonism continued to be represented as a dangerous, virus-like insurgent that spread rapidly through devious means, evangelicals increasingly characterized Catholicism as containing essential, if sometimes corrupted, truths. That evangelicalism had sprung directly from the Catholic Church meant the faith had always had to recognize to some extent the correct precepts and presumptions at the heart of Catholicism. But the presence of Mormonism and other competing "cults," like the growing Church of Scientology in the 1990s, in combination with the increasing orthodoxy of the Vatican shown best through the election of the arch-conservative Cardinal Joseph Ratzinger to Pope Benedict XVI in 2005, demonstrated again to many evangelicals that they shared a true history and values system with Catholics, while any admissions of the same with Mormons were judged as perversions of orthodox convictions and were deemed as permitting a dangerous false religion to continue its increase, often at the expense of evangelicalism.[86] Evangelical reactions to Benedict's installation—the *Baptist Standard* headlined an article "Conservative Evangelicals Hope for Ally in New Pope Benedict XVI" upon his election—demonstrated how far evangelical-Catholic relations had come, seeing Benedict more for his potential as a fellow cultural guardian and conservative stalwart than as an occasion for another round of anti-papal screeds.[87] But they also highlighted the persistent distance between evangelicals and Mormons. Evangelicals had never expressed any similar hopes about the election of a new Mormon prophet, no matter how reliably the LDS Church had defended the same political and cultural values evangelicals held dear.

Conclusion

Although far less robust than their evangelical counterparts, Catholic critics of Mormonism continued to launch their own challenges to the faith. Isaiah

Bennett, a former Catholic priest who converted to Mormonism before returning to his former faith, published two books in 1999 that promised an "inside" view of a mysterious religion.[88] While Bennett resisted identifying the LDS Church as a cult, his hook as a former Mormon who had pierced the veil of a secretive religion drew from many of evangelical anti-Mormonism's most prominent tropes.[89] In fact, Bennett noted that there was "not much written about Mormonism from a Catholic perspective," so he had relied more on evangelical treatments of the faith to supplement his personal account.[90] In an exhaustive eighty-one-page response to the two books, one LDS scholar from BYU lamented that Bennett had "uncritically accepted the charges of other anti-Mormon writers."[91]

Other Catholic investigations seemed almost unserious in their treatments of Mormonism. The bishop of San Diego, for example, endeavored to explain the "Distinctive Beliefs of the Mormon Church," which included such "curious" things as the outright abstention from alcohol and the more common critique that the church was guided by continuous revelations through its prophets.[92] As Donald Westbrook has argued, Catholicism's general treatment of Mormonism has been to ignore opportunities for direct engagement and to instead simply offer responses as issues arise. Such an occasion happened twice in the early twenty-first century when the Vatican announced in 2001 that Mormon baptisms were invalid for any Mormons converting to Catholicism and in 2008 when the Vatican declared the Genealogical Society of Utah could not have the records of any diocese, since the LDS Church was using these materials to perform baptism rituals for deceased Catholics.[93] The U.S. Conference of Catholic Bishops' Secretariat for Ecumenical and Interreligious Affairs also continued to avoid any meaningful or engaged dialogue with the LDS Church.[94]

While the Catholic-Mormon dialogue remained strained or nonexistent, the issue of gay marriage had provided some moments of cooperation as the two churches coordinated anti-same-sex marriage efforts in states like Hawaii.[95] Additional opportunities for collaborative work against gay marriage, including some coordination with evangelicals, would continue in the years ahead, particularly in California's Proposition 8 battle in 2008. But the presidential campaigns of 2008 and 2012, when Mitt Romney bid for the White House, would reveal the lingering challenges Mormonism still faced in the nation's public square, particularly from evangelicals.

Conclusion: 2012 and Beyond

ON A THURSDAY night late in August 2012, Mitt Romney strode across a large stage in the Tampa Bay Times Forum to accept the nomination as the Republican Party's candidate for president. Behind Romney, a digitized screen sparkled with an American flag and a campaign slogan emblazoned across it: "We Believe in America." That generic patriotic expression may have been typical campaign pabulum, but its bland vagueness echoed a persistent dimension of the Romney campaign: the candidate's unwillingness to speak directly and openly about his Mormon faith. On the campaign trail, Romney instead had emphasized his service to his church, its particular name left unsaid, and had focused on his love for God and country rather than engaging questions about LDS theology or history.

Romney campaign officials insisted their candidate's reticence and indirectness regarding his religious faith represented a conscious strategy to wait until Tampa to introduce Romney's Mormon faith into his campaign story. "The convention is a good platform for telling all dimensions of Romney's life," including Mormonism, a senior Romney adviser explained to the website BuzzFeed.[1] Still, if GOP delegates in Tampa or Americans watching at home hoped to at last hear a sustained discussion of Mormonism, they came away disappointed as the convention primarily depicted Romney as a deeply religious man rather than a devout Mormon. In convention speeches and media appearances, Republican operatives, conservative pundits, and Romney campaign officials all heralded Romney as a "man of faith" and "man of God," while avoiding talk of Mormonism. The night before Romney's speech his vice presidential pick, Paul Ryan, drew on American traditions of pluralism and Judeo-Christian identity as he explained that though he and Romney belonged to "different churches," their faiths shared the "same moral creed." For religious conservatives listening, Ryan characterized their common morality in political rather than theological terms: both he and Romney believed in traditional marriage and the sanctity of life. The Romney he had come to know, Ryan said to the crowd, was "prayerful and faithful and honorable."[2]

Romney's Mormonism could not be ignored entirely, of course, but it was dramatically left to the last night of the convention. Leading into that evening, pundits speculated that Romney might connect his own bid to the White House to the larger Mormon story, linking themes of persistence, hard work, humility, and virtue while conjuring images of Mormon caravans crossing a vast American landscape. Perhaps Romney would note the persecution and violence his own Mormon forebears had endured, suffering mightily for the sake of a cherished belief. In doing so, Romney would not only attach himself to a story resonant with deeply American themes but also soften his own image as the aloof multimillionaire born in privilege. Or maybe Romney would bear his own personal testimony—a common practice not only of Mormonism but especially of evangelicals. A clear elaboration of his religious beliefs might not only clarify the welter of misleading ideas Americans had about Mormonism but could also demonstrate that his faith represented just another branch of Christianity.

Neither story would be told that Thursday night. Instead, the Republican National Convention closed with more talk that skirted outright discussion of Mormonism while continuing to cultivate Romney's image as a decent, churchgoing man. First, two of Romney's fellow church members, Kenneth Hutchins and Grant Bennett, spoke of their time leading the church in Boston with him, emphasizing the voluntary nature of leadership in the LDS Church. Romney had previously served both as bishop for his Belmont, Massachusetts, ward and as stake president for Boston, and the two speakers stressed the humanitarian nature of those roles rather than the spiritual. "He didn't discuss questions of theology," Grant Bennett said of Romney's approach for dealing with Mormons who sought his counsel, a description of Romney's leadership style that once again sidestepped the pesky question of Mormon beliefs. Instead, Romney displayed a "pure religion" that amounted to caring for "the widows and the fatherless in their moments of affliction." Two more Mormons from Boston, both recipients of Romney's charitable leadership, also spoke. "I know him to be a loving father, a man of faith, and a caring and compassionate friend," Pam Finlayson said of the man who had comforted her after her daughter died.[3]

After all the buildup for a great Mormon moment in the campaign, an expectation that the evening's speeches had engaged and left unfulfilled, Romney at last stood before the American people in a crisp blue suit and bright red tie. But his faith garnered only one small mention in his acceptance speech, a comment that rendered the most controversial element of his presidential bid as an insignificant biographical detail. "We were Mormons and growing up in Michigan," Romney said with a relaxed smile. "That might have seemed unusual or out of place but I really don't remember it that way. My friends cared more about what sports teams we followed than what church we went to."[4]

****

Considering how enthusiastically Religious Right activists and voters had supported George W. Bush in two elections and how fulsomely the president had courted and embraced those same supporters, religious conservatives were remarkably confused and conflicted about their political future as the 2008 election approached. Some of that ambivalence stemmed from Bush's presidency itself, a time that had at first seemed bright with promise for achieving significant conservative goals but that had become significantly hampered by an unpopular war and the disastrous handling of Hurricane Katrina's devastation of New Orleans. Bruised and almost embarrassed by the Bush years, religious conservatives began to question their place within a Republican Party that many worried depended on them as a reliable voting bloc but ignored their political goals.[5] That worry, of course, had bounded about religious conservative circles since the Reagan years, but each repeat of that drama seemed to enhance political convictions far more than it suggested a conservative crackup. Still, the 2008 GOP field did little to set aside lingering questions and concerns. In a race that included Rudy Giuliani, John McCain, Mitt Romney, Mike Huckabee, Fred Thompson, Sam Brownback, and Ron Paul, among others, the quick unity religious conservatives—not to mention the entire Republican electorate—had established behind Bush in 2000 seemed as unlikely in the early campaign months of 2007 as Hillary Clinton losing the Democratic nomination to an upstart first-term senator from Illinois.

Mormons, not surprisingly, rallied enthusiastically behind Romney's campaign. Catholics showed less unity, but Giuliani captured their early support.[6] Evangelical Republicans, however, could not agree on a candidate. Some of the most attractive candidates, like former Baptist minister Mike Huckabee and the pro-life stalwart Sam Brownback, an evangelical turned ardent Catholic, raised interest, but evangelicals worried that supporting these clearly second-tier choices would just hand the White House over to Democrats. The frontrunners—Giuliani, McCain, and Romney—elicited too many questions for evangelicals even if they seemed like formidable candidates. Giuliani had a liberal social record and a messy personal life.

McCain struck evangelicals as unreliably conservative, had coauthored the loathed McCain-Feingold campaign reform act, and was known for his nasty temper and salty tongue. Evangelicals faulted Romney for his about-face on the litmus test issues of abortion and gay rights, but it was clear Romney's Mormon faith remained his biggest handicap with evangelical voters.[7]

Actually, Romney's Mormonism proved a liability with voters in general. In a poll conducted by the Pew Research Center, 25 percent said they were "less likely" to vote for a Mormon presidential candidate. Only atheists (61 percent) and Muslims (45 percent) fared worse. Evangelicals, however, demonstrated a greater aversion to Mormonism with 36 percent—more than a third—saying the LDS faith of a candidate would give them pause. Forty-five percent of those evangelicals answered negatively to a question regarding whether Mormons were Christians; 39 percent confessed they held an "unfavorable" view toward Mormons.[8] Considering their substantial presence in the Republican electorate, especially the GOP primaries, evangelicals posed a problem for his presidential ambitions that Romney could not ignore.

Considering these results, Romney's Mormonism quickly became one of the 2008 campaign's leading stories. While Romney had an impressive resume to tout—a wildly successful and lucrative career in private industry, an unlikely election as a Republican to the governorship of largely Democratic Massachusetts, a sterling reputation as the aboveboard reformer of the scandal-plagued 2002 Winter Games in Salt Lake City—Romney's Mormonism dominated the public conversation about his political future. Newspapers and magazines filled their pages with stories about the LDS Church, accounts of its history, and discussions of its theology. Pollsters tracked American attitudes about Mormonism. Campaign strategists obsessed over the results, looking to them for some indication of Romney's prospects with voters.

Early signs from the Romney camp indicated they hoped his religious beliefs would ultimately prove inconsequential to an American public more concerned with questions about the nation's plummeting economy and the unending Iraq War. But polling continued to reveal Republican hesitation, especially from the critical evangelical bloc, about supporting a Mormon candidate. Any hope Romney had of sidestepping the issue of his faith ignored the basic expectations of the American electorate who wanted to know everything about a candidate from his health record to tax returns as much as it overlooked the modern history of the Republican Party and its relationship to religious conservatism. In an attempt to quiet the chatter and also court Republican evangelicals, Romney reached out to influential outlets, including a sit-down interview with *Christianity Today*, where he acknowledged that though "the doctrines of my church are quite different from evangelical Christian doctrines, the values of our faiths are very much the same."[9] A conversation with the leading evangelical magazine was hardly the place for Romney to minimize theological differences between Mormonism and evangelicalism, but at other points along the campaign trail Romney seemed, especially to evangelical critics, too eager to present himself as a traditional Christian.

As the campaign accelerated in the fall of 2007, Romney worked overtime to land some key endorsements from evangelical leaders. Earlier in the year, he had earned the backing of two important evangelical politicos, the Christian public relations mastermind Rick DeMoss, and Jay Sekulow of the American Center for Law and Justice, a Christian legal group founded by Pat Robertson. DeMoss tried to convince a group of Religious Right activists that Romney was their man by introducing the candidate to them in a private session. "I've found the answer to the question of whether you can support a Mormon," DeMoss declared. "It depends on who the Mormon is."[10] Most evangelical leaders and, more importantly, evangelical pastors and voters remained unconvinced, however. For them, Romney's efforts were in vain largely because of his questionable assertions about his faith rather than his political positions. Bob Inglis, a conservative evangelical Republican congressman from South Carolina, told reporters he had offered Romney the hard truth about those appeals. "I told him," Inglis explained, "you cannot equate Mormonism with Christianity; you cannot say, 'I am a Christian just like you.'" "When he goes around and says Jesus Christ is my Lord and Savior, he ticks off at least half the evangelicals," Richard Land, president of the Southern Baptist Conference's Ethics and Religious Liberty Commission, concurred. "He's picking a fight he's going to lose."[11]

Recognizing that his religious comments had enflamed rather than satisfied his critics, Romney's campaign admitted their candidate needed to directly address the country much as a Catholic candidate for the White House had nearly fifty years before. In early December, with the critical Iowa caucuses looming, Romney traveled to College Station, Texas, to deliver his "Faith in America" speech at Texas A&M University's George H. W. Bush Presidential Library. After the library's namesake warmly introduced him, Romney stepped behind a podium bearing the presidential seal to deliver his speech. While the presence of the Bush family and the accoutrements of a presidential library bestowed a certain executive aura to Romney, his speech intended not to convince Americans to see him as presidential but rather to ensure his faith did not bar them from granting him that privilege. Like John F. Kennedy had argued in his Texas speech before the 1960 election—a moment Romney referenced in his own talk—Romney based his appeal to the American public on the cherished value of religious liberty. "A person should not be elected because of his faith nor should he be rejected because of his faith," Romney declared.[12] As JFK had, Romney also promised that no church authorities would exercise any influence over his presidency.

Because of Americans' general unfamiliarity with Mormonism, Romney had to directly address some of the questions and rumors he knew often attended his faith. Yet Romney's discussion of Mormonism felt more like political spin than theological explication. Ignoring questions of Mormon history or LDS theology, Romney instead focused on the tradition of American pluralism and the vibrancy of the nation's religious diversity. Romney said he had been asked "one fundamental question" repeatedly regarding what he believed about Jesus. "I believe that Jesus Christ is the Son of God and the Savior of mankind," he responded. Quickly noting that the particulars of his "church's beliefs about Christ may not all be the same as those of other faiths," Romney minimized these theological discrepancies—in short, the very reason why he needed to make the speech in the first place—in light of the more important value of religious tolerance. Because Americans respected religious diversity, Romney argued, what mattered most was the "common creed of moral convictions" that united all the religions, rather than the doctrinal points that might separate them. Americans had understood that Romney had intended to speak about his Mormon faith, but his speech was instead a rousing endorsement of civil religion and the American Judeo-Christian tradition in place of any substantive conversation about Mormonism. Indeed, Romney uttered only one direct mention of his particular faith in his speech, confessing he believed in "my Mormon faith" and tried to live by it. "Some believe that such a confession of my faith will sink my candidacy. If they are right, so be it," Romney dramatically remarked, but his talk struck most as far more bold in its promise than in its execution.[13]

While Americans of all different stripes admired Romney for deciding to speak out about his faith, the Texas speech and other religious declarations Romney made on the campaign trail left most of them flummoxed. Some of the most surprising responses came from fellow Mormons who found Romney on shaky theological grounds in his desire for evangelical acceptance. Romney's continual assertion of his salvation based only on his relationship with Jesus Christ—at times Romney even referred to Jesus as his "personal savior"—sounded like born-again talk and a contradiction of LDS teaching. Romney also offered strange thoughts on the Bible. At a GOP debate in St. Petersburg, Florida, a week before Romney's Texas speech, a video questioner asked the candidates if they believed every word of the Bible.

"I believe the Bible is the word of God, absolutely," Romney responded. The debate's moderator, Anderson Cooper, then repeated the inquiry, asking if Romney really believed every word. "Yeah, I believe it's the word of God," Romney continued. "The Bible is the word of God. I mean, I might interpret the word differently than you interpret the word, but I read the Bible and I believe the Bible is the word of God. I don't disagree with the Bible."[14]

Sounding almost like an evangelical defender of inerrancy, Romney's statement violated one of Mormonism's most foundational beliefs about the nature of the Bible as an imperfect, incomplete text—a teaching from the LDS Church's earliest days by which Joseph Smith had justified his new scriptures and a belief that Mormon leaders had continually reaffirmed right up to the time of Romney's comments. Just a few weeks before the St. Petersburg debate, M. Russell Ballard, one of the LDS Church's highest-ranking authorities, had explained to *U.S. News and World Report* that Mormons used the Bible and the Book of Mormon "hand in hand as Scripture and guidance and doctrine."[15] The day after the debate, the *New York Times* noted that the LDS Church's website clearly stated that Mormons regarded the Bible as "the word of God" but did not believe that it "as it is currently available, is without error." "As the Bible was compiled, organized, translated and transcribed," LDS.org continued, "many errors entered the text."[16] Other comments Romney made on the campaign trail, including saying that he couldn't "imagine anything more awful than polygamy," insisting that Jesus would return to Jerusalem rather than Jackson County, Missouri, as Mormons believe, and diminishing the LDS practice of baptism for the dead, a vital Mormon ritual, struck Romney's fellow Mormons as insensitive remarks at best and, in many cases, heretical statements. Increasingly, many Mormons felt as one LDS man from Wyoming did that Romney's discussion of his religious beliefs left them "very, very queasy."[17]

Unsurprisingly, evangelicals found Romney's words suspicious because they sounded too much like their own theological positions. As David Brody, the chief political correspondent for Pat Robertson's Christian Broadcasting Network, put it, "It's not like he's fooling Evangelicals. . . . They know the deal."[18] Brody suggested Romney "just recognize the differences between the two religions and then pivot to higher ground by saying this election shouldn't be about a religious test for office."[19] While Romney's Texas speech had tried to claim that higher ground of American religious tolerance, evangelicals felt he still had evaded a real acknowledgment of the critical differences between Mormonism and evangelical Christianity. *Christianity Today* welcomed Romney's Texas talk for endorsing many points evangelicals held dear, including the importance of religion in the nation's public life and the tradition of religious liberty. The magazine also praised the strength of Romney's religious convictions, unlike those Americans from mainline denominations who believed in a "wishy-washy religion." "If we are going to engage in interreligious conversation," the magazine explained, "we want to do it with people who believe what they believe." Still, *Christianity Today* observed that the particulars of Romney's beliefs remained unclear. "Romney refused to address the specifics of his religion," the magazine noted of his speech. Further, the magazine explained that most evangelicals considering Mormonism's "continued rejection of historic Christian truths" would have a hard time accepting Romney's contention that he depended on Jesus for his salvation. While evangelicals sympathized with Romney's request to be assessed on political rather than theological terms, the magazine admitted that lingering doubts about Mormonism overshadowed evangelical sensitivities to fairness and tolerance, especially since electing a Mormon to the nation's highest office would go far in "mainstreaming . . . a marginal faith" whose growth and expansion evangelicals had long worried about. "It's one thing to listen to the Mormon Tabernacle Choir or to elect Harry Reid or Orrin Hatch," *Christianity Today* explained. "It is quite something else to elect a Mormon president."[20]

Worries about Mormonism's greater visibility should he occupy the White House represented one of the biggest reasons evangelicals remained reluctant to support Romney. In a three-part series, "Is Mormonism Christian?," published on the website for the Southern Baptist Convention's North American Mission Board at the same time as Romney's speech in Texas, the SBC's director of apologetics and interfaith evangelism, Mike Licona, worried that a Mormon president would increase the LDS Church's presence and benefit its missionary efforts, a prospect evangelicals had warily watched for more than fifty years.[21] Yet, the series also noted that Romney's positions on abortion and gay marriage might make him the most attractive candidate to evangelical voters and reminded its readers that Americans were electing a president, not a pastor. Importantly, the articles focused on the question of Mormonism as a Christian religion. Licona pointed out that LDS missionaries would ignore the aspects of Mormon theology that "are fundamentally different from those found in biblical Christianity," including that God had once been a human, that humans themselves could become a god, and that Mormons disavowed the Trinity. Instead, Mormons sharing their faith had been trained to focus on the "common ground" they held with "biblical Christians," something evangelicals could see more publicly in Romney's appeals for their support.[22] But Christians should not be hoodwinked by these similarities, Licona warned. "Despite the fact that the Mormon church [*sic*] embraces a few beliefs in line with biblical Christianity it is demonstrably a false religion," he explained.[23] In the last article, appearing the day following Romney's Texas speech, Licona took up the question of whether Mormonism was a cult. While evangelicals, and particularly Southern Baptists, had routinely ascribed a cult status to Mormonism since the 1950s, Licona's answer revealed a subtle but important adjustment to that broad-brushed descriptor. Licona parsed the meaning of cult and concluded that Mormonism was a "theological cult" rather than a "sociological cult" because the LDS Church's extra-biblical doctrines meant Mormons believed a theology fundamentally different from orthodox Christianity. Yet it could not be considered a "sociological cult," Licona reasoned, because Mormons were not "sociologically or culturally deviant," such as the Moonies or Branch Davidians, nor were they commanded by a controlling leader who required outrageous acts of devotion from them, such as Jim Jones or David Koresh had.[24]

Significantly, evangelical commentary on Mormonism in the twenty-first century usually unreservedly praised Mormons as good and decent people, a notable change from nearly fifty years of evangelical anti-Mormonism that had suspiciously regarded Mormons' squeaky-clean image as a subterfuge masking aberrant beliefs and practices. (This may have been driven in part by their awareness that the news media were now closely examining evangelical-Mormon relations.) The SBC web series specifically noted that Mormons were not "sociologically or culturally deviant." Instead, Licona described Mormons as "wonderful people who are very sincere about their faith and are generally very caring."[25] That sentiment echoed through other evangelical commentary about Mormonism through the 2008 election. On the Christian Broadcasting Network's webpage, Pat Robertson's network included Mormonism in a short article entitled, "How Do I Recognize a Cult?" The piece praised Mormons as "the most exemplary human beings, especially in regards to their behavior patterns and their adherence to the fundamental values of society." Still, their religious beliefs were "simply, wrong. . . . when it comes to spiritual matters, the Mormons are far from the truth."[26]

Catholics generally seemed unconcerned with Romney's Mormon faith, but this didn't mean they lacked religious objections to Mormonism. A complimentary article in the conservative Catholic periodical, *Crisis Magazine*, explained why Romney was the "Best Choice for Catholic Conservatives," in spite of his religious faith. The piece admitted Mormonism's "bizarre doctrines" and objected to the LDS Church's "infiltration of third-world Catholic cultures" through its missionary efforts, but reminded readers they were electing a president rather than a religious leader. Some of this same argumentation had been made by evangelicals supportive of Romney (and would become a much more prominent evangelical argument in 2012), but Catholic discussion of Mormonism during the campaign seemed perfunctory rather than anguished as most evangelical commentary did. *Crisis* described Mormonism as a "corrupted religion . . . but it's a corruption of familiar American Christianity," suggesting the LDS faith was not that different from Protestantism's shortcomings.[27] In most Catholic corners, it seemed pointless to worry about Romney's Mormonism any more than the non-Catholic faiths of all the other inhabitants of the White House.

For some of his GOP opponents, however, Romney's Mormonism offered a useful issue to poke at, hoping that by keeping the topic alive Romney would be unable to take the lead in the GOP primaries that drew from a disproportionately evangelical electorate. Mike Huckabee, the former governor of Arkansas who had first begun as a Baptist preacher, especially cultivated a subtle but persistent queasiness about Mormonism from campaign voters. In the critical opening Iowa Caucus, where nearly 60 percent of Republican voters described themselves as evangelicals, Huckabee touted his authentic Christian credentials and slyly suggested Mormonism had connections to the occult, a historic accusation of evangelical anti-Mormonism but a charge that by 2008 had disappeared almost entirely from evangelical commentary on the LDS Church.[28]

Falling in early December, the Iowa Caucus commingled with preparations for Christmas. Republican candidates, particularly concerned with capturing support from Iowa's large base of religious conservatives, sprinkled "Merry Christmas" tidings amid their campaign speeches, spreading not only a typical yuletide greeting but also coyly tapping into conservative Christian fears, stoked by right-wing media outlets each December, about a liberal "War on Christmas." To say "Merry Christmas" was not merely a holiday pleasantry; it was another lob to the secular Left in the nation's ongoing culture war. As the nation looked on to see who would emerge victorious from Iowa, Mike Huckabee pretended to pause from the campaign with a television advertisement that drew Iowans back to the more important Christmas season. Huckabee's ad, "What Matters," found the candidate sitting in front of a Christmas tree in a warmly lit living room. As the soft strains of "Silent Night" played in the background, Huckabee dressed in a comfortable red sweater wondered aloud if those watching were "worn out" from all the commercials playing, especially those about politics. "I don't blame you," Huckabee commiserated. Amid all the rush and commotion of the season, Huckabee suggested that "sometimes it's nice to pull aside from all of that and just remember that what really matters is the celebration of the birth of Christ."[29]

Most observers saw the ad for what it was—a political move disguised as a nonpolitical offering, a candidate's attempt to assert the sacred over the political for his own electoral gain. But a smaller crowd spotted something more subliminal and subversive in Huckabee's commercial. As the camera panned across the living room, a bookcase over Huckabee's shoulder appeared to have been lighted in just such a way to make one section of the shelves glow as a bright white cross, standing out against an otherwise darkly lit background. Instantly, Huckabee's Christmas ad (which was also playing in New Hampshire and South Carolina in anticipation of their upcoming primaries and was being viewed by millions of Americans on YouTube) grabbed all the coverage of the Iowa campaign. The cable news outlets assembled the usual suspects of pundits and partisans to debate again whether or not a cross floated behind Huckabee's head as they repeatedly replayed the commercial. Huckabee expectedly claimed innocence, laughed off the controversy, and tried to steer the conversation back to his "War on Christmas" talking points. "I know this is probably a very controversial thing, but may I say to you, Merry Christmas," Huckabee took to exclaiming in his speeches throughout Iowa in the days that followed.[30] But a growing crowd started to contend that Huckabee's ad had crossed the line.

Predictably, Democrats had a field day with the ad, many seeing it as yet more proof of the theocratic intentions of the Republican Party. Some of Huckabee's fellow challengers for the GOP nomination also jumped at the chance to use the ad against Huckabee, now surging ahead in the Iowa polls. Ron Paul, the libertarian firebrand, said the ad reminded him of the famous Sinclair Lewis line, "When fascism comes to this country, it will be wrapped in a flag, carrying a cross." Paul growled that the floating cross was Huckabee's attempt to suggest he was the only Christian in the race.[31] Many GOP insiders saw the ad as embarrassing and a distraction from a campaign that ought to focus on serious economic and foreign policy concerns. Peggy Noonan devoted an entire article of her *Wall Street Journal* column to the floating cross controversy, deeming it "creepy."[32] But Huckabee's fiercest critics came from non-evangelical religious conservatives, most of whom shared his traditional social positions but recoiled at the cross imagery they interpreted as a dog-whistle to evangelical voters rather than an expression of conservative Christian ecumenism. Bill Donahue, president of the Catholic League for Religious and Civil Liberties, took to the morning television show, "Fox and Friends," to accuse the ad of that very sinister purpose. "You know what," Donahue scolded, "sell yourself on your issues, not on what your religion is."[33] The Catholic news network EWTN pondered the ad and suggested that Huckabee had "exploited his faith."[34]

Among Republican religious conservatives, however, Mormons reacted most negatively to Huckabee's Christmas ad. Modern Mormons generally avoid the symbol of the cross, yet another practice that Mormon critics pointed to as evidence of Mormonism's non-Christian status. Mormon buildings never display a cross; Mormons never wear a cross around their necks.[35] As LDS President Gordon B. Hinckley had explained in 2005, Mormons saw the cross as a "symbol of the dying Christ, while our message is a declaration of the Living Christ."[36] If Huckabee's Christmas ad indeed contained a planted cross in it, it was unlikely that Huckabee meant anything more by it than an expression of his Christian faith, but Mormon viewers were convinced the cross, especially coming from Huckabee, was an intentional anti-Mormon gesture. Leaders of the LDS Church unsurprisingly remained mute on the floating cross controversy; Romney's presence in the race meant LDS officials were particularly committed to appearing neutral during the campaign season. But the Mormon blogosphere erupted with chatter over Huckabee's anti-Mormon Christmas ad. As one blogger from Utah wrote, Huckabee's commercial with its "Anti-Mormon Cross" was "just the latest of his stunts to try and convince the voting populace that Mitt Romney is a member of a cult."[37]

Though Huckabee offered the most socially conservative positions of the major Republican candidates for the 2008 election, positions that marked him clearly to the right of Mitt Romney and aligned Huckabee more closely with most Mormons politically, Mormons resisted supporting Huckabee not only because of strong allegiances they felt toward Romney but also because of a growing sense among them of Huckabee's unabashed anti-Mormonism. Even before the Christmas commercial could confirm those fears, Huckabee had a number of strikes against him as far as Mormons were concerned. As a former Southern Baptist pastor, Huckabee's church affiliation represented one of the most stridently anti-Mormon denominations in LDS minds. Mormons knew well the history of Southern Baptist–LDS relations and they couldn't help but see Huckabee, a man who had not only pastored a church but also served as president of the Arkansas Baptist State Convention before becoming governor, as somehow complicit in propagating a Southern Baptist anti-Mormonism.

An extended profile of Huckabee in the *New York Times Magazine* offered additional proof for his questionable reputation among Mormons. Just days before the release of Huckabee's Christmas ad, the Sunday magazine's cover article, "The Huckabee Factor," legitimated the one-time dark-horse candidate who now seemed poised to win Iowa and perhaps even the GOP nomination, but a small comment Huckabee made soon became the only topic of conversation among those watching the race. Asked by the reporter if he considered Mormonism a cult, Huckabee feigned ignorance. "I think it's a religion," Huckabee responded. "I really don't know much about it."[38] Had Huckabee stopped there, his comment would have likely attracted no attention. It was a doubtful claim, of course. Huckabee, as a Southern Baptist pastor and state convention president, would have encountered Baptist teachings about Mormonism in various spots throughout his ministry, including seminary. As one Baptist pastor from North Carolina had recently explained to a different reporter, part of his training for the ministry had involved studying Mormonism in a course called "Cults and False Religions."[39] It was very likely Huckabee had done the same while in seminary, and even if he hadn't it would have been almost impossible to miss the steady stream of anti-Mormon materials the Southern Baptist Convention had produced through the years. In fact, Huckabee had delivered the keynote speech at the SBC's annual meeting in 1998 that, because of its convening in Salt Lake City, had given special attention to educating Baptists about the false religion of Mormonism and to proselytizing Mormons. Yet rather than maintaining an air of unfamiliarity—not a rare move for politicians during a campaign season—Huckabee pushed his conversation with the *Times'* reporter to an unexpected place. "Don't Mormons believe that Jesus and the devil are brothers?" Huckabee asked aloud.[40]

Predictably, Huckabee's suggestive question drew outrage from all corners. The LDS Church rushed to clarify Mormon theology regarding the devil in the aftermath of Huckabee's words. An LDS spokesperson explained to the Associated Press, "Satan is the exact opposite of who Christ is and what he stands for."[41] The website of Mormonism Research Ministry, an evangelical group devoted to converting LDS members into evangelical Christians, pointed out the LDS spokesperson's comments still hadn't addressed the question of Jesus and Satan's relationship in Mormon theology, and it cited an impressive collection of LDS scripture, documents, and statements that described them as siblings, including a passage from the *Journal of Discourses*, a 26-volume series of early LDS sermons, that described the devil as "the mighty Lucifer, the great prince of the angels, and the brother of Jesus."[42]

Though the controversy hurt Huckabee's reputation, it couldn't dim his prospects in Iowa. Buoyed by evangelical voters who dominated the state's Republican Party, Mike Huckabee pulled off an upset victory in the Iowa Caucus. But Huckabee's aspirations—and those of Romney—soon grew dim as Senator John McCain of Arizona marched to the GOP nomination and, in doing so, put to rest for the moment questions about the evangelical–Mormon political relationship. McCain, a man who seemed uncomfortable talking about any Christian faith he may have had and who was known more for his national security expertise than for leading any culture war battles, had tried for the presidency eight years earlier, but George W. Bush, aided by a battalion of conservative religious voters, had quickly nabbed the Republican nomination. McCain's victory in 2008 over Huckabee and Romney and coming at the conclusion of a Bush presidency widely regarded at the moment as a failure, led election observers to interpret the results as a repudiation by Republican voters of the Religious Right's prominent position in the party. With Barack Obama's historic win in the general election, the prognostications of the Religious Right's demise grew loud once again.

Some of the Religious Right's most important voices aided the doomsday talk. Cal Thomas, as he had done near the end of the Clinton presidency, once again urged Christians to abandon politics for proselytizing—a vision that privileged sectarianism over conservative ecumenism. "Thirty years of trying to use government to stop abortion, preserve opposite-sex marriage, improve television and movie content and transform culture into the conservative Evangelical image has failed," Thomas pronounced. "Evangelicals are at a junction. They can take the path that will lead them to more futility and ineffective attempts to reform culture through government, or they can embrace the far more powerful methods outlined by the One they claim to follow. By following His example, they will decrease, but He will increase. They will get no credit, but they will see results. If conservative Evangelicals choose obscurity and seek to glorify God, they will get much of what they hope for, but can never achieve, in and through politics."[43]

But not all conservative Christians were willing to abandon the public square altogether. Many believed Obama's victory required pro-family forces to join together again across denominational lines and theological boundaries united in their defense of traditional values against the proponents of secular liberalism and its ills. Some of these people met in the fall of 2009 to draft the Manhattan Declaration, a 4,700-word document that reaffirmed their common conservative stances on abortion, gay marriage, and religious freedom. Citing their "2,000 year tradition," these leaders from across Christianity wrote they had gathered together "to proclaim the Gospel of costly grace, to protect the intrinsic dignity of the human person and to stand for the common good." Affirming three points of agreement, the declaration lamented that the lives of the unborn were "severely threatened" in a nation that continued to allow abortions; rejected "accommodat[ing] fashionable ideologies" to allow gay marriage while defining marriage as "a conjugal union of man and woman, ordained by God from creation"; and defended "religious liberty, which is grounded in the character of God, the example of Christ, and the inherent freedom and dignity of human beings created in the divine image."[44] Led by Charles "Chuck" Colson, the Watergate ex-con turned evangelical culture warrior; Timothy George, the dean of a Southern Baptist seminary; and Robert George, a constitutional scholar at Princeton University and a devout Catholic, the Manhattan Declaration included the signatures of 125 evangelical, Catholic, and Orthodox leaders. No Mormon representatives appeared as signatories, however—a curious omission given the LDS Church's influential role in the recent passing of ballot Proposition 8 that overturned California's brief legalization of same-sex marriage.[45]

In addition to the 125 original signatories, Americans had the opportunity to add their name to the Manhattan Declaration on the group's website. After one week, more than one hundred and fifty thousand Americans had signed their name in support.[46] Less than two weeks later, that number had grown to more than two hundred and sixty thousand.[47] Most observers, and likely many of those who provided their signatures of support, saw the Manhattan Declaration as a political statement and the latest battle cry of the Religious Right. Yet its creators, and, importantly, its critics in evangelical circles, understood the document as a religious statement—a text more concerned with outlining biblical truth, Christian morality, and the sovereignty of God than in mobilizing political action. A few days after the Manhattan Declaration's public release, Chuck Colson took to his blog to emphasize its religious meaning, calling the document "a form of catechism for the foundational truths of the faith." Colson also celebrated the ecumenical group that had introduced it to the public at Washington, D.C.'s National Press Club. "It was a foretaste of what we're all going to see in heaven," Colson described the interfaith assembly, "when those of us who can truly trust the Bible, who love Christ with all our hearts, minds, and souls, are re-united in the presence of our gracious and loving God."[48]

Such comments made the exclusion of LDS participation from the Manhattan Declaration all the clearer. While an increasing community of evangelicals and Catholics could imagine spending eternity with one another in heaven based on a shared biblical understanding of salvation, accepting that any Mormons had also found salvation remained impossible for almost all of them. Although the LDS Church kept silent on its exclusion from the Manhattan Declaration, the church had made a few tentative outreaches to evangelicals and Catholics that must have made their absence in this important ecumenical statement all the more painful. One year earlier, LDS representatives had joined in an ecumenical religious service for the first time as two members of the church's Quorum of the Twelve Apostles had participated in a papal prayer service at New York's St. Joseph's Church. The Mormon leaders had asked if they could attend—a significant move considering how vigorously the LDS Church had opposed ecumenical efforts and how rarely ecumenists had sought Mormon involvement. But leaders in the LDS Church worried about how poorly Mormonism had fared in Romney's recent run for the GOP nomination, and some church authorities thought its image might be repaired through closer relations with other faiths and a less-separatist identity. Father James Massa, the Catholic Church's executive director for the Secretariat of Ecumenical and Interreligious Affairs, welcomed the Mormons. "We're not making any theological statements today," Massa told reporters, acknowledging that Catholic ecumenism had always meant far more theologically for other faiths than it had for the Catholic Church. "This is a very big statement they are making."[49] The day of the prayer service, the LDS Church released a statement regarding "Respect for Diversity of Faiths" on its website. The document urged Mormons to respect and seek to understand other faiths while also working with them to alleviate the world's ills, but to remember that joint charitable work didn't compromise theological integrity or religious autonomy. "It is necessary to maintain a separation between charitable efforts and doctrinal tenets," the document explained, "while at the same time sharing mutual concern for those in need. People of good faith do not need to have the same exact beliefs in order to accomplish great things in service of their fellow human beings."[50]

While the LDS statement mentioned only charitable partnerships, the "Respect for Diversity of Faiths" might also have pointed to shared political objectives, like the recent battle for Prop 8. Similarly, had the Manhattan Declaration's creators envisioned themselves as cultural polemicists, they likely would have drawn a much wider circle, inclusive of Mormons. But the declaration's organizers, many of them participants in "Evangelicals and Catholics Together" more than ten years before, instead wanted to assert a particular Christian conscience that drew on a shared history and biblical tradition. While the declaration's opening line had presented its backers as "Orthodox, Catholic, and Evangelical Christians," those designations dropped away as the document continued, replaced with the simple descriptive of "Christians." "We are Christians who have joined together across historic lines of ecclesial difference to affirm our right—and more importantly, to embrace our obligation—to speak and act in defense of these truths," the declaration explained. The Manhattan Declaration presented Christian division as merely ecclesiastical, the product of historical events disconnected from questions of theology or doctrine. (Indeed, the word "theology" never appeared in the document; "doctrine" merited two mentions but these referred to eugenicists' beliefs.)[51]

Evangelical critics of the Manhattan Declaration, who tended to come primarily from the Reformed wing of American evangelicalism, objected to its vague notion of the gospel, exhibited by its inclusive ecumenism and reaffirmed in Colson's expansive vision of heaven. The very religious nature of the document—rather than its political contents—troubled Reformed leaders like Mike Horton, Alistair Begg, and R. C. Sproul, who worried that the gospel was being reduced to shared cultural concerns. Horton charged that the declaration continued the "tendency to define 'the gospel' as something other than the specific announcement of the forgiveness of sins and declarations of righteousness solely by Christ's merits"—a precedent he'd noted and disparaged in "Evangelicals and Catholics Together." Because the declaration continually invoked the "gospel" but never defined it, Horton and others argued that its meaning had been confused and conflated with "Western Civilization" and "the law."[52] Begg offered an even more pointed attack at what he saw as the declaration's ecumenical emphasis over theological precision and purity. In a letter to Colson, which he republished on his blog, Begg declared he could not join in signing the declaration along "with those with whom I have fundamental disagreements on the nature of the Gospel." Begg further elaborated to his blog readers that he respected cobelligerency as a political tactic but that it had to be recognized as separate from any discussion of Christian conviction. "The activity of the Christian as a citizen engaging in co-belligerency over civic and moral issues is not the same as the declaration of Christians mutually recognizing the reality of each other's faiths," Begg explained. "I do not believe it is possible to embrace the premises of ecumenical strategy and still draw the conclusions of evangelical orthodoxy," he continued. Reminiscent of the "spiritual unity" that leading evangelical institutions like *Christianity Today* and the NAE had once championed as the sole ecumenical conception for conservative Protestants, Begg suggested evangelicals band together "rather than seeking cooperation with segments from Rome" or with any others who belonged to churches whose teachings were "a denial of the biblical gospel."[53] Sproul echoed such concerns. "How could I sign something that confuses the gospel and obscures the very definition of who is and who is not a Christian?" he asked on his blog. "While I would march with the bishop of Rome and an Orthodox prelate to resist the slaughter of innocents in the womb," Sproul explained, "I could never ground that cobelligerency on the assumption that we share a common faith and a unified understanding of the gospel."[54] Other corners of the evangelical community were even blunter. The Christian Apologetics and Research Ministry (CARM), an evangelical organization in Idaho, explained it could not join in the Manhattan Declaration "for one significant reason: it includes Roman

Catholics as Christians." "More important than Christian unity," CARM's president, Matt Slick explained, "is the truth of God's word."[55]

Those voices withstanding, the Manhattan Declaration displayed the increasing interfaith allegiances between Catholics and evangelicals. While the document strove to reflect common Christian convictions, it also contained particular Catholic ideas that evangelicals had typically disagreed with. Most notably, the declaration repeatedly affirmed the power of human reason as a basis for morality alongside Scripture. "What the Bible and the light of reason make clear," the declaration announced, "we must make clear." In its opening lines, the declaration had defined truth as "grounded in Holy Scripture" and "in natural human reason"—a twin basis for truth that departed from the evangelical belief of *sola scriptura*.[56] Robert George, the lone Catholic of the three-person drafting committee, had pushed for the inclusion of reason, a critical component of Catholic natural law theory. George saw himself in the tradition of Thomas Aquinas who had argued that reason allows humans to understand and identify an objective moral order. But evangelicals typically distrusted human reason as a guide to moral authority. The human mind was so corrupt, Martin Luther had argued, that faith alone, not reason, could bring salvation. Despite that historic resistance, George had convinced his evangelical coauthors of his case. "I sold my view about reason!" he boasted to the *New York Times* shortly after the declaration's release.[57]

Although Mormons had been left out of the Manhattan Declaration, their prominence in the movement against same-sex marriage in California in 2008 had earned them the respect of those same religious conservatives. That year, California voters considered a state ballot proposition that would amend California's constitution to define marriage as between a man and a woman. Earlier that year, California's Supreme Court had overruled two statutes prohibiting same-sex marriage. In the months after that ruling, thousands of gay and lesbian couples rushed to city halls across the state to have their unions legalized. While commentators cited the California decision as a harbinger for marriage equality across the nation—"as California goes, so goes the nation" became a favorite talking point from the chattering classes—opponents of same-sex marriage refused to accept the California ruling as settled law. Even before the court had issued its decision, pro-family activists had already collected almost one million signatures to guarantee the constitutional amendment proposal, named the California Marriage Protection Act, would be on the ballots for voters to consider that fall—far more than the seven hundred thousand signatures California required.[58]

After guaranteeing its inclusion on the November ballot, anti–gay marriage activists concentrated on ensuring California voters would support

Proposition 8. A broad coalition of religious activists, pro-family political groups, and churches emerged to mobilize voters, but the LDS Church quickly took the lead as the most powerful force for Prop 8. In June, the church's First Presidency sent a letter to all its congregations. Citing the church's "unequivocal" teachings on marriage and the family, LDS leaders implored the Saints to "do all you can to support the proposed constitutional amendment by donating of your means and time."[59] Donate they did. By September, LDS members had given nearly $5 million to the cause.[60] By election day, Protect Marriage, the leading organization supporting Prop 8 in California, estimated that Mormons had contributed at least half of the more than $40 million raised by their side.[61] (Another estimate, from a leading figure against Prop 8, pegged the Mormon contribution as closer to $30 million of the $42 million collected.)[62] With Mormons making up only about 2 percent of California's population, much of that LDS money turned out later to have come from out of state, particularly from members in Utah.[63] Yet despite their small presence in California, Mormons dominated the door-to-door canvassing, the phone banks, and other volunteer efforts on behalf of Prop 8. To cite one figure, Mormons made up 80 to 90 percent of the volunteers who visited each home in election precincts across the state.[64]

All along the way, the LDS Church continued encouraging its members across the nation to maintain their work for Prop 8's passage. Similar constitutional amendments in Arizona and Florida also received the church's attention—LDS members there were urged to assist the battles in their home states—but the focus remained on California since LDS leaders and others saw it as the bellwether scenario for the nation's marriage equality question. The church created a website, PreservingMarriage.org, where its members could learn more about the church's position on marriage and Proposition 8.[65] In August, LDS leaders released "The Divine Institution of Marriage," a robust elaboration of marriage's sacred nature and its essential role in "the plan of salvation," a fundamental Mormon teaching that had always drawn criticism from Mormonism's detractors, especially evangelicals. The document also warned against the "harmful consequences" that would arise from the legalization of gay marriage. These included requiring public schools to instruct students about marriage and sexuality in ways that contradicted conservative parents' beliefs, diminishing further the family unit in American society and culture, and eroding the "social identity, gender development, and moral character of children."[66] The document stopped short of claiming the legalization of same-sex marriage would force churches to change their beliefs or practices, but Prop 8 advertisements and materials frequently suggested churches might lose their tax-exempt status or face other punishments if they refused to accept the legal change.[67] One Mormon woman at a Prop 8 rally in Oakland told a reporter that without the amendment "there will be gay marriage in my church."[68]

In the final weeks before the election, the LDS Church spearheaded a vigorous effort on behalf of Prop 8 that in many ways resembled the work it had once conducted against the Equal Rights Amendment. Church officials traveled constantly from Salt Lake City to California to oversee the groundwork. Additional volunteers were bused in from Utah to aid California Mormons in their door-to-door canvassing. Direct mail sponsored by the church flooded Californians' mailboxes.[69] In October, Mormon officials requested that California Saints living outside of the state make calls to friends and family back home urging their support for Prop 8.[70] By saying that only California citizens living outside of the state should make those calls, church leaders were probably hoping to ensure that all their actions looked aboveboard. But a reporter in Rexburg, Idaho, where 97 percent of the thirty thousand residents belonged to the LDS Church, found the call center of a health-products company packed with Mormons phoning voters in California. All across the nation, Mormons staffed phone banks set up in similar locations, usually at the offices of a Mormon-owned business. It was unlikely that all those callers were displaced Californians.[71]

Going into election day, most polling suggested that Californians would defeat Prop 8. But long after Barack Obama had captured the White House, political watchers continued to wait on results from California. For much of the evening, the Prop 8 race remained too tight to call. Yet when all the precincts were reported in, the amendment had tallied a solid victory, garnering more than 52 percent of the vote.[72] (Voters in Florida and Arizona provided even larger margins for the anti–gay marriage bills under consideration there.) In light of Obama's historic victory that same night, not a few commentators noted the irony in an election that had cracked the racial barrier to the nation's highest office while also rolling back the civil rights of thousands of Californians. That irony seemed especially cruel to many considering Obama had grabbed a hearty 61 percent of the vote in California.[73] In the days following the election, gay marriage supporters organized protest rallies against Prop 8's passage in cities across the nation. Many of those rallies took place outside LDS temples as protesters focused their rage on the institution they believed responsible for the amendment's passage.

While thousands gathered outside their temples—an estimated ten thousand New Yorkers protested in front of the LDS temple near Lincoln Square—LDS leaders tried to shift attention away from their church. Noting that a majority of Californians had voted for Prop 8, LDS Church spokesman Michael Otterson also pointed to the "very broad-based coalition" of faiths that had worked on behalf of the amendment. "It's a little disturbing to see these protestors singling out the Mormon Church. What exactly are they protesting?" Otterson asked.[74] In the weeks and months following the protests against Prop 8 and the LDS Church, evangelicals and Catholics offered their support. The U.S. Conference of Catholic Bishops sent a letter to LDS President Thomas S. Monson thanking him for his church's leadership role on behalf of Prop 8 and offering "prayerful support and solidarity" with LDS efforts against same-sex marriage.[75] That same day, the National Organization for Marriage (NOM), a lobbying group that supported legislation against same-sex marriage across the country, also sent a letter to Monson, signed by dozens of prominent Catholic and evangelical activists, including James Dobson, Chuck Colson, the SBC's Richard Land, and Tony Perkins of the Family Research Council.[76] The letter began "We write firstly to express our deep gratitude to you and the entire LDS community for the large and impressive contributions of your church and its members in protecting marriage." More than thanking the LDS Church, the letter expressed "outrage at the vile and indecent attacks directed specifically and uniquely at the Church of Jesus Christ of Latter-day Saints and its members because of your courage in standing up for marriage."[77] More than four thousand supporters soon added their name to the letter on a website created by NOM, abovethehate.com.[78]

In naming the website "Above the Hate," Prop 8's supporters sought to reset the conversation on marriage equality. Opponents of Prop 8 in California had branded the measure as an act of odious vengeance against gays and lesbians—supporting Prop 8 equated to hating your gay friends, family, and fellow citizens. Prop 8's backers hoped instead that somehow voters would not see gays as the amendment's target. "It is not our goal in this campaign to attack the homosexual lifestyle . . . the less we refer to homosexuality, the better," a training document circulated among Mormon volunteers had explained. "We are pro-marriage, not anti-gay."[79] But after the election, many Americans had difficulty separating Prop 8's defense of traditional marriage from their conviction that gays had been unfairly persecuted. A wildly successful media campaign launched by a group called the NoH8 Campaign in the days following Prop 8's passage capitalized on those sentiments as it formed a photographic record of protest. Thousands of Americans, including dozens of celebrities, posed for NoH8's signature photograph. With silver duct tape covering their mouths, the subjects stared at the camera with "NoH8" emblazoned in black and red makeup across their cheeks.[80]

Yet the protests outside LDS temples, some of which turned violent and destructive, and boycotts against businesses owned by people who had donated money for Prop 8 allowed the amendment's supporters to claim their status as the real victims of hate and intolerance.[81] Branded as hateful and intolerant, Prop 8's supporters turned the script. "So Much for Tolerance," ran the headline of Chuck Colson's editorial in the *Christian Post*.[82] An ad taken out in the *New York Times* by a diverse group, including leaders of the National Association of Evangelicals, the Catholic League for Religious and Civil Rights, and Chuck Colson, acknowledged the "fundamental disagreements" among them, but deplored the "anti-religious bigotry" Mormons and other defenders of traditional marriage faced.[83] Religious conservatives argued that they, not gays and lesbians, suffered the true persecution and vilification; that they were not the bigots in this battle, but that their foes who sought to silence religious voices were. In supporting Prop 8, they claimed, they had not sought to deny anyone their rights but instead simply defend a traditional foundation of society in heterosexual marriage. Now they were being attacked, threatened, and intimidated by the forces who claimed their own campaign was one of love and acceptance. Though typically critical of minority claims of victimization, Prop 8's supporters relished adopting the identity for themselves and delighted in pointing out what they saw as the hypocrisy of their foes. The attacks on the LDS Church were also useful in recasting the conversation about the minority class under attack by Prop 8. While the amendment's passage seemed to its opponents a clear affront to the civil rights of the minority group of gay and lesbian Californians, Prop 8's supporters highlighted Mormons' status as a "minority religion" to heighten sympathy in the weeks following the election. Depicted as a small, earnest group of devout Americans, Mormons' defenders hardly saw the LDS Church as the powerful political force gay marriage advocates accused it of being.[84]

Of course, seeing the LDS Church as a potent and outsized force bent on controlling its members and growing its authority had long been the way Mormonism's religious critics, particularly evangelicals, had viewed the church's activities. The *National Review* pointed to the historical fact that "anti-Mormon bigotry is unfortunately common" to explain why Mormons had become an "easy target" of Prop 8's opponents, but such comments ignored the obvious point that the fiercest anti-Mormonism had always come from those now claiming to be the LDS Church's closest allies.[85] But as evangelicals in the wake of Prop 8 defended Mormons and declared their alliance with the LDS Church, they did so in a way that drew sharp distinctions between sociopolitical and theological agreement, an emphasis that evangelicals now rarely felt needed to be made in discussions about their shared political values with Catholics. In an article defending the "small religious group" that had been instrumental to Prop 8's win, John Mark Reynolds, a philosopher at California's fundamentalist Biola University, credited Mormons as not only the force behind Prop 8 but also as the best friends "traditional Christians" had in defending the family. Reynolds deplored the "false attacks on Mormon faith and family" and also lamented that Mitt Romney had endured "unfair religious scrutiny" during his 2008 campaign, though Reynolds failed to mention that scrutiny had come almost entirely from evangelical circles. Yet in praising Mormons' family values, Reynolds reminded his readers of the "deep and important" differences between Mormon and evangelical theology, including the nature of God and his plan of salvation, and encouraged evangelicals to continue theological discussions over those disagreements while also standing closely with Mormons against attacks from their political foes.[86]

Although evangelicals and conservative Catholics obviously agreed with LDS positions on same-sex marriage, the ensuing fracas over Mormon leadership in the Prop 8 victory shifted and enlarged the conversation in conservative religious circles from the particular topic of marriage to larger questions about religious liberty. Evangelicals and Catholics had to stand with Mormons not merely because they agreed on a traditional definition of marriage or a host of other particular issues, they reasoned, but because of the larger threat to represent their values and convictions in the public square. In witnessing the attacks on the LDS Church for its involvement in the Prop 8 battle, conservative Catholics and evangelicals imagined their own vulnerability. Even more than recognizing common social and political positions, evangelicals, Mormons, and Catholics saw in one another their deepest worries about cultural marginalization and political silencing. Increasing unity among evangelicals, Mormons, and Catholics was born from this shared concern over religious liberty. While political issues like the ERA, abortion, and gay marriage had drawn them to the same sides of the battlefield, the issue of religious liberty provided a powerful unifying logic. Of course, those shared political and social positions were not insignificant. Rather, they were the means by which they might view one another charitably and familiarly. (Religious conservatives, it should be noted, seldom fretted about the religious liberty of liberal religionists or even less of non-Christian religious minorities, particularly Muslims.)

Worries over religious liberty knitted the conservative ecumenical alliance together tightly in ways that issue politics and, more strongly, theology could not. Politics could be unifying at the level of opposition or endorsement, but the pesky particularities of the legislative process had often proved far too insurmountable. Theology in the hands of religious conservatives sought to heighten the distinctions among religious faiths over the many commonalities and points of agreement in order to bolster the exclusive truth claims of each. While political victories often stalled at points where compromise broke down, theology started from a position of intractable orthodoxy against any hints of conciliation. But the cause of religious liberty evaded the challenges posed by both politics and theology. In utilizing arguments about religious liberty as a way to defend their unique political and cultural positions, conservative ecumenists imagined a shared status that drew from but remained above the particularities of politics even as it elided doctrinal distinctions in favor of a common "religious" identity.[87] Such a vision was evident in the visit of Cardinal Francis George, archbishop of Chicago and president of the United States Conference of Catholic Bishops, to the campus of Brigham Young University in 2010. Addressing a Mormon audience of more than twenty thousand, with many more watching on the LDS Church's website, George's talk, "Catholics and Latter-day Saints: Partners in the Defense of Religious Freedom," called on Catholics and Mormons to band together more closely as a "vital bulwark" against societal and political forces that sought to make religion no more than a private, personal affair and a matter of individual conscience. Religious freedom, as Catholics understood it, George explained, meant the right to influence the public square. Any efforts to minimize that conception of religious freedom contradicted America's political tradition and resembled Lenin's Soviet Union. "The lesson of American history," George contended, "is that churches and other religious bodies prosper in a nation and in a social order that respects religious freedom and recognizes that civil government should never stand between the consciences and the religious practice of its citizens and Almighty God."[88]

George admitted that his own church had not always respected religious freedom as a hallmark of democracy, but he pointed to the Second Vatican Council's reforms as the moment when the Catholic Church fully embraced religious liberty, particularly as expressed in the landmark "Declaration on Religious Liberty." But while LDS leaders had hardly viewed Vatican II favorably at the time, George's presence at BYU signaled a growing sympathy and alliance between the two faiths, strengthened by collaborative anti-poverty work and efforts against pornography, abortion, and same-sex marriage. As the first ever cardinal to speak at BYU (and a rare Catholic before Mormon audiences), George recognized the significance of his visit while also acknowledging that the two faiths historically had had little to do with each other. "I'm personally grateful that, after 180 years of living mostly apart from one another, Catholics and Latter-day Saints have begun to see one another as trustworthy partners in the defense of shared moral principles," he noted of recent developments. Yet history also provided important lessons for Mormons and Catholics about each other. Both had risen from small, persecuted religious sects to become major faiths in the United States; that shared experience ought to be a powerful bond for Mormons and Catholics to face together the contemporary threats against religious actors, George argued. "It is . . . true especially of our two groups . . . that the defense of religious liberty affirms what is deepest in our self-identity," George declared.[89]

Through the first Obama administration and into the 2012 election, religious conservatives warned of the threats posed to religious liberty by the new president's policies, but especially in terms of his landmark Affordable Care Act, derisively tagged "Obamacare" by its foes before being embraced as the preferred moniker by the president himself.[90] Catholics stepped to the forefront of the religious liberty fight because they opposed Obamacare's contraception mandate requiring all health care plans to provide contraception free of charge. Although the mandate provided a religious exception that excluded churches, all other employers were required to participate, including Catholic schools, agencies, and hospitals. The Obama administration defended this arrangement, pointing out that many of the employees of Catholic institutions were not members of the church but had been denied access to free contraception in their health care plans because of Catholic objection to birth control. Though health care reform advocates felt the religious exception struck a reasonable compromise, Catholic leaders protested the contraception mandate that they believed circumscribed their own moral influence at the church door. "Never before," declared Archbishop Timothy Dolan, president of the USCCB, in a video posted on the conference's website, "has the federal government forced individuals and organizations to go out into the marketplace and buy a product that violates our conscience. This shouldn't happen in a land where free exercise of religion ranks first in the Bill of Rights." Other Catholic leaders mounted a rising chorus of protest. Across the nation, 147 bishops authored their own letters regarding religious liberty, posting them on their websites, distributing them in parish newsletters, and having priests read them aloud in Sunday services.[91]

Given the quick and vigorous, though also expected, objections from Catholic leaders, the Obama administration sought to strike another compromise by announcing that insurance companies, rather than Catholic institutions themselves, would have to take on the burden of paying for the contraception, but the bishops immediately rejected this offer too.[92] While the White House saw the health care debate in political terms—a legislative challenge where victory would be achieved through careful compromise and tweaking of the bill's language—for Catholic leaders and their allies the question of a contraception mandate transcended the particulars of health care reform, an issue that the church largely supported, to the bigger matter of religious liberty. Evangelicals rushed in to offer their support, providing vigorous defense of the Catholic Church's position. Throughout President Obama's first term, evangelicals and Catholics had joined together to defend religious liberty at the local level in regard to same-sex marriage and abortion. In New Mexico, for example, a pro-life, pro-marriage rally brought thousands of Catholics and evangelicals together to hear from local Catholic and evangelical clergy. After the speeches, the Catholics and evangelicals divided for separate religious services at their respective houses of worship, but they then rejoined to march together to the state capitol.[93] Now the contraception mandate provided a national issue that linked evangelical and Catholic leaders even more closely. Although evangelicals did not share Catholic opposition to birth control—and had, in fact, taunted Catholics for their anti–birth control views in the past—they stressed that their support for Catholics did not have to come from a shared political position but instead depended on their own worries about religious liberty. "We evangelicals must stand unequivocally with our Roman Catholic brothers and sisters," the culture warriors Chuck Colson and Timothy George wrote. "Because when the government violates the religious liberty of one group, it threatens the religious liberty of all."[94] Although evangelicals had long used arguments about religious liberty to limit Catholic presence in the public sphere, nearly a half century of cultural transformation and theological reform had shifted the meaning of the term and evangelicals' relationship with it. Whereas Protestants had once claimed religious liberty meant the freedom *from* Catholic domination of the nation and the protection of religious pluralism, in an age that they believed had become totally secularized and hostile to religion religious liberty now meant the basic freedom of expression and public influence.

Although Mormons typically defended religious liberty as a cherished value, the LDS Church remained remarkably silent during the birth control mandate fracas of 2012. Some suspected that LDS reticence on the issue owed to the church's permissive attitude about birth control, believing it was a personal matter for each married couple to decide.[95] Yet evangelicals largely held the same belief about contraception but had supported the Catholic Church's defending itself against government interference. More likely, the LDS Church ignored the health care debate exciting most religious conservatives as part of their larger commitment to avoid the political spotlight in 2012 because one of their own, Mitt Romney, had once again entered the race for the Republican nomination for president.

Having run for the nomination four years before, Romney hoped to benefit from Republican tradition that tended to give previous near-winners the nomination on their second go-around. Yet while Romney had clearly made important inroads with the party four years before, he remained hampered by a religious affiliation that continued to pose real problems for a significant number of GOP voters. On the day Romney announced his entry into the Republican race, the Pew Research Center released polling results that showed Romney's Mormonism remained a political liability for his White House chances. Twenty-three percent of GOP voters indicated they would be "less likely" to vote for a Mormon presidential candidate, but that number rose to 34 percent of white evangelical Republican voters—a critical bloc in the GOP primaries. Only 16 percent of white Catholic Republicans said the same.[96]

As Pew pointed out, those numbers hadn't changed much from four years before, and the Romney camp knew what it was up against again. "If Romney were Presbyterian," one GOP political veteran remarked, "he would be the Republican nominee."[97] Such was the political wisdom of 2012, yet evangelical candidates like Rick Perry and Michelle Bachmann also failed to gain much traction with GOP voters. While Republicans were unified in their opposition to President Obama, they could not agree on a single GOP candidate to back. In a crowded field that also included Ron Paul, Herman Cain, John Huntsman, and Newt Gingrich, nearly every candidate enjoyed a brief moment in the lead before fizzling out. None seemed capable of moving permanently to the front of the pack, but the inability of any of them, particularly the hard-right candidates, to draw the Religious Right's favor meant no clear frontrunner could emerge.

Many evangelical activists and voters felt that if they could not unite behind a candidate it would not only hand Mitt Romney the nomination but also further demonstrate their waning influence in the party. In an effort to reverse that trend, 125 evangelical leaders convened at a Texas ranch in early 2012 to see if they could agree on a candidate to back before the primaries got away from them. *Time* magazine joked that the gathering should be called "Operation What To Do About Mitt Romney," but the evangelical attendees insisted they hadn't set out to stop Romney's bid. Still the invitation to the meeting seemed to belie that claim as it asked attendees if they would be "willing to compromise and change your choice to one that the body as a whole supports in order to not divide our strength."[98] Taking place just days before the South Carolina primary where most observers believed Romney's chances were slim, the Texas gathering clearly meant to coalesce behind one rival candidate who could deliver Romney a devastating blow in the Palmetto

State. While the call for agreement and unity had brought them together, the Texas meeting revealed instead the lingering divisions that were also apparent in the larger Religious Right electorate. After three ballots, Rick Santorum, the firebrand Catholic conservative and former Pennsylvania Senator, finally captured the group's endorsement, but many attendees later complained that rigged voting had led to his win.[99] When Newt Gingrich won the South Carolina primary a week later, over a third place finish from Santorum, the disunity of religious conservatives appeared all the more visible.[100]

Given the divided electorate and the flash-in-the-pan nature of several of his opponents' campaigns, Romney grinded out a victory and secured the GOP nomination by winning the Texas primary in late May 2012.[101] While evangelicals had been reluctant to support Romney wholeheartedly through the primaries, there had been a clear indication they would eventually rally behind him if need be to prevent a second term for Obama. Just before the primaries began, the Pew Research Center conducted another poll that revealed some hopeful news for Romney. Like another poll taken by Pew half a year before, results from this poll demonstrated that Romney's Mormonism continued to be a problem with some GOP voters. Only 17 percent of white evangelical Republicans named Romney as their first choice to win the GOP nomination, and 53 percent answered that Mormonism was "not Christian." Yet the poll found that if Romney were to win the Republican nomination he would also then capture the enthusiastic support of these reluctant primary voters. Faced with an election between Obama and Romney, 91 percent of white evangelical Republicans said they would support Romney with 79 percent of them declaring they would "strongly" do so. This number exceeded all Republican voters combined where 87 percent said they would back Romney in a head-to-head race with Obama, showing that anti-Obama passions ran strongest among evangelicals in the Republican Party.[102]

Still, once Romney secured the Republican nomination, there was a lingering concern that evangelical disappointment could lead to low voter turnout and an Obama win. Both the Romney campaign team and key evangelical leaders now focused on ensuring strong engagement from evangelical voters for the November election. Romney did his part by a set of carefully orchestrated overtures to the evangelical community, including his commencement address at Jerry Falwell's Liberty University in May 2012. Notably, Romney's Liberty speech espoused conservative Christian values and name-checked beloved evangelical institutions, like the fast food chain Chick-fil-A, and people, including Billy Graham, C. S. Lewis, and Chuck Colson. Importantly, Romney avoided ever calling himself a Christian or suggesting close similarities between Mormonism and evangelical Christianity, as he had done four years earlier. Romney's attempts to talk about his faith in the language of evangelical Christianity and to pass himself off as born-again believer had backfired disastrously in 2008, drawing the ire of evangelical leaders, but the candidate had learned his lesson. In his Liberty address, Romney instead depicted his own Mormonism and the religion of his listeners as distinctly different, though he never mentioned his faith by name. "People of different faiths, like yours and mine," Romney told the crowd, "sometimes wonder where we can meet in common purpose, when there are so many differences in creed and theology." Romney suggested that "shared moral convictions . . . stemming from a common worldview" could provide the uniting force. Abandoning any appeals tied to a common Christian identity, Romney instead offered a unity based on conservative convictions and the values of "faith, family, work, and service."[103]

Evangelical leaders appreciated that in Romney's Liberty speech and other appeals to evangelicals he had presented himself as a good and decent man of moral convictions, but not as a Christian just like them. John Mark Reynolds, the provost of Houston Baptist University, praised Romney's speech in Lynchburg, Virginia, for not pretending "to agree with the theology of the Liberty University audience."[104] Tony Perkins of the Family Research Council appreciated the speech's attention to the defense of religious freedom and that Romney recognized "the shared values while acknowledging the theological differences."[105] Still, Romney's appearance at Liberty had stirred controversy among the student body, many of whom felt the university shouldn't provide a Mormon, even one who might be the next president, with the opportunity to offer the last words on their evangelical education. That divide among the student body appeared on the university newspaper's editorial page where "pro" and "con" editorials ran side by side about the upcoming Romney visit. Speaking for the "con" side, the editorial reminded its readers of Romans 12's admonition to not be conformed to the patterns of the world. "It is cool and progressively academic to have a potential future president speak at commencement—but is it Christ-honoring?" the editorial asked. "Everyone on the other side of the fence is calling out for tolerance, including Romney himself—but biblically there is no such thing as tolerance," the editorial concluded.[106]

While the Liberty students were offering a theological objection to Romney's appearance at Liberty rather than a political opposition to his potential presidency, that unresolved tension remained a sticking point among evangelicals when considering Romney as a candidate. But now that Romney had captured the nomination, evangelical leaders sought to smooth over whatever resistance remained among their followers despite the fact that many of them had helped create and nurture an evangelical aversion to Mormonism through the years. Robert Jeffress, pastor of First Baptist Dallas, had called Mormonism a cult and said Romney was "not a Christian" during the primaries, charges that he had also made four years before.[107] But Jeffress soon endorsed Romney "in spite of his Mormon faith" because he stood for biblical principles regarding abortion and marriage rather than the non-biblical values Jeffress argued Obama extolled.[108]

In endorsing Romney, Jeffress argued that Christians could support a cult member who defended biblical traditionalism, but the 2012 election notably signaled a larger evangelical disavowal of cult terminology in reference to Mormonism. This language hadn't entirely exited the evangelical conversation about Mormonism, as comments from Jeffress and a few other evangelical leaders indicated, but they had been marginalized and even repudiated by the larger evangelical mainstream.[109] Tellingly, the same evangelical institutions—*Christianity Today*, the Southern Baptist Convention, the Billy Graham Evangelistic Association, and others—that had been at the forefront of shaping and spreading more than a half-century of anti-Mormon teachings redirected their efforts to supporting Romney's candidacy and remaking their own positions on Mormonism. Some of this involved a thoughtful reconsideration that continued to emphasize key theological differences while also highlighting shared political and moral convictions between evangelicalism and Mormonism, such as in a series of articles published just before the election in *Christianity Today*.[110] Yet even this reevaluation involved drastic alterations in long-standing evangelical positions on Mormonism. One article published a month before the election contended that "evangelicals have been wrong in their reasons" for believing that the LDS faith is different from traditional Christianity. Yet the misconceptions that *Christianity Today* contended evangelicals held regarding Mormonism were the same beliefs the magazine had propagated for most of its history. In its most stunning example, the article contended that evangelicals falsely believed Mormons subscribed to a salvation by works theology—what dozens of articles in the magazine had historically argued. But now the magazine posited that "the Book of Mormon teaches salvation by Christ's work of grace."[111] Gone were any references to the "Mormon maze" that trapped Mormons in a futile life of effort and an allegiance to unbiblical lies that had so long characterized evangelical treatment of Mormonism. Evangelicals had reprimanded Romney's 2008 attempts to pass himself off as another orthodox Christian and they appreciated his refusal to do the same in 2012, yet in the last months of the election some of these same evangelicals strangely seemed to suggest that Mormonism offered an almost evangelical notion of salvation.

While evangelicals described some Mormon beliefs as Christian, they still did not consider Mormonism part of Christianity, but they significantly altered their placement of the LDS faith in the religious spectrum, moving it away from "cult" status. Parting from its historic insistence on Mormonism as a cult, the Southern Baptist Convention's Richard Land now said Mormonism was merely "another religion," an increasingly popular designation from evangelical leaders throughout the 2012 campaign.[112] Earlier in the campaign, after Rev. Jeffress had called Mormonism a cult, Dr. Land authored an editorial for the evangelical publication *Christian Post* where he chided Jeffress for saying such things aloud to secular newspaper reporters. Land acknowledged that while Mormonism "may technically be a cult theologically... it does not behave as a cult culturally or socially," a distinction he said that evangelical Christians could understand but that the liberal media would not.[113] This parsing, of course, was in keeping with the SBC's treatment of Mormonism established in the 2008 campaign, but Jeffress's refusal to mince his words showed not all Southern Baptists were willing to soften their language on Mormonism. In many ways, the disagreement between Land and Jeffress represented a divide that had often emerged among Southern Baptist denominational leaders and the Convention's pastors and laypersons over issues of theology and politics, not to mention the larger divisions often apparent between prominent evangelicals and the greater community of churches and believers. While Land and other prominent figureheads sought to change the evangelical conversation about Mormonism—Land suggested that instead of calling Mormonism a cult, it might be described as "a new religion," "not a particular branch of the Christian faith" but rather "the Fourth Abrahamic religion"—Jeffress and other pastors continued to insist in their sermons and interviews with reporters that Mormonism was, as one South Carolina Baptist pastor said, "a cult, most definitely."[114]

Other evangelical efforts regarding Mormonism involved the literal deleting of history. Just three weeks before the election, the Billy Graham Evangelistic Association (BGEA) released a picture of the nation's most famous evangelist meeting with Mitt Romney. Romney had journeyed to Graham's North Carolina home to pray about the election, but he walked away with an even bigger blessing. After their meeting, Graham issued a statement that all but endorsed Romney's presidential bid, as he praised Romney's "values and strong moral convictions." The photo and statement quickly became full-page ads paid for by Graham's organization and published in newspapers across the country as part of a last-ditch effort to ensure heavy evangelical turnout for Romney on November 6.[115] "I hope millions of Americans will join me," Graham wrote, "in praying for our nation and to vote for candidates who will support the biblical definition of marriage, protect the sanctity of life and defend our religious freedoms."[116] Shortly after the release of Billy Graham's photo with Romney, Graham's organization removed all its references to Mormonism as a cult from its website.[117] But this may have been a step too far for many evangelicals, particularly pastors, to go. While it was one thing to refrain from the use of cult terminology, particularly with secular reporters, in political discussions about Romney, for many evangelical pastors the BGEA's erasure of Mormonism's designation as a cult reflected a dangerous theological development that had to be rebuked. Not surprisingly, Rev. Jeffress rushed forward to offer his condemnations. "It is unfortunate that the BGEA chose to remove the cult designation describing Mormonism . . . ," Jeffress lamented. "It is possible to endorse Mitt Romney, as I have done, and yet maintain that Mormonism is a false religion that leads people away from the one true God."[118] Howell Scott, a Baptist pastor from New Mexico, warned that the declassification would "have disastrous unintended consequences," including the "acceptance and approval of Mormonism as a legitimate Christian 'denomination' or faith group." Another Baptist minister, Bart Barber of Farmersville, Texas, declared the BGEA's decision probably meant he would not vote for Romney now and that he would certainly continue to preach about Mormonism's cultic status. "For the sake of my congregation," Rev. Barber explained, "when Billy Graham is muddying the waters of the gospel, I have an obligation to provide clarity." "My question to Billy Graham is, What's more important for the kingdom of God: politics or the message of Jesus Christ?" a Methodist Church leader from North Carolina asked.[119]

Other evangelicals, however, supported the BGEA's decision in light of the growing friendship between evangelicals and Mormons. These evangelicals argued that as friends they needed to speak with a civil dialogue that reflected that affinity. "I don't believe this is a cause of concern, but rather one that will lead to discussions focusing on dialogue that has the flavor and content of grace," Jerry Root, the director of Wheaton College's Evangelism Institute explained. That dialogue, of course, always had the ultimate goal of seeking conversion, so evangelicals who accepted the BGEA's changes did so with the understanding that it would facilitate proselytizing efforts rather than alter theological truths. Not surprisingly given his own conciliatory work with the LDS Church, Richard Mouw praised Graham's organization for "setting aside a word that is designed to shut down serious, friendly explorations of the meaning of the gospel." Mouw's position clearly represented his conviction that evangelicals had work to do to make Mormons more open to the gospel. The use of "cult" terminology by the BGEA or any other evangelical group to describe Mormonism was "needlessly setting up a barrier" to "folks who are open to hearing Billy's message," Mouw argued. Ed Stetzer, president of the SBC's LifeWay Research, echoed Mouw's sentiments, contending that for the purposes of proselytizing it was "more helpful to call it a religion, like Islam and Judaism, and to share the gospel of Jesus with them accordingly."[120]

For evangelical politicians and activists, however, their clear goal remained ensuring Romney's victory rather than worrying about how Mormons received the gospel message. Prominent evangelical Republicans, like Mike Huckabee and Joe Scarborough, suggested Romney's faith was inconsequential with American voters who cared far more about character and competency. Scarborough, a Southern Baptist conservative who had served Congress from Florida before becoming a popular cable network morning television host, declared on his MSNBC show *Morning Joe* that growing up in the South he had always been taught that Mormons were good people, a perhaps unusual memory given the SBC's historical treatment of Mormonism.[121] Huckabee, who had cynically exploited evangelical discomfort with Mormonism in his presidential bid four years before, swiped away any concerns with Romney's faith during his speech to Republican delegates at the party's convention in Tampa. "I care far less as to where Mitt Romney takes his family to church," Huckabee declared to the crowd, "than I do about where he takes this country."[122]

Catholic leaders largely watched the evangelical debate over Mormonism during the 2012 election from a distance, generally unexcited by the concerns roiling the evangelical community over Romney's candidacy. A handful of influential Catholics, including the Rev. Frank Pavone, national director of Priests for Life, had signed on with evangelical leaders to a letter to Romney's campaign team that pledged to no longer let theological differences dampen their support for Romney in the remaining months of the campaign, but there was little evidence that Romney's Mormonism proved a significant barrier for Catholics, laypersons and leaders alike, to overcome.[123] The Archdiocese of Washington, D.C., chided any Catholics who might call Mormonism a cult, reminding them of their own faith's history of persecution by people who had distorted their beliefs, while also describing Mormonism as a "false religion, or at least a heretical offshoot of Christianity."[124] Other Catholic descriptions of Mormonism during the 2012 election displayed a much more thoroughly positive take on the faith than evangelical treatments, such as an article by a Catholic professor in the conservative ecumenical journal *First Things* that praised Mormonism for being "obsessed with Christ" and Mormons as "more Christian than many mainstream Christians who do not take seriously the astounding claim that Jesus is the Son of God."[125] For others, like the conservative Catholic publication *Crisis Magazine*, Romney's Mormonism posed no theological quandary but instead displayed Romney's leadership strengths and solid moral character. A family man married to his high school sweetheart who had held leadership positions in his church while also achieving wild success in his business career, "Romney is someone Catholics know," the magazine enthused in an article entitled "Why Catholics Love Mitt Romney."[126]

Throughout the campaign season, Republican activists had worried that conservative apathy, particularly from evangelicals, would prevent Romney from winning the election, but when the votes were tallied it was clear that a sustained excitement for Barack Obama among voters and a changing electorate whose demographics benefitted the Democrats had been the key to the president's reelection. Indeed, white evangelical support for Romney equaled their backing of Bush's reelection bid in 2004, giving both men 79 percent of their votes, and notably exceeded their support in 2008 for McCain, who drew only 73 percent of the evangelical electorate. Though party activists had worried about voter turnout for Romney, evangelicals' share of the electorate remained consistent with the past two elections, claiming 23 percent in both 2012 and 2008 and 21 percent in 2004. After all the handwringing over possible evangelical apathy—or even antipathy—toward Romney, evangelicals showed up as consistently as they had before. Surprisingly, white evangelical backing of Romney even exceeded Mormons' support for him by one percentage point. Mormons' 78 percent support for Romney had actually declined from 2004 numbers when they had given Bush 80 percent of their votes, though it was unlikely these voters had troubles with Romney's faith. Though providing a smaller margin of support, white Catholics still gave Romney far more of their votes than they had given to McCain or to Bush in his two elections, with 59 percent supporting Romney compared to only 52 percent and 56 percent for Bush in 2000 and 2004, respectively, and 52 percent for McCain in 2008.[127]

While religious conservatives' support remained solid for a Republican presidential nominee, it alone could not propel Romney to victory. Once again, predictions of the Religious Right's demise from both secular and religious observers proliferated in the wake of a Republican defeat.[128] On his popular blog for *Christianity Today*, Ed Stetzer voiced a comment religious conservatives had made in other moments of defeat: "We must face the reality that we may be on the losing side of the culture war."[129] In the months that followed, conservative religious leaders turned from lamenting their electoral impotency to decrying threats to religious liberty. A rallying cry during the election, religious liberty now became the leading issue for conservative ecumenists, who admitted the 2012 election may have marked their permanent defeat on culture war issues like abortion and gay rights. Obama's Affordable Care Act, however, offered continued opportunities for conservative ecumenists to warn about the increasing limits on religious liberty, which they presented as a violation of constitutional protections and of human rights. After the Obama administration said that nonprofit religious groups could hire a third party to provide their employees birth control through their health care plans, religious conservatives gathered to oppose the latest accommodation from the White House. Led by the Catholic bishops and leaders from the Southern Baptist Convention, the group produced "Standing Together for Religious Freedom," an open letter directed to "all Americans." Signed by more than one hundred religious leaders, the letter acknowledged that many of its supporters did not "hold doctrinal objections to the use of contraception. Yet we stand united in protest to this mandate, recognizing the encroachment on the conscience of our fellow citizens."[130]

Signatories to the letter primarily drew from evangelical and Catholic circles, but a representative from the LDS Church signed on, in addition to a handful of Jewish and Orthodox Christian leaders and even one leader from the International Society for Krishna Consciousness. Wanting to remain out of the election fray with one of their members running for the presidency, the LDS Church had absented itself from the religious liberty debates of the 2012 campaign. But the benefit of Romney's defeat meant a new freedom to address public issues, and the LDS Church mounted a vigorous public relations campaign on behalf of religious liberty in the summer of 2013. A church website archived resources Mormons could use to learn more about religious freedom and how to defend it in their communities and country. The website argued that Mormons had defended religious liberty throughout their nearly two-hundred-year history, but "this freedom is eroding."[131] The LDS Church also invited Richard Land, past president of the Southern Baptist Convention's Ethics and Religious Liberty Commission, to visit Salt Lake City to discuss with church leaders their common concerns about religious liberty. Land's designation of Mormonism as the "fourth Abrahamic religion" had been instrumental in recent evangelical reevaluations of Mormonism, but it also made cautious LDS leaders more comfortable with closer connections with evangelicals like Land who had foresworn the cult label for Mormonism.[132] Land was not alone. In a five-month period, he was one of five evangelical leaders who traveled to Utah to meet with LDS officials and speak to Mormon audiences about their shared work of protecting religious liberty, often sketching the battle in aggrieved and slightly paranoid terms popular in conservative circles. "We may go to jail together," the president of Southern Baptist Theological Seminary, Albert Mohler, warned an audience of nearly three thousand at BYU. "We are now called to defend religious liberty for each other, so that when they come for you, we are there, and so that when they come for us, you are there."[133]

In signing on to "Standing Together for Religious Freedom" earlier that summer, the LDS Church explained in a statement that commitment to defending religious liberty overshadowed theological divisions and united people of all faiths in support of a basic human right, a view echoed by evangelicals and Catholics.[134] While conservative ecumenists had made similar arguments for coming together on issues like school prayer, the ERA, abortion, and gay marriage, they had always admitted that those alliances united just conservative faiths. But with religious liberty, conservative ecumenists argued that people of all religious faiths shared their concern and remained above partisanship. "We don't think in those terms," an LDS leader said, dismissing suggestions that the religious liberty cause was a mask for conservative political objectives. "We look at the issues of preserving religious freedom . . . and think about it topically rather than on a partisan basis."[135] Still, there were battle lines to be drawn, and conservative ecumenists targeted "secularists" as the enemy of religious liberty. "People of all faiths had better stand together, because the secularists are after us," Richard Land argued during his visit to Utah. "When it comes to religious freedom, we all hang together or separately. We are common targets in this. The secularists are out to circumscribe our constitutional rights."[136] The letter's backers continued to tout the wide-ranging coalition. But as the religion professor and popular blogger Mark Silk pointed out, no names from any Protestant mainline denominations nor any Muslims, Buddhists, or Sikhs appeared among the more than one hundred signatories. Instead, the letter represented the usual suspects of Religious Right actors—a symbolic triumph of conservative ecumenism, perhaps, but hardly a truly interfaith expression. Or, as Silk put it, a "right wing flapping" rather than "a united front."[137]

Since mid-century, evangelicals, Mormons, and Catholics had debated the question of unity—sometimes with each other, always with themselves. Amid the heyday of liberal ecumenism, Catholics, evangelicals, and Mormons had stood apart and alone, unwilling to compromise their singular messages. They responded to cries for Christian unity with their own arguments about what it meant to be unified. For Mormons and Catholics, unity required right standing in the one true church; for evangelicals, unity depended on a shared understanding of salvation and a common conviction of scripture's perfection and authority. Cultural and political forces helped these three faiths see they were closer to each other than they had often realized, but internal religious developments also shaped that understanding, particularly the democratizing reforms of the Second Vatican Council and the Catholic Church's increased emphasis on the Bible. Still, the moments of political affinity brought new questions and concerns. Grouped together, often by religious leaders turned political activists, as the pillars of the Religious Right who were unified by their social and political positions, Mormon, evangelical, and Catholic officials and theologians pushed back, asserting their religious distinctions and expanding their evangelistic outreaches toward each other. At mid-century, they had warned about liberal ecumenism's watering down of religious truth for the sake of meaningless unity; with the rise of the Religious Right, they defined and emphasized their differences from each other so as to clarify their unique religious messages against the perception of political unity.

The day after the 2012 election, a disappointed *Christianity Today* surveyed the results and their meaning for evangelicals. The magazine also looked to the future, encouraging continued involvement in politics, urging a recommitment to the fight for the unborn, and advising "we need to be prepared to defend the protection of religious liberty as we move into the future." Nowhere did the magazine call for closer ties with conservative Catholics and Mormons to bring about these political changes and respond to a second Obama administration. Rather, the piece exhorted evangelicals to maintain their first priority of evangelizing the lost, specifically recommending evangelicals not let the "Mormon moment" pass but instead keep presenting the gospel to LDS friends and neighbors. "Just because the [political] conversations die down doesn't mean that the mission goes away," the magazine reminded. Far above and beyond politics, that mission continues for evangelicals, but also for Catholics and Mormons, to present their gospel messages to the world and to each other. "Regardless of who sits in the Oval Office," the *Christianity Today* piece concluded, "our King is still sitting on His throne."[138] No matter how politically and socially aligned they find themselves, Mormons, Catholics, and evangelicals will continue to argue to each other that they have the only true access to that throne.

Notes

INTRODUCTION

1. John Dart, "Interreligious Council Still Far From Goal," *Los Angeles Times*, November 29, 1970.
2. "Church Group Issues Holiday Proclamation," *Los Angeles Times*, November 24, 1970.
3. Dart, "Interreligious Council Still Far From Goal."
4. Ibid.
5. Kevin M. Schultz, *Tri-Faith America: How Catholics and Jews Held Postwar America to Its Protestant Promise* (New York: Oxford University Press, 2011); Will Herberg, *Protestant, Catholic, Jew: An Essay in American Religious Sociology* (Garden City, NY: Doubleday, 1955).
6. Jerry Falwell, *Listen, America!* (Garden City, NY: Doubleday & Company, Inc., 1980), 244.
7. Schultz, *Tri-Faith America*. On American pluralism, see William R. Hutchison, *Religious Pluralism in America: The Contentious History of a Founding Ideal* (New Haven, CT: Yale University Press, 2003); Diana Eck, *A New Religious America: How a "Christian Country" Became the World's Most Religiously Diverse Nation* (New York: HarperOne, 2001); and Noah Feldman, *Divided by God: America's Church-State Problem—and What We Should Do About It* (New York: Farrar, Straus and Giroux, 2005).
8. David A. Hollinger, "After Cloven Tongues of Fire: Ecumenical Protestantism and the Modern American Encounter with Diversity," *Journal of American History* 98, no. 1 (June 2011): 21–48; William R. Hutchison, ed., *Between the Times: The Travail of the Protestant Establishment in America, 1900–1960* (New York: Cambridge University Press, 1989); Heather A. Warren, *Theologians of a New World Order: Reinhold Niebuhr and the Christian Realists, 1920–1948* (New

York: Oxford University Press, 1997). See also, John S. Nurser, *For All Peoples and All Nations: The Ecumenical Church and Human Rights* (Washington, D.C.: Georgetown University Press, 2005).

9. Scholars have examined twentieth-century evangelical-Catholic, evangelical-Mormon, and Catholic-Mormon relations, but a treatment of relations among Catholics, Mormons, and evangelicals, the three major components of anti-ecumenism and the three pillars of the Religious Right coalition, has not been made. See John-Charles Duffy, "Conservative Pluralists: The Cultural Politics of Mormon-Evangelical Dialogue in the United States at the Turn of the Twenty-First Century" (Ph.D. diss., University of North Carolina at Chapel Hill, 2011); Mark A. Noll and Carolyn Nystrom, *Is the Reformation Over?: An Evangelical Assessment of Contemporary Roman Catholicism* (Grand Rapids, MI: Baker Academic, 2005); William M. Shea, *The Lion and the Lamb: Evangelicals and Catholics in America* (New York: Oxford University Press, 2004); and Donald Westbrook, "Catholic-Mormon Relations," *Religious Educator* 13, no. 1 (2012): 35–53.

10. While the Religious Right did include some Orthodox Jews, they were a small component with minor influence. For my study, I mean the Religious Right to be synonymous with the Christian Right—a movement of conservative Christian actors—namely, Catholics, evangelicals, and Mormons. Because I see the Religious Right as related to and in some ways growing out of the resistance of conservative Christians to the ecumenical movement, my study remains focused on these three major Christian faiths and how they responded to and organized around the religious question of Christian ecumenism, the rise of secularism, and the nation's changing political and social contexts. On the place of conservative Jews in the Religious Right and modern conservatism, see the special issue on "American Jewish Political Conservatism" in *American Jewish History* 87, no. 2 and 87, no. 3 (June and September 1999), especially Jonathan D. Sarna, "American Jewish Political Conservatism in Historical Perspective," 113–122. See also, Marshall J. Breger, "Jewish Activism in the Washington 'Square': An Analysis and Prognosis," in *Jews and the American Public Square: Debating Religion and Republic*, eds., Alan Mittleman, Jonathan D. Sarna, and Robert Licht (Lanham, MD: Rowman & Littlefield, 2002), 153–186; Nancy Maclean, *Freedom Is Not Enough: The Opening of the American Workplace* (Cambridge, MA: Harvard University Press, 2006), Chapter 6, "Jewish Americans Divide over Justice," 185–224; Kenneth D. Wald and Lee Sigelman, "Romancing the Jews: The Christian Right in Search of Strange Bedfellows," in *Sojourners in the Wilderness: The Christian Right in Comparative Perspective*, eds., Corwin E. Smidt and James M. Penning (Lanham, MD: Rowman & Littlefield, 1997), 139–168. On evangelical-Jewish relations, particularly around issues of Israel, see Zev Chafets, *A Match Made in Heaven:*

American Jews, Christian Zionists, and One Man's Exploration of the Weird and Wonderful Judeo-Christian Alliance (New York: HarperCollins, 2007); Melani McAlister, *Epic Encounters: Culture, Media, and U.S. Interests in the Middle East since 1945* (Berkeley: University of California Press, 2005), especially 165–197; Stephen Spector, *Evangelicals and Israel: The Story of American Christian Zionism* (New York: Oxford University Press, 2009); and Timothy P. Weber, *On the Road to Armageddon: How Evangelicals Became Israel's Best Friend* (Grand Rapids, MI: Baker Academic, 2004).

11. On the Religious Right, see Randall Balmer, *Thy Kingdom Come: How the Religious Right Distorts Faith and Threatens America, An Evangelical's Lament* (New York: Basic Books, 2006); David G. Bromley and Anson Shupe, eds., *New Christian Politics* (Macon, GA: Mercer University Press, 1984); Ruth Murray Brown, *For A "Christian America": A History of the Religious Right* (Amherst, MA: Prometheus Books, 2002); Steve Bruce, *The Rise and Fall of the New Christian Right: Conservative Protestant Politics in America, 1978–1988* (Oxford: Clarendon Press, 1988); Darren Dochuk, *From Bible Belt to Sunbelt: Plain-Folk Religion, Grassroots Politics, and the Rise of Evangelical Conservatism* (New York: W. W. Norton & Company, Inc., 2011); Kenneth J. Heineman, *God Is a Conservative: Religion, Politics, and Morality in Contemporary America* (New York: New York University Press, 1998); Samuel S. Hill and Dennis E. Owen, *The New Religious Political Right in America* (Nashville, TN: Abingdon, 1982); Erling Jorstad, *The New Christian Right, 1981–1988: Prospects for the Post-Reagan Decade* (Lewiston, ME: The Edwin Mellen Press, 1987); Kevin M. Kruse, *One Nation under God: How Corporate America Invented Christian America* (New York: Basic Books, 2015); Robert C. Liebman and Robert Wuthnow, eds., *The New Christian Right: Mobilization and Legitimation* (New York: Aldine Publishing Company, 1983); Michael Lienesch, *Redeeming America: Piety and Politics in the New Christian Right* (Chapel Hill: University of North Carolina Press, 1993); William Martin, *With God on Our Side: The Rise of the Religious Right in America* (New York: Broadway Books, 1996); Matthew Moen, *The Transformation of the Christian Right* (Tuscaloosa: University of Alabama Press, 1992); Duane Murray Oldfield, *The Right and the Righteous: The Christian Right Confronts the Republican Party* (Lanham, MD: Rowman & Littlefield, 1996); Clyde Wilcox, *God's Warriors: The Christian Right in Twentieth-Century America* (Baltimore: Johns Hopkins University Press, 1992); Daniel K. Williams, *God's Own Party: The Making of the Christian Right* (New York: Oxford University Press, 2010); and Garry Wills, *Under God: Religion and American Politics* (New York: Simon and Schuster, 1990).
12. Robert Wuthnow, *The Restructuring of American Religion: Society and Faith Since World War II* (Princeton, NJ: Princeton University Press, 1988).
13. Heineman, *God Is a Conservative*, 10.

14. Hutchison, *Religious Pluralism in America*, 2.
15. Both evangelicals and their scholars have wrestled over the question of how to define evangelicalism. See William J. Abraham, *The Coming Great Revival: Recovering the Full Evangelical Tradition* (San Francisco: Harper & Row Publishers, 1984); Nancy T. Ammerman, "Operationalizing Evangelicalism: An Amendment," *Sociological Analysis* 43, no. 2 (Summer 1982): 170–171; Randall Balmer, *Blessed Assurance: A History of Evangelicalism in America* (Boston: Beacon Press, 1999), and *The Making of Evangelicalism: From Revivalism to Politics and Beyond* (Waco, TX: Baylor University Press, 2010); James Davison Hunter, "Operationalizing Evangelicalism: A Review, Critique and Proposal," *Sociological Analysis* 42, no. 4 (Winter 1982): 363–372, *American Evangelicalism: Conservative Religion and the Quandary of Modernity* (New Brunswick, NJ: Rutgers University Press, 1983), and *Evangelicalism: The Coming Generation* (Chicago: University of Chicago Press, 1987); George M. Marsden, "From Fundamentalism to Evangelicalism: A Historical Analysis," in *The Evangelicals*, eds. David F. Wells and John D. Woodbridge (Grand Rapids, MI: Baker Book House, 1977), 142–162, *Evangelicalism and Modern America*, ed. (Grand Rapids, MI: Wm. B. Eerdmans Publishing, 1984), and *Understanding Fundamentalism and Evangelicalism* (Grand Rapids, MI: Wm. B. Eerdmans Publishing, 1991); and Richard Quebedeaux, *The Young Evangelicals: Revolution in Orthodoxy* (New York: Harper & Row, 1974), and *The Worldly Evangelicals* (San Francisco: Harper & Row, 1978). See also Steven P. Miller, *The Age of Evangelicalism: America's Born Again Years* (New York: Oxford University Press, 2014); Matthew Avery Sutton, *American Apocalypse: A History of Modern Evangelicalism* (Cambridge, MA: The Belknap Press of Harvard University Press, 2014); and Jon R. Stone, *On the Boundaries of American Evangelicalism: The Postwar Evangelical Coalition* (New York: St. Martin's Press, 1997), especially 23–49. Recently, Molly Worthen has offered a useful new way of defining evangelicals. Rather than looking to a shared set of beliefs and doctrines, as most scholars have, Worthen argues that evangelicals "share a set of fundamental questions": "how to repair the fracture between spiritual and rational knowledge; how to assure salvation and a true relationship with God; and how to resolve the tension between the demands of personal belief and the constraints of a secularized public square." Molly Worthen, *Apostles of Reason: The Crisis of Authority in American Evangelicalism* (New York: Oxford University Press, 2014), 4.

    For this book, I join with other scholars in defining evangelicalism by three characteristics: belief in the Holy Bible as God's inspired and revealed Word; experience of a "born again" conversion through belief in the divinity of Jesus Christ and acceptance of his atoning sacrifice on the cross; and the commitment to proselytizing others to the Christian faith. I also mean evangelicals to be a particular group of conservative Protestants who self-consciously constituted themselves after World War II as "New Evangelicals" or "neo-evangelicals" to distinguish themselves from fundamentalists, whom they saw as aggressively militant and separatist. These "new evangelicals" crossed denominational lines and linked together through new institutions they founded like the National Association of Evangelicals (1942), Fuller Theological Seminary (1947), and *Christianity Today* (1956).

For this work, evangelicalism and fundamentalism will sometimes be used interchangeably, but more often they will represent distinct traditions, sometimes in opposition to each other. These different usages should be clear from the context. By fundamentalist, I mean the historical American Protestant phenomenon originating in controversies over biblicism, science, and modernity in the early twentieth century and distinguished by both its biblical literalism and its separatist impulses. As Joel Carpenter has written, "Fundamentalists are evangelicals, but not all evangelicals are fundamentalists." Joel A. Carpenter, *Revive Us Again: The Reawakening of American Fundamentalism* (New York: Oxford University Press, 1997), 8. For other works that grapple with the definition of fundamentalism, see, Nancy Ammerman, "North American Protestant Fundamentalism," in *Fundamentalisms Observed*, eds. Martin E. Marty and R. Scott Appleby (Chicago: University of Chicago Press, 1991), 36–38; Joel A. Carpenter, "Fundamentalist Institutions and the Rise of Evangelical Protestantism, 1929–1942," *Church History* 49, no. 1 (March 1980): 62–76; George Marsden, *Fundamentalism and American Culture: The Shaping of Twentieth-Century Evangelicalism* (New York: Oxford University Press, 1980), *Reforming Fundamentalism: Fuller Seminary and the New Evangelicalism* (Grand Rapids, MI: Wm. B. Eerdmans Publishing Co., 1987), and *Understanding Fundamentalism and Evangelicalism*.

16. Miller, *The Age of Evangelicalism*, 16; Worthen, *Apostles of Reason*, 5.
17. Ecclesiastes 4:12 (KJV).

CHAPTER 1

1. Sydney Ahlstrom, *A Religious History of the American People*, 2nd ed. (New Haven, CT: Yale University Press, 2004), 952.
2. Kevin M. Schultz, *Tri-Faith America: How Catholics and Jews Held Postwar America to Its Protestant Promise* (New York: Oxford University Press, 2011), 73.
3. Schultz, *Tri-Faith America*, 3–96. On the history of American pluralism, see William R. Hutchison, *Religious Pluralism in America: The Contentious History of a Founding Ideal* (New Haven, CT: Yale University Press, 2003).
4. Heather A. Warren, *Theologians of a New World Order: Reinhold Niebuhr and the Christian Realists, 1920–1948* (New York: Oxford University Press, 1997);

Molly Worthen, *Apostles of Reason: The Crisis of Authority in American Evangelicalism* (New York: Oxford University Press, 2014), 167–173. See also Ruth Rouse and Stephen Neill, eds., *A History of the Ecumenical Movement, 1517–1948* (Philadelphia: Fortress Press, 1968).

5. David A. Hollinger, "After Cloven Tongues of Fire: Ecumenical Protestantism and the Modern American Encounter with Diversity," *Journal of American History* 98, no. 1 (June 2011): 25.
6. On the Protestant establishment, see William R. Hutchison, ed., *Between the Times: The Travail of the Protestant Establishment in America, 1900–1960* (New York: Cambridge University Press, 1989).
7. On neo-evangelical responses to liberal Protestantism, see Joel A. Carpenter, *Revive Us Again: The Reawakening of American Fundamentalism* (New York: Oxford University Press, 1997).
8. *Evangelical Action! A Report of the Organization of the National Association of Evangelicals for United Action* (Boston: United Action Press, 1942), v.
9. Neo-evangelicals returned to calling themselves evangelicals around the mid-1950s, when the distinction between evangelicals and fundamentalists had become generally understood. Notably, *Christianity Today* described itself as "evangelical." Harold Ockenga claimed that he had first coined the term "new evangelicalism." For his claim, see Harold J. Ockenga, "From Fundamentalism, Through New Evangelicalism, to Evangelicalism," in *Evangelical Roots: A Tribute to Wilbur Smith*, ed. Kenneth S. Kantzer (Nashville: Thomas Nelson, 1978), 38–40. On neo-evangelicalism, see Carpenter, *Revive Us Again*, 141–232; Jon R. Stone, *On the Boundaries of American Evangelicalism: The Postwar Evangelical Coalition* (New York: St. Martin's Press, 1997), especially 73–116; and Douglas A. Sweeney, "The Essential Evangelicalism Dialectic: The Historiography of the Early Neo-Evangelical Movement and the Observer-Participant Dilemma," *Church History* 60, no. 1 (March 1991): 70–84.
10. Stone, *On the Boundaries of American Evangelicalism*, 108.
11. Ibid., 120.
12. John Abernathy Smith, "Ecclesiastical Politics and the Founding of the Federal Council of Churches," *Church History* 43, no. 3 (September 1974): 350–365.
13. Stone, *On the Boundaries of American Evangelicalism*, 74–75. On Carl McIntire, see Heather Hendershot, "God's Angriest Man: Carl McIntire, Cold War Fundamentalism, and Right-Wing Broadcasting," *American Quarterly* 59, no. 2 (June 2007): 373–396.
14. *Evangelical Action!*, vi.
15. James DeForest Murch, *Cooperation Without Compromise: A History of the National Association of Evangelicals* (Grand Rapids, MI: Wm. B. Eerdmans Publishing Co., 1956), 19–47. Murch was active in the NAE and served as an editor

of the NAE's magazine, *United Evangelical Action*, for fifteen years. His account of the early history of the organization often reflects his personal sympathies. A more recent account of the NAE, commissioned by the organization and written by a senior editor at the evangelical magazine, *World*, offers an updated but hagiographic take on the organization: Arthur H. Matthews, *Standing Up, Standing Together: The Emergence of the National Association of Evangelicals* (Carol Stream, IL: National Association of Evangelicals, 1992). See also D. G. Hart, "The NAE and American Evangelicalism: The Dilemma of Institutionalization," in Box 164, Folder 2, National Association of Evangelicals (NAE) Records, Special Collections, Wheaton College (hereafter, NAE.) On NAE, see also Carpenter, *Revive Us Again*, 141–160; Bruce L. Shelley, *Evangelicalism in America* (Grand Rapids, MI: Wm. B. Eerdmans Publishing Co., 1967); and Worthen, *Apostles of Reason*, 25–27, 33–38. See also the documents in *A New Evangelical Coalition: Early Documents of the National Association of Evangelicals*, ed. Joel A. Carpenter (New York: Garland, 1988). On Murch, see William R. Baker, "Why Can't We Be Comfortable as Evangelicals?," *Christian Standard*, March 16, 2003, 196–201.

16. Stone, *On the Boundaries of American Evangelicalism*, 78.
17. "Statement of Faith" in Murch, *Cooperation Without Compromise*, 65–66.
18. Hart, "The NAE and American Evangelicalism," 15; Murch, *Cooperation Without Compromise*, 202; "History," National Association of Evangelicals, http://www.nae.net/about-us/history/62.
19. Carpenter, *Revive Us Again*, 158–159; Matthews, *Standing Up, Standing Together*, 86; Worthen, *Apostles of Reason*, 37–38. Barry Hankins observes that unlike northern fundamentalists (and the neo-evangelicals who followed), who endured a minority status not only within their region but even inside their denominations, Southern Baptists who enjoyed predominance across the South did not have to build the trans-denominational alliances that northern fundamentalists did in order to survive. Instead, well into the twentieth century Southern Baptists still reflected the prevailing culture of their surroundings as northern fundamentalists once had during the height of nineteenth-century evangelical dominance, "Southern Baptists and Northern Evangelicals: Cultural Factors and the Nature of Religious Alliances," *Religion and American Culture: A Journal of Interpretation* 7, no. 2 (Summer 1997): 271–298. See also, Glenn T. Miller, "Baptists and Neo-Evangelical Theology," *Baptist History and Heritage* 35, no. 1 (Winter 2000): 20–38. The question of whether Southern Baptists are evangelicals has animated and sometimes confounded both Southern Baptists and their scholars. In 1976, Foy Valentine, a leading SBC official, famously declared evangelical a "Yankee word." However, this ultimately represented a losing position among Baptists, just as Valentine's moderate theology was also on

the way out in a denomination that grew increasingly conservative after the fundamentalists took control of the SBC in 1979. Valentine quoted in Kenneth L. Woodward, "Born Again!," *Newsweek*, October 25, 1976, 76. Hankins argues that a younger, more conservative generation of Baptist leaders, many educated at evangelical seminaries outside of the South, came to see themselves as "distinctly evangelical and Baptist instead of just Baptist," a view that gained increasing currency among lay Baptists amid the larger social, political, and religious realignments taking place in the nation after the 1960s, *Uneasy in Babylon: Southern Baptist Conservatives and American Culture* (Tuscaloosa: University of Alabama Press, 2002), 22 and passim, particularly, 14–40. See also, James Leo Garret, Jr., E. Glenn Hinson, and James E. Tull, *Are Southern Baptists Evangelicals?* (Macon, GA: Mercer University Press, 1983); and the essays in David S. Dockery, ed., *Southern Baptists and American Evangelicals: The Conversation Continues* (Nashville: Broadman and Holman, 1993).

20. Memo, "Editorial Objectives," n.d., Records of Christianity Today International, Box 15, Folder 11, Billy Graham Center Archives (hereafter, BGCA).
21. Billy Graham (interview), "In the Beginning . . . ," *Christianity Today*, July 17, 1981, 26. On *Christianity Today*, see Phyllis Elaine Alsdurf, "Christianity Today Magazine and Late Twentieth-Century Evangelicalism" (Ph.D. diss., University of Minnesota, 2004); J. David Fairbanks, "The Politics of *Christianity Today*: 1956–1986," in *Contemporary Evangelical Political Involvement*, ed. Corwin E. Smidt (Lanham, MD: University Press of America, 1989), 25–43; Mark G. Toulouse, "*Christianity Today* and American Public Life: A Case Study," *Journal of Church and State* 35, no. 2 (Spring 1993): 241–284; and Worthen, *Apostles of Reason*, 56–72. The definitive biography of Billy Graham remains William Martin, *A Prophet with Honor: The Billy Graham Story* (New York: William Morrow and Company, Inc., 1991); see pages 211 through 217 on the founding of *Christianity Today*. On Graham, see his autobiography, Billy Graham *Just as I Am: The Autobiography of Billy Graham* (San Francisco: HarperSanFrancisco/Zondervan, 1997). See also Denton Lotz, "Billy Graham: An Appreciation," *Baptist History and Heritage* 41, no. 3 (Summer/Fall 2006): 49–65; Steven P. Miller, *Billy Graham and the Rise of the Republican South* (Philadelphia: University of Pennsylvania Press, 2009); and Grant Wacker, "Billy Graham's America," *Church History* 78, no. 3 (September 2009): 489–511, and *America's Pastor: Billy Graham and the Shaping of a Nation* (Cambridge, MA: The Belknap Press of Harvard University Press, 2014).
22. "In the Beginning . . . ," 26, 27; Memo, "Christianity Today," and "Memo to Contributors," n.d., both in Records of Christianity Today International, Box 15, Folder 11, BGCA. Underlining in the original.

23. Letter to Dr. Basil F. C. Atkinson, December 22, 1955, Records of Christianity Today International, Box 15, Folder 11, BGCA; Memo, "Christianity Today." On the emergence of a politicized evangelicalism in the Cold War years, see Angela M. Lahr, *Millennial Dreams and Apocalyptic Nightmares: The Cold War Origins of Political Evangelicalism* (New York: Oxford University Press, 2007). The scholar Dennis P. Hollinger found that from 1956 to 1976, *Christianity Today* addressed the issue of Communism more than any other political matter. Dennis P. Hollinger, *Individualism and Social Ethics: An Evangelical Syncretism* (Lanham, MD: University Press of America, 1983), 187–190.
24. Heather A. Warren, "The Theological Discussion Group and Its Impact on American and Ecumenical Theology, 1920–1945," *Church History* 62, no. 4 (December 1993): 537. On ecumenism's anti-Communist, anti-totalitarian outlook, see also Mark Thomas Edwards, "'God's Totalitarianism': Ecumenical Protestant Discourse During the Good War, 1941–45," *Totalitarian Movements and Political Religions* 10, no. 3–4 (September–December 2009): 285–302.
25. Letter, Marcellus Kik to Nelson Bell and Carl Henry, October 3, 1955, Records of Christianity Today International, Box 15, Folder 11, BGCA.
26. Nancy Ammerman, "North American Protestant Fundamentalism," in *Fundamentalisms Observed*, eds. Martin E. Marty and R. Scott Appleby (Chicago: University of Chicago Press, 1991), 36–38.
27. Henry biographical information taken from his autobiography: Carl F. H. Henry, *Confessions of a Theologian: An Autobiography* (Waco, TX: Word Books, 1986). For his views on the founding of *Christianity Today* and its influence, see pages 141–219. On Henry, see also *God and Culture: Essays in Honor of Carl F. H. Henry*, eds. D. A. Carson and John D. Woodbridge (Grand Rapids, MI: Wm. B. Eerdmans Publishing Co., 1993); Augustus Cerillo, Jr., and Murray W. Dempster, "Carl F. H. Henry's Early Apologetic for an Evangelical Social Ethic, 1942–1956," *Journal of the Evangelical Theological Society* 34, no. 3 (September 1991): 365–379; and R. Albert Mohler, Jr., "Carl F. H. Henry," *Theologians of the Baptist Tradition*, eds. Timothy George and David S. Dockery (Nashville: Broadman & Holman Publishers, 2001), 279–296. The chapter, "Carl F. H. Henry's Uneasy Conscience" in Peter Goodwin Herzel, *Jesus and Justice: Evangelicals, Race, and American Politics* (New Haven, CT: Yale University Press, 2009), 71–88, explores Henry's concern with racial justice and evangelical Christianity, a preoccupation of Henry's in the 1950s and 1960s. See also the essays in the Carl Henry tribute edition of *The Southern Baptist Journal of Theology* 8, no. 4 (Winter 2004).
28. On Fuller Theological Seminary, see George Marsden, *Reforming Fundamentalism: Fuller Seminary and the New Evangelicalism* (Grand Rapids, MI: Wm. B. Eerdmans Publishing Co., 1987).

29. Carl F. H. Henry, *The Uneasy Conscience of Modern Fundamentalism* (Grand Rapids, MI: Wm. B. Eerdmans Publishing Co., 1947, rev. ed. 2003).
30. Harold J. Ockenga, "Introduction," in Henry, *Uneasy Conscience*, xxi–xxii.
31. Martin, *A Prophet with Honor*, 212–215.
32. "The Perils of Independency," *Christianity Today*, November 12, 1956, 20, 21. As an editorial, the piece had no byline, but Henry authored it. See Stone, *On the Boundaries of American Evangelicalism*, 105–111.
33. "The Perils of Ecumenicity," *Christianity Today*, November 26, 1956, 20.
34. "The Perils of Independency," 20.
35. Ibid., 21, 22.
36. "The Perils of Ecumenicity," 21, 22.
37. "The Perils of Independency," 22.
38. Carl F. H. Henry, "Dare We Renew the Controversy? II: The Fundamentalist Reduction," *Christianity Today*, June 24, 1957, 26.
39. "The Perils of Independency," 22.
40. The anthropologist Susan Friend Harding has written about the "shared elementary language" among evangelical and fundamentalist Christians that helps them understand themselves—and recognize each other—as "Christian." Susan Friend Harding, *The Book of Jerry Falwell: Fundamentalist Language and Politics* (Princeton, NJ: Princeton University Press, 2000), 19.
41. Patrick Allitt, *Catholic Intellectual and Conservative Politics in America, 1950–1985* (Ithaca, NY: Cornell University Press, 1993), 16–48; James Hennesey, S.J., "Roman Catholics and American Politics, 1900–1960: Altered Circumstances, Continuing Patterns," in *Religion and American Politics: From the Colonial Period to the Present*, eds. Mark A. Noll and Luke E. Harlow (New York: Oxford University Press, 2007), 247–265. On Cold War pronatalism, see Elaine Tyler May, *Homeward Bound: American Families in the Cold War Era* (New York: Basic Books, 1988), 129–152.
42. Will Herberg, *Protestant, Catholic, Jew: An Essay in American Religious Sociology* (Garden City, NY: Doubleday, 1955), 169. On Herberg and *Protestant, Catholic, Jew*, see Hutchison, *Religious Pluralism in America*, 196–218; and Schultz, *Tri-Faith America*, 85–89.
43. Allitt, *Catholic Intellectuals and Conservative Politics*, 17–18.
44. Paul Blanshard, *American Freedom and Catholic Power* (Boston: Beacon Press, 1949), 9.
45. The reviewer for the *New York Times* found "little . . . that is not on a prejudiced plane" in the book. John W. Chase, "Expanded Articles; American Freedom and Catholic Power," *New York Times*, May 15, 1949. Kevin Schultz notes the persistence of anti-Catholicism in the tri-faith era, *Tri-Faith America*, 94–96.
46. John T. McGreevy, *Catholicism and American Freedom: A History* (New York: W. W. Norton & Company, 2003), 167.

47. Mark Massa, "Catholic-Protestant Tensions in Post-War America: Paul Blanshard, John Courtney Murray, and the 'Religious Imagination,'" *Harvard Theological Review* 95, no. 3 (July 2002): 319.
48. W. E. Garrison, "Catholic Plan for U.S.," *Christian Century*, June 8, 1949, 709, 710. Italics in the original.
49. Tully Nettleton, "A Book That 'May Prove Historic'," *Christian Science Monitor*, April 28, 1949.
50. Patrick Allitt, "American Catholics and the New Conservatism of the 1950s," *U.S. Catholic Historian* 7, no. 1 (Winter 1988): 26–27.
51. Letter, Rev. John E. Kelly to Editor, February 21, 1957, Records of Christianity Today International, Box 16, Folder 4, BGCA; C. Stanley Lowell, "Rising Tempo of Rome's Demands," *Christianity Today*, January 7, 1957, 11, 13.
52. Letters, Carl Henry to Rev. John E. Kelly, February 27 and March 19, 1957; and Letter, C. Stanley Lowell to Carl Henry, March 4, 1957, all in Records of Christianity Today International, Box 16, Folder 4, BGCA.
53. Philip Edgcumbe Hughes, "Review of Current Religious Thought," *Christianity Today*, April 1, 1957, 39.
54. On the New York crusade, see Martin, *A Prophet with Honor*, 225–238.
55. George Dugan, "Billy Graham Opens His Crusade Here," *New York Times*, May 16, 1957.
56. Martin, *A Prophet with Honor*, 229–230, 236.
57. "'Danger to the Faith'," *Christianity Today*, May 13, 1957, 30–31; Martin, *A Prophet with Honor*, 229–230.
58. "Billy Graham and the Pope's Legions," *Christianity Today*, July 22, 1957, 20, 21. Italics in the original.
59. John B. Sheerin, C.S.P., "American Catholics and Ecumenism," in *Contemporary Catholicism in the United States*, ed. Philip Gleason (Notre Dame, IN: University of Notre Dame Press, 1969), 74–75.
60. Cover, *Time*, December 12, 1960.
61. McGreevy, *Catholicism and American Freedom*, 189–190. On Murray, see also Patrick Allitt, "The Significance of John Courtney Murray," in *Church Polity and American Politics: Issues in Contemporary American Catholicism*, ed. Mary C. Segers (New York: Garland Publishing, Inc., 1990), 51–65; Thomas P. Ferguson, *Catholic and American: The Political Theology of John Courtney Murray* (Kansas City, MO: Sheed & Ward, 1993); Thomas Hughson, S.J., *The Believer as Citizen: John Courtney Murray in a New Context* (New York: Paulist Press, 1993); Thomas T. Love, "John Courtney Murray, S.J.: Liberal Roman Catholic Church-State Theory," *Journal of Religion* 45, no. 3 (July 1965): 211–224; Robert W. McElroy, *The Search for an American Public Theology: The Contribution of John Courtney Murray* (New York: Paulist Press, 1989); and Todd David Whitmore, "Immunity or Empowerment:

John Courtney Murray and the Question of Religious Liberty," *Journal of Religious Ethics* 21, no. 2 (Fall 1993): 247–273.

62. *McCollum v. Board of Education*, 333 U.S. 203 (1948).
63. John Courtney Murray, "Separation of Church and State: True and False Concepts," *America*, February 15, 1947, 545, quoted in McElroy, *The Search for an American Public Theology*, 112–113.
64. R. Scott Appleby and John H. Haas, "The Last Supernaturalists: Fenton, Connell, and the Threat of Catholic Indifferentism," *U.S. Catholic Historian* 13, no. 2 (Spring 1995): 32.
65. Patrick W. Collins, "Gustave Weigel, S.J.: The Ecumenical Preparations," *U.S. Catholic Historian* 7, no. 1 (Winter 1988): 114.
66. *Humani Generis*, August 12, 1950, http://www.vatican.va/holy_father/pius_xii/encyclicals/documents/hf_p-xii_enc_12,081,950_humani-generis_en.html.
67. Appleby and Haas, "The Last Supernaturalists," 32; Schultz, *Tri-Faith America*, 90–91.
68. Joseph Clifford Fenton, "The Status of a Controversy," *American Ecclesiastical Review* 124 (June 1951): 453, quoted in Appleby and Haas, "The Last Supernaturalists," 38.
69. Appleby and Haas, "The Last Supernaturalists," 32.
70. For example, see John Courtney Murray, "Crisis in the History of Trent," *Thought* 7 (December 1932): 463–473; John Courtney Murray, "The Catholic Position: A Reply," *The American Mercury* 69 (September 1949): 274–283; and John Courtney Murray, "Hopes and Misgivings for Dialogue," *America*, January 14, 1961, 459–460. J. Leon Hubbard, "John Courtney Murray, SJ (1904–67): Working with God," *Theology Today* 62 (October 2005): 342–351.
71. Letter, John Courtney Murray, S.J., to Mrs. Richard Thomas Reddington, August 1, 1956, Box 2, Folder 204, The Rev. John Courtney Murray, S.J. Papers, Special Collections, Georgetown University Library, Washington, D.C. (hereafter, Murray).
72. Ferguson, *Catholic and American*, 89–94.
73. Joseph A. Komonchak, "Catholic Principle and the American Experiment: The Silencing of John Courtney Murray," *U.S. Catholic Historian* 17, no. 1 (Winter 1999): 28–44.
74. McGreevy, *Catholicism and American Freedom*, 208.
75. On the Mormon settlement of Utah, see Leonard Arrington, *Great Basin Kingdom: An Economic History of the Latter-day Saints, 1830–1900* (Cambridge, MA: Harvard University Press, 1958).
76. David O. McKay biographic information taken from the following: James B. Allen, "David O. McKay," in *The Presidents of the Church*, ed. Leonard J.

Arrington (Salt Lake City, UT: Deseret Book Company, 1986), 275–313; Newell G. Bringhurst, "The Private versus the Public David O. McKay: Profile of a Complex Personality," *Dialogue: A Journal of Mormon Thought* 31, no. 3 (Fall 1998): 11–32; and Gregory A. Prince and Wm. Robert Wright, *David O. McKay and the Rise of Modern Mormonism* (Salt Lake City: University of Utah Press, 2005). See also, "David O. McKay, Mormon Leader, Is Dead at 96," *New York Times*, January 19, 1970. On McKay's leadership style as LDS president, see Gary James Bergera, "Tensions in David O. McKay's First Presidencies," *Journal of Mormon History* 33, no. 1 (Spring 2007): 179–246.

77. Prince and Wright, *David O. McKay*.
78. Ibid., 199–255.
79. Allen, "David O. McKay," 302.
80. William R. Hutchison, *Errand to the World: American Protestant Thought and Foreign Missions* (Chicago: University of Chicago Press, 1987); Grant Wacker, "Second Thoughts on the Great Commission: Liberal Protestants and Foreign Missions, 1890–1940," in *Earthen Vessels: American Evangelicals and Foreign Missions, 1880–1980*, eds. Joel A. Carpenter and Wilbert R. Shenk (Grand Rapids, MI: Wm. B. Eerdmans Publishing Co., 1990), 281–300.
81. David O. McKay, "The Church—A Worldwide Movement," *The Improvement Era*, December 1966, 1132.
82. Gregory A. Prince, "David O. McKay and the 'Twin Sisters': Free Agency and Tolerance," *Dialogue: A Journal of Mormon Thought* 33, no. 4 (Winter 2000): 1–13.
83. D. Michael Quinn, *The Mormon Hierarchy: Extensions of Power* (Salt Lake City, UT: Signature Books, 1997), 363–365; M. Dallas Burnett, "Conferences: General Conference," in *Encyclopedia of Mormonism: The History, Scripture, Doctrine, and Procedures of the Church of Jesus Christ of Latter-day Saints*, ed. Daniel H. Ludlow (5 vols., New York: Macmillan, 1992), vol. 2, 307–308. In 1953, television broadcasts brought the General Conferences to a national audience (as opposed to just the 7500 attendees who could fit in the Mormon Tabernacle in Salt Lake City where General Conferences were held), thus increasing the General Conferences' influence on church members.
84. The multitude of General Conference speeches, all reprinted in the church magazine *Ensign*, devoted to the president as "Prophet" in connection with the death and/or presidential ascendancy of Joseph Fielding Smith, Harold Lee, and Spencer Kimball between 1970 and 1973 is impressive. See Harold B. Lee, "The President—Prophet, Seer, and Revelator," *Ensign*, August 1972, 35–39; N. Eldon Tanner, "Warnings from Outer Space," *Ensign*, January 1973, 26–29; Spencer W. Kimball, "We Thank Thee, O God, for a Prophet," *Ensign*, January

1973, 33–35; Ezra Taft Benson, "Listen to a Prophet's Voice," *Ensign*, January 1973, 57–59; Mark E. Petersen, "Another Prophet Now Has Come!," *Ensign*, January 1973, 116–118; A. Theodore Tuttle, "What Is a Living Prophet?," *Ensign*, July 1973, 18–20; Harold B. Lee, "Follow the Leadership of the Church," *Ensign*, July 1973, 95–99; Joseph Anderson, "The Rock of Revelation," *Ensign*, July 1973, 105–107; Mark E. Petersen, "Salvation Comes Through the Church," *Ensign*, July 1973, 108–111; N. Eldon Tanner, "Obedience," *Ensign*, January 1974, 92–95; Theodore M. Burton, "The Need for Total Commitment," *Ensign*, January 1974, 114–116; Gordon B. Hinckley, "We Thank Thee, O God, for a Prophet," *Ensign*, January 1974, 122–125; Bruce R. McConkie, "God Foreordains His Prophets and His People," *Ensign*, May 1974, 71–73; N. Eldon Tanner, "Chosen of the Lord," *Ensign*, May 1974, 82–85; and LeGrand Richards, "Prophecy," *Ensign*, May 1974, 115–118.

85. Joseph Smith, *The Pearl of Great Price* (Salt Lake City, UT: The Deseret News, 1917), 85.
86. G. Homer Durham, "The Ecumenical Movement," *The Improvement Era*, April 1961, 210.
87. J. Reuben Clark, Jr., "All Roads Lead to Rome," *The Improvement Era*, June 1960, 399.
88. Ibid., 398.
89. McKay's biographers devote a chapter to what they call "Ecumenical Outreach." However, the nature of the examples they provide cannot be seen as ecumenical activity but rather, as I contend, expressions of increased neighborliness. Prince and Wright, *David O. McKay*, 106–123.
90. "Mormons See No Hope of Denominational Merger," *New York Times*, August 26, 1962.
91. Ezra Taft Benson, "Three Threatening Dangers," *The Improvement Era*, December 1964, 1067.
92. Prince and Wright, *David O. McKay*, 121.
93. Gregory A. Prince and Gary Topping, "A Turbulent Coexistence: Duane Hunt, David O. McKay, and a Quarter-Century of Catholic-Mormon Relations," *Journal of Mormon History* 31, no. 1 (Spring 2005): 159.
94. Carl Henry, "Three Threats to Our American Way of Life," *United Evangelical Action*, January 1, 1952, 3–4.
95. G. Earl Guinn, "Contemporary Threats to Freedom," May 18, 1964, in Southern Baptist Convention Presskit Collection, AR 375, Box 1, Folder 37, Southern Baptist Historical Library and Archives. (Hereafter, SBHLA.)
96. On Catholic anti-Communism, see McGreevy, *Catholicism and American Freedom*, 211–215. See also Donald F. Crosby, S.J., *God, Church, and Flag: Senator Joseph R. McCarthy and the Catholic Church, 1950–1957* (Chapel Hill: University of North Carolina Press, 1978); Thomas C. Reeves, *America's Bishop: The*

Life and Times of Fulton J. Sheen (San Francisco: Encounter Books, 2001), especially 206–211.

97. Raymond Tennies, Letter to the Editor, "Durable Dialogue," *Christianity Today*, June 21, 1963, 19.
98. James DeForest Murch, "Shall America Bow to the Pope of Rome?" 1951, in Box 65, Folder 19, NAE.

CHAPTER 2

1. "Protestant Preview of Second Vatican Council," *Christianity Today*, September 28, 1962, 36.
2. John O'Malley, S.J., "Reform, Historical Consciousness, and Vatican II's *Aggiornamento*," *Theological Studies* 32, no. 4 (December 1971): 573–601.
3. John W. O'Malley, *What Happened at Vatican II* (Cambridge, MA: Harvard University Press, 2008), 2, 23, 121–122, 295.
4. Arnaldo Cortesi, "Cardinal Roncalli Elected Pope," *New York Times*, October 29, 1958.
5. The best recent work on the Second Vatican Council is John W. O'Malley's aptly named *What Happened at Vatican II*. On the effects of the Second Vatican Council on the lives, beliefs, and practices of American Catholics, see Andrew M. Greeley, *American Catholics Since the Council: An Unauthorized Report* (Chicago: The Thomas More Press, 1985); and Joseph A. Komonchak, "Interpreting the Council: Catholic Attitudes Toward Vatican II," in *Being Right: Conservative Catholics in America*, eds. Mary Jo Weaver and R. Scott Appleby (Bloomington: Indiana University Press, 1995), 17–36.
6. O'Malley, *What Happened at Vatican II*, 1, 15–18, 82; Joseph P. Chinnici, O.F.M., "Ecumenism, Civil Rights, and the Second Vatican Council: The American Experience," *U.S. Catholic Historian* 30, no. 3 (Summer 2012): 25; Kevin M. Schultz, *Tri-Faith America: How Catholics and Jews Held Postwar America to Its Protestant Promise* (New York: Oxford University Press, 2011), 33.
7. John B. Sheerin, C.S.P., "American Catholics and Ecumenism," in *Contemporary Catholicism in the United States*, ed. Philip Gleason (Notre Dame, IN: University of Notre Dame Press, 1969), 75.
8. "Ecumenical Council Date 3 Years Off," *Boston Globe*, October 31, 1959.
9. Joseph A. Komonchak notes that of the 117 American bishops who sent letters regarding the upcoming council, 48 of them discussed ecumenical matters in their responses. Of those 48, Komonchak counts 40 as positive in their discussion of ecumenism. Komonchak, "U.S. Bishops' Suggestions for Vatican II," 3, 33, http://jakomonchak.files.wordpress.com/2012/01/us-bishops-suggestions-for-vatican-ii.pdf. This article originally appeared in Italian in *Cristianesimo nella Storia* 15 (1994) : 313–371.

10. Ibid., 33.
11. Ibid., 34.
12. *Ecumenism and Vatican II*, ed. Charles O'Neill, S.J. (Milwaukee, WI: The Bruce Publishing Company, 1964).
13. Camilla J. Kari, *Public Witness: The Pastoral Letters of the American Catholic Bishops* (Collegeville, MN: Liturgical Press, 2004), 57.
14. "Statement on the Ecumenical Council," August 18, 1962, in *Pastoral Letters of the United States Catholic Bishops: Volume III, 1962–1974*, ed. Hugh J. Nolan (Washington, D.C.: United States Catholic Conference, 1983), 12, 13.
15. Ibid., 15.
16. Neil J. Young, "'A Saga of Sacrilege': Evangelicals Respond to the Second Vatican Council," in *American Evangelicals and the 1960s*, ed. Axel Schäfer (Madison: University of Wisconsin Press, 2013), 255–279.
17. Frank Farrell, "Rome Projects Strategy for a World Church," *Christianity Today*, February 16, 1959, 27–28.
18. Leslie R. Keylock, "The Ecumenical Atmosphere: An Evangelical View of Vatican II," *Christianity Today*, April 12, 1963, 32.
19. "Catholic World Council Delayed Two Years," *Christian Century*, February 18, 1959, 189. Italics in the original.
20. C. Gregg Singer, "Agreements and Differences," *Christianity Today*, October 12, 1962, 14–18; Henry A. Buchanan and Bob W. Brown, "The Ecumenical Movement Threatens Protestantism," *Christianity Today*, November 20, 1964, 21–23.
21. "The Perils of Ecumenicity," *Christianity Today*, November 26, 1956, 21, 22.
22. Benjamin B. Sharp, Letter to the Editor, "Durable Dialogue," *Christianity Today*, June 21, 1963, 19.
23. G. C. Berkouwer, "Review of Current Religious Thought," *Christianity Today*, September 28, 1959, 33. Italics in the original.
24. Wilton M. Nelson, "Is the Roman Catholic Church Changing?," *Eternity*, October 1963, 22. Italics in the original.
25. Berkouwer, "Review of Current Religious Thought," 33.
26. "Evangelicals and Unity," *Christianity Today*, October 26, 1962, 34.
27. "What Will Happen in Rome?," *Eternity*, November 1962, 34.
28. Francis K. Hornicek, Letter to the Editor, "Durable Dialogue," *Christianity Today*, June 21, 1963, 19. Italics in the original.
29. Herbert Henry Ehrenstein, "Peter, the Pope, and the Vatican," *Eternity*, November 1962, 18.
30. Ibid., 20.
31. "The Constitution on Sacred Liturgy," December 4, 1963, in *Vatican Council II: The Basic Sixteen Documents*, ed. Austin Flannery (Northport, NY: Costello Publishing Company, 1996), 117–161; George Dugan, "Study of

Liturgy Begun at Council," *New York Times*, October 23, 1962; Milton Bracker, "Council Favors Administering Sacraments in the Vernacular," *New York Times*, October 16, 1963; O'Malley, *What Happened at Vatican II*, 129–141.

32. O'Malley, *What Happened at Vatican II*, 6.
33. "Vatican Council Recessed in 1962," *New York Times*, June 4, 1963.
34. O'Malley, *What Happened at Vatican II*, 194–198; Charles Morerod, O.P., "The Decree on Ecumenism, *Unitatis Redintegratio*," in *Vatican II: Renewal Within Tradition*, eds. Matthew L. Lamb and Matthew Levering (New York: Oxford University Press, 2008), 314.
35. "Decree on Ecumenism," November 21, 1964, in Flannery, ed., *Vatican Council II*, 506.
36. Ibid., 511.
37. Ibid., 507.
38. In its original Latin, the document referred to "fratres seiunctos." See *Unitatis Redintegratio*, http://www.ewtn.com/library/councils/v2unilat.htm. Scholars have tended to translate this as "separated brethren," although Austin Flannery prefers phrases like "separated christian [*sic*] communities," "separated churches," and "separated sisters and brothers." Flannery, ed., *Vatican Council II*, 499, 503.
39. G. Earl Guinn, "Contemporary Threats to Freedom," May 18, 1964, in Southern Baptist Convention Presskit Collection, AR 375, Box 1, Folder 37, SBHLA.
40. "Decree on Ecumenism," 503.
41. Ibid., 504.
42. Ibid., 512.
43. Ibid., 512.
44. Ibid., 509.
45. Ibid., 505.
46. Ibid., 511.
47. Ibid., 511.
48. O'Malley, *What Happened at Vatican II*, 195.
49. "Decree on Ecumenism," 499.
50. Ibid., 505.
51. Ibid., 522.
52. Buchanan and Brown, "The Ecumenical Movement Threatens Protestantism," 21.
53. Ibid., 22.
54. Timothy A. Byrnes, *Catholic Bishops in American Politics* (Princeton, NJ: Princeton University Press, 1991), 39.
55. "Pastoral Constitution on the Church in the Modern World," December 7, 1965, in Flannery, ed., *Vatican Council II*, 163.

56. O'Malley, *What Happened at Vatican II*, 258, 288.
57. "Pastoral Constitution on the Church in the Modern World," 217.
58. Byrnes, *Catholic Bishops in American Politics*, 41.
59. "Pastoral Constitution on the Church in the Modern World," 225.
60. Ibid., 209.
61. "Declaration on Religious Liberty," December 7, 1965, in Flannery, ed., *Vatican Council II*, 556.
62. "Pastoral Constitution on the Church in the Modern World," 280–281.
63. John Tracy Ellis, "Religious Freedom: An American Reaction," in *Vatican II: By Those Who Were There*, ed. Alberic Stacpoole (London: Geoffrey Chapman, 1986), 292–294.
64. Thomas P. Ferguson, *Catholic and American: The Political Theology of John Courtney Murray* (Kansas City, MO: Sheed & Ward, 1993), 75.
65. Buchanan and Brown, "The Ecumenical Movement Threatens Protestantism," 22.
66. "Rome and Saigon," *Christian Century*, September 4, 1963, 1068.
67. "Declaration on Religious Liberty," 552.
68. Ralph L. Keiper, "The Catholic Church and Religious Liberty," *Eternity*, March 1966, 17.
69. "Rome and Religious Liberty," *Christianity Today*, October 8, 1965, 36.
70. "1965: Religion in Review," *Christianity Today*, January 7, 1966, 52.
71. "Imperious Ecumenism," *Christian Century*, December 8, 1965, 1500.
72. See description of Murray addressing a group of Protestant and Mormon leaders in G. Homer Durham, "Ecumenical Change," *The Improvement Era*, July 1966, 606–607, 652.
73. Leslie R. Keylock, "Echoes of Vatican II at Notre Dame," *Christianity Today*, April 15, 1966, 43.
74. Manuscript, "Chicago Lecture," December, 1964, in Box 6, Folder 461, Murray.
75. John Courtney Murray, S.J., "Our Response to the Ecumenical Movement," *Religious Education* 42 (March–April 1967): 91.
76. Klaas Runia, "The Church of Rome and the Reformation Churches," *Christianity Today*, June 18, 1965, 17.
77. Buchanan and Brown, "The Ecumenical Movement Threatens Protestantism," 23.
78. J. D. Douglas, "Plea for 'Unity' Pervades Vatican Council," *Christianity Today*, October 26, 1962, 34.
79. "Study the Bible with Roman Catholics," *Eternity*, November 1963, 6, 8.
80. Edward Palmer, "A is for Aggiornamento," *Eternity*, September 1965, 45.
81. Chinnici, "Ecumenism, Civil Rights, and the Second Vatican Council," 48.
82. Lawrence E. Webb, "American Mosaic," *Contempo*, April 1971, 27–28.

83. Joseph R. Estes, "Outreach to Catholics," 1969, Pamphlets Collection, #2116, SBHLA.
84. "Baptist-Catholic Relations," 1968, Pamphlets Collection, #3346, SBHLA. Italics in the original. Other pamphlets produced included "'Talking Religion' with Catholics," "A Baptist Look at Roman Catholicism," and "Witnessing to Catholics." See also, William E. Burke, "What Does the Roman Catholic Bible Say?" 1965, Pamphlets Collection, #124, SBHLA.
85. "The Vernacular and the Bible in Rome," *Christianity Today*, November 8, 1963, 31.
86. Nelson, "Is the Roman Catholic Church Changing?," 20.
87. "The Vernacular and the Bible in Rome," 30.
88. "Dogmatic Constitution on Divine Revelation," November 18, 1965, in Flannery, ed., *Vatican Council II*, 97–115. On the bishops' debates over *Dei Verbum*, see O'Malley, *What Happened at Vatican II*, 226–229.
89. Ralph L. Keiper, "The Catholic Church and the Bible," *Eternity*, February 1966, 11.
90. "Dogmatic Constitution on Divine Revelation," 102–103.
91. Keiper, "The Catholic Church and the Bible," 12.
92. Ibid., 13.
93. "Dogmatic Constitution on Divine Revelation," 112.
94. Hugh Nibley, "Since Cumorah," *The Improvement Era*, December 1966, 1085.
95. G. Homer Durham, "Church Ceremonial," *The Improvement Era*, August 1968, 85–87.
96. Durham, "Ecumenical Change."
97. "Loss by Kennedy in Utah Expected," *New York Times*, October 9, 1960.
98. "Mormon's Backing of Nixon 'Personal'," *New York Times*, October 13, 1960. On Mormons' reaction to McKay's pronouncement, see Dean E. Mann, "Mormon Attitudes Toward the Political Roles of Church Leaders," *Dialogue: A Journal of Mormon Thought* 2, no. 2 (Summer 1967): 32–48.
99. "Loss by Kennedy in Utah Expected."
100. Durham, "Ecumenical Change," 652.
101. Mark E. Petersen, "The Christian Reformation," *The Improvement Era*, June 1964, 467.
102. Boyd K. Packer, "A Call to the Christian Clergy," *The Improvement Era*, June 1967, 107.
103. Mark E. Petersen, "A Divided Christianity," *The Improvement Era*, December 1969, 100.
104. Runia, "The Church of Rome and the Reformation Churches," 17.
105. "The Vernacular and the Bible in Rome," 31.
106. "Tenth Anniversary of Vatican II," *Christianity Today*, October 13, 1972, 35.

107. David Kucharsky and Edward E. Plowman, "An Evangelical Awakening in the Catholic Church?," *Christianity Today*, December 7, 1973, 47.
108. Nelson, "Is the Roman Catholic Church Changing?," 22. Italics in the original.
109. Hugh B. Brown, "This Church Is Christianity Restored," *The Improvement Era*, June 1965, 489–491.
110. LeGrand Richards, "One Lord, One Faith, One Baptism," *The Improvement Era*, December 1961, 950.
111. Pope Paul VI, "Ecclesiam Suam," August 6, 1964, quoted in Nibley, "Since Cumorah," 1085. For full text of "Ecclesiam Suam," see http://www.vatican.va/holy_father/paul_vi/encyclicals/documents/hf_p-vi_enc_06,081,964_ecclesiam_en.html.
112. Nibley, "Since Cumorah," 1085.
113. Brown, "This Church Is Christianity Restored," 469.
114. Petersen, "A Divided Christianity," 101.
115. Nibley, "Since Cumorah," 1162.
116. Ibid., 1163.
117. Ibid., 1085.
118. Ibid., 1164.
119. Memo, Carl F. H. Henry, "Report of the Editor," January 12, 1967, Box 4, Folder 4, Papers of Harold Lindsell, BGCA.
120. Guinn, "Contemporary Threats to Freedom."
121. National Association of Evangelicals, "Roman Catholic Church" in "Resolutions Adopted in 1964," in Box 43, Folder 6, Papers of Thomas Fletcher Zimmerman, BGCA.
122. National Association of Evangelicals, "Ecumenical Relations of the Church" in "Resolutions Adopted in 1964," in Box 43, Folder 6, Papers of Thomas Fletcher Zimmerman, BGCA.
123. National Association of Evangelicals, "Resolution on Christian Unity," in Minutes of General Convention Business Section, National Association of Evangelicals, April 20, 1966, in Box 9, Folder 14, Papers of Harold Lindsell, BGCA.
124. Editorial, *Ensign*, January 1971, https://www.lds.org/ensign/1971/01/editorial.

CHAPTER 3

1. Daniel K. Williams, *God's Own Party: The Making of the Christian Right* (New York: Oxford University Press, 2010), 62.
2. *Engel v. Vitale*, 370 U.S. 421 (1962); *Abington Township School District v. Schempp*, and *Murray v. Curlett*, 372 U.S. 203 (1963). On *Abington v. Schempp*, see Stephen D. Solomon, *Ellery's Protest: How One Young Man Defied Tradition and Sparked the Battle over School Prayer* (Ann Arbor: University of Michigan Press, 2007).

3. Frank S. Ravitch, *School Prayer and Discrimination: The Civil Rights of Religious Minorities and Dissenters* (Boston: Northeastern University Press, 1999), 4–6.
4. Solomon, *Ellery's Protest*, 118–119.
5. Donald D. Reich, "The Supreme Court and Public Policy: The School Prayer Cases," *Phi Delta Kappan* 48, no. 1 (September 1966): 29.
6. Robert E. Riggs, "Government-Sponsored Prayer in the Classroom," *Dialogue* 18, no. 3 (Fall 1985): 56.
7. Solomon, *Ellery's Protest*, 125–130. Solomon notes that 77 percent of Southern school systems and 68 percent in the Northeast had Bible readings compared to only 18 percent in the Midwest and 11 percent in the West.
8. Reich, "The Supreme Court and Public Policy," 29. A 1961 survey found only 41.7 percent of the nation's school systems conducted a daily Bible reading.
9. Ibid., 30.
10. Wallace Turner, "Pike Sees U.S. 'Deconsecrated' by Decision on School Prayer," *New York Times*, July 14, 1962.
11. Patrick Allitt, *Catholic Intellectual and Conservative Politics in America, 1950–1985* (Ithaca, NY: Cornell University Press, 1993), 106–110; Kevin M. Schultz, *Tri-Faith America: How Catholics and Jews Held Postwar America to Its Protestant Promise* (New York: Oxford University Press, 2011), 136.
12. "Tempest over School Prayer Ban," *Christianity Today*, July 20, 1962, 46.
13. Schultz, *Tri-Faith America*, 136.
14. "Parental Responsibility," *Relief Society Magazine*, December 1962, 878, quoted in Dallin H. Oaks, "Religion in Public Life," *Ensign*, July 1990, 10.
15. "Church News," *Deseret News*, June 22, 1963.
16. "Tempest over School Prayer Ban," 46.
17. Steven K. Green, "Evangelicals and the Becker Amendment: A Lesson in Church-State Moderation," *Journal of Church and State* 33, no. 3 (Summer 1991): 549.
18. Shem Peachey, Letter to the Editor, "Where God Is Banished," *Christianity Today*, July 20, 1962, 38.
19. Donald T. Critchlow, *The Conservative Ascendancy: How the GOP Right Made Political History* (Cambridge, MA: Harvard University Press, 2007), 133. On the emergence of a politicized evangelicalism in the Cold War years, see Angela M. Lahr, *Millennial Dreams and Apocalyptic Nightmares: The Cold War Origins of Political Evangelicalism* (New York: Oxford University Press, 2007).
20. "What Churchmen Are Saying," *Christianity Today*, August 3, 1962, 25.
21. "Tempest over School Prayer Ban," 46.
22. "Supreme Court Prayer Ban: Where Will It Lead?," *Christianity Today*, July 20, 1962, 25.
23. Williams, *God's Own Party*, 63.

24. Ibid., 63.
25. "Supreme Court Prayer Ban: Where Will it Lead?," 25.
26. "Church-State Separation: A Serpentine Wall?," *Christianity Today*, July 20, 1962, 31.
27. "What Churchmen Are Saying," 25.
28. "Repercussions of Supreme Court Prayer Ruling," *Christianity Today*, August 3, 1962, 25.
29. "Supreme Court Prayer Ban," 26.
30. Williams, *God's Own Party*, 64.
31. "Response to Bible-Prayer Ban," *Christianity Today*, July 5, 1963, 47.
32. "Is the Supreme Court on Trial?," *Christianity Today*, March 1, 1963, 28.
33. "Religion in the Public Schools," *Christianity Today*, August 30, 1963, 30, 31.
34. "The Role of Religion in Civic Life," *Christianity Today*, March 29, 1963, 21.
35. "Religion in the Public Schools," 30. Italics in the original. Williams, *God's Own Party*, 63, 66.
36. Green, "Evangelicals and the Becker Amendment," 548.
37. Ibid., 548, 551.
38. Reich, "The Supreme Court and Public Policy," 30; Green, "Evangelicals and the Becker Amendment," 552.
39. "Amendment Sought on School Prayers," *New York Times*, September 11, 1963.
40. Green, "Evangelicals and the Becker Amendment," 558–559.
41. "Catholic, Methodist Hit School Prayer Change," *Los Angeles Times*, May 9, 1964; Richard L. Lyons, "Sentiment for School Prayer Is Seen Waning," *Washington Post*, May 24, 1964; Kevin M. Kruse, *One Nation under God: How Corporate America Invented Christian America* (New York: Basic Books, 2015), 221.
42. "Catholic Caution Urged on School Prayer Issue," *Los Angeles Times*, June 22, 1964.
43. Green, "Evangelicals and the Becker Amendment," 563.
44. "What About the Becker Amendment?," *Christianity Today*, June 19, 1964, 22.
45. Ibid., 21.
46. Pamphlet, George E. Reed, "Prayer Amendment Controversy," Box 10, Folder 10 (Church: Church and State 1864, Jan.–June Folder), Records of the Office of the General Secretary, The American Catholic History Research Center and University Archives, The Catholic University of America, Washington, D.C. (hereafter, ACUA).
47. G. Homer Durham, "The State, Prayer, and the Public Schools," *The Improvement Era*, September 1962, 668.
48. Max B. Zimmer, Letter to the Editor, "Letters and Reports," *The Improvement Era*, January 1963, 10.

49. President J. Reuben Clark, Jr., "All Roads Lead to Rome," *The Improvement Era*, June 1960, 398.
50. LeGrand Richards, "One Lord, One Faith, One Baptism," *The Improvement Era*, December 1961, 951.
51. Clark, "All Roads Lead to Rome," 398.
52. Eighth Article of Faith, Articles of Faith, the Church of Jesus Christ of Latter-day Saints, http://www.mormon.org/beliefs/articles-of-faith. Joseph Smith recorded thirteen articles of faith.
53. Robert J. Matthews, "The Inspired Revision of the Bible," *The Improvement Era*, February 1965, 104.
54. Robert J. Matthews, "The Inspired Revision of the Bible: Part Two," *The Improvement Era*, March 1965, 217. See also Matthews, "The Inspired Revision of the Bible: Part Three," *The Improvement Era*, April 1965, 302–305, 352; and Matthews, "The Inspired Revision of the Bible: Part Four," *The Improvement Era*, May 1965, 404–405, 431–435.
55. Matthews, "The Inspired Revision of the Bible: Part Four," 435.
56. Ibid., 405.
57. Mark E. Petersen, "The Christian Reformation," *The Improvement Era*, June 1964, 469.
58. Dallin H. Oaks, "Antidotes for the School Prayer Cases," *The Improvement Era*, December 1963, 1048, 1050. Italics in the original.
59. Ibid., 1135.
60. Ibid, 1135.
61. "What About the Becker Amendment?," 20.
62. Green, "Evangelicals and the Becker Amendment," 563–564.
63. Critchlow, *The Conservative Ascendancy*, 129, 134; Williams, *God's Own Party*, 67.
64. "Christian Atheism: The 'God Is Dead' Movement," *Time*, October 22, 1965, 61. The article also profiled Paul Van Buren of Temple University, William Hamilton of Colgate Rochester Divinity School, and Gabriel Vahanian of Syracuse University.
65. Thomas J. J. Altizer, "Word and History," *Theology Today* 22, no. 3 (October 1965): 380–393. Edward B. Fiske, "Theology Without God," *New York Times*, November 7, 1965. For Altizer's account of the event, see Thomas J. J. Altizer, *Living the Death of God: A Theological Memoir* (Albany: State University Press of New York, 2006). See also, Lissa McCullough, "Historical Introduction," in *Thinking Through the Death of God: A Critical Companion to Thomas J. J. Altizer*, eds. Lissa McCullough and Brian Schroeder (Albany: State University of New York Press, 2004), xv–xxvii.
66. Fiske, "Theology Without God"; Walter Rugaber, "'God Is Dead' View Arouses College," *New York Times*, November 5, 1965.

67. "The Living God and the Atheist Theologians," *Christianity Today*, November 5, 1965, 35.
68. Cover, *Christianity Today*, December 17, 1965.
69. "Shadows of the Antichrist in the Decline of Western Theism," *Christianity Today*, December 17, 1965, 23.
70. Bernhard M. Auer, "A Letter from the Publisher," *Time*, April 8, 1966, 21. Easter 1966 took place on April 10.
71. "Toward a Hidden God," *Time*, April 8, 1966, 82–87.
72. See Kenneth Dole, "Worshippers Rejoice: 'God Lives!,'" *Washington Post*, April 11, 1966.
73. Will Oursler, "The 'God-Is-Dead' Controversy," *Boston Globe*, May 8, 1966.
74. "Why This Non-God-Talk?," *Christian Century*, December 1, 1965, 1468.
75. Albert Outler, "Veni, Creator Spiritus: The Doctrine of the Holy Spirit," *Perkins School of Theology Journal* 19, no. 3 (Spring 1966): 35.
76. Linda Charlton, "The 'God Is Dead' Controversy," *Newsday*, March 19, 1966.
77. Carl Henry, "A Reply to the God-Is-Dead Mavericks," *Christianity Today*, May 27, 1966, 37.
78. Addison H. Leitch, "Results of a Half-Truth," *Christianity Today*, April 1, 1966, 55.
79. Robert Wuthnow, *The Restructuring of American Religion: Society and Faith Since World War II* (Princeton, NJ: Princeton University Press, 1988), 164.
80. C. Gregg Singer, "Agreements and Differences," *Christianity Today*, October 12, 1962, 14.
81. Mary Maher, "Aggiornamento in the United States—I," *Irish Times*, February 6, 1967.
82. "Another Era Underway in the American Venture," *Christianity Today*, November 21, 1960, 21. Italics in the original.
83. Henry, "A Reply to the God-Is-Dead Mavericks," 37.
84. "Pope Decries Extremism in Church," *Washington Post*, April 26, 1968.
85. Dan L. Thrapp, "Nearly All Americans Reveal Belief in God," *Los Angeles Times*, December 31, 1967.
86. Memo, Carl F. H. Henry, "Report of the Editor," January 12, 1967, Box 4, Folder 4, Papers of Harold Lindsell, BGCA.
87. Harold O. J. Brown, "Your Theology Is Too Small," *Christianity Today*, April 15, 1966, 5. Italics added.
88. M. S. Handler, "Baptists Prepare for a 'Crusade'," *New York Times*, May 26, 1966.
89. Robert C. Doty, "Vatican Report Opens Way for New Synod Issues," *New York Times*, October 2, 1967; "Document on Doctrine Before Synod of Bishops," *Irish Times*, October 9, 1967.
90. "Action on Atheism," *Newsday*, October 9, 1967.

91. "Some Catholics Carry Modernization Too Far, Pope Says," *Boston Globe,* April 26, 1968.
92. Ibid.
93. "Pope Denounces 'Excessive Haste' to Unity," *Irish Times,* November 14, 1968.
94. See President Hugh G. Brown, "He Lives—All Glory to His Name," *The Improvement Era,* June 1966, 493–495.
95. G. Homer Durham, "God Is Not Dead," *The Improvement Era,* December 1967, 126.
96. President N. Eldon Tanner, "He Is Not Dead," *The Improvement Era,* June 1966, 496.
97. Ibid., 497.
98. Ibid., 498.
99. Durham, "God Is Not Dead," 126.
100. Ibid., 127.
101. Ibid., 126.
102. Ibid, 126.
103. Ibid., 127.
104. Tanner, "He Is Not Dead," 498.
105. Joseph Smith, *Documentary History of the Church,* Vol. 6, p. 474, as quoted in Durham, "God Is Not Dead," 126.
106. Gregory A. Prince and Wm. Robert Wright, *David O. McKay and the Rise of Modern Mormonism* (Salt Lake City: University of Utah Press, 2005), 199–255.
107. James B. Allen, "David O. McKay," in *The Presidents of the Church,* ed. Leonard J. Arrington (Salt Lake City, UT: Deseret Book Company, 1986), 302.
108. Matthew J. Grow, "The Whore of Babylon and the Abomination of Abominations: Nineteenth-Century Catholic and Mormon Mutual Perceptions and Religious Identity," *Church History* 73, no. 1 (March 2004): 139–167.
109. Ibid.
110. Verses using this descriptive include 1 Nephi 13:6, 13:8, 13:26, 13:28, 14:3, 14:9, 14:15; 14:17; 22:13; 22:14; 2 Nephi 6:12; and, 28:18.
111. 1 Nephi 13:7.
112. 1 Nephi 14:3; 14:10. Other verses that allude to the Catholic Church as the "whore of all the earth" include 1 Nephi 14:11; 14:12; 22:13; 22:14; 2 Nephi 10:16; 28:18.
113. 1 Nephi 13:5.
114. Bruce R. McConkie, *Mormon Doctrine* (Salt Lake City, UT: Bookcraft, 1958), 108, 129 as cited in Gregory A. Prince and Gary Topping, "A Turbulent Coexistence: Duane Hunt, David O. McKay, and a Quarter-Century of Catholic-Mormon Relations," *Journal of Mormon History* 31, no. 1 (Spring 2005): 161.
115. Prince and Topping, "A Turbulent Coexistence," 160–161.

116. Duane Hunt, *The Continuity of the Catholic Church* (Wrexham: Ecclesia Press, 1996), 7.
117. Audra Hendrickson, "Those Mystifying Mormons," *Extension*, July 1967, 24–26.
118. Ibid., 24.
119. Ibid., 24.
120. Ibid., 26.
121. Advertisement, "The Rising Threat of the Cults," *Christianity Today*, November 12, 1956, 35.
122. Dick Ostling, "The Mormon Surge," *Christianity Today*, August 28, 1964, 42.
123. John R. Richardson, "A Great Gulf," *Christianity Today*, July 6, 1962, 43.
124. Ostling, "The Mormon Surge," 42.
125. M. Thomas Starkes, "Latter-day Saints and the Baptist Witness," 1968, Pamphlets Collection, #1752, SBHLA.
126. Starkes, "Latter-day Saints and the Baptist Witness"; Lawrence E. Webb, "American Mosaic," *Contempo*, April 1971, 29.
127. Ostling, "The Mormon Surge," 43.
128. Wesley P. Walters, "Mormonism," *Christianity Today*, December 19, 1960, 8.
129. J. K. Van Baalen, "The Latter-day Saints Today," *Christianity Today*, June 19, 1964, 27.
130. "Mormons and Blacks," *Christianity Today*, January 30, 1970, 22. Blacks could be members of the LDS Church, but black men could not hold the priesthood, a requirement for exaltation in the afterlife, until President Spencer Kimball issued a change in church policy through a prophecy in June 1978.
131. Walters, "Mormonism," 10.
132. Van Baalen, "The Latter-day Saints Today," 27.
133. Walters, "Mormonism," 10.
134. Kate Ellen Gruver, "The Menace of Mormonism," 1954, Pamphlets Collection, Baptist History File, Mormonism folder, #2553, SBHLA.
135. Walters, "Mormonism," 8.
136. Van Baalen, "The Latter-day Saints Today," 27. Van Baalen was also author of the popular book *The Chaos of the Cults*, which included a section on the LDS Church.
137. Harold Lindsell, "The Four Major Cults: Christian Science, Jehovah's Witnesses, Mormonism, Seventh-Day Adventism," *Christianity Today*, January 31, 1964, 27–28.
138. Walters, "Mormonism," 8.
139. Richardson, "A Great Gulf," 43.
140. Ostling, "The Mormon Surge," 42.
141. Walters, "Mormonism," 9, 10. Italics in the original.

142. "Church Extension & Home Missions Commission Report to the NAE Board of Administration," April 1966, Folder 14, Box 9, Papers of Harold Lindsell, BGCA.
143. "Course Information – M839-CH859x – Cults and Sects," Folder 2, Box 13, Papers of Paul Eagleson Little, BGCA. Little was a professor at Trinity Evangelical Divinity School outside of Chicago. His course, "Cults and Sects," studied Mormonism, Jehovah's Witnesses, Christian Science, and Seventh Day Adventism.
144. John A. Witmer, "The Truth about Error," *Bibliotheca Sacra* 124, no. 495 (July 1967): 253.
145. John Dart, "Conservative and Liberal Split in Religion Widens," *Los Angeles Times*, December 7, 1969
146. Robert D. Putnam and David E. Campbell, *American Grace: How Religion Divides and Unites Us* (New York: Simon & Schuster, 2010), 91–100.
147. Susan Friend Harding, *The Book of Jerry Falwell: Fundamentalist Language and Politics* (Princeton, NJ: Princeton University Press, 2000), 19.
148. W. A. Criswell, *Look Up Brother!* (Nashville, TN: Broadman Press, 1970), 125, quoted in C. Allyn Russell, "W. A. Criswell: A Case Study in Fundamentalism," *Review and Expositor* 81, no. 1 (Winter 1984): 112.
149. Quoted in Dart, "Conservative and Liberal Split in Religion Widens."
150. Gregory A. Wills, "Progressive Theology and Southern Baptist Controversies of the 1950s and 1960s," *Southern Baptist Journal of Theology* 7, no. 1 (Spring 2003): 22.
151. Henry, "Report of the Editor."

CHAPTER 4

1. *Roe* challenged a Texas law from the nineteenth century outlawing abortion; *Doe* challenged a 1968 Georgia law that allowed abortion in three situations: the life of the mother, the possibility of mental or major physical defect in the child, and cases of rape. Kristin Luker, *Abortion and the Politics of Motherhood* (Berkeley: University of California Press, 1984), 126; "Abortion Ruling: Mother Knows Best," *Los Angeles Times*, January 22, 1973.
2. "Abortion Ruling: Mother Knows Best;" Dallas A. Blanchard, *The Anti-Abortion Movement and the Rise of the Religious Right: From Polite to Fiery Protest* (New York: Twayne Publishers, 1994), 28–30; Luker, *Abortion and the Politics of Motherhood*, 143; Warren Weaver, "National Guidelines Set by 7-to-2 Vote," *New York Times*, January 23, 1973. See also Karlyn Barker, "Abortion Backers Hail Ruling; Foes Pledge Continued Fight," *Washington Post*, January

23, 1973; John Dart, "Abortion Decision Expected to Have Little Effect in California," *Los Angeles Times*, January 23, 1973; Glen Elsasser, "Top Court Strikes Down Abortion Laws," *Chicago Tribune*, January 23, 1973; John P. MacKenzie, "Supreme Court Allows Early-Stage Abortions," *Washington Post*, January 23, 1973; and Linda Mathews, "Supreme Court Rule Gives Women Right to Have Abortions," *Los Angeles Times*, January 23, 1973.

3. William Martin, *With God on Our Side: The Rise of the Religious Right in America* (New York: Broadway Books, 1996), 192.
4. Luker, *Abortion and the Politics of Motherhood*, 142.
5. Connie Paige, *The Right to Lifers: Who They Are, How They Operate, Where They Get Their Money* (New York: Summit Books, 1983), 11. William Ray Arney and William H. Trescher, "Trends in Attitudes Toward Abortion, 1972–1975," *Family Planning Perspectives* 8, no. 3 (May–June 1976): 117. For other studies of attitudes toward abortion during the 1970s, see Elizabeth Adell Cook, Ted G. Jelen, and Clyde Wilcox, *Between Two Absolutes: Public Opinion and the Politics of Abortion* (Boulder, CO: Westview Press, 1992); Helen Rose Fuchs Ebaugh and C. Allen Haney, "Shifts in Abortion Attitudes: 1972–1978," *Journal of Marriage and the Family* 42, no. 3 (August 1980): 491–499; Donald Granberg and Beth Wellman Granberg, "Abortion Attitudes, 1965–1980: Trends and Determinants," *Family Planning Perspectives* 12, no. 5 (September–October 1980): 250–261; Richard J. Harris and Edgar W. Mills, "Religion, Values and Attitudes Toward Abortion," *Journal for the Scientific Study of Religion* 24, no. 2 (June 1985): 137–154; Bradley Hertel, Gerry E. Hendershot, and James W. Grimm, "Religion and Attitudes Toward Abortion: A Study of Nurses and Social Workers," *Journal for the Scientific Study of Religion* 13, no. 1 (March 1974): 23–34; and Frederick S. Jaffe, Barbara L. Lindheim, and Philip R. Lee, *Abortion Politics: Private Morality and Public Policy* (New York: McGraw-Hill, 1981), 99–109.
6. Much of the literature of the anti-abortion movement has focused on the social conditions that produce both anti-abortion positions and pro-life activists themselves. Overwhelmingly, these studies find that the role of religion, particularly Catholicism and conservative evangelical and fundamentalist Protestantism, and the extent to which people participate in those religious communities and adhere to their beliefs, influence their pro-life positions and encourage their activism in the movement. See, for example, Helen Rose Fuchs Ebaugh and C. Allen Haney, "Church Attendance and Attitudes Toward Abortion: Differentials in Liberal and Conservative Churches," *Journal for the Scientific Study of Religion* 17, no. 4 (December 1978): 407–413; Donald Granberg, "The Abortion Activists," *Family Planning Perspectives* 13, no. 4 (July–August 1981): 157–163; James L. Guth, Corwin E. Smidt, Lyman A. Kellstedt, and John C. Green, "The Sources of Antiabortion Attitudes: The Case of

Religious Political Activists," in *Understanding the New Politics of Abortion*, ed. Malcolm L. Goggin (Newbury Park, CA: Sage Publications, 1993), 44–56; Ted G. Jelen, "Respect for Life, Sexual Morality, and Opposition to Abortion," *Review of Religious Research* 25, no. 3 (March 1984): 220–231; Carol J. C. Maxwell, *Pro-Life Activists: Meaning, Motivation, and Direct Action* (Cambridge: Cambridge University Press, 2002); Mary Jo Neitz, "Family, State, and God: Ideologies of the Right-to-Life Movement," *Sociological Analysis* 42, no. 3 (Autumn 1981): 265–276; and Joseph B. Tamney, Stephen D. Johnson, and Ronald Burton, "The Abortion Controversy: Conflicting Beliefs and Values in American Society," *Journal for the Scientific Study of Religion* 31, no. 1 (March 1992): 32–46.

7. The scholarship that has examined the anti-abortion movement's history has tended to present a particular historical path where Catholics, through the auspices of the Catholic Church and the National Right to Life Committee, dominated the pro-life cause before *Roe v. Wade* and for most of the 1970s. This Catholic control of the movement lessened, the standard argument goes, as evangelical and fundamentalist Protestants in the 1980s awakened to the abortion issue at the prodding of their pastors and New Right political operatives and joined the fight to oppose abortion rights, thereby producing a new ecumenical movement. See Michael W. Cuneo, "Life Battles: The Rise of Catholic Militancy Within the American Pro-Life Movement," in *Being Right: Conservative Catholics in America*, eds. Mary Jo Weaver and R. Scott Appleby (Bloomington: Indiana University Press, 1995), 270–299; Cynthia Gorney, *Articles of Faith: A Frontline History of the Abortion Wars* (New York: Simon & Schuster, 1998); George Grant, *Third Time Around: A History of the Pro-Life Movement from the First Century to the Present* (Brentwood, TN: Wolgemuth & Hyatt, 1991); Kerry N. Jacoby, *Souls, Bodies, Spirits: The Drive to Abolish Abortion Since 1973* (Westport, CT: Praeger, 1998); Robert N. Karrer, "The National Right to Life Committee: Its Founding, Its History, and the Emergence of the Pro-Life Movement Prior to *Roe v. Wade*," *Catholic Historical Review* 97, no. 3 (July 2011): 527–557; James R. Kelly, "Learning and Teaching Consistency: Catholics and the Right-to-Life Movement," in *The Catholic Church and the Politics of Abortion: A View from the States*, eds. Timothy A. Byrnes and Mary C. Segers (Boulder, CO: Westview Press, 1992), 152–168; Daniel K. Williams, *God's Own Party: The Making of the Christian Right* (New York: Oxford University Press, 2010), 111–120.
8. Jacoby, *Souls, Bodies, Spirits*, 189.
9. For an overview, see John T. Noonan, Jr., "Abortion and the Catholic Church: A Summary History," *Natural Law Forum* 12 (1967), 85–131.
10. Blanchard, *The Anti-Abortion Movement and the Rise of the Religious Right*, 11.

11. Luker, *Abortion and the Politics of Motherhood*, 58–59. On nineteenth-century Catholic prohibitions of birth control, see Leslie Woodcock Tentler, *Catholics and Contraception: An American History* (Ithaca, NY: Cornell University Press, 2004), 15–42.
12. "Pastoral Constitution on the Church in the Modern World," 12/7/65, in *Vatican Council II: The Basic Sixteen Documents*, ed. Austin Flannery (Northport, NY: Costello Publishing Company, 1996), 193.
13. David J. Garrow, *Liberty and Sexuality: The Right to Privacy and the Making of Roe v. Wade* (Berkeley: University of California Press, 1998), 300–301; Luker, *Abortion and the Politics of Motherhood*, 80–87. On abortion before *Roe v. Wade*, see Donald T. Critchlow, *Intended Consequences: Birth Control, Abortion, and the Federal Government in Modern America* (New York: Oxford University Press, 1999), 3–183; Luker, *Abortion and the Politics of Motherhood*, 11–39; James C. Mohr, *Abortion in America: The Origins of National Policy, 1800–1900* (New York: Oxford University Press, 1978); Martin Olasky, *Abortion Rites: A Social History of Abortion in America* (Wheaton: Crossway Books, 1992); and Leslie J. Reagan, *When Abortion Was a Crime: Women, Medicine, and Law in the United States, 1867–1973* (Berkeley: University of California Press, 1997).
14. Garrow, *Liberty and Sexuality*, 290–307, 330–332; Williams, *God's Own Party*, 112–113.
15. "Pastoral Constitution on the Church in the Modern World," 280–281.
16. See, for example, Henry A. Buchanan and Bob W. Brown, "The Ecumenical Movement Threatens Protestantism," *Christianity Today*, November 20, 1964, 21–23; and "1965: Religion in Review," *Christianity Today*, January 7, 1966, 52.
17. Critchlow, *Intended Consequences*, 134. These fourteen states were Arkansas, California, Colorado, Delaware, Florida, Georgia, Kansas, Maryland, Mississippi, North Carolina, New Mexico, Oregon, South Carolina, and Virginia. Critchlow, *Intended Consequences*, 270 footnote 72.
18. Richley H. Crapo, "Grass-Roots Deviance from Official Doctrine: A Study of Latter-Day [*sic*] Saint (Mormon) Folk-Beliefs," *Journal for the Scientific Study of Religion* 26, no. 4 (December 1987): 473.
19. Byron Wilford Daynes and Raymond Tatalovich, "Mormons and Abortion Politics in the United States," *International Review of History and Political Science* 23, no. 2 (May 1986): 4.
20. James T. Richardson and Sandie Wightman Fox, "Religious Affiliation as a Predictor of Voting Behavior in Abortion Reform Legislation," *Journal for the Scientific Study of Religion* 11, no. 4 (December 1972): 351.
21. Ibid., 354–356.
22. "Abortion," *Priesthood Bulletin*, June 1972, in Salt Lake Public Communications Council Files, 1976–1977, Archives, Family and Church History Department of The Church of Jesus Christ of Latter-day Saints, Salt Lake City, Utah (hereafter, LDS Archives).

23. Crapo, "Grass-Roots Deviance from Official Doctrine," 474.
24. Crapo, "Grass-Roots Deviance from Official Doctrine," 474; Jeffrey E. Keller, "When Does the Spirit Enter the Body?" *Sunstone* 10, no. 2 (March 1985): 43.
25. "Abortion," *Priesthood Bulletin*. On LDS theology regarding abortion, see also Mary K. Beard, "Abortion" in *Encyclopedia of Mormonism: The History, Scripture, Doctrine, and Procedures of the Church of Jesus Christ of Latter-day Saints*, ed. Daniel H. Ludlow (5 vols., New York: Macmillan, 1992), vol. 1, 7.
26. Lynn Taylor, "But None Take It Lightly: Churches Not United on Question of Abortions," *Chicago Tribune*, February 12, 1973; John T. McGreevy, *Catholicism and American Freedom: A History* (New York: W. W. Norton & Company, 2003), 261; Critchlow, *Intended Consequences*, 168.
27. Raymond Tatalovich and Byron W. Daynes, *The Politics of Abortion: A Study of Community Conflict in Public Policy Making* (New York: Praeger, 1981), 112.
28. "Convention Circuit," *Christianity Today*, July 28, 1972, 38.
29. See, for example, "Abortion Made Easier," *Christianity Today*, March 27, 1970, 36.
30. "Capital Consistency," *Christianity Today*, June 20, 1969, 21.
31. "The War on the Womb," *Christianity Today*, June 5, 1970, 24–25. Daniel Williams argues that *Christianity Today*'s quick move from equivocation to a staunch anti-abortion position as exhibited in "The War on the Womb" came about because its editors realized "therapeutic" abortions were being used for more than just rare medical procedures and were resulting in far more abortions than they originally imagined would take place under the law. Yet in 1970, there was little abortion data to alarm evangelicals. The publication of the rather ambivalent editorial, "Abortion Made Easier," in March 1970, less than three months before the June 1970 publication of "The War on the Womb" suggests that an alarm over abortion rates was not behind the magazine's abrupt hardening of its abortion stance. Instead, the shift seems a clear response to New York's abortion reform law passed directly between the two editorials on April 10, 1970. As the first sentence of "The War on the Womb" read: "The drive to repeal and relax abortion laws is proving remarkably, if not startlingly, successful." If anything, the editors understood that such laws would bring about an upsurge in abortion numbers thanks to the widening legal provisions of the New York state law, but they weren't reacting to such a reality in 1970 as much as they were anticipating it. Williams, *God's Own Party*, 114–115.
32. "Financing Murder," *Christianity Today*, January 29, 1971, 22.
33. Harold B. Kuhn, "Now-Generation Churchmen and the Unborn," *Christianity Today*, January 29, 1971, 38; David Kucharsky, "The Abortion Issue," *Christianity Today*, April 23, 1971, 36–37.
34. "Social Action Aborning," *Christianity Today*, May 7, 1971, 26.
35. "Newly Published," *Christianity Today*, November 10, 1972, 29. For a background on the Willkes becoming involved in the abortion fight and the NRLC,

see "Teaching Pro-Life Story Is Subject of Newest Willke Book," *National Right to Life News*, November 1973, in Box 9, Folder 6, Joseph A. Breig Papers, University of Notre Dame Archives (hereafter, UNDA).

36. Kuhn, "Now-Generation Churchmen and the Unborn," 38. *Christianity Today* had regularly advocated contraception for married couples. One article maintained, "Contraception in Christian marriage not only is permissible but has a very significant value. This point should be made firmly, clearly, and loudly, for the benefit of all Christians who may have lingering doubts." M. O. Vincent, "A Christian View of Contraception," *Christianity Today*, November 8, 1968, 15.
37. In addition to the articles already mentioned, see also, L. Nelson Bell, "An Alternative to Abortion," *Christianity Today*, June 18, 1971, 17–18; "No Right to Be Born?," *Christianity Today*, November 10, 1972, 34, for pre-1973 *Christianity Today* pieces about abortion. This number would radically change in the coming years. Robert Johnston found that from 1972 to 1977, more than one-third of the magazine's seven hundred editorials concerned public issues, with abortion ranking as the favorite topic, though as I have indicated, the vast bulk of those occurred after the *Roe* decision, *Evangelicals at an Impasse: Biblical Authority in Practice* (Atlanta: John Knox Press, 1979), 85, cited in David R. Swartz, "Left Behind: The Evangelical Left and the Limits of Evangelical Politics, 1965–1988" (Ph.D. diss, University of Notre Dame, 2008), 519 footnote 108.
38. John Dart, "Catholic Church United by Opposition to Abortion Issue," *Los Angeles Times*, April 4, 1971.
39. Robert D. Visscher, "Therapeutic Abortion: Blessing or Murder?," *Christianity Today*, September 27, 1968, 7.
40. Paul K. Jewett, "The Relation of the Soul to the Fetus," *Christianity Today*, November 8, 1968, 8.
41. Nancy Hardesty, "Should Anyone Who Wants an Abortion Have One?," *Eternity*, June 1967, 32.
42. "The Abortion Debate," Letter to the Editor, C. E. Cerling, Jr., *Christianity Today*, June 19, 1970, 16.
43. Letters to Editor, Grenville A. Daun and John H. Tegenfeldt, *Christianity Today*, February 26, 1971, 22.
44. "On Law and Grace," Letter to the Editor, Rodney Juell, November 10, 1972, 49.
45. Jacoby, *Souls, Bodies, Spirits*, 28–40. See also, Michele Dillon, "Religion and Culture in Tension: The Abortion Discourses of the U.S. Catholic Bishops and the Southern Baptist Convention," *Religion and American Culture: A Journal of Interpretation* 5, no. 2 (Summer 1995): 159–180. Dillon explores the differences between natural law and biblical authority as the basis for Roman Catholic and Southern Baptist objections to abortion, respectively.

46. Steven P. Miller correctly points out that evangelical hesitancy to take up pro-life activism did not equate to any sort of pro-choice support, *The Age of Evangelicalism: America's Born Again Years* (New York: Oxford University Press, 2014), 54. But the apathy and even resistance to *Christianity Today*'s activist pro-life position from its readers suggests a more complicated relationship for lay evangelicals to the question of abortion reform than Miller suggests. More commonly, many evangelicals initially responded to abortion as they looked on other social ills like gambling or drinking: as lamentable evidence of the fallen world they lived in, but still something they were to personally avoid rather than seek to publically regulate. Some Southern Baptists even saw drinking and gambling as far more important political issues than abortion. Robert Holbrook, the founder of Baptists for Life, chastised this feeling among Southern Baptists, writing in 1973, "Surely the killing of the unborn is a more pressing issue of morality than 'betting on a horse.'" Quoted in Williams, *God's Own Party*, 118.
47. Williams rightly argues that northern evangelicals were more attuned to and worried about the fairly liberal abortion laws passing in their states, though their proximity to a vibrant Catholic anti-abortion opposition to that legislative reform in their backyards certainly played a part as well. With their more persistent anti-Catholic feelings, Southern Baptists tolerated abortion in part because of Catholic opposition to it, but also because Southern state legislatures that had passed abortion law reform had done so with little political turmoil—perhaps in part because of a diminished Catholic presence in the region—and had tended to more conservatively extend abortion rights only to cases of rape, incest, fetal defects, and threats to a woman's health. Williams, *God's Own Party*, 114–117.
48. Paul L. Sadler, "The Abortion Issue Within the Southern Baptist Convention, 1969–1988" (Ph.D. diss., Baylor University, 1991), 16. On Finkbine, see Garrow, *Liberty and Sexuality*, 285–291; Luker, *Abortion and the Politics of Motherhood*, 62–65; and Tatalovich and Daynes, *The Politics of Abortion*, 45–46.
49. "Resolution on Population Explosion," June 1967, http://www.sbc.net/resolutions/amResolution.asp?ID=799.
50. "Resolution on Abortion," June 1971, http://www.sbc.net/resolutions/amResolution.asp?ID=13.
51. Jerry Sutton, *A Matter of Conviction: A History of Southern Baptist Social Engagement with the Culture* (Nashville: B&H Publishing Group, 2008), 195. Scholars have noted that the seemingly moderate support some evangelicals gave abortion reform only extended to scenarios related to medical exceptions and never spoke of abortion as an individual right. Importantly, these evangelicals were advocating for the "reform" of abortion laws to allow for therapeutic abortion rather than, as pro-choice advocates usually argued, the

"right" of women to elective abortion. Miller, *The Age of Evangelicalism*, 54; Williams, *God's Own Party*, 112–115.

52. See letters in Carl Bates Papers, AR 298, Folder 7, SBHLA.
53. Letter, Carl E. Bates to William R. Stringer, 6/7/71, Carl Bates Papers, AR 298, Folder 7, SBHLA.
54. Letter, Carl E. Bates to The Reverend Ed Gardner, 3/21/72, Carl Bates Papers, AR 298, Folder 7, SBHLA.
55. Kenneth Hayes, "Baptist Leaders Favor Revision of Abortion Laws," *Baptist Press*, September 9, 1970, in Christian Life Commission Resource Files, 1955–1990, AR 138–2, Box 8, Folder 3, SBHLA.
56. Andrew D. Lester, "The Abortion Dilemma," *Review & Expositor* 68, no. 2 (Spring 1971): 233. On Lester, see Sadler, "The Abortion Issue Within the Southern Baptist Convention," 47–48.
57. Hayes, "Baptist Leaders Favor Revision of Abortion Laws."
58. Sadler rightly points out that Southern Baptists during the 1970s cultivated a conversation on abortion that kept alive "as many competing values as possible," but found consensus in rejecting abortion on demand. Sadler, "The Abortion Issue Within the Southern Baptist Convention," 69. Sadler, however, largely sees this as a temporary theological diversity that was soon replaced with a hardline theological and political uniformity opposing abortion brought about by changing social and political conditions. However, I argue that what remains remarkable about Southern Baptist responses to abortion during the 1970s is not merely the diversity of beliefs but, more importantly, the lack of a settled biblical position. This is particularly true around the question of personhood, as compared to clear doctrinal teachings that predate *Roe v. Wade* from not only the Catholic Church, but also some Protestant denominations whether opposing or supporting abortion law reform.
59. Keith Cassidy, "The Right to Life Movement: Sources, Development, and Strategies," in *The Politics of Abortion and Birth Control in Historical Perspective*, ed. Donald T. Critchlow (University Park: Pennsylvania State University Press, 1996), 139.
60. Critchlow, *Intended Consequences*, 137; McGreevy, *Catholicism and American Freedom*, 268–269.
61. McGreevy, *Catholicism and American Freedom*, 266.
62. Linda Greenhouse and Reva B. Segal, "Before (and After) *Roe v. Wade*: New Questions About Backlash," *Yale Law Journal* 120, no. 8 (June 2011): 2049.
63. Ibid., 2050–2051.
64. James DeForest Murch, "The Protestant Position Today," in "National Conference on Church-State Relations," National Association of Evangelicals, Winona Lake, Indiana, March 6–8, 1963, in Box 40, Folder 6, NAE.

65. Letter, (Rev.) James T. McHugh to Rev. John Courtney Murray, S.J., March 2, 1967, Box 12, Folder 778, the Rev. John Courtney Murray, S.J. Papers, Murray.
66. Cassidy, "The Right to Life Movement," 139; Critchlow, *Intended Consequences*, 138; Faye D. Ginsburg, *Contested Lives: The Abortion Debate in an American Community* (Berkeley: University of California Press, 1989), 44; Greenhouse and Segal, "Before (and After) *Roe v. Wade*," 2047–2049; Jaffe, Lindheim, and Lee, *Abortion Politics*, 74; Karrer, "The National Right to Life Committee," 537–539; Kelly, "Learning and Teaching Consistency," 154; Louis Kohlmeier, "Women's Lobby vs. Right to Life," *Chicago Tribune*, June 3, 1974.
67. Cassidy, "The Right to Life Movement," 139–140. The southern states that had liberalized their abortion laws for various exceptions were Arkansas, Florida, Georgia, Mississippi, North Carolina, South Carolina, and Virginia. Critchlow, *Intended Consequences*, 270 footnote 72.
68. "Abortion Charade Exposed," *The Pilot*, reprinted in *Boston Globe*, March 27, 1971.
69. "A Catholic Abortion," *Triumph*, April 1971, 7–12, details the attempt at establishing the National Right to Life Congress. The article also includes letters between Congress's organizers and Catholic Church officials.
70. Letter, (Rev.) James T. McHugh to Your Excellency, February 9, 1971, in "A Catholic Abortion," 9.
71. Letter, Charles E. Rice to Your Excellency, February 18, 1971, in "A Catholic Abortion," 10.
72. Pamphlet, Edward J. Melvin, C.M., "Abortion," (Huntington: Our Sunday Visitor, Inc., n.d.), 35, 36, 39, in Box 54, Folder 1, Paul Marx Papers, UNDA.
73. Pamphlet, "The Trouble with Abortion," n.d., Box 1, Folder 1, John F. Cronin Papers, UNDA.
74. Paige, *The Right to Lifers*, 91.
75. "Vatican's Radio Criticizes Abortion Ruling by Court," *New York Times*, January 24, 1973.
76. "Statements by 2 Cardinals," *New York Times*, January 23, 1973.
77. Sheila Wolfe and Richard Philbrick, "Cody to Continue Abortion Fight," *Chicago Tribune*, January 24, 1973.
78. "Statement of the Committee for Pro-Life Affairs of the National Conference of Catholic Bishops," January 23, 1973, in folder "Pro-Life – General (by year)," Box 1/1/1973 to 12/31/1978, Administrative Records—Subject Files—Communications, Archives of the Archdiocese of Chicago.
79. "Cardinal Calls for Abortion Sermons," *Los Angeles Times*, January 25, 1973; Marjorie Hyer, "Cardinal O'Boyle Asks Pastors to Preach Against Abortion Rule," *Washington Post*, January 25, 1973.
80. See Letter, Rev. John J. Quinn to Dear Father, January 24, 1973, and attached "Respect Life Program 1973 Liturgical Suggestions," in folder "Abortion," Respect Life Records, Archives of the Archdiocese of Chicago.

81. Lynn Taylor, "But None Take It Lightly: Churches Not United on Question of Abortions," *Chicago Tribune*, February 12, 1973.
82. Ibid.
83. Crapo, "Grass-Roots Deviance from Official Doctrine," 474.
84. Taylor, "But None Take It Lightly."
85. National Association of Evangelicals, "Resolution on Abortion," 1973, in Box 43, Folder 3, Papers of Thomas Fletcher Zimmerman, BGCA.
86. Lawrence Van Gelder, "Cardinals Shocked—Reaction Mixed," *New York Times*, January 23, 1973.
87. Gorney, *Articles of Faith*, 188.
88. "Two Rulings Criticized by Baptists," *Washington Post*, June 15, 1973. In 1972, the Supreme Court had banned capital punishment in *Furman v. Georgia*. The Court reinstated the death penalty, however, during its 1976 session.
89. "Resolution on Abortion and Sanctity of Human Life," June 1974, http://www.sbc.net/resolutions/amResolution.asp?ID=14.
90. "Abortion Newsletter," *Christian Faith in Action*, July 1973 in Christian Life Commission Resource Files, 1955–1990, AR 138–2, Box 92, Folder 11, SBHLA.
91. For example, see W. A. Criswell, "Religious Freedom, the Church, the State, and Senator Kennedy," http://contentdm.baylor.edu/cdm4/document.php?CISOROOT=/04wood&CISOPTR=7637&REC. See also, "Kennedy Is Attacked," *New York Times*, July 4, 1960.
92. "Abortion Decision: A Death Blow?," *Christianity Today*, February 16, 1973, 48.
93. J. Claude Evans, "Defusing the Abortion Debate," *Christian Century*, January 31, 1973, 117, quoted in Tatalovich and Daynes, *The Politics of Abortion*, 112.
94. Martin, *With God on Our Side*, 193.
95. "Abortion and the Court," *Christianity Today*, February 16, 1973, 32. Italics in the original. While the editorial was unsigned, William Martin and other scholars have identified Brown as the author. Martin, *With God on Our Side*, 193.
96. "A License to Live," *Christianity Today*, July 26, 1974, 22.
97. K. D. Whitehead, "From Abortion to Sex Education," *Homiletic & Pastoral Review*, November 1973, enclosed with Letter to Dear Father, March 17, 1971, Box 39, Folder 22, Rose Eileen Masterman Papers, UNDA.
98. "Abortion and the Court," 33.
99. George L. Norris, Letter to the Editor, "A Question of Liberty," *Christianity Today*, March 16, 1973, 21.
100. Nancy Hardesty, Letter to the Editor, "A Question of Liberty," *Christianity Today*, March 16, 1973, 20.
101. "What Price Abortion?," *Christianity Today*, March 2, 1973, 39.
102. Quotation from review of *Mormonism and American Culture*, eds. Marvin Hill and James Allen, in "Newly Published," *Christianity Today*, January 19, 1973, 32.

See also, review of Thomas Starkes, *Confronting Popular Cults* in "Newly Published," *Christianity Today*, October 27, 1972, 25.

103. Donald P. Shoemaker, "Why Your Neighbor Joined the Mormon Church," *Christianity Today*, October 11, 1974, 11.
104. "Abortion Decision: A Death Blow?," 48.
105. David Kucharsky and Edward E. Plowman, "An Evangelical Awakening in the Catholic Church?," *Christianity Today*, December 7, 1973, 47.
106. Advertisement for *A Prejudiced Protestant Takes a New Look at the Catholic Church*, *Christianity Today*, January 21, 1972, 44; review of James C. Hefley, *A Prejudiced Protestant Takes a New Look at the Catholic Church*, in "Newly Published," *Christianity Today*, March 17, 1972, 20.
107. "Roman Catholics—Ready to Hear," *Christianity Today*, December 7, 1973, 31.
108. Kucharsky and Plowman, "An Evangelical Awakening in the Catholic Church?," 46.
109. Ibid., 47.
110. For example, see "Review of Current Religious Thought," *Christianity Today*, October 29, 1956, 38; and "Giving Goals Soar," *Christianity Today*, January 7, 1957, 32.
111. "Religion in Transit," *Christianity Today*, January 21, 1972, 39. The exact number of baptisms reported for 1971 by the SBC was 412,600. Other than the year 1959, this stood as the most baptisms the SBC had recorded in one year.
112. "A License to Live," 23.
113. Letter, Harold O. J. Brown to The Reverend Dr. Foy Valentine, July 29, 1974, Box 17, Folder 107, Records of Christianity Today International, BGCA.
114. Letter, Foy Valentine to Dr. Harold Lindsell, August 30, 1974, Box 17, Folder 107, Records of Christianity Today International, BGCA.
115. Foy Valentine, Letter to the Editor, "Setting Straight?," *Christianity Today*, September 13, 1974, 37; and editor's response following Valentine letter, pp. 37–38.
116. Letter, Brown to Valentine, July 29, 1974.
117. Sutton, *A Matter of Conviction*, 212–213.
118. "Resolution on Abortion and Sanctity of Human Life," June 1974, http://www.sbc.net/resolutions/amResolution.asp?ID=14.
119. Paul Sadler argues that "evangelical writers and movements exerted increasing influence on Southern Baptist thought and action" on abortion during the 1970s, "The Abortion Issue Within the Southern Baptist Convention," 58. The contretemps between Foy Valentine and the editors of *Christianity Today* and the magazine's critical coverage of the SBC throughout the 1970s seems to suggest instead a different relationship between at least one major evangelical organ and the SBC over the issue of abortion. As a separatist denomination with its own robust network of seminaries, publications, and agencies, many

Southern Baptists, particularly of an older generation as represented by Foy Valentine, resisted outside influences, including the strong anti-abortion positions of northern evangelicals. But as the SBC spread beyond its historic base in the American South to the West and the Midwest, Southern Baptist pastors in places like California and Ohio were often in closer contact with evangelical associations than with their own denomination. Additionally, many younger Southern Baptist ministers had attended northern evangelical seminaries, making them more aware of evangelical theological debates over culture war issues like abortion that many parts of the Deep South of the 1960s and 1970s had yet to confront. Williams, *God's Own Party*, 157.

120. Gorney, *Articles of Faith*, 178.
121. Karrer, "The National Right to Life Committee," 543.
122. Ibid., 538.
123. Letter, Marjory Mecklenburg and Joseph Lampe to Father McHugh and Mike, July 11, 1972, folder: "NRLC 1972," Box 4, American Citizens Concerned for Life, Inc. Records, Gerald R. Ford Library (hereafter, Ford).
124. Karrer, "The National Right to Life Committee," 548–555.
125. Blanchard, *The Anti-Abortion Movement and the Rise of the Religious Right*, 32, 72; Paige, *The Right to Lifers*, 31, 51, 57–58.
126. Christopher Lyndon, "Abortion Is Big Issue in the Primaries in Massachusetts and New Hampshire," *New York Times*, February 4, 1976.
127. Luker, *Abortion and the Politics of Motherhood*, 127–128.
128. Greenhouse and Segal, "Before (and After) *Roe v. Wade*," 2050 footnote 79.
129. Marion K. Sanders, "Enemies of Abortion," *Harper's*, March 1974, 30.
130. Granberg, "The Abortion Activists," 157–163.
131. Luker, *Abortion and the Politics of Motherhood*, 196.
132. Letter, Russell Shaw to Editors, News Directors, March 22, 1973, Box 9, Folder 5, Joseph A. Breig Papers, UNDA.
133. Sanders, "Enemies of Abortion," 26.
134. Kelly, "Learning and Teaching Consistency," 156.
135. Critchlow, *Intended Consequences*, 137–138; Karrer, "The National Right to Life Committee," 540–541. For an excellent treatment of Minnesota Citizens Concerned for Life, see Julia Vill, "Abortion as a 'Medical Problem Broadly Defined': Grassroots Activist Beginnings and the Minnesota Story of the Pro-Life Movement, From Nineteenth Century State Anti-Abortion Legislation to 1980s Pro-Life National Politics" (Senior Thesis, Princeton University, 2012).
136. See "Articles of Incorporation of National Right to Life Committee, Inc." and "Revised Bylaws – The National Right to Life Committee, Inc.," both in folder: "NRLC 1973 Bylaws," Box 6, American Citizens Concerned for Life, Inc. Records, Ford. Also, "NRLC, Inc. Puts It All Together," *National Right to Life News*, November 1973, in National Right to Life News Collection, Wilcox

Collection, Spencer Research Library, University of Kansas (hereafter, Wilcox Collection). Paige, *The Right to Lifers*, 83–84.

137. Karrer, "The National Right to Life Committee," 541, 546, 556.
138. Paper, Judy Fink, "Alliances From NRLC Inc. with Protestant Judicatories," n.d., folder: "NRLC nd (2)," Box 4, American Citizens Concerned for Life, Inc., Ford.
139. Mary Ziegler accounts for the role of "moderates" in the early history of the NRLC like Fink, Mecklenburg, and Schaller in contrast to the "conservatives" who wanted the NRLC to oppose all forms of birth control, "The Possibility of Compromise: Antiabortion Moderates after *Roe v. Wade*, 1973–1980," *Chicago-Kent Law Review* 87, no. 2 (January 2012): 571–590. Yet rather than seeing the division in the NRLC along political categories of "moderate" and "conservative," I argue that the organization largely split along religious lines between Catholics and Protestants, as seen in the birth control debate and in other questions about the NRLC's management and public outreach, particularly to non-Catholics.
140. Memo, Judy Fink, "In Re: Policy Statement of the NRLC concerning 'birth control,'" 5/15/73, folder: "NRLC 1973 (2)," Box 4, American Citizens Concerned for Life, Inc. Records, Ford.
141. Cuneo, "Life Battles," 274. On the "contraceptive mentality" within the NRLC, see Cuneo, "Life Battles," 278–282.
142. Dillon, "Religion and Culture in Tension."
143. In addition to the Catholic William Hunt, the four Protestant members of the ILC were Jean Garton, a member of the Lutheran Church—Missouri Synod; Rev. Robert Holbrook, a minister of a Southern Baptist church in Texas; Rev. Rod Fink, a Lutheran pastor in Connecticut; and Judy Fink, a member of an Independent Baptist church in Pittsburgh. (I am unaware if Rod Fink and Judy Fink were related.) I have not been able to confirm the church membership of the last member of the ILC, Rev. Dwayne Summers.
144. Paper, "Intergroup Liaison Committee," folder: "NRLC 1973 Mid-Year Report (2)," Box 6, American Citizens Concerned for Life, Inc. Records, Ford.
145. Memo, Judith Fink to Intergroup Liaison Committee, NRLC Inc., 9/7/73, folder: "NRLC 1973 (5)," Box 4, American Citizens Concerned for Life, Inc. Records, Ford.
146. Paper, Judith Fink, "Midyear Report of the Intergroup Liaison Committee of National Right to Life Committee, Inc.," folder: "NRLC 1973 Mid-Year Report (2)," Box 6, American Citizens Concerned for Life, Inc. Records, Ford.
147. "Mormons Endorse Willkes' Speaking Tour in Utah," *National Right to Life News*, November 1973, National Right to Life News Collection, Wilcox Collection.
148. Fink, "Midyear Report of the Intergroup Liaison Committee of National Right to Life Committee, Inc." See also, Minutes of National Right to Life

Committee, Inc., Executive Committee Meeting, 10/26–27/73, folder: "NRLC 1973 (6)," Box 5, American Citizens Concerned for Life, Inc. Records, Ford.

149. Fink, "Midyear Report of the Intergroup Liaison Committee of National Right to Life Committee, Inc."

150. Ibid.

151. Paper, Robert Holbrook, "Proposed Plan for Pro-Life Ads in State Baptist Papers," n.d., folder: "NRLC 1973 Mid-Year Report (2)," Box 6, American Citizens Concerned for Life, Inc. Records, Ford.

152. Robert Holbrook, "Court Ruling Forces Issue," *Baptist Standard*, May 16, 1973, 13, cited in Sadler, "The Abortion Issue Within the Southern Baptist Convention," 122.

153. Ibid.

154. Letter, Bob Holbrook to Laird M. Wilcox, 10/5/76, and attached pages, Ephemeral Materials, Baptists for Life Collection, Wilcox Collection; Minutes of National Right to Life Committee, Inc., Executive Committee Meeting, 1/4–5/74, folder: "NLRC 1974 Board and Executive Committee (1)," Box 7, American Citizens Concerned for Life, Inc. Records, Ford; and Precis, "Review of Baptists for Life Activities and Future Plans," n.d., folder: "ACCL – Admin File – Office Admin – Fundraising," Box 19, American Citizens Concerned for Life, Inc. Records, Ford; "Rev. Holbrook Moves," *National Right to Life News*, August 1977 in National Right to Life News Collection, Wilcox Collection.

155. Sadler, "The Abortion Issue Within the Southern Baptist Convention," 122.

156. Paper, Paulette Standefer, "Establishing a Pro-Life Group on an Inter-Denominational Theme," n.d., folder: "NRLC 1973 Mid-Year Report (2)," Box 6, American Citizens Concerned for Life, Inc. Records, Ford.

157. Ibid.

158. Ibid.

159. Memo, Marjory Mecklenburg to the Executive Committee—NRLC, 7/18/74, folder: "NRLC – 1974 Board and Executive Committee (9)," Box 8, American Citizens Concerned for Life, Inc. Records, Ford. Underlining in the original.

160. Harold O. J. Brown, "In Defense of Life," *Christianity Today*, July 26, 1974, 39.

161. Sanders, "Enemies of Abortion," 28.

162. Linda Charlton, "Start of Life Debated at Abortion Hearing," *New York Times*, May 21, 1974; Marjorie Hyer, "Senators Hear 4 Cardinals Argue for Strict Abortion Ban," *Washington Post*, March 8, 1974; Nick Thimmesch, "The Battle over Abortion Heats Up Again," *Chicago Tribune*, April 28, 1974; Jaffe, Lindheim, and Lee, *Abortion Politics*, 113.

163. Copy of Robert Holbrook's testimony, March 7, 1974, in Christian Life Commission Resource Files, 1955–1990, AR 138–2, Box 79, Folder 1, SBHLA.

164. Carlton Sherwood, "Conflicts Lead to Forming of New Right-to-life Unit," *Catholic Star Herald*, August 30, 1974, in folder: "NRLC – 1974 (5)," Box 7, American Citizens Concerned for Life, Inc. Records, Ford.

165. James J. Diamond, "The Troubled Anti-Abortion Camp," *America*, August 10, 1974, 53, 54.
166. Karrer, "The National Right to Life Committee," 538.
167. Memo, n.d., folder: "NRLC nd (2)," Box 4, American Citizens Concerned for Life, Inc. Records, Ford.
168. Lester Kinsolving, "Anti-abortion Crusade Crumbling," *The Free Lance-Star*, June 24, 1974.
169. Memo, Judith Fink to Professor Joseph Witherspoon, 7/1/73, folder: "NRLC – 1973 – Board and Executive Committee (4)," Box 5, American Citizens Concerned for Life, Inc. Records, Ford.
170. Letter, Marjory Mecklenburg to Martin Ryan Haley, 9/3/73, quoted in Vill, "Abortion as a 'Medical Problem Broadly Defined'," 75–76.
171. Sherwood, "Conflicts Lead to Forming of New Right-to-life Unit." See also Vill, "Abortion as a 'Medical Problem Broadly Defined'," 76–93.
172. Paige, *The Right to Lifers*, 84–85; Sherwood, "Conflicts Lead to Forming of New Right-to-life Unit."
173. Paper, Mary Ann Henry, "Reaching Non-Catholics: the Catholic Problem," n.d., folder: "NRLC 1973 Mid-Year Report (2)," Box 6, American Citizens Concerned for Life, Inc. Records, Ford.
174. "Cardinal's Annual Luncheon Address to A.C.C.W. – September 22, 1973," enclosed with Letter, Rev. James J. Murtaugh to His Eminence John Cardinal Cody, October 2, 1973, CBC Agency Files—Council of Catholic Women, Box 2, Folder 1, Archives of the Archdiocese of Chicago.
175. Newsletter, Archdiocesan Office for Pro Life Activities, August 1973, in folder "Respect Life Newsletter 1973," Respect Life Records, Archives of the Archdiocese of Chicago. Underlining in the original.
176. Newsletter, Archdiocesan Office for Pro Life Activities, September 1973, in folder "Respect Life Newsletter 1973," Respect Life Records, Archives of the Archdiocese of Chicago.
177. Memorandum, "Specific Internal Planning Requirements – Supreme Court Decision on Abortion," March 6, 1973, Folder 15, Box 70, George Gilmary Higgins Papers, ACUA.
178. Newsletter, Archdiocesan Office for Pro Life Activities, August 1973.
179. "Background Material for Homily," enclosed with Letter, Reverend Monsignor Francis A. Brackin to Dear Father, January 15, 1974, in folder "Pro-Life Office and Activities," Box 1/1/1973 to 12/31/1978, Administrative Records—Subject Files—Communications, Archives of the Archdiocese of Chicago.

CHAPTER 5

1. Southern Baptist Convention and United States Catholic Conference, *Speeches from a Baptist-Catholic Regional Conference at Daytona Beach, Florida, February*

1–3, 1971 (Washington, D.C.: United States Catholic Conference, 1972); United States Catholic Conference, "Baptist-Catholic Conference Is Scheduled For October," August 28, 1975, http://www.usccb.org/beliefs-and-teachings/ecumenical-and-interreligious/ecumenical/southern-baptist/upload/sb2.pdf.

2. "Dean M. Kelley," in *Encyclopedia of Religion in American Politics*, eds. Jeffrey D. Schultz, John G. West, Jr., and Iain Maclean (Phoenix, AZ: Oryx Press, 1999), 136.
3. Steve Bruce, *The Rise and Fall of the New Christian Right: Conservative Protestant Politics in America, 1978–1988* (Oxford: Clarendon Press, 1988), 47.
4. Dean M. Kelley, *Why Conservative Churches Are Growing: A Study in Sociology of Religion* (New York: Harper & Row, 1972), 6. These five Protestant bodies were the United Methodist Church, the Episcopal Church, the United Presbyterian Church in the USA, the Lutheran Church in America, and the United Church of Christ.
5. Ibid., 21, 22.
6. Nancy Ammerman, *Baptist Battles: Social Change and Religious Conflict in the Southern Baptist Convention* (New Brunswick, NJ: Rutgers University Press, 1990), 52.
7. Darren Dochuk, *From Bible Belt to Sunbelt: Plain-Folk Religion, Grassroots Politics, and the Rise of Evangelical Conservatism* (New York: W. W. Norton & Company, Inc., 2011), 341.
8. Kelley, *Why Conservative Churches Are Growing*, 28, 29.
9. John E. Wagner, "How to Grow a Church," *Christianity Today*, October 13, 1972, 26.
10. Carl Bangs, "Deceptive Statistics," *Christian Century*, August 30, 1972, 852.
11. Kelley, *Why Conservative Churches Are Growing*, 55.
12. Ibid., 100.
13. Elmer L. Towns, *America's Fastest Growing Churches; Why 10 Sunday Schools are Growing Fast* (Nashville, TN: Impact Books, 1972).
14. Steven P. Miller, *The Age of Evangelicalism: America's Born Again Years* (New York: Oxford University Press, 2014), 15–16.
15. William Martin, *With God on Our Side: The Rise of the Religious Right in America* (New York: Broadway Books, 1996), 149.
16. Kenneth A. Briggs, "Carter's Evangelism Putting Religion into Politics for First Time since '60," *New York Times*, April 11, 1976. On Jimmy Carter and the 1976 election, see, Miller, *The Age of Evangelicalism*, 40–49; Daniel K. Williams, *God's Own Party: The Making of the Christian Right* (New York: Oxford University Press, 2010), 125–132. On the role of Carter's religious faith in his politics, see Dan Arial and Cheryl Heckler-Feltz, *The Carpenter's Apprentice: The Spiritual Biography of Jimmy Carter* (Grand Rapids, MI: Zondervan Publishing House, 1996); Randall Balmer, *God in the White House: A History: How*

Faith Shaped the Presidency from John F. Kennedy to George W. Bush (New York: HarperOne, 2008), 79–108, and *Redeemer: The Life of Jimmy Carter* (New York: Basic Books, 2014); E. Brooks Holifield, "The Three Strands of Jimmy Carter's Religion," *New Republic*, June 15, 1976, 15–17; Leo P. Ribuffo, "God and Jimmy Carter," in *Transforming Faith: The Sacred and Secular in Modern American History*, eds. M. L. Bradbury and James B. Gilbert (New York: Greenwood Press, 1989), 141–159; and Gary Scott Smith, *Faith and the Presidency: From George Washington to George W. Bush* (New York: Oxford University Press, 2006), 293–324.

17. Kenneth L. Woodward, "Born Again!," *Newsweek*, October 25, 1976, 68.
18. On the growth of evangelical churches in the 1970s and 1980s, see Robert D. Putnam and David E. Campbell, *American Grace: How Religion Divides and Unites Us* (New York: Simon & Schuster, 2010), 100–120.
19. Woodward, "Born Again!," 68–78.
20. Ibid., 78.
21. Dochuk, *From Bible Belt to Sunbelt*, 326–329; John G. Turner, *Bill Bright and Campus Crusade for Christ: The Renewal of Evangelicalism in Postwar America* (Chapel Hill: University of North Carolina Press, 2008), 93–146.
22. Erling Jorstad, *The New Christian Right, 1981–1988: Prospects for the Post-Reagan Decade* (Lewiston, ME: The Edwin Mellen Press, 1987), 97.
23. On the rise of televangelism, see Jeffrey K. Hadden and Charles E. Swann, *Prime Time Preachers: The Rising Power of Televangelism* (Reading, MA: Addison-Wesley, 1981).
24. Sara Diamond, *Roads to Dominion: Right-Wing Movements and Political Power in the United States* (New York: The Guilford Press, 1995), 162–163.
25. James Feron, "Growing Publishing Empire Is Built on Religion," *New York Times*, November 6, 1977.
26. Dochuk, *From Bible Belt to Sunbelt*, 365–368; Miller, *The Age of Evangelicalism*, 19–31; Bruce J. Schulman, *The Seventies: The Great Shift in American Culture, Society, and Politics* (Cambridge, MA: Da Capo Press, 2001), 92–96; Williams, *God's Own Party*, 160–162. See also Paul Boyer, "The Evangelical Resurgence in 1970s American Protestantism," in Bruce Schulman and Julian Zelizer, eds., *Rightward Bound: Making America Conservative in the 1970s* (Cambridge, MA: Harvard University Press, 2008), 29–51.
27. Donald G. Bloesch, *The Evangelical Renaissance* (Grand Rapids, MI: Zondervan, 1976), 18, quoted in Miller, *The Age of Evangelicalism*, 30.
28. James Daane, "Pentecostalism . . . and Reformation Faith," *The Reformed Journal* 24, no. 4 (April 1974): 17–20; Erling Jorstad, "Gifts of the Spirit and the Body of Christ: Perspectives on the Charismatic Movement," *Christianity Today*, October 26, 1973, 44; Edward E. Plowman, "Deepening Rift in the Charismatic Movement," *Christianity Today*, October 10, 1975, 52–54;

J. Rodman Williams, "Profile of the Charismatic Movement," *Christianity Today*, February 28, 1975, 9–13. For a more sympathetic response, see Donald G. Bloesch, "The Wind of the Spirit: Thoughts on a Doctrinal Controversy," *The Reformed Journal* 23, no. 8 (October 1973): 11–16.

29. Larry W. Hurtado, "The Charismatic Movement: What's Ahead," *Trinity Journal* 3 (Spring 1974): 70.
30. Dochuk, *From Bible Belt to Sunbelt*, 281–285; Miller, *The Age of Evangelicalism*, 16; Molly Worthen, *Apostles of Reason: The Crisis of Authority in American Evangelicalism* (New York: Oxford University Press, 2014), 138–147. See also Larry Eskridge, *God's Forever Family: The Jesus People Movement in America* (New York: Oxford University Press, 2013).
31. Walter A. Maier, "Charismatic Renewal in the Lutheran Church: 'Renewal in Missouri,'" *Concordia Theological Quarterly* 53, no. 1–2 (January–April 1989): 22.
32. Miller, *The Age of Evangelicalism*, 16. Miller also points out that these divisions "did not dilute the influence of evangelicalism . . . they simply dispersed it," 30. This was certainly true for evangelicalism's public influence, and divisions had always been part of the evangelical model. But many moderate neo-evangelicals still worried about what the rise of charismatics posed for traditional evangelical identity and theology. This tension would find some resolution in the 1980s, as Chapter 6 explores, but even in the 1970s' heyday of evangelical power and visibility, the question of charismatic Christianity continued to gnaw at many an evangelical's conscience and convictions.
33. On ecumenical-charismatic discussions, see Dorothy Mills Parker, "Ecumenical Conferees Explore the Charismatic Movement," *Christian Century*, February 27, 1974, 243–244.
34. David E. Kucharsky, "Obituary: CT Editor Emeritus Lindsell," *Christianity Today*, March 2, 1998, 67.
35. George Marsden, *Reforming Fundamentalism: Fuller Seminary and the New Evangelicalism* (Grand Rapids, MI: Wm. B. Eerdmans Publishing Co., 1987), 260; Worthen, *Apostles of Reason*, 66. For Henry's account of this period, see Carl F. H. Henry, *Confessions of a Theologian: An Autobiography* (Waco, TX: Word Books, 1986), 279–287.
36. L. Nelson Bell, "The Bible and Sex Education," *Christianity Today*, September 15, 1972, 38–39; "Sex Rights and Wrongs," *Christianity Today*, April 13, 1973, 31–32.
37. Marsden, *Reforming Fundamentalism*, 277.
38. Harold Lindsell, *The Battle for the Bible* (Grand Rapids, MI: Zondervan Publishing House, 1976), 203.
39. "Bible Battles," *Time*, May 10, 1976, 57.

40. Donald W. Dayton, "The Battle for the Bible: Renewing the Inerrancy Debate," *Christian Century*, November 10, 1976, 980.
41. Francis Rue Steele, "Inerrancy Is Indispensable," *Christianity Today*, April 9, 1976, 35.
42. Clark Pinnock, "Acrimonious Debate on Inerrancy," *Eternity*, June 1976, 40.
43. "Religion in Transit," *Christianity Today*, November 19, 1976, 60.
44. Worthen, *Apostles of Reason*, 202. See also Marsden, *Reforming Fundamentalism*, 279–282.
45. "Bible Battles," 57.
46. See Carl F. H. Henry, "The Battle for the Bible," *New Review of Books and Religion* 1, no. 1 (Spring 1976): 7, and "Conflict over Biblical Inerrancy," *Christianity Today*, May 7, 1976, 23–25. See also Dayton, "The Battle for the Bible," 980.
47. Marsden, *Reforming Fundamentalism*, 287.
48. Dayton, "The Battle for the Bible," 976.
49. Molly Worthen rightly argues for the role of the inerrancy debate in the rise of the Religious Right alongside religious conservatives' responses to the liberalizing culture and politics of the 1960s and 1970s, *Apostles of Reason*, 200–202. I contend, however, that the inerrancy debate and the relative triumph of biblical inerrantists in 1970s American evangelicalism shaped and utilized the political response to issues like abortion, gay rights, and the Equal Rights Amendment as a visible signifier of the inerrancy position and a basis of evangelical belief and identity. I make this argument more fully through the example of the Southern Baptist Convention in "'Worse than cancer and worse than snakes': Jimmy Carter's Southern Baptist Problem and the 1980 Election," *Journal of Policy History* 26, no. 4 (October 2014): 479–508.
50. Kelley, *Why Conservative Churches Are Growing*, 25–26.
51. Spencer W. Kimball, "A Report and a Challenge," *Ensign*, November 1976, 4.
52. Harold B. Lee, "Strengthen the Stakes of Zion," *Ensign*, July 1973, https://www.lds.org/ensign/1973/07/strengthen-the-stakes-of-zion.
53. "Editorial," *Ensign*, January 1971, https://www.lds.org/ensign/1971/01/editorial.
54. Douglas F. Tobler, quoted in "Selected Remarks: Excerpts from 'The Expanding Church' Symposium," *Ensign*, December 1976, https://www.lds.org/ensign/1976/12/selected-remarks-excerpts-from-the-expanding-church-symposium.
55. Chauncey C. Riddle, "Letter to Michael," *Ensign*, September 1975, https://www.lds.org/ensign/1975/09/letter-to-michael. See also Delbert L. Stapley, "What Constitutes the True Church," *Ensign*, May 1977, 21; Mark E. Petersen, "Signs of the True Church," *Ensign*, May 1979, 21.

56. "Chair of Christian Understanding Founded," *Ensign*, January 1973, 138; Steven David Grover, "Building Bridges: The Richard L. Evans Chair of Religious Understanding," *Religious Educator* 9, no. 2 (2008): 45–56.
57. Truman G. Madsen, "The Highest in Us," BYU Devotional, March 3, 1974, http://speeches.byu.edu/?act=viewitem&id=1020.
58. Dan L. Thrapp, "Philosopher Explains Controversial Status of Mormonism," *Los Angeles Times*, July 28, 1974.
59. Robert O. Self, *All in the Family: The Realignment of American Democracy since the 1960s* (New York: Hill and Wang, 2012), 344–345.
60. The definitive work on Francis Schaeffer is by Barry Hankins, *Francis Schaeffer and the Shaping of Evangelical America* (Grand Rapids, MI: Wm. B. Eerdmans Publishing Co., 2008). See also Williams, *God's Own Party*, 137–143; and Worthen, *Apostles of Reason*, 209–223. On L'Abri, see the accounts by Schaeffer's wife, Edith, and son, Frank: Edith Schaeffer, *L'Abri* (Carol Stream, IL: Tyndale House Publishers, 1969), and Frank Schaeffer, *Crazy for God: How I Grew Up as One of the Elect, Helped Found the Religious Right, and Lived to Take All (or Almost All) of It Back* (Cambridge, MA: Da Capo Press, 2007), especially pp. 1–152.
61. "Religious Best Sellers," *New York Times*, March 12, 1978.
62. Francis A. Schaeffer, *How Should We Then Live? The Rise and Decline of Western Thought and Culture* ([1976] Wheaton: Crossway Books, rev. ed. 2005), 19. Italics in the original.
63. Ibid., 22.
64. Ibid., 32.
65. Ibid., 209.
66. Ibid., 218.
67. Hankins, *Francis Schaeffer and the Shaping of Evangelical America*, 177.
68. Schaeffer, *Crazy for God*, 266.
69. On Franky's influence on the book and film of *How Should We Then Live?*, see Schaeffer, *Crazy for God*, 253–270; and Hankins, *Francis Schaeffer and the Shaping of Evangelical America*, 165–180.
70. Schaeffer, *Crazy for God*, 269–270; Mark Stegall, "God Land's Saving Grace, Author Says," *Dallas Morning News*, July 31, 1976.
71. Russell Chandler, "Schaeffer Sees Perils in Humanism," *Los Angeles Times*, March 5, 1977.
72. See ad for services at Moody Church in *Chicago Tribune*, October 8, 1977.
73. See ad for services at Church of Northern Virginia in *The Washington Post*, September 30, 1977; "Film Series Scheduled," *Trenton Evening Times*, September 24, 1977; and, "Religion Roundup," *Dallas Morning News*, October 8, 1977.
74. Mary Frances Berry, *Why ERA Failed: Politics, Women's Rights and the Amending Process of the Constitution* (Bloomington: University of Indiana Press,

1986), 63–67. See also Donald G. Matthews and Jane Sherron De Hart, *Sex, Gender, and the Politics of the ERA: A State and the Nation* (New York: Oxford University Press, 1990).

75. Seth Dowland, "'Family Values' and the Formation of a Christian Right Nation," *Church History* 78, no. 3 (September 2009): 607–610; Schulman, *The Seventies*, 168–171; Self, *All in the Family*, 276–283, 328–332. See also Matthew D. Lassiter, "Inventing Family Values," and Marjorie J. Spruill, "Gender and America's Right Turn," both in Schulman and Zelizer, eds., *Rightward Bound*, 13–28, and 71–89, respectively.

76. Bobby Joe Sims, "The American Right-Wing: A Case Study of the Political Role and Ideas of Phyllis Schlafly" (Ph.D. diss., Southern Illinois University, 1973), 137. See also Donald T. Critchlow, *Phyllis Schlafly and Grassroots Conservatism: A Woman's Crusade* (Princeton, NJ: Princeton University Press, 2005); Dowland, "'Family Values' and the Formation of a Christian Right Nation," 618–624; Carol Felsenthal, *The Sweetheart of the Silent Majority: The Biography of Phyllis Schlafly* (Garden City, NY: Doubleday, 1981); Self, *All in the Family*, 291–296; Patricia A. Tillson, "The Defeat of the Equal Rights Amendment: A Propaganda Analysis of Phyllis Schlafly's STOP ERA Campaign" (M.A. thesis, University of Houston, 1996); Williams, *God's Own Party*, 106–111.

77. Much has been written about the women who joined STOP ERA and other anti-ERA organizations. This literature has found a high correlation between religious fundamentalism, heavy religious participation, and committed anti-ERA activism; see Theodore S. Arrington and Patricia A. Kyle, "Equal Rights Amendment Activists in North Carolina," *Signs* 3, no. 3 (Spring 1978): 666–680; David W. Brady and Kent L. Tedin, "Ladies in Pink: Religion and Political Ideology in the Anti-ERA Movement," *Social Science Quarterly* 56, no. 4 (March 1976): 564–575; Iva E. Deutchman and Sandra Prince-Embury, "Political Ideology and Pro- and Anti-ERA Women," in *The Equal Rights Amendment: The Politics and Process of Ratification of the 27th Amendment to the Constitution*, ed. Sarah Slavin (New York: The Haworth Press, 1982), 39–55; Donald G. Mathews, "'Spiritual Warfare': Cultural Fundamentalism and the Equal Rights Amendment," *Religion and American Culture* 3, no. 2 (Summer 1993): 129–154; Kent L. Tedin, "Religious Preference and Pro/Anti Activism on the Equal Rights Amendment Issue," *Pacific Sociological Review* 21, no. 1 (January 1978): 55–66; and Kent L. Tedin, David W. Brady, Mary E. Buxton, Barbara M. Gorman, and Judy L. Thompson, "Social Background and Political Differences Between Pro- and Anti-ERA Activists," *American Politics Quarterly* 5, no. 3 (1977): 395–408.

78. *Eagle Forum Newsletter*, December 1975, Eagle Forum Collection, Wilcox Collection.

79. Rosemary Thomson, "A Christian View of the Equal Rights Amendment," 1975, quoted in Critchlow, *Phyllis Schlafly and Grassroots Conservatism*, 235–236.
80. Scholars have cited the ecumenical nature of the anti-ERA coalition, but I argue below for a more complicated understanding of that ecumenical relationship. See Williams, *God's Own Party*, 110–111.
81. Critchlow, *Phyllis Schlafly and Grassroots Conservatism*, 222.
82. Ibid., 67, 80.
83. *Eagle Forum Newsletter*, April 1976, Eagle Forum Collection, Wilcox Collection.
84. Schedule, Eagle Council IX, September 19–21, 1980, St. Louis, in Jaynann Morgan Payne Papers, L. Tom Perry Special Collections, Harold B. Lee Library, Brigham Young University.
85. Pamphlet, Eagle Forum, n.d., Folder 2, Box 1, Elaine Chenevert Donnelly Papers, Bentley Historical Library, University of Michigan.
86. Flyer, "Brief History of the W's," n.d., folder: "Miscellaneous, 1979–1983," Ephemeral Materials, Pro-Family Forum (U.S.), Wilcox Collection; Ruth Murray Brown, *For A "Christian America": A History of the Religious Right* (Amherst, NY: Prometheus Books, 2002), 61–65. Also Kyle Goyette, "The Politics of Rhetoric: Texas, the ERA, and the Defense of Family Values," talk delivered at the Policy History Conference, Columbus, Ohio, June 6, 2010. Copy of talk in my possession.
87. See materials in *Everyone is Listening to Women Aware* Newsletter Collection, Wilcox Collection.
88. Eileen Shanahan, "Opposition Rises to Amendment on Equal Rights," *New York Times*, January 15, 1973.
89. Louise Farr, "Peddling the Pedestal," *New Times*, October 17, 1975, 52.
90. The historiography of the Equal Rights Amendment has largely ignored the LDS Church's role in the political battle. Jane J. Mansbridge's study references the church in just one sentence when she locates anti-ERA opposition in "the fundamentalist South . . . and in the Mormon states of Utah and Nevada, where the Mormon church [*sic*] actively fought the ERA." Jane J. Mansbridge, *Why We Lost the ERA* (Chicago: University of Chicago Press, 1986), 3. Mary Frances Berry notes the church president's official opposition to the amendment, but fails to examine any organized role the church played in the ERA's defeat, *Why ERA Failed*, 76. Mormon-centered studies, however, have offered notable supplements to the ERA's historiography. These works have attributed the LDS Church's part in preventing the amendment's ratification to its hierarchal nature and Mormons' solid deference to that hierarchy. See D. Michael Quinn, "The LDS Church's Campaign Against the Equal Rights Amendment," *Journal of Mormon History* 20, no. 2 (Fall 1994): 85–155, and *The*

Mormon Hierarchy: Extensions of Power (Salt Lake City, UT: Signature Books, 1997), 373–406; O. Kendall White, Jr., "Overt and Covert Policies: The Mormon Church's Anti-ERA Campaign in Virginia," *Virginia Social Science Journal* 19 (Winter 1984): 11–16, and "Mormonism and the Equal Rights Amendment," *Journal of Church and State* 31, no. 2 (Spring 1989): 249–267; Marilyn Warenski, *Patriarchs and Politics: The Plight of the Mormon Woman* (New York: McGraw-Hill, 1978), 181–224; James Coates, *In Mormon Circles: Gentiles, Jack Mormons, and Latter-day Saints* (Reading: Addison-Wesley Publishing, 1991), 127–134; and Robert Gottlieb and Peter Wiley, *America's Saints: The Rise of Mormon Power* (New York: G.P. Putnam's Sons, 1984), 201–213. I have argued for understanding the role of LDS women in the anti-ERA fight. See "'The ERA Is a Moral Issue': The Mormon Church, LDS Women, and the Defeat of the Equal Rights Amendment," *American Quarterly* 59, no. 3 (September 2007): 623–644.

91. Victor L. Brown, "The Meaning of Morality," *Ensign*, June 1971, 55.
92. Harold B. Lee, "Maintain Your Place As a Woman," *Ensign*, February 1972, 48–56. On Mormonism's increasing conservatism in the 1970s regarding the role of women, see Laurence R. Iannaccone and Carrie A. Miles, "Dealing with Social Change: The Mormon Church's Response to Change in Women's Roles," *Social Forces* 68, no. 4 (June 1990): 1231–1250.
93. "First Presidency Reaffirms Opposition to ERA," *Ensign*, October 1978, 63.
94. "LDS Leaders Oppose ERA," *Deseret News*, October 22, 1976.
95. Memo, Ezra Taft Benson to "All Stake and Mission Presidents in the United States," December 29, 1976, quoted in Quinn, *The Mormon Hierarchy*, 377. Italics in the original. A "stake" is made up of a group of wards. A ward is the term Mormons use for a church congregation. Stakes, then, are the Mormon equivalent of dioceses.
96. Lisa Cronin Wohl, "A Mormon Connection? – The Defeat of the ERA in Nevada," *Ms.*, July 1977, 83.
97. Phyllis Schlafly, "A Viewpoint on Women's Issues," in *Outstanding Lectures, 1978–79* (Provo, UT: ASBYU Academics Office, 1979), 31–37.
98. James T. Richardson, "The 'Old Right' in Action: Mormon and Catholic Involvement in an Equal Rights Amendment Referendum," in *New Christian Politics*, eds. David G. Bromley and Anson Shupe (Macon, GA: Mercer University Press, 1984), 213–233.
99. Quinn, *The Mormon Hierarchy*, 387.
100. Richardson, "The 'Old Right' in Action," 222–223.
101. Sonia Johnson, *From Housewife to Heretic* (Garden City, NY: Doubleday, 1981), 101,102–105, 359; O. Kendall White, Jr., "A Feminist Challenge: 'Mormons for ERA' as an Internal Social Movement," *Journal of Ethnic Studies* 13, no. 1 (Spring 1985): 34–35; Quinn, *The Mormon Hierarchy*, 390, 395.

102. William Ray Arney and William H. Trescher, "Trends in Attitudes Toward Abortion, 1972–1975," *Family Planning Perspectives* 8, no. 3 (May–June 1976): 117.
103. "Religion in Transit," *Christianity Today*, November 5, 1976, 86.
104. Donald Granberg and Beth Wellman Granberg, "Abortion Attitudes, 1965–1980: Trends and Determinants," *Family Planning Perspectives* 12, no. 5 (September–October 1980): 252.
105. Scholars tend to agree that the knowledge of more than 1 million abortions performed each year profoundly influenced evangelical pro-life opinions and activism. Steven P. Miller quotes Harold O. J. Brown remarking in 1976, "the primary cause of death in the United States last year was abortion," and evangelicals after 1975 consistently shifted their discussion of abortion away from a complicated medical question to decrying it as an act of murder used as a form of birth control by a promiscuous American public, *The Age of Evangelicalism*, 55.
106. George Grant, *Third Time Around: A History of the Pro-Life Movement from the First Century to the Present* (Brentwood: Wolgemuth & Hyatt Publishers, 1991), 145; Martin, *With God on Our Side*, 193.
107. Harold O. J. Brown, "News Release," July 7, 1975, folder: "Abortion (1)," Box 1, Theodore C. Marrs Files, Ford.
108. Letter, Harold O. J. Brown to Dear Christian Friend, November 18, 1978, folder: "Letters, 1978–1983," Ephemeral Materials, Christian Action Council, Wilcox Collection.
109. Dowland, "'Family Values' and the Formation of a Christian Right Agenda," 612–613; Hankins, *Francis Schaeffer and the Shaping of Evangelical America*, 180–181; Miller, *The Age of Evangelicalism*, 52–53; Schaeffer, *Crazy for God*, 271–272; Williams, *God's Own Party*, 154–156.
110. *Whatever Happened to the Human Race?*, video 1 (Franky Schaeffer V Productions, Gospel Films, Inc., 1980).
111. C. Everett Koop, M.D., and Francis A. Schaeffer, *Whatever Happened to the Human Race?* ([1979] Wheaton: Crossway Books, rev. ed. 1983), 135.
112. Ibid., 27.
113. Schaeffer, *Crazy for God*, 283.
114. Hankins, *Francis Schaeffer and the Shaping of Evangelical America*, 199.
115. 1964 quotation in Gary North, "Analyzing the Changes in Catholicism," *Wall Street Journal*, October 25, 1972.
116. "Bottom-Line Theology: An Interview With Fulton J. Sheen," *Christianity Today*, June 3, 1977, 9.
117. Schaeffer, *Crazy for God*, 283–284.
118. Williams, *God's Own Party*, 155.
119. *Whatever Happened to the Human Race?*, video 1 (Franky Schaeffer V Productions, Gospel Films, Inc., 1980).

120. Hankins, *Francis Schaeffer and the Shaping of Evangelical America*, 182.
121. http://www.sbc.net/resolutions/amResolution.asp?ID=19. On the SBC's abortion resolutions in the 1970s and 1980s, see Paul L. Sadler, "The Abortion Issue Within the Southern Baptist Convention, 1969–1988" (Ph.D. diss., Baylor University, 1991), 89–98.
122. Barry Hankins, *Uneasy in Babylon: Southern Baptist Conservatives and American Culture* (Tuscaloosa: University of Alabama Press, 2002), 185.
123. James L. Franklin, "Southern Baptist Abortion Stance Sends Shock Waves," *Dallas Herald*, June 12, 1980, in Christian Life Commission Resource Files, 1955–1990, AR 138–2, Box 79, Folder 4, SBHLA.
124. Alan Crawford, *Thunder on the Right: The "New Right" and the Politics of Resentment* (New York: Pantheon Books, 1980), 273–274; Cynthia Gorney, *Articles of Faith: A Frontline History of the Abortion Wars* (New York: Simon & Schuster, 1998), 330–332; Michelle McKeegan, *Abortion Politics: Mutiny in the Ranks of the Right* (New York: The Free Press, 1992), 11; Williams, *God's Own Party*, 154.
125. McKeegan, *Abortion Politics*, 11.
126. Crawford, *Thunder on the Right*, 276.
127. Self, *All in the Family*, 370.
128. Byron Wilford Daynes and Raymond Tatalovich, "Mormons and Abortion Politics in the United States," *International Review of History and Political Science* 23, no. 2 (May 1986): 9.
129. "Mormons endorse Willkes' speaking tour in Utah," *National Right to Life News*, November 1973, National Right to Life News Collection, Wilcox Collection.
130. Memo, Wendell J. Ashton to Heber G. Wolsey, May 4, 1977, Salt Lake Public Communications Council Files, 1976–1977, LDS Archives.
131. "Abortions Rise 15 Pct.," *Deseret News*, September 20, 1977, in Salt Lake Public Communications Council Files, 1976–1977, LDS Archives.
132. Memo, L. Darrel Welling to Wendell J. Ashton, "Subject: Initiative Referendum to Restore Utah's Abortion Law," May 6, 1977, Salt Lake Public Communications Council Files, 1976–1977, LDS Archives.
133. Ibid.
134. Memo, L. Darrel Welling to Wendell J. Ashton, "Subject: Initiative Referendum to Restore Utah's Abortion Law," May 17, 1977, Salt Lake Public Communications Council Files, 1976–1977, LDS Archives.
135. 1978 Utah election results: http://elections.utah.gov/Results/Election%20Results%20General%201,978.pdf.
136. Richard Sherlock, "A Deafening Silence in the Church: Is the LDS Position Prolife Enough?," *Sunstone* 6, no. 4 (July–August 1981): 19.
137. "Political Responsibility: Reflections on an Election Year," February 12, 1976, in *Pastoral Letters of the United States Catholic Bishops: Vol. IV, 1975–1983*, ed.

Hugh J. Nolan (Washington, D.C.: United States Catholic Conference, 1984), 129–137.

138. Ibid., 132.

139. Dochuk, *From Bible Belt to Sunbelt*, 383–387; Self, *All in the Family*, 351–356; Williams, *God's Own Party*, 167–171.

140. On the New Right, see Crawford, *Thunder on the Right*; Thomas J. McIntyre and John C. Obert, *The Fear Brokers: Peddling the Hate Politics of the New Right* (New York: The Pilgrim Press, 1979); Gillian Peele, *Revival and Reaction: The Right in Contemporary America* (Oxford: Clarendon Press, 1984); Schulman, *The Seventies*, 194–205; Richard A. Viguerie, *The New Right: We're Ready to Lead* (Falls Church, VA: Viguerie Co., 1980); and John Kenneth White, *The New Politics of Old Values* (Lanham, MD: University Press of America, Inc., 1998).

141. Dinesh D'Souza, *Falwell, Before the Millennium: A Critical Biography* (Chicago: Regnery Gateway, 1984), 80–81. Susan Harding notes that Falwell's "disavowal of ministerial activism . . . was itself an instance of a preacher extending his reach beyond the gospel," and notes that at other times in the 1950s Falwell had directly advocated racial segregation in his sermons. Susan Friend Harding, *The Book of Jerry Falwell: Fundamentalist Language and Politics* (Princeton, NJ: Princeton University Press, 2000), 22. Harding also notes that around 1970, when Falwell began to build a national audience through his growing media empire, he recalled all his sermons so that none of his words could be used against him. However, because "Ministers and Marches" had been made into a pamphlet and distributed so widely, it was the lone sermon that escaped the recall. Harding, *The Book of Jerry Falwell*, 112.

142. Harding, *The Book of Jerry Falwell*, 105.

143. David Harrington Watt, "The Private Hopes of American Fundamentalists and Evangelicals, 1925–1975," *Religion and American Culture: A Journal of Interpretation* 1, no. 2 (Summer 1991): 164.

144. Harding, *The Book of Jerry Falwell*, 107–108.

145. Ibid., 22.

146. Ibid., 20.

147. Ibid., 128.

148. Dochuk, *From Bible Belt to Sunbelt*, 385; Williams, *God's Own Party*, 172.

149. Martin, *With God on Our Side*, 200. See also Daniel K. Williams, "Jerry Falwell's Sunbelt Politics: The Regional Origins of the Moral Majority," *Journal of Policy History* 22, no. 2 (April 2010): 125–147, and *God's Own Party*, 171–174. Dinesh D'Souza, however, contends that Ed McAteer jumped on Weyrich's words and claimed them as the name for the new organization. D'Souza, *Falwell*, 111. For Weyrich's account of the organization's creation, see Paul Weyrich, "Building the Moral Majority," *Conservative Digest*, August 1979, 18–19.

150. Weyrich, "Building the Moral Majority," 19.
151. Jerry Falwell, *Listen, America!* (Garden City, NY: Doubleday & Company, Inc., 1980), 255.
152. Ibid., 256.
153. Ibid., 256–257.
154. Williams, *God's Own Party*, 173.
155. Franky Schaeffer, *Bad News for Modern Man: An Agenda for Christian Activism* (Westchester, NY: Crossway, 1984), 93, quoted in Miller, *The Age of Evangelicalism*, 70.
156. Martin, *With God on Our Side*, 197.
157. Ibid., 197.
158. Dudley Clendinen, "'Christian New Right's' Rush to Power," *New York Times*, August 18, 1980.
159. "Political Responsibility," 131–132.
160. David B. Haight, "The Keys of the Kingdom," General Conference, October 1980, https://www.lds.org/general-conference/1980/10/the-keys-of-the-kingdom.
161. Williams, *God's Own Party*, 173–174.
162. Bob Jones III, *The Moral Majority* (Greenville, SC: Bob Jones University Press, 1980), 1–3, in Bruce, *The Rise and Fall of the New Christian Right*, 173.
163. William B. Prendergast, *The Catholic Voter in American Politics: The Passing of the Democratic Monolith* (Washington, D.C.: Georgetown University Press, 1999), 185–86.
164. Ibid., 137.
165. James Mann, "Preachers in Politics: Decisive Force in 1980?" *U.S. News and World Report*, September 15, 1980, 24.
166. Albert J. Menendez, *Evangelicals At the Ballot Box* (Amherst, NY: Prometheus Books, 1996), 135–138.
167. Ed Briggs, "Reagan Held Cooling on Morality Groups," *Times-Dispatch*, n.d., in Scrapbook 9, p. 48, Box 126, Records of National Religious Broadcasters, BGCA.

CHAPTER 6

1. Donald Alvin Eagle, "One Community's Reaction to *The Godmakers*," *Dialogue: A Journal of Mormon Thought* 18, no. 2 (Summer 1985): 34–35. Eagle biographic information from Randall A. Mackey, "Introduction," *Dialogue: A Journal of Mormon Thought* 18, no. 2 (Summer 1985): 15.
2. Erling Jorstad, *The New Christian Right, 1981–1988: Prospects for the Post-Reagan Decade* (Lewiston, ME: The Edwin Mellen Press, 1987), 108.
3. Jerry Falwell, Ed Dobson, and Ed Hindson, eds. *The Fundamentalist Phenomenon: The Resurgence of Conservative Christianity* (Garden City, NY: Doubleday, 1981), 221.

4. Ibid., 222.
5. Letter, Robert P. Dugan, Jr., to Dr. Jerry Falwell, August 26, 1981, Box 144, Folder 113, NAE.
6. Francis A. Schaeffer, *A Christian Manifesto* (Wheaton, IL: Crossway Books, 1981), 46.
7. Kenneth Woodward, "Guru of Fundamentalism," *Newsweek*, November 1, 1982, 88, quoted in Barry Hankins, *Francis Schaeffer and the Shaping of Evangelical America* (Grand Rapids: Wm. B. Eerdmans Publishing Co., 2008), 199.
8. Schaeffer, *A Christian Manifesto*, 54. Schaeffer cited the 1961 Supreme Court case, *Torcaso v. Watkins*, as evidence for this claim. *Torcaso* overturned a Maryland law requiring public officials believe in God, thus unconstitutionally establishing theism over non-theist belief. A footnote in the case included "secular humanism" among a list of non-theist options. Schaeffer interpreted this footnote as the state's establishment of secular humanism as its official religion. Hankins, *Francis Schaeffer and the Shaping of Evangelical America*, 200.
9. Schaeffer, *A Christian Manifesto*, 73.
10. Molly Worthen, *Apostles of Reason: The Crisis of Authority in American Evangelicalism* (New York: Oxford University Press, 2014), 219, 308–309 footnote 37.
11. Some media recognized the splintered world of 1980s evangelicalism. For one account written shortly after the meeting at Carl Henry's house, see Kenneth L. Woodward, "The Split-Up Evangelicals," *Newsweek*, April 26, 1982, 88–91.
12. While acknowledging the theological differences that existed among evangelicals, fundamentalists, and charismatics, Daniel Williams points to their victorious political coalition in the early 1980s as proof that "the evangelical unity that had seemed impossible to imagine only two years earlier had become reality," *God's Own Party: The Making of the Christian Right* (New York: Oxford University Press, 2010), 184. I concur, however, with Molly Worthen's assessment that this "illusion of solidarity" was not "reality," Worthen, *Apostles of Reason*, 240.
13. Richard N. Ostling, "Jerry Falwell's Crusade," *Time*, September 2, 1985, 50.
14. Memo, Kenneth S. Kantzer, "Meeting of Fundamentalists and Evangelicals in Response to the Invitation Given by Jerry Falwell in His Volume, The Fundamentalist Phenomenon," February 1, 1982, Box 144, Folder 1, NAE.
15. Ibid.
16. Schaeffer, *A Christian Manifesto*, 61, 62.
17. Hankins, *Francis Schaeffer and the Shaping of Evangelical America*, 202.
18. Francis Schaeffer's son, Frank, asserts in his memoir that Carl Henry "became bitterly jealous of my father in later years." Frank Schaeffer, *Crazy for God: How I Grew Up as One of the Elect, Helped Found the Religious Right, and Lived to Take All (or Almost All) of It Back* (Cambridge, MA: Da Capo Press, 2007), 117.

19. Kantzer, "Meeting of Fundamentalists and Evangelicals."
20. Susan Friend Harding, *The Book of Jerry Falwell: Fundamentalist Language and Politics* (Princeton, NJ: Princeton University Press, 2000), 150.
21. Kantzer, "Meeting of Fundamentalists and Evangelicals."
22. Kantzer, "Meeting of Fundamentalists and Evangelicals."
23. The Third Wave followed the First Wave that produced the Pentecostal movement out of the 1906 Azusa Street revivals and the Second Wave charismatic renewal movement of the 1950s and 1960s. For a diverse sampling of cautiously supportive treatments in evangelical outlets of charismatic renewal and the "Signs and Wonders" movement in the 1980s, see "A Third Wave?: An Interview with C. Peter Wagner," *Pastoral Renewal* 8, no. 1 (July–August 1983): 1–5; "Charisphobia," *Christianity Today*, January 7, 1983, 4; Kenneth S. Kantzer, "The Charismatics among Us," *Christianity Today*, February 22, 1980, 25–29; Tim Stafford, "Testing the Wine from John Wimber's Vineyard," *Christianity Today*, August 8, 1986, 18–22; Grant Wacker, "Wimber and Wonders – What About Miracles Today?," *The Reformed Journal* 37, no. 4 (April 1987): 16–19; John White, *When the Spirit Comes with Power: Signs and Wonders among God's People* (Downers Grove, IL: Intervarsity Press, 1988). See also Thomas F. Zimmerman, "Priorities and Beliefs of Pentecostals," *Christianity Today*, September 4, 1981, 36–37. For a more critical response, see Ben Patterson, "Cause for Concern," *Christianity Today*, August 8, 1986, 20; and Ken L. Sarles, "An Appraisal of the Signs and Wonders Movement," *Bibliotheca Sacra* 145, no. 577 (January–March 1988): 57–82.
24. See Dean Merrill, "The Fastest-growing American Denomination," *Christianity Today*, January 7, 1983, 28–34. For examples of evangelical treatments of glossolalia in the 1980s, see J. W. MacGorman, "Glossolalic Errors and Its Correction: 1 Corinthians 12–14," *Review & Expositor* 80, no. 3 (Summer 1983): 389–400; and Phillip H. Wiebe, "The Pentecostal Initial Evidence Doctrine," *Journal of the Evangelical Theological Society* 27, no. 4 (December 1984): 465–472.
25. Merrill McLoughlin, "From Revival Tent to Mainstream," *U.S. News and World Report*, December 19, 1988, 55.
26. Kantzer, "The Charismatics among Us," 28.
27. See "A Third Wave?," 5. See also C. Peter Wagner, *The Third Wave: Encountering the Power of Signs and Wonders Today* (Ann Arbor, MI: Servant Publications, 1988).
28. "A Third Wave?," 1, 3.
29. "A Third Wave?," 1, 3. See also C. Peter Wagner, "The Greatest Church Growth Is Beyond Our Shores," *Christianity Today*, May 18, 1984, 24–31, and "Supernatural Power in World Missions," *Evangelical Missions Quarterly* 20, no. 4 (October 1984): 398–400.

30. On the Church Growth movement, see Worthen, *Apostles of Reason*, 128–32.
31. Darren Dochuk, *From Bible Belt to Sunbelt: Plain-Folk Religion, Grassroots Politics, and the Rise of Evangelical Conservatism* (New York: W. W. Norton & Company, Inc., 2011), 313–314; T. M. Luhrmann, *When God Talks Back: Understanding the American Evangelical Relationship with God* (New York: Knopf, 2012), 27–33; Lisa McGirr, *Suburban Warriors: The Origins of the New American Right* (Princeton, NJ: Princeton University Press, 2001), 243–249; White, *When the Spirit Comes with Power*, 160–166; Worthen, *Apostles of Reason*, 145. See also Thomas W. Higgins, "Kenn Gulliksen, John Wimber, and the Founding of the Vineyard Movement," *Pneuma: The Journal of the Society for Pentecostal Studies* 34, no. 2 (2012): 208–228; and Bill Jackson, *The Quest for the Radical Middle: A History of the Vineyard* (Cape Town: Vineyard International Publishing, 1999).
32. "A Third Wave?," 1.
33. George Marsden, *Reforming Fundamentalism: Fuller Seminary and the New Evangelicalism* (Grand Rapids, MI: Wm. B. Eerdmans Publishing Co., 1987), 305.
34. Marsden, *Reforming Fundamentalism*, 292–295; Worthen, *Apostles of Reason*, 146–147.
35. John Wimber, *Power Evangelism* (San Francisco: Harper & Row, 1986). On Bill Bright's Four Spiritual Laws, see John G. Turner, *Bill Bright and Campus Crusade for Christ: The Renewal of Evangelicalism in Postwar America* (Chapel Hill: University of North Carolina Press, 2008), 99–103.
36. See Sarles, "An Appraisal of the Signs and Wonders Movement," 76–82; White, *When the Spirit Comes with Power*, 178–182; Worthen, *Apostles of Reason*, 145–146.
37. Steven P. Miller, *The Age of Evangelicalism: America's Born Again Years* (New York: Oxford University Press, 2014), 81–83.
38. Turner, *Bill Bright and Campus Crusade for Christ*, 173–175.
39. David P. Scaer, "The Charismatic Movement as Ecumenical Phenomenon," *Concordia Theological Quarterly* 45, no. 1–2 (January–April 1981): 81.
40. Doran McCarty, "Spirituality: A Southern Baptist Perspective," *Review & Expositor* 79, no. 2 (Spring 1982): 310.
41. Nancy Ammerman, *Baptist Battles: Social Change and Religious Conflict in the Southern Baptist Convention* (New Brunswick, NJ: Rutgers University Press, 1990), 224.
42. Toby Druin, "Robison-Green Ministry Causes SBC Controversy," *Baptist Press*, April 12, 1984, http://media.sbhla.org.s3.amazonaws.com/5826,12-Apr-1984.pdf; Art Toalston, "A Fiery Baptist Evangelist Adopts Some New Doctrines," *Christianity Today*, June 15, 1984, 69–70.

43. Scaer, "The Charismatic Movement as Ecumenical Phenomenon," 81, 83. For other critical treatments of the charismatic movement from Lutheran Church—Missouri Synod writers, see Thomas Bird, "Experience over Scripture in Charismatic Exegesis," *Concordia Theological Quarterly* 45, no. 1–2 (January–April 1981): 5–11; and Walter A. Maier, "Charismatic Renewal in the Lutheran Church: 'Renewal in Missouri'," *Concordia Theological Quarterly* 53, no. 1–2 (January–April 1989): 21–37.
44. Toalston, "A Fiery Baptist Evangelist Adopts Some New Doctrines," 70.
45. Molly Worthen argues that evangelical-charismatic tensions arose from the clash between evangelicals' rational approach to the Gospel and the anti-rational, Spirit-focused religious experience of charismatics, *Apostles of Reason*, 147. I contend, however, that evangelicals' historical anti-ecumenism and their real fears that charismatics sought Christian unity through shared supernatural experience rather than (and in spite of) common theological conviction drove evangelicals who responded negatively, or at least suspiciously, to charismatics and the Third Wave movement of the 1980s.
46. Worthen, *Apostles of Reason*, 148–62.
47. "What Separates Evangelicals and Catholics?" *Christianity Today*, October 23, 1981, 12.
48. Ibid., 15.
49. Ibid., 14.
50. Ibid., 13.
51. Ibid., 12.
52. Mother Teresa as metaphor and model of Christian charity and faithful devotion abounds in 1980s evangelical literature. See, for examples, Charles Lloyd, "Having Found the Truth," *Christianity Today*, March 13, 1981, 15; John R. W. Stott, "Setting the Spirit Free," *Christianity Today*, June 12, 1981, 17–21; Robert E. Frykenberg, "World Hunger: Food Is Not the Answer," *Christianity Today*, December 11, 1981, 36–39; Richard J. Foster, "The Celebration of Meditative Prayer," *Christianity Today*, October 7, 1983; Daniel Pawley, "The Year of Living Dangerously," *Christianity Today*, February 1, 1985, 35–36; Marjorie Hope and James Young, "The Homeless Poor," *Christianity Today*, October 4, 1985, 30–35; Gregg Lewis, "The Return of Apathy," *Christianity Today*, October 18, 1985, 19–25.
53. Mother Teresa, "Nobel Lecture," December 11, 1979, http://www.nobelprize.org/nobel_prizes/peace/laureates/1979/teresa-lecture.html.
54. Albert Mohler, "Faith Without Works Is Dead: An Evangelical Meditation on Mother Teresa," July 16, 2009, http://www.albertmohler.com/2009/07/16/faith-without-works-is-dead-an-evangelical-meditation-on-mother-teresa/. For Mother Teresa's address, see Mother Teresa, "Whatsoever You Do . . .,"

February 3, 1994, Washington, D.C., Priests for Life, http://www.priestsforlife.org/brochures/mtspeech.html.

55. "A Nobel Laureate Speaks in Defense of Unborn Life," *Christianity Today*, September 6, 1985, 62–63.
56. George De Vries, Jr., "The Pope in Des Moines," *The Reformed Journal* 29, no. 11 (November 1979): 4–5; Harry R. Boer, "An Authoritative Voice," *The Reformed Journal* 37, no. 10 (October 1987): 3–4.
57. "The Pope Draws the Theological Line," *Christianity Today*, January 25, 1980, 38–39; Harry Genet with Royal Peck, "Reining in the Jesuits," *Christianity Today*, April 9, 1982, 48–49.
58. Kenneth S. Kantzer, "A Man Under Orders," *Christianity Today*, September 6, 1985, 15.
59. Harry R. Boer, "Pastor and Teacher," *The Reformed Journal* 29, no. 11 (November 1979): 5.
60. Kantzer, "A Man Under Orders," 15.
61. David P. Scaer, "The Pope as Antichrist: An Anachronism?," *Christianity Today*, October 23, 1981, 66. In some evangelical communities, the view that the pope was the antichrist persisted. As recently as 1979, the Wisconsin Evangelical Lutheran Synod had reaffirmed its 1959 *Statement on the Antichrist* that named the pope as such. Lance Morrow, "The Rise and Fall of Anti-Catholicism," *Time*, October 15, 1979, 38.
62. Stephen E. Robinson, "Warring Against the Saints of God," *Ensign*, January 1988, https://www.lds.org/ensign/1988/01/warring-against-the-saints-of-god.
63. Scaer, "The Pope as Antichrist," 66.
64. Statement, National Association of Evangelicals, September 3, 1987, Box 177, Folder 2, NAE.
65. See Mark A. Noll, "Are Protestants and Catholics Really that Different," *Christianity Today*, April 18, 1980, 28–31; J. D. Douglas, "The Evangelist and the Pope Confer Privately in Rome," *Christianity Today*, February 6, 1981, 88–89; Marshall Shelley, "What Catholics and Evangelicals Have in Common," *Christianity Today*, November 26, 1982, 66; John Van Engen, "Catholicism 20 Years after Vatican II," *Christianity Today*, February 18, 1983, 50; and John D. Woodbridge, "Is Evangelical Faith Enough?," *Christianity Today*, May 17, 1985, 58–62.
66. Randy Frame, "Well-known Evangelical Author Thomas Howard Converts to Catholicism," *Christianity Today*, May 17, 1985, 47.
67. Evangelicals still worried about LDS success in foreign missions in the 1980s. See, for example, Ruth A. Tucker, "Foreign Missionaries with a False Message," *Evangelical Missions Quarterly* 20, no. 4 (October 1984): 327–332. But these older concerns about Mormonism's growth overseas were largely replaced by a

sense of crisis among American evangelicals about the LDS Church's increase in the United States, particularly from Christian converts.

68. Robert Wuthnow, *The Restructuring of American Religion: Society and Faith Since World War II* (Princeton, NJ: Princeton University Press, 1988), 85.
69. Bernard Quinn et al., *Churches and Church Membership in the United States 1980: An Enumeration by Region, State and County Based on Data Reported by 111 Church Bodies* (Atlanta: Glenmary Research Center, 1982), 1, 14, 19.
70. Beth Spring, "Refugees: Off Sinking Boats into American Churches," *Christianity Today*, June 15, 1984, 28; "Mormons and Scouts: A Happy Mix," *Christianity Today*, October 2, 1981, 72–73.
71. Rodney Stark, "The Rise of a New World Faith," *Review of Religious Research* 26, no. 1 (September 1984): 18–27.
72. Joseph M. Hopkins, "Cult Specialists Assess Nontraditional Religions in the Mid-eighties," *Christianity Today*, August 9, 1985, 54.
73. "Religionists, Witnessing to Us," *Royal Service*, March 1982, 17–18.
74. See Carlos E. Asay, "How to Help Fulfill Daniel's Prophecy," *Ensign*, October 1977, https://www.lds.org/ensign/1977/10/how-to-help-fulfill-daniels-prophecy; and James H. Young, "When Thou Art Converted," *New Era*, March 1977, https://www.lds.org/new-era/1977/03/when-thou-art-converted.
75. Kenneth L. Woodward and Barbara Burgower, "Bible-Belt Confrontation," *Newsweek*, March 4, 1985, 65.
76. Wuthnow, *The Restructuring of American Religion*, 192.
77. Mike Creswell, "Mormons: Challenge on the Mission Field," *The Commission*, January 1982, 43–44.
78. See, for example, Luman John Gilaman, "Assisting Evangelicals in Presenting a Positive Witness to Mormons" (D.Min. project in ministry report, Golden Gate Baptist Theological Seminary, 1983).
79. *The Christian Confronting the Cults* (Nashville, TN: The Sunday School Board of the Southern Baptist Convention, 1979), 10.
80. Ibid., 25.
81. Creswell, "Mormons," 43–44.
82. Press Release, Linda Lawson, "Two Films Withdrawn from Baptist Centers," 2/26/82, Baptist Press, News Service of the Southern Baptist Convention, Nashville, in Darrell Jay Stoddard Papers, LDS Archives.
83. Creswell, "Mormons," 43.
84. See "The Mormon Illusion: What the Bible Says about the Latter-day Saints," "The Maze of Mormonism," and "The Changing World of Mormonism" all in *Christianity Today*, August 8, 1980, 35; Dale Sanders, "Filmstrips about Cults and the Bible," *Christianity Today*, June 26, 1981, 27; "Keeping the Cults Away," *Christianity Today*, May 21, 1982, 45–46; Rodney Clapp, "Fighting Mormonism in Utah," *Christianity Today*, July 16, 1982, 30–31, 47–48; "Mormons and

Christ," *Christianity Today*, July 16, 1982, 31–32; and "Why Cults Succeed Where the Church Fails," *Christianity Today*, March 16, 1984, 14–21.

85. Ronald Enroth, "The Empire Strikes Gold," *Christianity Today*, September 5, 1986, 29, 30.
86. Ex-Mormons for Jesus advertisement, "Is the Mormon Plan for America," *Christianity Today*, July 17, 1981, 99.
87. Walter R. Martin, *The Maze of Mormonism* (Santa Ana, CA: Vision House, 1980). See also Anthony A. Hoekema, *The Four Major Cults: Christian Science, Jehovah's Witnesses, Mormonism, Seventh-day Adventism* (Grand Rapids, MI: Wm. B. Eerdmans Publishing Co., 1984), and *Mormonism* (Grand Rapids, MI: Wm. B. Eerdmans Publishing Co., 1981); and J. Gordon Melton and Robert L. Moore, *The Cult Experience: Responding to the New Religious Pluralism* (New York: The Pilgrim Press, 1982).
88. Ed Decker and Dave Hunt, *The God Makers* (Eugene, OR: Harvest House Publishers, 1984), 16.
89. Tim Slover, "Anti-Mormons Gather for Testimonial," *Sunstone* 3 (July/August 1983): 3–4. This is not to say that Decker and Baer were the only ex-Mormons to produce anti-Mormon literature after their conversion to evangelical Christianity. Jerald and Sandra Tanner were ex-Mormons who ran the evangelical Utah Lighthouse Ministry in Salt Lake City and published dozens of books critical of Mormon theology and history. Many other ex-Mormon converts to evangelicalism have published their own personal memoirs of leaving the faith, but Decker's works remain the most widely known ex-Mormon production in the evangelical world.
90. Sara M. Patterson, "The Ex Factor: Constructing a Religious Mission in the Ex-Mormons for Jesus/Saints Alive in Jesus, 1975–1990," in *New Perspectives in Mormon Studies: Creating and Crossing Boundaries*, eds. Quincy D. Newell and Eric F. Mason (Norman: University of Oklahoma Press, 2013), 119–144.
91. For example, see a notice in the *Los Angeles Times* announcing that two representatives from the Christian Research Institute will hold a "question-and-answer session" after a viewing at the Faith Lutheran Church in Anaheim. Mary E. Gilstrap, "Orange County Religion Notes," *Los Angeles Times*, November 16, 1985.
92. Of course, *The God Makers* was not the first or only anti-cult movie about Mormonism. Other small films like *Conspiracy Cults* and *Journey to Kolob* had been made. But *The God Makers* was the first film to gain a huge audience. Sharon Lee Swenson, "Does the Camera Lie?: A Structural Analysis of *The Godmakers*," *Dialogue: A Journal of Mormon Thought* 18, no. 2 (Summer 1985): 16.
93. *The God Makers* (Jeremiah Films, 1982).
94. Mackey, "Introduction," 14.

95. *The God Makers.*
96. *The God Makers.*
97. H. F., "Salt Lake City Diarist: This is the Place," *New Republic*, March 2, 1987, 42.
98. *The God Makers.*
99. Swenson, "Does the Camera Lie?," 17.
100. Patterson, "The Ex Factor," 132–133.
101. *The God Makers.*
102. Patterson, "The Ex Factor," 133.
103. J. B. Haws, *The Mormon Image in the American Mind: Fifty Years of Public Perception* (New York: Oxford University Press, 2013), 74–125; Jan Shipps, "'Is Mormonism Christian?': Reflections on a Complicated Question," *BYU Studies* 33, no. 3 (1993): 452.
104. "Mormons Add a Twist to Their Holy Book," *Christianity Today*, November 12, 1982, 91. Italics in the original. On other evangelical reactions to the LDS Church's increasing emphasis on Jesus Christ, see "Mormons and Christ," *Christianity Today*, July 16, 1982, 31–32.
105. *The God Makers.*
106. Massimo Introvigne, "The Devil-Makers: Contemporary Evangelical Fundamentalist Anti-Mormonism," *Dialogue: A Journal of Mormon Thought* 27, no. 1 (Spring 1994): 153–169. Conservative evangelicals became particularly concerned with the idea of "spiritual warfare" in the 1980s thanks in large part to the popular fiction books by the author Frank E. Peretti, a former Assembly of God pastor. These books included such titles as *This Present Darkness* (1986) and *Piercing the Darkness* (1988). On the 1980s "satanic panic," see Miller, *The Age of Evangelicalism*, 78–81.
107. *The God Makers.*
108. For example, see James Bjornstad, "America's Spiritual, Sometimes Satanic, Smorgasbord," *Christianity Today*, October 23, 1981, 28–29. On evangelical apocalypticism in the 1970s and 1980s and Reagan's deft use of premillennialism in his political rhetoric, see Matthew Avery Sutton, *American Apocalypse: A History of Modern Evangelicalism* (Cambridge, MA: The Belknap Press of Harvard University Press, 2014), 345–360.
109. Decker and Hunt, *The God Makers.*
110. Swenson, "Does the Camera Lie?," 17.
111. Bruce R. McConkie, "What Think Ye of Salvation by Grace?," BYU Devotional, January 10, 1984, http://speeches.byu.edu/?act=viewitem&id=597.
112. *Sacramento Union*, April 2, 1983, in Public Communications Directors' Files, 1979–1989, El Dorado, California Stake Records, LDS Archives.
113. Woodward and Burgower, "Bible-Belt Confrontation."
114. Mackey, "Introduction," 14.

115. Robert Lindsey, "Testing the Persuasive Powers of VCRs," *New York Times*, April 6, 1986.
116. Patterson, "The Ex Factor," 130.
117. Gordon B. Hinckley, "Let Us Go Forward!," General Conference, October 1983, https://www.lds.org/general-conference/1983/10/let-us-go-forward.
118. Haws, *The Mormon Image in the American Mind*, 119.
119. Ibid., 118.
120. Rex C. Reeve, "The Lord's Strange Act," BYU Devotional, February 25, 1986, http://speeches.byu.edu/?act=viewitem&id=1268; M. Russell Ballard, "Unlocking the Doors," BYU Devotional, November 14, 1989, http://speeches.byu.edu/?act=viewitem&id=46.
121. Erlend Peterson, "Anxiously Engaged in a Good Cause," BYU Devotional, March 17, 1998, http://speeches.byu.edu/?act=viewitem&id=528.
122. John Dart, "Mormon Church Sued for Criticism of Polemic Film," *Los Angeles Times*, March 16, 1985. Pamphlet available at: http://www.shields-research.org/Critics/GMErrors.htm.
123. See Mackey, "Introduction," 14–16; Swenson, "Does the Camera Lie?," 16–23; Allen D. Roberts, "*The Godmakers*: Shadow or Reality? A Content Analysis," *Dialogue: A Journal of Mormon Thought* 18, no. 2 (Summer 1985): 24–33; and Eagle, "One Community's Reaction to *The Godmakers*," 34–39.
124. Eagle, "One Community's Reaction to *The Godmakers*," 36.
125. Ibid., 37. Italics in the original.
126. Ibid, 37.
127. Ibid., 38.
128. Mackey, "Introduction," 14.
129. See, for example, Bill Peterson and Barry Sussman, "Moral Majority Is Growing in Recognition, But It Remains Unknown to Half the Public," *Washington Post*, June 13, 1981.
130. Moral Majority brochure, c. 1983, in Steve Bruce, *The Rise and Fall of the New Christian Right: Conservative Protestant Politics in America, 1978–1988* (Oxford: Clarendon Press, 1988), 81.
131. Sociologists and political scientists began giving great attention to the Moral Majority in the mid-1980s, hoping to understand why people were drawn to it and to what extent it influenced the American political process. These studies surveyed members and leaders of the Moral Majority, compiling socio-demographic characteristics of the group and outlining the political and theological orientations of the members. However, these studies did not deeply examine why the Moral Majority could not transcend denominational divisions and what this meant for understanding the nature and function of the Religious Right. See Emmett H. Buell, Jr. and Lee Sigelman, "An Army That Meets Every Sunday? Popular Support for the Moral Majority in 1980," *Social*

Science Quarterly 66, no. 2 (June 1985): 426–434; Sharon Linzey Georgianna, *The Moral Majority and Fundamentalism: Plausibility and Dissonance* (Lewiston, ME: The Edwin Mellen Press, 1989); James L. Guth and John C. Green, "The Moralizing Minority: Christian Right Support among Political Contributors," in *Religion and the Culture Wars: Dispatches from the Front*, eds. John C. Green, James L. Guth, Corwin E. Smidt and Lyman A. Kellstedt (Lanham: Rowman & Littlefield Publishers, Inc., 1996), 30–43; Stephen D. Johnson and Joseph P. Tamney, "Support for the Moral Majority: A Test of a Model," *Journal for the Scientific Study of Religion* 23, no. 2 (June 1984): 183–196; Robert C. Liebman, "Mobilizing the Moral Majority," in *The New Christian Right: Mobilization and Legitimation*, eds. Robert C. Liebman and Robert Wuthnow (New York: Aldine Publishing Company, 1983), 50–73; Richard V. Pierard and James L. Wright, "No Hoosier Hospitality for Humanism: The Moral Majority in Indiana," in *New Christian Politics*, eds. David G. Bromley and Anson Shupe (Macon: Mercer University Press, 1984), 195–212; Anson Shupe and William Stacey, "The Moral Majority Constituency," in Liebman and Wuthnow, eds., *The New Christian Right*, 103–116, and "Public and Clergy Sentiments Toward the Moral Majority: Evidence from the Dallas-Fort Worth Metroplex," in Bromley and Shupe, eds., *New Christian Politics*, 91–100; Lee Sigelman, Clyde Wilcox, and Emmett H. Buell, Jr., "An Unchanging Minority: Popular Support for the Moral Majority, 1980 and 1984," *Social Science Quarterly* 68, no. 4 (December 1987): 876–884; John H. Simpson, "Moral Issues and Status Politics," in Liebman and Wuthnow, eds., *The New Christian Right*, 187–205, and "Support for the Moral Majority and Its Sociomoral Platform," in Bromley and Shupe, eds., *New Christian Politics*, 65–68; Joseph P. Tamney and Stephen D. Johnson, "The Moral Majority in Middletown," *Journal for the Scientific Study of Religion* 22, no. 2 (June 1983): 145–157; Clyde Wilcox, "Evangelicals and Fundamentalists in the New Christian Right: Religious Differences in the Ohio Moral Majority," *Journal for the Scientific Study of Religion* 25, no. 3 (September 1986): 355–363, "Evangelicals and the Moral Majority," *Journal for the Scientific Study of Religion* 28, no. 4 (December 1989): 400–414, "Popular Support for the Moral Majority in 1980: A Second Look," *Social Science Quarterly* 68, no. 1 (March 1987): 157–166, and "Religious Orientations and Political Attitudes: Variations Within the New Christian Right," *American Politics Quarterly* 15, no. 2 (April 1987): 274–296; Clyde Wilcox, Sharon Linzey, and Ted G. Jelen, "Reluctant Warriors: Premillennialism and Politics in the Moral Majority," *Journal for the Scientific Study of Religion* 30, no. 3 (September 1991): 245–258; and, J. Milton Yinger and Stephen J. Cutler, "The Moral Majority Viewed Sociologically," in Bromley and Shupe, eds., *New Christian Politics*, 69–90.

132. Williams, *God's Own Party*, 177–178. Williams contends that Falwell's difficulty in attracting Christians besides fundamentalist Baptists to Moral Majority

owed to the perception that Falwell was a political extremist, even if those Christian conservatives tended to agree with Falwell's political views. While many Americans saw Falwell as an extremist, that extremism, I argue instead, was perceived particularly by Catholics and Mormons, but also by evangelicals, as a function of his outspoken, exclusivist, and often antagonistic views toward anything outside of fundamentalist Christianity. While Falwell certainly softened these views as he rose to political prominence, he could not escape his religious reputation as a hardline, anti-ecumenical fundamentalist that he had cultivated for more than two decades.

133. William Martin, *With God on Our Side: The Rise of the Religious Right in America* (New York: Broadway Books, 1996), 258–259.
134. "An Interview with the Lone Ranger of American Fundamentalism," *Christianity Today*, September 4, 1981, as quoted in Haws, *The Mormon Image in the American Mind*, 110.
135. Megan Rosenfeld, "The New Moral America and the War of the Religicos," *Washington Post*, August 24, 1980.
136. Anson Shupe and John Heinerman, "Mormonism and the New Christian Right: An Emerging Coalition?," *Review of Religious Research* 27, no. 2 (December 1985): 155.
137. Ex-Mormons for Jesus advertisement, "Is the Mormon Plan for America."
138. David B. Haight, "The Keys of the Kingdom," General Conference, October 1980, https://www.lds.org/general-conference/1980/10/the-keys-of-the-kingdom; Royden G. Derrick, "Valiance in the Drama of Life," General Conference, April 1983, https://www.lds.org/general-conference/1983/04/valiance-in-the-drama-of-life.
139. Boyd K. Packer, "The Only True Church," General Conference, October 1985, https://www.lds.org/general-conference/1985/10/the-only-true-church.
140. Merlin B. Brinkerhoff, Jeffrey C. Jacob, and Marlene M. Mackie, "Mormonism and the Moral Majority Make Strange Bedfellows?: An Exploratory Critique," *Review of Religious Research* 28, no. 3 (March 1987): 243.
141. Liebman, "Mobilizing the Moral Majority," 61–65. See also Georgianna, *The Moral Majority and Fundamentalism*, Appendix C for a table of the denominational makeup of Indiana Moral Majority's membership, showing 119 of 162 members, or nearly 75 percent, belonged to independent Baptist congregations. All of the forty-three other members belonged to only Protestant denominations and churches. There Georgianna concludes, "These findings *do not support* Jerry Falwell's claim that the Moral Majority is made up not only of fundamentalist Christians, but also Catholics, Jews, and Mormons." Italics are mine.
142. Dinesh D'Souza, *Falwell, Before the Millennium: A Critical Biography* (Chicago: Regnery Gateway, 1984), 32; Kantzer, "Meeting of Fundamentalists and

Evangelicals." Susan Harding rightly calls Falwell's claim of Moral Majority representing an ecumenical coalition "dubious." Harding, *The Book of Jerry Falwell*, 299 footnote 13.

143. Wilcox, Linzey, and Jelen, "Reluctant Warriors," 250.
144. Shupe and Stacey, "The Moral Majority Constituency," 114.
145. D'Souza, *Falwell, Before the Millennium*, 95.
146. Ibid., 154–155.
147. Leo P. Ribuffo, *The Old Christian Right: The Protestant Far Right from the Great Depression to the Cold War* (Philadelphia: Temple University Press, 1983), 267.
148. D'Souza, *Falwell, Before the Millennium*, 34–35.
149. Wilcox, "Evangelicals and Fundamentalists in the New Christian Right," 356, 360.
150. Letter, John Prewett, n.d., Box 144, Folder 5, NAE.
151. Letter, Steven Scott to John Prewett, July 20, 1983, Box 144, Folder 5, NAE.
152. Tom Greenley, "Anti-Catholic Rhetoric Heightens Religious Tensions," *Los Angeles Times*, December 13, 1981.
153. Jorstad, *The New Christian Right*, 108.
154. Anthony E. Gilles, *Fundamentalism—What Every Catholic Needs To Know* (Cincinnati: St. Anthony Messenger Press, 1985), 4.
155. Ibid., 61.
156. Jones was especially outraged that Falwell had introduced Schlafly as a "great Christian woman," something Schlafly could not be, Jones contended, because she was "a devout Roman Catholic." Mark Taylor Dalhouse, *An Island in the Lake of Fire: Bob Jones University, Fundamentalism and the Separatist Movement* (Athens: University of Georgia Press, 1996), 108.
157. Phyllis Schlafly, "A Viewpoint on Women's Issues," in *Outstanding Lectures, 1978–1979* (Provo, UT: ASBYU Academics Office, 1979), 31–37.
158. Shupe and Heinerman, "Mormonism and the New Christian Right," 153.

CHAPTER 7

1. Lou Cannon, *Reagan* (New York: Putnam, 1982), 316. On the Reagan years, see Haynes Johnson, *Sleepwalking Through History: America in the Reagan Years* (New York: Norton, 1991); Gil Troy, *Morning in America: How Ronald Reagan Invented the 1980s* (Princeton, NJ: Princeton University Press, 2005); and Sean Wilentz, *Age of Reagan: A History, 1974–2008* (New York: Harper, 2008). On the Reagan administration's often-strained relationship with the Religious Right, see David John Marley, "Ronald Reagan and the Splintering of the Christian Right," *Journal of Church and State* 48, no. 4 (Autumn 2006): 851–868.
2. William Martin, *With God on Our Side: The Rise of the Religious Right in America* (New York: Broadway Books, 1996), 223.

3. Sidney Blumenthal, "The Righteous Empire," *New Republic*, October 22, 1984, quoted in Richard V. Pierard, "Religion and the 1984 Election Campaign," *Review of Religious Research* 27, no. 2 (December 1985): 100. See also, Steven P. Miller, *The Age of Evangelicalism: America's Born Again Years* (New York: Oxford University Press, 2014), 64–68; Robert O. Self, *All in the Family: The Realignment of American Democracy Since the 1960s* (New York: Hill and Wang, 2012), 358–361; and Daniel K. Williams, *God's Own Party: The Making of the Christian Right* (New York: Oxford University Press, 2010), 194–198.
4. Letter, Morton C. Blackwell to Cal Thomas, April 6, 1982, folder "Moral Majority (3 of 4)," Box OA 9079, Morton C. Blackwell Files, Ronald Reagan Library (hereafter, RRL). Blackwell also sent a blind carbon copy of the letter to Religious Roundtable's Ed McAteer and to leading New Right figures including Paul Weyrich, Howard Phillips, Richard Viguerie, and Terry Dolan.
5. Martin, *With God on Our Side*, 216.
6. Robert D. Linder and Richard V. Pierard, "Ronald Reagan, Civil Religion and the New Religious Right in America," *Fides et Historia* 23 (Fall 1991): 70. The other three evangelical members who served at some point in Reagan's cabinet were Secretary of the Interior Donald Hodel, Secretary of Transportation Elizabeth Dole, and Attorney General Edwin Meese.
7. Richard V. Pierard, "Reagan and the Evangelicals: The Making of a Love Affair," *Christian Century*, December 21–28, 1983, 1185.
8. William Bole, "Reagan Aide Still Thinks Advisers Should 'Get Saved or Get Out'," *Religion News Service*, February 17, 1984, in folder "School Prayer (2 of 5)," Box 14 F, Faith Ryan Whittlesey Files, RRL; Williams, *God's Own Party*, 195.
9. Michelle McKeegan, *Abortion Politics: Mutiny in the Ranks of the Right* (New York: The Free Press, 1992), 132–133.
10. Letter, Curtis J. Young to Dear Christian Friend, 7/9/81, Folder: "Letters, 1978–1983," Ephemeral Materials, Christian Action Council, Wilcox Collection.
11. Memo, Morton Blackwell to Elizabeth H. Dole, "Conservative Organization Reaction to Sandra O'Connor Nomination," folder "Conservatives—General," OA 6386, Elizabeth Dole Files, RRL.
12. "Hyde, Helms, the Human Life Bill, the Hatch Compromise, and More . . . ," *Action Line: Christian Action Council Newsletter*, December 3, 1981, folder: "ACCL Political File: Political—Hatch Amendment Clippings (2)," Box 44, American Citizens Concerned for Life, Inc., Ford. Underlining in the original.
13. Bill Keller and Nadine Cohodas, "Tactical Errors, Disunity Blunt New Right Social Legislation," *Congressional Quarterly*, October 16, 1982, 2676.
14. Terrence Cardinal Cooke, "Statement," November 18, 1981, Box 32, Folder 5, John F. Dearden, Papers, UNDA; "Statement of Father Charles Fiore, O.P. Chairman, National Pro-Life Political Action Committee on SJR 110," December 7,

1981, in folder "National Pro-Life Action Committee: POTUS – Pro-Life Coalition – Cabinet Room – January 23, 1984 (2)," Box OA 9079, Morton C. Blackwell Files, RRL.

15. "The Bishops and the Abortion Amendment," *America*, November 21, 1981, 312. For the Catholic Church's objections to the Helms Bill, see Memo, Wilfred R. Caron to Father Bryce, "Human Life Bills, S.158 and H.R.900," in folder "Abortion – Helms Bill," Box OA 11,309, Stephen H. Galebach Files, RRL.
16. John J. Mulloy, "Bishops' Position on Hatch Is in a Moral Vacuum," *The Wanderer*, December 10, 1981, in folder: "ACCL Admin File: Political – Hatch Amendment Clippings (4)," Box 44, American Citizens Concerned for Life, Inc., Ford.
17. Robert L. Mauro, "Bishops Seeking to Mobilize Catholics to Support Hatch," *The Wanderer*, January 14, 1982, in folder: "ACCL Admin File: Political – Hatch Amendment Clippings (3)," Box 44, American Citizens Concerned for Life, Inc., Ford.
18. Ibid.
19. News Release, "Deepening Division in Pro-Life Ranks Dims Hopes for Hatch Amendment," Christian Action Council, 12/16/81, folder: "ACCL Political File: Political – Hatch Amendment Clippings (2)," Box 44, American Citizens Concerned for Life, Inc., Ford.
20. "Catholic Bishops Plunge Into Politics," *Eagle Forum Newsletter*, May 1983, Wilcox Collection.
21. See, for example, Charles W. Bell, "Did Catholics Goof on Abortion?," *New York Daily News*, November 29, 1981; Richard C. Dujardin, "Anti-abortion Movement Splits over Movement," *Providence Journal-Bulletin*, November 10, 1981; Myron S. Waldman, "Abortion Foes Split over Means to End," *Long Island Newsday*, December 21, 1981, all in folder: "ACCL Political File: Political – Hatch Amendment Clippings (2)," Box 44, American Citizens Concerned for Life, Inc., Ford. See also, Leslie Bennetts, "Antiabortion Forces in Disarray Less Than a Year after Victories in Election," *New York Times*, November 22, 1981.
22. Bennetts, "Antiabortion Forces in Disarray Less Than a Year after Victories in Election."
23. Connie Paige, *The Right to Lifers: Who They Are, How They Operate, Where They Get Their Money* (New York: Summit Books, 1983), 226.
24. Memo, Morton Blackwell to Elizabeth H. Dole, "Pro-Life Status Report," January 12, 1982, and "Talking Points for Meeting with Pro-Life Leadership" attached to Memo, Elizabeth H. Dole, "Meeting with Pro-Life Leadership," January 21, 1982, both in folder "Pro-Life Organizations – Friday, January 22 – 10:30 am – 15 min," Box OA 5233, Elizabeth Dole Files, RRL.

25. Letter, J. C. Willke, M.D., to President Reagan, April 7, 1982, folder "[Pro-Life (Continued – #2)] (2)," and Memo, Morton C. Blackwell to Elizabeth H. Dole, "Presidential Support for Cloture on Helms Amendment," folder "Pro-Family Activists (3)," both in Box OA 9081, Morton C. Blackwell Files, RRL; Memo, Edwin L. Harper to Elizabeth Dole, "Abortion Decision Paper," September 7, 1982, folder "Abortion 1982 (2 of 6)," Box 1, Elizabeth Dole Files, RRL; Memo, Morton C. Blackwell to Red Cavaney, "Participants at Jim Baker Meeting 2:00 p.m. September 14, 1982," September 14, 1982, folder "Abortion 1982 (1 of 6)," Elizabeth Dole Files, RRL.
26. Memo, Gary L. Bauer to Edwin L. Harper, June 18, 1982, folder "[Pro-Life (Continued – #2)] (2)," Box OA 9081, Morton C. Blackwell Files, RRL; Memo, Red Cavaney to Edwin Harper, "Abortion – Impact on our Coalition," folder "Abortion 1982 (5 of 6)," Box 1, Elizabeth Dole Files, RRL.
27. Tape, "Morton Blackwell Exit Interview," January 27, 1984, in Morton C. Blackwell Files, RRL.
28. Gary Scott Smith, *Faith and the Presidency: From George Washington to George W. Bush* (New York: Oxford University Press, 2006), 349.
29. Beth Spring, "Rating Reagan," *Christianity Today*, October 7, 1983, 50.
30. Bennetts, "Antiabortion Forces in Disarray Less Than a Year after Victories in Election."
31. Paige, *The Right to Lifers*, 225.
32. Ibid., 146–150.
33. Karl Keating, *Catholicism and Fundamentalism: The Attack on "Romanism" by "Bible Christians"* (San Francisco: Ignatius Press, 1988), 80–81.
34. Bennetts, "Antiabortion Forces in Disarray Less Than a Year after Victories in Election."
35. E. E. McAteer, "In Support of the Voluntary School Prayer Amendment," in folder "Prayer in Schools (5)," Box OA 9081, Morton C. Blackwell Files, RRL. All caps in the original.
36. Marjorie Hyer, "Conservatives Predict Return of Prayer to School," *Washington Post*, September 17, 1983.
37. Don Irwin, "Reagan Urges 'Voluntary' School Prayer," *Los Angeles Times*, May 24, 1983.
38. Steve Neal, "Reagan Will Propose Prayer Amendment," *Chicago Tribune*, May 7, 1982.
39. Memo, Gary L. Bauer to Edwin L. Harper, April 29, 1982, ID #071719PD, RM020, WHORM: Subject File, RRL.
40. Memo, Elizabeth H. Dole to Edwin L. Harper, April 26, 1982, ID #071796PD, RM020, WHORM: Subject File, RRL.
41. Memo, Fred F. Fielding to Richard G. Darman, May 5, 1982, ID #065026PD, RM020, WHORM: Subject File, RRL.

42. George Skelton, "Reagan Urges School Prayer Amendment," *Los Angeles Times*, May 7, 1982.
43. Handout, "Questions and Answer on the President's Proposed Voluntary School Prayer Amendment," May 6, 1982, ID #089709PD, RM020, WHORM: Subject File, RRL.
44. "Reagan Proposes School Prayer Amendment," *New York Times*, May 18, 1982.
45. Lou Cannon, "Hill Gets Reagan's Prayer Amendment," *Washington Post*, May 18, 1982.
46. Letter, Reverend Daniel F. Hoye to Mr. President, May 13, 1982, ID #078,474, RM020, WHORM: Subject File, RRL. See also, Kenneth A. Briggs, "Doubts on School Prayer," *New York Times*, May 8, 1982.
47. Robert F. Drinan, "School Prayer: 'An Emotionally Explosive Question'," *National Catholic Reporter*, May 14, 1982, 6.
48. Herbert H. Denton and Marjorie Hyer, "President to Ask Hill for Prayer Amendment," *Washington Post*, May 7, 1982.
49. Wesley Pruden, Jr., "Letters to the Editor: School Prayer in a Pluralistic Society?," *Washington Post*, May 15, 1982.
50. Williams, *God's Own Party*, 200–201. On the political implications of the SBC's fundamentalist turn in 1979, see Neil J. Young, "'Worse than cancer and worse than snakes': Jimmy Carter's Southern Baptist Problem and the 1980 Election," *Journal of Policy History* 26, no. 4 (October 2014): 479–508.
51. Michael Clark, "Southern Baptists Switch, Back Prayer in Schools," *Washington Times*, June 18, 1982; "Resolution on Prayer in Schools," June 1982, http://www.sbc.net/resolutions/amResolution.asp?ID=862.
52. "Resolution on Voluntary Prayer in Public School," June 1980, http://www.sbc.net/resolutions/amResolution.asp?ID=861.
53. Tom Wicker, "The Baptist Switch," *New York Times*, June 22, 1982.
54. "Resolution on Tuition Tax Credit," June 1982, http://www.sbc.net/resolutions/amResolution.asp?ID=1012.
55. Memo, Gary L. Bauer to Edwin L. Harper, June 22, 1982, ID #072601PD, RM020, WHORM: Subject File, RRL.
56. Letter, Adrian Rogers to Morton Blackwell, July 13, 1982, folder "Prayer in Schools (11)," Box OA 9081, Morton C. Blackwell Files, RRL.
57. "Invitees to Tuesday, July 15, 1982 Meeting on School Prayer," n.d., folder "[School Prayer – II]," Box OA 9081, Morton C. Blackwell Files, RRL. It is unclear from White House records who actually attended the meeting.
58. Robert P. Dugan, Jr., "NAE Office of Public Affairs Annual Report to the Board of Administration," March 7, 1983, Box 38, Folder 4, Papers of Thomas Fletcher Zimmerman, BGCA.

59. Memo, Gary Jarmin to Faith Whittlesey, Morton Blackwell, Dee Jepsen, Steven Gailebach, Kenn Cribb, April 15, 1983, ID #143783PD, RM020, WHORM: Subject File, RRL.
60. Robert E. Riggs, "Government-Sponsored Prayer in the Classroom," *Dialogue* 18, no. 3 (Fall 1985): 62.
61. See White House collection of statements on silent prayer amendment in folder "[School Prayer: Constitutional Amendment]," Box OA 9081, Morton C. Blackwell Files, RRL.
62. Memo, April 21, 1983, enclosed in Memo, Gary Jarmin to Ed Meese et al., June 13, 1983, in folder "[School Prayer: Constitutional Amendment]," Box OA 9081, Morton C. Blackwell Files, RRL.
63. Ibid.
64. Memo, Ken Duberstein to Faith Whittlesey, June 20, 1983, in folder "[School Prayer] (7)," Box OA 9081, Morton C. Blackwell Files, RRL.
65. Letter, Morton C. Blackwell to Gary L. Jarmin, June 24, 1983, in folder "Prayer in Schools (1)," Box OA 9081, Morton C. Blackwell Files, RRL.
66. Letter, James T. Draper, Jr., to President Ronald Reagan, July 8, 1983, ID #154465PL, RM020, WHORM: Subject File, RRL.
67. "Does Religion Belong in School?," *Christianity Today*, September 3, 1982, 12–15.
68. Letter, Morton C. Blackwell to George P. McDonnell, February 23, 1983, in folder "Prayer in Schools (8)," Box OA 9081, Morton C. Blackwell Files, RRL.
69. Letter, Morton C. Blackwell to Grover J. Reese, III, April 21, 1983, in folder "Prayer in Schools (1)," Box OA 9081, Morton C. Blackwell Files, RRL.
70. Beth Spring, "Rating Reagan," *Christianity Today*, October 7, 1983, 50.
71. "Reagan Address: America Is Strong but 'Economy Is Troubled'," *Los Angeles Times*, January 26, 1983.
72. Beth Spring, "An All-Court Press for School Prayer," *Christianity Today*, April 6, 1984, 60. Baker's proposed constitutional amendment would have prohibited the restriction of any prayer conducted in public buildings. Many pro-prayer forces believed Baker intended his bill to prevent any of the constitutional amendments from having enough support to pass.
73. Steven V. Roberts, "2 School Prayer Amendments Sent to Senate Floor by Panel," *New York Times*, July 15, 1983.
74. Charles Krauthammer, "America's Holy War," *New Republic*, April 9, 1984, 15.
75. Beth Spring, "School Prayer Fails, but Equal Access Gets a Boost in Congress," *Christianity Today*, April 20, 1984, 37.
76. "Congress Gives Student Religious Groups Access to Public Secondary Schools," *Christianity Today*, September 7, 1984, 77–79.
77. Francis X. Cline, "Preachers Hail Reagan on Abortion and Prayer," *New York Times*, February 1, 1983; "Bible Reading is Urged for Country by Reagan," *Boston Globe*, February 3, 1983.

78. John G. Turner, *Bill Bright and Campus Crusade for Christ: The Renewal of Evangelicalism in Postwar America* (Chapel Hill: University of North Carolina Press, 2008), 200.
79. Resolutions passed in October 1982 in both the House and Senate authorized the president to sign a proclamation making 1983 the Year of the Bible. The congressional resolutions described the Bible as the "word of God," though the presidential proclamation dropped that language. Paula Herbut, "Bible Year Hailed with Varying Degrees of Enthusiasm," *Washington Post*, February 12, 1983.
80. See Letter, Bill Bright to His Eminence John Cardinal Krol, October 29, 1982, Box 87, Folder 10, Records of National Religious Broadcasters, BGCA; Letter, Bill Bright to Dr. Thomas Zimmerman, November 2, 1982, Box 56, Folder 1, Papers of Thomas Fletcher Zimmerman, BGCA.
81. Letter, Ben Armstrong to John M. Jones, Jr., November 29, 1982, Box 87, Folder 10, Records of National Religious Broadcasters, BGCA; Letter, Bill Bright to Dr. Thomas F. Zimmerman, December 2, 1982, Box 56, Folder 1, Papers of Thomas Fletcher Zimmerman, BGCA; Letter, Bright to Zimmerman, November 2, 1982.
82. See Year of the Bible letterhead in Box 56, Folder 4, Papers of Thomas Fletcher Zimmerman, BGCA.
83. Letter, John MacArthur to Dr. William R. Bright, January 21, 1983, Box 56, Folder 2, Papers of Thomas Fletcher Zimmerman, BGCA. Revelation 22:18–19 (KJV) reads: "For I testify unto every man that heareth the words of the prophecy of this book, If any man shall add unto these things, God shall add unto him the plagues that are written in this book: And if any man shall take away from the words of the book of this prophecy, God shall take away his part out of the book of life, and out of the holy city, and from the things which are written in this book."
84. Minutes of the First Meeting, The Year of the Bible Media Committee, March 4, 1983, Box 56, Folder 2, Papers of Thomas Fletcher Zimmerman, BGCA; Minutes, National Committee, Year of the Bible, June 30, 1983, Box 56, Folder 3, Papers of Thomas Fletcher Zimmerman, BGCA.
85. "Civil Liberties Union Calls Reagan's 'Year of the Bible' Illegal," *New York Times*, November 25, 1983.
86. Memo, Michael P. Farris, "Proposal for Legal Response to ACLU Suit," Box 56, Folder 3, Papers of Thomas Fletcher Zimmerman, BGCA.
87. "U.S. Judge Upholds Bible Proclamation," *New York Times*, December 23, 1983.
88. "Year of the Bible Fact Sheet," n.d., Box 56, Folder 3, Papers of Thomas Fletcher Zimmerman, BGCA.
89. Letter, Bill Bright to Dr. Thomas F. Zimmerman, December 23, 1983, Box 56, Folder 3, Papers of Thomas Fletcher Zimmerman, BGCA.
90. "The Bible: Highly Revered but Seldom Read," *Christianity Today*, March 21, 1980, 13.

91. Peter Binzen, "DeMoss Foundation Puts Its Money Behind Evangelism," *Philadelphia Inquirer*, November 26, 1984; "Minutes of the Board of Directors' Meeting of Year of the Bible Foundation, Inc.," July 24, 1984, Box 56, Folder 4, Papers of Thomas Fletcher Zimmerman, BGCA. See also, Randy Frame, "Millions Respond to National Evangelistic Media Blitz," *Christianity Today*, February 3, 1984, 40, 43.
92. "Minutes of the Board of Directors' Meeting of Year of the Bible Foundation, Inc."
93. On the Reagan White House's efforts with evangelical voters for the 1984 campaign, see Memo, Morton C. Blackwell to Faith Whittlesey, "The Fundamentalist and Evangelical Voters," October 3, 1983, folder "Evangelicals," Box 12 F, Faith Ryan Whittlesey Files, RRL; Memo, Carl A. Anderson to John A. Svahn, "Meese/Baker Meeting with Evangelical Leaders," January 16, 1984, ID #201660PD, RM, WHORM: Subject File, RRL. See also various White House documents in coordination with evangelical organizations in Box 48, Folders 11 and 14, NAE. On coordination with LDS officials, see Memo, Faith Ryan Whittlesey to the Vice President, "Blunting Allegations of Inordinant [*sic*] Influence of Far Right Religious Groups upon White House Policy," October 10, 1984, folder "Religion/Politics," Box 14 F, Faith Ryan Whittlesey Files, RRL. For the White House's Catholic strategy, see Memo, Thomas Patrick Melady to Michael A. McManus, Jr., "Comments on Obtaining the Catholic Ethnic Vote in 1984 (No. 59)," folder "Catholic Strategy [1 of 3]," Box OH12418, Robert R. Reilly Files, RRL; Memo, Morton Blackwell, "General Plan of Appeal to Catholics," folder "Catholic Strategy," Box OA 12,450, Morton C. Blackwell Files, RRL. See also Pierard, "Religion and the 1984 Election Campaign," 98–114.
94. Morton Blackwell distributed a copy of Adam Walinsky's 1976 memo to Jimmy Carter about capturing the Catholic vote with the hopes that the Reagan team could seize on the "growing instability of the old Democratic coalition" Walinsky's memo had worried over. Memo, Morton C. Blackwell to Linas Kojelis, "Attached Carter Campaign Documents," August 26, 1983, folder "Catholic Strategy [1 of 3]," Box OH12418, Robert R. Reilly Files, RRL.
95. Memo, Morton Blackwell, "General Plan of Appeal to Catholics," folder "Catholic Strategy," Box OA 12,450, Morton C. Blackwell Files, RRL, quoted in Smith, *Faith and the Presidency*, 347.
96. Pierard, "Religion and the 1984 Election Campaign," 109.
97. McKeegan, *Abortion Politics*, 100.
98. Andrew M. Essig and Jennifer L. Moore, "U.S.-Holy See Diplomacy: The Establishment of Formal Relations, 1984," *Catholic Historical Review* 95, no. 4 (October 2009): 741–764; and Marie Gayte, "The American Reception of the Establishment of Diplomatic Relations Between the United States and the

Vatican in 1984," talk delivered at the Annual Meeting of the American Historical Association, San Diego, California, January 9, 2010. Copy of talk in my possession.

99. Letter, Bob Jones to President Ronald Reagan, December 30, 1983, folder "Bob Jones University," Box OA 12,756, Carolyn Sundseth Files, RRL.
100. Kenneth A. Briggs, "Church Groups Denounce Reagan Move," *New York Times*, January 11, 1984.
101. "Resolution on a U.S. Ambassador to the Vatican," June 1984, http://www.sbc.net/resolutions/amResolution.asp?ID=1072.
102. Letter, Billy A. Melvin, February 15, 1984, Box 133, Folder 20, NAE; Testimony of Robert P. Dugan, Jr., before the Committee on Foreign Relations, United States Senate, February 2, 1984, and Testimony of Forest D. Montgomery before the Subcommittee on Commerce, Justice, State, the Judiciary and Related Agencies Appropriations Committee, House of Representatives, February 9, 1984, both in Box 133, Folder 20, NAE. For editions of *Insight* pertaining to the issue of a Vatican ambassador, see copies in same folder.
103. Letter, Robert P. Dugan, Jr., to The Hon. James A. Baker III, December 9, 1983, Box 95, Folder 13, NAE.
104. Kenneth Kantzer and Gilbert Beers, "That Controversial Appointment," *Christianity Today*, March 16, 1984, 13.
105. "The Pope in Poland," *Christianity Today*, June 29, 1979, 11. For other selected examples of *Christianity Today*'s admiration of Pope John Paul II, see "Pope John Paul II: The Game of the Name," *Christianity Today*, September 22, 1978, 46–47; Jack Houston, "The Pope's Presence: Enough to Sell His Unpopular Stand?," *Christianity Today*, November 2, 1979, 64–69; "Society's Yearnings Surface," *Christianity Today*, November 16, 1979, 12; "The Evangelist and the Pope Confer Privately in Rome," *Christianity Today*, February 6, 1981, 88–89; "What Separates Evangelicals and Catholics?," *Christianity Today*, October 23, 1981, 12–15; David P. Scaer, "The Pope as Antichrist: An Anachronism?," *Christianity Today*, October 23, 1981, 66; and, Stephen Sywulka, "The Pope in Central America," *Christianity Today*, April 8, 1983, 42–44.
106. Montgomery, "Testimony before the House of Representatives."
107. Gayte, "The American Reception of the Establishment of Diplomatic Relations Between the United States and the Vatican in 1984."
108. "Appointment of an Ambassador to the Vatican Meets Mild Opposition," *Christianity Today*, February 17, 1984, 41.
109. Ibid.
110. Gayte, "The American Reception of the Establishment of Diplomatic Relations Between the United States and the Vatican in 1984."
111. Arthur Jones, "Reagan Pushes Full Vatican Ties," *National Catholic Reporter*, October 21, 1983.

112. "An Ambassador to the Vatican?," *America*, December 24, 1983, 401.
113. Peter Hebblethwaite, "US-Vatican Relations, Hemisphere Policy Tied," *National Catholic Reporter*, January 27, 1984, 5.
114. Memo, Linas to Jonathan, August 23, 1983, folder "Vatican – U.S. Diplomatic Relations," Box OA 12,420, Robert R. Reilly Files, RRL.
115. Pierard, "Religion and the 1984 Election Campaign," 110.
116. Letter, Gommar A. DePauw to The Honorable Ronald Reagan, February 18, 1985, ID #289,155, RM, WHORM: Subject File, RRL.
117. Pierard, "Religion and the 1984 Election Campaign," 111.
118. "Church Representatives at Reagan Inauguration," *Ensign*, March 1981, https://www.lds.org/ensign/1981/03/news-of-the-church/church-representatives-at-reagan-inauguration.
119. Robert Lindsey, "The Mormons: Growth, Prosperity, and Controversy," *New York Times Magazine*, January 12, 1986, 24.
120. "Latter-day Saints Appointed to Reagan Cabinet and White House Team," *Ensign*, March 1981, https://www.lds.org/ensign/1981/03/news-of-the-church; Robert Gottlieb and Peter Wiley, *America's Saints: The Rise of Mormon Power* (New York: G.P. Putnam's Sons, 1984), 14, 21–22, 87–90; D. Michael Quinn, *The Mormon Hierarchy: Extensions of Power* (Salt Lake City, UT: Signature Books, 1997), 111–113.
121. Gottlieb and Wiley, *America's Saints*, 89.
122. Susan L. M. Huck, "Good Work: How Mormons Solve the Welfare Problem," *American Opinion*, April 1975, 17.
123. "U.S. President Reagan Praises Church for Taking Care of Its Own," *Ensign*, November 1982, https://www.lds.org/ensign/1982/11/news-of-the-church/us-president-reagan-praises-church-for-taking-care-of-its-own.
124. See Spencer W. Kimball, "A Report of My Stewardship," *Ensign*, April 1981, https://www.lds.org/general-conference/1981/04/a-report-of-my-stewardship; Thomas S. Monson, "A Provident Plan – A Precious Promise," *Ensign*, April 1986, https://www.lds.org/general-conference/1986/04/a-provident-plan-a-precious-promise.
125. "President Benson Addresses Members in Utah, California," *Ensign*, September 1987, https://www.lds.org/ensign/1987/09/news-of-the-church/president-benson-addresses-members-in-utah-california; Gregory A. Prince and Wm. Robert Wright, *David O. McKay and the Rise of Modern Mormonism* (Salt Lake City, UT: University of Utah Press, 2005), 288. Marion G. Romney explained that the Mormon Welfare Plan was not socialism because it was not run by the state and was a voluntary program that depended on individual contributions and stressed personal responsibility. Marion G. Romney, "The Purpose of Church Welfare Services," General Conference, April 1977, https://www.lds.org/general-conference/1977/04/the-purpose-of-church-welfare-services.

126. Monson, "A Provident Plan – A Precious Promise."
127. See, for example, J. K. Van Baalen, "The Latter-day Saints Today," *Christianity Today*, June 19, 1964, 27.
128. Jerry Falwell, *Listen, America!* (Garden City, NY: Doubleday & Company, Inc., 1980).
129. Klaus Bockmuhl, "The Socialist Ideal: Some Soul-Searching Constraints," *Christianity Today*, May 23, 1980, 53, 56.
130. Steven Cory, "Rerouting Ayn Rand's 'Virtue of Selfishness'," *Christianity Today*, June 18, 1982, 72.
131. Rodney Clapp, "Where Capitalism and Christianity Meet," *Christianity Today*, February 4, 1983, 23.
132. Larissa MacFarquhar, "The Gilder Effect," *New Yorker*, May 29, 2000, 103.
133. George Gilder, *Wealth and Poverty* (New York: Basic Books, 1981).
134. Clapp, "Where Capitalism and Christianity Meet," 27.
135. R. C. Sproul, "Biblical Economics: Equity or Equality?," *Christianity Today*, March 5, 1982, 94.
136. David L. Weeks, "Capitalism: For Good or Evil?," *Christianity Today*, October 7, 1983, 81.
137. David R. Swartz, *Moral Minority: The Evangelical Left in an Age of Conservatism* (Philadelphia: University of Pennsylvania Press, 2012), 153–169, 233–254.
138. Carl Horn III, "Christianity and Capitalism: New Light in an Old Debate," *Christianity Today*, January 21, 1983, 43.
139. Clapp, "Where Capitalism and Christianity Meet," 25.
140. Ibid., 26.
141. Ibid., 25.
142. Ibid., 26.
143. James R. Dickerson, "President Welcomes Draft of Bishops' Pastoral Letter," *Washington Post*, November 14, 1984; Letter, Thomas J. Donahue to The Honorable Edwin Meese, III, February 7, 1984, ID #206,964, RM Box 1, File 204,001–211,000, WHORM: Subject File, RRL.
144. "U.S. Catholic Bishops Call Poverty a National Scandal," *Christianity Today*, December 14, 1984, 67.
145. "Excerpts from Draft of Bishops' Letter on the U.S. Economy," *New York Times*, November 12, 1984.
146. Ibid.
147. Dickerson, "President Welcomes Draft of Bishops' Pastoral Letter."
148. "U.S. Catholic Bishops Call Poverty a National Scandal"; Randy Frame, "Leading Evangelical Scholars Trade Their Latest Insights," *Christianity Today*, April 19, 1985, 56.
149. Kenneth S. Kantzer, "Pastoral Letters and the Realities of Life," *Christianity Today*, March 1, 1985, 12.

150. John T. McGreevy, *Catholicism and American Freedom: A History* (New York: W. W. Norton & Company, 2003), 285. See also, Samuel S. Kim, "The U.S. Catholic Bishops and the Nuclear Crisis," *Journal of Peace Research* 22, no. 4 (December 1985): 321–333.
151. National Conference of Catholic Bishops, "The Challenge of Peace: God's Promise and Our Response," May 3, 1983, http://www.usccb.org/issues-and-action/human-life-and-dignity/war-and-peace/nuclear-weapons/upload/statement-the-challenge-of-peace-1983–05–03.pdf.
152. Kenneth A. Briggs, "Roman Catholic Bishops Toughen Stance Against Nuclear Weapons," *New York Times*, May 3, 1983.
153. Ibid.
154. Kenneth L. Woodward and Jane Whitmore, "Challenging the Bishops," *Newsweek*, November 8, 1982, 78; Gerald F. Powers, "The U.S. Bishops and War since the Peace Pastoral," *U.S. Catholic Historian* 27, no. 3 (Winter 2009): 73.
155. Kenneth D. Wald, "Religious Elites and Public Opinion: The Impact of the Bishops' Peace Pastoral," *Review of Politics* 54, no. 1 (Winter 1992): 126, 135.
156. Powers, "The U.S. Bishops and War since the Peace Pastoral," 76.
157. Woodward and Whitmore, "Challenging the Bishops," 78.
158. McGreevy, *Catholicism and American Freedom*, 285.
159. "Catholic Bishops Strongly Denounce Nuclear Weapons," *Christianity Today*, January 1, 1982, 42.
160. Frances Fitzgerald, *Way Out There in the Blue: Reagan, Star Wars and the End of the Cold War* (New York: Simon & Schuster, 2000), 118.
161. "Mormon Church Opposes Placing MX Missiles in Utah and Nevada," *New York Times*, May 6, 1981.
162. "First Presidency Statement on Basing of MX Missile," *Ensign*, June 1981, 76.
163. "Christmas Message from the First Presidency," *Church News, Deseret News*, December 20, 1983, quoted in Steven A. Hildreth, "The First Presidency Statement on MX in Perspective," *BYU Studies* 22, vol. 2 (Spring 1982): 222; "Easter Message – A Plea for Peace," *Deseret News*, April 18, 1981.
164. William Appleman Williams, "Regional Resistance: Backyard Autonomy," *The Nation*, September 5, 1981, 179.
165. "First Presidency Statement on Basing of MX Missile." On church leaders' discussions that led to their decision on the MX system and the creation of the First Presidency statement opposing it, see Jacob W. Olmstead, "The Mormon Hierarchy and the MX," *Journal of Mormon History* 33, no. 3 (Fall 2007): 1–30.
166. "Mormon Church Opposes Placing MX Missiles in Utah and Nevada"; Gottlieb and Wiley, *America's Saints*, 92–93; Quinn, *The Mormon Hierarchy*,

366–367; "MX Opposition Soars Since LDS Statement," *Deseret News*, May 25, 1981, quoted in Quinn, *The Mormon Hierarchy*, 366.

167. J. B. Haws, *The Mormon Image in the American Mind: Fifty Years of Public Perception* (New York: Oxford University Press, 2013), 346 footnote 12.
168. Kenneth A. Briggs, "Hatfield's Arms Stand: Evangelical Influence," *New York Times*, April 1, 1982. See also, Swartz, *Moral Minority*, 68–85.
169. Angela M. Lahr, *Millennial Dreams and Apocalyptic Nightmares: The Cold War Origins of Political Evangelicalism* (New York: Oxford University Press, 2007), 196–198.
170. Richard V. Pierard, "Mending the Fence: Reagan and the Evangelicals," *The Reformed Journal* 33, no. 6 (June 1983): 20.
171. "Resolution on Peace and National Security," 1981, http://www.sbc.net/resolutions/832/resolution-on-peace-and-national-security; see also, "Resolution on Peace and National Security," 1980, http://www.sbc.net/resolutions/831/resolution-on-peace-and-national-security; "Resolution on Peace with Justice," 1982, http://www.sbc.net/resolutions/833/resolution-on-peace-with-justice; and "Resolution on Peace with Justice," 1983, http://www.sbc.net/resolutions/834/resolution-on-peace-with-justice.
172. See Robert D. Culver, "Justice Is Something Worth Fighting For," and John Drescher, "Why Christians Shouldn't Carry Swords," both in *Christianity Today*, November 7, 1980, 14–25. See also, Robert Culver, "Between War and Peace: Old Debate in a New Age," *Christianity Today*, October 24, 1980, 30–34, 51.
173. "SALT II: The Only Alternative to Annihilation?," *Christianity Today*, March 27, 1981, 14.
174. "A Proposal to Tilt the Balance of Terror," *Christianity Today*, April 9, 1982, 16–19; Kenneth S. Kantzer, "What Shall We Do About the Nuclear Problem?," *Christianity Today*, January 21, 1983, 9–11. See also, Stephen S. Talbott, "Can We Transcend the Nuclear Stalemate?," *Christianity Today*, August 10, 1984, 30–33.
175. Ronald Reagan, "Remarks at the Annual Convention of the National Association of Evangelicals in Orlando, Florida," March 8, 1983, http://www.reagan.utexas.edu/archives/speeches/1983/30883b.htm; Francis X. Clines, "Reagan Denounces Ideology of Soviet as 'Focus of Evil'," *New York Times*, March 9, 1983; Charles Austin, "Divided Evangelicals Avoid a Policy Stand on Nuclear Freeze," *New York Times*, March 12, 1983; Beth Spring, "Reagan Courts Evangelical Clout Against Nuclear Freeze," *Christianity Today*, April 8, 1983, 44–48; Fitzgerald, *Way Out There in the Blue*, 25–27; Matthew Avery Sutton, *American Apocalypse: A History of Modern Evangelicalism* (Cambridge, MA: The Belknap Press of Harvard University Press, 2014), 355–360; Williams, *God's Own Party*, 203–205.

176. Pierard, "Mending the Fence," 21.
177. Kantzer, "Pastoral Letters and the Realities of Life," 12. See also, Beth Spring, "The Bishops Debate the Bomb," *Christianity Today*, December 17, 1982, 32–33, 48–49.
178. "Reagan by a Landslide, Pro-Life Gains in Congress!," *Action Line: Christian Action Council Newsletter*, November 16, 1984, Wilcox Collection.
179. Smith, *Faith and the Presidency*, 349.
180. Wayne King, "Falwell Quits as Moral Majority Head," *New York Times*, November 4, 1987.
181. Marley, "Ronald Reagan and the Splintering of the Christian Right," 859.
182. Laura Sessions Stepp, "Falwell Says Moral Majority To Be Dissolved," *Washington Post*, June 12, 1989.
183. Randy Frame, "Were Christians Courted for Their Votes or Beliefs?," *Christianity Today*, February 17, 1989, 38.
184. "Lost Momentum: Carl F. H. Henry Looks at the Future of the Religious Right," *Christianity Today*, September 4, 1987, 32.
185. David Shribman, "Going Mainstream: Religious Right Drops High-Profile Tactics, Works on Local Level," *Wall Street Journal*, September 26, 1989.
186. E. J. Dionne, Jr., "Bloom Is Off Religious Right, Scholars at Conference Agree," *Washington Post*, November 30, 1990.

CHAPTER 8

1. John C. Green, "Pat Robertson and the Latest Crusade: Religious Resources and the 1988 Presidential Campaign," *Social Science Quarterly* 74, no. 1 (March 1993): 156–168; John C. Green and James L. Guth, "The Christian Right in the Republican Party: The Case of Pat Robertson's Supporters," *Journal of Politics* 50, no. 1 (February 1988): 150–165; Stephen D. Johnson, Joseph B. Tamney, and Ronald Burton, "Pat Robertson: Who Supported His Candidacy for President?," *Journal for the Scientific Study of Religion* 28, no. 4 (December 1989): 387–399; Lisa Langenbach and John C. Green, "Hollow Core: Evangelical Clergy and the 1988 Robertson Campaign," *Polity* 25, no. 1 (Autumn 1992): 147–158; Steven P. Miller, *The Age of Evangelicalism: America's Born Again Years* (New York: Oxford University Press, 2014), 84–85; James M. Penning, "Pat Robertson and the GOP: 1988 and Beyond," *Sociology of Religion* 55, no. 3 (Fall 1994): 327–335; Justin Watson, *The Christian Coalition: Dreams of Restoration, Demands for Recognition* (New York: St. Martin's Griffin, 1999), 35–42; and Daniel K. Williams, *God's Own Party: The Making of the Christian Right* (New York: Oxford University Press, 2010), 213–220. See also, Corwin Smidt and Paul Kellstedt, "Evangelicals in the Post-Reagan Era: An Analysis of Evangelical Voters in the 1988 Presidential Election," *Journal for*

the Scientific Study of Religion 31, no. 3 (September 1992): 330–338. On Pat Robertson, see Robert Boston, *The Most Dangerous Man in America? Pat Robertson and the Rise of the Christian Coalition* (Amherst, NY: Prometheus Books, 1993); David Edwin Harrell, Jr., *Pat Robertson: A Life and Legacy* (Grand Rapids, MI: Wm. B. Eerdmans Publishing Co., 2010); and David John Marley, *Pat Robertson: An American Life* (Lanham, MD: Rowman & Littlefield Publishers, Inc., 2007).

2. Sean Wilentz, "God and Man at Lynchburg," *New Republic*, April 25, 1988, 30, quoted in Watson, *The Christian Coalition*, 51.
3. Ralph Reed, *Active Faith: How Christians Are Changing the Soul of American Politics* (New York: Free Press, 1996), 12.
4. Reed, *Active Faith*, 12–13. See also, Frederick Clarkson, "The Christian Coalition: On the Road to Victory?," *Church and State* 44, no. 1 (January 1992): 4–7.
5. Clyde Wilcox, "Laying Up Treasures in Washington and in Heaven: the Christian Right and Evangelical Politics in the Twentieth Century and Beyond," *OAH Magazine of History* 17, no. 2 (January 2003): 23.
6. Miller, *The Age of Evangelicalism*, 107–108; Reed, *Active Faith*, 13–14, 129; Williams, *God's Own Party*, 227–228.
7. Watson, *The Christian Coalition*, 53–54; Williams, *God's Own Party*, 228.
8. Watson, *The Christian Coalition*, 57.
9. "Robertson Regroups 'Invisible Army' into New Coalition," *Christianity Today*, April 23, 1990, 35.
10. Watson, *The Christian Coalition*, 46.
11. Frank S. Ravitch, *School Prayer and Discrimination: The Civil Rights of Religious Minorities and Dissenters* (Boston: Northeastern University Press, 1999), 33.
12. Ibid., 63.
13. Maralee Schwartz and Paul Taylor, "Ex-Candidate Robertson Creates New Christian Political Group," *Washington Post*, March 14, 1990.
14. Ravitch, *School Prayer and Discrimination*, 58.
15. On the Christian Coalition's strategy for how precincts would operate, see "Christian Coalition Ten-Year Plan 1991–2000," Presented to the Christian Coalition Board of Directors, January 25, 1991, in Box 164, Folder 7, NAE.
16. Miller, *The Age of Evangelicalism*, 109; Williams, *God's Own Party*, 228.
17. Clarkson, "The Christian Coalition," 4; Miller, *The Age of Evangelicalism*, 108–109.
18. Clarkson, "The Christian Coalition," 4–5.
19. "American Congress of Christian Citizens Planning Meeting Summary of Proceedings," February 1, 1990, Box 54, Folder 34, NAE. The Christian Coalition went by the name American Congress of Christian Citizens at first.
20. "Christian Coalition Ten-Year Plan."
21. Wilcox, "Laying Up Treasures in Washington and in Heaven," 27.

22. John G. Pottenger, *Reaping the Whirlwind: Liberal Democracy and the Religious Axis* (Washington, D.C.: Georgetown University Press, 2007), 149.
23. Wilcox, "Laying Up Treasures in Washington and in Heaven," 27.
24. "Christian Coalition Ten-Year Plan."
25. Gustav Niebuhr, "The Christian Coalition Sees Recruiting Possibilities Arising from the Pope's Visit," *New York Times*, October 7, 1995.
26. Watson, *The Christian Coalition*, 67.
27. Reed, *Active Faith*, 219.
28. "Mostly Protestant Christian Coalition Gains Catholic Alliance," *New York Times*, December 10, 1995.
29. Niebuhr, "Christian Coalition."
30. Laurie Goodstein, "Secure at the Helm," *New York Times*, May 12, 2000.
31. Frank Rich, "Christian Coalition Chutzpah," *New York Times*, December 20, 1995.
32. "Bishops Issue Warning on Catholic Alliance," *Christian Century*, February 7–14, 1996, 125.
33. Rich, "Christian Coalition Chutzpah."
34. Laurie Goodstein, "Catholics Prove Hard to Convert to the Politics of the Coalition," *Washington Post*, September 2, 1996; Heidi Schlumpf, "How Catholic Is the Catholic Alliance?" *Christianity Today*, May 20, 1996, 76.
35. Peter Steinfels, "Bishops Steer Middle Course on Politics," *New York Times*, November 5, 1995.
36. Laurie Goodstein, "Religious Right, Frustrated, Trying New Tactic on G.O.P.," *New York Times*, March 23, 1998. Steven Miller notes the Christian Coalition's ecumenism and Reed's "big-tent approach" to cross-denominational coalition building, *The Age of Evangelicalism*, 111. But the example of the Catholic Alliance and, especially, the Catholic bishops' response reveal a more complicated picture of the organization's attempts to foster a movement beyond the group's evangelical base and the consistent challenges the Catholic Church raised to ecumenical political efforts organized outside of its leadership.
37. Mary E. Bendyna, R. S. M., John C. Green, Mark J. Rozell, and Clyde Wilcox, "Uneasy Alliance: Conservative Catholics and the Christian Right," *Sociology of Religion* 62, no. 1 (Spring 2001): 62. See also, Mary Bendyna, John C. Green, Mark J. Rozell, and Clyde Wilcox, "Catholics and the Christian Right: A View from Four States," *Journal for the Scientific Study of Religion* 39, no. 3 (September 2000): 321–332; and Paul Perl and Mary Bendyna, "Perceptions of Anti-Catholic Bias and Political Party Identification among U.S. Catholics," *Journal for the Scientific Study of Religion* 41, no. 4 (December 2002): 653–668.
38. Gustav Niebuhr, "Ray Flynn to Head Catholic Group with Conservative Roots," *New York Times*, March 13, 1999.
39. Williams, *God's Own Party*, 231–233.

40. "Mr. Bush, Crossing the Line," *New York Times*, August 26, 1992. On religious conservatives' influence on the 1992 Republican Party platform, see Duane M. Oldfield, *The Right and the Righteous* (Lanham, MD: Rowman & Littlefield Publishers, Inc., 1996), 197–207.
41. Reed, *Active Faith*, 137.
42. Ibid., 150.
43. Watson, *The Christian Coalition*, 64.
44. Ibid., 81.
45. Ibid., 83.
46. Ibid., 81.
47. Ibid., 85.
48. Wilcox, "Laying Up Treasures in Washington and in Heaven," 23.
49. Cal Thomas and Ed Dobson, *Blinded By Might: Can the Religious Right Save America?* (Grand Rapids, MI: Zondervan Publishing House, 1999), 24.
50. Miller, *The Age of Evangelicalism*, 99–101; Molly Worthen, *Apostles of Reason: The Crisis of Authority in American Evangelicalism* (New York: Oxford University Press, 2014), 245–249.
51. Peter Steinfels, "Catholic and Evangelical: Seeking a Middle Ground," *New York Times*, March 30, 1994. See also, William M. Shea, *The Lion and the Lamb: Evangelicals and Catholics in America* (New York: Oxford University Press, 2004), 155–158, 181–185; and Jonathan Aitken, *Charles W. Colson: A Life Redeemed* (Colorado Springs: WaterBrook Press, 2005), 378–388.
52. "Evangelicals and Catholics Together: The Christian Mission in the Third Millennium," *First Things*, May 1994, http://www.firstthings.com/article/1994/05/evangelicals--catholics-together-the-christian-mission-in-the-third-millennium-2.
53. Ibid.
54. Ibid.
55. "Evangelicals and Catholics Together"; Shea, *The Lion and the Lamb*, 182.
56. Memo, Billy A. Melvin to NAE Executive Committee, "Re: Recent publicity regarding Evangelicals and Roman Catholics," April 6, 1994, Box 177, Folder 2, NAE.
57. "Dallas Theological Seminary's Response to the Discussion of Evangelical/Roman Catholic Cooperation," Fall 1995, available at http://bible.org/seriespage/dallas-theological-seminary%E2%80%99s-response-discussion-evangelicalroman-catholic-cooperation.
58. Statement available at http://www.waysidechurch.org/pcadoc.htm.
59. John Dart, "Protestant Minister's Remarks Create Divisions with Catholics," *Los Angeles Times*, March 18, 1995.
60. John F. MacArthur, Jr., "Evangelicals and Catholics Together," *The Master's Seminary Journal* 6, no. 1 (Spring 1995): 36.

61. "Evangelicals and Catholics Together."
62. R. C. Sproul, "After Light, Darkness," *Tabletalk*, November 1994, 5–7, 52, copy in Box 177, Folder 2, NAE.
63. R. C. Sproul, *Faith Alone: The Evangelical Doctrine of Justification* (Grand Rapids, MI: Baker Books, 1995).
64. Kenneth S. Kantzer, "Should Roman Catholics and Evangelicals Join Ranks?," *Christianity Today*, July 18, 1994, 17.
65. "The Gift of Salvation," *First Things* 79 (January 1998): 22.
66. Ibid., 21.
67. Shea, *The Lion and the Lamb*, 184–185.
68. Don Lattin, "Proselytizing Baptists Hit Salt Lake," Sfgate.com, June 6, 1998, http://articles.sfgate.com/1998–1906-06/news/17724138_1_mormon-church-southern-baptists-latter-day-saints.
69. Patrick O' Driscoll, "20,000 Southern Baptists Knocking on Mormons' Doors," *USA Today*, June 9, 1998.
70. Gustav Niebuhr, "In Face-Off of Faiths, Kindness Is Winner," *New York Times*, June 14, 1998.
71. Katharine Biele, "Baptist Meeting in Mormon Utah Leads to 'Battle of the Bibles'," *Christian Science Monitor*, June 11, 1998.
72. John W. Kennedy, "Southern Baptists Take up the Mormon Challenge," *Christianity Today*, June 15, 1998, 25–30.
73. Patricia Rice, "Even in Land of Mormons, Baptists Proselytize," *St. Louis Post-Dispatch*, June 14, 1998.
74. Dallin H. Oaks, "Have You Been Saved?," *Ensign*, April 1998, https://www.lds.org/general-conference/1998/04/have-you-been-saved.
75. Niebuhr, "In Face-Off of Faiths."
76. Linda Caillouet, "Huckabee: U.S. Gave Up on Religion," *Arkansas Democrat-Gazette*, June 8, 1998.
77. "Resolution on the True Christian Gospel," June 1998, http://www.sbc.net/resolutions/amResolution.asp?ID=315.
78. "The Baptist Faith and Message," 1925, amended and revised 1963, 1998, and 2000, http://www.sbc.net/bfm/bfm2000.asp#xviii.
79. Gustav Niebuhr, "Southern Baptists Declare Wife Should 'Submit' to Her Husband," *New York Times*, June 10, 1998.
80. O' Driscoll, "20,000 Southern Baptists Knocking on Mormons' Doors."
81. Niebuhr, "In Face-Off of Faiths."
82. Biele, "Baptist Meeting in Mormon Utah."
83. Pottenger, *Reaping the Whirlwind*, 152. See also, Carrie Moore, "Evangelical Preaches at Salt Lake Temple," *Deseret News*, November 15, 2004. For a rich and detailed examination of "An Evening of Friendship" and the larger evangelical-Mormon dialogue of the late 1990s, see John-Charles Duffy, "Conservative

Pluralists: The Cultural Politics of Mormon-Evangelical Dialogue in the United States at the Turn of the Twenty-First Century" (Ph.D. diss, University of North Carolina at Chapel Hill, 2011), especially p. xii–xxvi and passim.

84. "Fuller Seminary President Stirs Mormon Controversy," *Florida Baptist Witness*, December 7, 2004, http://www.gofbw.com/news.asp?ID=3580.
85. Ibid.
86. For further evangelical discussion of how seeing Mormonism as a cult or "non-religion" influenced softer evangelical reflections on both Catholicism and liberal Protestantism, see Ted Olsen, "Latter-day Complaints," *Christianity Today*, July 2006, 50.
87. Greg Warner, "Conservative Evangelicals Hope for Ally in New Pope Benedict XVI," *Baptist Standard*, April 22, 2005, https://www.baptiststandard.com/resources/archives/45–2005-archives/3440-conservative-evangelicals-hope-for-ally-in-new-pope-benedict-xvi50205.
88. Isaiah Bennett, *Inside Mormonism: What Mormons Really Believe* (El Cajon, CA: Catholic Answers, Inc., 1999), and *When Mormon Missionaries Call: Answering Mormon Missionaries at Your Door* (El Cajon, CA: Catholic Answers, Inc., 1999).
89. Bennett, *Inside Mormonism*, 15.
90. Ibid., 513.
91. Barry R. Bickmore, "A Passion for Faultfinding: The Deconversion of a Catholic Priest," *FARMS Review of Books* 13, no. 2 (2001): 202.
92. Robert H. Brom, "Distinctive Beliefs of the Mormon Church," *Catholic Answers*, August 10, 2004, http://www.catholic.com/tracts/distinctive-beliefs-of-the-mormon-church.
93. Donald Westbrook, "Catholic-Mormon Relations," *Religious Educator* 13, no. 1 (2012): 47.
94. Ibid., 37.
95. Mike Cannon, "LDS and Catholic Coalition Opposes Hawaii Legislation," *Deseret News*, February 21, 1996.

CONCLUSION

1. McKay Coppins, "How Mitt Romney Decided to Start Talking about Mormonism Again," *BuzzFeed*, August 29, 2012, http://www.buzzfeed.com/mckaycoppins/how-mitt-romney-decided-to-start-talking-about-mor.
2. "Transcript of Paul Ryan's Speech at the RNC," August 29, 2012, http://www.foxnews.com/politics/2012/08/29/transcript-paul-ryan-speech-at-rnc/.
3. Jason Horowitz, "Romney Friends Open Up on Mormon Faith," *Washington Post*, August 30, 2012, http://www.washingtonpost.com/blogs/post-politics/wp/2012/08/30/church-members-on-the-real-romney.

4. Mitt Romney, Republican nomination acceptance speech, August 30, 2012, http://mittromneycentral.com/speeches/2012-speeches/083012-romney-accepts-the-gop-nomination-in-tampa.
5. Laurie Goodstein, "For a Trusty Voting Bloc, a Faith Shaken," *New York Times*, October 7, 2007, http://www.nytimes.com/2007/10/07/weekinreview/07goodstein.html; Kevin M. Kruse, "Compassionate Conservatism: Religion in the Age of George W. Bush," in Julian Zelizer, ed., *The Presidency of George W. Bush: A First Historical Assessment* (Princeton, NJ: Princeton University Press, 2010), 227–251; Steven P. Miller, *The Age of Evangelicalism: America's Born Again Years* (New York: Oxford University Press, 2014), 117–144; and, Daniel K. Williams, *God's Own Party: The Making of the Christian Right* (New York: Oxford University Press, 2010), 245–268.
6. "White, Non-Hispanic Catholics and Republican Presidential Candidates," Pew Research Religion and Public Life Project, June 4, 2007, http://www.pewforum.org/2007/06/04/publicationpage-aspxid815.
7. See Dan Gilgoff, "Keeping the Faith," *U.S. News & World Report*, February 25, 2007, http://www.usnews.com/usnews/news/articles/070225/5evangelicals.htm; David D. Kirkpatrick, "Christian Right Labors to Find '08 Candidate," *New York Times*, February 25, 2007, http://www.nytimes.com/2007/02/25/us/politics/25secret.html; Michael Luo, "Evangelicals See Dilemmas in G.O.P. Field," *New York Times*, July 8, 2007, http://www.nytimes.com/2007/07/08/us/politics/08conservatives.html; Michael Finnegan, "Evangelicals Split on GOP Field," *Washington Post*, October 1, 2007, http://articles.latimes.com/2007/oct/01/nation/na-evangelicals1; and, David D. Kirkpatrick, "The Evangelical Crackup," *New York Times Magazine*, October 28, 2007, http://www.nytimes.com/2007/10/28/magazine/28Evangelicals-t.html. Williams, *God's Own Party*, 272–273.
8. "How the Public Perceives Romney, Mormons," Pew Research Religion and Public Life Project, December 4, 2007, http://www.pewforum.org/2007/12/04/how-the-public-perceives-romney-mormons.
9. "Latter-day Politics," *Christianity Today*, September 2007, 77.
10. Gilgoff, "Keeping the Faith."
11. Hans Nichols and Christopher Stern, "Romney Shouldn't Equate Mormons, Christians, Evangelicals Say," *Bloomberg News*, October 30, 2007, http://www.bloomberg.com/apps/news?pid=newsarchive&sid=aU_vOirVlXhY&refer=home.
12. Mitt Romney, "Faith in America," December 6, 2007, full transcript at http://www.npr.org/templates/story/story.php?storyId=16,969,460.
13. Ibid.
14. Transcript, "The Republican Debate," St. Petersburg, Florida, November 28, 2007, http://www.nytimes.com/2007/11/28/us/politics/28debate-transcript.html?pagewanted=all.

15. Jay Tolson, "QA: Elder M. Russell Ballard on the Mormon Way," *U.S. News and World Report*, November 1, 2007, http://www.usnews.com/news/national/articles/2007/11/01/qa-elder-m-russell-ballard-on-the-mormon-way.
16. Michael Luo, "Mormons and the Bible, Every Word," *New York Times*, December 1, 2007, http://www.nytimes.com/2007/12/01/us/politics/01romney.html?ref=politics.
17. Jonathan Stein, "Mormons Against Romney," *Mother Jones*, November 20, 2007, http://www.motherjones.com/mojo/2007/11/mormons-against-romney. See also Laurie Goodstein, "Romney's Run Has Mormons Wary of Scrutiny," *New York Times*, June 11, 2007, http://www.nytimes.com/2007/06/11/us/politics/11mormons.html.
18. David Brody, "Bible Lesson, Republican Style," quoted in "Brody: Romney's Answer to Bible Question 'Problematic'," November 30, 2007, http://dotan.wordpress.com/2007/11/30/brody-romneys-answer-to-bible-question-problematic.
19. Ibid.
20. David Neff, "What Evangelicals Heard in Romney's 'Faith in America' Speech," *Christianity Today*, December 6, 2007, http://www.christianitytoday.com/ct/2007/decemberweb-only/149–142.0.html?paging=off.
21. Mike Licona, "Is Mormonism Christian?," Part 1, *Baptist Press*, December 5, 2007, http://www.bpnews.net/26976/is-mormonism-christian-part-1, Part 2, December 6, 2007, http://www.bpnews.net/26978/is-mormonism-christian-part-2, Part 3, December 7, 2007, http://www.bpnews.net/26994/is-mormonism-christian-part-3.
22. Licona, "Is Mormonism Christian?," Part 1.
23. Licona, "Is Mormonism Christian?," Part 2.
24. Licona, "Is Mormonism Christian?," Part 3.
25. Licona, "Is Mormonism Christian?," Part 1.
26. "How Do I Recognize a Cult?," *CBN.com*, circa 2007, http://www.cbn.com/spirituallife/cbnteachingsheets/faq_cult.aspx. CBN article mentioned in Perry Bacon, Jr., "Romney Reaches to the Religious Right," *Washington Post*, May 6, 2007, http://www.washingtonpost.com/wp-dyn/content/article/2007/05/05/AR2007050501081.html.
27. Todd M. Aglialoro, "Why Mitt Romney Is the Best Choice for Catholic Conservatives," *Crisis Magazine*, January 17, 2008, http://www.crisismagazine.com/2008/why-mitt-romney-is-the-best-choice-for-catholic-conservatives.
28. On the Iowa caucus's evangelical makeup, see Kimberly H. Conger, "Evangelicals, Issues, and the 2008 Iowa Caucuses," *Politics and Religion* 3, no. 1 (March 2010): 130–149.
29. Mike Huckabee, "What Matters," http://www.youtube.com/watch?v=8xn7uSHtkuA.

30. Paul Vitello, "Huckabee, Back in Iowa, Brings Christmas Message," *New York Times*, December 21. 2007.
31. Will Thomas, "Huckabee's Christmas Ad, Ron Paul Fires Back," *Huffington Post*, http://www.huffingtonpost.com/2007/12/18/huckabees-christmas-ad-ro_n_77,315.html.
32. Peggy Noonan, "American Pastoral," *Wall Street Journal*, December 22, 2007.
33. Deacon Keith Fournier, "Governor Huckabee's Christmas Ad Controversy," *Catholic Online*, December 19, 2007, http://www.catholic.org/national/national_story.php?id=26,229.
34. http://www.youtube.com/watch?v=4T7vjaB2QxQ.
35. For an excellent history of Mormonism's relationship to the symbol of the cross, see Michael G. Reed, *Banishing the Cross: The Emergence of a Mormon Taboo* (Independence, MO: John Whitmer Books, 2012).
36. Reed, *Banishing the Cross*, 2.
37. Frank Staheli, "Mike Huckabee and that Anti-Mormon Cross in the Window," *Simple Utah Mormon Politics*, December 23, 2007, http://frankstaheli.blogspot.com/2007/12/mike-huckabee-and-that-non-mormon-cross.html.
38. Zev Chafets, "The Huckabee Factor," *New York Times Sunday Magazine*, December 12, 2007, http://www.nytimes.com/2007/12/12/magazine/16huckabee.html.
39. Nichols and Stern, "Romney Shouldn't Equate Mormons, Christians, Evangelicals Say."
40. Chafets, "The Huckabee Factor."
41. Libby Quaid, "Huckabee Asks If Mormons Believe Jesus, Satan Are Brothers," *Deseret News*, December 11, 2007, http://www.deseretnews.com/article/695235240/Huckabee-asks-if-Mormons-believe-Jesus-Satan-are-brothers.html.
42. *Journal of Discourses* 6:207 quoted in Bill McKeever, "The Relationship Between Jesus and Lucifer in a Mormon Context," *Mormonism Research Ministry*, n.d., http://www.mrm.org/lucifers-brother.
43. Cal Thomas, "Religious Right R.I.P," November 5, 2008, http://www.calthomas.com/index.php?news=2419.
44. "Manhattan Declaration: A Call of Christian Conscience," November 20, 2009, http://www.manhattandeclaration.org/man_dec_resources/Manhattan_Declaration_full_text.pdf. See also Laurie Goodstein, "Christian Leaders Unite on Political Issues," *New York Times*, November 20, 2009.
45. "Manhattan Declaration."
46. Lillian Kwon, "Over 150,000 Americans Sign Manhattan Declaration," *Christian Post*, November 26, 2009, http://www.christianpost.com/news/over-150–000-americans-sign-manhattan-declaration-42,026.
47. Ed Stetzer, "The Manhattan Declaration," *The Exchange, a Blog by Ed Stetzer*, December 6, 2009, http://www.christianitytoday.com/edstetzer/2009/december/manhattan-declaration.html.

48. Chuck Colson, "Just the Beginning," *The BreakPoint Blog*, November 25, 2009, http://www.breakpoint.org/commentaries/13626-just-the-beginning.
49. Beth Griffin, "Ecumenical Meeting Marks First Time Mormons Join in Papal Gathering," *Catholic News Service*, April 19, 2008, http://www.catholicnews.com/data/stories/cns/0802159.htm.
50. "Respect for Diversity of Faiths," *Mormon Newsroom*, April 18, 2008, http://www.mormonnewsroom.org/article/respect-for-diversity-of-faiths.
51. "The Manhattan Declaration."
52. Mike Horton, "A Review of the Manhattan Declaration," *Out of the Horse's Mouth*, December 1, 2009, http://www.whitehorseinn.org/blog/2009/12/01/a-review-of-the-manhattan-declaration.
53. Alistair Begg, "The Manhattan Declaration," *Truth for Life Blog*, November 23, 2009, http://www.truthforlife.org/blog/manhattan-declaration.
54. R. C. Sproul, "The Manhattan Declaration: Why Didn't You Sign It, R. C.?," *Ligonier Blog*, December 8, 2009, http://www.ligonier.org/blog/the-manhattan-declaration.
55. Matt Slick, "Manhattan Declaration," *Christian Apologetics and Research Ministry*, n.d., http://carm.org/manhattan-declaration.
56. "Manhattan Declaration."
57. David D. Kirkpatrick, "The Conservative-Christian Big Thinker," *New York Times Sunday Magazine*, December 16, 2009, http://www.nytimes.com/2009/12/20/magazine/20george-t.html.
58. Alexander J. Sheffrin, "Pro-Family Group Says Effort to Ban Calif. Gay 'Marriage' Looks 'Strong,'" *Christian Post*, April 5, 2008, http://www.christianpost.com/news/pro-family-group-says-effort-to-ban-calif-gay-marriage-looks-strong-31,814.
59. "California and Same-Sex Marriage," *Mormon Newsroom*, June 30, 2008, http://www.mormonnewsroom.org/article/california-and-same-sex-marriage. Copy of original letter at http://messengerandadvocate.files.wordpress.com/2008/06/fp-letter.pdf.
60. Joe Pyrah, "LDS Donate Millions to Fight Gay Marriage," *Daily Herald*, September 15, 2008, http://www.heraldextra.com/news/local/lds-donate-millions-to-fight-gay-marriage/article_84a8a9bf-6851-56a1-8c36-f170e8cd9f13.html.
61. Jessie McKinley and Kirk Johnson, "Mormons Tipped Scale in Ban on Gay Marriage," *New York Times*, November 14, 2008, http://www.nytimes.com/2008/11/15/us/politics/15marriage.html.
62. Stephanie Mencimer, "Of Mormons and (Gay) Marriage," *Mother Jones*, March/April 2010, http://www.motherjones.com/politics/2010/02/fred-karger-save-gay-marriage.
63. James Kirchick, "The New Religious Right," *The Advocate*, December 3, 2008, http://www.advocate.com/news/2008/12/03/new-religious-right.

64. McKinley and Johnson, "Mormons Tipped Scale in Ban on Gay Marriage."
65. "Same-Sex Marriage and Proposition 8," *Mormon Newsroom*, October 16, 2008, http://www.mormonnewsroom.org/ldsnewsroom/eng/commentary/same-sex-marriage-and-proposition-8.
66. "The Divine Institution of Marriage," *Mormon Newsroom*, August 13, 2008, http://www.mormonnewsroom.org/article/the-divine-institution-of-marriage.
67. McKinley and Johnson, "Mormons Tipped Scale in Ban on Gay Marriage."
68. Elizabeth Gettelman, "Mormon Church GOTV for Prop 8: 'Do All You Can'," *Mother Jones*, October 22, 2008, http://www.motherjones.com/mojo/2008/10/mormon-church-gotv-prop-8-do-all-you-can.
69. Arleen Garcia-Herbst, "California Ethics Commission Finds Mormons Guilty on 13 Counts of Late Prop 8 Campaign Reporting," *Examiner.com*, June 15, 2010, http://www.examiner.com/article/california-ethics-commission-finds-mormons-guilty-on-13-counts-of-late-prop-8-campaign-reporting.
70. "Church Readies Members on Proposition 8," *Mormon Newsroom*, October 8, 2008, http://www.mormonnewsroom.org/article/church-readies-members-on-proposition-8.
71. Ray Ring, "Prophets and Politics," *High Country News*, October 27, 2008, http://www.hcn.org/issues/40.19/prophets-and-politics.
72. Jessie McKinley and Laurie Goodstein, "Bans in 3 States on Gay Marriage," *New York Times*, November 5, 2008, http://www.nytimes.com/2008/11/06/us/politics/06marriage.html?ref=californiasproposition8samesexmarriage.
73. 2008 Election Map, *NPR.org*, http://www.npr.org/news/specials/election2008/2008-election-map.html.
74. "New Yorkers Protest Gay Marriage Ban Outside Mormon Church," *Fox News*, November 13, 2008, http://www.foxnews.com/story/0,2933,451446,00.html.
75. USCCB News Release, "U.S. Bishops Offer Support to Mormons Targeted for Defending Marriage, Backing California's Proposition Eight," United States Conference of Catholic Bishops, November 25, 2008, http://old.usccb.org/comm/archives/2008/08–187.shtml.
76. Peggy Fletcher Stack, "Online Petition Thanks LDS Church for Prop. 8 Support," *Salt Lake Tribune*, November 25, 2008, http://www.sltrib.com/ci_11,071,617.
77. Letter quoted at Kyle Mantyla, "Anti-Gay Forces Pretend to Rise 'Above the Hate'," *Right Wing Watch*, November 25, 2008, http://www.rightwingwatch.org/content/anti-gay-forces-pretend-rise-above-hate.
78. Sarah Pulliam, "A Latter-day Alliance," *Christianity Today*, December 2, 2008, http://www.christianitytoday.com/ct/2008/decemberweb-only/149–22.0.html.
79. McKinley and Johnson, "Mormons Tipped Scale in Ban on Gay Marriage."

80. See NoH8 Campaign website, http://www.noh8campaign.com.
81. Alexandra Zavis, Gale Holland, and Shelby Grad, "Gay Marriage Backers Threaten Boycotts of Pro-Prop. 8 Restaurants," *L.A. Now*, November 12, 2008, http://latimesblogs.latimes.com/lanow/2008/11/gay-marriage-ba.html.
82. Chuck Colson, "So Much for Tolerance," *Christian Post*, November 15, 2008, http://www.christianpost.com/news/so-much-for-tolerance-35,425.
83. "Full-Page Ad Calls Gay Rallies 'Mob Veto'," *Gay Salt Lake*, December 5, 2008, http://gaysaltlake.com/news/2008/12/05/full-page-ad-calls-gay-rallies-qmob-vetoq. Link to advertisement at http://gaysaltlake.com/wp-content/uploads/2008/12/nytimes-no_mob_veto1.jpg.
84. See, for example, Maggie Gallagher, "Above the Hate," *Real Clear Politics*, November 26, 2008, http://www.realclearpolitics.com/articles/2008/11/above_the_hate.html; and Jonah Goldberg, "An Ugly Attack on Mormons," *Los Angeles Times*, December 2, 2008, http://www.latimes.com/la-oe-goldberg2-2008dec02-column.html.
85. "Legislating Immorality," *National Review*, November 24, 2008, http://www.nationalreview.com/articles/226374/legislating-immorality/editors.
86. John Mark Reynolds, "California and Thank-A-Mormon Day," *Conversant Life*, November 7, 2008, http://www.conversantlife.com/morality/california-and-thank-a-mormon-day.
87. Steven Miller argues that in the 1990s Ralph Reed had shifted Religious Right discourse away from issue-based political objections to the language of "religious freedom," in part to unite diverse religious actors who felt increasingly threatened to exert their influence in American public life, *The Age of Evangelicalism*, 108–109.
88. Cardinal Francis George, O.M.I., "Catholics and Latter-Day Saints: Partners in the Defense of Religious Freedom," February 23, 2010, http://www.jrcls.org/first_amendment/Cardinal%20George%20talk-BYU%2023feb10.pdf; "Cardinal George Addresses Religious Freedom in Speech at BYU," *Mormon Newsroom*, February 23, 2010, http://www.mormonnewsroom.org/article/cardinal-george-addresses-religious-freedom-in-speech-at-byu; "Cardinal: Catholics, Mormons Must Defend Religious Freedom Together," *Catholic News Service*, February 23, 2010, http://www.catholicnews.com/data/stories/cns/1000780.htm. Full video of George's speech available at http://www.byutv.org/watch/13b3f5f2-725f-4c24-a5ae-aafd756a09b6.
89. George, "Catholics and Latter-Day Saints."
90. Miller, *The Age of Evangelicalism*, 161.
91. Laurie Goodstein, "Bishops Were Prepared for Battle over Birth Control Coverage," *New York Times*, February 9, 2012, http://www.nytimes.com/2012/02/10/us/bishops-planned-battle-on-birth-control-coverage-rule.html.

92. Laurie Goodstein, "Bishops Reject White House's New Plan on Contraception," *New York Times*, February 11, 2012, http://www.nytimes.com/2012/02/12/us/catholic-bishops-criticize-new-contraception-proposal.html.
93. Chuck Colson and Timothy George, "An Improbable Alliance," *Christianity Today*, April 11, 2011, http://www.christianitytoday.com/ct/2011/april/improbablealliance.html.
94. Timothy George and Chuck Colson, "First They Came for the Catholics: Obama's Contraceptive Mandate," *Christianity Today*, February 8, 2012, http://www.christianitytoday.com/ct/2012/februaryweb-only/catholics-contraceptive-mandate.html.
95. Thomas Burr, "Romney, LDS Church Align on Contraception Issue," *Salt Lake Tribune*, March 4, 2012, http://www.sltrib.com/sltrib/huntsman/53634462–188/romney-church-religious-birth.html.csp.
96. Pew Research Center for the People and the Press, "Republican Candidates Stir Little Enthusiasm," June 2, 2011, http://www.people-press.org/2011/06/02/section-2-candidate-traits-and-experience. See also Neil J. Young, "Romney's Evangelical Problem," *Huffington Post*, June 7, 2011, http://www.huffingtonpost.com/neil-j-young/romney-evangelical-problem_b_872,240.html.
97. Jared Whitley, "'Excommunicated' by GOP, Bob Bennett Says Romney, Religion, Economy Make 2012 Election Unique," *Deseret News*, February 25, 2012, http://www.deseretnews.com/article/765554199/Excommunicated-by-GOP-Bob-Bennett-says-Romney-religion-economy-make-2012-election-unique.html.
98. Elizabeth Dias, "Evangelicals' Last-Ditch Effort to Unite in the GOP Race," *Time*, January 11, 2012, http://swampland.time.com/2012/01/11/evangelicals-last-ditch-effort-to-unite-in-the-gop-race.
99. Ralph Z. Hallow, "Conservatives Feud over Santorum Endorsement," *Washington Times*, January 16, 2012, http://www.washingtontimes.com/news/2012/jan/16/activists-say-pro-santorum-vote-was-rigged.
100. Jim Rutenberg, "Gingrich Wins South Carolina Primary, Upending G.O.P. Race," *New York Times*, January 21, 2012, http://www.nytimes.com/2012/01/22/us/politics/south-carolina-republican-primary.html.
101. "Romney Clinches GOP Nomination with Texas Primary Win," *FoxNews.com*, May 30, 2012, http://www.foxnews.com/politics/2012/05/29/romney-clinches-gop-nomination-with-texas-primary-win.
102. Pew Research Center, "Romney and the 2012 Election: Romney's Mormon Faith Likely a Factor in Primaries, Not in a General Election," November 23, 2011, http://www.pewforum.org/files/2011/11/Religion-Report-FINAL.pdf. See also, Neil J. Young, "Evangelical Good News for Romney?," *Huffington Post*, November 28, 2011, http://www.huffingtonpost.com/neil-j-young/evangelical-good-news-for_b_1,115,594.html.

103. "Text of Mitt Romney's Commencement Address at Liberty University," *CNN Belief Blog*, May 12, 2012, http://religion.blogs.cnn.com/2012/05/12/text-of-mitt-romneys-commencement-address-at-liberty-university.
104. John Mark Reynolds, "How Romney Wooed Evangelicals," *Guest Voices*, May 14, 2012, http://www.washingtonpost.com/blogs/guest-voices/post/how-romney-wooed-evangelicals/2012/05/14/gIQAKPYuPU_blog.html.
105. Ashley Parker, "Romney Tells Evangelicals Their Values Are His, Too," *New York Times*, May 12, 2012, http://www.nytimes.com/2012/05/13/us/politics/romney-woos-evangelicals-treading-lightly-on-gay-marriage.html.
106. "Commencement Commentary," *Liberty Champion*, April 24, 2012, http://www.liberty.edu/champion/2012/04/commencement-commentary.
107. Richard A. Oppel, Jr. and Erik Eckholm, "Prominent Pastor Calls Romney's Church a Cult," *New York Times*, October 7, 2011, http://www.nytimes.com/2011/10/08/us/politics/prominent-pastor-calls-romneys-church-a-cult.html.
108. Steve Coleman, "Robert Jeffress, Southern Baptist Pastor Who Called Mormonism a 'Cult,' Endorses Romney," *Huffington Post*, April 17, 2012, http://www.huffingtonpost.com/2012/04/17/robert-jeffress-mitt-romney-endorsement_n_1,433,215.html.
109. For another example of evangelical leaders describing Mormonism as a cult, see Joseph Walker, "Rick Santorum-Backing Pastor Plays the 'Mormon Cult' Card," *Deseret News*, January 20, 2012, http://www.deseretnews.com/article/700217469/Rick-Santorum-backing-pastor-plays-the-Mormon-cult-card.html.
110. Ed Stetzer, "Morning Roundup 10/16/12: Are Mormons Christians?," *The Exchange, a Blog by Ed Stetzer*, October 31, 2012, http://www.christianitytoday.com/edstetzer/2012/october/morning-roundup-101,612-are-mormons-christians.html; Ed Stetzer, "Dealing with the 'Mormon Moment': Cults, Truth, and Grace," *The Exchange, a Blog by Ed Stetzer*, October 31, 2012, http://www.christianitytoday.com/edstetzer/2012/october/dealing-with-this-mormon-moment-cults-truth-and-grace.html. See also article series, Stephen Mansfield, Mollie Ziegler Hemmingway, and Richard Mouw, "Is There Anything Wrong With Voting for a Mormon for President?" *Christianity Today*, September 2012, http://www.christianitytoday.com/ct/2012/september/is-it-wrong-to-vote-for-mormon-president.html.
111. Gerald R. McDermott, "The Real Differences Between Mormons and Orthodox Christians," *Christianity Today*, October 12, 2012, http://www.christianitytoday.com/ct/2012/october-web-only/differences-between-mormonism-christianity.html.
112. "With Santorum Out, Will Evangelicals Back Romney?," *NPR*, April 12, 2012, http://www.npr.org/2012/04/12/150516905/after-santorum-will-evangelicals-find-ally-in-romney.

113. Richard D. Land, "Editorial: Mormons, Christianity and Presidential Elections," *CP Opinion*, October 18, 2011, http://www.christianpost.com/news/editorial-mormons-christianity-and-presidential-elections-58,423.
114. Land, "Editorial: Mormons, Christianity and Presidential Elections"; Walker, "Rick Santorum-Backing Pastor Plays the 'Mormon Cult' Card."
115. Eric Marrapodi, "Billy Graham Buys Election Ads after Romney Meeting," *CNN Belief Blog*, October 18, 2012, http://religion.blogs.cnn.com/2012/10/18/billy-graham-buys-election-ads-after-romney-meeting.
116. Mitchell Landsberg, "Evangelist Billy Graham All but Endorses Mitt Romney," *Los Angeles Times*, October 12, 2012, http://www.latimes.com/news/politics/la-pn-billy-graham-romney-endorsement-2,012,101,102,827,291.story.
117. Eric Marrapodi, "Billy Graham Site Removes Mormon 'Cult' Reference after Romney Meeting," *CNN Belief Blog*, October 16, 2012, http://religion.blogs.cnn.com/2012/10/16/billy-grahams-group-removes-mormon-cult-reference-from-website-after-romney-meeting.
118. Ruth Moon, "Should the Billy Graham Evangelistic Association Have Removed Mormons from 'Cult' List?," *Christianity Today*, October 19, 2012, http://www.christianitytoday.com/ct/2012/october-web-only/should-billy-graham-have-removed-mormons-from-cult-list.html.
119. Daniel Burke, "Billy Graham Faces Backlash over Mormon 'Cult' Removal," *On Faith Blog*, October 24, 2012, http://www.washingtonpost.com/national/on-faith/billy-graham-faces-backlash-over-mormoncult-removal/2012/10/24/2f9ca0c6-1e1b-11e2-8817-41b9a7aaabc7_story.html.
120. Moon, "Should the Billy Graham Evangelistic Association Have Removed Mormons from 'Cult' List?"
121. Neil J. Young, "Romney Finds Religion," *Huffington Post*, August 31, 2012, http://www.huffingtonpost.com/neil-j-young/romney-finds-religion_b_1,846,542.html.
122. Emily Schultheis, "Huckabee: I Don't Care Where Romney Goes to Church," *Burns & Haberman on 2012 Blog*, August 29, 2012, http://www.politico.com/blogs/burns-haberman/2012/08/huckabee-i-dont-care-where-romney-goes-to-church-133,774.html.
123. Adelle M. Banks, "Conservative Christian Leaders Focus on Romney's Policies, Not Faith," *Religion News Service*, September 11, 2012, http://www.religionnews.com/2012/09/11/conservative-christian-leaders-urge-focus-on-romneys-policies-not-faith.
124. Msgr. Charles Pope, "Chris Matthews Says Evangelicals See Catholics (and Mormons) as Cultists. Is He Right or Wrong?," *Archdiocese of Washington Blog*, March 14, 2012, http://blog.adw.org/2012/03/chris-matthews-says-evangelicals-see-catholics-and-mormons-as-cultists-is-he-right-or-wrong.

125. Stephen H. Webb, "Mormonism Obsessed with Christ," *First Things*, February 2012, http://www.firstthings.com/article/2012/01/mormonism-obsessed-with-christ.
126. Nicholas G. Hahn III, "Why Catholics Love Mitt Romney," *Crisis*, March 27, 2012, http://www.crisismagazine.com/2012/why-catholics-love-mitt-romney.
127. "How the Faithful Voted: 2012 Preliminary Analysis," Pew Research Religion and Public Life Project, November 7, 2012, http://www.pewforum.org/2012/11/07/how-the-faithful-voted-2012-preliminary-exit-poll-analysis. See also, "Election 2012 Post Mortem: White Evangelicals and Support for Romney," Pew Research Religion and Public Life Project, December 7, 2012, http://www.pewforum.org/2012/12/07/election-2012-post-mortem-white-evangelicals-and-support-for-romney/.
128. See Laurie Goodstein, "Christian Right Failed to Sway Voters on Issues," *New York Times*, November 9, 2012, http://www.nytimes.com/2012/11/10/us/politics/christian-conservatives-failed-to-sway-voters.html; Albert Mohler, "Aftermath: Lessons from the 2012 Election," *AlbertMohler.com*, November 7, 2012, http://www.albertmohler.com/2012/11/07/aftermath-lessons-from-the-2012-election/; Peter J. Leithart, "The Religious Right after Reaganism," *On the Square Blog*, November 9, 2012, http://www.firstthings.com/onthesquare/2012/11/the-religious-right-after-reaganism; and Tobin Grant, "Post-Election Fight over the 'Evangelical' Brand," *Christianity Today*, November 20, 2012, http://www.christianitytoday.com/ct/2012/november-web-only/post-election-fight-over-evangelical-brand.html. For an alternate view, see pragmaticidealist, "In Defeat, Expect the Religious Right to Get Louder," *DailyKos.com*, November 10, 2012, http://www.dailykos.com/story/2012/11/10/1160219/-In-Defeat-Expect-the-Religious-Right-to-Get-Louder.
129. Ed Stetzer, "The People Have Spoken – What Should Christians Do Now?" *The Exchange, a Blog by Ed Stetzer*, November 7, 2012, http://www.christianitytoday.com/edstetzer/2012/november/people-have-spoken--what-should-christians-do-now.html.
130. "Stand Together for Religious Freedom," July 2, 2013, http://www.usccb.org/issues-and-action/religious-liberty/upload/standing-together-for-religious-freedom.pdf; "Catholic, Southern Baptist Religious Liberty Leaders Lead Open Letter Effort for Conscience Protection Given HHS Mandate," July 2, 2013, http://www.usccb.org/news/2013/13–134.cfm.
131. "Religious Freedom," *Mormon Newsroom*, http://www.mormonnewsroom.org/official-statement/religious-freedom; "Church Launches New Resources on Freedom of Religion," *Mormon Newsroom*, September 10, 2013, http://www.mormonnewsroom.org/article/religious-freedom-resources.
132. Matthew Brown, "Q&A: Evangelical Leader Richard Land Shares Views on LDS Church, Threats to Religious Liberty, Other Issues," *Deseret News*,

September 6, 2013, http://www.deseretnews.com/article/865585938/QA-Evangelical-leader-Richard-Land-shares-views-on-LDS-Church-threats-to-religious-liberty-other.html.

133. Tad Walch, "Mohler Returns to BYU, Says Mormons, Evangelicals 'May Go to Jail Together' Sooner Than He Thought," *Deseret News*, February 25, 2014, http://www.deseretnews.com/article/865597349/Mohler-returns-to-BYU-says-Mormons-evangelicals-may-go-to-jail-together-sooner-than-he-thought.html.
134. Matthew Brown, "Coalition of Religious Groups Signs Open Letter for Religious Liberty," *Deseret News*, July 8, 2013, http://www.deseretnews.com/article/865582788/Religious-groups-including-LDS-Church-sign-open-letter-against-birth-control-mandate.html.
135. Matthew Brown, "LDS Church Joins 'Growing Chorus' of Faiths Asking Followers to Defend Religious Liberty," *Deseret News*, September 15, 2013, http://www.deseretnews.com/article/865586460/LDS-join-growing-chorus-of-faiths-asking-followers-to-defend-religious-liberty.html.
136. Brown, "Q&A."
137. Mark Silk, "Bishop Lori's Odd Company," *Spiritual Politics Blog*, July 3, 2013, http://marksilk.religionnews.com/2013/07/03/bishop-loris-odd-company.
138. Stetzer, "The People Have Spoken – What Should Christians Do Now?"

Index

Note: locators followed by n refer to notes